SELECTED INTERNATIONAL HUMAN RIGHTS INSTRUMENTS, AND BIBLIOGRAPHY FOR RESEARCH ON INTERNATIONAL HUMAN RIGHTS

Fourth Edition

SELECTED INTERNATIONAL HUMAN RIGHTS INSTRUMENTS AND BIBLIOGRAPHY FOR RESEARCH ON INTERNATIONAL HUMAN RIGHTS

Fourth Edition

David Weissbrodt
Regents Professor of Law and
Fredrikson & Byron Professor of Law
University of Minnesota Law School

Fionnuala Ní Aoláin
Dorsey & Whitney Professor of Law
University of Minnesota Law School

Mary Rumsey
Jeffrey & Susan Brotman Professor of Law
University of Minnesota Law School

Marci Hoffman
Associate Director, International and Foreign Law Librarian
University of California Law School, Berkeley

Joan Fitzpatrick (1950–2003)
Jeffrey & Susan Brotman Professor of Law
University of Washington School of Law

CAROLINA ACADEMIC PRESS

Durham, North Carolina

ISBN: 978-1-4224-1174-2

Carolina Academic Press, LLC
700 Kent Street
Durham, North Carolina 27701
Telephone (919) 489-7486
Fax (919) 493-5668
www.caplaw.com

Printed in the United States of America
2018 Printing

TABLE OF CONTENTS

SELECTED INTERNATIONAL HUMAN RIGHTS INSTRUMENTS

Page

A.   UNITED NATIONS DOCUMENTS

B.   OTHER UNITED NATIONS INSTRUMENTS

C.   REGIONAL INSTRUMENTS

BIBLIOGRAPHY FOR RESEARCH ON INTERNATIONAL HUMAN RIGHTS LAW

TABLE OF CONTENTS

SELECTED INTERNATIONAL HUMAN RIGHTS
INSTRUMENTS   PAGE

A. UNITED NATIONS DOCUMENTS

CHARTER OF THE UNITED NATIONS, June 26, 1945, 59 Stat. 1031, T.S. NO. 993, 3 Bevans 1153, *entered into force* **Oct. 24, 1945:**

Preamble

WE THE PEOPLES OF THE UNITED NATIONS DETERMINED

to save succeeding generations from the scourge of war, which twice in our lifetime has brought untold sorrow to mankind, and

to reaffirm faith in fundamental human rights, in the dignity and worth of the human person, in the equal rights of men and women and of nations large and small, and

to establish conditions under which justice and respect for the obligations arising from treaties and other sources of international law can be maintained, and

to promote social progress and better standards of life in larger freedom,

AND FOR THESE ENDS

to practice tolerance and live together in peace with one another as good neighbors, and

to unite our strength to maintain international peace and security, and

to ensure, by the acceptance of principles and the institution of methods, that armed force shall not be used, save in the common interest, and

to employ international machinery for the promotion of the economic and social advancement of all peoples,

HAVE RESOLVED TO COMBINE OUR EFFORTS TO ACCOMPLISH THESE AIMS.

Accordingly, our respective Governments, through representatives assembled in the city of San Francisco, who have exhibited their full powers found to be in good and due form, have agreed to the present Charter of the United Nations and do hereby establish an international organization to be known as the United Nations.

CHAPTER I
PURPOSES AND PRINCIPLES

Article 1

The Purposes of the United Nations are:

1. To maintain international peace and security, and to that end: to take effective collective measures for the prevention and removal of threats to the peace, and for the suppression of acts of aggression or other breaches of the peace, and to bring about by peaceful means, and in conformity with the principles of justice and international law, adjustment or settlement of international disputes or situations which might lead to a breach of the peace;

2. To develop friendly relations among nations based on respect for the principle of equal rights and self-determination of peoples, and to take other appropriate measures to strengthen universal peace;

3. To achieve international cooperation in solving international problems of an economic, social, cultural, or humanitarian character, and in promoting and encouraging respect for human rights and for fundamental freedoms for all without distinction as to race, sex, language, or religion; and

4. To be a center for harmonizing the actions of nations in the attainment of these common ends.

Article 2

The Organization and its Members, in pursuit of the Purposes stated in Article 1, shall act in accordance with the following Principles.

1. The Organization is based on the principle of the sovereign equality of all its Members.

2. All Members, in order to ensure to all of them the rights and benefits resulting from membership, shall fulfill in good faith the obligations assumed by them in accordance with the present Charter.

3. All Members shall settle their international disputes by peaceful means in such a manner that international peace and security, and justice, are not endangered.

4. All Members shall refrain in their international relations from the threat or use of force against the territorial integrity or political independence of any state, or in any other manner inconsistent with the Purposes of the United Nations.

5. All Members shall give the United Nations every assistance in any action it takes in accordance with the present Charter, and shall refrain from giving assistance to any state against which the United Nations is taking preventive or enforcement action.

6. The Organization shall ensure that states which are not Members of the United Nations act in accordance with these Principles so far as may be necessary for the maintenance of international peace and security.

7. Nothing contained in the present Charter shall authorize the United Nations to intervene in matters which are essentially within the domestic jurisdiction of any state or shall require the Members to submit such matters to settlement under the present Charter; but this principle shall not prejudice the application of enforcement measures under Chapter VII.

CHAPTER II
MEMBERSHIP

Article 3

The original Members of the United Nations shall be the states which, having participated in the United Nations Conference on International

Organization at San Francisco, or having previously signed the Declaration by United Nations of January 1, 1942, sign the present Charter and ratify it in accordance with Article 110.

Article 4

1. Membership in the United Nations is open to all other peace-loving states which accept the obligations contained in the present Charter and, in the judgment of the Organization, are able and willing to carry out these obligations.

2. The admission of any such state to membership in the United Nations will be effected by a decision of the General Assembly upon the recommendation of the Security Council.

Article 5

A member of the United Nations against which preventive or enforcement action has been taken by the Security Council may be suspended from the exercise of the rights and privileges of membership by the General Assembly upon the recommendation of the Security Council. The exercise of these rights and privileges may be restored by the Security Council.

Article 6

A Member of the United Nations which has persistently violated the Principles contained in the present Charter may be expelled from the Organization by the General Assembly upon the recommendation of the Security Council.

CHAPTER III
ORGANS

Article 7

1. There are established as the principal organs of the United Nations: a General Assembly, a Security Council, an Economic and Social Council, a Trusteeship Council, an International Court of Justice, and a Secretariat.

2. Such subsidiary organs as may be found necessary may be established in accordance with the present Charter.

Article 8

The United Nations shall place no restrictions on the eligibility of men and women to participate in any capacity and under conditions of equality in its principal and subsidiary organs.

CHAPTER IV
THE GENERAL ASSEMBLY

Composition

Article 9

1. The General Assembly shall consist of all the Members of the United Nations.

2. Each member shall have not more than five representatives in the General Assembly.

Functions and Powers

Article 10

The General Assembly may discuss any questions or any matters within the scope of the present Charter or relating to the powers and functions of any organs provided for in the present Charter, and, except as provided in Article 12, may make recommendations to the Members of the United Nations or to the Security Council or to both on any such questions or matters.

Article 11

1. The General Assembly may consider the general principles of cooperation in the maintenance of international peace and security, including the principles governing disarmament and the regulation of armaments, and may make recommendations with regard to such principles to the Members or to the Security Council or to both.

2. The General Assembly may discuss any questions relating to the maintenance of international peace and security brought before it by any Member of the United Nations, or by the Security Council, or by a state which is not a Member of the United Nations in accordance with Article 35, paragraph 2, and, except as provided in Article 12, may make recommendations with regard to any such questions to the state or states concerned or to the Security Council or to both. Any such question on which action is necessary shall be referred to the Security Council by the General Assembly either before or after discussion.

3. The General Assembly may call the attention of the Security Council to situations which are likely to endanger international peace and security.

4. The powers of the General Assembly set forth in this Article shall not limit the general scope of Article 10.

Article 12

1. While the Security Council is exercising in respect of any dispute or situation the functions assigned to it in the present Charter, the General Assembly shall not make any recommendation with regard to that dispute or situation unless the Security Council so requests.

2. The Secretary-General, with the consent of the Security Council, shall notify the General Assembly at each session of any matters relative to the maintenance of international peace and security which are being dealt with by the Security Council and shall similarly notify the General Assembly, or the Members of the United Nations if the General Assembly is not in session, immediately the Security Council ceases to deal with such matters.

Article 13

1. The General Assembly shall initiate studies and make recommendations for the purpose of:

a. promoting international cooperation in the political field and encouraging the progressive development of international law and its codification;

b. promoting international cooperation in the economic, social, cultural, educational, and health fields, and assisting in the realization of human rights and fundamental freedoms for all without distinction as to race, sex, language, or religion.

2. The further responsibilities, functions and powers of the General Assembly with respect to matters mentioned in paragraph 1(b) above are set forth in Chapters IX and X.

Article 14

Subject to the provisions of Article 12, the General Assembly may recommend measures for the peaceful adjustment of any situation, regardless of origin, which it deems likely to impair the general welfare or friendly relations among nations, including situations resulting from a violation of the provisions of the present Charter setting forth the Purposes and Principles of the United Nations.

Article 15

1. The General Assembly shall receive and consider annual and special reports from the Security Council; these reports shall include an account of the measures that the Security Council has decided upon or taken to maintain international peace and security.

2. The General Assembly shall receive and consider reports from the other organs of the United Nations.

Article 16

The General Assembly shall perform such functions with respect to the international trusteeship system as are assigned to it under Chapters XII and XIII, including the approval of the trusteeship agreements for areas not designated as strategic.

Article 17

1. The General Assembly shall consider and approve the budget of the Organization.

2. The expenses of the Organization shall be borne by the Members as apportioned by the General Assembly.

3. The General Assembly shall consider and approve any financial and budgetary arrangements with specialized agencies referred to in Article 57 and shall examine the administrative budgets of such specialized agencies with a view to making recommendations to the agencies concerned.

Voting

Article 18

1. Each member of the General Assembly shall have one vote.

2. Decisions of the General Assembly on important questions shall be made by a two-thirds majority of the members present and voting. These questions shall include: recommendations with respect to the maintenance of international peace and security, the election of the non-permanent members of the Security Council, the election of the members of the Economic and Social Council, the election of members of the Trusteeship Council in accordance with paragraph 1(c) of Article 86, the admission of new Members to the United Nations, the suspension of the rights and privileges of membership, the expulsion of Members, questions relating to the operation of the trusteeship system, and budgetary questions.

3. Decisions on other questions, including the determination of additional categories of questions to be decided by a two-thirds majority, shall be made by a majority of the members present and voting.

Article 19

A Member of the United Nations which is in arrears in the payment of its financial contributions to the Organization shall have no vote in the General Assembly if the amount of its arrears equals or exceeds the amount of the contributions due from it for the preceding two full years. The General Assembly may, nevertheless, permit such a Member to vote if it is satisfied that the failure to pay is due to conditions beyond the control of the Member.

Procedure

Article 20

The General Assembly shall meet in regular annual sessions and in such special sessions as occasion may require. Special sessions shall be convoked by the Secretary-General at the request of the Security Council or of a majority of the Members of the United Nations.

Article 21

The General Assembly shall adopt its own rules of procedure. It shall elect its President for each session.

Article 22

The General Assembly may establish such subsidiary organs as it deems necessary for the performance of its functions.

CHAPTER V
THE SECURITY COUNCIL

Composition

Article 23

1. The Security Council shall consist of fifteen Members of the United Nations. The Republic of China, France, the Union of Soviet Socialist Republics, the United Kingdom of Great Britain and Northern Ireland, and the United

States of America shall be permanent members of the Security Council. The General Assembly shall elect ten other Members of the United Nations to be non-permanent members of the Security Council, due regard being specially paid, in the first instance to the contribution of Members of the United Nations to the maintenance of international peace and security and to the other purposes of the Organization, and also to equitable geographical distribution.

2. The non-permanent members of the Security Council shall be elected for a term of two years. In the first election of the non-permanent members after the increase of the membership of the Security Council from eleven to fifteen, two of the four additional members shall be chosen for a term of one year. A retiring member shall not be eligible for immediate re-election.

3. Each member of the Security Council shall have one representative.

Functions and Powers

Article 24

1. In order to ensure prompt and effective action by the United Nations, its Members confer on the Security Council primary responsibility for the maintenance of international peace and security, and agree that in carrying out its duties under this responsibility the Security Council acts on their behalf.

2. In discharging these duties the Security Council shall act in accordance with the Purposes and Principles of the United Nations. The specific powers granted to the Security Council for the discharge of these duties are laid down in Chapters VI, VII, VIII and XII.

3. The Security Council shall submit annual and, when necessary, special reports to the General Assembly for its consideration.

Article 25

The Members of the United Nations agree to accept and carry out the decisions of the Security Council in accordance with the present Charter.

Article 26

In order to promote the establishment and maintenance of international peace and security with the least diversion for armaments of the world's human and economic resources, the Security Council shall be responsible for formulating, with the assistance of the Military Staff Committee referred to in Article 47, plans to be submitted to the Members of the United Nations for the establishment of a system for the regulation of armaments.

Voting

Article 27

1. Each member of the Security Council shall have one vote.

2. Decisions of the Security Council on procedural matters shall be made by an affirmative vote of nine members.

3. Decisions of the Security Council on all other matters shall be made by an affirmative vote of nine members including the concurring votes of the permanent members; provided that, in decisions under Chapter VI, and under paragraph 3 of Article 52, a party to a dispute shall abstain from voting.

Procedure

Article 28

1. The Security Council shall be so organized as to be able to function continuously. Each member of the Security Council shall for this purpose be represented at all times at the seat of the Organization.

2. The Security Council shall hold periodic meetings at which each of its members may, if it so desires, be represented by a member of the government or by some other specially designated representative.

3. The Security Council may hold meetings at such places other than the seat of the Organization as in its judgment will best facilitate its work.

Article 29

The Security Council may establish such subsidiary organs as it deems necessary for the performance of its functions.

Article 30

The Security Council shall adopt its own rules of procedure, including the method of selecting its President.

Article 31

Any Member of the United Nations which is not a member of the Security Council may participate, without vote, in the discussion of any question brought before the Security Council whenever the latter considers that the interests of that Member are specially affected.

Article 32

Any Member of the United Nations which is not a member of the Security Council or any state which is not a Member of the United Nations, if it is a party to a dispute under consideration by the Security Council, shall be invited to participate, without vote, in the discussion relating to the dispute. The Security Council shall lay down such conditions as it deems just for the participation of a state which is not a Member of the United Nations.

CHAPTER VI
PACIFIC SETTLEMENT OF DISPUTES

Article 33

1. The parties to any dispute, the continuance of which is likely to endanger the maintenance of international peace and security, shall, first of all, seek

a solution by negotiation, enquiry, mediation, conciliation, arbitration, judicial settlement, resort to regional agencies or arrangements, or other peaceful means of their own choice.

2. The Security Council shall, when it deems necessary, call upon the parties to settle their dispute by such means.

Article 34

The Security Council may investigate any dispute, or any situation which might lead to international friction or give rise to a dispute, in order to determine whether the continuance of the dispute or situation is likely to endanger the maintenance of international peace and security.

Article 35

1. Any Member of the United Nations may bring any dispute, or any situation of the nature referred to in Article 34, to the attention of the Security Council or of the General Assembly.

2. A state which is not a Member of the United Nations may bring to the attention of the Security Council or of the General Assembly any dispute to which it is a party if it accepts in advance, for the purposes of the dispute, the obligations of pacific settlement provided in the present Charter.

3. The proceedings of the General Assembly in respect of matters brought to its attention under this Article will be subject to the provisions of Articles 11 and 12.

Article 36

1. The Security Council may, at any stage of a dispute of the nature referred to in Article 33 or of a situation of like nature, recommend appropriate procedures or methods of adjustment.

2. The Security Council should take into consideration any procedures for the settlement of the dispute which have already been adopted by the parties.

3. In making recommendations under this Article the Security Council should also take into consideration that legal disputes should as a general rule be referred by the parties to the International Court of Justice in accordance with the provisions of the Statute of the Court.

Article 37

1. Should the parties to a dispute of the nature referred to in Article 33 fail to settle it by the means indicated in that Article, they shall refer it to the Security Council.

2. If the Security Council deems that the continuance of the dispute is in fact likely to endanger the maintenance of international peace and security, it shall decide whether to take action under Article 36 or to recommend such terms of settlement as it may consider appropriate.

Article 38

Without prejudice to the provisions of Articles 33 to 37, the Security Council may, if all the parties to any dispute so request, make recommendations to the parties with a view to a pacific settlement of the dispute.

CHAPTER VII
ACTION WITH RESPECT TO THREATS TO THE PEACE, BREACHES OF THE PEACE, AND ACTS OF AGGRESSION

Article 39

The Security Council shall determine the existence of any threat to the peace, breach of the peace, or act of aggression and shall make recommendations, or decide what measures shall be taken in accordance with Articles 41 and 42, to maintain or restore international peace and security.

Article 40

In order to prevent an aggravation of the situation, the Security Council may, before making the recommendations or deciding upon the measures provided for in Article 39, call upon the parties concerned to comply with such provisional measures as it deems necessary or desirable. Such provisional measures shall be without prejudice to the rights, claims, or position of the parties concerned. The Security Council shall duly take account of failure to comply with such provisional measures.

Article 41

The Security Council may decide what measures not involving the use of armed force are to be employed to give effect to its decisions, and it may call upon the Members of the United Nations to apply such measures. These may include complete or partial interruption of economic relations and of rail, sea, air, postal, telegraphic, radio, and other means of communication, and the severance of diplomatic relations.

Article 42

Should the Security Council consider that measures provided for in Article 41 would be inadequate or have proved to be inadequate, it may take such action by air, sea, or land forces as may be necessary to maintain or restore international peace and security. Such action may include demonstrations, blockade, and other operations by air, sea or land forces of Members of the United Nations.

Article 43

1. All Members of the United Nations, in order to contribute to the maintenance of international peace and security, undertake to make available to the Security Council, on its call and in accordance with a special agreement or agreements, armed forces, assistance, and facilities, including rights of

passage, necessary for the purpose of maintaining international peace and security.

2. Such agreement or agreements shall govern the numbers and types of forces, their degree of readiness and general location, and the nature of the facilities and assistance to be provided.

3. The agreement or agreements shall be negotiated as soon as possible on the initiative of the Security Council. They shall be concluded between the Security Council and Members or between the Security Council and groups of Members and shall be subject to ratification by the signatory states in accordance with their respective constitutional processes.

Article 44

When the Security Council has decided to use force it shall, before calling upon a Member not represented on it to provide armed forces in fulfillment of the obligations assumed under Article 43, invite that Member, if the Member so desires, to participate in the decisions of the Security Council concerning the employment of contingents of that Member's armed forces.

Article 45

In order to enable the United Nations to take urgent military measures Members shall hold immediately available national air-force contingents for combined international enforcement action. The strength and degree of readiness of these contingents and plans for their combined action shall be determined, within the limits laid down in the special agreement or agreements referred to in Article 43, by the Security Council with the assistance of the Military Staff Committee.

Article 46

Plans for the application of armed force shall be made by the Security Council with the assistance of the Military Staff Committee.

Article 47

1. There shall be established a Military Staff Committee to advise and assist the Security Council on all questions relating to the Security Council's military requirements for the maintenance of international peace and security, the employment and command of forces placed at its disposal, the regulation of armaments, and possible disarmament.

2. The Military Staff Committee shall consist of the Chiefs of Staff of the permanent members of the Security Council or their representatives. Any Member of the United Nations not permanently represented on the Committee shall be invited by the Committee to be associated with it when the efficient discharge of the Committee's responsibilities requires the participation of that Member in its work.

3. The Military Staff Committee shall be responsible under the Security Council for the strategic direction of any armed forces placed at the disposal of the Security Council. Questions relating to the command of such forces shall be worked out subsequently.

4. The Military Staff Committee, with the authorization of the Security Council and after consultation with appropriate regional agencies, may establish regional subcommittees.

Article 48

1. The action required to carry out the decisions of the Security Council for the maintenance of international peace and security shall be taken by all the Members of the United Nations or by some of them, as the Security Council may determine.

2. Such decisions shall be carried out by the Members of the United Nations directly and through their action in the appropriate international agencies of which they are members.

Article 49

The Members of the United Nations shall join in affording mutual assistance in carrying out the measures decided upon by the Security Council.

Article 50

If preventive or enforcement measures against any state are taken by the Security Council, any other state, whether a Member of the United Nations or not, which finds itself confronted with special economic problems arising from the carrying out of those measures shall have the right to consult the Security Council with regard to a solution of those problems.

Article 51

Nothing in the present Charter shall impair the inherent right of individual or collective self-defence if an armed attack occurs against a Member of the United Nations, until the Security Council has taken measures necessary to maintain international peace and security. Measures taken by Members in the exercise of this right of self-defence shall be immediately reported to the Security Council and shall not in any way affect the authority and responsibility of the Security Council under the present Charter to take at any time such action as it deems necessary in order to maintain or restore international peace and security.

CHAPTER VIII
REGIONAL ARRANGEMENTS

Article 52

1. Nothing in the present Charter precludes the existence of regional arrangements or agencies for dealing with such matters relating to the maintenance of international peace and security as are appropriate for regional action, provided that such arrangements or agencies and their activities are consistent with the Purposes and Principles of the United Nations.

2. The Members of the United Nations entering into such arrangements or constituting such agencies shall make every effort to achieve pacific

settlement of local disputes through such regional arrangements or by such regional agencies before referring them to the Security Council.

3. The Security Council shall encourage the development of pacific settlement of local disputes through such regional arrangements or by such regional agencies either on the initiative of the states concerned or by reference from the Security Council.

4. This Article in no way impairs the application of Articles 34 and 35.

Article 53

1. The Security Council shall, where appropriate, utilize such regional arrangements or agencies for enforcement action under its authority. But no enforcement action shall be taken under regional arrangements or by regional agencies without the authorization of the Security Council, with the exception of measures against any enemy state, as defined in paragraph 2 of this Article, provided for pursuant to Article 107 or in regional arrangements directed against renewal of aggressive policy on the part of any such state, until such time as the Organization may, on request of the Governments concerned, be charged with the responsibility for preventing further aggression by such a state.

2. The term enemy state as used in paragraph 1 of this Article applies to any state which during the Second World War has been an enemy of any signatory of the present Charter.

Article 54

The Security Council shall at all times be kept fully informed of activities undertaken or in contemplation under regional arrangements or by regional agencies for the maintenance of international peace and security.

CHAPTER IX
INTERNATIONAL ECONOMIC AND SOCIAL CO-OPERATION

Article 55

With a view to the creation of conditions of stability and well-being which are necessary for peaceful and friendly relations among nations based on respect for the principle of equal rights and self-determination of peoples, the United Nations shall promote:

a. higher standards of living, full employment, and conditions of economic and social progress and development;

b. solutions of international economic, social, health, and related problems; and international cultural and educational co-operation; and

c. universal respect for, and observance of, human rights and fundamental freedoms for all without distinction as to race, sex, language or religion.

Article 56

All Members pledge themselves to take joint and separate action in cooperation with the Organization for the achievement of the purposes set forth in Article 55.

Article 57

1. The various specialized agencies, established by intergovernmental agreement and having wide international responsibilities, as defined in their basic instruments, in economic, social, cultural, educational, health, and related fields, shall be brought into relationship with the United Nations in accordance with the provisions of Article 63.

2. Such agencies thus brought into relationship with the United Nations are hereinafter referred to as specialized agencies.

Article 58

The Organization shall make recommendations for the coordination of the policies and activities of the specialized agencies.

Article 59

The Organization shall, where appropriate, initiate negotiations among the states concerned for the creation of any new specialized agencies required for the accomplishment of the purposes set forth in Article 55.

Article 60

Responsibility for the discharge of the functions of the Organization set forth in this Chapter shall be vested in the General Assembly and, under the authority of the General Assembly, in the Economic and Social Council, which shall have for this purpose the powers set forth in Chapter X.

CHAPTER X
THE ECONOMIC AND SOCIAL COUNCIL

Composition

Article 61

1. The Economic and Social Council shall consist of fifty-four Members of the United Nations elected by the General Assembly.

2. Subject to the provisions of paragraph 3, eighteen members of the Economic and Social Council shall be elected each year for a term of three years. A retiring member shall be eligible for immediate re-election.

3. At the first election after the increase in the membership of the Economic and Social Council from twenty-seven to fifty-four members, in addition to the members elected in place of the nine members whose term of office expires at the end of that year, twenty-seven additional members shall be elected. Of these twenty-seven additional members, the term of office of nine

members so elected shall expire at the end of one year, and of nine other members at the end of two years, in accordance with arrangements made by the General Assembly.

4. Each member of the Economic and Social Council shall have one representative.

Functions and Powers

Article 62

1. The Economic and Social Council may make or initiate studies and reports with respect to international economic, social, cultural, educational, health, and related matters and may make recommendations with respect to any such matters to the General Assembly, to the Members of the United Nations, and to the specialized agencies concerned.

2. It may make recommendations for the purpose of promoting respect for, and observance of, human rights and fundamental freedoms for all.

3. It may prepare draft conventions for submission to the General Assembly, with respect to matters falling within its competence.

4. It may call, in accordance with the rules prescribed by the United Nations, international conferences on matters falling within its competence.

Article 63

1. The Economic and Social Council may enter into agreements with any of the agencies referred to in Article 57, defining the terms on which the agency concerned shall be brought into relationship with the United Nations. Such agreements shall be subject to approval by the General Assembly.

2. It may coordinate the activities of the specialized agencies through consultation with and recommendations to such agencies and through recommendations to the General Assembly and to the Members of the United Nations.

Article 64

1. The Economic and Social Council may take appropriate steps to obtain regular reports from the specialized agencies. It may make arrangements with the Members of the United Nations and with the specialized agencies to obtain reports on the steps taken to give effect to its own recommendations and to recommendations on matters falling within its competence made by the General Assembly.

2. It may communicate its observations on these reports to the General Assembly.

Article 65

The Economic and Social Council may furnish information to the Security Council and shall assist the Security Council upon its request.

Article 66

1. The Economic and Social Council shall perform such functions as fall within its competence in connection with the carrying out of the recommendations of the General Assembly.

2. It may, with the approval of the General Assembly, perform services at the request of Members of the United Nations and at the request of specialized agencies.

3. It shall perform such other functions as are specified elsewhere in the present Charter or as may be assigned to it by the General Assembly.

Article 67

1. Each member of the Economic and Social Council shall have one vote.

2. Decisions of the Economic and Social Council shall be made by a majority of the members present and voting.

Procedure

Article 68

The Economic and Social Council shall set up commissions in economic and social fields and for the promotion of human rights, and such other commissions as may be required for the performance of its functions.

Article 69

The Economic and Social Council shall invite any Member of the United Nations to participate, without vote, in its deliberations on any matter of particular concern to that Member.

Article 70

The Economic and Social Council may make arrangements for representatives of the specialized agencies to participate, without vote, in its deliberations and in those of the commissions established by it, and for its representatives to participate in the deliberations of the specialized agencies.

Article 71

The Economic and Social Council may make suitable arrangements for consultation with non-governmental organizations which are concerned with matters within its competence. Such arrangements may be made with international organizations and, where appropriate, with national organizations after consultation with the Member of the United Nations concerned.

Article 72

1. The Economic and Social Council shall adopt its own rules of procedure, including the method of selecting its President.

2. The Economic and Social Council shall meet as required in accordance with its rules, which shall include provision for the convening of meetings on the request of a majority of its members.

CHAPTER XI
DECLARATION REGARDING NON-SELF-GOVERNING TERRITORIES

Article 73

Members of the United Nations which have or assume responsibilities for the administration of territories whose peoples have not yet attained a full measure of self-government recognize the principle that the interests of the inhabitants of these territories are paramount, and accept as a sacred trust the obligation to promote to the utmost, within the system of international peace and security established by the present Charter, the well-being of the inhabitants of these territories, and, to this end:

a. to ensure, with due respect for the culture of the peoples concerned, their political, economic, social, and educational advancement, their just treatment, and their protection against abuses;

b. to develop self-government, to take due account of the political aspirations of the peoples, and to assist them in the progressive development of their free political institutions, according to the particular circumstances of each territory and its peoples and their varying stages of advancement;

c. to further international peace and security;

d. to promote constructive measures of development, to encourage research, and to cooperate with one another and, when and where appropriate, with specialized international bodies with a view to the practical achievement of the social, economic, and scientific purposes set forth in this Article; and

e. to transmit regularly to the Secretary-General for information purposes, subject to such limitation as security and constitutional considerations may require, statistical and other information of a technical nature relating to economic, social, and educational conditions in the territories for which they are respectively responsible other than those territories to which Chapters XII and XIII apply.

Article 74

Members of the United Nations also agree that their policy in respect of the territories to which this Chapter applies, no less than in respect of their metropolitan areas, must be based on the general principle of good-neighborliness, due account being taken of the interests and well-being of the rest of the world, in social, economic, and commercial matters.

CHAPTER XII
INTERNATIONAL TRUSTEESHIP SYSTEM

Article 75

The United Nations shall establish under its authority an international trusteeship system for the administration and supervision of such territories as may be placed thereunder by subsequent individual agreements. These territories are hereinafter referred to as trust territories.

Article 76

The basic objectives of the trusteeship system, in accordance with the Purposes of the United Nations laid down in Article 1 of the present Charter, shall be:

a. to further international peace and security;

b. to promote the political, economic, social, and educational advancement of the inhabitants of the trust territories, and their progressive development towards self-government or independence as may be appropriate to the particular circumstances of each territory and its peoples and the freely expressed wishes of the peoples concerned, and as may be provided by the terms of each trusteeship agreement;

c. to encourage respect for human rights and for fundamental freedoms for all without distinction as to race, sex, language, or religion, and to encourage recognition of the interdependence of the peoples of the world; and

d. to ensure equal treatment in social, economic, and commercial matters for all Members of the United Nations and their nationals and also equal treatment for the latter in the administration of justice without prejudice to the attainment of the foregoing objectives and subject to the provisions of Article 80.

Article 77

1. The trusteeship system shall apply to such territories in the following categories as may be placed thereunder by means of trusteeship agreements:

a. territories now held under mandate;

b. territories which may be detached from enemy states as a result of the Second World War, and

c. territories voluntarily placed under the system by states responsible for their administration.

2. It will be a matter for subsequent agreement as to which territories in the foregoing categories will be brought under the trusteeship system and upon what terms.

Article 78

The trusteeship system shall not apply to territories which have become Members of the United Nations, relationship among which shall be based on respect for the principle of sovereign equality.

Article 79

The terms of trusteeship for each territory to be placed under the trusteeship system, including any alteration or amendment, shall be agreed upon by the states directly concerned, including the mandatory power in the case of territories held under mandate by a Member of the United Nations, and shall be approved as provided for in Articles 83 and 85.

Article 80

1. Except as may be agreed upon in individual trusteeship agreements, made under Articles 77, 79, and 81, placing each territory under the trusteeship system, and until such agreements have been concluded, nothing in this Chapter shall be construed in or of itself to alter in any manner the rights whatsoever of any states or any peoples or the terms of existing international instruments to which Members of the United Nations may respectively be parties.

2. Paragraph 1 of this Article shall not be interpreted as giving grounds for delay or postponement of the negotiation and conclusion of agreements for placing mandated and other territories under the trusteeship system as provided for in Article 77.

Article 81

The trusteeship agreement shall in each case include the terms under which the trust territory will be administered and designate the authority which will exercise the administration of the trust territory. Such authority, hereinafter called the administering authority, may be one or more states or the Organization itself.

Article 82

There may be designated, in any trusteeship agreement, a strategic area or areas which may include part or all of the trust territory to which the agreement applies, without prejudice to any special agreement or agreements made under Article 43.

Article 83

1. All functions of the United Nations relating to strategic areas, including the approval of the terms of the trusteeship agreements and of their alteration or amendment, shall be exercised by the Security Council.

2. The basic objectives set forth in Article 76 shall be applicable to the people of each strategic area.

3. The Security Council shall, subject to the provisions of the trusteeship agreements and without prejudice to security considerations, avail itself of the assistance of the Trusteeship Council to perform those functions of the United Nations under the trusteeship system relating to political, economic, social and educational matters in the strategic areas.

Article 84

It shall be the duty of the administering authority to ensure that the trust territory shall play its part in the maintenance of international peace and security. To this end the administering authority may make use of volunteer forces, facilities, and assistance from the trust territory in carrying out the obligations towards the Security Council undertaken in this regard by the administering authority, as well as for local defense and the maintenance of law and order within the trust territory.

Article 85

1. The functions of the United Nations with regard to trusteeship agreements for all areas not designated as strategic, including the approval of the terms of the trusteeship agreements and of their alteration or amendment, shall be exercised by the General Assembly.

2. The Trusteeship Council, operating under the authority of the General Assembly, shall assist the General Assembly in carrying out these functions.

CHAPTER XIII
THE TRUSTEESHIP COUNCIL

Composition

Article 86

1. The Trusteeship Council shall consist of the following Members of the United Nations:

a. those Members administering trust territories;

b. such of those Members mentioned by name in Article 23 as are not administering trust territories; and

c. as many other Members elected for three-year terms by the General Assembly as may be necessary to ensure that the total number of members of the Trusteeship Council is equally divided between those Members of the United Nations which administer trust territories and those which do not.

2. Each member of the Trusteeship Council shall designate one specially qualified person to represent it therein.

Functions and Powers

Article 87

The General Assembly and, under its authority, the Trusteeship Council, in carrying out their functions, may:

a. consider reports submitted by the administering authority;

b. accept petitions and examine them in consultation with the administering authority;

c. provide for periodic visits to the respective trust territories at times agreed upon with the administering authority; and

d. take these and other actions in conformity with the terms of the trusteeship agreements.

Article 88

The Trusteeship Council shall formulate a questionnaire on the political, economic, social, and educational advancement of the inhabitants of each trust territory, and the administering authority for each trust territory within the competence of the General Assembly shall make an annual report to the General Assembly upon the basis of such questionnaire.

Voting

Article 89

1. Each member of the Trusteeship Council shall have one vote.

2. Decisions of the Trusteeship Council shall be made by a majority of the members present and voting.

Procedure

Article 90

1. The Trusteeship Council shall adopt its own rules of procedure, including the method of selecting its President.

2. The Trusteeship Council shall meet as required in accordance with its rules, which shall include provision for the convening of meetings on the request of a majority of its members.

Article 91

The Trusteeship Council shall, when appropriate, avail itself of the assistance of the Economic and Social Council and of the specialized agencies in regard to matters with which they are respectively concerned.

CHAPTER XIV
THE INTERNATIONAL COURT OF JUSTICE

Article 92

The International Court of Justice shall be the principal judicial organ of the United Nations. It shall function in accordance with the annexed Statute which is based upon the Statute of the Permanent Court of International Justice and forms an integral part of the present Charter.

Article 93

1. All Members of the United Nations are *ipso facto* parties to the Statute of the International Court of Justice.

2. A state which is not a Member of the United Nations may become a party to the Statute of the International Court of Justice on conditions to be determined in each case by the General Assembly upon the recommendation of the Security Council.

Article 94

1. Each Member of the United Nations undertakes to comply with the decision of the International Court of Justice in any case to which it is a party.

2. If any party to a case fails to perform the obligations incumbent upon it under a judgment rendered by the Court, the other party may have recourse to the Security Council, which may, if it deems necessary, make recommendations or decide upon measures to be taken to give effect to the judgment.

Article 95

Nothing in the present Charter shall prevent Members of the United Nations from entrusting the solution of their differences to other tribunals by virtue of agreements already in existence or which may be concluded in the future.

Article 96

1. The General Assembly or the Security Council may request the International Court of Justice to give an advisory opinion on any legal question.

2. Other organs of the United Nations and specialized agencies, which may at any time be so authorized by the General Assembly, may also request advisory opinions of the Court on legal questions arising within the scope of their activities.

CHAPTER XV
THE SECRETARIAT

Article 97

The Secretariat shall comprise a Secretary-General and such staff as the Organization may require. The Secretary-General shall be appointed by the General Assembly upon the recommendation of the Security Council. He shall be the chief administrative officer of the Organization.

Article 98

The Secretary-General shall act in that capacity in all meetings of the General Assembly, of the Security Council, of the Economic and Social Council, and of the Trusteeship Council, and shall perform such other functions as are entrusted to him by these organs. The Secretary-General shall make an annual report to the General Assembly on the work of the Organization.

Article 99

The Secretary-General may bring to the attention of the Security Council any matter which in his opinion may threaten the maintenance of international peace and security.

Article 100

1. In the performance of their duties the Secretary-General and the staff shall not seek or receive instructions from any government or from any other

authority external to the Organization. They shall refrain from any action which might reflect on their position as international officials responsible only to the Organization.

2. Each Member of the United Nations undertakes to respect the exclusively international character of the responsibilities of the Secretary-General and the staff and not to seek to influence them in the discharge of their responsibilities.

Article 101

1. The staff shall be appointed by the Secretary-General under regulations established by the General Assembly.

2. Appropriate staffs shall be permanently assigned to the Economic and Social Council, the Trusteeship Council, and, as required, to other organs of the United Nations. These staffs shall form a part of the Secretariat.

3. The paramount consideration in the employment of the staff and in the determination of the conditions of service shall be the necessity of securing the highest standards of efficiency, competence, and integrity. Due regard shall be paid to the importance of recruiting the staff on as wide a geographical basis as possible.

CHAPTER XVI
MISCELLANEOUS PROVISIONS

Article 102

1. Every treaty and every international agreement entered into by any Member of the United Nations after the present Charter comes into force shall as soon as possible be registered with the Secretariat and published by it.

2. No party to any such treaty or international agreement which has not been registered in accordance with the provisions of paragraph 1 of this Article may invoke that treaty or agreement before any organ of the United Nations.

Article 103

In the event of a conflict between the obligations of the Members of the United Nations under the present Charter and their obligations under any other international agreement, their obligations under the present Charter shall prevail.

Article 104

The Organization shall enjoy in the territory of each of its Members such legal capacity as may be necessary for the exercise of its functions and the fulfillment of its purposes.

Article 105

1. The Organization shall enjoy in the territory of each of its Members such privileges and immunities as are necessary for the fulfillment of its purposes.

2. Representatives of the Members of the United Nations and officials of the Organization shall similarly enjoy such privileges and immunities as are necessary for the independent exercise of their functions in connection with the Organization.

3. The General Assembly may make recommendations with a view to determining the details of the application of paragraphs 1 and 2 of this Article or may propose conventions to the Members of the United Nations for this purpose.

CHAPTER XVII
TRANSITIONAL SECURITY ARRANGEMENTS

Article 106

Pending the coming into force of such special agreements referred to in Article 43 as in the opinion of the Security Council enable it to begin the exercise of its responsibilities under Article 42, the parties to the Four-Nation Declaration, signed at Moscow October 30, 1943, and France, shall, in accordance with the provisions of paragraph 5 of that Declaration, consult with one another and as occasion requires with other Members of the United Nations with a view to such joint action on behalf of the Organization as may be necessary for the purpose of maintaining international peace and security.

Article 107

Nothing in the present Charter shall invalidate or preclude action, in relation to any state which during the Second World War has been an enemy of any signatory to the present Charter, taken or authorized as a result of that war by the Governments having responsibility for such action.

CHAPTER XVIII
AMENDMENTS

Article 108

Amendments to the present Charter shall come into force for all Members of the United Nations when they have been adopted by a vote of two thirds of the members of the General Assembly and ratified in accordance with their respective constitutional processes by two thirds of the Members of the United Nations, including all the permanent members of the Security Council.

Article 109

1. A General Conference of the Members of the United Nations for the purpose of reviewing the present Charter may be held at a date and place to be fixed by a two-thirds vote of the members of the General Assembly and by a vote of any seven members of the Security Council. Each Member of the United Nations shall have one vote in the conference.

2. Any alteration of the present Charter recommended by a two-thirds vote of the conference shall take effect when ratified in accordance with their respective constitutional processes by two thirds of the Members of the United Nations including all the permanent members of the Security Council.

3. If such a conference has not been held before the tenth annual session of the General Assembly following the coming into force of the present Charter, the proposal to call such a conference shall be placed on the agenda of that session of the General Assembly, and the conference shall be held if so decided by a majority vote of the members of the General Assembly and by a vote of any seven members of the Security Council.

CHAPTER XIX
RATIFICATION AND SIGNATURE

Article 110

1. The present Charter shall be ratified by the signatory states in accordance with their respective constitutional processes.

2. The ratifications shall be deposited with the Government of the United States of America, which shall notify all the signatory states of each deposit as well as the Secretary-General of the Organization when he has been appointed.

3. The present Charter shall come into force upon the deposit of ratifications by the Republic of China, France, the Union of Soviet Socialist Republics, the United Kingdom of Great Britain and Northern Ireland, and the United States of America, and by a majority of the other signatory states. A protocol of the ratifications deposited shall thereupon be drawn up by the Government of the United States of America which shall communicate copies thereof to all the signatory states.

4. The states signatory to the present Charter which ratify it after it has come into force will become original Members of the United Nations on the date of the deposit of their respective ratifications.

Article 111

The present Charter, of which the Chinese, French, Russian, English, and Spanish texts are equally authentic, shall remain deposited in the archives of the Government of the United States of America. Duly certified copies thereof shall be transmitted by that Government to the Governments of the other signatory states.

IN FAITH WHEREOF the representatives of the Governments of the United Nations have signed the present Charter.

DONE at the city of San Francisco the twenty-sixth day of June, one thousand nine hundred and forty-five.

THE INTERNATIONAL BILL OF HUMAN RIGHTS

UNIVERSAL DECLARATION OF HUMAN RIGHTS, G.A. res. 217 A(III), U.N. Doc. A/810 at 71 (1948):

Preamble

Whereas recognition of the inherent dignity and of the equal and inalienable rights of all members of the human family is the foundation of freedom, justice and peace in the world,

Whereas disregard and contempt for human rights have resulted in barbarous acts which have outraged the conscience of mankind, and the advent of a world in which human beings shall enjoy freedom of speech and belief and freedom from fear and want has been proclaimed as the highest aspiration of the common people,

Whereas it is essential, if man is not to be compelled to have recourse, as a last resort, to rebellion against tyranny and oppression, that human rights should be protected by the rule of law,

Whereas it is essential to promote the development of friendly relations between nations,

Whereas the peoples of the United Nations have in the Charter reaffirmed their faith in fundamental human rights, in the dignity and worth of the human person and in the equal rights of men and women and have determined to promote social progress and better standards of life in larger freedom,

Whereas Member States have pledged themselves to achieve, in co-operation with the United Nations, the promotion of universal respect for and observance of human rights and fundamental freedoms,

Whereas a common understanding of these rights and freedoms is of the greatest importance for the full realization of this pledge,

Now, therefore,

The General Assembly

Proclaims this Universal Declaration of Human Rights as a common standard of achievement for all peoples and all nations, to the end that every individual and every organ of society, keeping this Declaration constantly in mind, shall strive by teaching and education to promote respect for these rights and freedoms and by progressive measures, national and international, to secure their universal and effective recognition and observance, both among the peoples of Member States themselves and among the peoples of territories under their jurisdiction.

Article 1

All human beings are born free and equal in dignity and rights. They are endowed with reason and conscience and should act towards one another in a spirit of brotherhood.

Article 2

Everyone is entitled to all the rights and freedoms set forth in this Declaration, without distinction of any kind, such as race, colour, sex, language, religion, political or other opinion, national or social origin, property, birth or other status.

Furthermore, no distinction shall be made on the basis of the political, jurisdictional or international status of the country or territory to which a person belongs, whether it be independent, trust, non-self-governing or under any other limitation of sovereignty.

Article 3

Everyone has the right to life, liberty and the security of person.

Article 4

No one shall be held in slavery or servitude; slavery and the slave trade shall be prohibited in all their forms.

Article 5

No one shall be subjected to torture or to cruel, inhuman or degrading treatment or punishment.

Article 6

Everyone has the right to recognition everywhere as a person before the law.

Article 7

All are equal before the law and are entitled without any discrimination to equal protection of the law. All are entitled to equal protection against any discrimination in violation of this Declaration and against any incitement to such discrimination.

Article 8

Everyone has the right to an effective remedy by the competent national tribunals for acts violating the fundamental rights granted him by the constitution or by law.

Article 9

No one shall be subjected to arbitrary arrest, detention or exile.

Article 10

Everyone is entitled in full equality to a fair and public hearing by an independent and impartial tribunal, in the determination of his rights and obligations and of any criminal charge against him.

Article 11

1. Everyone charged with a penal offence has the right to be presumed innocent until proved guilty according to law in a public trial at which he has had all the guarantees necessary for his defence.

2. No one shall be held guilty of any penal offence on account of any act or omission which did not constitute a penal offence, under national or international law, at the time when it was committed. Nor shall a heavier penalty be imposed than the one that was applicable at the time the penal offence was committed.

Article 12

No one shall be subjected to arbitrary interference with his privacy, family, home or correspondence, nor to attacks upon his honour and reputation. Everyone has the right to the protection of the law against such interference or attacks.

Article 13

1. Everyone has the right to freedom of movement and residence within the borders of each State.

2. Everyone has the right to leave any country, including his own, and to return to his country.

Article 14

1. Everyone has the right to seek and to enjoy in other countries asylum from persecution.

2. This right may not be invoked in the case of prosecutions genuinely arising from non-political crimes or from acts contrary to the purposes and principles of the United Nations.

Article 15

1. Everyone has the right to a nationality.

2. No one shall be arbitrarily deprived of his nationality nor denied the right to change his nationality.

Article 16

1. Men and women of full age, without any limitation due to race, nationality or religion, have the right to marry and to found a family. They are entitled to equal rights as to marriage, during marriage and at its dissolution.

2. Marriage shall be entered into only with the free and full consent of the intending spouses.

3. The family is the natural and fundamental group unit of society and is entitled to protection by society and the State.

Article 17

1. Everyone has the right to own property alone as well as in association with others.

2. No one shall be arbitrarily deprived of his property.

Article 18

Everyone has the right to freedom of thought, conscience and religion; this right includes freedom to change his religion or belief, and freedom, either alone or in community with others and in public or private, to manifest his religion or belief in teaching, practice, worship and observance.

Article 19

Everyone has the right to freedom of opinion and expression; this right includes freedom to hold opinions without interference and to seek, receive and impart information and ideas through any media and regardless of frontiers.

Article 20

1. Everyone has the right to freedom of peaceful assembly and association.

2. No one may be compelled to belong to an association.

Article 21

1. Everyone has the right to take part in the government of his country, directly or through freely chosen representatives.

2. Everyone has the right of equal access to public service in his country.

3. The will of the people shall be the basis of the authority of government; this will shall be expressed in periodic and genuine elections which shall be by universal and equal suffrage and shall be held by secret vote or by equivalent free voting procedures.

Article 22

Everyone, as a member of society, has the right to social security and is entitled to realization, through national effort and international co-operation and in accordance with the organization and resources of each State, of the economic, social and cultural rights indispensable for his dignity and the free development of his personality.

Article 23

1. Everyone has the right to work, to free choice of employment, to just and favourable conditions of work and to protection against unemployment.

2. Everyone, without any discrimination, has the right to equal pay for equal work.

3. Everyone who works has the right to just and favourable remuneration ensuring for himself and his family an existence worthy of human dignity, and supplemented, if necessary, by other means of social protection.

4. Everyone has the right to form and to join trade unions for the protection of his interests.

Article 24

Everyone has the right to rest and leisure, including reasonable limitation of working hours and periodic holidays with pay.

Article 25

1. Everyone has the right to a standard of living adequate for the health and well-being of himself and of his family, including food, clothing, housing and medical care and necessary social services, and the right to security in the event of unemployment, sickness, disability, widowhood, old age or other lack of livelihood in circumstances beyond his control.

2. Motherhood and childhood are entitled to special care and assistance. All children, whether born in or out of wedlock, shall enjoy the same social protection.

Article 26

1. Everyone has the right to education. Education shall be free, at least in the elementary and fundamental stages. Elementary education shall be compulsory. Technical and professional education shall be made generally available and higher education shall be equally accessible to all on the basis of merit.

2. Education shall be directed to the full development of the human personality and to the strengthening of respect for human rights and fundamental freedoms. It shall promote understanding, tolerance and friendship among all nations, racial or religious groups, and shall further the activities of the United Nations for the maintenance of peace.

3. Parents have a prior right to choose the kind of education that shall be given to their children.

Article 27

1. Everyone has the right freely to participate in the cultural life of the community, to enjoy the arts and to share in scientific advancement and its benefits.

2. Everyone has the right to the protection of the moral and material interests resulting from any scientific, literary or artistic production of which he is the author.

Article 28

Everyone is entitled to a social and international order in which the rights and freedoms set forth is this Declaration can be fully realized.

Article 29

1. Everyone has duties to the community in which alone the free and full development of his personality is possible.

2. In the exercise of his rights and freedoms, everyone shall be subject only to such limitations as are determined by law solely for the purpose of

securing due recognition and respect for the rights and freedoms of others and of meeting the just requirements of morality, public order and the general welfare in a democratic society.

3. These rights and freedoms may in no case be exercised contrary to the purposes and principles of the United Nations.

Article 30

Nothing in this Declaration may be interpreted as implying for any State, group or person any right to engage in any activity or to perform any act aimed at the destruction of any of the rights and freedoms set forth herein.

INTERNATIONAL COVENANT ON ECONOMIC, SOCIAL AND CULTURAL RIGHTS, G.A. res. 2200A (XXI), 21 U.N. GAOR Supp. (No. 16) at 49, U.N. Doc. A/6316 (1966), 993 U.N.T.S. 3, *entered into force* January 3, 1976:

Preamble

The States Parties to the present Covenant,

Considering that, in accordance with the principles proclaimed in the Charter of the United Nations, recognition of the inherent dignity and of the equal and inalienable rights of all the members of the human family is the foundation of freedom, justice and peace in the world,

Recognizing that these rights derive from the inherent dignity of the human person,

Recognizing that, in accordance with the Universal Declaration of Human Rights, the ideal of free human beings enjoying freedom from fear and want can only be achieved if conditions are created whereby everyone may enjoy his economic, social and cultural rights, as well as his civil and political rights,

Considering the obligation of States under the Charter of the United Nations to promote universal respect for, and observance of, human rights and freedoms,

Realizing that the individual, having duties to other individuals and to the community to which he belongs, is under a responsibility to strive for the promotion and observance of the rights recognized in the present Covenant,

Agree upon the following articles:

PART I

Article 1

1. All peoples have the right of self-determination. By virtue of that right they freely determine their political status and freely pursue their economic, social and cultural development.

2. All peoples may, for their own ends, freely dispose of their natural wealth and resources without prejudice to any obligations arising out of international economic co-operation, based upon the principle of mutual benefit, and international law. In no case may a people be deprived of its own means of subsistence.

3. The States Parties to the present Covenant, including those having responsibility for the administration of Non-Self-Governing and Trust Territories, shall promote the realization of the right of self-determination, and shall respect that right, in conformity with the provisions of the Charter of the United Nations.

PART II

Article 2

1. Each State Party to the present Covenant undertakes to take steps, individually and through international assistance and co-operation, especially economic and technical, to the maximum of its available resources, with a view to achieving progressively the full realization of the rights recognized in the present Covenant by all appropriate means, including particularly the adoption of legislative measures.

2. The States Parties to the present Covenant undertake to guarantee that the rights enunciated in the present Covenant will be exercised without discrimination of any kind as to race, colour, sex, language, religion, political or other opinion, national or social origin, property, birth or other status.

3. Developing countries, with due regard to human rights and their national economy, may determine to what extent they would guarantee the economic rights recognized in the present Covenant to non-nationals.

Article 3

The States Parties to the present Covenant undertake to ensure the equal right of men and women to the enjoyment of all economic, social and cultural rights set forth in the present Covenant.

Article 4

The States Parties to the present Covenant recognize that, in the enjoyment of those rights provided by the State in conformity with the present Covenant, the State may subject such rights only to such limitations as are determined by law only in so far as this may be compatible with the nature of these rights and solely for the purpose of promoting the general welfare in a democratic society.

Article 5

1. Nothing in the present Covenant may be interpreted as implying for any State, group or person any right to engage in any activity or to perform any act aimed at the destruction of any of the rights or freedoms recognized herein,

or at their limitation to a greater extent than is provided for in the present Covenant.

2. No restriction upon or derogation from any of the fundamental human rights recognized or existing in any country in virtue of law, conventions, regulations or custom shall be admitted on the pretext that the present Covenant does not recognize such rights or that it recognizes them to a lesser extent.

PART III

Article 6

1. The States Parties to the present Covenant recognize the right to work, which includes the right of everyone to the opportunity to gain his living by work which he freely chooses or accepts, and will take appropriate steps to safeguard this right.

2. The steps to be taken by a State Party to the present Covenant to achieve the full realization of this right shall include technical and vocational guidance and training programmes, policies and techniques to achieve steady economic, social and cultural development and full and productive employment under conditions safeguarding fundamental political and economic freedoms to the individual.

Article 7

The States Parties to the present Covenant recognize the right of everyone to the enjoyment of just and favourable conditions of work which ensure, in particular:

(a) Remuneration which provides all workers, as a minimum, with:

(i) Fair wages and equal remuneration for work of equal value without distinction of any kind, in particular women being guaranteed conditions of work not inferior to those enjoyed by men, with equal pay for equal work;

(ii) A decent living for themselves and their families in accordance with the provisions of the present Covenant;

(b) Safe and healthy working conditions;

(c) Equal opportunity for everyone to be promoted in his employment to an appropriate higher level, subject to no considerations other than those of seniority and competence;

(d) Rest, leisure and reasonable limitation of working hours and periodic holidays with pay, as well as remuneration for public holidays.

Article 8

1. The States Parties to the present Covenant undertake to ensure:

(a) The right of everyone to form trade unions and join the trade union of his choice, subject only to the rules of the organization concerned, for the promotion and protection of his economic and social interests. No restrictions may be placed on the exercise of this right other than those prescribed by law and which are necessary in a democratic society in the interests of national security or public order or for the protection of the rights and freedoms of others;

(b) The right of trade unions to establish national federations or confederations and the right of the latter to form or join international trade-union organizations;

(c) The right of trade unions to function freely subject to no limitations other than those prescribed by law and which are necessary in a democratic society in the interests of national security or public order or for the protection of the rights and freedoms of others;

(d) The right to strike, provided that it is exercised in conformity with the laws of the particular country.

2. This article shall not prevent the imposition of lawful restrictions on the exercise of these rights by members of the armed forces or of the police or of the administration of the State.

3. Nothing in this article shall authorize States Parties to the International Labour Organisation Convention of 1948 concerning Freedom of Association and Protection of the Right to Organise to take legislative measures which would prejudice, or apply the law in such a manner as would prejudice, the guarantees provided for in that Convention.

Article 9

The States Parties to the present Covenant recognize the right of everyone to social security, including social insurance.

Article 10

The States Parties to the present Covenant recognize that:

1. The widest possible protection and assistance should be accorded to the family, which is the natural and fundamental group unit of society, particularly for its establishment and while it is responsible for the care and education of dependent children. Marriage must be entered into with the free consent of the intending spouses.

2. Special protection should be accorded to mothers during a reasonable period before and after childbirth. During such period working mothers should be accorded paid leave or leave with adequate social security benefits.

3. Special measures of protection and assistance should be taken on behalf of all children and young persons without any discrimination for reasons of parentage or other conditions. Children and young persons should be protected from economic and social exploitation. Their employment in work harmful to their morals or health or dangerous to life or likely to hamper their normal development should be punishable by law. States should also set age limits below which the paid employment of child labour should be prohibited and punishable by law.

Article 11

1. The States Parties to the present Covenant recognize the right of everyone to an adequate standard of living for himself and his family, including adequate food, clothing and housing, and to the continuous improvement of living conditions. The States Parties will take appropriate steps to ensure the realization of this right, recognizing to this effect the essential importance of international co-operation based on free consent.

2. The States Parties to the present Covenant, recognizing the fundamental right of everyone to be free from hunger, shall take, individually and through international co-operation, the measures, including specific programmes, which are needed:

(a) To improve methods of production, conservation and distribution of food by making full use of technical and scientific knowledge, by disseminating knowledge of the principles of nutrition and by developing or reforming agrarian systems in such a way as to achieve the most efficient development and utilization of natural resources;

(b) Taking into account the problems of both food-importing and food-exporting countries, to ensure an equitable distribution of world food supplies in relation to need.

Article 12

1. The States Parties to the present Covenant recognize the right of everyone to the enjoyment of the highest attainable standard of physical and mental health.

2. The steps to be taken by the States Parties to the present Covenant to achieve the full realization of this right shall include those necessary for:

(a) The provision for the reduction of the stillbirth-rate and of infant mortality and for the healthy development of the child;

(b) The improvement of all aspects of environmental and industrial hygiene;

(c) The prevention, treatment and control of epidemic, endemic, occupational and other diseases;

(d) The creation of conditions which would assure to all medical service and medical attention in the event of sickness.

Article 13

1. The States Parties to the present Covenant recognize the right of everyone to education. They agree that education shall be directed to the full development of the human personality and the sense of its dignity, and shall strengthen the respect for human rights and fundamental freedoms. They further agree that education shall enable all persons to participate effectively in a free society, promote understanding, tolerance and friendship among all nations and all racial, ethnic or religious groups, and further the activities of the United Nations for the maintenance of peace.

2. The States Parties to the present Covenant recognize that, with a view to achieving the full realization of this right:

(a) Primary education shall be compulsory and available free to all;

(b) Secondary education in its different forms, including technical and vocational secondary education, shall be made generally available and accessible to all by every appropriate means, and in particular by the progressive introduction of free education;

(c) Higher education shall be made equally accessible to all, on the basis of capacity, by every appropriate means, and in particular by the progressive introduction of free education;

(d) Fundamental education shall be encouraged or intensified as far as possible for those persons who have not received or completed the whole period of their primary education;

(e) The development of a system of schools at all levels shall be actively pursued, an adequate fellowship system shall be established, and the material conditions of teaching staff shall be continuously improved.

3. The States Parties to the present Covenant undertake to have respect for the liberty of parents and, when applicable, legal guardians to choose for their children schools, other than those established by the public authorities, which conform to such minimum educational standards as may be laid down or approved by the State and to ensure the religious and moral education of their children in conformity with their own convictions.

4. No part of this article shall be construed so as to interfere with the liberty of individuals and bodies to establish and direct educational institutions, subject always to the observance of the principles set forth in paragraph 1 of this article and to the requirement that the education given in such institutions shall conform to such minimum standards as may be laid down by the State.

Article 14

Each State Party to the present Covenant which, at the time of becoming a Party, has not been able to secure in its metropolitan territory or other territories under its jurisdiction compulsory primary education, free of charge, undertakes, within two years, to work out and adopt a detailed plan of action for the progressive implementation, within a reasonable number of years, to be fixed in the plan, of the principle of compulsory education free of charge for all.

Article 15

1. The States Parties to the present Covenant recognize the right of everyone:

(a) To take part in cultural life;

(b) To enjoy the benefits of scientific progress and its applications;

(c) To benefit from the protection of the moral and material interests resulting from any scientific, literary or artistic production of which he is the author.

2. The steps to be taken by the States Parties to the present Covenant to achieve the full realization of this right shall include those necessary for the conservation, the development and the diffusion of science and culture.

3. The States Parties to the present Covenant undertake to respect the freedom indispensable for scientific research and creative activity.

4. The States Parties to the present Covenant recognize the benefits to be derived from the encouragement and development of international contacts and co-operation in the scientific and cultural fields.

PART IV

Article 16

1. The States Parties to the present Covenant undertake to submit in conformity with this part of the Covenant reports on the measures which they have adopted and the progress made in achieving the observance of the rights recognized herein.

2. (a) All reports shall be submitted to the Secretary-General of the United Nations, who shall transmit copies to the Economic and Social Council for consideration in accordance with the provisions of the present Covenant;

(b) The Secretary-General of the United Nations shall also transmit to the specialized agencies copies of the reports, or any relevant parts therefrom, from States Parties to the present Covenant which are also members of these specialized agencies in so far as these reports, or parts therefrom, relate to any matters which fall within the responsibilities of the said agencies in accordance with their constitutional instruments.

Article 17

1. The States Parties to the present Covenant shall furnish their reports in stages, in accordance with a programme to be established by the Economic and Social Council within one year of the entry into force of the present Covenant after consultation with the States Parties and the specialized agencies concerned.

2. Reports may indicate factors and difficulties affecting the degree of fulfillment of obligations under the present Covenant.

3. Where relevant information has previously been furnished to the United Nations or to any specialized agency by any State Party to the present Covenant, it will not be necessary to reproduce that information, but a precise reference to the information so furnished will suffice.

Article 18

Pursuant to its responsibilities under the Charter of the United Nations in the field of human rights and fundamental freedoms, the Economic and Social Council may make arrangements with the specialized agencies in respect of their reporting to it on the progress made in achieving the observance of the provisions of the present Covenant falling within the scope of their activities. These reports may include particulars of decisions and recommendations on such implementation adopted by their competent organs.

Article 19

The Economic and Social Council may transmit to the Commission on Human Rights for study and general recommendation or, as appropriate, for information the reports concerning human rights submitted by States in accordance with articles 16 and 17, and those concerning human rights submitted by the specialized agencies in accordance with article 18.

Article 20

The States Parties to the present Covenant and the specialized agencies concerned may submit comments to the Economic and Social Council on any general recommendation under article 19 or reference to such general recommendation in any report of the Commission on Human Rights or any documentation referred to therein.

Article 21

The Economic and Social Council may submit from time to time to the General Assembly reports with recommendations of a general nature and a summary of the information received from the States Parties to the present Covenant and the specialized agencies on the measures taken and the progress made in achieving general observance of the rights recognized in the present Covenant.

Article 22

The Economic and Social Council may bring to the attention of other organs of the United Nations, their subsidiary organs and specialized agencies concerned with furnishing technical assistance any matters arising out of the reports referred to in this part of the present Covenant which may assist such bodies in deciding, each within its field of competence, on the advisability of international measures likely to contribute to the effective progressive implementation of the present Covenant.

Article 23

The States Parties to the present Covenant agree that international action for the achievement of the rights recognized in the present Covenant includes such methods as the conclusion of conventions, the adoption of recommendations, the furnishing of technical assistance and the holding of regional meetings and technical meetings for the purpose of consultation and study organized in conjunction with the Governments concerned.

Article 24

Nothing in the present Covenant shall be interpreted as impairing the provisions of the Charter of the United Nations and of the constitutions of the specialized agencies which define the respective responsibilities of the various organs of the United Nations and of the specialized agencies in regard to the matters dealt with in the present Covenant.

Article 25

Nothing in the present Covenant shall be interpreted as impairing the inherent right of all peoples to enjoy and utilize fully and freely their natural wealth and resources.

PART V

Article 26

1. The present Covenant is open for signature by any State Member of the United Nations or member of any of its specialized agencies, by any State Party to the Statute of the International Court of Justice, and by any other State which has been invited by the General Assembly of the United Nations to become a party to the present Covenant.

2. The present Covenant is subject to ratification. Instruments of ratification shall be deposited with the Secretary-General of the United Nations.

3. The present Covenant shall be open to accession by any State referred to in paragraph 1 of this article.

4. Accession shall be effected by the deposit of an instrument of accession with the Secretary-General of the United Nations.

5. The Secretary-General of the United Nations shall inform all States which have signed the present Covenant or acceded to it of the deposit of each instrument of ratification or accession.

Article 27

1. The present Covenant shall enter into force three months after the date of the deposit with the Secretary-General of the United Nations of the thirty-fifth instrument of ratification or instrument of accession.

2. For each State ratifying the present Covenant or acceding to it after the deposit of the thirty-fifth instrument of ratification or instrument of accession, the present Covenant shall enter into force three months after the date of the deposit of its own instrument of ratification or instrument of accession.

Article 28

The provisions of the present Covenant shall extend to all parts of federal States without any limitations or exceptions.

Article 29

1. Any State Party to the present Covenant may propose an amendment and file it with the Secretary-General of the United Nations. The Secretary-General shall thereupon communicate any proposed amendments to the States Parties to the present Covenant with a request that they notify him whether they favour a conference of States Parties for the purpose of considering and voting upon the proposals. In the event that at least one third of the States Parties favours such a conference, the Secretary-General shall convene the conference under the auspices of the United Nations. Any amendment adopted by a majority of the States Parties present and voting at the conference shall be submitted to the General Assembly of the United Nations for approval.

2. Amendments shall come into force when they have been approved by the General Assembly of the United Nations and accepted by a two-thirds majority of the States Parties to the present Covenant in accordance with their respective constitutional processes.

3. When amendments come into force they shall be binding on those States Parties which have accepted them, other States Parties still being bound by the provisions of the present Covenant and any earlier amendment which they have accepted.

Article 30

Irrespective of the notifications made under article 26, paragraph 5, the Secretary-General of the United Nations shall inform all States referred to in paragraph 1 of the same article of the following particulars:

(a) Signatures, ratifications and accessions under article 26;

(b) The date of the entry into force of the present Covenant under article 27 and the date of the entry into force of any amendments under article 29.

Article 31

1. The present Covenant, of which the Chinese, English, French, Russian and Spanish texts are equally authentic, shall be deposited in the archives of the United Nations.

2. The Secretary-General of the United Nations shall transmit certified copies of the present Covenant to all States referred to in article 26.

INTERNATIONAL COVENANT ON CIVIL AND POLITICAL RIGHTS, G.A. res. 2200A (XXI), 21 U.N. GAOR Supp. (No. 16) at 52, U.N. Doc. A/6316 (1966), 999 U.N.T.S. 171, *entered into force* March 23, 1976:

Preamble

The States Parties to the present Covenant,

Considering that, in accordance with the principles proclaimed in the Charter of the United Nations, recognition of the inherent dignity and of the equal and inalienable rights of all members of the human family is the foundation of freedom, justice and peace in the world,

Recognizing that these rights derive from the inherent dignity of the human person,

Recognizing that, in accordance with the Universal Declaration of Human Rights, the ideal of free human beings enjoying civil and political freedom and freedom from fear and want can only be achieved if conditions are created whereby everyone may enjoy his civil and political rights, as well as his economic, social and cultural rights.

Considering the obligation of States under the Charter of the United Nations to promote universal respect for, and observance of, human rights and freedoms,

Realizing that the individual, having duties to other individuals and to the community to which he belongs, is under a responsibility to strive for the promotion and observance of the rights recognized in the present Covenant,

Agree upon the following articles:

PART I

Article 1

1. All peoples have the right of self-determination. By virtue of that right they freely determine their political status and freely pursue their economic, social and cultural development.

2. All peoples may, for their own ends, freely dispose of their natural wealth and resources without prejudice to any obligations arising out of international economic co-operation, based upon the principle of mutual benefit, and international law. In no case may a people be deprived of its own means of subsistence.

3. The States Parties to the present Covenant, including those having responsibility for the administration of Non-Self-Governing and Trust Territories, shall promote the realization of the right of self-determination, and shall respect that right, in conformity with the provisions of the Charter of the United Nations.

PART II

Article 2

1. Each State Party to the present Covenant undertakes to respect and to ensure to all individuals within its territory and subject to its jurisdiction the rights recognized in the present Covenant, without distinction of any kind, such as race, colour, sex, language, religion, political or other opinion, national or social origin, property, birth or other status.

2. Where not already provided for by existing legislative or other measures, each State Party to the present Covenant undertakes to take the necessary steps, in accordance with its constitutional processes and with the provisions of the present Covenant, to adopt such legislative or other measures as may be necessary to give effect to the rights recognized in the present Covenant.

3. Each State Party to the present Covenant undertakes:

(a) To ensure that any person whose rights or freedoms as herein recognized are violated shall have an effective remedy, notwithstanding that the violation has been committed by persons acting in an official capacity;

(b) To ensure that any person claiming such a remedy shall have his right thereto determined by competent judicial, administrative or legislative authorities, or by any other competent authority provided for by the legal system of the State, and to develop the possibilities of judicial remedy;

(c) To ensure that the competent authorities shall enforce such remedies when granted.

Article 3

The States Parties to the present Covenant undertake to ensure the equal right of men and women to the enjoyment of all civil and political rights set forth in the present Covenant.

Article 4

1. In time of public emergency which threatens the life of the nation and the existence of which is officially proclaimed, the States Parties to the present Covenant may take measures derogating from their obligations under the present Covenant to the extent strictly required by the exigencies of the situation, provided that such measures are not inconsistent with their other obligations under international law and do not involve discrimination solely on the ground of race, colour, sex, language, religion or social origin.

2. No derogation from articles 6, 7, 8 (paragraphs 1 and 2), 11, 15, 16 and 18 may be made under this provision.

3. Any State Party to the present Covenant availing itself of the right of derogation shall immediately inform the other States Parties to the present Covenant, through the intermediary of the Secretary-General of the United Nations, of the provisions from which it has derogated and of the reasons by which it was actuated. A further communication shall be made, through the same intermediary, on the date on which it terminates such derogation.

Article 5

1. Nothing in the present Covenant may be interpreted as implying for any State, group or person any right to engage in any activity or perform any act aimed at the destruction of any of the rights and freedoms recognized herein

or at their limitation to a greater extent than is provided for in the present Covenant.

2. There shall be no restriction upon or derogation from any of the fundamental human rights recognized or existing in any State Party to the present Covenant pursuant to law, conventions, regulations or custom on the pretext that the present Covenant does not recognize such rights or that it recognizes them to a lesser extent.

PART III

Article 6

1. Every human being has the inherent right to life. This right shall be protected by law. No one shall be arbitrarily deprived of his life.

2. In countries which have not abolished the death penalty, sentence of death may be imposed only for the most serious crimes in accordance with the law in force at the time of the commission of the crime and not contrary to the provisions of the present Covenant and to the Convention on the Prevention and Punishment of the Crime of Genocide. This penalty can only be carried out pursuant to a final judgement rendered by a competent court.

3. When deprivation of life constitutes the crime of genocide, it is understood that nothing in this article shall authorize any State Party to the present Covenant to derogate in any way from any obligation assumed under the provisions of the Convention on the Prevention and Punishment of the Crime of Genocide.

4. Anyone sentenced to death shall have the right to seek pardon or commutation of the sentence. Amnesty, pardon or commutation of the sentence of death may be granted in all cases.

5. Sentence of death shall not be imposed for crimes committed by persons below eighteen years of age and shall not be carried out on pregnant women.

6. Nothing in this article shall be invoked to delay or to prevent the abolition of capital punishment by any State Party to the present Covenant.

Article 7

No one shall be subjected to torture or to cruel, inhuman or degrading treatment or punishment. In particular, no one shall be subjected without his free consent to medical or scientific experimentation.

Article 8

1. No one shall be held in slavery; slavery and the slave-trade in all their forms shall be prohibited.

2. No one shall be held in servitude.

3. *(a)* No one shall be required to perform forced or compulsory labour;

(b) Paragraph 3*(a)* shall not be held to preclude, in countries where imprisonment with hard labour may be imposed as a punishment for a crime, the performance of hard labour in pursuance of a sentence to such punishment by a competent court;

(c) For the purpose of this paragraph the term "forced or compulsory labour" shall not include:

(i) Any work or service, not referred to in subparagraph *(b)*, normally required of a person who is under detention in consequence of a lawful order of a court, or of a person during conditional release from such detention;

(ii) Any service of a military character and, in countries where conscientious objection is recognized, any national service required by law of conscientious objectors;

(iii) Any service exacted in cases of emergency or calamity threatening the life or well-being of the community;

(iv) Any work or service which forms part of normal civil obligations.

Article 9

1. Everyone has the right to liberty and security of person. No one shall be subjected to arbitrary arrest or detention. No one shall be deprived of his liberty except on such grounds and in accordance with such procedure as are established by law.

2. Anyone who is arrested shall be informed, at the time of arrest, of the reasons for his arrest and shall be promptly informed of any changes against him.

3. Anyone arrested or detained on a criminal charge shall be brought promptly before a judge or other officer authorized by law to exercise judicial power and shall be entitled to trial within a reasonable time or to release. It shall not be the general rule that persons awaiting trial shall be detained in custody, but release may be subject to guarantees to appear for trial, at any other stage of the judicial proceedings, and, should occasion arise, for execution of the judgement.

4. Anyone who is deprived of his liberty by arrest or detention shall be entitled to take proceedings before a court, in order that that court may decide without delay on the lawfulness of his detention and order his release if the detention is not lawful.

5. Anyone who has been the victim of unlawful arrest or detention shall have an enforceable right to compensation.

Article 10

1. All persons deprived of their liberty shall be treated with humanity and with respect for the inherent dignity of the human person.

2. *(a)* Accused persons shall, save in exceptional circumstances, be segregated from convicted persons and shall be subject to separate treatment appropriate to their status as unconvicted persons;

(b) Accused juvenile persons shall be separated from adults and brought as speedily as possible for adjudication.

3. The penitentiary system shall comprise treatment of prisoners the essential aim of which shall be their reformation and social rehabilitation. Juvenile offenders shall be segregated from adults and be accorded treatment appropriate to their age and legal status.

Article 11

No one shall be imprisoned merely on the ground of inability to fulfill a contractual obligation.

Article 12

1. Everyone lawfully within the territory of a State shall, within that territory, have the right to liberty of movement and freedom to choose his residence.

2. Everyone shall be free to leave any country, including his own.

3. The above-mentioned rights shall not be subject to any restrictions except those which are provided by law, are necessary to protect national security, public order (*ordre public*), public health or morals or the rights and freedoms of others, and are consistent with the other rights recognized in the present Covenant.

4. No one shall be arbitrarily deprived of the right to enter his own country.

Article 13

An alien lawfully in the territory of a State Party to the present Covenant may be expelled therefrom only in pursuance of a decision reached in accordance with law and shall, except where compelling reasons of national security otherwise require, be allowed to submit the reasons against his expulsion and to have his case reviewed by, and be represented for the purpose before, the competent authority or a person or persons especially designated by the competent authority.

Article 14

1. All persons shall be equal before the courts and tribunals. In the determination of any criminal charge against him, or of his rights and obligations in a suit at law, everyone shall be entitled to a fair and public hearing by a competent, independent and impartial tribunal established by law. The Press and the public may be excluded from all or part of a trial for reasons of morals, public order (*ordre public*) or national security in a democratic society, or when the interest of the private lives of the parties so requires, or to the extent

strictly necessary in the opinion of the court in special circumstances where publicity would prejudice the interests of justice; but any judgement rendered in a criminal case or in a suit at law shall be made public except where the interest of juvenile persons otherwise requires or the proceedings concern matrimonial disputes or the guardianship of children.

2. Everyone charged with a criminal offence shall have the right to be presumed innocent until proved guilty according to law.

3. In the determination of any criminal charge against him, everyone shall be entitled to the following minimum guarantees, in full equality:

(a) To be informed promptly and in detail in a language which he understands of the nature and cause of the charge against him;

(b) To have adequate time and facilities for the preparation of his defence and to communicate with counsel of his own choosing;

(c) To be tried without undue delay;

(d) To be tried in his presence, and to defend himself in person or through legal assistance of his own choosing; to be informed, if he does not have legal assistance, of this right; and to have legal assistance assigned to him, in any case where the interests of justice so require, and without payment by him in any such case if he does not have sufficient means to pay for it;

(e) To examine, or have examined, the witnesses against him and to obtain the attendance and examination of witnesses on his behalf under the same conditions as witnesses against him;

(f) To have the free assistance of an interpreter if he cannot understand or speak the language used in court;

(g) Not to be compelled to testify against himself or to confess guilt.

4. In the case of juvenile persons, the procedure shall be such as will take account of their age and the desirability of promoting their rehabilitation.

5. Everyone convicted of a crime shall have the right to his conviction and sentence being reviewed by a higher tribunal according to law.

6. When a person has by a final decision been convicted of a criminal offence and when subsequently his conviction has been reversed or he has been pardoned on the ground that a new or newly discovered fact shows conclusively that there has been a miscarriage of justice, the person who has suffered punishment as a result of such conviction shall be compensated according to law, unless it is proved that the non-disclosure of the unknown fact in time is wholly or partly attributable to him.

7. No one shall be liable to be tried or punished again for an offence for which he has already been finally convicted or acquitted in accordance with the law and penal procedure of each country.

Article 15

1. No one shall be held guilty of any criminal offence on account of any act or omission which did not constitute a criminal offence, under national or international law, at the time when it was committed. Nor shall a heavier penalty be imposed than the one that was applicable at the time when the criminal offence was committed. If, subsequent to the commission of the offence, provision is made by law for the imposition of a lighter penalty, the offender shall benefit thereby.

2. Nothing in this article shall prejudice the trial and punishment of any person for any act or omission which, at the time when it was committed, was criminal according to the general principles of law recognized by the community of nations.

Article 16

Everyone shall have the right to recognition everywhere as a person before the law.

Article 17

1. No one shall be subjected to arbitrary or unlawful interference with his privacy, family, home or correspondence, nor to unlawful attacks on his honour and reputation.

2. Everyone has the right to the protection of the law against such interference or attacks.

Article 18

1. Everyone shall have the right to freedom of thought, conscience and religion. This right shall include freedom to have or to adopt a religion or belief of his choice, and freedom, either individually or in community with others and in public or private, to manifest his religion or belief in worship, observance, practice and teaching.

2. No one shall be subject to coercion which would impair his freedom to have or to adopt a religion or belief of his choice.

3. Freedom to manifest one's religion or beliefs may be subject only to such limitations as are prescribed by law and are necessary to protect public safety, order, health, or morals or the fundamental rights and freedoms of others.

4. The States Parties to the present Covenant undertake to have respect for the liberty of parents and, when applicable, legal guardians to ensure the religious and moral education of their children in conformity with their own convictions.

Article 19

1. Everyone shall have the right to hold opinions without interference.

2. Everyone shall have the right to freedom of expression; this right shall include freedom to seek, receive and impart information and ideas of all kinds, regardless of frontiers, either orally, in writing or in print, in the form of art, or through any other media of his choice.

3. The exercise of the rights provided for in paragraph 2 of this article carries with it special duties and responsibilities. It may therefore be subject to certain restrictions, but these shall only be such as are provided by law and are necessary:

(a) For respect of the rights or reputations of others;

(b) For the protection of national security or of public order (*ordre public*), or of public health or morals.

Article 20

1. Any propaganda for war shall be prohibited by law.

2. Any advocacy of national, racial or religious hatred that constitutes incitement to discrimination, hostility or violence shall be prohibited by law.

Article 21

The right of peaceful assembly shall be recognized. No restrictions may be placed on the exercise of this right other than those imposed in conformity with the law and which are necessary in a democratic society in the interests of national security or public safety, public order (*ordre public*), the protection of public health or morals or the protection of the rights and freedoms of others.

Article 22

1. Everyone shall have the right to freedom of association with others, including the right to form and join trade unions for the protection of his interests.

2. No restrictions may be placed on the exercise of this right other than those which are prescribed by law and which are necessary in a democratic society in the interests of national security or public safety, public order (*ordre public*), the protection of public health or morals or the protection of the rights and freedoms of others. This article shall not prevent the imposition of lawful restrictions on members of the armed forces and of the police in their exercise of this right.

3. Nothing in this article shall authorize States Parties to the International Labour Organisation Convention of 1948 concerning Freedom of Association and Protection of the Right to Organise to take legislative measures which would prejudice, or to apply the law in such a manner as to prejudice, the guarantees provided for in that Convention.

Article 23

1. The family is the natural and fundamental group unit of society and is entitled to protection by society and the State.

2. The right of men and women of marriageable age to marry and to found a family shall be recognized.

3. No marriage shall be entered into without the free and full consent of the intending spouses.

4. States Parties to the present Covenant shall take appropriate steps to ensure equality of rights and responsibilities of spouses as to marriage, during marriage and at its dissolution. In the case of dissolution, provision shall be made for the necessary protection of any children.

Article 24

1. Every child shall have, without any discrimination as to race, colour, sex, language, religion, national or social origin, property or birth, the right to such measures of protection as are required by his status as a minor, on the part of his family, society and the State.

2. Every child shall be registered immediately after birth and shall have a name.

3. Every child has the right to acquire a nationality.

Article 25

Every citizen shall have the right and the opportunity, without any of the distinctions mentioned in article 2 and without unreasonable restrictions:

(a) To take part in the conduct of public affairs, directly or through freely chosen representatives;

(b) To vote and to be elected at genuine periodic elections which shall be by universal and equal suffrage and shall be held by secret ballot, guaranteeing the free expression of the will of the electors;

(c) To have access, on general terms of equality, to public service in his country.

Article 26

All persons are equal before the law and are entitled without any discrimination to the equal protection of the law. In this respect, the law shall prohibit any discrimination and guarantee to all persons equal and effective protection against discrimination on any ground such as race, colour, sex, language, religion, political or other opinion, national or social origin, property, birth or other status.

Article 27

In those States in which ethnic, religious or linguistic minorities exist, persons belonging to such minorities shall not be denied the right, in community with the other members of their group, to enjoy their own culture, to profess and practise their own religion, or to use their own language.

PART IV

Article 28

1. There shall be established a Human Rights Committee (hereafter referred to in the present Covenant as the Committee). It shall consist of eighteen members and shall carry out the functions hereinafter provided.

2. The Committee shall be composed of nationals of the States Parties to the present Covenant who shall be persons of high moral character and recognized competence in the field of human rights, consideration being given to the usefulness of the participation of some persons having legal experience.

3. The members of the Committee shall be elected and shall serve in their personal capacity.

Article 29

1. The members of the Committee shall be elected by secret ballot from a list of persons possessing the qualifications prescribed in article 28 and nominated for the purpose by the States Parties to the present Covenant.

2. Each State Party to the present Covenant may nominate not more than two persons. These persons shall be nationals of the nominating State.

3. A person shall be eligible for renomination.

Article 30

1. The initial election shall be held no later than six months after the date of the entry into force of the present Covenant.

2. At least four months before the date of each election to the Committee, other than an election to fill a vacancy declared in accordance with article 34, the Secretary-General of the United Nations shall address a written invitation to the States Parties to the present Covenant to submit their nominations for membership of the Committee within three months.

3. The Secretary-General of the United Nations shall prepare a list in alphabetical order of all the persons thus nominated, with an indication of the States Parties which have nominated them, and shall submit it to the States Parties to the present Covenant no later than one month before the date of each election.

4. Elections of the members of the Committee shall be held at a meeting of the States Parties to the present Covenant convened by the Secretary-General of the United Nations at the Headquarters of the United Nations. At that meeting, for which two thirds of the States Parties to the present Covenant shall constitute a quorum, the persons elected to the Committee shall be those nominees who obtain the largest number of votes and an absolute majority of the votes of the representatives of States Parties present and voting.

Article 31

1. The Committee may not include more than one national of the same State.

2. In the election of the Committee, consideration shall be given to equitable geographical distribution of membership and to the representation of the different forms of civilization and of the principal legal systems.

Article 32

1. The members of the Committee shall be elected for a term of four years. They shall be eligible for re-election if renominated. However, the terms of nine of the members elected at the first election shall expire at the end of two years; immediately after the first election, the names of these nine members shall be chosen by lot by the Chairman of the meeting referred to in article 30, paragraph 4.

2. Elections at the expiry of office shall be held in accordance with the preceding articles of this part of the present Covenant.

Article 33

1. If, in the unanimous opinion of the other members, a member of the Committee has ceased to carry out his functions for any cause other than absence of a temporary character, the Chairman of the Committee shall notify the Secretary-General of the United Nations, who shall then declare the seat of that member to be vacant.

2. In the event of the death or the resignation of a member of the Committee, the Chairman shall immediately notify the Secretary-General of the United Nations, who shall declare the seat vacant from the date of death or the date on which the resignation takes effect.

Article 34

1. When a vacancy is declared in accordance with article 33 and if the term of office of the member to be replaced does not expire within six months of the declaration of the vacancy, the Secretary-General of the United Nations shall notify each of the States Parties to the present Covenant, which may within two months submit nominations in accordance with article 29 for the purpose of filling the vacancy.

2. The Secretary-General of the United Nations shall prepare a list in alphabetical order of the persons thus nominated and shall submit it to the States Parties to the present Covenant. The election to fill the vacancy shall then take place in accordance with the relevant provisions of this part of the present Covenant.

3. A member of the Committee elected to fill a vacancy declared in accordance with article 33 shall hold office for the remainder of the term of the member who vacated the seat on the Committee under the provisions of that article.

Article 35

The members of the Committee shall, with the approval of the General Assembly of the United Nations, receive emoluments from United Nations resources on such terms and conditions as the General Assembly may decide, having regard to the importance of the Committee's responsibilities.

Article 36

The Secretary-General of the United Nations shall provide the necessary staff and facilities for the effective performance of the functions of the Committee under the present Covenant.

Article 37

1. The Secretary-General of the United Nations shall convene the initial meeting of the Committee at the Headquarters of the United Nations.

2. After its initial meeting, the Committee shall meet at such times as shall be provided in its rules of procedure.

3. The Committee shall normally meet at the Headquarters of the United Nations or at the United Nations Office at Geneva.

Article 38

Every member of the Committee shall, before taking up his duties, make a solemn declaration in open committee that he will perform his functions impartially and conscientiously.

Article 39

1. The Committee shall elect its officers for a term of two years. They may be re-elected.

2. The Committee shall establish its own rules of procedure, but these rules shall provide, inter alia, that:

(a) Twelve members shall constitute a quorum;

(b) Decisions of the Committee shall be made by a majority vote of the members present.

Article 40

1. The States Parties to the present Covenant undertake to submit reports on the measures they have adopted which give effect to the rights recognized herein and on the progress made in the enjoyment of those rights:

(a) Within one year of the entry into force of the present Covenant for the States Parties concerned;

(b) Thereafter whenever the Committee so requests.

2. All reports shall be submitted to the Secretary-General of the United Nations, who shall transmit them to the Committee for consideration. Reports shall indicate the factors and difficulties, if any, affecting the implementation of the present Covenant.

3. The Secretary-General of the United Nations may, after consultation with the Committee, transmit to the specialized agencies concerned copies of such parts of the reports as may fall within their field of competence.

4. The Committee shall study the reports submitted by the States Parties to the present Covenant. It shall transmit its reports, and such general

comments as it may consider appropriate, to the States Parties. The Committee may also transmit to the Economic and Social Council these comments along with the copies of the reports it has received from States Parties to the present Covenant.

5. The States Parties to the present Covenant may submit to the Committee observations on any comments that may be made in accordance with paragraph 4 of this article.

Article 41

1. A State Party to the present Covenant may at any time declare under this article that it recognizes the competence of the Committee to receive and consider communications to the effect that a State Party claims that another State Party is not fulfilling its obligations under the present Covenant. Communications under this article may be received and considered only if submitted by a State Party which has made a declaration recognizing in regard to itself the competence of the Committee. No communication shall be received by the Committee if it concerns a State Party which has not made such a declaration. Communications received under this article shall be dealt with in accordance with the following procedure:

(a) If a State Party to the present Covenant considers that another State Party is not giving effect to the provisions of the present Covenant, it may, by written communication, bring the matter to the attention of that State Party. Within three months after the receipt of the communication, the receiving State shall afford the State which sent the communication an explanation or any other statement in writing clarifying the matter, which should include, to the extent possible and pertinent, reference to domestic procedures and remedies taken, pending, or available in the matter.

(b) If the matter is not adjusted to the satisfaction of both States Parties concerned within six months after the receipt by the receiving State of the initial communication, either State shall have the right to refer the matter to the Committee, by notice given to the Committee and to the other State.

(c) The Committee shall deal with a matter referred to it only after it has ascertained that all available domestic remedies have been invoked and exhausted in the matter, in conformity with the generally recognized principles of international law. This shall not be the rule where the application of the remedies is unreasonably prolonged.

(d) The Committee shall hold closed meetings when examining communications under this article.

(e) Subject to the provisions of subparagraph *(c)*, the Committee shall make available its good offices to the States Parties concerned with a view to a friendly solution of the matter on the basis of respect for human rights and fundamental freedoms as recognized in the present Covenant.

(f) In any matter referred to it, the Committee may call upon the States Parties concerned, referred to in subparagraph *(b)*, to supply any relevant information.

(g) The States Parties concerned, referred to in subparagraph *(b)*, shall have the right to be represented when the matter is being considered in the Committee and to make submissions orally and/or in writing.

(h) The Committee shall, within twelve months after the date of receipt of notice under subparagraph *(b)*, submit a report:

(i) If a solution within the terms of subparagraph *(e)* is reached, the Committee shall confine its report to a brief statement of the facts and of the solution reached;

(ii) If a solution within the terms of subparagraph *(e)* is not reached, the Committee shall confine its report to a brief statement of the facts; the written submissions and record of the oral submissions made by the States Parties concerned shall be attached to the report. In every matter, the report shall be communicated to the States Parties concerned.

2. The provisions of this article shall come into force when ten States Parties to the present Covenant have made declarations under paragraph 1 of this article. Such declarations shall be deposited by the States Parties with the Secretary-General of the United Nations, who shall transmit copies thereof to the other States Parties. A declaration may be withdrawn at any time by notification to the Secretary-General. Such a withdrawal shall not prejudice the consideration of any matter which is the subject of a communication already transmitted under this article; no further communication by any State Party shall be received after the notification of withdrawal of the declaration has been received by the Secretary-General, unless the State Party concerned has made a new declaration.

Article 42

1. *(a)* If a matter referred to the Committee in accordance with article 41 is not resolved to the satisfaction of the States Parties concerned, the Committee may, with the prior consent of the States Parties concerned, appoint an ad hoc Conciliation Commission (hereinafter referred to as the Commission). The good offices of the Commission shall be made available to the States Parties concerned with a view to an amicable solution of the matter on the basis of respect for the present Covenant;

(b) The Commission shall consist of five persons acceptable to the States Parties concerned. If the States Parties concerned fail to reach agreement within three months on all or part of the composition of the Commission, the members of the Commission concerning whom no agreement has been reached shall be elected by secret ballot by a two-thirds majority vote of the Committee from among its members.

2. The members of the Commission shall serve in their personal capacity. They shall not be nationals of the States Parties concerned, or of a State not

party to the present Covenant, or of a State Party which has not made a declaration under article 41.

3. The Commission shall elect its own Chairman and adopt its own rules of procedure.

4. The meetings of the Commission shall normally be held at the Headquarters of the United Nations or at the United Nations Office at Geneva. However, they may be held at such other convenient places as the Commission may determine in consultation with the Secretary-General of the United Nations and the States Parties concerned.

5. The secretariat provided in accordance with article 36 shall also service the commissions appointed under this article.

6. The information received and collated by the Committee shall be made available to the Commission and the Commission may call upon the States Parties concerned to supply any other relevant information.

7. When the Commission has fully considered the matter, but in any event not later than twelve months after having been seized of the matter, it shall submit to the Chairman of the Committee a report for communication to the States Parties concerned:

(a) If the Commission is unable to complete its consideration of the matter within twelve months, it shall confine its report to a brief statement of the status of its consideration of the matter;

(b) If an amicable solution to the matter on the basis of respect for human rights as recognized in the present Covenant is reached, the Commission shall confine its report to a brief statement of the facts and of the solution reached;

(c) If a solution within the terms of subparagraph *(b)* is not reached, the Commission's report shall embody its findings on all questions of fact relevant to the issues between the States Parties concerned, and its views on the possibilities of an amicable solution of the matter. This report shall also contain the written submissions and a record of the oral submissions made by the States Parties concerned;

(d) If the Commission's report is submitted under subparagraph *(c)*, the States Parties concerned shall, within three months of the receipt of the report, notify the Chairman of the Committee whether or not they accept the contents of the report of the Commission.

8. The provisions of this article are without prejudice to the responsibilities of the Committee under article 41.

9. The States Parties concerned shall share equally all the expenses of the members of the Commission in accordance with estimates to be provided by the Secretary-General of the United Nations.

10. The Secretary-General of the United Nations shall be empowered to pay the expenses of the members of the Commission, if necessary, before reim-

bursement by the States Parties concerned, in accordance with paragraph 9 of this article.

Article 43

The members of the Committee, and of the ad hoc conciliation commissions which may be appointed under article 42, shall be entitled to the facilities, privileges and immunities of experts on mission for the United Nations as laid down in the relevant sections of the Convention on the Privileges and Immunities of the United Nations.

Article 44

The provisions for the implementation of the present Covenant shall apply without prejudice to the procedures prescribed in the field of human rights by or under the constituent instruments and the conventions of the United Nations and of the specialized agencies and shall not prevent the States Parties to the present Covenant from having recourse to other procedures for settling a dispute in accordance with general or special international agreements in force between them.

Article 45

The Committee shall submit to the General Assembly of the United Nations, through the Economic and Social Council, an annual report on its activities.

Article 46

Nothing in the present Covenant shall be interpreted as impairing the provisions of the Charter of the United Nations and of the constitutions of the specialized agencies which define the respective responsibilities of the various organs of the United Nations and of the specialized agencies in regard to the matters dealt with in the present Covenant.

Article 47

Nothing in the present Covenant shall be interpreted as impairing the inherent right of all peoples to enjoy and utilize fully and freely their natural wealth and resources.

PART VI

Article 48

1. The present Covenant is open for signature by any State Member of the United Nations or member of any of its specialized agencies, by any State Party to the Statute of the International Court of Justice, and by any other State which has been invited by the General Assembly of the United Nations to become a party to the present Covenant.

2. The present Covenant is subject to ratification. Instruments of ratification shall be deposited with the Secretary-General of the United Nations.

3. The present Covenant shall be open to accession by any State referred to in paragraph 1 of this article.

4. Accession shall be effected by the deposit of an instrument of accession with the Secretary-General of the United Nations.

5. The Secretary-General of the United Nations shall inform all States which have signed this Covenant or acceded to it of the deposit of each instrument of ratification or accession.

Article 49

1. The present Covenant shall enter into force three months after the date of the deposit with the Secretary-General of the United Nations of the thirty-fifth instrument of ratification or instrument of accession.

2. For each State ratifying the present Covenant or acceding to it after the deposit of the thirty-fifth instrument of ratification or instrument of accession, the present Covenant shall enter into force three months after the date of the deposit of its own instrument of ratification or instrument of accession.

Article 50

The provisions of the present Covenant shall extend to all parts of federal States without any limitations or exceptions.

Article 51

1. Any State Party to the present Covenant may propose an amendment and file it with the Secretary-General of the United Nations. The Secretary-General of the United Nations shall thereupon communicate any proposed amendments to the States Parties to the present Covenant with a request that they notify him whether they favour a conference of States Parties for the purpose of considering and voting upon the proposals. In the event that at least one third of the States Parties favours such a conference, the Secretary-General shall convene the conference under the auspices of the United Nations. Any amendment adopted by a majority of the States Parties present and voting at the conference shall be submitted to the General Assembly of the United Nations for approval.

2. Amendments shall come into force when they have been approved by the General Assembly of the United Nations and accepted by a two-thirds majority of the States Parties still being bound by the provisions of the present Covenant and any earlier amendment which they have accepted.

Article 52

Irrespective of the notifications made under article 48, paragraph 5, the Secretary-General of the United Nations shall inform all States referred to in paragraph 1 of the same article of the following particulars:

(a) Signatures, ratifications and accessions under article 48:

(b) The date of the entry into force of the present Covenant under article 49 and the date of the entry into force of any amendments under article 51.

Article 53

1. The present Covenant, of which the Chinese, English, French, Russian and Spanish texts are equally authentic, shall be deposited in the archives of the United Nations.

2. The Secretary-General of the United Nations shall transmit certified copies of the present Covenant to all States referred to in article 48.

OPTIONAL PROTOCOL TO THE INTERNATIONAL COVENANT ON CIVIL AND POLITICAL RIGHTS, G.A. res. 2200A (XXI), 21 UN GAOR Supp. (No. 16) at 59, U.N. Doc. A/6316, 999 U.N.T.S. 302, *entered into force* March 23, 1976:

The States Parties to the present Protocol,

Considering that in order further to achieve the purposes of the Covenant on Civil and Political Rights (hereinafter referred to as the Covenant) and the implementation of its provisions it would be appropriate to enable the Human Rights Committee set up in part IV of the Covenant (hereinafter referred to as the Committee) to receive and consider, as provided in the present Protocol, communications from individuals claiming to be victims of violations of any of the rights set forth in the Covenant,

Have agreed as follows:

Article 1

A State Party to the Covenant that becomes a party to the present Protocol recognizes the competence of the Committee to receive and consider communications from individuals subject to its jurisdiction who claim to be victims of a violation by that State Party of any of the rights set forth in the Covenant. No communication shall be received by the Committee if it concerns a State Party to the Covenant which is not a party to the present Protocol.

Article 2

Subject to the provisions of article 1, individuals who claim that any of their rights enumerated in the Covenant have been violated and who have exhausted all available domestic remedies may submit a written communication to the Committee for consideration.

Article 3

The Committee shall consider inadmissible any communication under the present Protocol which is anonymous, or which it considers to be an abuse of the right of submission of such communications or to be incompatible with the provisions of the Covenant.

Article 4

1. Subject to the provisions of article 3, the Committee shall bring any communications submitted to it under the present Protocol to the attention of

the State Party to the present Protocol alleged to be violating any provision of the Covenant.

2. Within six months, the receiving State shall submit to the Committee written explanations or statements clarifying the matter and the remedy, if any, that may have been taken by that State.

Article 5

1. The Committee shall consider communications received under the present Protocol in the light of all written information made available to it by the individual and by the State Party concerned.

2. The Committee shall not consider any communication from an individual unless it has ascertained that:

(a) The same matter is not being examined under another procedure of international investigation or settlement;

(b) The individual has exhausted all available domestic remedies. This shall not be the rule where the application of the remedies is unreasonably prolonged.

3. The Committee shall hold closed meetings when examining communications under the present Protocol.

4. The Committee shall forward its views to the State Party concerned and to the individual.

Article 6

The Committee shall include in its annual report under article 45 of the Covenant a summary of its activities under the present Protocol.

Article 7

Pending the achievement of the objectives of resolution 1514(XV) adopted by the General Assembly of the United Nations on 14 December 1960 concerning the Declaration on the Granting of Independence to Colonial Countries and Peoples, the provisions of the present Protocol shall in no way limit the right of petition granted to these peoples by the Charter of the United Nations and other international conventions and instruments under the United Nations and its specialized agencies.

Article 8

1. The present Protocol is open for signature by any State which has signed the Covenant.

2. The present Protocol is subject to ratification by any State which has ratified or acceded to the Covenant. Instruments of ratification shall be deposited with the Secretary-General of the United Nations.

3. The present Protocol shall be open to accession by any State which has ratified or acceded to the Covenant.

4. Accession shall be effected by the deposit of an instrument of accession with the Secretary-General of the United Nations.

5. The Secretary-General of the United Nations shall inform all States which have signed the present Protocol or acceded to it of the deposit of each instrument of ratification or accession.

Article 9

1. Subject to the entry into force of the Covenant, the present Protocol shall enter into force three months after the date of the deposit with the Secretary-General of the United Nations of the tenth instrument of ratification or instrument of accession.

2. For each State ratifying the present Protocol or acceding to it after the deposit of the tenth instrument of ratification or instrument of accession, the present Protocol shall enter into force three months after the date of the deposit of its own instrument of ratification or instrument of accession.

Article 10

The provisions of the present Protocol shall extend to all parts of federal States without any limitations or exceptions.

Article 11

1. Any State Party to the present Protocol may propose an amendment and file it with the Secretary-General of the United Nations. The Secretary-General shall thereupon communicate any proposed amendments to the States Parties to the present Protocol with a request that they notify him whether they favour a conference of States Parties for the purpose of considering and voting upon the proposal. In the event that at least one third of the States Parties favours such a conference, the Secretary-General shall convene the conference under the auspices of the United Nations. Any amendment adopted by a majority of the States Parties present and voting at the conference shall be submitted to the General Assembly of the United Nations for approval.

2. Amendments shall come into force when they have been approved by the General Assembly of the United Nations and accepted by a two-thirds majority of the States Parties to the present Protocol in accordance with their respective constitutional processes.

3. When amendments come into force, they shall be binding on those States Parties which have accepted them, other States Parties still being bound by the provisions of the present Protocol and any earlier amendment which they have accepted.

Article 12

1. Any State Party may denounce the present Protocol at any time by written notification addressed to the Secretary-General of the United Nations.

Denunciation shall take effect three months after the date of receipt of the notification by the Secretary-General.

2. Denunciation shall be without prejudice to the continued application of the provisions of the present Protocol to any communication submitted under article 2 before the effective date of denunciation.

Article 13

Irrespective of the notifications made under article 8, paragraph 5, of the present Protocol, the Secretary-General of the United Nations shall inform all States referred to in article 48, paragraph 1, of the Covenant of the following particulars:

(a) Signatures, ratifications and accessions under article 8;

(b) The date of the entry into force of the present Protocol under article 9 and the date of the entry into force of any amendments under article 11;

(c) Denunciations under article 12.

Article 14

1. The present Protocol, of which the Chinese, English, French, Russian and Spanish texts are equally authentic, shall be deposited in the archives of the United Nations.

2. The Secretary-General of the United Nations shall transmit certified copies of the present Protocol to all States referred to in article 48 of the Covenant.

SECOND OPTIONAL PROTOCOL TO THE INTERNATIONAL COVENANT ON CIVIL AND POLITICAL RIGHTS, AIMING AT ABOLITION OF THE DEATH PENALTY, G.A. res. 44/128, 44 UN GAOR Supp. (No. 49) at 207, U.N. Doc. A/44/49, *entered into force* July 11, 1991:

The States parties to the present Protocol,

Believing that abolition of the death penalty contributes to enhancement of human dignity and progressive development of human rights,

Recalling article 3 of the Universal Declaration of Human Rights adopted on 10 December 1948 and article 6 of the International Covenant on Civil and Political Rights adopted on 16 December 1966,

Noting that article 6 of the International Covenant on Civil and Political Rights refers to abolition of the death penalty in terms that strongly suggest that abolition is desirable,

Convinced that all measures of abolition of the death penalty should be considered as progress in the enjoyment of the right to life,

Desirous to undertake hereby an international commitment to abolish the death penalty,

Have agreed as follows:

Article 1

1. No one within the jurisdiction of a State party to the present Optional Protocol shall be executed.

2. Each State party shall take all necessary measures to abolish the death penalty within its jurisdiction.

Article 2

1. No reservation is admissible to the present Protocol, except for a reservation made at the time of ratification or accession that provides for the application of the death penalty in time of war pursuant to a conviction for a most serious crime of a military nature committed during wartime.

2. The State party making such a reservation shall at the time of ratification or accession communicate to the Secretary-General of the United Nations the relevant provisions of its national legislation applicable during wartime.

3. The State party having made such a reservation shall notify the Secretary-General of the United Nations of any beginning or ending of a state of war applicable to its territory.

Article 3

The States parties to the present Protocol shall include in the reports they submit to the Human Rights Committee, in accordance with article 40 of the Covenant, information on the measures that they have adopted to give effect to the present Protocol.

Article 4

With respect to the States parties to the Covenant that have made a declaration under article 41, the competence of the Human Rights Committee to receive and consider communications when a State party claims that another State party is not fulfilling its obligations shall extend to the provisions of the present Protocol, unless the State party concerned has made a statement to the contrary at the moment of ratification or accession.

Article 5

With respect to the States parties to the (First) Optional Protocol to the International Covenant on Civil and Political Rights adopted on 16 December 1966, the competence of the Human Rights Committee to receive and consider communications from individuals subject to its jurisdiction shall extend to the provisions of the present Protocol, unless the State party concerned has made a statement to the contrary at the moment of ratification or accession.

Article 6

1. The provisions of the present Protocol shall apply as additional provisions to the Covenant.

2. Without prejudice to the possibility of a reservation under article 2 of the present Protocol, the right guaranteed in article 1, paragraph 1, of the present Protocol shall not be subject to any derogation under article 4 of the Covenant.

Article 7

1. The present Protocol is open for signature by any State that has signed the Covenant.

2. The present Protocol is subject to ratification by any State that has ratified the Covenant or acceded to it. Instruments of ratification shall be deposited with the Secretary-General of the United Nations.

3. The present Protocol shall be open to accession by any State that has ratified the Covenant or acceded to it.

4. Accession shall be effected by the deposit of an instrument of accession with the Secretary-General of the United Nations.

5. The Secretary-General of the United Nations shall inform all States that have signed the present Protocol or acceded to it of the deposit of each instrument of ratification or accession.

Article 8

1. The present Protocol shall enter into force three months after the date of the deposit with the Secretary-General of the United Nations of the tenth instrument of ratification or accession.

2. For each State ratifying the present Protocol or acceding to it after the deposit of the tenth instrument of ratification or accession, the present Protocol shall enter into force three months after the date of the deposit of its own instrument of ratification or accession.

Article 9

The provisions of the present Protocol shall extend to all parts of federal States without any limitations or exceptions.

Article 10

The Secretary-General of the United Nations shall inform all States referred to in article 48, paragraph 1, of the Covenant of the following particulars:

(a) Reservations, communications and notifications under article 2 of the present Protocol;

(b) Statements made under its articles 4 or 5;

(c) Signatures, ratifications and accessions under its article 7;

(d) The date of the entry into force of the present Protocol under its article 8.

Article 11

1. The present Protocol, of which the Arabic, Chinese, English, French, Russian and Spanish texts are equally authentic, shall be deposited in the archives of the United Nations.

2. The Secretary-General of the United Nations shall transmit certified copies of the present Protocol to all States referred to in article 48 of the Covenant.

OPTIONAL PROTOCOL TO THE INTERNATIONAL COVENANT ON ECONOMIC, SOCIAL AND CULTURAL RIGHTS, H.R.C. res. 8/2, U.N. Doc. A/HRC/8/2 (2008):

Preamble

The States Parties to the present Protocol,

Considering that, in accordance with the principles proclaimed in the Charter of the United Nations, recognition of the inherent dignity and of the equal and inalienable rights of all members of the human family is the foundation of freedom, justice and peace in the world,

Noting that the Universal Declaration of Human Rights proclaims that all human beings are born free and equal in dignity and rights and that everyone is entitled to all the rights and freedoms set forth therein, without distinction of any kind, such as race, colour, sex, language, religion, political or other opinion, national or social origin, property, birth or other status,

Recalling that the Universal Declaration of Human Rights and the International Covenants on Human Rights recognize that the ideal of free human beings enjoying freedom from fear and want can only be achieved if conditions are created whereby everyone may enjoy civil, cultural, economic, political and social rights,

Reaffirming the universality, indivisibility, interdependence and interrelatedness of all human rights and fundamental freedoms,

Recalling that each State Party to the International Covenant on Economic, Social and Cultural Rights (hereinafter referred to as the Covenant) undertakes to take steps, individually and through international assistance and cooperation, especially economic and technical, to the maximum of its available resources, with a view to achieving progressively the full realization of the rights recognized in the Covenant by all appropriate means, including particularly the adoption of legislative measures,

Considering that, in order further to achieve the purposes of the Covenant and the implementation of its provisions, it would be appropriate to enable the Committee on Economic, Social and Cultural Rights (hereinafter referred to as the Committee) to carry out the functions provided for in the present Protocol,

Have agreed as follows:

Article 1

Competence of the Committee to receive and consider communications

1. A State Party to the Covenant that becomes a Party to the present Protocol recognizes the competence of the Committee to receive and consider communications as provided for by the provisions of the present Protocol.

2. No communication shall be received by the Committee if it concerns a State Party to the Covenant which is not a Party to the present Protocol.

Article 2

Communications

Communications may be submitted by or on behalf of individuals or groups of individuals, under the jurisdiction of a State Party, claiming to be victims of a violation of any of the economic, social and cultural rights set forth in the Covenant by that State Party. Where a communication is submitted on behalf of individuals or groups of individuals, this shall be with their consent unless the author can justify acting on their behalf without such consent.

Article 3

Admissibility

1. The Committee shall not consider a communication unless it has ascertained that all available domestic remedies have been exhausted. This shall not be the rule where the application of such remedies is unreasonably prolonged.

2. The Committee shall declare a communication inadmissible when:

(*a*) It is not submitted within one year after the exhaustion of domestic remedies, except in cases where the author can demonstrate that it had not been possible to submit the communication within that time limit;

(*b*) The facts that are the subject of the communication occurred prior to the entry into force of the present Protocol for the State Party concerned unless those facts continued after that date;

(*c*) The same matter has already been examined by the Committee or has been or is being examined under another procedure of international investigation or settlement;

(*d*) It is incompatible with the provisions of the Covenant;

(*e*) It is manifestly ill-founded, not sufficiently substantiated or exclusively based on reports disseminated by mass media;

(*f*) It is an abuse of the right to submit a communication; or when

(*g*) It is anonymous or not in writing.

Article 4

Communications not revealing a clear disadvantage

The Committee may, if necessary, decline to consider a communication where it does not reveal that the author has suffered a clear disadvantage, unless the Committee considers that the communication raises a serious issue of general importance.

Article 5

Interim measures

1. At any time after the receipt of a communication and before a determination on the merits has been reached, the Committee may transmit to the

State Party concerned for its urgent consideration a request that the State Party take such interim measures as may be necessary in exceptional circumstances to avoid possible irreparable damage to the victim or victims of the alleged violations.

2. Where the Committee exercises its discretion under paragraph 1 of the present article, this does not imply a determination on admissibility or on the merits of the communication.

Article 6

Transmission of the communication

1. Unless the Committee considers a communication inadmissible without reference to the State Party concerned, the Committee shall bring any communication submitted to it under the present Protocol confidentially to the attention of the State Party concerned.

2. Within six months, the receiving State Party shall submit to the Committee written explanations or statements clarifying the matter and the remedy, if any, that may have been provided by that State Party.

Article 7

Friendly settlement

1. The Committee shall make available its good offices to the parties concerned with a view to reaching a friendly settlement of the matter on the basis of the respect for the obligations set forth in the Covenant.

2. An agreement on a friendly settlement closes consideration of the communication under the present Protocol.

Article 8

Examination of communications

1. The Committee shall examine communications received under article 2 of the present Protocol in the light of all documentation submitted to it, provided that this documentation is transmitted to the parties concerned.

2. The Committee shall hold closed meetings when examining communications under the present Protocol.

3. When examining a communication under the present Protocol, the Committee may consult, as appropriate, relevant documentation emanating from other United Nations bodies, specialized agencies, funds, programmes and mechanisms, and other international organizations, including from regional human rights systems, and any observations or comments by the State Party concerned.

4. When examining communications under the present Protocol, the Committee shall consider the reasonableness of the steps taken by the State Party in accordance with Part II of the Covenant. In doing so, the Committee shall bear in mind that the State Party may adopt a range of possible policy measures for the implementation of the rights set forth in the Covenant.

Article 9

Follow-up to the views of the Committee

1. After examining a communication, the Committee shall transmit its views on the communication, together with its recommendations, if any, to the parties concerned.

2. The State Party shall give due consideration to the views of the Committee, together with its recommendations, if any, and shall submit to the Committee, within six months, a written response, including information on any action taken in the light of the views and recommendations of the Committee.

3. The Committee may invite the State Party to submit further information about any measures the State Party has taken in response to its views or recommendations, if any, including as deemed appropriate by the Committee, in the State Party's subsequent reports under articles 16 and 17 of the Covenant.

Article 10

Inter-State communications

1. A State Party to the present Protocol may at any time declare under this article that it recognizes the competence of the Committee to receive and consider communications to the effect that a State Party claims that another State Party is not fulfilling its obligations under the Covenant. Communications under this article may be received and considered only if submitted by a State Party that has made a declaration recognizing in regard to itself the competence of the Committee. No communication shall be received by the Committee if it concerns a State Party which has not made such a declaration. Communications received under this article shall be dealt with in accordance with the following procedure:

(*a*) If a State Party to the present Protocol considers that another State Party is not fulfilling its obligations under the Covenant, it may, by written communication, bring the matter to the attention of that State Party. The State Party may also inform the Committee of the matter. Within three months after the receipt of the communication the receiving State shall afford the State that sent the communication an explanation, or any other statement in writing clarifying the matter which should include, to the extent possible and pertinent, reference to domestic procedures and remedies taken, pending or available in the matter;

(*b*) If the matter is not settled to the satisfaction of both States Parties concerned within six months after the receipt by the receiving State of the initial communication, either State shall have the right to refer the matter to the Committee, by notice given to the Committee and to the other State;

(*c*) The Committee shall deal with a matter referred to it only after it has ascertained that all available domestic remedies have been invoked and exhausted in the matter. This shall not be the rule where the application of the remedies is unreasonably prolonged;

(*d*) Subject to the provisions of subparagraph (*c*) of the present paragraph the Committee shall make available its good offices to the States Parties concerned with a view to a friendly solution of the matter on the basis of the respect for the obligations set forth in the Covenant;

(*e*) The Committee shall hold closed meetings when examining communications under the present article;

(*f*) In any matter referred to it in accordance with subparagraph (*b*) of the present paragraph, the Committee may call upon the States Parties concerned, referred to in subparagraph (*b*), to supply any relevant information;

(*g*) The States Parties concerned, referred to in subparagraph (*b*) of the present paragraph, shall have the right to be represented when the matter is being considered by the Committee and to make submissions orally and/or in writing;

(*h*) The Committee shall, with all due expediency after the date of receipt of notice under subparagraph (*b*) of the present paragraph, submit a report, as follows:

(i) If a solution within the terms of subparagraph (*d*) of the present paragraph is reached, the Committee shall confine its report to a brief statement of the facts and of the solution reached;

(ii) If a solution within the terms of subparagraph (*d*) is not reached, the Committee shall, in its report, set forth the relevant facts concerning the issue between the States Parties concerned. The written submissions and record of the oral submissions made by the States Parties concerned shall be attached to the report. The Committee may also communicate only to the States Parties concerned any views that it may consider relevant to the issue between them.

In every matter, the report shall be communicated to the States Parties concerned.

2. A declaration under paragraph 1 of the present article shall be deposited by the States Parties with the Secretary-General of the United Nations, who shall transmit copies thereof to the other States Parties. A declaration may be withdrawn at any time by notification to the Secretary-General. Such a withdrawal shall not prejudice the consideration of any matter that is the subject of a communication already transmitted under the present article; no further communication by any State Party shall be received under the present article after the notification of withdrawal of the declaration has been received by the Secretary-General, unless the State Party concerned has made a new declaration.

Article 11

Inquiry procedure

1. A State Party to the present Protocol may at any time declare that it recognizes the competence of the Committee provided for under this article.

2. If the Committee receives reliable information indicating grave or systematic violations by a State Party of any of the economic, social and cultural rights set forth in the Covenant, the Committee shall invite that State Party to cooperate in the examination of the information and to this end to submit observations with regard to the information concerned.

3. Taking into account any observations that may have been submitted by the State Party concerned as well as any other reliable information available to it, the Committee may designate one or more of its members to conduct an inquiry and to report urgently to the Committee. Where warranted and with the consent of the State Party, the inquiry may include a visit to its territory.

4. Such an inquiry shall be conducted confidentially and the cooperation of the State Party shall be sought at all stages of the proceedings.

5. After examining the findings of such an inquiry, the Committee shall transmit these findings to the State Party concerned together with any comments and recommendations.

6. The State Party concerned shall, within six months of receiving the findings, comments and recommendations transmitted by the Committee, submit its observations to the Committee.

7. After such proceedings have been completed with regard to an inquiry made in accordance with paragraph 2, the Committee may, after consultations with the State Party concerned, decide to include a summary account of the results of the proceedings in its annual report provided for in article 15.

8. Any State Party having made a declaration in accordance with paragraph 1 of the present article may, at any time, withdraw this declaration by notification to the Secretary-General.

Article 12

Follow-up to the inquiry procedure

1. The Committee may invite the State Party concerned to include in its report under articles 16 and 17 of the Covenant details of any measures taken in response to an inquiry conducted under article 11 of the present Protocol.

2. The Committee may, if necessary, after the end of the period of six months referred to in article 11, paragraph 6, invite the State Party concerned to inform it of the measures taken in response to such an inquiry.

Article 13

Protection measures

A State Party shall take all appropriate measures to ensure that individuals under its jurisdiction are not subjected to any form of ill-treatment or intimidation as a consequence of communicating with the Committee pursuant to the present Protocol.

Article 14

International assistance and cooperation

1. The Committee shall transmit, as it may consider appropriate, and with the consent of the State Party concerned, to United Nations specialized agencies, funds and programmes and other competent bodies, its views or recommendations concerning communications and inquiries that indicate a need for technical advice or assistance, along with the State Party's observations and suggestions, if any, on these views or recommendations.

2. The Committee may also bring to the attention of such bodies, with the consent of the State Party concerned, any matter arising out of communications considered under the present Protocol which may assist them in deciding, each within its field of competence, on the advisability of international measures likely to contribute to assisting States Parties in achieving progress in implementation of the rights recognized in the Covenant.

3. A trust fund shall be established in accordance with the relevant procedures of the General Assembly, to be administered in accordance with the financial regulations and rules of the United Nations, with a view to providing expert and technical assistance to States Parties, with the consent of the State Party concerned, for the enhanced implementation of the rights contained in the Covenant, thus contributing to building national capacities in the area of economic, social and cultural rights in the context of the present Protocol.

4. The provisions of this article are without prejudice to the obligations of each State Party to fulfil its obligations under the Covenant.

Article 15

Annual report

The Committee shall include in its annual report a summary of its activities under the present Protocol.

Article 16

Dissemination and information

Each State Party undertakes to make widely known and to disseminate the Covenant and the present Protocol and to facilitate access to information about the views and recommendations of the Committee, in particular, on matters involving that State Party, and to do so in accessible formats for persons with disabilities.

Article 17

Signature, ratification and accession

1. The present Protocol is open for signature by any State that has signed, ratified or acceded to the Covenant.

2. The present Protocol is subject to ratification by any State that has ratified or acceded to the Covenant. Instruments of ratification shall be deposited with the Secretary-General of the United Nations.

3. The present Protocol shall be open to accession by any State that has ratified or acceded to the Covenant.

4. Accession shall be effected by the deposit of an instrument of accession with the Secretary-General of the United Nations.

Article 18

Entry into force

1. The present Protocol shall enter into force three months after the date of the deposit with the Secretary-General of the United Nations of the tenth instrument of ratification or accession.

2. For each State ratifying or acceding to the present Protocol, after the deposit of the tenth instrument of ratification or accession, the protocol shall enter into force three months after the date of the deposit of its instrument of ratification or accession.

Article 19

Amendments

1. Any State Party may propose an amendment to the present Protocol and submit it to the Secretary-General of the United Nations. The Secretary-General shall communicate any proposed amendments to States Parties, with a request to be notified whether they favour a meeting of States Parties for the purpose of considering and deciding upon the proposals. In the event that, within four months from the date of such communication, at least one third of the States Parties favour such a meeting, the Secretary-General shall convene the meeting under the auspices of the United Nations. Any amendment adopted by a majority of two thirds of the States Parties present and voting shall be submitted by the Secretary-General to the General Assembly for approval and thereafter to all States Parties for acceptance.

2. An amendment adopted and approved in accordance with paragraph 1 of this article shall enter into force on the thirtieth day after the number of instruments of acceptance deposited reaches two thirds of the number of States Parties at the date of adoption of the amendment. Thereafter, the amendment shall enter into force for any State Party on the thirtieth day following the deposit of its own instrument of acceptance. An amendment shall be binding only on those States Parties which have accepted it.

Article 20

Denunciation

1. Any State Party may denounce the present Protocol at any time by written notification addressed to the Secretary-General of the United Nations. Denunciation shall take effect six months after the date of receipt of the notification by the Secretary-General.

2. Denunciation shall be without prejudice to the continued application of the provisions of the present Protocol to any communication submitted under

articles 2 and 10 or to any procedure initiated under article 11 before the effective date of denunciation.

Article 21

Notification by the Secretary-General

The Secretary-General of the United Nations shall notify all States referred to in article 26, paragraph 1 of the Covenant of the following particulars:

(*a*) Signatures, ratifications and accessions under the present Protocol;

(*b*) The date of entry into force of the present Protocol and of any amendment under article 19;

(*c*) Any denunciation under article 20.

Article 22

Official languages

1. The present Protocol, of which the Arabic, Chinese, English, French, Russian and Spanish texts are equally authentic, shall be deposited in the archives of the United Nations.

2. The Secretary-General of the United Nations shall transmit certified copies of the present Protocol to all States referred to in article 26 of the Covenant.

CONVENTION ON THE PREVENTION AND PUNISHMENT OF THE CRIME OF GENOCIDE, 78 U.N.T.S. 277, *entered into force* Dec. 9, 1948:

The Contracting Parties,

Having considered the declaration made by the General Assembly of the United Nations in its resolution 96(I) dated 11 December 1946 that genocide is a crime under international law, contrary to the spirit and aims of the United Nations and condemned by the civilized world,

Recognizing that at all periods of history genocide has inflicted great losses on humanity, and

Being convinced that, in order to liberate mankind from such an odious scourge, international co-operation is required,

Hereby agree as hereinafter provided:

Article I

The Contracting Parties confirm that genocide, whether committed in time of peace or in time of war, is a crime under international law which they undertake to prevent and to punish.

Article II

In the present Convention, genocide means any of the following acts committed with intent to destroy, in whole or in part, a national, ethnical, racial or religious group, as such:

(a) Killing members of the group;

(b) Causing serious bodily or mental harm to members of the group;

(c) Deliberately inflicting on the group conditions of life calculated to bring about its physical destruction in whole or in part;

(d) Imposing measures intended to prevent births within the group.

(e) Forcibly transferring children of the group to another group.

Article III

The following acts shall be punishable:

(a) Genocide;

(b) Conspiracy to commit genocide;

(c) Direct and public incitement to commit genocide;

(d) Attempt to commit genocide;

(e) Complicity in genocide.

Article IV

Persons committing genocide or any of the other acts enumerated in article III shall be punished, whether they are constitutionally responsible rulers, public officials or private individuals.

Article V

The Contracting Parties undertake to enact, in accordance with their respective Constitutions, the necessary legislation to give effect to the provisions of the present Convention, and, in particular, to provide effective penalties for persons guilty of genocide or any of the other acts enumerated in article III.

Article VI

Persons charged with genocide or any of the other acts enumerated in article III shall be tried by a competent tribunal of the State in the territory of which the act was committed, or by such international penal tribunal as may have jurisdiction with respect to those Contracting Parties which shall have accepted its jurisdiction.

Article VII

Genocide and the other acts enumerated in article III shall not be considered as political crimes for the purpose of extradition.

The Contracting Parties pledge themselves in such cases to grant extradition in accordance with their laws and treaties in force.

Article VIII

Any Contracting Party may call upon the competent organs of the United Nations to take such action under the Charter of the United Nations as they consider appropriate for the prevention and suppression of acts of genocide or any of the other acts enumerated in article III.

Article IX

Disputes between the Contracting Parties relating to the interpretation, application or fulfilment of the present Convention, including those relating to the responsibility of a State for genocide or for any of the other acts enumerated in article III, shall be submitted to the International Court of Justice at the request of any of the parties to the dispute.

Article X

The present Convention, of which the Chinese, English, French, Russian and Spanish texts are equally authentic, shall bear the date of 9 December 1948.

Article XI

The present Convention shall be open until 31 December 1949 for signature on behalf of any Member of the United Nations and of any non-member State to which an invitation to sign has been addressed by the General Assembly.

The present Convention shall be ratified, and the instruments of ratification shall be deposited with the Secretary-General of the United Nations.

After 1 January 1950, the present Convention may be acceded to on behalf of any Member of the United Nations and of any non-member State which has received an invitation as aforesaid.

Instruments of accession shall be deposited with the Secretary-General of the United Nations.

Article XII

Any Contracting Party may at any time, by notification addressed to the Secretary-General of the United Nations, extend the application of the present Convention to all or any of the territories for the conduct of whose foreign relations that Contracting Party is responsible.

Article XIII

On the day when the first twenty instruments of ratification or accession have been deposited, the Secretary-General shall draw up a *procès-verbal* and transmit a copy thereof to each Member of the United Nations and to each of the non-member States contemplated in article XI.

The present Convention shall come into force on the ninetieth day following the date of deposit of the twentieth instrument of ratification or accession.

Any ratification or accession effected, subsequent to the latter date shall become effective on the ninetieth day following the deposit of the instrument of ratification or accession.

Article XIV

The present Convention shall remain in effect for a period of ten years as from the date of its coming into force.

It shall thereafter remain in force for successive periods of five years for such Contracting Parties as have not denounced it at least six months before the expiration of the current period.

Denunciation shall be effected by a written notification addressed to the Secretary-General of the United Nations.

Article XV

If, as a result of denunciations, the number of Parties to the present Convention should become less than sixteen, the Convention shall cease to be in force as from the date on which the last of these denunciations shall become effective.

Article XVI

A request for the revision of the present Convention may be made at any time by any Contracting Party by means of a notification in writing addressed to the Secretary-General.

The General Assembly shall decide upon the steps, if any, to be taken in respect of such request.

Article XVII

The Secretary-General of the United Nations shall notify all Members of the United Nations and the non-member States contemplated in article XI of the following:

(a) Signatures, ratifications and accessions received in accordance with article XI;

(b) Notifications received in accordance with article XII;

(c) The date upon which the present Convention comes into force in accordance with article XIII;

(d) Denunciations received in accordance with article XIV;

(e) The abrogation of the Convention in accordance with article XV;

(f) Notifications received in accordance with article XVI.

Article XVIII

The original of the present Convention shall be deposited in the archives of the United Nations.

A certified copy of the Convention shall be transmitted to each Member of the United Nations and to each of the non-member States contemplated in article XI.

Article XIX

The present Convention shall be registered by the Secretary-General of the United Nations on the date of its coming into force.

INTERNATIONAL CONVENTION ON THE ELIMINATION OF ALL FORMS OF RACIAL DISCRIMINATION, 660 U.N.T.S. 195, *entered into force* **Jan. 4, 1969:**

The States Parties to this Convention,

Considering that the Charter of the United Nations is based on the principles of the dignity and equality inherent in all human beings, and that all Member States have pledged themselves to take joint and separate action, in co-operation with the Organization, for the achievement of one of the purposes of the United Nations which is to promote and encourage universal respect for and observance of human rights and fundamental freedoms for all, without distinction as to race, sex, language or religion,

Considering that the Universal Declaration of Human Rights proclaims that all human beings are born free and equal in dignity and rights and that everyone is entitled to all the rights and freedoms set out therein, without distinction of any kind, in particular as to race, colour or national origin,

Considering that all human beings are equal before the law and are entitled to equal protection of the law against any discrimination and against any incitement to discrimination,

Considering that the United Nations has condemned colonialism and all practices of segregation and discrimination associated therewith, in whatever form and wherever they exist, and that the Declaration on the Granting of Independence to Colonial Countries and Peoples of 14 December 1960 (General Assembly resolution 1514 (XV)) has affirmed and solemnly proclaimed the necessity of bringing them to a speedy and unconditional end,

Considering that the United Nations Declaration on the Elimination of All Forms of Racial Discrimination of 20 November 1963 (General Assembly resolution 1904 (XVIII)) solemnly affirms the necessity of speedily eliminating racial discrimination throughout the world in all its forms and manifestations and of securing understanding of and respect for the dignity of the human person,

Convinced that any doctrine of superiority based on racial differentiation is scientifically false, morally condemnable, socially unjust and dangerous, and that there is no justification for racial discrimination, in theory or in practice, anywhere,

Reaffirming that discrimination between human beings on the grounds of race, colour or ethnic origin is an obstacle to friendly and peaceful relations among nations and is capable of disturbing peace and security among peoples and the harmony of persons living side by side even within one and the same State,

Convinced that the existence of racial barriers is repugnant to the ideals of any human society,

Alarmed by manifestations of racial discrimination still in evidence in some areas of the world and by governmental policies based on racial superiority or hatred, such as policies of *apartheid*, segregation or separation,

Resolved to adopt all necessary measures for speedily eliminating racial discrimination in all its forms and manifestations, and to prevent and combat racist doctrines and practices in order to promote understanding between races and to build an international community free from all forms of racial segregation and racial discrimination,

Bearing in mind the Convention concerning Discrimination in respect of Employment and Occupation adopted by the International Labour Organisation in 1958, and the Convention against Discrimination in Education adopted by the United Nations Educational, Scientific and Cultural Organisation in 1960,

Desiring to implement the principles embodied in the United Nations Declaration on the Elimination of All Forms of Racial Discrimination and to secure the earliest adoption of practical measures to that end,

Have agreed as follows:

PART I

Article 1

1. In this Convention, the term "racial discrimination" shall mean any distinction, exclusion, restriction or preference based on race, colour, descent, or national or ethnic origin which has the purpose or effect of nullifying or impairing the recognition, enjoyment or exercise, on an equal footing, of human rights and fundamental freedoms in the political, economic, social, cultural or any other field of public life.

2. This Convention shall not apply to distinctions, exclusions, restrictions or preferences made by a State Party to this Convention between citizens and non-citizens.

3. Nothing in this Convention may be interpreted as affecting in any way the legal provisions of States Parties concerning nationality, citizenship or naturalization, provided that such provisions do not discriminate against any particular nationality.

4. Special measures taken for the sole purpose of securing adequate advancement of certain racial or ethnic groups or individuals requiring such protection as may be necessary in order to ensure such groups or individuals equal enjoyment or exercise of human rights and fundamental freedoms shall not be deemed racial discrimination, provided, however, that such measures do not, as a consequence, lead to the maintenance of separate rights or different racial groups and that they shall not be continued after the objectives for which they were taken have been achieved.

Article 2

1. States Parties condemn racial discrimination and undertake to pursue by all appropriate means and without delay a policy of eliminating racial discrimination in all its forms and promoting understanding among all races, and, to this end:

(a) Each State Party undertakes to engage in no act or practice of racial discrimination against persons, groups of persons or institutions and to ensure that all public authorities and public institutions, national and local, shall act in conformity with this obligation;

(b) Each State Party undertakes not to sponsor, defend or support racial discrimination by any persons or organizations;

(c) Each State Party shall take effective measures to review governmental, national and local policies, and to amend, rescind or nullify any laws and regulations which have the effect of creating or perpetuating racial discrimination wherever it exists;

(d) Each State Party shall prohibit and bring to an end, by all appropriate means, including legislation as required by circumstances, racial discrimination by any persons, group or organization;

(e) Each State Party undertakes to encourage, where appropriate, integrationist multiracial organizations and movements and other means of eliminating barriers between races, and to discourage anything which tends to strengthen racial division.

2. States Parties shall, when the circumstances so warrant, take, in the social, economic, cultural and other fields, special and concrete measures to ensure the adequate development and protection of certain racial groups or individuals belonging to them, for the purpose of guaranteeing them the full and equal enjoyment of human rights and fundamental freedoms. These measures shall in no case entail as a consequence the maintenance of unequal or separate rights for different racial groups after the objectives for which they were taken have been achieved.

Article 3

States Parties particularly condemn racial segregation and apartheid and undertake to prevent, prohibit and eradicate all practices of this nature in territories under their jurisdiction.

Article 4

States Parties condemn all propaganda and all organizations which are based on ideas or theories of superiority of one race or group of persons of one colour or ethnic origin, or which attempt to justify or promote racial hatred and discrimination in any form, and undertake to adopt immediate and positive measures designed to eradicate all incitement to, or acts of, such discrimination and, to this end, with due regard to the principles embodied in the Universal Declaration of Human Rights and the rights expressly set forth in article 5 of this Convention, inter alia:

(a) Shall declare an offence punishable by law all dissemination of ideas based on racial superiority or hatred, incitement to racial discrimination, as well as all acts of violence or incitement to such acts against any race or group of persons of another colour or ethnic origin, and also the provision of any assistance to racist activities, including the financing thereof;

(b) Shall declare illegal and prohibit organizations, and also organized and all other propaganda activities, which promote and incite racial discrimination, and shall recognize participation in such organizations or activities as an offence punishable by law;

(c) Shall not permit public authorities or public institutions, national or local, to promote or incite racial discrimination.

Article 5

In compliance with the fundamental obligations laid down in article 2 of this Convention, States Parties undertake to prohibit and to eliminate racial discrimination in all its forms and to guarantee the right of everyone, without distinction as to race, colour, or national or ethnic origin, to equality before the law, notably in the enjoyment of the following rights:

(a) The right to equal treatment before the tribunals and all other organs administering justice;

(b) The right to security of person and protection by the State against violence or bodily harm, whether inflicted by government officials or by any individual group or institution;

(c) Political rights, in particular the rights to participate in elections -- to vote and to stand for election -- on the basis of universal and equal suffrage, to take part in the Government as well as in the conduct of public affairs at any level and to have equal access to public service;

(d) Other civil rights, in particular:

(i) The right to freedom of movement and residence within the border of the State;

(ii) The right to leave any country, including one's own, and to return to one's country;

(iii) The right to nationality;

(iv) The right to marriage and choice of spouse;

(v) The right to own property alone as well as in association with others;

(vi) The right to inherit;

(vii) The right to freedom of thought, conscience and religion;

(viii) The right to freedom of opinion and expression;

(ix) The right to freedom of peaceful assembly and association;

(e) Economic, social and cultural rights, in particular:

(i) The rights to work, to free choice of employment, to just and favourable conditions of work, to protection against unemployment, to equal pay for equal work, to just and favourable remuneration;

(ii) The right to form and join trade unions;

(iii) The right to housing;

(iv) The right to public health, medical care, social security and social services;

(v) The right to education and training;

(vi) The right to equal participation in cultural activities;

(f) The right of access to any place or service intended for use by the general public, such as transport, hotels, restaurants, cafes, theatres and parks.

Article 6

States Parties shall assure to everyone within their jurisdiction effective protection and remedies, through the competent national tribunals and other State institutions, against any acts of racial discrimination which violate his human rights and fundamental freedoms contrary to this Convention, as well as the right to seek from such tribunals just and adequate reparation or satisfaction for any damage suffered as a result of such discrimination.

Article 7

States Parties undertake to adopt immediate and effective measures, particularly in the fields of teaching, education, culture and information, with a view to combating prejudices which lead to racial discrimination and to promoting understanding, tolerance and friendship among nations and racial or ethnical groups, as well as to propagating the purposes and principles of the Charter of the United Nations, the Universal Declaration of Human Rights, the United Nations Declaration on the Elimination of All Forms of Racial Discrimination, and this Convention.

PART II

Article 8

1. There shall be established a Committee on the Elimination of Racial Discrimination (hereinafter referred to as the Committee) consisting of eighteen experts of high moral standing and acknowledged impartiality elected by States Parties from among their nationals, who shall serve in their personal capacity, consideration being given to equitable geographical distribution and to the representation of the different forms of civilization as well as of the principal legal systems.

2. The members of the Committee shall be elected by secret ballot from a list of persons nominated by the States Parties. Each State Party may nominate one person from among its own nationals.

3. The initial election shall be held six months after the date of the entry into force of this Convention. At least three months before the date of each election the Secretary-General of the United Nations shall address a letter to the States Parties inviting them to submit their nominations within two months. The Secretary-General shall prepare a list in alphabetical order of all persons thus nominated, indicating the States Parties which have nominated them, and shall submit it to the States Parties.

4. Elections of the members of the Committee shall be held at a meeting of States Parties convened by the Secretary-General at United Nations Headquarters. At that meeting, for which two thirds of the States Parties shall constitute a quorum, the persons elected to the Committee shall be those nominees who obtain the largest number of votes and an absolute majority of the votes of the representatives of States Parties present and voting.

5. *(a)* The members of the Committee shall be elected for a term of four years. However, the terms of nine of the members elected at the first election shall expire at the end of two years; immediately after the first election the names of these nine members shall be chosen by lot by the Chairman of the Committee.

(b) For the filling of casual vacancies, the State Party whose expert has ceased to function as a member of the Committee shall appoint another expert from among its nationals, subject to the approval of the Committee.

6. States Parties shall be responsible for the expenses of the members of the Committee while they are in performance of Committee duties.

Article 9

1. States Parties undertake to submit to the Secretary-General of the United Nations, for consideration by the Committee, a report on the legislative, judicial, administrative or other measures which they have adopted and which give effect to the provisions of this Convention: (a) within one year after the entry into force of the Convention for the State concerned; and (b) thereafter every two years and whenever the Committee so requests. The Committee may request further information from the States Parties.

2. The Committee shall report annually, through the Secretary-General, to the General Assembly of the United Nations on its activities and may make suggestions and general recommendations based on the examination of the reports and information received from the States Parties. Such suggestions and general recommendations shall be reported to the General Assembly together with comments, if any, from States Parties.

Article 10

1. The Committee shall adopt its own rules of procedure.

2. The Committee shall elect its officers for a term of two years.

3. The secretariat of the Committee shall be provided by the Secretary-General of the United Nations.

4. The meetings of the Committee shall normally be held at United Nations Headquarters.

Article 11

1. If a State Party considers that another State Party is not giving effect to the provisions of this Convention, it may bring the matter to the attention of the Committee. The Committee shall then transmit the communication to the State Party concerned. Within three months, the receiving State shall submit to the Committee written explanations or statements clarifying the matter and the remedy, if any, that may have been taken by that State.

2. If the matter is not adjusted to the satisfaction of both parties, either by bilateral negotiations or by any other procedure open to them, within six months after the receipt by the receiving State of the initial communication, either State shall have the right to refer the matter again to the Committee by notifying the Committee and also the other State.

3. The Committee shall deal with a matter referred to it in accordance with paragraph 2 of this article after it has ascertained that all available domestic remedies have been invoked and exhausted in the case, in conformity with the generally recognized principles of international law. This shall not be the rule where the application of the remedies is unreasonably prolonged.

4. In any matter referred to it, the Committee may call upon the States Parties concerned to supply any other relevant information.

5. When any matter arising out of this article is being considered by the Committee, the States Parties concerned shall be entitled to send a representative to take part in the proceedings to the Committee, without voting rights, while the matter is under consideration.

Article 12

1. *(a)* After the Committee has obtained and collated all the information it deems necessary, the Chairman shall appoint an ad hoc Conciliation Commission (hereinafter referred to as the Commission) comprising five persons who may or may not be members of the Committee. The members of the Commission shall be appointed with the unanimous consent of the parties to the dispute, and its good offices shall be made available to the States concerned with a view to an amicable solution of the matter on the basis of respect for this Convention.

(b) If the States Parties to the dispute fail to reach agreement within three months on all or part of the composition of the Commission, the members of the Commission not agreed upon by the States parties to the dispute shall be elected by secret ballot by a two-thirds majority vote of the Committee from among its own members.

2. The members of the Commission shall serve in their personal capacity. They shall not be nationals of the States Parties to the dispute or of a State not Party to this Convention.

3. The Commission shall elect its own Chairman and adopt its own rules of procedure.

4. The meetings of the Commission shall normally be held at United Nations Headquarters or at any other convenient place as determined by the Commission.

5. The secretariat provided in accordance with article 10, paragraph 3, of this Convention shall also service the Commission whenever a dispute among States Parties brings the Commission into being.

6. The States Parties to the dispute shall share equally all the expenses of the members of the Commission in accordance with estimates to be provided by the Secretary-General of the United Nations.

7. The Secretary-General shall be empowered to pay the expenses of the members of the Commission, if necessary, before reimbursement by the States Parties to the dispute in accordance with paragraph 6 of this article.

8. The information obtained and collated by the Committee shall be made available to the Commission, and the Commission may call upon the States concerned to supply any other relevant information.

Article 13

1. When the Commission has fully considered the matter, it shall prepare and submit to the Chairman of the Committee a report embodying its findings on all questions of fact relevant to the issue between the parties and containing such recommendations as it may think proper for the amicable solution of the dispute.

2. The Chairman of the Committee shall communicate the report of the Commission to each of the States Parties to the dispute. These States shall, within three months, inform the Chairman of the Committee whether or not they accept the recommendations contained in the report of the Commission.

3. After the period provided for in paragraph 2 of this article, the Chairman of the Committee shall communicate the report of the Commission and the declarations of the States Parties concerned to the other States Parties to this Convention.

Article 14

1. A State Party may at any time declare that it recognizes the competence of the Committee to receive and consider communications from individuals or groups of individuals within its jurisdiction claiming to be victims of a violation by that State Party of any of the rights set forth in this Convention. No communication shall be received by the Committee if it concerns a State Party which has not made such a declaration.

2. Any State Party which makes a declaration as provided for in paragraph 1 of this article may establish or indicate a body within its national legal order which shall be competent to receive and consider petitions from individuals and groups of individuals within its jurisdiction who claim to be victims of a violation of any of the rights set forth in this Convention and who have exhausted other available local remedies.

3. A declaration made in accordance with paragraph 1 of this article and the name of any body established or indicated in accordance with paragraph 2 of this article shall be deposited by the State Party concerned with the Secretary-General of the United Nations, who shall transmit copies thereof to the other States Parties. A declaration may be withdrawn at any time by notification to the Secretary General but such a withdrawal shall not affect communications pending before the Committee.

4. A register of petitions shall be kept by the body established or indicated in accordance with paragraph 2 of this Article, and certified copies of the register shall be filed annually through appropriate channels with the Secretary-General on the understanding that the contents shall not be publicly disclosed.

5. In the event of failure to obtain satisfaction from the body established or indicated in accordance with paragraph 2 of this Article, the petitioner shall have the right to communicate the matter to the Committee within six months.

6. *(a)* The Committee shall confidentially bring any communication referred to it to the attention of the State Party alleged to be violating any provision of this Convention, but the identity of the individual or groups of individuals concerned shall not be revealed without his or their express consent. The Committee shall not receive anonymous communications.

(b) Within three months, the receiving State shall submit to the Committee written explanations or statements clarifying the matter and the remedy, if any, that may have been taken by that State.

7. *(a)* The Committee shall consider communications in the light of all information made available to it by the State Party concerned and by the petitioner. The Committee shall not consider any communication from a petitioner unless it has ascertained that the petitioner has exhausted all available domestic remedies. However, this shall not be the rule where the application of the remedies is unreasonably prolonged.

(b) The Committee shall forward its suggestions and recommendations, if any, to the State Party concerned and to the petitioner.

8. The Committee shall include in its annual report a summary of such communications and, where appropriate, a summary of the explanations and statements of the States Parties concerned and of its own suggestions and recommendations.

9. The Committee shall be competent to exercise the functions provided for in this article only when at least ten States Parties to this Convention are bound by declarations in accordance with paragraph 1 of this article.

Article 15

1. Pending the achievement of the objectives of the Declaration on the Granting of Independence to Colonial Countries and Peoples, contained in General Assembly resolutions 1514 (XV) of 14 December 1960, the provisions of this Convention shall in no way limit the right of petition granted to these

peoples by other international instruments or by the United Nations and its specialized agencies.

2. *(a)* The Committee established under article 8, paragraph 1, of this Convention shall receive copies of the petitions from, and submit expressions of opinion and recommendations on these petitions to, the bodies of the United Nations which deal with matters directly related to the principles and objectives of this Convention in their consideration of petitions from the inhabitants of Trust and Non-Self-Governing Territories and all other territories to which General Assembly resolution 1514 (XV) applies, relating to matters covered by this Convention which are before these bodies.

(b) The Committee shall receive from the competent bodies of the United Nations copies of the reports concerning the legislative, judicial, administrative or other measures directly related to the principles and objectives of this Convention applied by the administering Powers within the Territories mentioned in subparagraph *(a)* of this paragraph, and shall express opinions and make recommendations to these bodies.

3. The Committee shall include in its report to the General Assembly a summary of the petitions and reports it has received from United Nations bodies, and the expressions of opinion and recommendations of the Committee relating to the said petitions and reports.

4. The Committee shall request from the Secretary-General of the United Nations all information relevant to the objectives of this Convention and available to him regarding the Territories mentioned in paragraph 2 *(a)* of this article.

Article 16

The provisions of this Convention concerning the settlement of disputes or complaints shall be applied without prejudice to other procedures for settling disputes or complaints in the field of discrimination laid down in the constituent instruments of, or in conventions adopted by, the United Nations and its specialized agencies, and shall not prevent the States Parties from having recourse to other procedures for settling a dispute in accordance with general or special international agreements in force between them.

PART III

Article 17

1. This Convention is open for signature by any State Member of the United Nations or member of any of its specialized agencies, by any State Party to the Statute of the International Court of Justice, and by any other State which has been invited by the General Assembly of the United Nations to become a Party to this Convention.

2. This Convention is subject to ratification. Instruments of ratification shall be deposited with the Secretary-General of the United Nations.

Article 18

1. This Convention shall be open to accession by any State referred to in article 17, paragraph 1, of the Convention.

2. Accession shall be effected by the deposit of an instrument of accession with the Secretary-General of the United Nations.

Article 19

1. This Convention shall enter into force on the thirtieth day after the date of the deposit with the Secretary-General of the United Nations of the twenty-seventh instrument of ratification or instrument of accession.

2. For each State ratifying this Convention or acceding to it after the deposit of the twenty-seventh instrument of ratification or instrument of accession, the Convention shall enter into force on the thirtieth day after the date of the deposit of its own instrument of ratification or instrument of accession.

Article 20

1. The Secretary-General of the United Nations shall receive and circulate to all States which are or may become Parties to this Convention reservations made by States at the time of ratification or accession. Any State which objects to the reservation shall, within a period of ninety days from the date of the said communication, notify the Secretary-General that it does not accept it.

2. A reservation incompatible with the object and purpose of this Convention shall not be permitted, nor shall a reservation the effect of which would inhibit the operation of any of the bodies established by this Convention be allowed. A reservation shall be considered incompatible or inhibitive if at least two thirds of the States Parties to this Convention object to it.

3. Reservations may be withdrawn at any time by notification to this effect addressed to the Secretary-General. Such notification shall take effect on the date on which it is received.

Article 21

A State Party may denounce this Convention by written notification to the Secretary-General of the United Nations. Denunciation shall take effect one year after the date of receipt of the notification by the Secretary-General.

Article 22

Any dispute between two or more States Parties with respect to the interpretation or application of this Convention, which is not settled by negotiation or by the procedures expressly provided for in this Convention, shall, at the request of any of the parties to the dispute, be referred to the International Court of Justice for decision, unless the disputants agree to another mode of settlement.

Article 23

1. A request for the revision of this Convention may be made at any time by any State Party by means of a notification in writing addressed to the Secretary-General of the United Nations.

2. The General Assembly of the United Nations shall decide upon the steps, if any, to be taken in respect of such a request.

Article 24

The Secretary-General of the United Nations shall inform all States referred to in article 17, paragraph 1, of this Convention of the following particulars:

(a) Signatures, ratifications and accessions under articles 17 and 18;

(b) The date of entry into force of this Convention under article 19;

(c) Communications and declarations received under articles 14, 20 and 23;

(d) Denunciations under article 21.

Article 25

1. This Convention, of which the Chinese, English, French, Russian and Spanish texts are equally authentic, shall be deposited in the archives of the United Nations.

2. The Secretary-General of the United Nations shall transmit certified copies of this Convention to all States belonging to any of the categories mentioned in article 17, paragraph l, of the Convention.

CONVENTION ON THE ELIMINATION OF ALL FORMS OF DISCRIMINATION AGAINST WOMEN, G.A. res. 34/180, U.N. GAOR Supp. (No. 46) at 193, U.N. Doc. A/34/180, *entered into force* Sept. 3, 1981:

The States Parties to the present Convention,

Noting that the Charter of the United Nations reaffirms faith in fundamental human rights, in the dignity and worth of the human person and in the equal rights of men and women,

Noting that the Universal Declaration of Human Rights affirms the principle of the inadmissibility of discrimination and proclaims that all human beings are born free and equal in dignity and rights and that everyone is entitled to all the rights and freedoms set forth therein, without distinction of any kind, including distinction based on sex,

Noting that the States Parties to the International Covenants on Human Rights have the obligation to ensure the equal rights of men and women to enjoy all economic, social, cultural, civil and political rights,

Considering the international conventions concluded under the auspices of the United Nations and the specialized agencies promoting equality of rights of men and women,

Noting also the resolutions, declarations and recommendations adopted by the United Nations and the specialized agencies promoting equality of rights of men and women,

Concerned, however, that despite these various instruments extensive discrimination against women continues to exist,

Recalling that discrimination against women violates the principles of equality of rights and respect for human dignity, is an obstacle to the participation of women, on equal terms with men, in the political, social, economic and cultural life of their countries, hampers the growth of the prosperity of society and the family and makes more difficult the full development of the potentialities of women in the service of their countries and of humanity,

Concerned that in situations of poverty women have the least access to food, health, education, training and opportunities for employment and other needs,

Convinced that the establishment of the new international economic order based on equity and justice will contribute significantly towards the promotion of equality between men and women,

Emphasizing that the eradication of apartheid, all forms of racism, racial discrimination, colonialism, neo-colonialism, aggression, foreign occupation and domination and interference in the internal affairs of States is essential to the full enjoyment of the rights of men and women,

Affirming that the strengthening of international peace and security, the relaxation of international tension, mutual co-operation among all States irrespective of their social and economic systems, general and complete disarmament, in particular nuclear disarmament under strict and effective international control, the affirmation of the principles of justice, equality and mutual benefit in relations among countries and the realization of the right of peoples under alien and colonial domination and foreign occupation to self-determination and independence, as well as respect for national sovereignty and territorial integrity, will promote social progress and development and as a consequence will contribute to the attainment of full equality between men and women,

Convinced that the full and complete development of a country, the welfare of the world and the cause of peace require the maximum participation of women on equal terms with men in all fields,

Bearing in mind the great contribution of women to the welfare of the family and to the development of society, so far not fully recognized, the social significance of maternity and the role of both parents in the family and in the upbringing of children, and aware that the role of women in procreation should not be a basis for discrimination but that the upbringing of children requires a sharing of responsibility between men and women and society as a whole,

Aware that a change in the traditional role of men as well as the role of women in society and in the family is needed to achieve full equality between men and women,

Determined to implement the principles set forth in the Declaration on the Elimination of Discrimination against Women and, for that purpose, to adopt the measures required for the elimination of such discrimination in all its forms and manifestations,

Have agreed on the following:

PART I

Article I

For the purposes of the present Convention, the term "discrimination against women" shall mean any distinction, exclusion or restriction made on the basis of sex which has the effect or purpose of impairing or nullifying the recognition, enjoyment or exercise by women, irrespective of their marital status, on a basis of equality of men and women, of human rights and fundamental freedoms in the political, economic, social, cultural, civil or any other field.

Article 2

States Parties condemn discrimination against women in all its forms, agree to pursue by all appropriate means and without delay a policy of eliminating discrimination against women and, to this end, undertake:

(a) To embody the principle of the equality of men and women in their national constitutions or other appropriate legislation if not yet incorporated therein and to ensure, through law and other appropriate means, the practical realization of this principle;

(b) To adopt appropriate legislative and other measures, including sanctions where appropriate, prohibiting all discrimination against women;

(c) To establish legal protection of the rights of women on an equal basis with men and to ensure through competent national tribunals and other public institutions the effective protection of women against any act of discrimination;

(d) To refrain from engaging in any act or practice of discrimination against women and to ensure that public authorities and institutions shall act in conformity with this obligation;

(e) To take all appropriate measures to eliminate discrimination against women by any person, organization or enterprise;

(f) To take all appropriate measures, including legislation, to modify or abolish existing laws, regulations, customs and practices which constitute discrimination against women;

(g) To repeal all national penal provisions which constitute discrimination against women.

Article 3

States Parties shall take in all fields, in particular in the political, social, economic and cultural fields, all appropriate measures, including legislation, to ensure the full development and advancement of women, for the purpose of guaranteeing them the exercise and enjoyment of human rights and fundamental freedoms on a basis of equality with men.

Article 4

1. Adoption by States Parties of temporary special measures aimed at accelerating de facto equality between men and women shall not be considered discrimination as defined in the present Convention, but shall in no way entail as a consequence the maintenance of unequal or separate standards; these measures shall be discontinued when the objectives of equality of opportunity and treatment have been achieved.

2. Adoption by States Parties of special measures, including those measures contained in the present Convention, aimed at protecting maternity, shall not be considered discriminatory.

Article 5

States Parties shall take all appropriate measures:

(a) To modify the social and cultural patterns of conduct of men and women, with a view to achieving the elimination of prejudices and customary and all other practices which are based on the idea of the inferiority or the superiority of either of the sexes or on stereotyped roles for men and women;

(b) To ensure that family education includes a proper understanding of maternity as a social function and the recognition of the common responsibility of men and women in the upbringing and development of their children, it being understood that the interest of the children is the primordial consideration in all cases.

Article 6

States Parties shall take all appropriate measures, including legislation, to suppress all forms of traffic in women and exploitation of prostitution of women.

PART II

Article 7

States Parties shall take all appropriate measures to eliminate discrimination against women in the political and public life of the country and, in particular, shall ensure to women, on equal terms with men, the right:

(a) To vote in all elections and public referenda and to be eligible for election to all publicly elected bodies;

(b) To participate in the formulation of government policy and the implementation thereof and to hold public office and perform all public functions at all levels of government;

(c) To participate in non-governmental organizations and associations concerned with the public and political life of the country.

Article 8

States Parties shall take all appropriate measures to ensure to women, on equal terms with men and without any discrimination, the opportunity to represent their Governments at the international level and to participate in the work of international organizations.

Article 9

1. States Parties shall grant women equal rights with men to acquire, change or retain their nationality. They shall ensure in particular that neither marriage to an alien nor change of nationality by the husband during marriage shall automatically change the nationality of the wife, render her stateless or force upon her the nationality of the husband.

2. States Parties shall grant women equal rights with men with respect to the nationality of their children.

PART III

Article 10

States Parties shall take all appropriate measures to eliminate discrimination against women in order to ensure to them equal rights with men in the field of education and in particular to ensure, on a basis of equality of men and women:

(a) The same conditions for career and vocational guidance, for access to studies and for the achievement of diplomas in educational establishments of all categories in rural as well as in urban areas; this equality shall be ensured in pre-school, general, technical, professional and higher technical education, as well as in all types of vocational training;

(b) Access to the same curricula, the same examinations, teaching staff with qualifications of the same standard and school premises and equipment of the same quality;

(c) The elimination of any stereotyped concept of the roles of men and women at all levels and in all forms of education by encouraging coeducation and other types of education which will help to achieve this aim and, in particular, by the revision of textbooks and school programmes and the adaptation of teaching methods;

(d) The same opportunities to benefit from scholarships and other study grants;

(e) The same opportunities for access to programmes of continuing education, including adult and functional literacy programmes, particularly those aimed at reducing, at the earliest possible time, any gap in education existing between men and women;

(f) The reduction of female student drop-out rates and the organization of programmes for girls and women who have left school prematurely;

(g) The same opportunities to participate actively in sports and physical education;

(h) Access to specific educational information to help to ensure the health and well-being of families, including information and advice on family planning.

Article 11

1. States Parties shall take all appropriate measures to eliminate discrimination against women in the field of employment in order to ensure, on a basis of equality of men and women, the same rights, in particular:

(a) The right to work as an inalienable right of all human beings;

(b) The right to the same employment opportunities, including the application of the same criteria for selection in matters of employment;

(c) The right to free choice of profession and employment, the right to promotion, job security and all benefits and conditions of service and the right to receive vocational training and retraining, including apprenticeships, advanced vocational training and recurrent training;

(d) The right to equal remuneration, including benefits, and to equal treatment in respect of work of equal value, as well as equality of treatment in the evaluation of the quality of work;

(e) The right to social security, particularly in cases of retirement, unemployment, sickness, invalidity and old age and other incapacity to work, as well as the right to paid leave;

(f) The right to protection of health and to safety in working conditions, including the safeguarding of the function of reproduction.

2. In order to prevent discrimination against women on the grounds of marriage or maternity and to ensure their effective right to work, States Parties shall take appropriate measures:

(a) To prohibit, subject to the imposition of sanctions, dismissal on the grounds of pregnancy or of maternity leave and discrimination in dismissals on the basis of marital status;

(b) To introduce maternity leave with pay or with comparable social benefits without loss of former employment, seniority or social allowances;

(c) To encourage the provision of the necessary supporting social services to enable parents to combine family obligations with work responsibilities and participation in public life, in particular through promoting the establishment and development of a network of child-care facilities;

(d) To provide special protection to women during pregnancy in types of work proved to be harmful to them.

3. Protective legislation relating to matters covered in this article shall be reviewed periodically in the light of scientific and technological knowledge and shall be revised, repealed or extended as necessary.

Article 12

1. States Parties shall take all appropriate measures to eliminate discrimination against women in the field of health care in order to ensure, on a basis of equality of men and women, access to health care services, including those related to family planning.

2. Notwithstanding the provisions of paragraph 1 of this article, States Parties shall ensure to women appropriate services in connection with pregnancy, confinement and the post-natal period, granting free services where necessary, as well as adequate nutrition during pregnancy and lactation.

Article 13

States Parties shall take all appropriate measures to eliminate discrimination against women in other areas of economic and social life in order to ensure, on a basis of equality of men and women, the same rights, in particular:

(a) The right to family benefits;

(b) The right to bank loans, mortgages and other forms of financial credit;

(c) The right to participate in recreational activities, sports and all aspects of cultural life.

Article 14

1. States Parties shall take into account the particular problems faced by rural women and the significant roles which rural women play in the economic survival of their families, including their work in the non-monetized sectors of the economy, and shall take all appropriate measures to ensure the application of the provisions of the present Convention to women in rural areas.

2. States Parties shall take all appropriate measures to eliminate discrimination against women in rural areas in order to ensure, on a basis of equality of men and women, that they participate in and benefit from rural development and, in particular, shall ensure to such women the right:

(a) To participate in the elaboration and implementation of development planning at all levels;

(b) To have access to adequate health care facilities, including information, counselling and services in family planning;

(c) To benefit directly from social security programmes;

(d) To obtain all types of training and education, formal and non-formal, including that relating to functional literacy, as well as, inter alia, the benefit of all community and extension services, in order to increase their technical proficiency;

(e) To organize self-help groups and co-operatives in order to obtain equal access to economic opportunities through employment or self-employment;

(f) To participate in all community activities;

(g) To have access to agricultural credit and loans, marketing facilities, appropriate technology and equal treatment in land and agrarian reform as well as in land resettlement schemes;

(h) To enjoy adequate living conditions, particularly in relation to housing, sanitation, electricity and water supply, transport and communications.

PART IV

Article 15

1. States Parties shall accord to women equality with men before the law.

2. States Parties shall accord to women, in civil matters, a legal capacity identical to that of men and the same opportunities to exercise that capacity. In particular, they shall give women equal rights to conclude contracts and to administer property and shall treat them equally in all stages of procedure in courts and tribunals.

3. States Parties agree that all contracts and all other private instruments of any kind with a legal effect which is directed at restricting the legal capacity of women shall be deemed null and void.

4. States Parties shall accord to men and women the same rights with regard to the law relating to the movement of persons and the freedom to choose their residence and domicile.

Article 16

1. States Parties shall take all appropriate measures to eliminate discrimination against women in all matters relating to marriage and family relations and in particular shall ensure, on a basis of equality of men and women:

(a) The same right to enter into marriage;

(b) The same right freely to choose a spouse and to enter into marriage only with their free and full consent;

(c) The same rights and responsibilities during marriage and at its dissolution;

(d) The same rights and responsibilities as parents, irrespective of their marital status, in matters relating to their children; in all cases the interests of the children shall be paramount;

(e) The same rights to decide freely and responsibly on the number and spacing of their children and to have access to the information, education and means to enable them to exercise these rights;

(f) The same rights and responsibilities with regard to guardianship, wardship, trusteeship and adoption of children, or similar institutions

where these concepts exist in national legislation; in all cases the interests of the children shall be paramount;

(g) The same personal rights as husband and wife, including the right to choose a family name, a profession and an occupation;

(h) The same rights for both spouses in respect of the ownership, acquisition, management, administration, enjoyment and disposition of property, whether free of charge or for a valuable consideration.

2. The betrothal and the marriage of a child shall have no legal effect, and all necessary action, including legislation, shall be taken to specify a minimum age for marriage and to make the registration of marriages in an official registry compulsory.

PART V

Article 17

1. For the purpose of considering the progress made in the implementation of the present Convention, there shall be established a Committee on the Elimination of Discrimination against Women (hereinafter referred to as the Committee) consisting, at the time of entry into force of the Convention, of eighteen and, after ratification of or accession to the Convention by the thirty-fifth State Party, of twenty-three experts of high moral standing and competence in the field covered by the Convention. The experts shall be elected by States Parties from among their nationals and shall serve in their personal capacity, consideration being given to equitable geographical distribution and to the representation of the different forms of civilization as well as the principal legal systems.

2. The members of the Committee shall be elected by secret ballot from a list of persons nominated by States Parties. Each State Party may nominate one person from among its own nationals.

3. The initial election shall be held six months after the date of the entry into force of the present Convention. At least three months before the date of each election the Secretary-General of the United Nations shall address a letter to the States Parties inviting them to submit their nominations within two months. The Secretary-General shall prepare a list in alphabetical order of all persons thus nominated, indicating the States Parties which have nominated them, and shall submit it to the States Parties.

4. Elections of the members of the Committee shall be held at a meeting of States Parties convened by the Secretary-General at United Nations Headquarters. At that meeting, for which two thirds of the States Parties shall constitute a quorum, the persons elected to the Committee shall be those nominees who obtain the largest number of votes and an absolute majority of the votes of the representatives of States Parties present and voting.

5. The members of the Committee shall be elected for a term of four years. However, the terms of nine of the members elected at the first election

shall expire at the end of two years; immediately after the first election the names of these nine members shall be chosen by lot by the Chairman of the Committee.

6. The election of the five additional members of the Committee shall be held in accordance with the provisions of paragraphs 2, 3 and 4 of this article, following the thirty-fifth ratification or accession. The terms of two of the additional members elected on this occasion shall expire at the end of two years, the names of these two members having been chosen by lot by the Chairman of the Committee.

7. For the filling of casual vacancies, the State Party whose expert has ceased to function as a member of the Committee shall appoint another expert from among its nationals, subject to the approval of the Committee.

8. The members of the Committee shall, with the approval of the General Assembly, receive emoluments from United Nations resources on such terms and conditions as the Assembly may decide, having regard to the importance of the Committee's responsibilities.

9. The Secretary-General of the United Nations shall provide the necessary staff and facilities for the effective performance of the functions of the Committee under the present Convention.

Article 18

1. States Parties undertake to submit to the Secretary-General of the United Nations, for consideration by the Committee, a report on the legislative, judicial, administrative or other measures which they have adopted to give effect to the provisions of the present Convention and on the progress made in this respect:

(a) Within one year after the entry into force for the State concerned;

(b) Thereafter at least every four years and further whenever the Committee so requests.

2. Reports may indicate factors and difficulties affecting the degree of fulfilment of obligations under the present Convention.

Article 19

1. The Committee shall adopt its own rules of procedure.

2. The Committee shall elect its officers for a term of two years.

Article 20

1. The Committee shall normally meet for a period of not more than two weeks annually in order to consider the reports submitted in accordance with article 18 of the present Convention.

2. The meetings of the Committee shall normally be held at United Nations Headquarters or at any other convenient place as determined by the Committee.

Article 21

1. The Committee shall, through the Economic and Social Council, report annually to the General Assembly of the United Nations on its activities and may make suggestions and general recommendations based on the examination of reports and information received from the States Parties. Such suggestions and general recommendations shall be included in the report of the Committee together with comments, if any, from States Parties.

2. The Secretary-General of the United Nations shall transmit the reports of the Committee to the Commission on the Status of Women for its information.

Article 22

The specialized agencies shall be entitled to be represented at the consideration of the implementation of such provisions of the present Convention as fall within the scope of their activities. The Committee may invite the specialized agencies to submit reports on the implementation of the Convention in areas falling within the scope of their activities.

PART VI

Article 23

Nothing in the present Convention shall affect any provisions that are more conducive to the achievement of equality between men and women which may be contained:

(a) In the legislation of a State Party; or

(b) In any other international convention, treaty or agreement in force for that State.

Article 24

States Parties undertake to adopt all necessary measures at the national level aimed at achieving the full realization of the rights recognized in the present Convention.

Article 25

1. The present Convention shall be open for signature by all States.

2. The Secretary-General of the United Nations is designated as the depositary of the present Convention.

3. The present Convention is subject to ratification. Instruments of ratification shall be deposited with the Secretary-General of the United Nations.

4. The present Convention shall be open to accession by all States. Accession shall be effected by the deposit of an instrument of accession with the Secretary-General of the United Nations.

Article 26

1. A request for the revision of the present Convention may be made at any time by any State Party by means of a notification in writing addressed to the Secretary-General of the United Nations.

2. The General Assembly of the United Nations shall decide upon the steps, if any, to be taken in respect of such a request.

Article 27

1. The present Convention shall enter into force on the thirtieth day after the date of deposit with the Secretary-General of the United Nations of the twentieth instrument of ratification or accession.

2. For each State ratifying the present Convention or acceding to it after the deposit of the twentieth instrument of ratification or accession, the Convention shall enter into force on the thirtieth day after the date of the deposit of its own instrument of ratification or accession.

Article 28

1. The Secretary-General of the United Nations shall receive and circulate to all States the text of reservations made by States at the time of ratification or accession.

2. A reservation incompatible with the object and purpose of the present Convention shall not be permitted.

3. Reservations may be withdrawn at any time by notification to this effect addressed to the Secretary-General of the United Nations, who shall then inform all States thereof. Such notification shall take effect on the date on which it is received.

Article 29

1. Any dispute between two or more States Parties concerning the interpretation or application of the present Convention which is not settled by negotiation shall, at the request of one of them, be submitted to arbitration. If within six months from the date of the request for arbitration the parties are unable to agree on the organization of the arbitration, any one of those parties may refer the dispute to the International Court of Justice by request in conformity with the Statute of the Court.

2. Each State Party may at the time of signature or ratification of the present Convention or accession thereto declare that it does not consider itself bound by paragraph 1 of this article. The other States Parties shall not be bound by that paragraph with respect to any State Party which has made such a reservation.

3. Any State Party which has made a reservation in accordance with paragraph 2 of this article may at any time withdraw that reservation by notification to the Secretary-General of the United Nations.

Article 30

The present Convention, the Arabic, Chinese, English, French, Russian and Spanish texts of which are equally authentic, shall be deposited with the Secretary-General of the United Nations.

OPTIONAL PROTOCOL TO THE CONVENTION ON THE ELIMINATION OF THE DISCRIMINATION AGAINST WOMEN, G.A. res. 54/4, annex, 54 U.N. GAOR Supp. (No. 49) at 5, U.N. Doc. A/54/49 (Vol. I) (2000), *entered into force* Dec. 22, 2000:

The States Parties to the present Protocol,

Noting that the Charter of the United Nations reaffirms faith in fundamental human rights, in the dignity and worth of the human person and in the equal rights of men and women,

Also noting that the Universal Declaration of Human Rights Resolution 217 A (III). proclaims that all human beings are born free and equal in dignity and rights and that everyone is entitled to all the rights and freedoms set forth therein, without distinction of any kind, including distinction based on sex,

Recalling that the International Covenants on Human Rights Resolution 2200 A (XXI), annex. and other international human rights instruments prohibit discrimination on the basis of sex,

Also recalling the Convention on the Elimination of All Forms of Discrimination against Women ("the Convention"), in which the States Parties thereto condemn discrimination against women in all its forms and agree to pursue by all appropriate means and without delay a policy of eliminating discrimination against women,

Reaffirming their determination to ensure the full and equal enjoyment by women of all human rights and fundamental freedoms and to take effective action to prevent violations of these rights and freedoms,

Have agreed as follows:

Article 1

A State Party to the present Protocol ("State Party") recognizes the competence of the Committee on the Elimination of Discrimination against Women ("the Committee") to receive and consider communications submitted in accordance with article 2.

Article 2

Communications may be submitted by or on behalf of individuals or groups of individuals, under the jurisdiction of a State Party, claiming to be victims of a violation of any of the rights set forth in the Convention by that State Party. Where a communication is submitted on behalf of individuals or groups of individuals, this shall be with their consent unless the author can justify acting on their behalf without such consent.

Article 3

Communications shall be in writing and shall not be anonymous. No communication shall be received by the Committee if it concerns a State Party to the Convention that is not a party to the present Protocol.

Article 4

1. The Committee shall not consider a communication unless it has ascertained that all available domestic remedies have been exhausted unless the application of such remedies is unreasonably prolonged or unlikely to bring effective relief.

2. The Committee shall declare a communication inadmissible where:

(a) The same matter has already been examined by the Committee or has been or is being examined under another procedure of international investigation or settlement;

(b) It is incompatible with the provisions of the Convention;

(c) It is manifestly ill-founded or not sufficiently substantiated;

(d) It is an abuse of the right to submit a communication;

(e) The facts that are the subject of the communication occurred prior to the entry into force of the present Protocol for the State Party concerned unless those facts continued after that date.

Article 5

1. At any time after the receipt of a communication and before a determination on the merits has been reached, the Committee may transmit to the State Party concerned for its urgent consideration a request that the State Party take such interim measures as may be necessary to avoid possible irreparable damage to the victim or victims of the alleged violation.

2. Where the Committee exercises its discretion under paragraph 1 of the present article, this does not imply a determination on admissibility or on the merits of the communication.

Article 6

1. Unless the Committee considers a communication inadmissible without reference to the State Party concerned, and provided that the individual or individuals consent to the disclosure of their identity to that State Party, the Committee shall bring any communication submitted to it under the present Protocol confidentially to the attention of the State Party concerned.

2. Within six months, the receiving State Party shall submit to the Committee written explanations or statements clarifying the matter and the remedy, if any, that may have been provided by that State Party.

Article 7

1. The Committee shall consider communications received under the present Protocol in the light of all information made available to it by or on behalf of individuals or groups of individuals and by the State Party concerned, provided that this information is transmitted to the parties concerned.

2. The Committee shall hold closed meetings when examining communications under the present Protocol.

3. After examining a communication, the Committee shall transmit its views on the communication, together with its recommendations, if any, to the parties concerned.

4. The State Party shall give due consideration to the views of the Committee, together with its recommendations, if any, and shall submit to the Committee, within six months, a written response, including information on any action taken in the light of the views and recommendations of the Committee.

5. The Committee may invite the State Party to submit further information about any measures the State Party has taken in response to its views or recommendations, if any, including as deemed appropriate by the Committee, in the State Party's subsequent reports under article 18 of the Convention.

Article 8

1. If the Committee receives reliable information indicating grave or systematic violations by a State Party of rights set forth in the Convention, the Committee shall invite that State Party to cooperate in the examination of the information and to this end to submit observations with regard to the information concerned.

2. Taking into account any observations that may have been submitted by the State Party concerned as well as any other reliable information available to it, the Committee may designate one or more of its members to conduct an inquiry and to report urgently to the Committee. Where warranted and with the consent of the State Party, the inquiry may include a visit to its territory.

3. After examining the findings of such an inquiry, the Committee shall transmit these findings to the State Party concerned together with any comments and recommendations.

4. The State Party concerned shall, within six months of receiving the findings,

comments and recommendations transmitted by the Committee, submit its observations to the Committee.

5. Such an inquiry shall be conducted confidentially and the cooperation of the State Party shall be sought at all stages of the proceedings.

Article 9

1. The Committee may invite the State Party concerned to include in its report under article 18 of the Convention details of any measures taken in response to an inquiry conducted under article 8 of the present Protocol.

2. The Committee may, if necessary, after the end of the period of six months referred to in article 8.4, invite the State Party concerned to inform it of the measures taken in response to such an inquiry.

Article 10

1. Each State Party may, at the time of signature or ratification of the present Protocol or accession thereto, declare that it does not recognize the competence of the Committee provided for in articles 8 and 9.

2. Any State Party having made a declaration in accordance with paragraph 1 of the present article may, at any time, withdraw this declaration by notification to the Secretary-General.

Article 11

A State Party shall take all appropriate steps to ensure that individuals under its jurisdiction are not subjected to ill treatment or intimidation as a consequence of communicating with the Committee pursuant to the present Protocol.

Article 12

The Committee shall include in its annual report under article 21 of the Convention a summary of its activities under the present Protocol.

Article 13

Each State Party undertakes to make widely known and to give publicity to the Convention and the present Protocol and to facilitate access to information about the views and recommendations of the Committee, in particular, on matters involving that State Party.

Article 14

The Committee shall develop its own rules of procedure to be followed when exercising the functions conferred on it by the present Protocol.

Article 15

1. The present Protocol shall be open for signature by any State that has signed, ratified or acceded to the Convention.

2. The present Protocol shall be subject to ratification by any State that has ratified or acceded to the Convention. Instruments of ratification shall be deposited with the Secretary-General of the United Nations.

3. The present Protocol shall be open to accession by any State that has ratified or acceded to the Convention.

4. Accession shall be effected by the deposit of an instrument of accession with the Secretary-General of the United Nations.

Article 16

1. The present Protocol shall enter into force three months after the date of the deposit with the Secretary-General of the United Nations of the tenth instrument of ratification or accession.

2. For each State ratifying the present Protocol or acceding to it after its entry into force, the present Protocol shall enter into force three months after the date of the deposit of its own instrument of ratification or accession.

Article 17

No reservations to the present Protocol shall be permitted.

Article 18

1. Any State Party may propose an amendment to the present Protocol and file it with the Secretary-General of the United Nations. The Secretary-General shall thereupon communicate any proposed amendments to the States Parties with a request that they notify her or him whether they favour a conference of States Parties for the purpose of considering and voting on the proposal. In the event that at least one third of the States Parties favour such a conference, the Secretary-General shall convene the conference under the auspices of the United Nations. Any amendment adopted by a majority of the States Parties present and voting at the conference shall be submitted to the General Assembly of the United Nations for approval.

2. Amendments shall come into force when they have been approved by the General Assembly of the United Nations and accepted by a two-thirds majority of the States Parties to the present Protocol in accordance with their respective constitutional processes.

3. When amendments come into force, they shall be binding on those States Parties that have accepted them, other States Parties still being bound by the provisions of the present Protocol and any earlier amendments that they have accepted.

Article 19

1. Any State Party may denounce the present Protocol at any time by written notification addressed to the Secretary-General of the United Nations. Denunciation shall take effect six months after the date of receipt of the notification by the Secretary-General.

2. Denunciation shall be without prejudice to the continued application of the provisions of the present Protocol to any communication submitted under article 2 or any inquiry initiated under article 8 before the effective date of denunciation.

Article 20

The Secretary-General of the United Nations shall inform all States of:

(a) Signatures, ratifications and accessions under the present Protocol;

(b) The date of entry into force of the present Protocol and of any amendment under article 18;

(c) Any denunciation under article 19.

Article 21

1. The present Protocol, of which the Arabic, Chinese, English, French, Russian and Spanish texts are equally authentic, shall be deposited in the archives of the United Nations.

2. The Secretary-General of the United Nations shall transmit certified copies of the present Protocol to all States referred to in article 25 of the Convention.

CONVENTION AGAINST TORTURE AND OTHER CRUEL, INHUMAN OR DEGRADING TREATMENT OR PUNISHMENT, G.A. res. 39/46, annex, 39 U.N. GAOR Supp. (No. 51) at 197, U.N. Doc. A/39/51 (1984), *entered into force* June 26, 1987:

The States Parties to this Convention,

Considering that, in accordance with the principles proclaimed in the Charter of the United Nations, recognition of the equal and inalienable rights of all members of the human family is the foundation of freedom, justice and peace in the world,

Recognizing that those rights derive from the inherent dignity of the human person,

Considering the obligation of States under the Charter, in particular Article 55, to promote universal respect for, and observance of, human rights and fundamental freedoms,

Having regard to article 5 of the Universal Declaration of Human Rights and article 7 of the International Covenant on Civil and Political Rights, both of which provide that no one shall be subjected to torture or to cruel, inhuman or degrading treatment or punishment,

Having regard also to the Declaration on the Protection of All Persons from Being Subjected to Torture and Other Cruel, Inhuman or Degrading Treatment or Punishment, adopted by the General Assembly on 9 December 1975,

Desiring to make more effective the struggle against torture and other cruel, inhuman or degrading treatment or punishment throughout the world,

Have agreed as follows:

PART I

Article 1

1. For the purposes of this Convention, the term "torture" means any act by which severe pain or suffering, whether physical or mental, is intentionally inflicted on a person for such purposes as obtaining from him or a third person

information or a confession, punishing him for an act he or a third person has committed or is suspected of having committed, or intimidating or coercing him or a third person, or for any reason based on discrimination of any kind, when such pain or suffering is inflicted by or at the instigation of or with the consent or acquiescence of a public official or other person acting in an official capacity. It does not include pain or suffering arising only from, inherent in or incidental to lawful sanctions.

2. This article is without prejudice to any international instrument or national legislation which does or may contain provisions of wider application.

Article 2

1. Each State Party shall take effective legislative, administrative, judicial or other measures to prevent acts of torture in any territory under its jurisdiction.

2. No exceptional circumstances whatsoever, whether a state of war or a threat of war, internal political instability or any other public emergency, may be invoked as a justification of torture.

3. An order from a superior officer or a public authority may not be invoked as a justification of torture.

Article 3

1. No State Party shall expel, return *("refouler")* or extradite a person to another State where there are substantial grounds for believing that he would be in danger of being subjected to torture.

2. For the purpose of determining whether there are such grounds, the competent authorities shall take into account all relevant considerations including, where applicable, the existence in the State concerned of a consistent pattern of gross, flagrant or mass violations of human rights.

Article 4

1. Each State Party shall ensure that all acts of torture are offences under its criminal law. The same shall apply to an attempt to commit torture and to an act by any person which constitutes complicity or participation in torture.

2. Each State Party shall make these offences punishable by appropriate penalties which take into account their grave nature.

Article 5

1. Each State Party shall take such measures as may be necessary to establish its jurisdiction over the offences referred to in article 4 in the following cases:

(a) When the offences are committed in any territory under its jurisdiction or on board a ship or aircraft registered in that State;

(b) When the alleged offender is a national of that State;

(c) When the victim is a national of that State if that State considers it appropriate.

2. Each State Party shall likewise take such measures as may be necessary to establish its jurisdiction over such offences in cases where the alleged offender is present in any territory under its jurisdiction and it does not extradite him pursuant to article 8 to any of the States mentioned in paragraph 1 of this article.

3. This Convention does not exclude any criminal jurisdiction exercised in accordance with internal law.

Article 6

1. Upon being satisfied, after an examination of information available to it, that the circumstances so warrant, any State Party in whose territory a person alleged to have committed any offence referred to in article 4 is present shall take him into custody or take other legal measures to ensure his presence. The custody and other legal measures shall be as provided in the law of that State but may be continued only for such time as is necessary to enable any criminal or extradition proceedings to be instituted.

2. Such State shall immediately make a preliminary inquiry into the facts.

3. Any person in custody pursuant to paragraph 1 of this article shall be assisted in communicating immediately with the nearest appropriate representative of the State of which he is a national, or, if he is a stateless person, with the representative of the State where he usually resides.

4. When a State, pursuant to this article, has taken a person into custody, it shall immediately notify the States referred to in article 5, paragraph 1, of the fact that such person is in custody and of the circumstances which warrant his detention. The State which makes the preliminary inquiry contemplated in paragraph 2 of this article shall promptly report its findings to the said States and shall indicate whether it intends to exercise jurisdiction.

Article 7

1. The State Party in the territory under whose jurisdiction a person alleged to have committed any offence referred to in article 4 is found shall in the cases contemplated in article 5, if it does not extradite him, submit the case to its competent authorities for the purpose of prosecution.

2. These authorities shall take their decision in the same manner as in the case of any ordinary offence of a serious nature under the law of that State. In the cases referred to in article 5, paragraph 2, the standards of evidence required for prosecution and conviction shall in no way be less stringent than those which apply in the cases referred to in article 5, paragraph 1.

3. Any person regarding whom proceedings are brought in connection with any of the offences referred to in article 4 shall be guaranteed fair treatment at all stages of the proceedings.

Article 8

1. The offences referred to in article 4 shall be deemed to be included as extraditable offences in any extradition treaty existing between States Parties.

States Parties undertake to include such offences as extraditable offences in every extradition treaty to be concluded between them.

2. If a State Party which makes extradition conditional on the existence of a treaty receives a request for extradition from another State Party with which it has no extradition treaty, it may consider this Convention as the legal basis for extradition in respect of such offences. Extradition shall be subject to the other conditions provided by the law of the requested State.

3. States Parties which do not make extradition conditional on the existence of a treaty shall recognize such offences as extraditable offences between themselves subject to the conditions provided by the law of the requested State.

4. Such offences shall be treated, for the purpose of extradition between States Parties, as if they had been committed not only in the place in which they occurred but also in the territories of the States required to establish their jurisdiction in accordance with article 5, paragraph 1.

Article 9

1. States Parties shall afford one another the greatest measure of assistance in connection with criminal proceedings brought in respect of any of the offences referred to in article 4, including the supply of all evidence at their disposal necessary for the proceedings.

2. States Parties shall carry out their obligations under paragraph 1 of this article in conformity with any treaties on mutual judicial assistance that may exist between them.

Article 10

1. Each State Party shall ensure that education and information regarding the prohibition against torture are fully included in the training of law enforcement personnel, civil or military, medical personnel, public officials and other persons who may be involved in the custody, interrogation or treatment of any individual subjected to any form of arrest, detention or imprisonment.

2. Each State Party shall include this prohibition in the rules or instructions issued in regard to the duties and functions of any such person.

Article 11

Each State Party shall keep under systematic review interrogation rules, instructions, methods and practices as well as arrangements for the custody and treatment of persons subjected to any form of arrest, detention or imprisonment in any territory under its jurisdiction, with a view to preventing any cases of torture.

Article 12

Each State Party shall ensure that its competent authorities proceed to a prompt and impartial investigation, wherever there is reasonable ground to believe that an act of torture has been committed in any territory under its jurisdiction.

Article 13

Each State Party shall ensure that any individual who alleges he has been subjected to torture in any territory under its jurisdiction has the right to complain to, and to have his case promptly and impartially examined by, its competent authorities. Steps shall be taken to ensure that the complainant and witnesses are protected against all ill-treatment or intimidation as a consequence of his complaint or any evidence given.

Article 14

1. Each State Party shall ensure in its legal system that the victim of an act of torture obtains redress and has an enforceable right to fair and adequate compensation, including the means for as full rehabilitation as possible. In the event of the death of the victim as a result of an act of torture, his dependents shall be entitled to compensation.

2. Nothing in this article shall affect any right of the victim or other persons to compensation which may exist under national law.

Article 15

Each State Party shall ensure that any statement which is established to have been made as a result of torture shall not be invoked as evidence in any proceedings, except against a person accused of torture as evidence that the statement was made.

Article 16

1. Each State Party shall undertake to prevent in any territory under its jurisdiction other acts of cruel, inhuman or degrading treatment or punishment which do not amount to torture as defined in article 1, when such acts are committed by or at the instigation of or with the consent or acquiescence of a public official or other person acting in an official capacity. In particular, the obligations contained in articles 10, 11, 12 and 13 shall apply with the substitution for references to torture of references to other forms of cruel, inhuman or degrading treatment or punishment.

2. The provisions of this Convention are without prejudice to the provisions of any other international instrument or national law which prohibits cruel, inhuman or degrading treatment or punishment or which relates to extradition or expulsion.

PART II

Article 17

1. There shall be established a Committee against Torture (hereinafter referred to as the Committee) which shall carry out the functions hereinafter provided. The Committee shall consist of ten experts of high moral standing and recognized competence in the field of human rights, who shall serve in their personal capacity. The experts shall be elected by the States

Parties, consideration being given to equitable geographical distribution and to the usefulness of the participation of some persons having legal experience.

2. The members of the Committee shall be elected by secret ballot from a list of persons nominated by States Parties. Each State Party may nominate one person from among its own nationals. States Parties shall bear in mind the usefulness of nominating persons who are also members of the Human Rights Committee established under the International Covenant on Civil and Political Rights and who are willing to serve on the Committee against Torture.

3. Elections of the members of the Committee shall be held at biennial meetings of States Parties convened by the Secretary-General of the United Nations. At those meetings, for which two thirds of the States Parties shall constitute a quorum, the persons elected to the Committee shall be those who obtain the largest number of votes and an absolute majority of the votes of the representatives of States Parties present and voting.

4. The initial election shall be held no later than six months after the date of the entry into force of this Convention. At least four months before the date of each election, the Secretary-General of the United Nations shall address a letter to the States Parties inviting them to submit their nominations within three months. The Secretary-General shall prepare a list in alphabetical order of all persons thus nominated, indicating the States Parties which have nominated them, and shall submit it to the States Parties.

5. The members of the Committee shall be elected for a term of four years. They shall be eligible for re-election if renominated. However, the term of five of the members elected at the first election shall expire at the end of two years; immediately after the first election the names of these five members shall be chosen by lot by the chairman of the meeting referred to in paragraph 3 of this article.

6. If a member of the Committee dies or resigns or for any other cause can no longer perform his Committee duties, the State Party which nominated him shall appoint another expert from among its nationals to serve for the remainder of his term, subject to the approval of the majority of the States Parties. The approval shall be considered given unless half or more of the States Parties respond negatively within six weeks after having been informed by the Secretary-General of the United Nations of the proposed appointment.

7. States Parties shall be responsible for the expenses of the members of the Committee while they are in performance of Committee duties.

Article 18

1. The Committee shall elect its officers for a term of two years. They may be re-elected.

2. The Committee shall establish its own rules of procedure, but these rules shall provide, inter alia, that:

(a) Six members shall constitute a quorum;

(b) Decisions of the Committee shall be made by a majority vote of the members present.

3. The Secretary-General of the United Nations shall provide the necessary staff and facilities for the effective performance of the functions of the Committee under this Convention.

4. The Secretary-General of the United Nations shall convene the initial meeting of the Committee. After its initial meeting, the Committee shall meet at such times as shall be provided in its rules of procedure.

5. The States Parties shall be responsible for expenses incurred in connection with the holding of meetings of the States Parties and of the Committee, including reimbursement to the United Nations for any expenses, such as the cost of staff and facilities, incurred by the United Nations pursuant to paragraph 3 of this article.

Article 19

1. The States Parties shall submit to the Committee, through the Secretary-General of the United Nations, reports on the measures they have taken to give effect to their undertakings under this Convention, within one year after the entry into force of the Convention for the State Party concerned. Thereafter the States Parties shall submit supplementary reports every four years on any new measures taken and such other reports as the Committee may request.

2. The Secretary-General of the United Nations shall transmit the reports to all States Parties.

3. Each report shall be considered by the Committee which may make such general comments on the report as it may consider appropriate and shall forward these to the State Party concerned. That State Party may respond with any observations it chooses to the Committee.

4. The Committee may, at its discretion, decide to include any comments made by it in accordance with paragraph 3 of this article, together with the observations thereon received from the State Party concerned, in its annual report made in accordance with article 24. If so requested by the State Party concerned, the Committee may also include a copy of the report submitted under paragraph 1 of this article.

Article 20

1. If the Committee receives reliable information which appears to it to contain well-founded indications that torture is being systematically practised in the territory of a State Party, the Committee shall invite that State Party to co-operate in the examination of the information and to this end to submit observations with regard to the information concerned.

2. Taking into account any observations which may have been submitted by the State Party concerned, as well as any other relevant information available to it, the Committee may, if it decides that this is warranted, designate one or more of its members to make a confidential inquiry and to report to the Committee urgently.

3. If an inquiry is made in accordance with paragraph 2 of this article, the Committee shall seek the co-operation of the State Party concerned. In agreement with that State Party, such an inquiry may include a visit to its territory.

4. After examining the findings of its member or members submitted in accordance with paragraph 2 of this article, the Commission shall transmit these findings to the State Party concerned together with any comments or suggestions which seem appropriate in view of the situation.

5. All the proceedings of the Committee referred to in paragraphs 1 to 4 of this article shall be confidential, and at all stages of the proceedings the co-operation of the State Party shall be sought. After such proceedings have been completed with regard to an inquiry made in accordance with paragraph 2, the Committee may, after consultations with the State Party concerned, decide to include a summary account of the results of the proceedings in its annual report made in accordance with article 24.

Article 21

1. A State Party to this Convention may at any time declare under this article that it recognizes the competence of the Committee to receive and consider communications to the effect that a State Party claims that another State Party is not fulfilling its obligations under this Convention. Such communications may be received and considered according to the procedures laid down in this article only if submitted by a State Party which has made a declaration recognizing in regard to itself the competence of the Committee. No communication shall be dealt with by the Committee under this article if it concerns a State Party which has not made such a declaration. Communications received under this article shall be dealt with in accordance with the following procedure:

(a) If a State Party considers that another State Party is not giving effect to the provisions of this Convention, it may, by written communication, bring the matter to the attention of that State Party. Within three months after the receipt of the communication the receiving State shall afford the State which sent the communication an explanation or any other statement in writing clarifying the matter, which should include, to the extent possible and pertinent, reference to domestic procedures and remedies taken, pending or available in the matter;

(b) If the matter is not adjusted to the satisfaction of both States Parties concerned within six months after the receipt by the receiving State of the initial communication, either State shall have the right to refer the matter to the Committee, by notice given to the Committee and to the other State;

(c) The Committee shall deal with a matter referred to it under this article only after it has ascertained that all domestic remedies have been invoked and exhausted in the matter, in conformity with the generally recognized principles of international law. This shall not be the rule where the application of the remedies is unreasonably prolonged or is unlikely to bring effective relief to the person who is the victim of the violation of this Convention;

(d) The Committee shall hold closed meetings when examining communications under this article;

(e) Subject to the provisions of subparagraph *(c)*, the Committee shall make available its good offices to the States Parties concerned with a view to a friendly solution of the matter on the basis of respect for the obligations provided for in this Convention. For this purpose, the Committee may, when appropriate, set up an ad hoc conciliation commission;

(f) In any matter referred to it under this article, the Committee may call upon the States Parties concerned, referred to in subparagraph *(b)*, to supply any relevant information;

(g) The States Parties concerned, referred to in subparagraph *(b)*, shall have the right to be represented when the matter is being considered by the Committee and to make submissions orally and/or in writing;

(h) The Committee shall, within twelve months after the date of receipt of notice under subparagraph *(b)*, submit a report:

(i) If a solution within the terms of subparagraph *(e)* is reached, the Committee shall confine its report to a brief statement of the facts and of the solution reached;

(ii) If a solution within the terms of subparagraph *(e)* is not reached, the Committee shall confine its report to a brief statement of the facts; the written submissions and record of the oral submissions made by the States Parties concerned shall be attached to the report. In every matter, the report shall be communicated to the States Parties concerned.

2. The provisions of this article shall come into force when five States Parties to this Convention have made declarations under paragraph 1 of this article. Such declarations shall be deposited by the States Parties with the Secretary-General of the United Nations, who shall transmit copies thereof to the other States Parties. A declaration may be withdrawn at any time by notification to the Secretary-General. Such a withdrawal shall not prejudice the consideration of any matter which is the subject of a communication already transmitted under this article; no further communication by any State Party shall be received under this article after the notification of withdrawal of the declaration has been received by the Secretary-General, unless the State Party concerned has made a new declaration.

Article 22

1. A State Party to this Convention may at any time declare under this article that it recognizes the competence of the Committee to receive and consider communications from or on behalf of individuals subject to its jurisdiction who claim to be victims of a violation by a State Party of the provisions of the Convention. No communication shall be received by the Committee if it concerns a State Party which has not made such a declaration.

2. The Committee shall consider inadmissible any communication under this article which is anonymous or which it considers to be an abuse of the right of submission of such communications or to be incompatible with the provisions of this Convention.

3. Subject to the provisions of paragraph 2, the Committee shall bring any communications submitted to it under this article to the attention of the State Party to this Convention which has made a declaration under paragraph 1 and is alleged to be violating any provisions of the Convention. Within six months, the receiving State shall submit to the Committee written explanations or statements clarifying the matter and the remedy, if any, that may have been taken by that State.

4. The Committee shall consider communications received under this article in the light of all information made available to it by or on behalf of the individual and by the State Party concerned.

5. The Committee shall not consider any communications from an individual under this article unless it has ascertained that:

(a) The same matter has not been, and is not being, examined under another procedure of international investigation or settlement;

(b) The individual has exhausted all available domestic remedies; this shall not be the rule where the application of the remedies is unreasonably prolonged or is unlikely to bring effective relief to the person who is the victim of the violation of this Convention.

6. The Committee shall hold closed meetings when examining communications under this article.

7. The Committee shall forward its views to the State Party concerned and to the individual.

8. The provisions of this article shall come into force when five States Parties to this Convention have made declarations under paragraph 1 of this article. Such declarations shall be deposited by the States Parties with the Secretary-General of the United Nations, who shall transmit copies thereof to the other States Parties. A declaration may be withdrawn at any time by notification to the Secretary-General. Such a withdrawal shall not prejudice the consideration of any matter which is the subject of a communication already transmitted under this article; no further communication by or on behalf of an individual shall be received under this article after the notification of withdrawal of the declaration has been received by the Secretary-General, unless the State Party has made a new declaration.

Article 23

The members of the Committee and of the ad hoc conciliation commissions which maybe appointed under article 21, paragraph 1 (e), shall be entitled to the facilities, privileges and immunities of experts on mission for the United Nations as laid down in the relevant sections of the Convention on the Privileges and Immunities of the United Nations.

Article 24

The Committee shall submit an annual report on its activities under this Convention to the States Parties and to the General Assembly of the United Nations.

PART III

Article 25

1. This Convention is open for signature by all States.

2. This Convention is subject to ratification. Instruments of ratification shall be deposited with the Secretary-General of the United Nations.

Article 26

This Convention is open to accession by all States. Accession shall be effected by the deposit of an instrument of accession with the Secretary-General of the United Nations.

Article 27

1. This Convention shall enter into force on the thirtieth day after the date of the deposit with the Secretary-General of the United Nations of the twentieth instrument of ratification or accession.

2. For each State ratifying this Convention or acceding to it after the deposit of the twentieth instrument of ratification or accession, the Convention shall enter into force on the thirtieth day after the date of the deposit of its own instrument of ratification or accession.

Article 28

1. Each State may, at the time of signature or ratification of this Convention or accession thereto, declare that it does not recognize the competence of the Committee provided for in article 20.

2. Any State Party having made a reservation in accordance with paragraph 1 of this article may, at any time, withdraw this reservation by notification to the Secretary-General of the United Nations.

Article 29

1. Any State Party to this Convention may propose an amendment and file it with the Secretary-General of the United Nations. The Secretary-General shall thereupon communicate the proposed amendment to the States Parties with a request that they notify him whether they favour a conference of States Parties for the purpose of considering and voting upon the proposal. In the event that within four months from the date of such communication at least one third of the States Parties favours such a conference, the Secretary-General shall convene the conference under the auspices of the United Nations. Any amendment adopted by a majority of the States Parties present and voting at the conference shall be submitted by the Secretary-General to all the States Parties for acceptance.

2. An amendment adopted in accordance with paragraph 1 of this article shall enter into force when two thirds of the States Parties to this Convention have notified the Secretary-General of the United Nations that they have accepted it in accordance with their respective constitutional processes.

3. When amendments enter into force, they shall be binding on those States Parties which have accepted them, other States Parties still being bound by the provisions of this Convention and any earlier amendments which they have accepted.

Article 30

1. Any dispute between two or more States Parties concerning the interpretation or application of this Convention which cannot be settled through negotiation shall, at the request of one of them, be submitted to arbitration. If within six months from the date of the request for arbitration the Parties are unable to agree on the organization of the arbitration, any one of those Parties may refer the dispute to the International Court of Justice by request in conformity with the Statute of the Court.

2. Each State may, at the time of signature or ratification of this Convention or accession thereto, declare that it does not consider itself bound by paragraph 1 of this article. The other States Parties shall not be bound by paragraph 1 of this article with respect to any State Party having made such a reservation.

3. Any State Party having made a reservation in accordance with paragraph 2 of this article may at any time withdraw this reservation by notification to the Secretary-General of the United Nations.

Article 31

1. A State Party may denounce this Convention by written notification to the Secretary-General of the United Nations. Denunciation becomes effective one year after the date of receipt of the notification by the Secretary-General.

2. Such a denunciation shall not have the effect of releasing the State Party from its obligations under this Convention in regard to any act or omission which occurs prior to the date at which the denunciation becomes effective, nor shall denunciation prejudice in any way the continued consideration of any matter which is already under consideration by the Committee prior to the date at which the denunciation becomes effective.

3. Following the date at which the denunciation of a State Party becomes effective, the Committee shall not commence consideration of any new matter regarding that State.

Article 32

The Secretary-General of the United Nations shall inform all States Members of the United Nations and all States which have signed this Convention or acceded to it of the following:

(a) Signatures, ratifications and accessions under articles 25 and 26;

(b) The date of entry into force of this Convention under article 27 and the date of the entry into force of any amendments under article 29;

(c) Denunciations under article 31.

Article 33

1. This Convention, of which the Arabic, Chinese, English, French, Russian and Spanish texts are equally authentic, shall be deposited with the Secretary-General of the United Nations.

2. The Secretary-General of the United Nations shall transmit certified copies of this Convention to all States.

OPTIONAL PROTOCOL TO CONVENTION AGAINST TORTURE AND OTHER CRUEL, INHUMAN OR DEGRADING TREATMENT OR PUNISHMENT, G.A. res. A/RES/57/199, *entered into force* June 22, 2006:

PART I

General principles

Article 1

The objective of this Protocol is to establish a system of regular visits undertaken by independent international and national bodies to places where people are deprived of their liberty, in order to prevent torture and other cruel, inhuman or degrading treatment or punishment.

Article 2

1. A Sub-Committee on Prevention of Torture and Other Cruel, Inhuman or Degrading Treatment or Punishment of the Committee against Torture (hereinafter referred to as the Sub-Committee on Prevention shall be established and shall carry out the functions laid down in the present Protocol.

2. The Sub-Committee on Prevention shall carry out its work within the framework of the Charter of the United Nations and will be guided by the purposes and principles thereof as well as the norms of the United Nations concerning the treatment of people deprived of their liberty.

3. Equally, the Sub-Committee on Prevention shall be guided by the principles of confidentiality, impartiality, non-selectivity, universality and objectivity.

4. The Sub-Committee on Prevention and the State parties shall cooperate in the implementation of the present Protocol.

Article 3

Each State party shall set up, designate or maintain at the domestic level one or several visiting bodies for the prevention of torture and other cruel, inhuman or degrading treatment or punishment (hereinafter referred to as the national preventive mechanism).

Article 4

1. Each State Party shall allow visits, in accordance with the present Protocol, by the mechanisms referred to in articles 2 and 3 to any place under its jurisdiction and control where persons are or may be deprived of their liberty, either by virtue of an order given by a public authority or at its instigation or with its consent or acquiescence (hereinafter referred to as places of detention). These visits shall be undertaken with a view to strengthening, if necessary, the protection of these persons against torture and other cruel, inhuman or degrading treatment or punishment.

2. For the purposes of the present Protocol deprivation of liberty means any form of detention or imprisonment or the placement of a person in a public or private custodial setting, from which this person is not permitted to leave at will by order of any judicial, administrative or other authority.

PART II

The Sub-Committee on Prevention

Article 5

1. The Sub-Committee on Prevention shall consist of ten members. After the fiftieth ratification or accession to the present Protocol, the number of the members of the Sub-Committee on Prevention shall increase to 25.

2. The members of the Sub-Committee shall be chosen from among persons of high moral character, having proven professional experience in the field of the administration of justice, in particular criminal law, prison or police administration or in the various fields relevant to the treatment of persons deprived of their liberty.

3. In the composition of the Sub-Committee due consideration shall be given to the equitable geographic distribution and to the representation of different forms of civilisation and legal systems of the States parties.

4. In this composition consideration shall also be given to the balanced gender representation on the basis of the principles of equality and non-discrimination.

5. No two members of the Sub-Committee on Prevention may be nationals of the same State.

6. The members of the Sub-Committee on Prevention shall serve in their individual capacity, shall be independent and impartial and shall be available to serve the Sub-Committee on Prevention efficiently.

Article 6

1. Each State party may nominate, in accordance with paragraph 2, up to two candidates possessing the qualifications and meeting the requirements set out in article 5, and in doing so shall provide detailed information on the qualifications of the nominees.

2. The nominees shall have the nationality of a State party to the present Protocol;

    a. At least one of the two candidates shall have the nationality of the nominating State party;

    b. No more than two nationals of a State party shall be nominated;

    c. Before a State party nominates a national of another State party, it shall seek and obtain the consent of that State party.

3. At least five months before the date of the meeting of the State parties during which the elections will be held, the Secretary-General of the United Nations shall address a letter to the States parties inviting them to submit their nominations within three months. The Secretary-General shall submit a list in alphabetical order of all persons thus nominated, indicating the States parties which have nominated them.

Article 7

1. The members of the Sub-Committee on Prevention shall be elected in the following manner:

    a. Primary consideration shall be given to the fulfilment of the requirements and criteria of article 5 of the present Protocol;

    b. The initial election shall be held no later than six months after the entry into force of the present Protocol;

    c. The State parties shall elect the members of the Sub-Committee by secret ballot;

    d. Elections of the members of the Sub-Committee shall be held at biennial meetings of the States parties convened by the Secretary-General of the United Nations. At those meetings, for which two thirds of the States parties shall constitute a quorum, the persons elected to the Sub-Committee shall be those who obtain the largest number of votes and an absolute majority of the votes of the representatives of the States parties present and voting;

2. If, during the election process, two nationals of a State party have become eligible to serve as members of the Sub-Committee on Prevention, the candidate receiving the higher number of votes shall serve as the member of the Sub-Committee. Where nationals have received the same number of votes, the following procedure applies:

    a. Where only one has been nominated by the State party of which he or she is a national, that national shall serve as the member of the Sub-Committee on Prevention;

    b. Where both nationals have been nominated by the State party of which they are nationals, a separate vote by secret ballot shall be held to determine which national shall become member;

    c. Where neither national has been nominated by the State party of which he or she is a national, a separate vote by secret ballot shall be held to determine which national shall be the member.

Article 8

If a member of the Sub-Committee on Prevention dies or resigns or for any cause can no longer perform his or her duties, the State party which nominated the member shall nominate another eligible person possessing the qualifications and meeting the requirements set out in article 5, taking into account the need for a proper balance among the various fields of competence, to serve until the next meeting of the States parties, subject to approval of the majority of the States parties. The approval shall be considered given unless half or more of the States parties respond negatively within six weeks after having been informed by the SecretaryGeneral of the United Nations of the proposed appointment.

Article 9

The members of the Sub-Committee on Prevention shall be elected for a term of four years. They shall be eligible for re-election once if renominated. The term of half the members elected at the first election shall expire at the end of two years; immediately after the first election the names of these members shall be chosen by lot by the Chairman of the meeting referred to in article 7 paragraph 1 d.

Article 10

1. The Sub-Committee on Prevention shall elect its officers for a term of two years. They may be re-elected.

2. The Sub-Committee on Prevention shall establish its own rules of procedure. These rules shall provide inter alia that:

   a. Half plus one members shall constitute a quorum;

   b. Decisions of the Sub-Committee on Prevention shall be made by a majority vote of the members present;

   c. The Sub-Committee on Prevention shall meet in camera.

3. The Secretary-General of the United Nations shall convene the initial meeting of the Sub-Committee on Prevention. After its initial meeting, the Sub-Committee on Prevention shall meet at such times as shall be provided by its rules of procedure. The Sub-Committee on Prevention and the Committee against Torture shall hold their sessions simultaneously at least once a year.

PART III

Mandate of the Sub-Committee on Prevention

Article 11

The Sub-Committee on Prevention shall:

1. Visit the places referred to in article 4 and make recommendations to States Parties concerning the protection of persons deprived of their liberty from torture and other cruel, inhuman or degrading treatment or punishment;

2. In regard to the national preventive mechanisms:

a. Advise and assist States Parties, when necessary, in their establishment;

b. Maintain direct, if necessary confidential, contact with the national preventive mechanisms and offer them training and technical assistance with a view to strengthening their capacities;

c. Advise and assist them in the evaluation of the needs and the means necessary to strengthen the protection of persons deprived of their liberty from torture and other cruel, inhuman or degrading treatment or punishment;

d. Make recommendations and observations to the States parties with a view to strengthening the capacity and the mandate of the national preventive mechanisms for the prevention of torture and other cruel, inhuman or degrading treatment or punishment;

3. Cooperate, for the prevention of torture in general, with the relevant United Nations organs and mechanisms as well as with the international, regional and national institutions or organisations working toward the strengthing of the protection of persons from torture and other cruel, inhuman or degrading treatment or punishment.

Article 12

In order to enable the Sub-Committee on Prevention to comply with its mandate as laid out in article 11, the State parties undertake to:

1. Receive the Sub-Committee on Prevention in its territory and grant it access to the places of detention as defined in article 4 of the present Protocol;

2. Share all relevant information the Sub-Committe on Prevention may request to evaluate the needs and measures that should be adopted in order to strengthen the protection of persons deprived of their liberty from torture and other cruel, inhuman or degrading treatment or punishment;

3. Encourage and facilitate contacts between the Sub-Committee on Prevention and the national preventive mechanisms;

4. Examine the recommendations of the Sub-Committee on Prevention and enter into dialogue with it on possible implementation measures.

Article 13

1. The Sub-Committee on Prevention shall establish, at first by lot, a programme of regular visits to the States Parties in order to fulfill its mandate as established in article 11.

2. After consultations, the Sub-Committe on Prevention shall notify its programme to the States Parties for them to, without delay, make the necessary practical arrangements for the visits to take place.

3. The visits shall be conducted by at least two members of the Sub-Committee on Prevention. These members can be accompanied if needed by

experts of demonstrated professional experience and knowledge in the fields covered by the present Protocol and shall be selected from a roster of experts prepared on the basis of proposals made by the States parties, the Office of the High Commissioner for Human Rights and the United Nations Centre for Crime Prevention. In preparing the roster, the States parties concerned shall propose no more than five national experts. The State party concerned may oppose the inclusion of a specific expert in the visit, whereupon the Sub-Committee on Prevention shall propose another expert.

4. If the Sub-Committee on Prevention considers it appropriate, it can propose a short follow-up visit to a regular visit.

Article 14

1. In order to enable the Sub-Committee on Prevention to fulfill its mandate the States Parties to the present Protocol undertake to grant it:

a. Unrestricted access to all information concerning the number of persons deprived of their liberty in places of detention as defined in article 4, as well as the number of places and their location;

b. Unrestricted access to all information referring to the treatment of these persons as well as their conditions of detention;

c. Subject to paragraph 2, unrestricted access to all places of detention and their installations and facilities;

d. The opportunity to have private interviews with the persons deprived of their liberty without witnesses, either personally or with a translator if deemed necessary, as well as with any other person whom the Sub-Committee on Prevention believes may supply relevant information;

e. The liberty to choose the places it wants to visit and the persons it wants to interview.

2. Objection to a visit to a particular place of detention can only be made on urgent and compelling grounds of national defence, public safety, natural disaster or serious disorder in the place to be visited, which temporarily prevent the carrying out of such a visit. The existence of a declaration of a State of Emergency as such shall not be invoked by a State Party as a reason to object a visit.

Article 15

No authority or official shall order, apply, permit or tolerate any sanction against any person or organisation for having communicated to the Sub-Committee on Prevention or to its delegates any information, whether true or false, and no such person or organisation shall be otherwise prejudiced in any way.

Article 16

1. The Sub-Committee on Prevention shall communicate its recommendations and observations confidentially to the State Party and, if relevant, to the national mechanism.

2. The Sub-Committee on Prevention shall publish its report, together with any comments of the State Patty concerned, whenever requested to do so by that State party. If the State Party makes part of the report public, the Sub-Committee on Prevention may publish the report in whole or in part. However, no personal data shall be published without the express consent of the person concerned.

3. The Sub-Committee on Prevention shall present a public annual report on its acitvities to the Committee against Torture.

4. If the State Party refuses to co-operate with the Sub-Committee on Prevention according to articles 12 and 14, or to take steps to improve the situation in the light of the Sub-Committee on Prevention's recommendations, the Committee against Torture may at the request of the Sub-Committee on Prevention decide by a majority of its members, after the State Party has had an opportunity to make its views known, to make a public statement on the matter or to publish the Sub-Committee on Prevention's report.

PART IV

National Preventive Mechanisms

Article 17

Each State Party shall maintain, designate or establish at the latest one year after the entry into force of the present Protocol or of its ratification or accession, one or several independent national preventive mechanisms for the prevention of torture at the domestic level. Mechanisms established by decentralised units may be designated as national preventive mechanisms for the purposes of the present Protocol, if they are in conformity with its provisions.

Article 18

1. The States Parties shall guarantee the functional independance of the national preventive mechanisms as well as the independence of their personnel.

2. The States Parties shall take the necessary measures in order for the experts of the national mechanism to have the required capabilities and professional knowledge. They shall strive for a gender balance and the adequate representation of ethnic and minority groups in the country.

3. The States Parties undertake to make available the necessary resources for the functioning of the national preventive mechanisms.

4. When establishing national preventive mechanisms, States Parties shall give due consideration to the Principles relating to the Status and Functioning of National Institutions for Protection and Promotion of Human Rights.

Article 19

The national preventive mechanisms shall be granted at least the powers to:

1. Regularly examine the treatment of the persons deprived of their liberty in places according to article 4, with a view to strengthening, if necessary,

their protection from torture, cruel, inhuman or degrading treatment or punishment;

2. Make recommendations to the relevant authorities with the aim of improving the treatment and the conditions of the persons deprived of their liberty and to prevent torture, cruel, inhuman or degrading treatment or punishment, taking into consideration the relevant norms of the United Nations;

3. Submit proposals and observations concerning existing or draft legislation.

Article 20

In order to enable the national preventive mechanisms to fulfill their mandate, the States Parties to the present Protocol undertake to grant them:

1. Access to all information concerning the number of persons deprived of their liberty in places of detention as defined in article 4, as well as the number of places and their location;

2. Access to all information referring to the treatment of these persons as well as their conditions of detention;

3. Access to all places of detention and their installations and facilities;

4. The opportunity to have private interviews with the persons deprived of their liberty without witnesses, either personally or with a translator if deemed necessary, as well as with any other person whom the national preventive mechanism believes may supply relevant information;

5. The liberty to choose the places it wants to visit and the persons it wants to interview;

6. The right to have contacts with the Sub-Committee on Prevention, to send it information and to meet with it.

Article 21

1. No authority or official shall order, apply, permit or tolerate any sanction against any person or organisation for having communicated to the national preventive mechanism any information, whether true or false, and no such person or organisation shall be otherwise prejudiced in any way.

2. Confidential information collected by the national preventive mechanism shall be privileged. No personal data shall be published without the express consent of the person concerned.

Article 22

The competent authorities of the State Party concerned shall examine the recommendations of the national preventive mechanism and enter into a dialogue with it on possible implementation measures.

Article 23

The States Parties to the present Protocol undertake to publish and disseminate the annual reports of the national preventive mechanisms.

PART V

Declaration

Article 24

1. Upon ratification States Parties can make a declaration postponing the implementation of their obligations either under Part III or under Part IV of the present Protocol.

2. This postponement shall be valid for a maximum of three years. After due representations made by the State Party and after consultation with the Sub-Committee on Prevention, the Committee against Torture may extend this period for an additional two year period.

PART VI

Financial provisions

Article 25

1. The expenditure incurred by the Sub-Committee in the implementation of the present Protocol shall be borne by the United Nations.

2. The Secretary-General of the United Nations shall provide the necessary staff and facilities for the effective performance of the functions of the Sub-Committee under the present Protocol.

Article 26

1. A Special Fund shall be set up in accordance with General Assembly procedures, to be administered in accordance with the financial regulations and rules of the United Nations, to help finance the implementation of the recommendations made by the Sub-Committee on Prevention to a State party after a visit, as well as education programmes of the national preventive mechanisms.

2. This Fund may be financed through voluntary contributions made by Governments, intergovernmental and non-governmental organizations and other private or public entities.

PART VII

Final provisions

Article 27

1. The present Protocol is open for signature by any State which has signed the Convention.

2. The present Protocol is subject to ratification by any State which has ratified or acceded to the Convention. Instruments of ratification shall be deposited with the Secretary-General of the United Nations.

3. The present Protocol shall be open to accession by any State which has ratified or acceded to the Convention.

4. Accession shall be effected by the deposit of an instrument of accession with the Secretary General of the United Nations.

5. The Secretary-General of the United Nations shall inform all States which have signed the present Protocol or acceded to it of the deposit of each instrument of ratification or accession.

Article 28

1. The present Protocol shall enter into force on the thirtieth day after the date of deposit with the Secretary-General of the United Nations of the twentieth instrument of ratification or accession.

2. For each State ratifying the present Protocol or acceding to it after the deposit with the Secretary-General of the United Nations of the twentieth instrument of ratification or accession, the present Protocol shall enter into force on the thirtieth day after the date of the deposit of its own instrument of ratification or accession.

Article 29

The provisions of the present Protocol shall extend to all parts of federal States without any limitations or exceptions.

Article 30

No reservations shall be made to the present Protocol.

Article 31

The provisions of the present Protocol shall not affect the obligations of States Parties under any regional convention instituting a system of visits to places of detention. The Sub-Committee on Prevention and the bodies established under such regional conventions are encouraged to consult and cooperate with a view to avoiding duplication and promoting effectively the objectives of the present Protocol.

Article 32

The provisions of the present Protocol shall not affect the obligations of States parties to the four Geneva Conventions of 12 August 1949 and their Additional Protocols of 8 June 1997, or the opportunity available to any State party to authorize the International Committee of the Red Cross to visit places of detention in situations not covered by international humanitarian law.

Article 33

1. Any State party may denounce the present Protocol at any time by written notification addressed to the Secretary-General of the United Nations, who shall thereafter inform the other States Parties to the present Protocol and the Convention. Denunciation shall take effect one year after the date of receipt of the notification by the Secretary-General.

2. Such a denunciation shall not have the effect of releasing the State party from its obligations under the present Protocol in regard to any act or situation which occurs prior to the date at which the denunciation becomes effective, or to the actions that the Sub-Committee on Prevention has decided or may decide to adopt with respect to the State Party concerned, nor shall denunciation prejudice in any way the continued consideration of any matter which is already under consideration by the Sub-Committee on Prevention prior to the date at which the denunciation becomes effective.

3. Following the date at which the denunciation of the State party becomes effective, the SubCommittee on Prevention shall not commence consideration of any new matter regarding that State.

Article 34

1. Any State party to the present Protocol may propose an amendment and file it with the Secretary General of the United Nations. The Secretary-General shall thereupon communicate the proposed amendment to the States parties to the present Protocol with a request that they notify him whether they favour a conference of States parties for the purpose of considering and voting upon the proposal. In the event that within four months from the date of such communication at least one third of the States parties favour such a conference, the Secretary-General shall convene the conference under the auspices of the United Nations. Any amendment adopted by a majority of two thirds of the States parties present and voting at the conference shall be submitted by the Secretary-General of the United Nations to all States parties for acceptance.

2. An amendment adopted in accordance with paragraph I of the present article shall come into force when it has been accepted by a two-thirds majority of the States parties to the present Protocol in accordance with their respective constitutional process.

3. When amendments come into force, they shall be binding on those States parties which have accepted them, other States parties still being bound by the provisions of the present Protocol and any earlier amendment which they have accepted.

Article 35

Members of the Sub-Committee on Prevention and of the national preventive mechanisms shall be accorded such privileges and immunities as are necessary for the independent exercise of their functions. Members of the Sub-Committee on Prevention shall be accorded the privileges and immunities specified in section 22 of the Convention on Privileges and Immunities of the United Nations of 13 February 1946, subject to the provisions of section 23 of that Convention.

Article 36

When visiting a State Party the members of the Sub-Committee on Prevention shall, without prejudice to the provisions and purposes of the present Protocol and such privileges and immunities as they may enjoy:

(a) Respect the laws and regulations of the visited State; and

(b) Refrain from any action or activity incompatible with the impartial and international nature of their duties.

Article 37

1. The present Protocol, of which the Arabic, Chinese, English, French, Russian and Spanish texts are equally authentic, shall be deposited with the Secretary-General of the United Nations.

2. The Secretary-General of the United Nations shall transmit certified copies of the present Protocol to all States.

CONVENTION ON THE RIGHTS OF THE CHILD, G.A. res. 44/25, annex, 44 U.N. GAOR Supp. (No. 49) at 167, U.N. Doc. A/44/49 (1989), *entered into force* September 2, 1990:

Preamble

The States Parties to the present Convention,

Considering that, in accordance with the principles proclaimed in the Charter of the United Nations, recognition of the inherent dignity and of the equal and inalienable rights of all members of the human family is the foundation of freedom, justice and peace in the world,

Bearing in mind that the peoples of the United Nations have, in the Charter, reaffirmed their faith in fundamental human rights and in the dignity and worth of the human person, and have determined to promote social progress and better standards of life in larger freedom,

Recognizing that the United Nations has, in the Universal Declaration of Human Rights and in the International Covenants on Human Rights, proclaimed and agreed that everyone is entitled to all the rights and freedoms set forth therein, without distinction of any kind, such as race, colour, sex, language, religion, political or other opinion, national or social origin, property, birth or other status,

Recalling that, in the Universal Declaration of Human Rights, the United Nations has proclaimed that childhood is entitled to special care and assistance,

Convinced that the family, as the fundamental group of society and the natural environment for the growth and well-being of all its members and particularly children, should be afforded the necessary protection and assistance so that it can fully assume its responsibilities within the community,

Recognizing that the child, for the full and harmonious development of his or her personality, should grow up in a family environment, in an atmosphere of happiness, love and understanding,

Considering that the child should be fully prepared to live an individual life in society, and brought up in the spirit of the ideals proclaimed in the Charter of the United Nations, and in particular in the spirit of peace, dignity, tolerance, freedom, equality and solidarity,

Bearing in mind that the need to extend particular care to the child has been stated in the Geneva Declaration of the Rights of the Child of 1924 and in the Declaration of the Rights of the Child adopted by the General Assembly on 20 November 1959 and recognized in the Universal Declaration of Human Rights, in the International Covenant on Civil and Political Rights (in particular in articles 23 and 24), in the International Covenant on Economic, Social and Cultural Rights (in particular in article 10) and in the statutes and relevant instruments of specialized agencies and international organizations concerned with the welfare of children,

Bearing in mind that, as indicated in the Declaration of the Rights of the Child, "the child, by reason of his physical and mental immaturity, needs special safeguards and care, including appropriate legal protection, before as well as after birth",

Recalling the provisions of the Declaration on Social and Legal Principles relating to the Protection and Welfare of Children, with Special Reference to Foster Placement and Adoption Nationally and Internationally; the United Nations Standard Minimum Rules for the Administration of Juvenile Justice (The Beijing Rules); and the Declaration on the Protection of Women and Children in Emergency and Armed Conflict,

Recognizing that, in all countries in the world, there are children living in exceptionally difficult conditions, and that such children need special consideration,

Taking due account of the importance of the traditions and cultural values of each people for the protection and harmonious development of the child,

Recognizing the importance of international co-operation for improving the living conditions of children in every country, in particular in the developing countries,

Have agreed as follows:

PART I

Article 1

For the purposes of the present Convention, a child means every human being below the age of eighteen years unless under the law applicable to the child, majority is attained earlier.

Article 2

1. States Parties shall respect and ensure the rights set forth in the present Convention to each child within their jurisdiction without discrimination of any kind, irrespective of the child's or his or her parent's or legal guardian's race, colour, sex, language, religion, political or other opinion, national, ethnic or social origin, property, disability, birth or other status.

2. States Parties shall take all appropriate measures to ensure that the child is protected against all forms of discrimination or punishment on the basis of the status, activities, expressed opinions, or beliefs of the child's parents, legal guardians, or family members.

Article 3

1. In all actions concerning children, whether undertaken by public or private social welfare institutions, courts of law, administrative authorities or legislative bodies, the best interests of the child shall be a primary consideration.

2. States Parties undertake to ensure the child such protection and care as is necessary for his or her well-being, taking into account the rights and duties of his or her parents, legal guardians, or other individuals legally responsible for him or her, and, to this end, shall take all appropriate legislative and administrative measures.

3. States Parties shall ensure that the institutions, services and facilities responsible for the care or protection of children shall conform with the standards established by competent authorities, particularly in the areas of safety, health, in the number and suitability of their staff, as well as competent supervision.

Article 4

States Parties shall undertake all appropriate legislative, administrative, and other measures for the implementation of the rights recognized in the present Convention. With regard to economic, social and cultural rights, States Parties shall undertake such measures to the maximum extent of their available resources and, where needed, within the framework of international co-operation.

Article 5

States Parties shall respect the responsibilities, rights and duties of parents or, where applicable, the members of the extended family or community as provided for by local custom, legal guardians or other persons legally responsible for the child, to provide, in a manner consistent with the evolving capacities of the child, appropriate direction and guidance in the exercise by the child of the rights recognized in the present Convention.

Article 6

1. States Parties recognize that every child has the inherent right to life.

2. States Parties shall ensure to the maximum extent possible the survival and development of the child.

Article 7

1. The child shall be registered immediately after birth and shall have the right from birth to a name, the right to acquire a nationality and, as far as possible, the right to know and be cared for by his or her parents.

2. States Parties shall ensure the implementation of these rights in accordance with their national law and their obligations under the relevant international instruments in this field, in particular where the child would otherwise be stateless.

Article 8

1. States Parties undertake to respect the right of the child to preserve his or her identity, including nationality, name and family relations as recognized by law without unlawful interference.

2. Where a child is illegally deprived of some or all of the elements of his or her identity, States Parties shall provide appropriate assistance and protection, with a view to re-establishing speedily his or her identity.

Article 9

1. States Parties shall ensure that a child shall not be separated from his or her parents against their will, except when competent authorities subject to judicial review determine, in accordance with applicable law and procedures, that such separation is necessary for the best interests of the child. Such determination may be necessary in a particular case such as one involving abuse or neglect of the child by the parents, or one where the parents are living separately and a decision must be made as to the child's place of residence.

2. In any proceedings pursuant to paragraph 1 of the present article, all interested parties shall be given an opportunity to participate in the proceedings and make their views known.

3. States Parties shall respect the right of the child who is separated from one or both parents to maintain personal relations and direct contact with both parents on a regular basis, except if it is contrary to the child's best interests.

4. Where such separation results from any action initiated by a State Party, such as the detention, imprisonment, exile, deportation or death (including death arising from any cause while the person is in the custody of the State) of one or both parents or of the child, that State Party shall, upon request, provide the parents, the child or, if appropriate, another member of the family with the essential information concerning the whereabouts of the absent member(s) of the family unless the provision of the information would be detrimental to the well-being of the child. States Parties shall further ensure that the submission of such a request shall of itself entail no adverse consequences for the person(s) concerned.

Article 10

1. In accordance with the obligation of States Parties under article 9, paragraph 1, applications by a child or his or her parents to enter or leave a State Party for the purpose of family reunification shall be dealt with by States Parties in a positive, humane and expeditious manner. States Parties shall further ensure that the submission of such a request shall entail no adverse consequences for the applicants and for the members of their family.

2. A child whose parents reside in different States shall have the right to maintain on a regular basis, save in exceptional circumstances personal relations and direct contacts with both parents. Towards that end and in accordance with the obligation of States Parties under article 9, paragraph 1, States Parties shall respect the right of the child and his or her parents to leave any country, including their own, and to enter their own country. The right to leave any country shall be subject only to such restrictions as are prescribed by law and which are necessary to protect the national security, public order (*ordre public*), public health or morals or the rights and freedoms of others and are consistent with the other rights recognized in the present Convention.

Article 11

1. States Parties shall take measures to combat the illicit transfer and non-return of children abroad.

2. To this end, States Parties shall promote the conclusion of bilateral or multilateral agreements or accession to existing agreements.

Article 12

1. States Parties shall assure to the child who is capable of forming his or her own views the right to express those views freely in all matters affecting the child, the views of the child being given due weight in accordance with the age and maturity of the child.

2. For this purpose, the child shall in particular be provided the opportunity to be heard in any judicial and administrative proceedings affecting the child, either directly, or through a representative or an appropriate body, in a manner consistent with the procedural rules of national law.

Article 13

1. The child shall have the right to freedom of expression; this right shall include freedom to seek, receive and impart information and ideas of all kinds, regardless of frontiers, either orally, in writing or in print, in the form of art, or through any other media of the child's choice.

2. The exercise of this right may be subject to certain restrictions, but these shall only be such as are provided by law and are necessary:

　　(a) For respect of the rights or reputations of others; or

　　(b) For the protection of national security or of public order (*ordre public*), or of public health or morals.

Article 14

1. States Parties shall respect the right of the child to freedom of thought, conscience and religion.

2. States Parties shall respect the rights and duties of the parents and, when applicable, legal guardians, to provide direction to the child in the exercise of his or her right in a manner consistent with the evolving capacities of the child.

3. Freedom to manifest one's religion or beliefs may be subject only to such limitations as are prescribed by law and are necessary to protect public safety, order, health or morals, or the fundamental rights and freedoms of others.

Article 15

1. States Parties recognize the rights of the child to freedom of association and to freedom of peaceful assembly.

2. No restrictions may be placed on the exercise of these rights other than those imposed in conformity with the law and which are necessary in a democratic society in the interests of national security or public safety, public order (*ordre public*), the protection of public health or morals or the protection of the rights and freedoms of others.

Article 16

1. No child shall be subjected to arbitrary or unlawful interference with his or her privacy, family, home or correspondence, nor to unlawful attacks on his or her honour and reputation.

2. The child has the right to the protection of the law against such interference or attacks.

Article 17

States Parties recognize the important function performed by the mass media and shall ensure that the child has access to information and material from a diversity of national and international sources, especially those aimed at the promotion of his or her social, spiritual and moral well-being and physical and mental health. To this end, States Parties shall:

(a) Encourage the mass media to disseminate information and material of social and cultural benefit to the child and in accordance with the spirit of article 29;

(b) Encourage international co-operation in the production, exchange and dissemination of such information and material from a diversity of cultural, national and international sources;

(c) Encourage the production and dissemination of children's books;

(d) Encourage the mass media to have particular regard to the linguistic needs of the child who belongs to a minority group or who is indigenous;

(e) Encourage the development of appropriate guidelines for the protection of the child from information and material injurious to his or her well-being, bearing in mind the provisions of articles 13 and 18.

Article 18

1. States Parties shall use their best efforts to ensure recognition of the principle that both parents have common responsibilities for the upbringing and development of the child. Parents or, as the case may be, legal guardians,

have the primary responsibility for the upbringing and development of the child. The best interests of the child will be their basic concern.

2. For the purpose of guaranteeing and promoting the rights set forth in the present Convention, States Parties shall render appropriate assistance to parents and legal guardians in the performance of their child-rearing responsibilities and shall ensure the development of institutions, facilities and services for the care of children.

3. States Parties shall take all appropriate measures to ensure that children of working parents have the right to benefit from child-care services and facilities for which they are eligible.

Article 19

1. States Parties shall take all appropriate legislative, administrative, social and educational measures to protect the child from all forms of physical or mental violence, injury or abuse, neglect or negligent treatment, maltreatment or exploitation, including sexual abuse, while in the care of parent(s), legal guardian(s) or any other person who has the care of the child.

2. Such protective measures should, as appropriate, include effective procedures for the establishment of social programmes to provide necessary support for the child and for those who have the care of the child, as well as for other forms of prevention and for identification, reporting, referral, investigation, treatment and follow-up of instances of child maltreatment described heretofore, and, as appropriate, for judicial involvement.

Article 20

1. A child temporarily or permanently deprived of his or her family environment, or in whose own best interests cannot be allowed to remain in that environment, shall be entitled to special protection and assistance provided by the State.

2. States Parties shall in accordance with their national laws ensure alternative care for such a child.

3. Such care could include, inter alia, foster placement, *kafalah* of Islamic law, adoption or if necessary placement in suitable institutions for the care of children. When considering solutions, due regard shall be paid to the desirability of continuity in a child's upbringing and to the child's ethnic, religious, cultural and linguistic background.

Article 21

States Parties that recognize and/or permit the system of adoption shall ensure that the best interests of the child shall be the paramount consideration and they shall:

(a) Ensure that the adoption of a child is authorized only by competent authorities who determine, in accordance with applicable law and procedures and on the basis of all pertinent and reliable information, that the adoption is permissible in view of the child's status concerning parents, relatives and legal guardians and that, if required, the persons concerned have given their

informed consent to the adoption on the basis of such counselling as may be necessary;

(b) Recognize that inter-country adoption may be considered as an alternative means of child's care, if the child cannot be placed in a foster or an adoptive family or cannot in any suitable manner be cared for in the child's country of origin;

(c) Ensure that the child concerned by inter-country adoption enjoys safeguards and standards equivalent to those existing in the case of national adoption;

(d) Take all appropriate measures to ensure that, in inter-country adoption, the placement does not result in improper financial gain for those involved in it;

(e) Promote, where appropriate, the objectives of the present article by concluding bilateral or multilateral arrangements or agreements, and endeavour, within this framework, to ensure that the placement of the child in another country is carried out by competent authorities or organs.

Article 22

1. States Parties shall take appropriate measures to ensure that a child who is seeking refugee status or who is considered a refugee in accordance with applicable international or domestic law and procedures shall, whether unaccompanied or accompanied by his or her parents or by any other person, receive appropriate protection and humanitarian assistance in the enjoyment of applicable rights set forth in the present Convention and in other international human rights or humanitarian instruments to which the said States are Parties.

2. For this purpose, States Parties shall provide, as they consider appropriate, co-operation in any efforts by the United Nations and other competent intergovernmental organizations or non-governmental organizations co-operating with the United Nations to protect and assist such a child and to trace the parents or other members of the family of any refugee child in order to obtain information necessary for reunification with his or her family. In cases where no parents or other members of the family can be found, the child shall be accorded the same protection as any other child permanently or temporarily deprived of his or her family environment for any reason, as set forth in the present Convention.

Article 23

1. States Parties recognize that a mentally or physically disabled child should enjoy a full and decent life, in conditions which ensure dignity, promote self-reliance and facilitate the child's active participation in the community.

2. States Parties recognize the right of the disabled child to special care and shall encourage and ensure the extension, subject to available resources, to the eligible child and those responsible for his or her care, of assistance for which application is made and which is appropriate to the child's condition and to the circumstances of the parents or others caring for the child.

3. Recognizing the special needs of a disabled child, assistance extended in accordance with paragraph 2 of the present article shall be provided free of charge, whenever possible, taking into account the financial resources of the parents or others caring for the child, and shall be designed to ensure that the disabled child has effective access to and receives education, training, health care services, rehabilitation services, preparation for employment and recreation opportunities in a manner conducive to the child's achieving the fullest possible social integration and individual development, including his or her cultural and spiritual development.

4. States Parties shall promote, in the spirit of international co-operation, the exchange of appropriate information in the field of preventive health care and of medical, psychological and functional treatment of disabled children, including dissemination of and access to information concerning methods of rehabilitation, education and vocational services, with the aim of enabling States Parties to improve their capabilities and skills and to widen their experience in these areas. In this regard, particular account shall be taken of the needs of developing countries.

Article 24

1. States Parties recognize the right of the child to the enjoyment of the highest attainable standard of health and to facilities for the treatment of illness and rehabilitation of health. States Parties shall strive to ensure that no child is deprived of his or her right of access to such health care services.

2. States Parties shall pursue full implementation of this right and, in particular, shall take appropriate measures:

(a) To diminish infant and child mortality;

(b) To ensure the provision of necessary medical assistance and health care to all children with emphasis on the development of primary health care;

(c) To combat disease and malnutrition, including within the framework of primary health care, through, inter alia, the application of readily available technology and through the provision of adequate nutritious foods and clean drinking-water, taking into consideration the dangers and risks of environmental pollution;

(d) To ensure appropriate pre-natal and post-natal health care for mothers;

(e) To ensure that all segments of society, in particular parents and children, are informed, have access to education and are supported in the use of basic knowledge of child health and nutrition, the advantages of breastfeeding, hygiene and environmental sanitation and the prevention of accidents;

(f) To develop preventive health care, guidance for parents and family planning education and services.

3. States Parties shall take all effective and appropriate measures with a view to abolishing traditional practices prejudicial to the health of children.

4. States Parties undertake to promote and encourage international co-operation with a view to achieving progressively the full realization of the right recognized in the present article. In this regard, particular account shall be taken of the needs of developing countries.

Article 25

States Parties recognize the right of a child who has been placed by the competent authorities for the purposes of care, protection or treatment of his or her physical or mental health, to a periodic review of the treatment provided to the child and all other circumstances relevant to his or her placement.

Article 26

1. States Parties shall recognize for every child the right to benefit from social security, including social insurance, and shall take the necessary measures to achieve the full realization of this right in accordance with their national law.

2. The benefits should, where appropriate, be granted, taking into account the resources and the circumstances of the child and persons having responsibility for the maintenance of the child, as well as any other consideration relevant to an application for benefits made by or on behalf of the child.

Article 27

1. States Parties recognize the right of every child to a standard of living adequate for the child's physical, mental, spiritual, moral and social development.

2. The parent(s) or others responsible for the child have the primary responsibility to secure, within their abilities and financial capacities, the conditions of living necessary for the child's development.

3. States Parties, in accordance with national conditions and within their means, shall take appropriate measures to assist parents and others responsible for the child to implement this right and shall in case of need provide material assistance and support programmes, particularly with regard to nutrition, clothing and housing.

4. States Parties shall take all appropriate measures to secure the recovery of maintenance for the child from the parents or other persons having financial responsibility for the child, both within the State Party and from abroad. In particular, where the person having financial responsibility for the child lives in a State different from that of the child, States Parties shall promote the accession to international agreements or the conclusion of such agreements, as well as the making of other appropriate arrangements.

Article 28

1. States Parties recognize the right of the child to education, and with a view to achieving this right progressively and on the basis of equal opportunity, they shall, in particular:

   (a) Make primary education compulsory and available free to all;

(b) Encourage the development of different forms of secondary education, including general and vocational education, make them available and accessible to every child, and take appropriate measures such as the introduction of free education and offering financial assistance in case of need;

(c) Make higher education accessible to all on the basis of capacity by every appropriate means;

(d) Make educational and vocational information and guidance available and accessible to all children;

(e) Take measures to encourage regular attendance at schools and the reduction of drop-out rates.

2. States Parties shall take all appropriate measures to ensure that school discipline is administered in a manner consistent with the child's human dignity and in conformity with the present Convention.

3. States Parties shall promote and encourage international co-operation in matters relating to education, in particular with a view to contributing to the elimination of ignorance and illiteracy throughout the world and facilitating access to scientific and technical knowledge and modern teaching methods. In this regard, particular account shall be taken of the needs of developing countries.

Article 29

1. States Parties agree that the education of the child shall be directed to:

(a) The development of the child's personality, talents and mental and physical abilities to their fullest potential;

(b) The development of respect for human rights and fundamental freedoms, and for the principles enshrined in the Charter of the United Nations;

(c) The development of respect for the child's parents, his or her own cultural identity, language and values, for the national values of the country in which the child is living, the country from which he or she may originate, and for civilizations different from his or her own;

(d) The preparation of the child for responsible life in a free society, in the spirit of understanding, peace, tolerance, equality of sexes, and friendship among all peoples, ethnic, national and religious groups and persons of indigenous origin;

(e) The development of respect for the natural environment.

2. No part of the present article or article 28 shall be construed so as to interfere with the liberty of individuals and bodies to establish and direct educational institutions, subject always to the observance of the principle set forth in paragraph 1 of the present article and to the requirements that the education given in such institutions shall conform to such minimum standards as may be laid down by the State.

Article 30

In those States in which ethnic, religious or linguistic minorities or persons of indigenous origin exist, a child belonging to such a minority or who is indigenous shall not be denied the right, in community with other members of his or her group, to enjoy his or her own culture, to profess and practise his or her own religion, or to use his or her own language.

Article 31

1. States Parties recognize the right of the child to rest and leisure, to engage in play and recreational activities appropriate to the age of the child and to participate freely in cultural life and the arts.

2. States Parties shall respect and promote the right of the child to participate fully in cultural and artistic life and shall encourage the provision of appropriate and equal opportunities for cultural, artistic, recreational and leisure activity.

Article 32

1. States Parties recognize the right of the child to be protected from economic exploitation and from performing any work that is likely to be hazardous or to interfere with the child's education, or to be harmful to the child's health or physical, mental, spiritual, moral or social development.

2. States Parties shall take legislative, administrative, social and educational measures to ensure the implementation of the present article. To this end, and having regard to the relevant provisions of other international instruments, States Parties shall in particular:

(a) Provide for a minimum age or minimum ages for admission to employment;

(b) Provide for appropriate regulation of the hours and conditions of employment;

(c) Provide for appropriate penalties or other sanctions to ensure the effective enforcement of the present article.

Article 33

States Parties shall take all appropriate measures, including legislative, administrative, social and educational measures, to protect children from the illicit use of narcotic drugs and psychotropic substances as defined in the relevant international treaties, and to prevent the use of children in the illicit production and trafficking of such substances.

Article 34

States Parties undertake to protect the child from all forms of sexual exploitation and sexual abuse. For these purposes, States Parties shall in particular take all appropriate national, bilateral and multilateral measures to prevent:

(a) The inducement or coercion of a child to engage in any unlawful sexual activity;

(b) The exploitative use of children in prostitution or other unlawful sexual practices;

(c) The exploitative use of children in pornographic performances and materials.

Article 35

States Parties shall take all appropriate national, bilateral and multilateral measures to prevent the abduction of, the sale of or traffic in children for any purpose or in any form.

Article 36

States Parties shall protect the child against all other forms of exploitation prejudicial to any aspects of the child's welfare.

Article 37

States Parties shall ensure that:

(a) No child shall be subjected to torture or other cruel, inhuman or degrading treatment or punishment. Neither capital punishment nor life imprisonment without possibility of release shall be imposed for offences committed by persons below eighteen years of age;

(b) No child shall be deprived of his or her liberty unlawfully or arbitrarily. The arrest, detention or imprisonment of a child shall be in conformity with the law and shall be used only as a measure of last resort and for the shortest appropriate period of time;

(c) Every child deprived of liberty shall be treated with humanity and respect for the inherent dignity of the human person, and in a manner which takes into account the needs of persons of his or her age. In particular, every child deprived of liberty shall be separated from adults unless it is considered in the child's best interest not to do so and shall have the right to maintain contact with his or her family through correspondence and visits, save in exceptional circumstances;

(d) Every child deprived of his or her liberty shall have the right to prompt access to legal and other appropriate assistance, as well as the right to challenge the legality of the deprivation of his or her liberty before a court or other competent, independent and impartial authority, and to a prompt decision on any such action.

Article 38

1. States Parties undertake to respect and to ensure respect for rules of international humanitarian law applicable to them in armed conflicts which are relevant to the child.

2. States Parties shall take all feasible measures to ensure that persons who have not attained the age of fifteen years do not take a direct part in hostilities.

3. States Parties shall refrain from recruiting any person who has not attained the age of fifteen years into their armed forces. In recruiting among

those persons who have attained the age of fifteen years but who have not attained the age of eighteen years, States Parties shall endeavour to give priority to those who are oldest.

4. In accordance with their obligations under international humanitarian law to protect the civilian population in armed conflicts, States Parties shall take all feasible measures to ensure protection and care of children who are affected by an armed conflict.

Article 39

States Parties shall take all appropriate measures to promote physical and psychological recovery and social reintegration of a child victim of: any form of neglect, exploitation, or abuse; torture or any other form of cruel, inhuman or degrading treatment or punishment; or armed conflicts. Such recovery and reintegration shall take place in an environment which fosters the health, self-respect and dignity of the child.

Article 40

1. States Parties recognize the right of every child alleged as, accused of, or recognized as having infringed the penal law to be treated in a manner consistent with the promotion of the child's sense of dignity and worth, which reinforces the child's respect for the human rights and fundamental freedoms of others and which takes into account the child's age and the desirability of promoting the child's reintegration and the child's assuming a constructive role in society.

2. To this end, and having regard to the relevant provisions of international instruments, States Parties shall, in particular, ensure that:

(*a*) No child shall be alleged as, be accused of, or recognized as having infringed the penal law by reason of acts or omissions that were not prohibited by national or international law at the time they were committed;

(*b*) Every child alleged as or accused of having infringed the penal law has at least the following guarantees:

(i) To be presumed innocent until proven guilty according to law;

(ii) To be informed promptly and directly of the charges against him or her, and, if appropriate, through his or her parents or legal guardians, and to have legal or other appropriate assistance in the preparation and presentation of his or her defence;

(iii) To have the matter determined without delay by a competent, independent and impartial authority or judicial body in a fair hearing according to law, in the presence of legal or other appropriate assistance and, unless it is considered not to be in the best interest of the child, in particular, taking into account his or her age or situation, his or her parents or legal guardians;

(iv) Not to be compelled to give testimony or to confess guilt; to examine or have examined adverse witnesses and to obtain the participation and examination of witnesses on his or her behalf under conditions of equality;

(v) If considered to have infringed the penal law, to have this decision and any measures imposed in consequence thereof reviewed by a higher competent, independent and impartial authority or judicial body according to law;

(vi) To have the free assistance of an interpreter if the child cannot understand or speak the language used;

(vii) To have his or her privacy fully respected at all stages of the proceedings.

3. States Parties shall seek to promote the establishment of laws, procedures, authorities and institutions specifically applicable to children alleged as, accused of, or recognized as having infringed the penal law, and, in particular:

(a) The establishment of a minimum age below which children shall be presumed not to have the capacity to infringe the penal law;

(b) Whenever appropriate and desirable, measures for dealing with such children without resorting to judicial proceedings, providing that human rights and legal safeguards are fully respected.

4. A variety of dispositions, such as care, guidance and supervision orders; counselling; probation; foster care; education and vocational training programmes and other alternatives to institutional care shall be available to ensure that children are dealt with in a manner appropriate to their well-being and proportionate both to their circumstances and the offence.

Article 41

Nothing in the present Convention shall affect any provisions which are more conducive to the realization of the rights of the child and which may be contained in:

(a) The law of a State party; or

(b) International law in force for that State.

PART II

Article 42

States Parties undertake to make the principles and provisions of the Convention widely known, by appropriate and active means, to adults and children alike.

Article 43

1. For the purpose of examining the progress made by States Parties in achieving the realization of the obligations undertaken in the present Convention, there shall be established a Committee on the Rights of the Child, which shall carry out the functions hereinafter provided.

2. The Committee shall consist of ten experts of high moral standing and recognized competence in the field covered by this Convention. The members of the Committee shall be elected by States Parties from among their nationals and shall serve in their personal capacity, consideration being given to equitable geographical distribution, as well as to the principal legal systems.

3. The members of the Committee shall be elected by secret ballot from a list of persons nominated by States Parties. Each State Party may nominate one person from among its own nationals.

4. The initial election to the Committee shall be held no later than six months after the date of the entry into force of the present Convention and thereafter every second year. At least four months before the date of each election, the Secretary-General of the United Nations shall address a letter to States Parties inviting them to submit their nominations within two months. The Secretary-General shall subsequently prepare a list in alphabetical order of all persons thus nominated, indicating States Parties which have nominated them, and shall submit it to the States Parties to the present Convention.

5. The elections shall be held at meetings of States Parties convened by the Secretary-General at United Nations Headquarters. At those meetings, for which two thirds of States Parties shall constitute a quorum, the persons elected to the Committee shall be those who obtain the largest number of votes and an absolute majority of the votes of the representatives of States Parties present and voting.

6. The members of the Committee shall be elected for a term of four years. They shall be eligible for re-election if renominated. The term of five of the members elected at the first election shall expire at the end of two years; immediately after the first election, the names of these five members shall be chosen by lot by the Chairman of the meeting.

7. If a member of the Committee dies or resigns or declares that for any other cause he or she can no longer perform the duties of the Committee, the State Party which nominated the member shall appoint another expert from among its nationals to serve for the remainder of the term, subject to the approval of the Committee.

8. The Committee shall establish its own rules of procedure.

9. The Committee shall elect its officers for a period of two years.

10. The meetings of the Committee shall normally be held at United Nations Headquarters or at any other convenient place as determined by the Committee. The Committee shall normally meet annually. The duration of the meetings of the Committee shall be determined, and reviewed, if necessary, by a meeting of the States Parties to the present Convention, subject to the approval of the General Assembly.

11. The Secretary-General of the United Nations shall provide the necessary staff and facilities for the effective performance of the functions of the Committee under the present Convention.

12. With the approval of the General Assembly, the members of the Committee established under the present Convention shall receive emoluments from United Nations resources on such terms and conditions as the Assembly may decide.

Article 44

1. States Parties undertake to submit to the Committee, through the Secretary-General of the United Nations, reports on the measures they have adopted which give effect to the rights recognized herein and on the progress made on the enjoyment of those rights:

(a) Within two years of the entry into force of the Convention for the State Party concerned;

(b) Thereafter every five years.

2. Reports made under the present article shall indicate factors and difficulties, if any, affecting the degree of fulfilment of the obligations under the present Convention. Reports shall also contain sufficient information to provide the Committee with a comprehensive understanding of the implementation of the Convention in the country concerned.

3. A State Party which has submitted a comprehensive initial report to the Committee need not, in its subsequent reports submitted in accordance with paragraph 1 (b) of the present article, repeat basic information previously provided.

4. The Committee may request from States Parties further information relevant to the implementation of the Convention.

5. The Committee shall submit to the General Assembly, through the Economic and Social Council, every two years, reports on its activities.

6. States Parties shall make their reports widely available to the public in their own countries.

Article 45

In order to foster the effective implementation of the Convention and to encourage international co-operation in the field covered by the Convention:

(a) The specialized agencies, the United Nations Children's Fund, and other United Nations organs shall be entitled to be represented at the consideration of the implementation of such provisions of the present Convention as fall within the scope of their mandate. The Committee may invite the specialized agencies, the United Nations Children's Fund and other competent bodies as it may consider appropriate to provide expert advice on the implementation of the Convention in areas falling within the scope of their respective mandates. The Committee may invite the specialized agencies, the United Nations Children's Fund, and other United Nations organs to submit reports on the implementation of the Convention in areas falling within the scope of their activities;

(b) The Committee shall transmit, as it may consider appropriate, to the specialized agencies, the United Nations Children's Fund and other competent bodies, any reports from States Parties that contain a request, or indicate a need, for technical advice or assistance, along with the Committee's observations and suggestions, if any, on these requests or indications;

(c) The Committee may recommend to the General Assembly to request the Secretary-General to undertake on its behalf studies on specific issues relating to the rights of the child;

(d) The Committee may make suggestions and general recommendations based on information received pursuant to articles 44 and 45 of the present Convention. Such suggestions and general recommendations shall be transmitted to any State Party concerned and reported to the General Assembly, together with comments, if any, from States Parties.

PART III

Article 46

The present Convention shall be open for signature by all States.

Article 47

The present Convention is subject to ratification. Instruments of ratification shall be deposited with the Secretary-General of the United Nations.

Article 48

The present Convention shall remain open for accession by any State. The instruments of accession shall be deposited with the Secretary-General of the United Nations.

Article 49

1. The present Convention shall enter into force on the thirtieth day following the date of deposit with the Secretary-General of the United Nations of the twentieth instrument of ratification or accession.

2. For each State ratifying or acceding to the Convention after the deposit of the twentieth instrument of ratification or accession, the Convention shall enter into force on the thirtieth day after the deposit by such State of its instrument of ratification or accession.

Article 50

1. Any State Party may propose an amendment and file it with the Secretary-General of the United Nations. The Secretary-General shall thereupon communicate the proposed amendment to States Parties, with a request that they indicate whether they favour a conference of States Parties for the purpose of considering and voting upon the proposals. In the event that, within four months from the date of such communication, at least one third of the States Parties favour such a conference, the Secretary-General shall convene

the conference under the auspices of the United Nations. Any amendment adopted by a majority of States Parties present and voting at the conference shall be submitted to the General Assembly for approval.

2. An amendment adopted in accordance with paragraph 1 of the present article shall enter into force when it has been approved by the General Assembly of the United Nations and accepted by a two-thirds majority of States Parties.

3. When an amendment enters into force, it shall be binding on those States Parties which have accepted it, other States Parties still being bound by the provisions of the present Convention and any earlier amendments which they have accepted.

Article 51

1. The Secretary-General of the United Nations shall receive and circulate to all States the text of reservations made by States at the time of ratification or accession.

2. A reservation incompatible with the object and purpose of the present Convention shall not be permitted.

3. Reservations may be withdrawn at any time by notification to that effect addressed to the Secretary-General of the United Nations, who shall then inform all States. Such notification shall take effect on the date on which it is received by the Secretary-General.

Article 52

A State Party may denounce the present Convention by written notification to the Secretary-General of the United Nations. Denunciation becomes effective one year after the date of receipt of the notification by the Secretary-General.

Article 53

The Secretary-General of the United Nations is designated as the depositary of the present Convention.

Article 54

The original of the present Convention, of which the Arabic, Chinese, English, French, Russian and Spanish texts are equally authentic, shall be deposited with the Secretary-General of the United Nations.

OPTIONAL PROTOCOL TO THE CONVENTION ON THE RIGHTS OF THE CHILD ON THE INVOLVEMENT OF CHILDREN IN ARMED CONFLICTS, G.A. res. 54/263, Annex I, 54 U.N. GAOR Supp. (No. 49) at 7, U.N. Doc. A/54/49 (2000), *entered into force* February 12, 2002:

The States Parties to the present Protocol,

Encouraged by the overwhelming support for the Convention on the Rights of the Child, demonstrating the widespread commitment that exists to strive for the promotion and protection of the rights of the child,

Reaffirming that the rights of children require special protection, and calling for continuous improvement of the situation of children without distinction, as well as for their development and education in conditions of peace and security,

Disturbed by the harmful and widespread impact of armed conflict on children and the long-term consequences this has for durable peace, security and development,

Condemning the targeting of children in situations of armed conflict and direct attacks on objects protected under international law, including places generally having a significant presence of children, such as schools and hospitals,

Noting the adoption of the Statute of the International Criminal Court2 and, in particular, its inclusion as a war crime of conscripting or enlisting children under the age of 15 years or using them to participate actively in hostilities in both international and non-international armed conflicts,

Considering, therefore, that to strengthen further the implementation of rights recognized in the Convention on the Rights of the Child there is a need to increase the protection of children from involvement in armed conflict,

Noting that article 1 of the Convention on the Rights of the Child specifies that, for the purposes of that Convention, a child means every human being below the age of 18 years unless, under the law applicable to the child, majority is attained earlier,

Convinced that an optional protocol to the Convention raising the age of possible recruitment of persons into armed forces and their participation in hostilities will contribute effectively to the implementation of the principle that the best interests of the child are to be a primary consideration in all actions concerning children,

Noting that the twenty-sixth international Conference of the Red Cross and Red Crescent in December 1995 recommended, inter alia, that parties to conflict take every feasible step to ensure that children under the age of 18 years do not take part in hostilities,

Welcoming the unanimous adoption, in June 1999, of International Labour Organization Convention No. 182 on the Prohibition and Immediate Action for the Elimination of the Worst Forms of Child Labour, which prohibits, inter alia, forced or compulsory recruitment of children for use in armed conflict,

Condemning with the gravest concern the recruitment, training and use within and across national borders of children in hostilities by armed groups distinct from the armed forces of a State, and recognizing the responsibility of those who recruit, train and use children in this regard,

Recalling the obligation of each party to an armed conflict to abide by the provisions of international humanitarian law,

Stressing that this Protocol is without prejudice to the purposes and principles contained in the Charter of the United Nations, including Article 51, and relevant norms of humanitarian law,

Bearing in mind that conditions of peace and security based on full respect of the purposes and principles contained in the Charter and observance of applicable human rights instruments are indispensable for the full protection of children, in particular during armed conflicts and foreign occupation,

Recognizing the special needs of those children who are particularly vulnerable to recruitment or use in hostilities contrary to this Protocol owing to their economic or social status or gender,

Mindful of the necessity of taking into consideration the economic, social and political root causes of the involvement of children in armed conflicts,

Convinced of the need to strengthen international cooperation in the implementation of this Protocol, as well as the physical and psychosocial rehabilitation and social reintegration of children who are victims of armed conflict,

Encouraging the participation of the community and, in particular, children and child victims in the dissemination of informational and educational programmes concerning the implementation of the Protocol,

Have agreed as follows:

Article 1

States Parties shall take all feasible measures to ensure that members of their armed forces who have not attained the age of 18 years do not take a direct part in hostilities.

Article 2

States Parties shall ensure that persons who have not attained the age of 18 years are not compulsorily recruited into their armed forces.

Article 3

1. States Parties shall raise the minimum age for the voluntary recruitment of persons into their national armed forces from that set out in article 38, paragraph 3, of the Convention on the Rights of the Child,1 taking account of the principles contained in that article and recognizing that under the Convention persons under 18 are entitled to special protection.

2. Each State Party shall deposit a binding declaration upon ratification of or accession to this Protocol that sets forth the minimum age at which it will permit voluntary recruitment into its national armed forces and a description of the safeguards that it has adopted to ensure that such recruitment is not forced or coerced.

3. States Parties that permit voluntary recruitment into their national armed forces under the age of 18 shall maintain safeguards to ensure, as a minimum, that:

(a) Such recruitment is genuinely voluntary;

(b) Such recruitment is done with the informed consent of the person's parents or legal guardians;

(c) Such persons are fully informed of the duties involved in such military service;

(d) Such persons provide reliable proof of age prior to acceptance into national military service.

4. Each State Party may strengthen its declaration at any time by notification to that effect addressed to the Secretary-General of the United Nations, who shall inform all States Parties. Such notification shall take effect on the date on which it is received by the Secretary-General.

5. The requirement to raise the age in paragraph 1 of the present article does not apply to schools operated by or under the control of the armed forces of the States Parties, in keeping with articles 28 and 29 of the Convention on the Rights of the Child.

Article 4

1. Armed groups that are distinct from the armed forces of a State should not, under any circumstances, recruit or use in hostilities persons under the age of 18 years.

2. States Parties shall take all feasible measures to prevent such recruitment and use, including the adoption of legal measures necessary to prohibit and criminalize such practices.

3. The application of the present article under this Protocol shall not affect the legal status of any party to an armed conflict.

Article 5

Nothing in the present Protocol shall be construed as precluding provisions in the law of a State Party or in international instruments and international humanitarian law that are more conducive to the realization of the rights of the child.

Article 6

1. Each State Party shall take all necessary legal, administrative and other measures to ensure the effective implementation and enforcement of the provisions of this Protocol within its jurisdiction.

2. States Parties undertake to make the principles and provisions of the present Protocol widely known and promoted by appropriate means, to adults and children alike.

3. States Parties shall take all feasible measures to ensure that persons within their jurisdiction recruited or used in hostilities contrary to this Protocol are demobilized or otherwise released from service. States Parties shall, when

necessary, accord to these persons all appropriate assistance for their physical and psychological recovery and their social reintegration.

Article 7

1. States Parties shall cooperate in the implementation of the present Protocol, including in the prevention of any activity contrary to the Protocol and in the rehabilitation and social reintegration of persons who are victims of acts contrary to this Protocol, including through technical cooperation and financial assistance. Such assistance and cooperation will be undertaken in consultation with concerned States Parties and relevant international organizations.

2. States Parties in a position to do so shall provide such assistance through existing multilateral, bilateral or other programmes, or, inter alia, through a voluntary fund established in accordance with the rules of the General Assembly.

Article 8

1. Each State Party shall submit, within two years following the entry into force of the Protocol for that State Party, a report to the Committee on the Rights of the Child providing comprehensive information on the measures it has taken to implement the provisions of the Protocol, including the measures taken to implement the provisions on participation and recruitment.

2. Following the submission of the comprehensive report, each State Party shall include in the reports they submit to the Committee on the Rights of the Child, in accordance with article 44 of the Convention, any further information with respect to the implementation of the Protocol. Other States Parties to the Protocol shall submit a report every five years.

3. The Committee on the Rights of the Child may request from States Parties further information relevant to the implementation of this Protocol.

Article 9

1. The present Protocol is open for signature by any State that is a party to the Convention or has signed it.

2. The present Protocol is subject to ratification and is open to accession by any State. Instruments of ratification or accession shall be deposited with the Secretary-General of the United Nations.

3. The Secretary-General, in his capacity as depositary of the Convention and the Protocol, shall inform all States Parties to the Convention and all States that have signed the Convention of each instrument of declaration pursuant to article 13.

Article 10

1. The present Protocol shall enter into force three months after the deposit of the tenth instrument of ratification or accession.

2. For each State ratifying the present Protocol or acceding to it after its entry into force, the present Protocol shall enter into force one month after the date of the deposit of its own instrument of ratification or accession.

Article 11

1. Any State Party may denounce the present Protocol at any time by written notification to the Secretary-General of the United Nations, who shall thereafter inform the other States Parties to the Convention and all States that have signed the Convention. The denunciation shall take effect one year after the date of receipt of the notification by the Secretary-General. If, however, on the expiry of that year the denouncing State Party is engaged in armed conflict, the denunciation shall not take effect before the end of the armed conflict.

2. Such a denunciation shall not have the effect of releasing the State Party from its obligations under the present Protocol in regard to any act that occurs prior to the date on which the denunciation becomes effective. Nor shall such a denunciation prejudice in any way the continued consideration of any matter that is already under consideration by the Committee prior to the date on which the denunciation becomes effective.

Article 12

1. Any State Party may propose an amendment and file it with the Secretary-General of the United Nations. The Secretary-General shall thereupon communicate the proposed amendment to States Parties, with a request that they indicate whether they favour a conference of States Parties for the purpose of considering and voting upon the proposals. In the event that, within four months from the date of such communication, at least one third of the States Parties favour such a conference, the Secretary-General shall convene the conference under the auspices of the United Nations. Any amendment adopted by a majority of States Parties present and voting at the conference shall be submitted to the General Assembly for approval.

2. An amendment adopted in accordance with paragraph 1 of the present article shall enter into force when it has been approved by the General Assembly of the United Nations and accepted by a two-thirds majority of States Parties.

3. When an amendment enters into force, it shall be binding on those States Parties that have accepted it, other States Parties still being bound by the provisions of the present Protocol and any earlier amendments that they have accepted.

Article 13

1. The present Protocol, of which the Arabic, Chinese, English, French, Russian and Spanish texts are equally authentic, shall be deposited in the archives of the United Nations.

2. The Secretary-General of the United Nations shall transmit certified copies of the present Protocol to all States Parties to the Convention and all States that have signed the Convention.

INTERNATIONAL CONVENTION FOR THE PROTECTION OF ALL PERSONS FROM ENFORCED DISAPPEARANCE, G.A. res. 61/177, U.N. Doc. A/RES/61/177 (2006), *adopted* **Dec. 20, 2006:**

Preamble

The States Parties to this Convention,

Considering the obligation of States under the Charter of the United Nations to promote universal respect for, and observance of, human rights and fundamental freedoms,

Having regard to the Universal Declaration of Human Rights,

Recalling the International Covenant on Economic, Social and Cultural Rights, the International Covenant on Civil and Political Rights and all other relevant international instruments in the fields of human rights, humanitarian law and international criminal law,

Recalling the Declaration on the Protection of All Persons from Enforced Disappearance adopted by the General Assembly of the United Nations in its resolution 47/133 of 18 December 1992,

Aware of the extreme seriousness of enforced disappearance, which constitutes a crime and, in certain circumstances defined in international law, a crime against humanity,

Determined to prevent enforced disappearances and combat impunity for the crime of enforced disappearance,

Considering the right of any person not to be subjected to an enforced disappearance, the right of victims to justice and to reparation and,

Affirming the right to know the truth about circumstances of an enforced disappearance and the fate of the disappeared person, and the respect of the right to freedom to seek, receive and impart information to this end.

Have agreed as follows:

Article 1

1. No one shall be subjected to enforced disappearance.

2. No exceptional circumstances whatsoever, whether a state of war or a threat of war, internal political instability or any other public emergency, may be invoked as a justification for enforced disappearance.

Article 2

For the purposes of this Convention, enforced disappearance is considered to be the arrest, detention, abduction or any other form of deprivation of liberty committed by agents of the State or by persons or groups of persons acting with the authorization, support or acquiescence of the State, followed by a refusal to acknowledge the deprivation of liberty or by concealment of the fate or whereabouts of the disappeared person, which place such a person outside the protection of the law.

Article 3

Each State Party shall take appropriate measures to investigate acts defined in article 2 committed by persons or groups of persons acting without the authorization, support or acquiescence of the State and to bring those responsible to justice.

Article 4

Each State Party shall take the necessary measures to ensure that enforced disappearance constitutes an offence under its criminal law.

Article 5

The widespread or systematic practice of enforced disappearance constitutes a crime against humanity as defined in applicable international law and shall attract the consequences provided for under such applicable international law.

Article 6

1. Each State Party shall take the necessary measures to hold criminally responsible at least:

(a) Any person who commits, orders, solicits or induces the commission of, attempts to commit, is an accomplice to or participates in an enforced disappearance;

(b) The superior who:

(i) Knew, or consciously disregarded information which clearly indicated, that subordinates under his or her effective authority and control were committing or about to commit a crime of enforced disappearance;

(ii) Exercised effective responsibility for and control over activities which were concerned with the crime of enforced disappearance; and

(iii) Failed to take all necessary and reasonable measures within his or her power to prevent or repress the commission of the enforced disappearance or to submit the matter to the competent authorities for investigation and prosecution;

(c) Subparagraph *(b)* above is without prejudice to the higher standards of responsibility applicable under relevant international law to a military commander or to a person effectively acting as a military commander.

2. No order or instruction from any public authority, civilian, military or other, may be invoked to justify an offence of enforced disappearance.

Article 7

1. Each State Party shall make the offence of enforced disappearance punishable by appropriate penalties which take into account its extreme seriousness.

2. Each State Party may establish:

(a) Mitigating circumstances, in particular for persons who, having been implicated in the commission of an enforced disappearance, effectively contribute to bringing the disappeared person forward alive or make it possible to clarify cases of enforced disappearance or to identify the perpetrators of an enforced disappearance;

(b) Without prejudice to other criminal procedures, aggravating circumstances, in particular in the event of the death of the disappeared person or the commission of an enforced disappearance in respect of pregnant women, minors, persons with disabilities or other particularly vulnerable persons.

Article 8

Without prejudice to article 5,

1. A State Party which applies a statute of limitations in respect of enforced disappearance shall take the necessary measures to ensure that the term of limitation for criminal proceedings:

(a) Is of long duration and is proportionate to the extreme seriousness of this offence;

(b) Commences from the moment when the offence of enforced disappearance ceases, taking into account its continuous nature.

2. Each State Party shall guarantee the right of victims of enforced disappearances to an effective remedy during the term of limitation.

Article 9

1. Each State Party shall take the necessary measures to establish its jurisdiction over the offence of enforced disappearance:

(a) When the offence is committed in any territory under its jurisdiction or on board a ship or aircraft registered in that State;

(b) When the alleged offender is one of its nationals;

(c) When the disappeared person is one of its nationals and the State Party considers it appropriate.

2. Each State Party shall likewise take such measures as may be necessary to establish its jurisdiction over the offence of enforced disappearance when the alleged offender is present in any territory under its jurisdiction, unless it extradites or surrenders him or her to another State in accordance with its international obligations or surrenders him or her to an international criminal tribunal whose jurisdiction it has recognized.

3. This Convention does not exclude any additional criminal jurisdiction exercised in accordance with national law.

Article 10

1. Upon being satisfied, after an examination of the information available to it, that the circumstances so warrant, any State Party in whose terri-

tory a person alleged to have committed an offence of enforced disappearance is present shall take him or her into custody or take such other legal measures as are necessary to ensure his or her presence. The custody and other legal measures shall be as provided for in the law of that State Party but may be continued only for such time as is necessary to ensure the person's presence at criminal, surrender or extradition proceedings.

2. A State Party which has taken the measures referred to in paragraph 1 shall immediately carry out a preliminary inquiry or investigations to establish the facts. It shall notify the States Parties referred to in article 9, paragraph 1, of the measures it has taken in pursuance of paragraph 1 of this article, including detention and the circumstances warranting detention, and the findings of its preliminary inquiry or its investigations, indicating whether it intends to exercise its jurisdiction.

3. Any person in custody pursuant to paragraph 1 shall be assisted in communicating immediately with the nearest appropriate representative of the State of which he or she is a national, or, if he or she is a stateless person, with the representative of the State where he or she usually resides.

Article 11

1. The State Party in the territory under whose jurisdiction a person alleged to have committed an offence of enforced disappearance is found shall, if it does not extradite that person or surrender him or her to another State in accordance with its international obligations or surrender him or her to an international criminal tribunal whose jurisdiction it has recognized, submit the case to its competent authorities for the purpose of prosecution.

2. These authorities shall take their decision in the same manner as in the case of any ordinary offence of a serious nature under the law of that State Party. In the cases referred to in article 9, paragraph 2, the standards of evidence required for prosecution and conviction shall in no way be less stringent than those which apply in the cases referred to in article 9, paragraph 1.

3. Any person against whom proceedings are brought in connection with an offence of enforced disappearance shall be guaranteed fair treatment at all stages of the proceedings. Any person tried for an offence of enforced disappearance shall benefit from a fair trail before a competent, independent and impartial court or tribunal established by law.

Article 12

1. Each State Party shall ensure that any individual who alleges that a person has been subjected to enforced disappearance has the right to report the facts to the competent authorities, which shall examine the allegation promptly and impartially and, where appropriate, undertake without delay a thorough and impartial investigation. Appropriate steps shall be taken, where necessary, to ensure that the complainant, witnesses, relatives of the disappeared person and their defence counsel, as well as persons participating in the investigation, are protected against all ill-treatment or intimidation as a consequence of the complaint or any evidence given.

2. Where there are reasonable grounds for believing that a person has been subjected to enforced disappearance, the authorities referred to in paragraph 1 shall undertake an investigation, even if there has been no formal complaint.

3. Each State Party shall ensure that the authorities referred to in paragraph 1:

(a) Have the necessary powers and resources to conduct the investigation effectively, including access to the documentation and other information relevant to their investigation;

(b) Have access, if necessary with the prior authorization of a judicial authority, which shall rule promptly on the matter, to any place of detention or any other place where there are reasonable grounds to believe that the disappeared person may be present.

4. Each State Party shall take the necessary measures to prevent and sanction acts that hinder the conduct of the investigations. It shall ensure in particular that persons suspected of having committed an offence of enforced disappearance are not in a position to influence the progress of the investigations by means of pressure or acts of intimidation or reprisal aimed at the complainant, witnesses, relatives of the disappeared person or their defence counsel, or at persons participating in the investigation.

Article 13

1. For the purposes of extradition between States Parties, the offence of enforced disappearance shall not be regarded as a political offence or as an offence connected with a political offence or as an offence inspired by political motives. Accordingly, a request for extradition based on such an offence may not be refused only on these grounds.

2. The offence of enforced disappearance shall be deemed to be included as an extraditable offence in any extradition treaty existing between States Parties before the entry into force of this Convention.

3. States Parties undertake to include the offence of enforced disappearance as an extraditable offence in any extradition treaty subsequently to be concluded between them.

4. If a State Party which makes extradition conditional on the existence of a treaty receives a request for extradition from another State Party with which it has no extradition treaty, it may consider this Convention as the necessary legal basis for extradition in respect of the offence of enforced disappearance.

5. States Parties which do not make extradition conditional on the existence of a treaty shall recognize the offence of enforced disappearance as an extraditable offence between themselves.

6. Extradition shall, in all cases, be subject to the conditions provided for by the law of the requested State Party or by applicable extradition treaties,

including, in particular, conditions relating to the minimum penalty requirement for extradition and the grounds upon which the requested State Party may refuse extradition or make it subject to certain conditions.

7. Nothing in this Convention shall be interpreted as imposing an obligation to extradite if the requested State Party has substantial grounds for believing that the request has been made for the purpose of prosecuting or punishing a person on account of that person's sex, race, religion, nationality, ethnic origin, membership of a particular social group or political opinions, or that compliance with the request would cause harm to that person for any one of these reasons.

Article 14

1. States Parties shall afford one another the greatest measure of mutual legal assistance in connection with criminal proceedings brought in respect of an offence of enforced disappearance, including the supply of all evidence at their disposal that is necessary for the proceedings.

2. Such legal assistance shall be subject to the conditions provided for by the domestic law of the requested State Party or by applicable treaties on mutual legal assistance, including, in particular, the conditions in relation to the grounds upon which the requested State Party may refuse to grant mutual legal assistance or may make it subject to conditions.

Article 15

States Parties shall cooperate with each other and shall afford one another the greatest measure of assistance with a view to assisting victims of enforced disappearance, and in searching for, locating and releasing disappeared persons and, in the event of death, in exhuming and identifying them and returning their remains.

Article 16

1. No State Party shall expel, return ("refouler"), surrender or extradite a person to another State where there are substantial grounds for believing that he or she would be in danger of being subjected to enforced disappearance.

2. For the purpose of determining whether there are such grounds, the competent authorities shall take into account all relevant considerations, including, where applicable, the existence in the State concerned of a consistent pattern of gross, flagrant or mass violations of human rights or of serious violations of international humanitarian law.

Article 17

1. No one shall be held in secret detention.

2. Without prejudice to other international obligations of the State Party with regard to the deprivation of liberty, each State Party shall, in its legislation:

   (*a*) Establish the conditions under which orders of deprivation of liberty may be given;

(b) Indicate those authorities authorized to order the deprivation of liberty;

(c) Guarantee that any person deprived of liberty shall be held solely in officially recognized and supervised places of deprivation of liberty;

(d) Guarantee that any person deprived of liberty shall be authorized to communicate with and be visited by his or her family, counsel or any other person of his or her choice, subject only to the conditions established by law, or, if he or she is a foreigner, to communicate with his or her consular authorities, in accordance with applicable international law;

(e) Guarantee access by the competent and legally authorized authorities and institutions to the places where persons are deprived of liberty, if necessary with the prior authorisation of a judicial authority;

(f) Guarantee that any person deprived of liberty and, in the case of a suspected enforced disappearance, the person deprived of liberty not being able to exercise this right, that any person with a legitimate interest, such as relatives of the person deprived of liberty, their representative or their counsel, in all circumstances, shall be entitled to take proceedings before a court, in order that that court may decide without delay on the lawfulness of the deprivation of liberty and order the release if that deprivation of liberty is not lawful.

3. Each State Party shall assure the compilation and maintenance of one or more up-to-date official registers and/or records of persons deprived of liberty, which shall be made promptly available, upon request, to any judicial or other competent authority or institution authorized for that purpose by the law of the State Party concerned or any relevant international legal instrument to which the State concerned is a party. The information contained therein shall include, as a minimum:

(a) The identity of the person deprived of liberty;

(b) The date, time and location where the person was deprived of liberty and the identity of the authority who deprived the person of liberty;

(c) The authority having decided the deprivation of liberty and the reasons for the deprivation of liberty;

(d) The authority controlling the deprivation of liberty;

(e) The place of deprivation of liberty, the date and time of admission to the place of deprivation of liberty and the authority responsible for the place of deprivation of liberty;

(f) Elements regarding the physical integrity of the person deprived of liberty;

(g) In the event of death during the deprivation of liberty, the circumstances and cause of death and the destination of the human remains;

(h) The date and time of release or transfer to another place of detention, the destination and the authority responsible for the transfer.

Article 18

1. Without prejudice to articles 19 and 20, each State Party shall guarantee to any person with a legitimate interest in this information, such as relatives of the person deprived of liberty, their representative or their counsel, access to at least the following information:

(*a*) The authority having decided the deprivation of liberty;

(*b*) The date, time and location where the person was deprived of liberty and admitted to the place of deprivation of liberty;

(*c*) The authority controlling the deprivation of liberty;

(*d*) The whereabouts of the person deprived of liberty, including, in the event of a transfer to another place of deprivation of liberty, the destination and the authority responsible for the transfer;

(*e*) The date, time and place of release;

(*f*) Elements regarding the physical integrity of the person deprived of liberty;

(*g*) In the event of death during the deprivation of liberty, the circumstances and cause of death and the destination of the human remains.

2. Appropriate measures shall be taken, where necessary, to protect the persons referred to in paragraph 1, as well as persons participating in the investigation, from any ill-treatment, intimidation or sanction as a result of the search for information concerning a person deprived of liberty.

Article 19

1. Personal information, including medical and genetic data, which are collected and/or transmitted within the framework of the search for a disappeared person shall not be used or made available for purposes other than the search for the disappeared person. This is without prejudice to the use of such information in criminal proceedings relating to an offence of enforced disappearance or the exercise of the right to obtain reparation.

2. The collection, processing, use and storage of personal information, including medical and genetic data, shall not infringe or have the effect of infringing the human rights, fundamental freedoms or human dignity of an individual.

Article 20

1. Only when a person is under the protection of the law and the deprivation of liberty is subject to judicial control, can the right to information referred to in Article 18 be restricted and only on an exceptional basis, where strictly necessary and provided for by law, and if the transmission of the information would undermine the privacy or safety of the person, hinder a criminal investigation, or for other equivalent reasons in accordance with the law, and in conformity with applicable international law and with the objectives of this

Convention. In no case shall there be restrictions to the right to information referred to in article 18 that could constitute conduct defined in article 2 or be in violation of article 17, paragraph 1.

2. Without prejudice to consideration of the lawfulness of the deprivation of a person's liberty, States Parties shall guarantee to the persons referred to in article 18, paragraph 1 the right to a prompt and effective judicial remedy as a means of obtaining without delay information referred to in article 18, paragraph 1. This right to a remedy may not be suspended or restricted in any circumstances.

Article 21

Each State Party shall take the necessary measures to ensure that persons deprived of liberty are released in a manner permitting reliable verification that they have actually been released. Each State Party shall also take the necessary measures to assure the physical integrity of such persons and their ability to exercise fully their rights at the time of release, without prejudice to any obligations to which such persons may be subject under national law.

Article 22

Without prejudice to article 6, each State Party shall take the necessary measures to prevent and impose sanctions for the following conduct:

(a) Delaying or obstructing the remedies referred to in article 17, paragraph 2 (f), and article 20, paragraph 2;

(b) Failure to record the deprivation of liberty of any person, or the recording of any information which the official responsible for the official register and/or records knew or should have known to be inaccurate;

(c) Refusal to provide information on the deprivation of liberty of a person, or the provision of inaccurate information, even though the legal requirements for providing such information have been met.

Article 23

1. Each State Party shall ensure that the training of law enforcement personnel, civil or military, medical personnel, public officials and other persons who may be involved in the custody or treatment of any person deprived of liberty includes the necessary education and information regarding the relevant provisions of this Convention, in order to:

(a) Prevent the involvement of such officials in enforced disappearances;

(b) Emphasize the importance of prevention and investigations in relation to enforced disappearances;

(c) Ensure that the urgent need to resolve cases of enforced disappearance is recognized.

2. Each State Party shall ensure that orders or instructions prescribing, authorizing or encouraging enforced disappearance are prohibited. Each State

Party shall guarantee that a person who refuses to obey such an order will not be punished.

3. Each State Party shall take the necessary measures to ensure that the persons referred to in paragraph 1 who have reason to believe that an enforced disappearance has occurred or is planned report the matter to their superiors and, where necessary, to the appropriate authorities or organs vested with reviewing or remedial powers.

Article 24

1. For the purposes of this Convention, "victim" means the disappeared person and any individual who has suffered harm as a direct result of an enforced disappearance.

2. Each victim has the right to know the truth regarding the circumstances of the enforced disappearance, the progress and results of the investigation and the fate of the disappeared person. Each State Party shall take appropriate measures in this regard.

3. Each State Party shall take all appropriate measures to search for, locate and release disappeared persons and, in the event of death, to locate, respect and return their remains.

4. Each State Party shall ensure in its legal system that the victims of enforced disappearance have the right to obtain reparation and prompt, fair and adequate compensation.

5. The right to obtain reparation referred to in paragraph 4 covers material and psychological harm and, where appropriate, other means of reparation such as:

(a) Restitution;

(b) Rehabilitation;

(c) Satisfaction, including restoration of dignity and reputation;

(d) Guarantees of non-repetition.

6. Without prejudice to the obligation to continue the investigation until the fate of the disappeared person has been clarified, each State Party shall take the appropriate steps with regard to the legal situation of the disappeared persons whose fate has not been clarified and that of their relatives, in fields such as social welfare, financial matters, family law and property rights.

7. Each State Party shall guarantee the right to form and participate freely in organizations and associations concerned with contributing to the establishment of the circumstances ofenforced disappearances and the fate of disappeared persons, and with assistance to victims of enforced disappearance.

Article 25

1. Each State Party shall take the necessary measures to prevent and punish under its criminal law:

(a) The wrongful removal of children who are subjected to enforced disappearance, children whose father, mother or legal guardian is subjected to enforced disappearance or children born during the captivity of a mother subjected to enforced disappearance;

(b) The falsification, concealment or destruction of documents attesting to the true identity of the children referred to in subparagraph (a).

2. Each State Party shall take the necessary measures to search for and identify the children referred to in paragraph 1 (a) and to return them to their families of origin, in accordance with legal procedures and applicable international agreements.

3. States Parties shall assist one another in searching for, identifying and locating the children referred to in paragraph 1 (a).

4. Given the need to protect the best interests of the children referred to in paragraph 1 (a) and their right to preserve, or to have re-established, their identity, including their nationality, name and family relations as recognized by law, States Parties which recognize a system of adoption or other form of placement of children shall have legal procedures in place to review the adoption or placement procedure, and, where appropriate, to annul any adoption or placement of children that stemmed from an enforced disappearance.

5. In all cases, and in particular in all matters relating to this article, the best interests of the child shall be a primary consideration, and a child who is capable of forming his or her own views shall have the right to express those views freely, the views of the child being given due weight in accordance with the age and maturity of the child.

Article 26

1. A Committee on Enforced Disappearances (hereafter referred to as the Committee) shall be established to carry out the functions provided for under this Convention. The Committee shall consist of 10 experts of high moral character and recognised competence in the field of human rights, who shall serve in their personal capacity and be independent and impartial. The members of the Committee shall be elected by the States Parties according to equitable geographical distribution. Consideration shall be given to the usefulness of the participation to the work of the Committee of persons having relevant legal experience and to balanced gender representation.

2. The members of the Committee shall be elected by secret ballot from a list of persons nominated by the States Parties from among their nationals, at biennial meetings of States Parties convened by the Secretary General of the United Nations for this purpose. At those meetings, for which two thirds of the States Parties shall constitute a quorum, the persons elected to the Committee shall be those who obtain the largest number of votes and an absolute majority of votes of the representatives of States Parties present and voting.

3. The initial election shall be held no later than six months after the date of entry into force of this Convention. At least four months before the date

of each election, the Secretary General of the United Nations shall address a letter to the States Parties inviting them to submit the nominations within three months. The Secretary General shall prepare a list in alphabetical order of all persons thus nominated, indicating the State Party which nominated each candidate. He/She shall submit this list to all States Parties.

4. The members of the Committee shall be elected for a term of four years. They shall be eligible for re-election once. However, the term of five of the members elected at the first election shall expire at the end of two years; immediately after the first election, the names of these five members shall be chosen by lot by the chairman of the meeting referred to in paragraph 2 of this article.

5. If a member of the Committee dies or resigns or for any other cause can no longer perform his/her committee duties, the State Party which nominated him/her shall, in accordance with the criteria set out in paragraph 1 of this article, appoint another candidate from among its nationals, to serve for the remainder of his/her term, subject to the approval of the majority of the States Parties. The approval shall be considered given unless half or more of the States Parties respond negatively within six weeks after having been informed by the Secretary General of the United Nations of the proposed appointment.

6. The Committee shall establish its own rules of procedure.

7. The Secretary General of the United Nations shall provide the necessary means, staff and facilities for the effective performance of the functions of the Committee. The Secretary General of the United Nations shall convene the initial meeting of the Committee.

8. The members of the Committee shall be entitled to the facilities, privileges and immunities of experts on mission for the United Nations as laid down in the relevant sections of the Convention on the Privileges and Immunities of the United Nations.

9. Each State Party shall co-operate with the Committee and assist its members in the fulfilment of their mandate, to the extent of the Committee's functions that the State Party has accepted.

Article 27

A Conference of States Parties will take place at the earliest four years and at the latest six years following the entry into force of this Convention to evaluate the functioning of the Committee and to decide, in accordance with the procedure described in article 44, paragraph 2, whether it is appropriate to transfer to another body – without excluding any possibility - the monitoring of this Convention, in accordance with the functions defined in articles 28 to 36.

Article 28

1. In the framework of the competencies granted by this Convention, the Committee shall co-operate with all relevant organs, offices and specialized agencies and funds of the United Nations, with the treaty bodies instituted by

international instruments, with the special procedures of the United Nations, and with the regional intergovernmental organizations or bodies concerned, as well as with all relevant State institutions, agencies or offices working toward the protection of all persons against enforced disappearances.

2. As it discharges its mandate, the Committee shall consult other treaty bodies instituted by relevant international human rights instruments, in particular the Human Rights Committee instituted by the International Covenant on Civil and Political Rights, with a view to ensuring the consistency of their respective observations and recommendations.

Article 29

1. Each State Party shall submit to the Committee, through the Secretary-General of the United Nations, a report on the measures taken to give effect to its obligations under this Convention, within two years after the entry into force of this Convention for the State Party concerned.

2. The Secretary-General of the United Nations shall make this report available to all States Parties.

3. Each report shall be considered by the Committee, which shall issue such comments, observations or recommendations as it may deem appropriate. The comments, observations or recommendations shall be communicated to the State Party concerned, which may respond to them, on its own initiative or at the request of the Committee.

4. The Committee may also request further information from State Parties relevant to the implementation of this Convention.

Article 30

1. A request that a disappeared person should be sought and found on an urgent basis may be submitted to the Committee by relatives of the disappeared person or their legal representatives, their counsel or any person authorized by them, as well as by any other person having a legitimate interest.

2. If the Committee considers that the request for urgent action submitted in pursuance of paragraph 1:

(a) Is not manifestly unfounded;

(b) Does not constitute an abuse of the right of submission of such requests;

(c) Has already been duly presented to the competent bodies of the State Party concerned, such as investigative authorities, when this possibility exists;

(d) Is not incompatible with the provisions of this Convention; and

(e) The same matter is not being examined under another procedure of international investigation or settlement of the same nature; it shall request the State Party concerned to provide it with information on the situation of the person concerned, within a time limit set by the Committee.

3. In the light of the information provided by the State Party concerned in accordance with paragraph 2, the Committee may transmit recommendations to the State Party including a request that the State Party take all appropriate measures, including interim measures, to locate and protect the person in accordance with this Convention and inform the Committee within a specified period of time, of measures taken, taking into account the urgency of the situation. The Committee shall inform the person submitting the urgent action request of its recommendations and of the information provided to it by the State as it becomes available.

4. The Committee shall continue its efforts to work with the State Party concerned for as long as the fate of the person sought remains unresolved. The person presenting the request shall be kept informed.

Article 31

1. A State Party may at the time of ratification or at any time afterwards declare that it recognises the competence of the Committee to receive and consider communications from or on behalf of individuals subject to its jurisdiction claiming to be victims of a violation by this State Party of the provisions of this Convention. No communication shall be received by the Committee if it concerns a State Party which has not made such a declaration.

2. The Committee shall consider a communication inadmissible when:

(a) The communication is anonymous;

(b) The communication constitutes an abuse of the right of submission of such communications or is incompatible with the provisions of this Convention;

(c) The same matter is being examined under another procedure of international investigation or settlement; or when

(d) All effective available domestic remedies have not been exhausted. This rule shall not apply where the application of the remedies is unreasonably prolonged.

3. If the Committee considers that the communication meets the requirements set out in paragraph 2, it shall transmit the communication to the State Party concerned, requesting it to provide observations and comments within a time limit set by the Committee

4. At any time after the receipt of a communication and before a determination on the merits has been reached, the Committee may transmit to the State Party concerned for its urgent consideration a request that the State Party take such interim measures as may be necessary to avoid possible irreparable damage to the victim or victims of the alleged violation. Where the Committee exercises its discretion, this does not imply a determination on admissibility or on the merits of the communication.

5. The Committee shall hold closed meetings when examining communications under the present article. It shall inform the author of the communication of the responses provided by the State Party concerned. When the

Committee decides to terminate the procedure it shall communicate its views to the State Party and to the author of the communication.

Article 32

1. If the Committee receives reliable information indicating grave violations by a State Party of this Convention, it may, after consultation with the State Party concerned, request one or more of its members to undertake a visit and report back to it without delay.

2. The Committee shall notify the State Party concerned in writing of its intention to organise a visit, indicating the composition of the delegation and the purpose of the visit. The State Party shall answer the Committee within a reasonable time.

3. Upon a substantiated request by the State Party, the Committee may decide to postpone or cancel its visit.

4. If the State Party agrees to the visit, the Committee and the State Party concerned shall work together to define the modalities of the visit and the State Party shall provide the Committee with all the facilities needed for the successful completion of the visit.

5. Following its visit, the Committee shall communicate to the State Party concerned its observations and recommendations.

Article 33

A State Party to this Convention may at any time declare that it recognises the competence of the Committee to receive and consider communications to the effect that a State Party claims that another State Party is not fulfilling its obligations under this Convention. The Committee shall not receive communications concerning a State Party which has not made such a declaration, nor communications from a State Party which has not made such a declaration.

Article 34

If the Committee receives information which appears to it to contain well-founded indications that enforced disappearance is being practised on a widespread or systematic basis in the territory under the jurisdiction of a State Party, it may, after seeking from the State Party concerned all relevant information on the situation, urgently bring the matter to the attention of the General Assembly of the United Nations, through the Secretary General of the United Nations.

Article 35

1. The Committee shall have competence solely in respect of enforced disappearances which commenced after the entry into force of this Convention.

2. If a State becomes a party to this Convention after its entry into force, the obligations of that State vis-à-vis the Committee shall relate only to enforced disappearances which commenced after the entry into force of this Convention for the State concerned.

Article 36

1. The Committee shall submit an annual report on its activities under this Convention to the States Parties and to the General Assembly of the United Nations.

2. Before an observation on a State Party is published in the annual report, the State Party concerned shall be informed in advance and shall be given reasonable time to answer. This State Party may request the publication of its comments or observations in the report.

Article 37

Nothing in this Convention shall affect any provisions which are more conducive to the protection of all persons from enforced disappearance and which may be contained in:

(a) the law of a State Party;

(b) International law in force for that State.

Article 38

1. This Convention is open for signature by all Member States of the United Nations Organisation.

2. This Convention is subject to ratification by all Member States of the United Nations Organisation. Instruments of ratification shall be deposited with the Secretary-General of the United Nations.

3. This Convention is open to accession by all Member States of the United Nations Organisation. Accession shall be effected by the deposit of an instrument of accession with the Secretary-General of the United Nations.

Article 39

1. This Convention shall enter into force on the thirtieth day after the date of deposit of the twentieth instrument of ratification or accession.

2. For each State ratifying this Convention or acceding to it after the deposit of the twentieth instrument of ratification or accession, this Convention shall enter into force on the thirtieth day after the date of the deposit of its own instrument of ratification or accession.

Article 40

The Secretary-General of the United Nations shall inform all States Members of the United Nations and all States which have signed this Convention or acceded to it of the following:

(a) Signatures, ratifications and accessions under article 38;

(b) The date of entry into force of this Convention under article 39.

Article 41

The provisions of this Convention shall extend to all parts of federal States without any limitations or exceptions.

Article 42

1. Any dispute between two or more States Parties concerning the interpretation or application of this Convention which cannot be settled through negotiation or by the procedures expressly provided for in this Convention shall, at the request of one of them, be submitted to arbitration. If within six months from the date of the request for arbitration the Parties are unable to agree on the organisation of the arbitration, any one of those Parties may refer the dispute to the International Court of Justice by request in conformity with the Statute of the Court.

2. Each State may, at the time of signature or ratification of this Convention or accession thereto, declare that it does not consider itself bound by paragraph 1 of this article. The other States Parties shall not be bound by paragraph 1 of this article with respect to any State Party having made such a declaration.

3. Any State Party having made a declaration in accordance with paragraph 2 of this article may at any time withdraw this declaration by notification to the Secretary-General of the United Nations. Article 43 This Convention is without prejudice to the provisions of international humanitarian law, including the obligations of the High Contracting Parties to the four Geneva Conventions of 12 August 1949 and the additional protocols thereto of 8 June 1977, or to the opportunity available to any State Party to authorize the International Committee of the Red Cross to visit places of detention in situations not covered by international humanitarian law.

Article 44

1. Any State Party to this Convention may propose an amendment and file it with the Secretary-General of the United Nations. The Secretary-General shall thereupon communicate the proposed amendment to the States Parties to this Convention with a request that they indicate whether they favour a conference of States Parties for the purpose of considering and voting upon the proposal. In the event that within four months from the date of such communication at least one third of the States Parties favour such a conference, the Secretary-General shall convene the conference under the auspices of the United Nations.

2. Any amendment adopted by a majority of two thirds of the States Parties present and voting at the conference shall be submitted by the Secretary-General to all the States Parties for acceptance.

3. An amendment adopted in accordance with paragraph 1 of this article shall enter into force when two thirds of the States Parties to this Convention have accepted it in accordance with their respective constitutional processes.

4. When amendments enter into force, they shall be binding on those States Parties which have accepted them, other States Parties still being bound by the provisions of this Convention and any earlier amendment which they have accepted.

Article 45

1. This Convention, of which the Arabic, Chinese, English, French, Russian and Spanish texts are equally authentic, shall be deposited with the Secretary-General of the United Nations.

2. The Secretary-General of the United Nations shall transmit certified copies of this Convention to all States.

INTERNATIONAL CONVENTION ON THE PROTECTION AND PROMOTION OF THE RIGHTS AND DIGNITY OF PERSONS WITH DISABILITIES, G.A. Res. 61/106, Annex I, U.N. GAOR, 61st Sess., Supp. No. 49, at 65, U.N. Doc. A/61/49 (2006), *entered into force* **May 3, 2008:**

Preamble

The States Parties to the present Convention,

(a) *Recalling* the principles proclaimed in the Charter of the United Nation which recognize the inherent dignity and worth and the equal and inalienable rights of all members of the human family as the foundation of freedom, justice and peace in the world,

(b) *Recognizing* that the United Nations, in the Universal Declaration of Human Rights and in the International Covenants on Human Rights, has proclaimed and agreed that everyone is entitled to all the rights and freedoms set forth therein, without distinction of any kind,

(c) *Reaffirming* the universality, indivisibility, interdependence and interrelatedness of all human rights and fundamental freedoms and the need for persons with disabilities to be guaranteed their full enjoyment without discrimination,

(d) *Recalling* the International Covenant on Economic, Social and Cultural Rights, the International Covenant on Civil and Political Rights, the International Convention on the Elimination of All Forms of Racial Discrimination, the Convention on the Elimination of All Forms of Discrimination against Women, the Convention against Torture and Other Cruel, Inhuman or Degrading Treatment or Punishment, the Convention on the Rights of the Child, and the International Convention on the Protection of the Rights of All Migrant Workers and Members of Their Families,

(e) *Recognizing* that disability is an evolving concept and that disability results from the interaction between persons with impairments and attitudinal and environmental barriers that hinders their full and effective participation in society on an equal basis with others,

(f) *Recognizing* the importance of the principles and policy guidelines contained in the World Programme of Action concerning Disabled Persons and in the Standard Rules on the Equalization of Opportunities for Persons with Disabilities in influencing the promotion, formulation and evaluation of the policies, plans, programmes and actions at the national, regional and international levels to further equalize opportunities for persons with disabilities,

(g) *Emphasizing* the importance of mainstreaming disability issues as an integral part of relevant strategies of sustainable development,

(h) *Recognizing also* that discrimination against any person on the basis of disability is a violation of the inherent dignity and worth of the human person,

(i) *Recognizing further* the diversity of persons with disabilities,

(j) *Recognizing* the need to promote and protect the human rights of all persons with disabilities, including those who require more intensive support,

(k) *Concerned* that, despite these various instruments and undertakings, persons with disabilities continue to face barriers in their participation as equal members of society and violations of their human rights in all parts of the world,

(l) *Recognizing* the importance of international cooperation for improving the living conditions of persons with disabilities in every country, particularly in developing countries,

(m) *Recognizing* the valued existing and potential contributions made by persons with disabilities to the overall well-being and diversity of their communities, and that the promotion of the full enjoyment by persons with disabilities of their human rights and fundamental freedoms and of full participation by persons with disabilities will result in their enhanced sense of belonging and in significant advances in the human, social and economic development of society and the eradication of poverty,

(n) *Recognizing* the importance for persons with disabilities of their individual autonomy and independence, including the freedom to make their own choices,

(o) *Considering* that persons with disabilities should have the opportunity to be actively involved in decision-making processes about policies and programmes, including those directly concerning them,

(p) *Concerned* about the difficult conditions faced by persons with disabilities who are subject to multiple or aggravated forms of discrimination on the basis of race, colour, sex, language, religion, political or other opinion, national, ethnic, indigenous or social origin, property, birth, age or other status,

(q) *Recognizing* that women and girls with disabilities are often at greater risk, both within and outside the home of violence, injury or abuse, neglect or negligent treatment, maltreatment or exploitation,

(r) *Recognizing* that children with disabilities should have full enjoyment of all human rights and fundamental freedoms on an equal basis with other children, and recalling obligations to that end undertaken by States Parties to the Convention on the Rights of the Child,

(s) *Emphasizing* the need to incorporate a gender perspective in all efforts to promote the full enjoyment of human rights and fundamental freedoms by persons with disabilities,

(t) *Highlighting* the fact that the majority of persons with disabilities live in conditions of poverty, and in this regard recognizing the critical need to address the negative impact of poverty on persons with disabilities,

(u) *Bearing in mind* that conditions of peace and security based on full respect for the purposes and principles contained in the Charter of the United Nations and observance of applicable human rights instruments are indispensable for the full protection of persons with disabilities, in particular during armed conflicts and foreign occupation,

(v) *Recognizing* the importance of accessibility to the physical, social, economic and cultural environment, to health and education and to information and communication, in enabling persons with disabilities to fully enjoy all human rights and fundamental freedoms,

(w) *Realizing* that the individual, having duties to other individuals and to the community to which he or she belongs, is under a responsibility to strive for the promotion and observance of the rights recognized in the International Bill of Human Rights,

(x) *Convinced* that the family is the natural and fundamental group unit of society and is entitled to protection by society and the State, and that persons with disabilities and their family members should receive the necessary protection and assistance to enable families to contribute towards the full and equal enjoyment of the rights of persons with disabilities,

(y) *Convinced* that a comprehensive and integral international convention to promote and protect the rights and dignity of persons with disabilities will make a significant contribution to redressing the profound social disadvantage of persons with disabilities and promote their participation in the civil, political, economic, social and cultural spheres with equal opportunities, in both developing and developed countries,

Have agreed as follows:

Article 1

Purpose

The purpose of the present Convention is to promote, protect and ensure the full and equal enjoyment of all human rights and fundamental freedoms by all persons with disabilities, and to promote respect for their inherent dignity. Persons with disabilities include those who have long-term physical, mental, intellectual or sensory impairments which in interaction with various barriers may hinder their full and effective participation in society on an equal basis with others.

Article 2

Definitions

For the purposes of the present Convention:

"Communication" includes languages, display of text, Braille, tactile communication, large print, accessible multimedia as well as written, audio, plain-language, human-reader and augmentative and alternative modes, means and formats of communication, including accessible information and communication technology;

"Language" includes spoken and signed languages and other forms of non-spoken languages;

"Discrimination on the basis of disability" means any distinction, exclusion or restriction on the basis of disability which has the purpose or effect of impairing or nullifying the recognition, enjoyment or exercise, on an equal basis with others, of all human rights and fundamental freedoms in the political, economic, social, cultural, civil or any other field. It includes all forms of discrimination, including denial of reasonable accommodation;

"Reasonable accommodation" means necessary and appropriate modification and adjustments not imposing a disproportionate or undue burden, where needed in a particular case, to ensure to persons with disabilities the enjoyment or exercise on an equal basis with others of all human rights and fundamental freedoms;

"Universal design" means the design of products, environments, programmes and services to be usable by all people, to the greatest extent possible, without the need for adaptation or specialized design. "Universal design" shall not exclude assistive devices for particular groups of persons with disabilities where this is needed.

Article 3

General principles

The principles of the present Convention shall be:

(a) Respect for inherent dignity, individual autonomy including the freedom to make one's own choices, and independence of persons;

(b) Non-discrimination;

(c) Full and effective participation and inclusion in society;

(d) Respect for difference and acceptance of persons with disabilities as part of human diversity and humanity;

(e) Equality of opportunity;

(f) Accessibility;

(g) Equality between men and women;

(h) Respect for the evolving capacities of children with disabilities and respect for the right of children with disabilities to preserve their identities.

Article 4

General obligations

1. States Parties undertake to ensure and promote the full realization of all human rights and fundamental freedoms for all persons with disabilities

without discrimination of any kind on the basis of disability. To this end, States Parties undertake:

(a) To adopt all appropriate legislative, administrative and other measures for the implementation of the rights recognized in the present Convention;

(b) To take all appropriate measures, including legislation, to modify or abolish existing laws, regulations, customs and practices that constitute discrimination against persons with disabilities;

(c) To take into account the protection and promotion of the human rights of persons with disabilities in all policies and programmes;

(d) To refrain from engaging in any act or practice that is inconsistent with the present Convention and to ensure that public authorities and institutions act in conformity with the present Convention;

(e) To take all appropriate measures to eliminate discrimination on the basis of disability by any person, organization or private enterprise;

(f) To undertake or promote research and development of universally designed goods, services, equipment and facilities, as defined in article 2 of the present Convention, which should require the minimum possible adaptation and the least cost to meet the specific needs of a person with disabilities, to promote their availability and use, and to promote universal design in the development of standards and guidelines;

(g) To undertake or promote research and development of, and to promote the availability and use of new technologies, including information and communications technologies, mobility aids, devices and assistive technologies, suitable for persons with disabilities, giving priority to technologies at an affordable cost;

(h) To provide accessible information to persons with disabilities about mobility aids, devices and assistive technologies, including new technologies, as well as other forms of assistance, support services and facilities;

(i) To promote the training of professionals and staff working with persons with disabilities in the rights recognized in this Convention so as to better provide the assistance and services guaranteed by those rights.

2. With regard to economic, social and cultural rights, each State Party undertakes to take measures to the maximum of its available resources and, where needed, within the framework of international cooperation, with a view to achieving progressively the full realization of these rights, without prejudice to those obligations contained in the present Convention that are immediately applicable according to international law.

3. In the development and implementation of legislation and policies to implement the present Convention, and in other decision-making processes concerning issues relating to persons with disabilities, States Parties shall closely consult with and actively involve persons with disabilities, including children with disabilities, through their representative organizations.

4. Nothing in the present Convention shall affect any provisions which are more conducive to the realization of the rights of persons with disabilities and which may be contained in the law of a State Party or international law in force for that State. There shall be no restriction upon or derogation from any of the human rights and fundamental freedoms recognized or existing in any State Party to the present Convention pursuant to law, conventions, regulation or custom on the pretext that the present Convention does not recognize such rights or freedoms or that it recognizes them to a lesser extent.

5. The provisions of the present Convention shall extend to all parts of federal states without any limitations or exceptions.

Article 5

Equality and non-discrimination

1. States Parties recognize that all persons are equal before and under the law and are entitled without any discrimination to the equal protection and equal benefit of the law.

2. States Parties shall prohibit all discrimination on the basis of disability and guarantee to persons with disabilities equal and effective legal protection against discrimination on all grounds.

3. In order to promote equality and eliminate discrimination, States Parties shall take all appropriate steps to ensure that reasonable accommodation is provided.

4. Specific measures which are necessary to accelerate or achieve de facto equality of persons with disabilities shall not be considered discrimination under the terms of the present Convention.

Article 6

Women with disabilities

1. States Parties recognize that women and girls with disabilities are subject to multiple discrimination, and in this regard shall take measures to ensure the full and equal enjoyment by them of all human rights and fundamental freedoms.

2. States Parties shall take all appropriate measures to ensure the full development, advancement and empowerment of women, for the purpose of guaranteeing them the exercise and enjoyment of the human rights and fundamental freedoms set out in the present Convention.

Article 7

Children with disabilities

1. States Parties shall take all necessary measures to ensure the full enjoyment by children with disabilities of all human rights and fundamental freedoms on an equal basis with other children.

2. In all actions concerning children with disabilities, the best interests of the child shall be a primary consideration.

3. States Parties shall ensure that children with disabilities have the right to express their views freely on all matters affecting them, their views being given due weight in accordance with their age and maturity, on an equal basis with other children, and to be provided with disability and age-appropriate assistance to realize that right.

Article 8

Awareness-raising

1. States Parties undertake to adopt immediate, effective and appropriate measures:

(a) To raise awareness throughout society, including at the family level, regarding persons with disabilities, and to foster respect for the rights and dignity of persons with disabilities;

(b) To combat stereotypes, prejudices and harmful practices relating to persons with disabilities, including those based on sex and age, in all areas of life;

(c) To promote awareness of the capabilities and contributions of persons with disabilities.

2. Measures to this end include:

(a) Initiating and maintaining effective public awareness campaigns designed:

(i) To nurture receptiveness to the rights of persons with disabilities;

(ii) To promote positive perceptions and greater social awareness towards persons with disabilities;

(iii) To promote recognition of the skills, merits and abilities of persons with disabilities, and of their contributions to the workplace and the labour market;

(b) Fostering at all levels of the education system, including in all children from an early age, an attitude of respect for the rights of persons with disabilities;

(c) Encouraging all organs of the media to portray persons with disabilities in a manner consistent with the purpose of the present Convention;

(d) Promoting awareness-training programmes regarding persons with disabilities and the rights of persons with disabilities.

Article 9

Accessibility

1. To enable persons with disabilities to live independently and participate fully in all aspects of life, States Parties shall take appropriate measures to ensure to persons with disabilities access, on an equal basis with others, to the physical environment, to transportation, to information and communications, including information and communications technologies and systems,

and to other facilities and services open or provided to the public, both in urban and in rural areas. These measures, which shall include the identification and elimination of obstacles and barriers to accessibility, shall apply to, inter alia:

(a) Buildings, roads, transportation and other indoor and outdoor facilities, including schools, housing, medical facilities and workplaces;

(b) Information, communications and other services, including electronic services and emergency services.

2. States Parties shall also take appropriate measures to:

(a) Develop, promulgate and monitor the implementation of minimum standards and guidelines for the accessibility of facilities and services open or provided to the public;

(b) Ensure that private entities that offer facilities and services which are open or provided to the public take into account all aspects of accessibility for persons with disabilities;

(c) Provide training for stakeholders on accessibility issues facing persons with disabilities;

(d) Provide in buildings and other facilities open to the public signage in Braille and in easy to read and understand forms;

(e) Provide forms of live assistance and intermediaries, including guides, readers and professional sign language interpreters, to facilitate accessibility to buildings and other facilities open to the public;

(f) Promote other appropriate forms of assistance and support to persons with disabilities to ensure their access to information;

(g) Promote access for persons with disabilities to new information and communications technologies and systems, including the Internet;

(h) Promote the design, development, production and distribution of accessible information and communications technologies and systems at an early stage, so that these technologies and systems become accessible at minimum cost.

Article 10

Right to life

States Parties reaffirm that every human being has the inherent right to life and shall take all necessary measures to ensure its effective enjoyment by persons with disabilities on an equal basis with others.

Article 11

Situations of risk and humanitarian emergencies

States Parties shall take, in accordance with their obligations under international law, including international humanitarian law and international human rights law, all necessary measures to ensure the protection and safety of persons with disabilities in situations of risk, including situations of armed conflict, humanitarian emergencies and the occurrence of natural disasters.

Article 12

Equal recognition before the law

1. States Parties reaffirm that persons with disabilities have the right to recognition everywhere as persons before the law.

2. States Parties shall recognize that persons with disabilities enjoy legal capacity on an equal basis with others in all aspects of life.

3. States Parties shall take appropriate measures to provide access by persons with disabilities to the support they may require in exercising their legal capacity.

4. States Parties shall ensure that all measures that relate to the exercise of legal capacity provide for appropriate and effective safeguards to prevent abuse in accordance with international human rights law. Such safeguards shall ensure that measures relating to the exercise of legal capacity respect the rights, will and preferences of the person, are free of conflict of interest and undue influence, are proportional and tailored to the person's circumstances, apply for the shortest time possible and are subject to regular review by a competent, independent and impartial authority or judicial body. The safeguards shall be proportional to the degree to which such measures affect the person's rights and interests.

5. Subject to the provisions of this article, States Parties shall take all appropriate and effective measures to ensure the equal right of persons with disabilities to own or inherit property, to control their own financial affairs and to have equal access to bank loans, mortgages and other forms of financial credit, and shall ensure that persons with disabilities are not arbitrarily deprived of their property.

Article 13

Access to justice

1. States Parties shall ensure effective access to justice for persons with disabilities on an equal basis with others, including through the provision of procedural and age-appropriate accommodations, in order to facilitate their effective role as direct and indirect participants, including as witnesses, in all legal proceedings, including at investigative and other preliminary stages.

2. In order to help to ensure effective access to justice for persons with disabilities, States Parties shall promote appropriate training for those working in the field of administration of justice, including police and prison staff.

Article 14

Liberty and security of the person

1. States Parties shall ensure that persons with disabilities, on an equal basis with others:

(a) Enjoy the right to liberty and security of person;

(b) Are not deprived of their liberty unlawfully or arbitrarily, and that any deprivation of liberty is in conformity with the law, and that the existence of a disability shall in no case justify a deprivation of liberty.

2. States Parties shall ensure that if persons with disabilities are deprived of their liberty through any process, they are, on an equal basis with others, entitled to guarantees in accordance with international human rights law and shall be treated in compliance with the objectives and principles of this Convention, including by provision of reasonable accommodation.

Article 15

Freedom from torture or cruel, inhuman or degrading treatment or punishment

1. No one shall be subjected to torture or to cruel, inhuman or degrading treatment or punishment. In particular, no one shall be subjected without his or her free consent to medical or scientific experimentation.

2. States Parties shall take all effective legislative, administrative, judicial or other measures to prevent persons with disabilities, on an equal basis with others, from being subjected to torture or cruel, inhuman or degrading treatment or punishment.

Article 16

Freedom from exploitation, violence and abuse

1. States Parties shall take all appropriate legislative, administrative, social, educational and other measures to protect persons with disabilities, both within and outside the home, from all forms of exploitation, violence and abuse, including their gender-based aspects.

2. States Parties shall also take all appropriate measures to prevent all forms of exploitation, violence and abuse by ensuring, inter alia, appropriate forms of gender- and age-sensitive assistance and support for persons with disabilities and their families and caregivers, including through the provision of information and education on how to avoid, recognize and report instances of exploitation, violence and abuse. States Parties shall ensure that protection services are age-, gender- and disability-sensitive.

3. In order to prevent the occurrence of all forms of exploitation, violence and abuse, States Parties shall ensure that all facilities and programmes designed to serve persons with disabilities are effectively monitored by independent authorities.

4. States Parties shall take all appropriate measures to promote the physical, cognitive and psychological recovery, rehabilitation and social reintegration of persons with disabilities who become victims of any form of exploitation, violence or abuse, including through the provision of protection services. Such recovery and reintegration shall take place in an environment that fosters the health, welfare, self-respect, dignity and autonomy of the person and takes into account gender- and age-specific needs.

5. States Parties shall put in place effective legislation and policies, including women- and child-focused legislation and policies, to ensure that instances of exploitation, violence and abuse against persons with disabilities are identified, investigated and, where appropriate, prosecuted.

Article 17

Protecting the integrity of the person

Every person with disabilities has a right to respect for his or her physical and mental integrity on an equal basis with others.

Article 18

Liberty of movement and nationality

1. States Parties shall recognize the rights of persons with disabilities to liberty of movement, to freedom to choose their residence and to a nationality, on an equal basis with others, including by ensuring that persons with disabilities:

(a) Have the right to acquire and change a nationality and are not deprived of their nationality arbitrarily or on the basis of disability;

(b) Are not deprived, on the basis of disability, of their ability to obtain, possess and utilize documentation of their nationality or other documentation of identification, or to utilize relevant processes such as immigration proceedings, that may be needed to facilitate exercise of the right to liberty of movement;

(c) Are free to leave any country, including their own;

(d) Are not deprived, arbitrarily or on the basis of disability, of the right to enter their own country.

2. Children with disabilities shall be registered immediately after birth and shall have the right from birth to a name, the right to acquire a nationality and, as far as possible, the right to know and be cared for by their parents.

Article 19

Living independently and being included in the community

States Parties to this Convention recognize the equal right of all persons with disabilities to live in the community, with choices equal to others, and shall take effective and appropriate measures to facilitate full enjoyment by persons with disabilities of this right and their full inclusion and participation in the community, including by ensuring that:

(a) Persons with disabilities have the opportunity to choose their place of residence and where and with whom they live on an equal basis with others and are not obliged to live in a particular living arrangement;

(b) Persons with disabilities have access to a range of in-home, residential and other community support services, including personal assistance necessary to support living and inclusion in the community, and to prevent isolation or segregation from the community;

(c) Community services and facilities for the general population are available on an equal basis to persons with disabilities and are responsive to their needs.

Article 20

Personal mobility

States Parties shall take effective measures to ensure personal mobility with the greatest possible independence for persons with disabilities, including by:

(a) Facilitating the personal mobility of persons with disabilities in the manner and at the time of their choice, and at affordable cost;

(b) Facilitating access by persons with disabilities to quality mobility aids, devices, assistive technologies and forms of live assistance and intermediaries, including by making them available at affordable cost;

(c) Providing training in mobility skills to persons with disabilities and to specialist staff working with persons with disabilities;

(d) Encouraging entities that produce mobility aids, devices and assistive technologies to take into account all aspects of mobility for persons with disabilities.

Article 21

Freedom of expression and opinion, and access to information

States Parties shall take all appropriate measures to ensure that persons with disabilities can exercise the right to freedom of expression and opinion, including the freedom to seek, receive and impart information and ideas on an equal basis with others and through all forms of communication of their choice, as defined in article 2 of the present Convention, including by:

(a) Providing information intended for the general public to persons with disabilities in accessible formats and technologies appropriate to different kinds of disabilities in a timely manner and without additional cost;

(b) Accepting and facilitating the use of sign languages, Braille, augmentative and alternative communication, and all other accessible means, modes and formats of communication of their choice by persons with disabilities in official interactions;

(c) Urging private entities that provide services to the general public, including through the Internet, to provide information and services in accessible and usable formats for persons with disabilities;

(d) Encouraging the mass media, including providers of information through the Internet, to make their services accessible to persons with disabilities;

(e) Recognizing and promoting the use of sign languages.

Article 22

Respect for privacy

1. No person with disabilities, regardless of place of residence or living arrangements, shall be subjected to arbitrary or unlawful interference with his or her privacy, family, home or correspondence or other types of communication or to unlawful attacks on his or her honour and reputation. Persons with disabilities have the right to the protection of the law against such interference or attacks.

2. States Parties shall protect the privacy of personal, health and rehabilitation information of persons with disabilities on an equal basis with others.

Article 23

Respect for home and the family

1. States Parties shall take effective and appropriate measures to eliminate discrimination against persons with disabilities in all matters relating to marriage, family, parenthood and relationships, on an equal basis with others, so as to ensure that:

(a) The right of all persons with disabilities who are of marriageable age to marry and to found a family on the basis of free and full consent of the intending spouses is recognized;

(b) The rights of persons with disabilities to decide freely and responsibly on the number and spacing of their children and to have access to age-appropriate information, reproductive and family planning education are recognized, and the means necessary to enable them to exercise these rights are provided;

(c) Persons with disabilities, including children, retain their fertility on an equal basis with others.

2. States Parties shall ensure the rights and responsibilities of persons with disabilities, with regard to guardianship, wardship, trusteeship, adoption of children or similar institutions, where these concepts exist in national legislation; in all cases the best interests of the child shall be paramount. States Parties shall render appropriate assistance to persons with disabilities in the performance of their childrearing responsibilities.

3. States Parties shall ensure that children with disabilities have equal rights with respect to family life. With a view to realizing these rights, and to

prevent concealment, abandonment, neglect and segregation of children with disabilities, States Parties shall undertake to provide early and comprehensive information, services and support to children with disabilities and their families.

4. States Parties shall ensure that a child shall not be separated from his or her parents against their will, except when competent authorities subject to judicial review determine, in accordance with applicable law and procedures, that such separation is necessary for the best interests of the child. In no case shall a child be separated from parents on the basis of a disability of either the child or one or both of the parents.

5. States Parties shall, where the immediate family is unable to care for a child with disabilities, undertake every effort to provide alternative care within the wider family, and failing that, within the community in a family setting.

Article 24

Education

1. States Parties recognize the right of persons with disabilities to education. With a view to realizing this right without discrimination and on the basis of equal opportunity, States Parties shall ensure an inclusive education system at all levelsand life long learning directed to:

(a) The full development of human potential and sense of dignity and selfworth, and the strengthening of respect for human rights, fundamental freedoms and human diversity;

(b) The development by persons with disabilities of their personality, talents and creativity, as well as their mental and physical abilities, to their fullest potential;

(c) Enabling persons with disabilities to participate effectively in a free society.

2. In realizing this right, States Parties shall ensure that:

(a) Persons with disabilities are not excluded from the general education system on the basis of disability, and that children with disabilities are not excluded from free and compulsory primary education, or from secondary education, on the basis of disability;

(b) Persons with disabilities can access an inclusive, quality and free primary education and secondary education on an equal basis with others in the communities in which they live;

(c) Reasonable accommodation of the individual's requirements is provided;

(d) Persons with disabilities receive the support required, within the general education system, to facilitate their effective education;

(e) Effective individualized support measures are provided in environments that maximize academic and social development, consistent with the goal of full inclusion.

3. States Parties shall enable persons with disabilities to learn life and social development skills to facilitate their full and equal participation in education and as members of the community. To this end, States Parties shall take appropriate measures, including:

(a) Facilitating the learning of Braille, alternative script, augmentative and alternative modes, means and formats of communication and orientation and mobility skills, and facilitating peer support and mentoring;

(b) Facilitating the learning of sign language and the promotion of the linguistic identity of the deaf community;

(c) Ensuring that the education of persons, and in particular children, who are blind, deaf or deafblind, is delivered in the most appropriate languages and modes and means of communication for the individual, and in environments which maximize academic and social development.

4. In order to help ensure the realization of this right, States Parties shall take appropriate measures to employ teachers, including teachers with disabilities, who are qualified in sign language and/or Braille, and to train professionals and staff who work at all levels of education. Such training shall incorporate disability awareness and the use of appropriate augmentative and alternative modes, means and formats of communication, educational techniques and materials to support persons with disabilities.

5. States Parties shall ensure that persons with disabilities are able to access general tertiary education, vocational training, adult education and lifelong learning without discrimination and on an equal basis with others. To this end, States Parties shall ensure that reasonable accommodation is provided to persons with disabilities.

Article 25

Health

States Parties recognize that persons with disabilities have the right to the enjoyment of the highest attainable standard of health without discrimination on the basis of disability. States Parties shall take all appropriate measures to ensure access for persons with disabilities to health services that are gender-sensitive, including health-related rehabilitation. In particular, States Parties shall:

(a) Provide persons with disabilities with the same range, quality and standard of free or affordable health care and programmes as provided to other persons, including in the area of sexual and reproductive health and population based public health programmes;

(b) Provide those health services needed by persons with disabilities specifically because of their disabilities, including early identification and intervention as appropriate, and services designed to minimize and prevent further disabilities, including among children and older persons;

(c) Provide these health services as close as possible to people's own communities, including in rural areas;

(d) Require health professionals to provide care of the same quality to persons with disabilities as to others, including on the basis of free and informed consent by, inter alia, raising awareness of the human rights, dignity, autonomy and needs of persons with disabilities through training and the promulgation of ethical standards for public and private health care;

(e) Prohibit discrimination against persons with disabilities in the provision of health insurance, and life insurance where such insurance is permitted by national law, which shall be provided in a fair and reasonable manner;

(f) Prevent discriminatory denial of health care or health services or food and fluids on the basis of disability.

Article 26

Habilitation and rehabilitation

1. States Parties shall take effective and appropriate measures, including through peer support, to enable persons with disabilities to attain and maintain maximum independence, full physical, mental, social and vocational ability, and full inclusion and participation in all aspects of life. To that end, States Parties shall organize, strengthen and extend comprehensive habilitation and rehabilitation services and programmes, particularly in the areas of health, employment, education and social services, in such a way that these services and programmes:

(a) Begin at the earliest possible stage, and are based on the multidisciplinary assessment of individual needs and strengths;

(b) Support participation and inclusion in the community and all aspects of society, are voluntary, and are available to persons with disabilities as close as possible to their own communities, including in rural areas.

2. States Parties shall promote the development of initial and continuing training for professionals and staff working in habilitation and rehabilitation services.

3. States Parties shall promote the availability, knowledge and use of assistive devices and technologies, designed for persons with disabilities, as they relate to habilitation and rehabilitation.

Article 27

Work and employment

1. States Parties recognize the right of persons with disabilities to work, on an equal basis with others; this includes the right to the opportunity to gain a living by work freely chosen or accepted in a labour market and work environment that is open, inclusive and accessible to persons with disabilities. States Parties shall safeguard and promote the realization of the right to

work, including for those who acquire a disability during the course of employment, by taking appropriate steps, including through legislation, to, inter alia:

(a) Prohibit discrimination on the basis of disability with regard to all matters concerning all forms of employment, including conditions of recruitment, hiring and employment, continuance of employment, career advancement and safe and healthy working conditions;

(b) Protect the rights of persons with disabilities, on an equal basis with others, to just and favourable conditions of work, including equal opportunities and equal remuneration for work of equal value, safe and healthy working conditions, including protection from harassment, and the redress of grievances;

(c) Ensure that persons with disabilities are able to exercise their labour and trade union rights on an equal basis with others;

(d) Enable persons with disabilities to have effective access to general technical and vocational guidance programmes, placement services and vocational and continuing training;

(e) Promote employment opportunities and career advancement for persons with disabilities in the labour market, as well as assistance in finding, obtaining, maintaining and returning to employment;

(f) Promote opportunities for self-employment, entrepreneurship, the development of cooperatives and starting one's own business;

(g) Employ persons with disabilities in the public sector;

(h) Promote the employment of persons with disabilities in the private sector through appropriate policies and measures, which may include affirmative action programmes, incentives and other measures;

(i) Ensure that reasonable accommodation is provided to persons with disabilities in the workplace;

(j) Promote the acquisition by persons with disabilities of work experience in the open labour market;

(k) Promote vocational and professional rehabilitation, job retention and return-to-work programmes for persons with disabilities.

2. States Parties shall ensure that persons with disabilities are not held in slavery or in servitude, and are protected, on an equal basis with others, from forced or compulsory labour.

Article 28

Adequate standard of living and social protection

1. States Parties recognize the right of persons with disabilities to an adequate standard of living for themselves and their families, including adequate food, clothing and housing, and to the continuous improvement of living

conditions, and shall take appropriate steps to safeguard and promote the realization of this right without discrimination on the basis of disability.

2. States Parties recognize the right of persons with disabilities to social protection and to the enjoyment of that right without discrimination on the basis of disability, and shall take appropriate steps to safeguard and promote the realization of this right, including measures:

(a) To ensure equal access by persons with disabilities to clean water services, and to ensure access to appropriate and affordable services, devices and other assistance for disability-related needs;

(b) To ensure access by persons with disabilities, in particular women and girls with disabilities and older persons with disabilities, to social protection programmes and poverty reduction programmes;

(c) To ensure access by persons with disabilities and their families living in situations of poverty to assistance from the State with disability-related expenses, including adequate training, counselling, financial assistance and respite care;

(d) To ensure access by persons with disabilities to public housing programmes;

(e) To ensure equal access by persons with disabilities to retirement benefits and programmes.

Article 29

Participation in political and public life

States Parties shall guarantee to persons with disabilities political rights and the opportunity to enjoy them on an equal basis with others, and shall undertake to:

(a) Ensure that persons with disabilities can effectively and fully participate in political and public life on an equal basis with others, directly or through freely chosen representatives, including the right and opportunity for persons with disabilities to vote and be elected, inter alia, by:

(i) Ensuring that voting procedures, facilities and materials are appropriate, accessible and easy to understand and use;

(ii) Protecting the right of persons with disabilities to vote by secret ballot in elections and public referendums without intimidation, and to stand for elections, to effectively hold office and perform all public functions at all levels of government, facilitating the use of assistive and new technologies where appropriate;

(iii) Guaranteeing the free expression of the will of persons with disabilities as electors and to this end, where necessary, at their request, allowing assistance in voting by a person of their own choice;

(b) Promote actively an environment in which persons with disabilities can effectively and fully participate in the conduct of public affairs, without discrimination and on an equal basis with others, and encourage their partici-pation in public affairs, including:

(i) Participation in non-governmental organizations and associa-tions concerned with the public and political life of the country, and in the activities and administration of political parties;

(ii) Forming and joining organizations of persons with disabilities to represent persons with disabilities at international, national, regional and local levels.

Article 30

Participation in cultural life, recreation, leisure and sport

1. States Parties recognize the right of persons with disabilities to take part on an equal basis with others in cultural life, and shall take all appropri-ate measures to ensure that persons with disabilities:

(a) Enjoy access to cultural materials in accessible formats;

(b) Enjoy access to television programmes, films, theatre and other cultural activities, in accessible formats;

(c) Enjoy access to places for cultural performances or services, such as theatres, museums, cinemas, libraries and tourism services, and, as far as possible, enjoy access to monuments and sites of national cultural importance.

2. States Parties shall take appropriate measures to enable persons with disabilities to have the opportunity to develop and utilize their creative, artis-tic and intellectual potential, not only for their own benefit, but also for the enrichment of society.

3. States Parties shall take all appropriate steps, in accordance with international law, to ensure that laws protecting intellectual property rights do not constitute an unreasonable or discriminatory barrier to access by persons with disabilities to cultural materials.

4. Persons with disabilities shall be entitled, on an equal basis with oth-ers, to recognition and support of their specific cultural and linguistic identity, including sign languages and deaf culture.

5. With a view to enabling persons with disabilities to participate on an equal basis with others in recreational, leisure and sporting activities, States Parties shall take appropriate measures:

(a) To encourage and promote the participation, to the fullest extent possible, of persons with disabilities in mainstream sporting activities at all levels;

(b) To ensure that persons with disabilities have an opportunity to organize, develop and participate in disability-specific sporting and recreational activities and, to this end, encourage the provision, on an equal basis with others, of appropriate instruction, training and resources;

(c) To ensure that persons with disabilities have access to sporting, recreational and tourism venues;

(d) To ensure that children with disabilities have equal access with other children to participation in play, recreation and leisure and sporting activities, including those activities in the school system;

(e) To ensure that persons with disabilities have access to services from those involved in the organization of recreational, tourism, leisure and sporting activities.

Article 31

Statistics and data collection

1. States Parties undertake to collect appropriate information, including statistical and research data, to enable them to formulate and implement policies to give effect to the present Convention. The process of collecting and maintaining this information shall:

(a) Comply with legally established safeguards, including legislation on data protection, to ensure confidentiality and respect for the privacy of persons with disabilities;

(b) Comply with internationally accepted norms to protect human rights and fundamental freedoms and ethical principles in the collection and use of statistics.

2. The information collected in accordance with this article shall be disaggregated, as appropriate, and used to help assess the implementation of States Parties' obligations under the present Convention and to identify and address the barriers faced by persons with disabilities in exercising their rights.

3. States Parties shall assume responsibility for the dissemination of these statistics and ensure their accessibility to persons with disabilities and others.

Article 32

International cooperation

1. States Parties recognize the importance of international cooperation and its promotion, in support of national efforts for the realization of the purpose and objectives of the present Convention, and will undertake appropriate and effective measures in this regard, between and among States and, as appropriate, in partnership with relevant international and regional organizations and civil society, in particular organizations of persons with disabilities. Such measures could include, inter alia:

(a) Ensuring that international cooperation, including international development programmes, is inclusive of and accessible to persons with disabilities;

(b) Facilitating and supporting capacity-building, including through the exchange and sharing of information, experiences, training programmes and best practices;

(c) Facilitating cooperation in research and access to scientific and technical knowledge;

(d) Providing, as appropriate, technical and economic assistance, including by facilitating access to and sharing of accessible and assistive technologies, and through the transfer of technologies.

2. The provisions of this article are without prejudice to the obligations of each State Party to fulfil its obligations under the present Convention.

Article 33

National implementation and monitoring

1. States Parties, in accordance with their system of organization, shall designate one or more focal points within government for matters relating to the implementation of the present Convention, and shall give due consideration to the establishment or designation of a coordination mechanism within government to facilitate related action in different sectors and at different levels.

2. States Parties shall, in accordance with their legal and administrative systems, maintain, strengthen, designate or establish within the State Party, a framework, including one or more independent mechanisms, as appropriate, to promote, protect and monitor implementation of the present Convention. When designating or establishing such a mechanism, States Parties shall take into account the principles relating to the status and functioning of national institutions for protection and promotion of human rights.

3. Civil society, in particular persons with disabilities and their representative organizations, shall be involved and participate fully in the monitoring process.

Article 34

Committee on the Rights of Persons with Disabilities

1. There shall be established a Committee on the Rights of Persons with Disabilities (hereafter referred to as "the Committee"), which shall carry out the functions hereinafter provided.

2. The Committee shall consist, at the time of entry into force of the present Convention, of twelve experts. After an additional sixty ratifications or accessions to the Convention, the membership of the Committee shall increase by six members, attaining a maximum number of eighteen members.

3. The members of the Committee shall serve in their personal capacity and shall be of high moral standing and recognized competence and experience in the field covered by the present Convention. When nominating their candidates, States Parties are invited to give due consideration to the provision set out in article 4.3 of the present Convention.

4. The members of the Committee shall be elected by States Parties, consideration being given to equitable geographical distribution, representation of the different forms of civilization and of the principal legal systems, balanced gender representation and participation of experts with disabilities.

5. The members of the Committee shall be elected by secret ballot from a list of persons nominated by the States Parties from among their nationals at meetings of the Conference of States Parties. At those meetings, for which two thirds of States Parties shall constitute a quorum, the persons elected to the Committee shall be those who obtain the largest number of votes and an absolute majority of the votes of the representatives of States Parties present and voting.

6. The initial election shall be held no later than six months after the date of entry into force of the present Convention. At least four months before the date of each election, the Secretary-General of the United Nations shall address a letter to the States Parties inviting them to submit the nominations within two months. The Secretary-General shall subsequently prepare a list in alphabetical order of all persons thus nominated, indicating the State Parties which have nominated them, and shall submit it to the States Parties to the present Convention.

7. The members of the Committee shall be elected for a term of four years. They shall be eligible for re-election once. However, the term of six of the members elected at the first election shall expire at the end of two years; immediately after the first election, the names of these six members shall be chosen by lot by the chairperson of the meeting referred to in paragraph 5 of this article.

8. The election of the six additional members of the Committee shall be held on the occasion of regular elections, in accordance with the relevant provisions of this article.

9. If a member of the Committee dies or resigns or declares that for any other cause she or he can no longer perform her or his duties, the State Party which nominated the member shall appoint another expert possessing the qualifications and meeting the requirements set out in the relevant provisions of this article, to serve for the remainder of the term.

10. The Committee shall establish its own rules of procedure.

11. The Secretary-General of the United Nations shall provide the necessary staff and facilities for the effective performance of the functions of the Committee under the present Convention, and shall convene its initial meeting.

12. With the approval of the General Assembly, the members of the Committee established under the present Convention shall receive emoluments from United Nations resources on such terms and conditions as the Assembly may decide, having regard to the importance of the Committee's responsibilities.

13. The members of the Committee shall be entitled to the facilities, privileges and immunities of experts on mission for the United Nations as laid down in the relevant sections of the Convention on the Privileges and Immunities of the United Nations.

Article 35

Reports by States Parties

1. Each State Party shall submit to the Committee, through the Secretary-General of the United Nations, a comprehensive report on measures taken to give effect to its obligations under the present Convention and on the progress made in that regard, within two years after the entry into force of the present Convention for the State Party concerned.

2. Thereafter, States Parties shall submit subsequent reports at least every four years and further whenever the Committee so requests.

3. The Committee shall decide any guidelines applicable to the content of the reports.

4. A State Party which has submitted a comprehensive initial report to the Committee need not, in its subsequent reports, repeat information previously provided. When preparing reports to the Committee, States Parties are invited to consider doing so in an open and transparent process and to give due consideration to the provision set out in article 4.3 of the present Convention.

5. Reports may indicate factors and difficulties affecting the degree of fulfilment of obligations under the present Convention.

Article 36

Consideration of reports

1. Each report shall be considered by the Committee, which shall make such suggestions and general recommendations on the report as it may consider appropriate and shall forward these to the State Party concerned. The State Party may respond with any information it chooses to the Committee. The Committee may request further information from States Parties relevant to the implementation of the present Convention.

2. If a State Party is significantly overdue in the submission of a report, the Committee may notify the State Party concerned of the need to examine the implementation of the present Convention in that State Party, on the basis of reliable information available to the Committee, if the relevant report is not submitted within three months following the notification. The Committee shall invite the State Party concerned to participate in such examination. Should the State Party respond by submitting the relevant report, the provisions of paragraph 1 of this article will apply.

3. The Secretary-General of the United Nations shall make available the reports to all States Parties.

4. States Parties shall make their reports widely available to the public in their own countries and facilitate access to the suggestions and general recommendations relating to these reports.

5. The Committee shall transmit, as it may consider appropriate, to the specialized agencies, funds and programmes of the United Nations, and other

competent bodies, reports from States Parties in order to address a request or indication of a need for technical advice or assistance contained therein, along with the Committee's observations and recommendations, if any, on these requests or indications.

Article 37

Cooperation between States Parties and the Committee

1. Each State Party shall cooperate with the Committee and assist its members in the fulfilment of their mandate.

2. In its relationship with States Parties, the Committee shall give due consideration to ways and means of enhancing national capacities for the implementation of the present Convention, including through international cooperation.

Article 38

Relationship of the Committee with other bodies

In order to foster the effective implementation of the present Convention and to encourage international cooperation in the field covered by the present Convention:

(a) The specialized agencies and other United Nations organs shall be entitled to be represented at the consideration of the implementation of such provisions of the present Convention as fall within the scope of their mandate. The Committee may invite the specialized agencies and other competent bodies as it may consider appropriate to provide expert advice on the implementation of the Convention in areas falling within the scope of their respective mandates. The Committee may invite specialized agencies and other United Nations organs to submit reports on the implementation of the Convention in areas falling within the scope of their activities;

(b) The Committee, as it discharges its mandate, shall consult, as appropriate, other relevant bodies instituted by international human rights treaties, with a view to ensuring the consistency of their respective reporting guidelines, suggestions and general recommendations, and avoiding duplication and overlap in the performance of their functions.

Article 39

Report of the Committee

The Committee shall report every two years to the General Assembly and to the Economic and Social Council on its activities, and may make suggestions and general recommendations based on the examination of reports and information received from the States Parties. Such suggestions and general recommendations shall be included in the report of the Committee together with comments, if any, from States Parties.

Article 40

Conference of States Parties

1. The States Parties shall meet regularly in a Conference of States Parties in order to consider any matter with regard to the implementation of the present Convention.

2. No later than six months after the entry into force of the present Convention, the Conference of the States Parties shall be convened by the Secretary-General of the United Nations. The subsequent meetings shall be convened by the Secretary-General of the United Nations biennially or upon the decision of the Conference of States Parties. The Secretary-General of the United Nations shall be the depositary of the present Convention.

Article 42

Signature

The present Convention shall be open for signature by all States and by regional integration organizations at United Nations Headquarters in New York as of 30 March 2007.

Article 43

Consent to be bound

The present Convention shall be subject to ratification by signatory States and to formal confirmation by signatory regional integration organizations. It shall be open for accession by any State or regional integration organization which has not signed the Convention.

Article 44

Regional integration organizations

1. "Regional integration organization" shall mean an organization constituted by sovereign States of a given region, to which its member States have transferred competence in respect of matters governed by this Convention. Such organizations shall declare, in their instruments of formal confirmation or accession, the extent of their competence with respect to matters governed by this Convention. Subsequently, they shall inform the depositary of any substantial modification in the extent of their competence.

2. References to "States Parties" in the present Convention shall apply to such organizations within the limits of their competence.

3. For the purposes of article 45, paragraph 1, and article 47, paragraphs 2 and 3, any instrument deposited by a regional integration organization shall not be counted.

4. Regional integration organizations, in matters within their competence, may exercise their right to vote in the Conference of States Parties, with a number of votes equal to the number of their member States that are Parties

to this Convention. Such an organization shall not exercise its right to vote if any of its member States exercises its right, and vice versa.

Article 45

Entry into force

1. The present Convention shall enter into force on the thirtieth day after the deposit of the twentieth instrument of ratification or accession.

2. For each State or regional integration organization ratifying, formally confirming or acceding to the Convention after the deposit of the twentieth such instrument, the Convention shall enter into force on the thirtieth day after the deposit of its own such instrument.

Article 46

Reservations

1. Reservations incompatible with the object and purpose of the present Convention shall not be permitted.

2. Reservations may be withdrawn at any time.

Article 47

Amendments

1. Any State Party may propose an amendment to the present Convention and submit it to the Secretary-General of the United Nations. The Secretary-General shall communicate any proposed amendments to States Parties, with a request to be notified whether they favour a conference of States Parties for the purpose of considering and deciding upon the proposals. In the event that, within four months from the date of such communication, at least one third of the States Parties favour such a conference, the Secretary-General shall convene the conference under the auspices of the United Nations. Any amendment adopted by a majority of two thirds of the States Parties present and voting shall be submitted by the Secretary-General to the General Assembly for approval and thereafter to all States Parties for acceptance.

2. An amendment adopted and approved in accordance with paragraph 1 of this article shall enter into force on the thirtieth day after the number of instruments of acceptance deposited reaches two thirds of the number of States Parties at the date of adoption of the amendment. Thereafter, the amendment shall enter into force for any State Party on the thirtieth day following the deposit of its own instrument of acceptance. An amendment shall be binding only on those States Parties which have accepted it.

3. If so decided by the Conference of States Parties by consensus, an amendment adopted and approved in accordance with paragraph 1 of this article which relates exclusively to articles 34, 38, 39 and 40 shall enter into force for all States Parties on the thirtieth day after the number of instruments of acceptance deposited reaches two thirds of the number of States Parties at the date of adoption of the amendment.

Article 48

Denunciation

A State Party may denounce the present Convention by written notification to the Secretary-General of the United Nations. The denunciation shall become effective one year after the date of receipt of the notification by the Secretary- General.

Article 49

Accessible format

The text of the present Convention shall be made available in accessible formats.

Article 50

Authentic texts

The Arabic, Chinese, English, French, Russian and Spanish texts of the present Convention shall be equally authentic.

In witness thereof the undersigned plenipotentiaries, being duly authorized thereto by their respective Governments, have signed the present Convention.

FIRST OPTIONAL PROTOCOL, INTERNATIONAL CONVENTION ON THE PROTECTION AND PROMOTION OF THE RIGHTS AND DIGNITY OF PERSONS WITH DISABILITIES, G.A. Res. 61/106, Annex II, U.N. GAOR, 61st Sess., Supp. No. 49, at 80, U.N. Doc. A/61/49 (2006), entered into force May 3, 2008:

The States Parties to the present Protocol have agreed as follows:

Article 1

1. A State Party to the present Protocol ("State Party") recognizes the competence of the Committee on the Rights of Persons with Disabilities ("the Committee") to receive and consider communications from or on behalf of individuals or groups of individuals subject to its jurisdiction who claim to be victims of a violation by that State Party of the provisions of the Convention.

2. No communication shall be received by the Committee if it concerns a State Party to the Convention that is not a party to the present Protocol.

Article 2

The Committee shall consider a communication inadmissible when:

(a) The communication is anonymous;

(b) The communication constitutes an abuse of the right of submission of such communications or is incompatible with the provisions of the Convention;

(c) The same matter has already been examined by the Committee or has been or is being examined under another procedure of international investigation or settlement;

(d) All available domestic remedies have not been exhausted. This shall not be the rule where the application of the remedies is unreasonably prolonged or unlikely to bring effective relief;

(e) It is manifestly ill-founded or not sufficiently substantiated; or when

(f) The facts that are the subject of the communication occurred prior to the entry into force of the present Protocol for the State Party concerned unless those facts continued after that date.

Article 3

Subject to the provisions of article 2 of the present Protocol, the Committee shall bring any communications submitted to it confidentially to the attention of the State Party. Within six months, the receiving State shall submit to the Committee written explanations or statements clarifying the matter and the remedy, if any, that may have been taken by that State.

Article 4

1. At any time after the receipt of a communication and before a determination on the merits has been reached, the Committee may transmit to the State Party concerned for its urgent consideration a request that the State Party take such interim measures as may be necessary to avoid possible irreparable damage to the victim or victims of the alleged violation.

2. Where the Committee exercises its discretion under paragraph 1 of this article, this does not imply a determination on admissibility or on the merits of the communication.

Article 5

The Committee shall hold closed meetings when examining communications under the present Protocol. After examining a communication, the Committee shall forward its suggestions and recommendations, if any, to the State Party concerned and to the petitioner.

Article 6

1. If the Committee receives reliable information indicating grave or systematic violations by a State Party of rights set forth in the Convention, the Committee shall invite that State Party to cooperate in the examination of the information and to this end submit observations with regard to the information concerned.

2. Taking into account any observations that may have been submitted by the State Party concerned as well as any other reliable information available to it, the Committee may designate one or more of its members to conduct an inquiry and to report urgently to the Committee. Where warranted and with the consent of the State Party, the inquiry may include a visit to its territory.

3. After examining the findings of such an inquiry, the Committee shall transmit these findings to the State Party concerned together with any comments and recommendations.

4. The State Party concerned shall, within six months of receiving the findings, comments and recommendations transmitted by the Committee, submit its observations to the Committee.

5. Such an inquiry shall be conducted confidentially and the cooperation of the State Party shall be sought at all stages of the proceedings.

Article 7

1. The Committee may invite the State Party concerned to include in its report under article 35 of the Convention details of any measures taken in response to an inquiry conducted under article 6 of the present Protocol.

2. The Committee may, if necessary, after the end of the period of six months referred to in article 6.4, invite the State Party concerned to inform it of the measures taken in response to such an inquiry.

Article 8

Each State Party may, at the time of signature or ratification of the present Protocol or accession thereto, declare that it does not recognize the competence of the Committee provided for in articles 6 and 7.

Article 9

The Secretary-General of the United Nations shall be the depositary of the present Protocol.

Article 10

The present Protocol shall be open for signature by signatory States and regional integration organizations of the Convention at United Nations Headquarters in New York as of 30 March 2007.

Article 11

The present Protocol shall be subject to ratification by signatory States of this Protocol which have ratified or acceded to the Convention. It shall be subject to formal confirmation by signatory regional integration organizations of this Protocol which have formally confirmed or acceded to the Convention. It shall be open for accession by any State or regional integration organization which has ratified, formally confirmed or acceded to the Convention and which has not signed the Protocol.

Article 12

1. "Regional integration organization" shall mean an organization constituted by sovereign States of a given region, to which its member States have transferred competence in respect of matters governed by the Convention and this Protocol. Such organizations shall declare, in their instruments of formal confirmation or accession, the extent of their competence with respect to matters governed by the Convention and this Protocol. Subsequently, they shall inform the depositary of any substantial modification in the extent of their competence.

2. References to "States Parties" in the present Protocol shall apply to such organizations within the limits of their competence.

3. For the purposes of article 13, paragraph 1, and article 15, paragraph 2, any instrument deposited by a regional integration organization shall not be counted.

4. Regional integration organizations, in matters within their competence, may exercise their right to vote in the meeting of States Parties, with a number of votes equal to the number of their member States that are Parties to this Protocol. Such an organization shall not exercise its right to vote if any of its member States exercises its right, and vice versa.

Article 13

1. Subject to the entry into force of the Convention, the present Protocol shall enter into force on the thirtieth day after the deposit of the tenth instrument of ratification or accession

2. For each State or regional integration organization ratifying, formally confirming or acceding to the Protocol after the deposit of the tenth such instrument, the Protocol shall enter into force on the thirtieth day after the deposit of its own such instrument.

Article 14

1. Reservations incompatible with the object and purpose of the present Protocol shall not be permitted.

2. Reservations may be withdrawn at any time.

Article 15

1. Any State Party may propose an amendment to the present Protocol and submit it to the Secretary-General of the United Nations. The Secretary-General shall communicate any proposed amendments to States Parties, with a request to be notified whether they favour a meeting of States Parties for the purpose of considering and deciding upon the proposals. In the event that, within four months from the date of such communication, at least one third of the States Parties favour such a meeting, the Secretary-General shall convene the meeting under the auspices of the United Nations. Any amendment adopted by a majority of two thirds of the States Parties present and voting shall be submitted by the Secretary-General to the General Assembly for approval and thereafter to all States Parties for acceptance.

2. An amendment adopted and approved in accordance with paragraph 1 of this article shall enter into force on the thirtieth day after the number of instruments of acceptance deposited reaches two thirds of the number of States Parties at the date of adoption of the amendment. Thereafter, the amendment shall enter into force for any State Party on the thirtieth day following the deposit of its own instrument of acceptance. An amendment shall be binding only on those States Parties which have accepted it.

Article 16

A State Party may denounce the present Protocol by written notification to the Secretary-

General of the United Nations. The denunciation shall become effective one year after the date of receipt of the notification by the Secretary-General.

Article 17

The text of the present Protocol shall be made available in accessible formats.

Article 18

The Arabic, Chinese, English, French, Russian and Spanish texts of the present Protocol shall be equally authentic.

In witness thereof the undersigned plenipotentiaries, being duly authorized thereto by their respective Governments, have signed the present Protocol.

INTERNATIONAL CONVENTION ON THE PROTECTION OF THE RIGHTS OF ALL MIGRANT WORKERS AND MEMBERS OF THEIR FAMILIES, G.A. res. 45/158, annex, 45 U.N. GAOR Supp. (No. 49A) at 262, U.N. Doc. A/45/49 (1990), *entered into force* July 1, 2003:

Preamble

1. The States Parties to the present Convention,

Taking into account the principles embodied in the basic instruments of the United Nations concerning human rights, in particular the Universal Declaration of Human Rights, the International Covenant on Economic, Social and Cultural Rights, the International Covenant on Civil and Political Rights, the International Convention on the Elimination of All Forms of Racial Discrimination, the Convention on the Elimination of All Forms of Discrimination against Women and the Convention on the Rights of the Child,

Taking into account also the principles and standards set forth in the relevant instruments elaborated within the framework of the International Labour Organisation, especially the Convention concerning Migration for Employment (No. 97), the Convention concerning Migrations in Abusive Conditions and the Promotion of Equality of Opportunity and Treatment of Migrant Workers (No. 143), the Recommendation concerning Migration for Employment (No. 86), the Recommendation concerning Migrant Workers (No. 151), the Convention concerning Forced or Compulsory Labour (No. 29) and the Convention concerning Abolition of Forced Labour (No. 105),

Reaffirming the importance of the principles contained in the Convention against Discrimination in Education of the United Nations Educational, Scientific and Cultural Organization,

Recalling the Convention against Torture and Other Cruel, Inhuman or Degrading Treatment or Punishment, the Declaration of the Fourth United

Nations Congress on the Prevention of Crime and the Treatment of Offenders, the Code of Conduct for Law Enforcement Officials, and the Slavery Conventions,

Recalling that one of the objectives of the International Labour Organisation, as stated in its Constitution, is the protection of the interests of workers when employed in countries other than their own, and bearing in mind the expertise and experience of that organization in matters related to migrant workers and members of their families,

Recognizing the importance of the work done in connection with migrant workers and members of their families in various organs of the United Nations, in particular in the Commission on Human Rights and the Commission for Social Development, and in the Food and Agriculture Organization of the United Nations, the United Nations Educational, Scientific and Cultural Organization and the World Health Organization, as well as in other international organizations,

Recognizing also the progress made by certain States on a regional or bilateral basis towards the protection of the rights of migrant workers and members of their families, as well as the importance and usefulness of bilateral and multilateral agreements in this field,

Realizing the importance and extent of the migration phenomenon, which involves millions of people and affects a large number of States in the international community,

Aware of the impact of the flows of migrant workers on States and people concerned, and desiring to establish norms which may contribute to the harmonization of the attitudes of States through the acceptance of basic principles concerning the treatment of migrant workers and members of their families,

Considering the situation of vulnerability in which migrant workers and members of their families frequently-find themselves owing, among other things, to their absence from their State of origin and to the difficulties they may encounter arising from their presence in the State of employment,

Convinced that the rights of migrant workers and members of their families have not been sufficiently recognized everywhere and therefore require appropriate international protection,

Taking into account the fact that migration is often the cause of serious problems for the members of the families of migrant workers as well as for the workers themselves, in particular because of the scattering of the family,

Bearing in mind that the human problems involved in migration are even more serious in the case of irregular migration and convinced therefore that appropriate action should be encouraged in order to prevent and eliminate clandestine movements and trafficking in migrant workers, while at the same time assuring the protection of their fundamental human rights,

Considering that workers who are non-documented or in an irregular situation are frequently employed under less favourable conditions of work than other workers and that certain employers find this an inducement to seek such labour in order to reap the benefits of unfair competition,

Considering also that recourse to the employment of migrant workers who are in an irregular situation will be discouraged if the fundamental human rights of all migrant workers are more widely recognized and, moreover, that granting certain additional rights to migrant workers and members of their families in a regular situation will encourage all migrants and employers to respect and comply with the laws and procedures established by the States concerned,

Convinced, therefore, of the need to bring about the international protection of the rights of all migrant workers and members of their families, reaffirming and establishing basic norms in a comprehensive convention which could be applied universally,

Have agreed as follows:

PART I—SCOPE AND DEFINITIONS

Article 1

1. The present Convention is applicable, except as otherwise provided hereafter, to all migrant workers and members of their families without distinction of any kind such as sex, race, colour, language, religion or conviction, political or other opinion, national, ethnic or social origin, nationality, age, economic position, property, marital status, birth or other status.

2. The present Convention shall apply during the entire migration process of migrant workers and members of their families, which comprises preparation for migration, departure, transit and the entire period of stay and remunerated activity in the State of employment as well as return to the State of origin or the State of habitual residence.

Article 2

For the purposes of the present Convention:

1. The term "migrant worker" refers to a person who is to be engaged, is engaged or has been engaged in a remunerated activity in a State of which he or she is not a national.

2. (a) The term "frontier worker" refers to a migrant worker who retains his or her habitual residence in a neighbouring State to which he or she normally returns every day or at least once a week;

(b) The term "seasonal worker" refers to a migrant worker whose work by its character is dependent on seasonal conditions and is performed only during part of the year;

(c) The term "seafarer", which includes a fisherman, refers to a migrant worker employed on board a vessel registered in a State of which he or she is not a national;

(d) The term "worker on an offshore installation" refers to a migrant worker employed on an offshore installation that is under the jurisdiction of a State of which he or she is not a national;

(e) The term "itinerant worker" refers to a migrant worker who, having his or her habitual residence in one State, has to travel to another State or States for short periods, owing to the nature of his or her occupation;

(f) The term "project-tied worker" refers to a migrant worker admitted to a State of employment for a defined period to work solely on a specific project being carried out in that State by his or her employer;

(g) The term "specified-employment worker" refers to a migrant worker:

(i) Who has been sent by his or her employer for a restricted and defined period of time to a State of employment to undertake a specific assignment or duty; or

(ii) Who engages for a restricted and defined period of time in work that requires professional, commercial, technical or other highly specialized skill; or

(iii) Who, upon the request of his or her employer in the State of employment, engages for a restricted and defined period of time in work whose nature is transitory or brief; and who is required to depart from the State of employment either at the expiration of his or her authorized period of stay, or earlier if he or she no longer undertakes that specific assignment or duty or engages in that work;

(h) The term "self-employed worker" refers to a migrant worker who is engaged in a remunerated activity otherwise than under a contract of employment and who earns his or her living through this activity normally working alone or together with members of his or her family, and to any other migrant worker recognized as self-employed by applicable legislation of the State of employment or bilateral or multilateral agreements.

Article 3

The present Convention shall not apply to:

(a) Persons sent or employed by international organizations and agencies or persons sent or employed by a State outside its territory to perform official functions, whose admission and status are regulated by general international law or by specific international agreements or conventions;

(b) Persons sent or employed by a State or on its behalf outside its territory who participate in development programmes and other co-operation programmes, whose admission and status are regulated by agreement with the State of employment and who, in accordance with that agreement, are not considered migrant workers;

(c) Persons taking up residence in a State different from their State of origin as investors;

(d) Refugees and stateless persons, unless such application is provided for in the relevant national legislation of, or international instruments in force for, the State Party concerned;

(e) Students and trainees;

(f) Seafarers and workers on an offshore installation who have not been admitted to take up residence and engage in a remunerated activity in the State of employment.

Article 4

For the purposes of the present Convention the term "members of the family" refers to persons married to migrant workers or having with them a relationship that, according to applicable law, produces effects equivalent to marriage, as well as their dependent children and other dependent persons who are recognized as members of the family by applicable legislation or applicable bilateral or multilateral agreements between the States concerned.

Article 5

For the purposes of the present Convention, migrant workers and members of their families:

(a) Are considered as documented or in a regular situation if they are authorized to enter, to stay and to engage in a remunerated activity in the State of employment pursuant to the law of that State and to international agreements to which that State is a party;

(b) Are considered as non-documented or in an irregular situation if they do not comply with the conditions provided for in subparagraph (a) of the present article.

Article 6

For the purposes of the present Convention:

(a) The term "State of origin" means the State of which the person concerned is a national;

(b) The term "State of employment" means a State where the migrant worker is to be engaged, is engaged or has been engaged in a remunerated activity, as the case may be;

(c) The term "State of transit," means any State through which the person concerned passes on any journey to the State of employment or from the State of employment to the State of origin or the State of habitual residence.

PART II—NON-DISCRIMINATION WITH RESPECT TO RIGHTS

Article 7

States Parties undertake, in accordance with the international instruments concerning human rights, to respect and to ensure to all migrant workers and members of their families within their territory or subject to their jurisdiction the rights provided for in the present Convention without distinction of any kind such as to sex, race, colour, language, religion or conviction, political or other opinion, national, ethnic or social origin, nationality, age, economic position, property, marital status, birth or other status.

PART III—HUMAN RIGHTS OF ALL MIGRANT WORKERS AND MEMBERS OF THEIR FAMILIES

Article 8

1. Migrant workers and members of their families shall be free to leave any State, including their State of origin. This right shall not be subject to any restrictions except those that are provided by law, are necessary to protect national security, public order (ordre public), public health or morals or the rights and freedoms of others and are consistent with the other rights recognized in the present part of the Convention.

2. Migrant workers and members of their families shall have the right at any time to enter and remain in their State of origin.

Article 9

The right to life of migrant workers and members of their families shall be protected by law.

Article 10

No migrant worker or member of his or her family shall be subjected to torture or to cruel, inhuman or degrading treatment or punishment.

Article 11

1. No migrant worker or member of his or her family shall be held in slavery or servitude.

2. No migrant worker or member of his or her family shall be required to perform forced or compulsory labour.

3. Paragraph 2 of the present article shall not be held to preclude, in States where imprisonment with hard labour may be imposed as a punishment for a crime, the performance of hard labour in pursuance of a sentence to such punishment by a competent court.

4. For the purpose of the present article the term "forced or compulsory labour" shall not include:

(a) Any work or service not referred to in paragraph 3 of the present article normally required of a person who is under detention in consequence of a lawful order of a court or of a person during conditional release from such detention;

(b) Any service exacted in cases of emergency or clamity threatening the life or well-being of the community;

(c) Any work or service that forms part of normal civil obligations so far as it is imposed also on citizens of the State concerned.

Article 12

1. Migrant workers and members of their families shall have the right to freedom of thought, conscience and religion. This right shall include freedom to have or to adopt a religion or belief of their choice and freedom either individually or in community with others and in public or private to manifest their religion or belief in worship, observance, practice and teaching.

2. Migrant workers and members of their families shall not be subject to coercion that would impair their freedom to have or to adopt a religion or belief of their choice.

3. Freedom to manifest one's religion or belief may be subject only to such limitations as are prescribed by law and are necessary to protect public safety, order, health or morals or the fundamental rights and freedoms of others.

4. States Parties to the present Convention undertake to have respect for the liberty of parents, at least one of whom is a migrant worker, and, when applicable, legal guardians to ensure the religious and moral education of their children in conformity with their own convictions.

Article 13

1. Migrant workers and members of their families shall have the right to hold opinions without interference.

2. Migrant workers and members of their families shall have the right to freedom of expression; this right shall include freedom to seek, receive and impart information and ideas of all kinds, regardless of frontiers, either orally, in writing or in print, in the form of art or through any other media of their choice.

3. The exercise of the right provided for in paragraph 2 of the present article carries with it special duties and responsibilities. It may therefore be subject to certain restrictions, but these shall only be such as are provided by law and are necessary:

(a) For respect of the rights or reputation of others;

(b) For the protection of the national security of the States concerned or of public order (ordre public) or of public health or morals;

(c) For the purpose of preventing any propaganda for war;

(d) For the purpose of preventing any advocacy of national, racial or religious hatred that constitutes incitement to discrimination, hostility or violence.

Article 14

No migrant worker or member of his or her family shall be subjected to arbitrary or unlawful interference with his or her privacy, family, home, correspondence or other communications, or to unlawful attacks on his or her honour and reputation. Each migrant worker and member of his or her family shall have the right to the protection of the law against such interference or attacks.

Article 15

No migrant worker or member of his or her family shall be arbitrarily deprived of property, whether owned individually or in association with others. Where, under the legislation in force in the State of employment, the assets of a migrant worker or a member of his or her family are expropriated in whole or in part, the person concerned shall have the right to fair and adequate compensation.

Article 16

1. Migrant workers and members of their families shall have the right to liberty and security of person.

2. Migrant workers and members of their families shall be entitled to effective protection by the State against violence, physical injury, threats and intimidation, whether by public officials or by private individuals, groups or institutions.

3. Any verification by law enforcement officials of the identity of migrant workers or members of their families shall be carried out in accordance with procedure established by law.

4. Migrant workers and members of their families shall not be subjected individually or collectively to arbitrary arrest or detention; they shall not be deprived of their liberty except on such grounds and in accordance with such procedures as are established by law.

5. Migrant workers and members of their families who are arrested shall be informed at the time of arrest as far as possible in a language they understand of the reasons for their arrest and they shall be promptly informed in a language they understand of any charges against them.

6. Migrant workers and members of their families who are arrested or detained on a criminal charge shall be brought promptly before a judge or other officer authorized by law to exercise judicial power and shall be entitled to trial within a reasonable time or to release. It shall not be the general rule that while awaiting trial they shall be detained in custody, but release may be subject to guarantees to appear for trial, at any other stage of the judicial proceedings and, should the occasion arise, for the execution of the judgement.

7. When a migrant worker or a member of his or her family is arrested or committed to prison or custody pending trial or is detained in any other manner:

(a) The consular or diplomatic authorities of his or her State of origin or of a State representing the interests of that State shall, if he or she so requests, be informed without delay of his or her arrest or detention and of the reasons therefor;

(b) The person concerned shall have the right to communicate with the said authorities. Any communication by the person concerned to the said authorities shall be forwarded without delay, and he or she shall also have the right to receive communications sent by the said authorities without delay;

(c) The person concerned shall be informed without delay of this right and of rights deriving from relevant treaties, if any, applicable between the States concerned, to correspond and to meet with representatives of the said authorities and to make arrangements with them for his or her legal representation.

8. Migrant workers and members of their families who are deprived of their liberty by arrest or detention shall be entitled to take proceedings before a court, in order that that court may decide without delay on the lawfulness of their detention and order their release if the detention is not lawful. When they attend such proceedings, they shall have the assistance, if necessary without cost to them, of an interpreter, if they cannot understand or speak the language used.

9. Migrant workers and members of their families who have been victims of unlawful arrest or detention shall have an enforceable right to compensation.

Article 17

1. Migrant workers and members of their families who are deprived of their liberty shall be treated with humanity and with respect for the inherent dignity of the human person and for their cultural identity.

2. Accused migrant workers and members of their families shall, save in exceptional circumstances, be separated from convicted persons and shall be subject to separate treatment appropriate to their status as unconvicted persons. Accused juvenile persons shall be separated from adults and brought as speedily as possible for adjudication.

3. Any migrant worker or member of his or her family who is detained in a State of transit or in a State of employment for violation of provisions relating to migration shall be held, in so far as practicable, separately from convicted persons or persons detained pending trial.

4. During any period of imprisonment in pursuance of a sentence imposed by a court of law, the essential aim of the treatment of a migrant worker or a member of his or her family shall be his or her reformation and social rehabilitation. Juvenile offenders shall be separated from adults and be accorded treatment appropriate to their age and legal status.

5. During detention or imprisonment, migrant workers and members of their families shall enjoy the same rights as nationals to visits by members of their families.

6. Whenever a migrant worker is deprived of his or her liberty, the competent authorities of the State concerned shall pay attention to the problems that may be posed for members of his or her family, in particular for spouses and minor children.

7. Migrant workers and members of their families who are subjected to any form of detention or imprisonment in accordance with the law in force in

the State of employment or in the State of transit shall enjoy the same rights as nationals of those States who are in the same situation.

8. If a migrant worker or a member of his or her family is detained for the purpose of verifying any infraction of provisions related to migration, he or she shall not bear any costs arising therefrom.

Article 18

1. Migrant workers and members of their families shall have the right to equality with nationals of the State concerned before the courts and tribunals. In the determination of any criminal charge against them or of their rights and obligations in a suit of law, they shall be entitled to a fair and public hearing by a competent, independent and impartial tribunal established by law.

2. Migrant workers and members of their families who are charged with a criminal offence shall have the right to be presumed innocent until proven guilty according to law.

3. In the determination of any criminal charge against them, migrant workers and members of their families shall be entitled to the following minimum guarantees:

(a) To be informed promptly and in detail in a language they understand of the nature and cause of the charge against them;

(b) To have adequate time and facilities for the preparation of their defence and to communicate with counsel of their own choosing;

(c) To be tried without undue delay;

(d) To be tried in their presence and to defend themselves in person or through legal assistance of their own choosing; to be informed, if they do not have legal assistance, of this right; and to have legal assistance assigned to them, in any case where the interests of justice so require and without payment by them in any such case if they do not have sufficient means to pay;

(e) To examine or have examined the witnesses against them and to obtain the attendance and examination of witnesses on their behalf under the same conditions as witnesses against them;

(f) To have the free assistance of an interpreter if they cannot understand or speak the language used in court;

(g) Not to be compelled to testify against themselves or to confess guilt.

4. In the case of juvenile persons, the procedure shall be such as will take account of their age and the desirability of promoting their rehabilitation.

5. Migrant workers and members of their families convicted of a crime shall have the right to their conviction and sentence being reviewed by a higher tribunal according to law.

6. When a migrant worker or a member of his or her family has, by a final decision, been convicted of a criminal offence and when subsequently his or her conviction has been reversed or he or she has been pardoned on the ground that a new or newly discovered fact shows conclusively that there has been a miscarriage of justice, the person who has suffered punishment as a result of such conviction shall be compensated according to law, unless it is proved that the non-disclosure of the unknown fact in time is wholly or partly attributable to that person.

7. No migrant worker or member of his or her family shall be liable to be tried or punished again for an offence for which he or she has already been finally convicted or acquitted in accordance with the law and penal procedure of the State concerned.

Article 19

1. No migrant worker or member of his or her family shall be held guilty of any criminal offence on account of any act or omission that did not constitute a criminal offence under national or international law at the time when the criminal offence was committed, nor shall a heavier penalty be imposed than the one that was applicable at the time when it was committed. If, subsequent to the commission of the offence, provision is made by law for the imposition of a lighter penalty, he or she shall benefit thereby.

2. Humanitarian considerations related to the status of a migrant worker, in particular with respect to his or her right of residence or work, should be taken into account in imposing a sentence for a criminal offence committed by a migrant worker or a member of his or her family.

Article 20

1. No migrant worker or member of his or her family shall be imprisoned merely on the ground of failure to fulfil a contractual obligation.

2. No migrant worker or member of his or her family shall be deprived of his or her authorization of residence or work permit or expelled merely on the ground of failure to fulfil an obligation arising out of a work contract unless fulfilment of that obligation constitutes a condition for such authorization or permit.

Article 21

It shall be unlawful for anyone, other than a public official duly authorized by law, to confiscate, destroy or attempt to destroy identity documents, documents authorizing entry to or stay, residence or establishment in the national territory or work permits. No authorized confiscation of such documents shall take place without delivery of a detailed receipt. In no case shall it be permitted to destroy the passport or equivalent document of a migrant worker or a member of his or her family.

Article 22

1. Migrant workers and members of their families shall not be subject to measures of collective expulsion. Each case of expulsion shall be examined and decided individually.

2. Migrant workers and members of their families may be expelled from the territory of a State Party only in pursuance of a decision taken by the competent authority in accordance with law.

3. The decision shall be communicated to them in a language they understand. Upon their request where not otherwise mandatory, the decision shall be communicated to them in writing and, save in exceptional circumstances on account of national security, the reasons for the decision likewise stated. The persons concerned shall be informed of these rights before or at the latest at the time the decision is rendered.

4. Except where a final decision is pronounced by a judicial authority, the person concerned shall have the right to submit the reason he or she should not be expelled and to have his or her case reviewed by the competent authority, unless compelling reasons of national security require otherwise. Pending such review, the person concerned shall have the right to seek a stay of the decision of expulsion.

5. If a decision of expulsion that has already been executed is subsequently annulled, the person concerned shall have the right to seek compensation according to law and the earlier decision shall not be used to prevent him or her from re-entering the State concerned.

6. In case of expulsion, the person concerned shall have a reasonable opportunity before or after departure to settle any claims for wages and other entitlements due to him or her and any pending liabilities.

7. Without prejudice to the execution of a decision of expulsion, a migrant worker or a member of his or her family who is subject to such a decision may seek entry into a State other than his or her State of origin.

8. In case of expulsion of a migrant worker or a member of his or her family the costs of expulsion shall not be borne by him or her. The person concerned may be required to pay his or her own travel costs.

9. Expulsion from the State of employment shall not in itself prejudice any rights of a migrant worker or a member of his or her family acquired in accordance with the law of that State, including the right to receive wages and other entitlements due to him or her.

Article 23

Migrant workers and members of their families shall have the right to have recourse to the protection and assistance of the consular or diplomatic authorities of their State of origin or of a State representing the interests of that State whenever the rights recognized in the present Convention are impaired. In particular, in case of expulsion, the person concerned shall be informed of this right without delay and the authorities of the expelling State shall facilitate the exercise of such right.

Article 24

Every migrant worker and every member of his or her family shall have the right to recognition everywhere as a person before the law.

Article 25

1. Migrant workers shall enjoy treatment not less favourable than that which applies to nationals of the State of employment in respect of remuneration and:

(a) Other conditions of work, that is to say, overtime, hours of work, weekly rest, holidays with pay, safety, health, termination of the employment relationship and any other conditions of work which, according to national law and practice, are covered by these terms;

(b) Other terms of employment, that is to say, minimum age of employment, restriction on home work and any other matters which, according to national law and practice, are considered a term of employment.

2. It shall not be lawful to derogate in private contracts of employment from the principle of equality of treatment referred to in paragraph 1 of the present article.

3. States Parties shall take all appropriate measures to ensure that migrant workers are not deprived of any rights derived from this principle by reason of any irregularity in their stay or employment. In particular, employers shall not be relieved of any legal or contractual obligations, nor shall their obligations be limited in any manner by reason of such irregularity.

Article 26

1. States Parties recognize the right of migrant workers and members of their families:

(a) To take part in meetings and activities of trade unions and of any other associations established in accordance with law, with a view to protecting their economic, social, cultural and other interests, subject only to the rules of the organization concerned;

(b) To join freely any trade union and any such association as aforesaid, subject only to the rules of the organization concerned;

(c) To seek the aid and assistance of any trade union and of any such association as aforesaid.

2. No restrictions may be placed on the exercise of these rights other than those that are prescribed by law and which are necessary in a democratic society in the interests of national security, public order (ordre public) or the protection of the rights and freedoms of others.

Article 27

1. With respect to social security, migrant workers and members of their families shall enjoy in the State of employment the same treatment granted to nationals in so far as they fulfil the requirements provided for by the applicable legislation of that State and the applicable bilateral and multilateral treaties. The competent authorities of the State of origin and the State of employment can at any time establish the necessary arrangements to determine the modalities of application of this norm.

2. Where the applicable legislation does not allow migrant workers and members of their families a benefit, the States concerned shall examine the possibility of reimbursing interested persons the amount of contributions made by them with respect to that benefit on the basis of the treatment granted to nationals who are in similar circumstances.

Article 28

Migrant workers and members of their families shall have the right to receive any medical care that is urgently required for the preservation of their life or the avoidance of irreparable harm to their health on the basis of equality of treatment with nationals of the State concerned. Such emergency medical care shall not be refused them by reason of any irregularity with regard to stay or employment.

Article 29

Each child of a migrant worker shall have the right to a name, to registration of birth and to a nationality.

Article 30

Each child of a migrant worker shall have the basic right of access to education on the basis of equality of treatment with nationals of the State concerned. Access to public pre-school educational institutions or schools shall not be refused or limited by reason of the irregular situation with respect to stay or employment of either parent or by reason of the irregularity of the child's stay in the State of employment.

Article 31

1. States Parties shall ensure respect for the cultural identity of migrant workers and members of their families and shall not prevent them from maintaining their cultural links with their State of origin.

2. States Parties may take appropriate measures to assist and encourage efforts in this respect.

Article 32

Upon the termination of their stay in the State of employment, migrant workers and members of their families shall have the right to transfer their earnings and savings and, in accordance with the applicable legislation of the States concerned, their personal effects and belongings.

Article 33

1. Migrant workers and members of their families shall have the right to be informed by the State of origin, the State of employment or the State of transit as the case may be concerning:

(a) Their rights arising out of the present Convention;

(b) The conditions of their admission, their rights and obligations under the law and practice of the State concerned and such other matters as will enable them to comply with administrative or other formalities in that State.

2. States Parties shall take all measures they deem appropriate to disseminate the said information or to ensure that it is provided by employers, trade unions or other appropriate bodies or institutions. As appropriate, they shall co-operate with other States concerned.

3. Such adequate information shall be provided upon request to migrant workers and members of their families, free of charge, and, as far as possible, in a language they are able to understand.

Article 34

Nothing in the present part of the Convention shall have the effect of relieving migrant workers and the members of their families from either the obligation to comply with the laws and regulations of any State of transit and the State of employment or the obligation to respect the cultural identity of the inhabitants of such States.

Article 35

Nothing in the present part of the Convention shall be interpreted as implying the regularization of the situation of migrant workers or members of their families who are non-documented or in an irregular situation or any right to such regularization of their situation, nor shall it prejudice the measures intended to ensure sound and equitable conditions for international migration as provided in part VI of the present Convention.

PART IV—OTHER RIGHTS OF MIGRANT WORKERS AND MEMBERS OF THEIR FAMILIES WHO ARE DOCUMENTED OR IN A REGULAR SITUATION

Article 36

Migrant workers and members of their families who are documented or in a regular situation in the State of employment shall enjoy the rights set forth in the present part of the Convention in addition to those set forth in part III.

Article 37

Before their departure, or at the latest at the time of their admission to the State of employment, migrant workers and members of their families shall have the right to be fully informed by the State of origin or the State of employment, as appropriate, of all conditions applicable to their admission and particularly those concerning their stay and the remunerated activities in which they may engage as well as of the requirements they must satisfy in the State of employment and the authority to which they must address themselves for any modification of those conditions.

Article 38

1. States of employment shall make every effort to authorize migrant workers and members of the families to be temporarily absent without effect upon their authorization to stay or to work, as the case may be. In doing so, States of employment shall take into account the special needs and obligations of migrant workers and members of their families, in particular in their States of origin.

2. Migrant workers and members of their families shall have the right to be fully informed of the terms on which such temporary absences are authorized.

Article 39

1. Migrant workers and members of their families shall have the right to liberty of movement in the territory of the State of employment and freedom to choose their residence there.

2. The rights mentioned in paragraph 1 of the present article shall not be subject to any restrictions except those that are provided by law, are necessary to protect national security, public order (ordre public), public health or morals, or the rights and freedoms of others and are consistent with the other rights recognized in the present Convention.

Article 40

1. Migrant workers and members of their families shall have the right to form associations and trade unions in the State of employment for the promotion and protection of their economic, social, cultural and other interests.

2. No restrictions may be placed on the exercise of this right other than those that are prescribed by law and are necessary in a democratic society in the interests of national security, public order (ordre public) or the protection of the rights and freedoms of others.

Article 41

1. Migrant workers and members of their families shall have the right to participate in public affairs of their State of origin and to vote and to be elected at elections of that State, in accordance with its legislation.

2. The States concerned shall, as appropriate and in accordance with their legislation, facilitate the exercise of these rights.

Article 42

1. States Parties shall consider the establishment of procedures or institutions through which account may be taken, both in States of origin and in States of employment, of special needs, aspirations and obligations of migrant workers and members of their families and shall envisage, as appropriate, the possibility for migrant workers and members of their families to have their freely chosen representatives in those institutions.

2. States of employment shall facilitate, in accordance with their national legislation, the consultation or participation of migrant workers and members

of their families in decisions concerning the life and administration of local communities.

3. Migrant workers may enjoy political rights in the State of employment if that State, in the exercise of its sovereignty, grants them such rights.

Article 43

1. Migrant workers shall enjoy equality of treatment with nationals of the State of employment in relation to:

(a) Access to educational institutions and services subject to the admission requirements and other regulations of the institutions and services concerned;

(b) Access to vocational guidance and placement services;

(c) Access to vocational training and retraining facilities and institutions;

(d) Access to housing, including social housing schemes, and protection against exploitation in respect of rents;

(e) Access to social and health services, provided that the requirements for participation in the respective schemes are met;

(f) Access to co-operatives and self-managed enterprises, which shall not imply a change of their migration status and shall be subject to the rules and regulations of the bodies concerned;

(g) Access to and participation in cultural life.

2. States Parties shall promote conditions to ensure effective equality of treatment to enable migrant workers to enjoy the rights mentioned in paragraph 1 of the present article whenever the terms of their stay, as authorized by the State of employment, meet the appropriate requirements.

3. States of employment shall not prevent an employer of migrant workers from establishing housing or social or cultural facilities for them. Subject to article 70 of the present Convention, a State of employment may make the establishment of such facilities subject to the requirements generally applied in that State concerning their installation.

Article 44

1. States Parties, recognizing that the family is the natural and fundamental group unit of society and is entitled to protection by society and the State, shall take appropriate measures to ensure the protection of the unity of the families of migrant workers.

2. States Parties shall take measures that they deem appropriate and that fall within their competence to facilitate the reunification of migrant workers with their spouses or persons who have with the migrant worker a relationship that, according to applicable law, produces effects equivalent to marriage, as well as with their minor dependent unmarried children.

3. States of employment, on humanitarian grounds, shall favourably consider granting equal treatment, as set forth in paragraph 2 of the present article, to other family members of migrant workers.

Article 45

1. Members of the families of migrant workers shall, in the State of employment, enjoy equality of treatment with nationals of that State in relation to:

(a) Access to educational institutions and services, subject to the admission requirements and other regulations of the institutions and services concerned;

(b) Access to vocational guidance and training institutions and services, provided that requirements for participation are met;

(c) Access to social and health services, provided that requirements for participation in the respective schemes are met;

(d) Access to and participation in cultural life.

2. States of employment shall pursue a policy, where appropriate in collaboration with the States of origin, aimed at facilitating the integration of children of migrant workers in the local school system, particularly in respect of teaching them the local language.

3. States of employment shall endeavour to facilitate for the children of migrant workers the teaching of their mother tongue and culture and, in this regard, States of origin shall collaborate whenever appropriate.

4. States of employment may provide special schemes of education in the mother tongue of children of migrant workers, if necessary in collaboration with the States of origin.

Article 46

Migrant workers and members of their families shall, subject to the applicable legislation of the States concerned, as well as relevant international agreements and the obligations of the States concerned arising out of their participation in customs unions, enjoy exemption from import and export duties and taxes in respect of their personal and household effects as well as the equipment necessary to engage in the remunerated activity for which they were admitted to the State of employment:

(a) Upon departure from the State of origin or State of habitual residence;

(b) Upon initial admission to the State of employment;

(c) Upon final departure from the State of employment;

(d) Upon final return to the State of origin or State of habitual residence.

Article 47

1. Migrant workers shall have the right to transfer their earnings and savings, in particular those funds necessary for the support of their families,

from the State of employment to their State of origin or any other State. Such transfers shall be made in conformity with procedures established by applicable legislation of the State concerned and in conformity with applicable international agreements.

2. States concerned shall take appropriate measures to facilitate such transfers.

Article 48

1. Without prejudice to applicable double taxation agreements, migrant workers and members of their families shall, in the matter of earnings in the State of employment:

(a) Not be liable to taxes, duties or charges of any description higher or more onerous than those imposed on nationals in similar circumstances;

(b) Be entitled to deductions or exemptions from taxes of any description and to any tax allowances applicable to nationals in similar circumstances, including tax allowances for dependent members of their families.

2. States Parties shall endeavour to adopt appropriate measures to avoid double taxation of the earnings and savings of migrant workers and members of their families.

Article 49

1. Where separate authorizations to reside and to engage in employment are required by national legislation, the States of employment shall issue to migrant workers authorization of residence for at least the same period of time as their authorization to engage in remunerated activity.

2. Migrant workers who in the State of employment are allowed freely to choose their remunerated activity shall neither be regarded as in an irregular situation nor shall they lose their authorization of residence by the mere fact of the termination of their remunerated activity prior to the expiration of their work permits or similar authorizations.

3. In order to allow migrant workers referred to in paragraph 2 of the present article sufficient time to find alternative remunerated activities, the authorization of residence shall not be withdrawn at least for a period corresponding to that during which they may be entitled to unemployment benefits.

Article 50

1. In the case of death of a migrant worker or dissolution of marriage, the State of employment shall favourably consider granting family members of that migrant worker residing in that State on the basis of family reunion an authorization to stay; the State of employment shall take into account the length of time they have already resided in that State.

2. Members of the family to whom such authorization is not granted shall be allowed before departure a reasonable period of time in order to enable them to settle their affairs in the State of employment.

3. The provisions of paragraphs I and 2 of the present article may not be interpreted as adversely affecting any right to stay and work otherwise granted to such family members by the legislation of the State of employment or by bilateral and multilateral treaties applicable to that State.

Article 51

Migrant workers who in the State of employment are not permitted freely to choose their remunerated activity shall neither be regarded as in an irregular situation nor shall they lose their authorization of residence by the mere fact of the termination of their remunerated activity prior to the expiration of their work permit, except where the authorization of residence is expressly dependent upon the specific remunerated activity for which they were admitted. Such migrant workers shall have the right to seek alternative employment, participation in public work schemes and retraining during the remaining period of their authorization to work, subject to such conditions and limitations as are specified in the authorization to work.

Article 52

1. Migrant workers in the State of employment shall have the right freely to choose their remunerated activity, subject to the following restrictions or conditions.

2. For any migrant worker a State of employment may:

(a) Restrict access to limited categories of employment, functions, services or activities where this is necessary in the interests of this State and provided for by national legislation;

(b) Restrict free choice of remunerated activity in accordance with its legislation concerning recognition of occupational qualifications acquired outside its territory. However, States Parties concerned shall endeavour to provide for recognition of such qualifications.

3. For migrant workers whose permission to work is limited in time, a State of employment may also:

(a) Make the right freely to choose their remunerated activities subject to the condition that the migrant worker has resided lawfully in its territory for the purpose of remunerated activity for a period of time prescribed in its national legislation that should not exceed two years;

(b) Limit access by a migrant worker to remunerated activities in pursuance of a policy of granting priority to its nationals or to persons who are assimilated to them for these purposes by virtue of legislation or bilateral or multilateral agreements. Any such limitation shall cease to apply to a migrant worker who has resided lawfully in its territory for the purpose of remunerated activity for a period of time prescribed in its national legislation that should not exceed five years.

4. States of employment shall prescribe the conditions under which a migrant worker who has been admitted to take up employment may be authorized to engage in work on his or her own account. Account shall be taken of the

period during which the worker has already been lawfully in the State of employment.

Article 53

1. Members of a migrant worker's family who have themselves an authorization of residence or admission that is without limit of time or is automatically renewable shall be permitted freely to choose their remunerated activity under the same conditions as are applicable to the said migrant worker in accordance with article 52 of the present Convention.

2. With respect to members of a migrant worker's family who are not permitted freely to choose their remunerated activity, States Parties shall consider favourably granting them priority in obtaining permission to engage in a remunerated activity over other workers who seek admission to the State of employment, subject to applicable bilateral and multilateral agreements.

Article 54

1. Without prejudice to the terms of their authorization of residence or their permission to work and the rights provided for in articles 25 and 27 of the present Convention, migrant workers shall enjoy equality of treatment with nationals of the State of employment in respect of:

(a) Protection against dismissal;

(b) Unemployment benefits;

(c) Access to public work schemes intended to combat unemployment;

(d) Access to alternative employment in the event of loss of work or termination of other remunerated activity, subject to article 52 of the present Convention.

2. If a migrant worker claims that the terms of his or her work contract have been violated by his or her employer, he or she shall have the right to address his or her case to the competent authorities of the State of employment, on terms provided for in article 18, paragraph 1, of the present Convention.

Article 55

Migrant workers who have been granted permission to engage in a remunerated activity, subject to the conditions attached to such permission, shall be entitled to equality of treatment with nationals of the State of employment in the exercise of that remunerated activity.

Article 56

1. Migrant workers and members of their families referred to in the present part of the Convention may not be expelled from a State of employment, except for reasons defined in the national legislation of that State, and subject to the safeguards established in part III.

2. Expulsion shall not be resorted to for the purpose of depriving a migrant worker or a member of his or her family of the rights arising out of the authorization of residence and the work permit.

3. In considering whether to expel a migrant worker or a member of his or her family, account should be taken of humanitarian considerations and of the length of time that the person concerned has already resided in the State of employment.

PART V—PROVISIONS APPLICABLE TO PARTICULAR CATEGORIES OF MIGRANT WORKERS AND OF THEIR FAMILIES

Article 57

The particular categories of migrant workers and members of their families specified in the present part of the Convention who are documented or in a regular situation shall enjoy the rights set forth in part m and, except as modified below, the rights set forth in part IV.

Article 58

1. Frontier workers, as defined in article 2, paragraph 2 (a), of the present Convention, shall be entitled to the rights provided for in part IV that can be applied to them by reason of their presence and work in the territory of the State of employment, taking into account that they do not have their habitual residence in that State.

2. States of employment shall consider favourably granting frontier workers the right freely to choose their remunerated activity after a specified period of time. The granting of that right shall not affect their status as frontier workers.

Article 59

1. Seasonal workers, as defined in article 2, paragraph 2 (b), of the present Convention, shall be entitled to the rights provided for in part IV that can be applied to them by reason of their presence and work in the territory of the State of employment and that are compatible with their status in that State as seasonal workers, taking into account the fact that they are present in that State for only part of the year.

2. The State of employment shall, subject to paragraph 1 of the present article, consider granting seasonal workers who have been employed in its territory for a significant period of time the possibility of taking up other remunerated activities and giving them priority over other workers who seek admission to that State, subject to applicable bilateral and multilateral agreements.

Article 60

Itinerant workers, as defined in article 2, paragraph 2 (A), of the present Convention, shall be entitled to the rights provided for in part IV that can be granted to them by reason of their presence and work in the territory of the State of employment and that are compatible with their status as itinerant workers in that State.

Article 61

1. Project-tied workers, as defined in article 2, paragraph 2 (of the present Convention, and members of their families shall be entitled to the rights provided for in part IV except the provisions of article 43, paragraphs I (b) and (c), article 43, paragraph I (d), as it pertains to social housing schemes, article 45, paragraph I (b), and articles 52 to 55.

2. If a project-tied worker claims that the terms of his or her work contract have been violated by his or her employer, he or she shall have the right to address his or her case to the competent authorities of the State which has jurisdiction over that employer, on terms provided for in article 18, paragraph 1, of the present Convention.

3. Subject to bilateral or multilateral agreements in force for them, the States Parties concerned shall endeavour to enable project-tied workers to remain adequately protected by the social security systems of their States of origin or habitual residence during their engagement in the project. States Parties concerned shall take appropriate measures with the aim of avoiding any denial of rights or duplication of payments in this respect.

4. Without prejudice to the provisions of article 47 of the present Convention and to relevant bilateral or multilateral agreements, States Parties concerned shall permit payment of the earnings of project-tied workers in their State of origin or habitual residence.

Article 62

1. Specified-employment workers as defined in article 2, paragraph 2 (g), of the present Convention, shall be entitled to the rights provided for in part IV, except the provisions of article 43, paragraphs I (b) and (c), article 43, paragraph I (d), as it pertains to social housing schemes, article 52, and article 54, paragraph 1 (d).

2. Members of the families of specified-employment workers shall be entitled to the rights relating to family members of migrant workers provided for in part IV of the present Convention, except the provisions of article 53.

Article 63

1. Self-employed workers, as defined in article 2, paragraph 2 (h), of the pre sent Convention, shall be entitled to the rights provided for in part IV with the exception of those rights which are exclusively applicable to workers having a contract of employment.

2. Without prejudice to articles 52 and 79 of the present Convention, the termination of the economic activity of the self-employed workers shall not in itself imply the withdrawal of the authorization for them or for the members of their families to stay or to engage in a remunerated activity in the State of employment except where the authorization of residence is expressly dependent upon the specific remunerated activity for which they were admitted.

PART VI—PROMOTION OF SOUND, EQUITABLE, HUMANE AND LAWFUL CONDITIONS CONNECTION WITH INTERNATIONAL MIGRATION OF WORKERS AND MEMBERS OF THEIR FAMILIES

Article 64

1. Without prejudice to article 79 of the present Convention, the States Parties concerned shall as appropriate consult and co-operate with a view to promoting sound, equitable and humane conditions in connection with international migration of workers and members of their families.

2. In this respect, due regard shall be paid not only to labour needs and resources, but also to the social, economic, cultural and other needs of migrant workers and members of their families involved, as well as to the consequences of such migration for the communities concerned.

Article 65

1. States Parties shall maintain appropriate services to deal with questions concerning international migration of workers and members of their families. Their functions shall include, inter alia:

(a) The formulation and implementation of policies regarding such migration;

(b) An exchange of information. consultation and co-operation with the competent authorities of other States Parties involved in such migration;

(c) The provision of appropriate information, particularly to employers, workers and their organizations on policies, laws and regulations relating to migration and employment, on agreements concluded with other States concerning migration and on other relevant matters;

(d) The provision of information and appropriate assistance to migrant workers and members of their families regarding requisite authorizations and formalities and arrangements for departure, travel, arrival, stay, remunerated activities, exit and return, as well as on conditions of work and life in the State of employment and on customs, currency, tax and other relevant laws and regulations.

2. States Parties shall facilitate as appropriate the provision of adequate consular and other services that are necessary to meet the social, cultural and other needs of migrant workers and members of their families.

Article 66

1. Subject to paragraph 2 of the present article, the right to undertake operations with a view to the recruitment of workers for employment in another State shall be restricted to:

(a) Public services or bodies of the State in which such operations take place;

(b) Public services or bodies of the State of employment on the basis of agreement between the States concerned;

(c) A body established by virtue of a bilateral or multilateral agreement.

2. Subject to any authorization, approval and supervision by the public authorities of the States Parties concerned as may be established pursuant to the legislation and practice of those States, agencies, prospective employers or persons acting on their behalf may also be permitted to undertake the said operations.

Article 67

1. States Parties concerned shall co-operate as appropriate in the adoption of measures regarding the orderly return of migrant workers and members of their families to the State of origin when they decide to return or their authorization of residence or employment expires or when they are in the State of employment in an irregular situation.

2. Concerning migrant workers and members of their families in a regular situation, States Parties concerned shall co-operate as appropriate, on terms agreed upon by those States, with a view to promoting adequate economic conditions for their resettlement and to facilitating their durable social and cultural reintegration in the State of origin.

Article 68

1. States Parties, including States of transit, shall collaborate with a view to preventing and eliminating illegal or clandestine movements and employ- ment of migrant workers in an irregular situation. The measures to be taken to this end within the jurisdiction of each State concerned shall include:

(a) Appropriate measures against the dissemination of misleading information relating to emigration and immigration;

(b) Measures to detect and eradicate illegal or clandestine movements of migrant workers and members of their families and to impose effective sanctions on persons, groups or entities which organize, operate or assist in organizing or operating such movements;

(c) Measures to impose effective sanctions on persons, groups or entities which use violence, threats or intimidation against migrant workers or members of their families in an irregular situation.

2. States of employment shall take all adequate and effective measures to eliminate employment in their territory of migrant workers in an irregular situation, including, whenever appropriate, sanctions on employers of such workers. The rights of migrant workers vis-a-vis their employer arising from employment shall not be impaired by these measures.

Article 69

1. States Parties shall, when there are migrant workers and members of their families within their territory in an irregular situation, take appropriate measures to ensure that such a situation does not persist.

2. Whenever States Parties concerned consider the possibility of regularizing the situation of such persons in accordance with applicable national legislation and bilateral or multilateral agreements, appropriate account shall be taken of the circumstances of their entry, the duration of their stay in the States of employment and other relevant considerations, in particular those relating to their family situation.

Article 70

States Parties shall take measures not less favourable than those applied to nationals to ensure that working and living conditions of migrant workers and members of their families in a regular situation are in keeping with the standards of fitness, safety, health and principles of human dignity.

Article 71

1. States Parties shall facilitate, whenever necessary, the repatriation to the State of origin of the bodies of deceased migrant workers or members of their families.

2. As regards compensation matters relating to the death of a migrant worker or a member of his or her family, States Parties shall, as appropriate _ provide assistance to the persons concerned with a view to the prompt settlement of such matters. Settlement of these matters shall be carried out on the basis of applicable national law in accordance with the provisions of the present Convention and any relevant bilateral or multilateral agreements.

PART VII—APPLICATION OF THE CONVENTION

Article 72

1. (a) For the purpose of reviewing the application of the present Convention, there shall be established a Committee on the Protection of the Rights of All Migrant Workers and Members of Their Families (hereinafter referred to as "the Committee");

(b) The Committee shall consist, at the time of entry into force of the present Convention, of ten and, after the entry into force of the Convention for the forty-first State Party, of fourteen experts of high moral standing, impartiality and recognized competence in the field covered by the Convention.

2. (a) Members of the Committee shall be elected by secret ballot by the States Parties from a list of persons nominated by the States Parties, due consideration being given to equitable geographical distribution, including both States of origin and States of employment, and to the representation of the principal legal system. Each State Party may nominate one person from among its own nationals;

(b) Members shall be elected and shall serve in their personal capacity.

3. The initial election shall be held no later than six months after the date of the entry into force of the present Convention and subsequent elections every second year. At least four months before the date of each election, the

Secretary-General of the United Nations shall address a letter to all States Parties inviting them to submit their nominations within two months. The Secretary-General shall prepare a list in alphabetical order of all persons thus nominated, indicating the States Parties that have nominated them, and shall submit it to the States Parties not later than one month before the date of the corresponding election, together with the curricula vitae of the persons thus nominated.

4. Elections of members of the Committee shall be held at a meeting of States Parties convened by the Secretary-General at United Nations Headquarters. At that meeting, for which two thirds of the States Parties shall constitute a quorum, the persons elected to the Committee shall be those nominees who obtain the largest number of votes and an absolute majority of the votes of the States Parties present and voting.

5. (a) The members of the Committee shall serve for a term of four years. However, the terms of five of the members elected in the first election shall expire at the end of two years; immediately after the first election, the names of these five members shall be chosen by lot by the Chairman of the meeting of States Parties;

(b) The election of the four additional members of the Committee shall be held in accordance with the provisions of paragraphs 2, 3 and 4 of the present article, following the entry into force of the Convention for the forty-first State Party. The term of two of the additional members elected on this occasion shall expire at the end of two years; the names of these members shall be chosen by lot by the Chairman of the meeting of States Parties;

(c) The members of the Committee shall be eligible for re-election if renominated.

6. If a member of the Committee dies or resigns or declares that for any other cause he or she can no longer perform the duties of the Committee, the State Party that nominated the expert shall appoint another expert from among its own nationals for the remaining part of the term. The new appointment is subject to the approval of the Committee.

7. The Secretary-General of the United Nations shall provide the necessary staff and facilities for the effective performance of the functions of the Committee.

8. The members of the Committee shall receive emoluments from United Nations resources on such terms and conditions as the General Assembly may decide.

9. The members of the Committee shall be entitled to the facilities, privileges and immunities of experts on mission for the United Nations as laid down in the relevant sections of the Convention on the Privileges and Immunities of the United Nations.

Article 73

1. States Parties undertake to submit to the Secretary-General of the United Nations for consideration by the Committee a report on the legislative,

judicial, administrative and other measures they have taken to give effect to the provisions of the present Convention:

      (a) Within one year after the entry into force of the Convention for the State Party concerned;

      (b) Thereafter every five years and whenever the Committee so requests.

2. Reports prepared under the present article shall also indicate factors and difficulties, if any, affecting the implementation of the Convention and shall include information on the characteristics of migration flows in which the State Party concerned is involved.

3. The Committee shall decide any further guidelines applicable to the content of the reports.

4. States Parties shall make their reports widely available to the public in their own countries.

Article 74

1. The Committee shall examine the reports submitted by each State Party and shall transmit such comments as it may consider appropriate to the State Party concerned. This State Party may submit to the Committee observations on any comment made by the Committee in accordance with the present article. The Committee may request supplementary information from States Parties when considering these reports.

2. The Secretary-General of the United Nations shall, in due time before the opening of each regular session of the Committee, transmit to the Director-General of the International Labour Office copies of the reports submitted by States Parties concerned and information relevant to the consideration of these reports, in order to enable the Office to assist the Committee with the expertise the Office may provide regarding those matters dealt with by the present Convention that fall within the sphere of competence of the International Labour Organisation. The Committee shall consider in its deliberations such comments and materials as the Office may provide.

3. The Secretary-General of the United Nations may also, after consultation with the Committee, transmit to other specialized agencies as well as to intergovernmental organizations, copies of such parts of these reports as may fall within their competence.

4. The Committee may invite the specialized agencies and organs of the United Nations, as well as intergovernmental organizations and other concerned bodies to submit, for consideration by the Committee, written information on such matters dealt with in the present Convention as fall within the scope of their activities.

5. The International Labour Office shall be invited by the Committee to appoint representatives to participate, in a consultative capacity, in the meetings of the Committee.

6. The Committee may invite representatives of other specialized agencies and organs of the United Nations, as well as of intergovernmental organizations, to be present and to be heard in its meetings whenever matters falling within their field of competence are considered.

7. The Committee shall present an annual report to the General Assembly of the United Nations on the implementation of the present Convention, containing its own considerations and recommendations, based, in particular, on the examination of the reports and any observations presented by States Parties.

8. The Secretary-General of the United Nations shall transmit the annual reports of the Committee to the States Parties to the present Convention, the Economic and Social Council, the Commission on Human Rights of the United Nations, the Director-General of the International Labour Office and other relevant organizations.

Article 75

1. The Committee shall adopt its own rules of procedure.

2. The Committee shall elect its officers for a term of two years.

3. The Committee shall normally meet annually.

4. The meetings of the Committee shall normally be held at United Nations Headquarters.

Article 76

1. A State Party to the present Convention may at any time declare under this article that it recognizes the competence of the Committee to receive and consider communications to the effect that a State Party claims that another State Party is not fulfilling its obligations under the present Convention. Communications under this article may be received and considered only if submitted by a State Party that has made a declaration recognizing in regard to itself the competence of the Committee. No communication shall be received by the Committee if it concerns a State Party which has not made such a declaration. Communications received under this article shall be dealt with in accordance with the following procedure:

(a) If a State Party to the present Convention considers that another State Party is not fulfilling its obligations under the present Convention, it may, by written communication, bring the matter to the attention of that State Party. The State Party may also inform the Committee of the matter. Within three months after the receipt of the communication the receiving State shall afford the State that sent the communication an explanation, or any other statement in writing clarifying the matter which should include, to the extent possible and pertinent, reference to domestic procedures and remedies taken, pending or available in the matter;

(b) If the matter is not adjusted to the satisfaction of both States Parties concerned within six months after the receipt by the receiving

State of the initial communication, either State shall have the right to refer the matter to the Committee, by notice given to the Committee and to the other State;

(c) The Committee shall deal with a matter referred to it only after it has ascertained that all available domestic remedies have been invoked and exhausted in the matter, in conformity with the generally recognized principles of international law. This shall not be the rule where, in the view of the Committee, the application of the remedies is unreasonably prolonged;

(d) Subject to the provisions of subparagraph (c) of the present paragraph, the Committee shall make available its good offices to the States Parties concerned with a view to a friendly solution of the matter on the basis of the respect for the obligations set forth in the present Convention;

(e) The Committee shall hold closed meetings when examining communications under the present article;

(f) In any matter referred to it in accordance with subparagraph (b) of the present paragraph, the Committee may call upon the States Parties concerned, referred to in subparagraph (b), to supply any relevant information;

(g) The States Parties concerned, referred to in subparagraph (b) of the present paragraph, shall have the right to be represented when the matter is being considered by the Committee and to make submissions orally and/or in writing;

(h) The Committee shall, within twelve months after the date of receipt of notice under subparagraph (b) of the present paragraph, submit a report, as follows:

(i) If a solution within the terms of subparagraph (d) of the present paragraph is reached, the Committee shall confine its report to a brief statement of the facts and of the solution reached; (ii) If a solution within the terms of subparagraph (d) is not reached, the Committee shall, in its report, set forth the relevant facts concerning the issue between the States Parties concerned. The written submissions and record of the oral submissions made by the States Parties concerned shall be attached to the report. The Committee may also communicate only to the States Parties concerned any views that it may consider relevant to the issue between them.In every matter, the report shall be communicated to the States Parties concerned.

2. The provisions of the present article shall come into force when ten States Parties to the present Convention have made a declaration under paragraph I of the present article. Such declarations shall be deposited by the States Parties with the Secretary-General of the United Nations, who shall transmit

copies thereof to the other States Parties. A declaration may be withdrawn at any time by notification to the Secretary-General. Such a withdrawal shall not prejudice the consideration of any matter that is the subject of a communication already transmitted under the present article; no further communication by any State Party shall be received under the present article after the notification of withdrawal of the declaration has been received by the Secretary-General, unless the State Party concerned has made a new declaration.

Article 77

1. A State Party to the present Convention may at any time declare under the present article that it recognizes the competence of the Committee to receive and consider communications from or on behalf of individuals subject to its jurisdiction who claim that their individual rights as established by the present Convention have been violated by that State Party. No communication shall be received by the Committee if it concerns a State Party that has not made such a declaration.

2. The Committee shall consider inadmissible any communication under the present article which is anonymous or which it considers to be an abuse of the right of submission of such communications or to be incompatible with the provisions of the present Convention.

3. The Committee shall not consider any communication from an individual under the present article unless it has ascertained that:

(a) The same matter has not been, and is not being, examined under another procedure of international investigation or settlement;

(b) The individual has exhausted all available domestic remedies; this shall not be the rule where, in the view of the Committee, the application of the remedies is unreasonably prolonged or is unlikely to bring effective relief to that individual.

4. Subject to the provisions of paragraph 2 of the present article, the Committee shall bring any communications submitted to it under this article to the attention of the State Party to the present Convention that has made a declaration under paragraph 1 and is alleged to be violating any provisions of the Convention. Within six months, the receiving State shall submit to the Committee written explanations or statements clarifying the matter and the remedy, if any, that may have been taken by that State.

5. The Committee shall consider communications received under the present article in the light of all information made available to it by or on behalf of the individual and by the State Party concerned.

6. The Committee shall hold closed meetings when examining communications under the present article.

7. The Committee shall forward its views to the State Party concerned and to the individual.

8. The provisions of the present article shall come into force when ten States Parties to the present Convention have made declarations under paragraph 1 of the present article. Such declarations shall be deposited by the States Parties with the Secretary-General of the United Nations, who shall transmit copies thereof to the other States Parties. A declaration may be withdrawn at any time by notification to the Secretary-General. Such a withdrawal shall not prejudice the consideration of any matter that is the subject of a communication already transmitted under the present article; no further communication by or on behalf of an individual shall be received under the present article after the notification of withdrawal of the declaration has been received by the Secretary-General, unless the State Party has made a new declaration.

Article 78

The provisions of article 76 of the present Convention shall be applied without prejudice to any procedures for settling disputes or complaints in the field covered by the present Convention laid down in the constituent instruments of, or in conventions adopted by, the United Nations and the specialized agencies and shall not prevent the States Parties from having recourse to any procedures for settling a dispute in accordance with international agreements in force between them.

PART VIII—GENERAL PROVISIONS

Article 79

Nothing in the present Convention shall affect the right of each State Party to establish the criteria governing admission of migrant workers and members of their families. Concerning other matters related to their legal situation and treatment as migrant workers and members of their families, States Parties shall be subject to the limitations set forth in the present Convention.

Article 80

Nothing in the present Convention shall be interpreted as impairing the provisions of the Charter of the United Nations and of the constitutions of the specialized agencies which define the respective responsibilities of the various organs of the United Nations and of the specialized agencies in regard to the matters dealt with in the present Convention.

Article 81

1. Nothing in the present Convention shall affect more favourable rights or freedoms granted to migrant workers and members of their families by virtue of:

(a) The law or practice of a State Party; or

(b) Any bilateral or multilateral treaty in force for the State Party concerned.

2. Nothing in the present Convention may be interpreted as implying for any State, group or person any right to engage in any activity or perform any act that would impair any of the rights and freedoms as set forth in the present Convention.

Article 82

The rights of migrant workers and members of their families provided for in the present Convention may not be renounced. It shall not be permissible to exert any form of pressure upon migrant workers and members of their families with a view to their relinquishing or foregoing any of the said rights. It shall not be possible to derogate by contract from rights recognized in the present Convention. States Parties shall take appropriate measures to ensure that these principles are respected.

Article 83

Each State Party to the present Convention undertakes:

(a) To ensure that any person whose rights or freedoms as herein recognized are violated shall have an effective remedy, notwithstanding that the violation has been committed by persons acting in an official capacity;

(b) To ensure that any persons seeking such a remedy shall have his or her claim reviewed and decided by competent judicial, administrative or legislative authorities, or by any other competent authority provided for by the legal system of the State, and to develop the possibilities of judicial remedy;

(c) To ensure that the competent authorities shall enforce such remedies when granted.

Article 84

Each State Party undertakes to adopt the legislative and other measures that are necessary to implement the provisions of the present Convention.

PART IX—FINAL PROVISIONS

Article 85

The Secretary-General of the United Nations is designated as the depositary of the present Convention.

Article 86

1. The present Convention shall be open for signature by all States. It is subject to ratification.

2. The present Convention shall be open to accession by any State.

3. Instruments of ratification or accession shall be deposited with the Secretary-General of the United Nations.

Article 87

1. The present Convention shall enter into force on the first day of the month following a period of three months after the date of the deposit of the twentieth instrument of ratification or accession.

2. For each State ratifying or acceding to the present Convention after its entry into force, the Convention shall enter into force on the first day of the month following a period of three months after the date of the deposit of its own instrument of ratification or accession.

Article 88

A State ratifying or acceding to the present Convention may not exclude the application of any Part of it, or, without prejudice to article 3, exclude any particular category of migrant workers from its application.

Article 89

1. Any State Party may denounce the present Convention, not earlier than five years after the Convention has entered into force for the State concerned, by means of a notification writing addressed to the Secretary-General of the United Nations.

2. Such denunciation shall become effective on the first day of the month following the expiration of a period of twelve months after the date of the receipt of the notification by the Secretary-General of the United Nations.

3. Such a denunciation shall not have the effect of releasing the State Party from its obligations under the present Convention in regard to any act or omission which occurs prior to the date at which the denunciation becomes effective, nor shall denunciation prejudice in any way the continued consideration of any matter which is already under consideration by the Committee prior to the date at which the denunciation becomes effective.

4. Following the date at which the denunciation of a State Party becomes effective, the Committee shall not commence consideration of any new matter regarding that State.

Article 90

1. After five years from the entry into force of the Convention a request for the revision of the Convention may be made at any time by any State Party by means of a notification in writing addressed to the Secretary-General of the United Nations. The Secretary-General shall thereupon communicate any proposed amendments to the States Parties with a request that they notify him whether the favour a conference of States Parties for the purpose of considering and voting upon the proposals. In the event that within four months from the date of such communication at least one third of the States Parties favours such a conference, the Secretary-General shall convene the conference under the auspices of the United Nations. Any amendment adopted by a majority of the States Parties present and voting shall be submitted to the General Assembly for approval.

2. Amendments shall come into force when they have been approved by the General Assembly of the United Nations and accepted by a two-thirds majority of the States Parties in accordance with their respective constitutional processes.

3. When amendments come into force, they shall be binding on those States Parties that have accepted them, other States Parties still being bound by the provisions of the present Convention and any earlier amendment that they have accepted.

Article 91

1. The Secretary-General of the United Nations shall receive and circulate to all States the text of reservations made by States at the time of signature, ratification or accession.

2. A reservation incompatible with the object and purpose of the present Convention shall not be permitted.

3. Reservations may be withdrawn at any time by notification to this effect addressed to the Secretary-General of the United Nations, who shall then inform all States thereof. S uch notification shall take effect on the date on which it is received.

Article 92

1. Any dispute between two or more States Parties concerning the interpretation or application of the present Convention that is not settled by negotiation shall, at the request of one of them, be submitted to arbitration. If within six months from the date of the request for arbitration the Parties are unable to agree on the organization of the arbitration, any one of those Parties may refer the dispute to the International Court of Justice by request in conformity with the Statute of the Court.

2. Each State Party may at the time of signature or ratification of the present Convention or accession thereto declare that it does not consider itself bound by paragraph 1 of the present article. The other States Parties shall not be bound by that paragraph with respect to any State Party that has made such a declaration.

3. Any State Party that has made a declaration in accordance with paragraph 2 of the present article may at any time withdraw that declaration by notification to the Secretary-General of the United Nations.

Article 93

1. The present Convention, of which the Arabic, Chinese, English, French, Russian and Spanish texts are equally authentic, shall be deposited with the Secretary-General of the United Nations.

2. The Secretary-General of the United Nations shall transmit certified copies of the present Convention to all States.

IN WITNESS WHEREOF the undersigned plenipotentiaries, being duly authorized thereto by their respective Governments, have signed the present Convention.

CONVENTION RELATING TO THE STATUS OF REFUGEES, 189 U.N.T.S. 150, *entered into force* April 22, 1954:

Preamble

The High Contracting Parties,

Considering that the Charter of the United Nations and the Universal Declaration of Human Rights approved on 10 December 1948 by the General Assembly have affirmed the principle that human beings shall enjoy fundamental rights and freedoms without discrimination,

Considering that the United Nations has, on various occasions, manifested its profound concern for refugees and endeavoured to assure refugees the widest possible exercise of these fundamental rights and freedoms,

Considering that it is desirable to revise and consolidate previous international agreements relating to the status of refugees and to extend the scope of and the protection accorded by such instruments by means of a new agreement,

Considering that the grant of asylum may place unduly heavy burdens on certain countries, and that a satisfactory solution of a problem of which the United Nations has recognized the international scope and nature cannot therefore be achieved without international co-operation,

Expressing the wish that all States, recognizing the social and humanitarian nature of the problem of refugees, will do everything within their power to prevent this problem from becoming a cause of tension between States,

Noting that the United Nations High Commissioner for Refugees is charged with the task of supervising international conventions providing for the protection of refugees, and recognizing that the effective co-ordination of measures taken to deal with this problem will depend upon the co-operation of States with the High Commissioner,

Have agreed as follows:

CHAPTER I
GENERAL PROVISIONS

Article 1

Definition of the term "refugee"

A. For the purposes of the present Convention, the term "refugee", shall apply to any person who:

(1) Has been considered a refugee under the Arrangements of 12 May 1926 and 30 June 1928 or under the Conventions of 28 October 1933 and 10 February 1938, the Protocol of 14 September 1939 or the Constitution of the

International Refugee Organization; Decisions of non-eligibility taken by the International Refugee Organization during the period of its activities shall not prevent the status of refugee being accorded to persons who fulfil the conditions of paragraph 2 of this section;

(2) As a result of events occurring before 1 January 1951 and owing to well-founded fear of being persecuted for reasons of race, religion, nationality, membership of a particular social group or political opinion, is outside the country of his nationality and is unable, or owing to such fear, is unwilling to avail himself of the protection of that country; or who, not having a nationality and being outside the country of his former habitual residence as a result of such events, is unable or, owing to such fear, is unwilling to return to it.

In the case of a person who has more than one nationality, the term "the country of his nationality" shall mean each of the countries of which he is a national, and a person shall not be deemed to be lacking the protection of the country of his nationality if, without any valid reason based on well-founded fear, he has not availed himself of the protection of one of the countries of which he is a national.

B. (1) For the purposes of this Convention, the words "events occurring before 1 January 1951" in article 1, section A, shall be understood to mean either (a) "events occurring in Europe before 1 January 1951"; or (b) "events occurring in Europe or elsewhere before 1 January 1951"; and each Contracting State shall make a declaration at the time of signature, ratification or accession, specifying which of these meanings it applies for the purpose of its obligations under this Convention.

(2) Any Contracting State which has adopted alternative (a) may at any time extend its obligations by adopting alternative (b) by means of a notification addressed to the Secretary-General of the United Nations.

C. This Convention shall cease to apply to any person falling under the terms of section A if:

(1) He has voluntarily re-availed himself of the protection of the country of his nationality; or

(2) Having lost his nationality, he has voluntarily reacquired it; or

(3) He has acquired a new nationality, and enjoys the protection of the country of his new nationality; or

(4) He has voluntarily re-established himself in the country which he left or outside which he remained owing to fear of persecution; or

(5) He can no longer, because the circumstances in connection with which he has been recognized as a refugee have ceased to exist, continue to refuse to avail himself of the protection of the country of his nationality; Provided that this paragraph shall not apply to a refugee falling under section A (1) of this article who is able to invoke compelling reasons arising out of previous persecution for refusing to avail himself of the protection of the country of nationality;

(6) Being a person who has no nationality he is, because the circumstances in connection with which he has been recognized as a refugee have ceased to exist, able to return to the country of his former habitual residence; Provided that this paragraph shall not apply to a refugee falling under section A (1) of this article who is able to invoke compelling reasons arising out of previous persecution for refusing to return to the country of his former habitual residence.

D. This Convention shall not apply to persons who are at present receiving from organs or agencies of the United Nations other than the United Nations High Commissioner for Refugees protection or assistance.

When such protection or assistance has ceased for any reason, without the position of such persons being definitively settled in accordance with the relevant resolutions adopted by the General Assembly of the United Nations, these persons shall *ipso facto* be entitled to the benefits of this Convention.

E. This Convention shall not apply to a person who is recognized by the competent authorities of the country in which he has taken residence as having the rights and obligations which are attached to the possession of the nationality of that country.

F. The provisions of this Convention shall not apply to any person with respect to whom there are serious reasons for considering that.

(a) He has committed a crime against peace, a war crime, or a crime against humanity, as defined in the international instruments drawn up to make provision in respect of such crimes;

(b) He has committed a serious non-political crime outside the country of refuge prior to his admission to that country as a refugee;

(c) He has been guilty of acts contrary to the purposes and principles of the United Nations.

Article 2

General obligations

Every refugee has duties to the country in which he finds himself, which require in particular that he conform to its laws and regulations as well as to measures taken for the maintenance of public order.

Article 3

Non-discrimination

The Contracting States shall apply the provisions of this Convention to refugees without discrimination as to race, religion or country of origin.

Article 4

Religion

The Contracting States shall accord to refugees within their territories treatment at least as favourable as that accorded to their nationals with respect to freedom to practise their religion and freedom as regards the religious education of their children.

Article 5

Rights granted apart from this Convention

Nothing in this Convention shall be deemed to impair any rights and benefits granted by a Contracting State to refugees apart from this Convention.

Article 6

The term "in the same circumstances"

For the purposes of this Convention, the term "in the same circumstances, implies that any requirements (including requirements as to length and conditions of sojourn or residence) which the particular individual would have to fulfil for the enjoyment of the right in question, if he were not a refugee, must be fulfilled by him, with the exception of requirements which by their nature a refugee is incapable of fulfilling.

Article 7

Exemption from reciprocity

1. Except where this Convention contains more favourable provisions, a Contracting State shall accord to refugees the same treatment as is accorded to aliens generally.

2. After a period of three years' residence, all refugees shall enjoy exemption from legislative reciprocity in the territory of the Contracting States.

3. Each Contracting State shall continue to accord to refugees the rights and benefits to which they were already entitled, in the absence of reciprocity, at the date of entry into force of this Convention for that State.

4. The Contracting States shall consider favourably the possibility of according to refugees, in the absence of reciprocity, rights and benefits beyond those to which they are entitled according to paragraphs 2 and 3, and to extending exemption from reciprocity to refugees who do not fulfil the conditions provided for in paragraphs 2 and 3.

5. The provisions of paragraphs 2 and 3 apply both to the rights and benefits referred to in articles 13, 18, 19, 21 and 22 of this Convention and to rights and benefits for which this Convention does not provide.

Article 8

Exemption from exceptional measures

With regard to exceptional measures which may be taken against the person, property or interests of nationals of a foreign State, the Contracting States shall not apply such measures to a refugee who is formally a national of the said State solely on account of such nationality. Contracting States which, under their legislation, are prevented from applying the general principle expressed in this article, shall, in appropriate cases, grant exemptions in favour of such refugees.

Article 9

Provisional measures

Nothing in this Convention shall prevent a Contracting State, in time of war or other grave and exceptional circumstances, from taking provisionally measures which it considers to be essential to the national security in the case of a particular person, pending a determination by the Contracting State that person is in fact a refugee and that the continuance of such measures is necessary in his case in the interests of national security.

Article 10

Continuity of residence

1. Where a refugee has been forcibly displaced during the Second World War and removed to the territory of a Contracting State, and is resident there, the period of such enforced sojourn shall be considered to have been lawful residence within that territory.

2. Where a refugee has been forcibly displaced during the Second World War from the territory of a Contracting State and has, prior to the date of entry into force of this Convention, returned there for the purpose of taking up residence, the period of residence before and after such enforced displacement shall be regarded as one uninterrupted period for any purposes for which uninterrupted residence is required.

Article 11

Refugee seamen

In the case of refugees regularly serving as crew members on board a ship flying the flag of a Contracting State, that State shall give sympathetic consideration to their establishment on its territory and the issue of travel documents to them or their temporary admission to its territory particularly with a view to facilitating their establishment in another country.

CHAPTER II
JURIDICAL STATUS

Article 12

Personal status

1. The personal status of a refugee shall be governed by the law of the country of his domicile or, if he has no domicile, by the law of the country of his residence.

2. Rights previously acquired by a refugee and dependent on personal status, more particularly rights attaching to marriage, shall be respected by a Contracting State, subject to compliance, if this be necessary, with the formalities required by the law of that State, provided that the right in question is one which would have been recognized by the law of that State had he not become a refugee.

Article 13

Movable and immovable property

The Contracting States shall accord to a refugee treatment as favourable as possible and, in any event, not less favourable than that accorded to aliens generally in the same circumstances, as regards the acquisition of movable and immovable property and other rights pertaining thereto, and to leases and other contracts relating to movable and immovable property.

Article 14

Artistic rights and industrial property

In respect of the protection of industrial property, such as inventions, designs or models, trade marks, trade names, and of rights in literary, artistic and scientific works, a refugee shall be accorded in the country in which he has his habitual residence the same protection as is accorded to nationals of that country. In the territory of any other Contracting States, he shall be accorded the same protection as is accorded in that territory to nationals of the country in which he has his habitual residence.

Article 15

Right of association

As regards non-political and non-profit-making associations and trade unions the Contracting States shall accord to refugees lawfully staying in their territory the most favourable treatment accorded to nationals of a foreign country, in the same circumstances.

Article 16

Access to courts

1. A refugee shall have free access to the courts of law on the territory of all Contracting States.

2. A refugee shall enjoy in the Contracting State in which he has his habitual residence the same treatment as a national in matters pertaining to access to the courts, including legal assistance and exemption from *cautio judicatum solvi*.

3. A refugee shall be accorded in the matters referred to in paragraph 2 in countries other than that in which he has his habitual residence the treatment granted to a national of the country of his habitual residence.

CHAPTER III
GAINFUL EMPLOYMENT

Article 17

Wage-earning employment

1. The Contracting States shall accord to refugees lawfully staying in their territory the most favourable treatment accorded to nationals of a foreign country in the same circumstances, as regards the right to engage in wage-earning employment.

2. In any case, restrictive measures imposed on aliens or the employment of aliens for the protection of the national labour market shall not be applied to a refugee who was already exempt from them at the date of entry into force of this Convention for the Contracting State concerned, or who fulfils one of the following conditions:

(a) He has completed three years' residence in the country;

(b) He has a spouse possessing the nationality of the country of residence. A refugee may not invoke the benefit of this provision if he has abandoned his spouse;

(c) He has one or more children possessing the nationality of the country of residence.

3. The Contracting States shall give sympathetic consideration to assimilating the rights of all refugees with regard to wage-earning employment to those of nationals, and in particular of those refugees who have entered their territory pursuant to programmes of labour recruitment or under immigration schemes.

Article 18

Self-employment

The Contracting States shall accord to a refugee lawfully in their territory treatment as favourable as possible and, in any event, not less favourable than that accorded to aliens generally in the same circumstances, as regards the right to engage on his own account in agriculture, industry, handicrafts and commerce and to establish commercial and industrial companies.

Article 19

Liberal professions

1. Each Contracting State shall accord to refugees lawfully staying in their territory who hold diplomas recognized by the competent authorities of that State, and who are desirous of practising a liberal profession, treatment as favourable as possible and, in any event, not less favourable than that accorded to aliens generally in the same circumstances.

2. The Contracting States shall use their best endeavours consistently with their laws and constitutions to secure the settlement of such refugees in the territories, other than the metropolitan territory, for whose international relations they are responsible.

CHAPTER IV
WELFARE

Article 20

Rationing

Where a rationing system exists, which applies to the population at large and regulates the general distribution of products in short supply, refugees shall be accorded the same treatment as nationals.

Article 21

Housing

As regards housing, the Contracting States, in so far as the matter is regulated by laws or regulations or is subject to the control of public authorities, shall accord to refugees lawfully staying in their territory treatment as favourable as possible and, in any event, not less favourable than that accorded to aliens generally in the same circumstances.

Article 22

Public education

1. The Contracting States shall accord to refugees the same treatment as is accorded to nationals with respect to elementary education.

2. The Contracting States shall accord to refugees treatment as favourable as possible, and, in any event, not less favourable than that accorded to aliens generally in the same circumstances, with respect to education other than elementary education and, in particular, as regards access to studies, the recognition of foreign school certificates, diplomas and degrees, the remission of fees and charges and the award of scholarships.

Article 23

Public relief

The Contracting States shall accord to refugees lawfully staying in their territory the same treatment with respect to public relief and assistance as is accorded to their nationals.

Article 24

Labour legislation and social security

1. The Contracting States shall accord to refugees lawfully staying in their territory the same treatment as is accorded to nationals in respect of the following matters;

(a) In so far as such matters are governed by laws or regulations or are subject to the control of administrative authorities: remuneration, including family allowances where these form part of remuneration, hours of work, overtime arrangements, holidays with pay, restrictions on home work, minimum age of employment, apprenticeship and training, women's work and the work of young persons, and the enjoyment of the benefits of collective bargaining;

(b) Social security (legal provisions in respect of employment injury, occupational diseases, maternity, sickness, disability, old age, death, unemployment, family responsibilities and any other contingency which, according to national laws or regulations, is covered by a social security scheme), subject to the following limitations:

(i) There may be appropriate arrangements for the maintenance of acquired rights and rights in course of acquisition;

(ii) National laws or regulations of the country of residence may prescribe special arrangements concerning benefits or portions of benefits which are payable wholly out of public funds, and concerning allowances paid to persons who do not fulfil the contribution conditions prescribed for the award of a normal pension.

2. The right to compensation for the death of a refugee resulting from employment injury or from occupational disease shall not be affected by the fact that the residence of the beneficiary is outside the territory of the Contracting State.

3. The Contracting States shall extend to refugees the benefits of agreements concluded between them, or which may be concluded between them in the future, concerning the maintenance of acquired rights and rights in the process of acquisition in regard to social security, subject only to the conditions which apply to nationals of the States signatory to the agreements in question.

4. The Contracting States will give sympathetic consideration to extending to refugees so far as possible the benefits of similar agreements which may at any time be in force between such Contracting States and non-contracting States.

CHAPTER V
ADMINISTRATIVE MEASURES

Article 25

Administrative assistance

1. When the exercise of a right by a refugee would normally require the assistance of authorities of a foreign country to whom he cannot have recourse, the Contracting States in whose territory he is residing shall arrange that such assistance be afforded to him by their own authorities or by an international authority.

2. The authority or authorities mentioned in paragraph I shall deliver or cause to be delivered under their supervision to refugees such documents or

certifications as would normally be delivered to aliens by or through their national authorities.

3. Documents or certifications so delivered shall stand in the stead of the official instruments delivered to aliens by or through their national authorities, and shall be given credence in the absence of proof to the contrary.

4. Subject to such exceptional treatment as may be granted to indigent persons, fees may be charged for the services mentioned herein, but such fees shall be moderate and commensurate with those charged to nationals for similar services.

5. The provisions of this article shall be without prejudice to articles 27 and 28.

Article 26

Freedom of movement

Each Contracting State shall accord to refugees lawfully in its territory the right to choose their place of residence and to move freely within its territory subject to any regulations applicable to aliens generally in the same circumstances.

Article 27

Identity papers

The Contracting States shall issue identity papers to any refugee in their territory who does not possess a valid travel document.

Article 28

Travel documents

1. The Contracting States shall issue to refugees lawfully staying in their territory travel documents for the purpose of travel outside their territory, unless compelling reasons of national security or public order otherwise require, and the provisions of the Schedule to this Convention shall apply with respect to such documents. The Contracting States may issue such a travel document to any other refugee in their territory; they shall in particular give sympathetic consideration to the issue of such a travel document to refugees in their territory who are unable to obtain a travel document from the country of their lawful residence.

2. Travel documents issued to refugees under previous international agreements by Parties thereto shall be recognized and treated by the Contracting States in the same way as if they had been issued pursuant to this article.

Article 29

Fiscal charges

1. The Contracting States shall not impose upon refugees duties, charges or taxes, of any description whatsoever, other or higher than those which are or may be levied on their nationals in similar situations.

2. Nothing in the above paragraph shall prevent the application to refugees of the laws and regulations concerning charges in respect of the issue to aliens of administrative documents including identity papers.

Article 30

Transfer of assets

1. A Contracting State shall, in conformity with its laws and regulations, permit refugees to transfer assets which they have brought into its territory, to another country where they have been admitted for the purposes of resettlement.

2. A Contracting State shall give sympathetic consideration to the application of refugees for permission to transfer assets wherever they may be and which are necessary for their resettlement in another country to which they have been admitted.

Article 31

Refugees unlawfully in the country of refuge

1. The Contracting States shall not impose penalties, on account of their illegal entry or presence, on refugees who, coming directly from a territory where their life or freedom was threatened in the sense of article 1, enter or are present in their territory without authorization, provided they present themselves without delay to the authorities and show good cause for their illegal entry or presence.

2. The Contracting States shall not apply to the movements of such refugees restrictions other than those which are necessary and such restrictions shall only be applied until their status in the country is regularized or they obtain admission into another country. The Contracting States shall allow such refugees a reasonable period and all the necessary facilities to obtain admission into another country.

Article 32

Expulsion

1. The Contracting States shall not expel a refugee lawfully in their territory save on grounds of national security or public order.

2. The expulsion of such a refugee shall be only in pursuance of a decision reached in accordance with due process of law. Except where compelling reasons of national security otherwise require, the refugee shall be allowed to submit evidence to clear himself, and to appeal to and be represented for the purpose before competent authority or a person or persons specially designated by the competent authority.

3. The Contracting States shall allow such a refugee a reasonable period within which to seek legal admission into another country. The Contracting States reserve the right to apply during that period such internal measures as they may deem necessary.

Article 33

Prohibition of expulsion or return ("refoulement")

1. No Contracting State shall expel or return ("refouler") a refugee in any manner whatsoever to the frontiers of territories where his life or freedom would be threatened on account of his race, religion, nationality, membership of a particular social group or political opinion.

2. The benefit of the present provision may not, however, be claimed by a refugee whom there are reasonable grounds for regarding as a danger to the security of the country in which he is, or who, having been convicted by a final judgement of a particularly serious crime, constitutes a danger to the community of that country.

Article 34

Naturalization

The Contracting States shall as far as possible facilitate the assimilation and naturalization of refugees. They shall in particular make every effort to expedite naturalization proceedings and to reduce as far as possible the charges and costs of such proceedings.

CHAPTER VI
EXECUTORY AND TRANSITORY PROVISIONS

Article 35

Co-operation of the national authorities with the United Nations

1. The Contracting States undertake to co-operate with the Office of the United Nations High Commissioner for Refugees, or any other agency of the United Nations which may succeed it, in the exercise of its functions, and shall in particular facilitate its duty of supervising the application of the provisions of this Convention.

2. In order to enable the Office of the High Commissioner or any other agency of the United Nations which may succeed it, to make reports to the competent organs of the United Nations, the Contracting States undertake to provide them in the appropriate form with information and statistical data requested concerning:

(a) The condition of refugees,

(b) The implementation of this Convention, and

(c) Laws, regulations and decrees which are, or may hereafter be, in force relating to refugees.

Article 36

Information on national legislation

The Contracting States shall communicate to the Secretary-General of the United Nations the laws and regulations which they may adopt to ensure the application of this Convention.

Article 37

Relation to previous conventions

Without prejudice to article 28, paragraph 2, of this Convention, this Convention replaces, as between Parties to it, the Arrangements of 5 July 1922, 31 May 1924, 12 May 1926, 30 June 1928 and 30 July 1935, the Conventions of 28 October 1933 and 10 February 1938, the Protocol of 14 September 1939 and the Agreement of 15 October 1946.

CHAPTER VII
FINAL CLAUSES

Article 38

Settlement of disputes

Any dispute between Parties to this Convention relating to its interpretation or application, which cannot be settled by other means, shall be referred to the International Court of Justice at the request of any one of the parties to the dispute.

Article 39

Signature, ratification and accession

1. This Convention shall be opened for signature at Geneva on 28 July 1951 and shall thereafter be deposited with the Secretary-General of the United Nations. It shall be open for signature at the European Office of the United Nations from 28 July to 31 August 1951 and shall be re-opened for signature at the Headquarters of the United Nations from 17 September 1951 to 31 December 1952.

2. This Convention shall be open for signature on behalf of all States Members of the United Nations, and also on behalf of any other State invited to attend the Conference of Plenipotentiaries on the Status of Refugees and Stateless Persons or to which an invitation to sign will have been addressed by the General Assembly. It shall be ratified and the instruments of ratification shall be deposited with the Secretary-General of the United Nations.

3. This Convention shall be open from 28 July 1951 for accession by the States referred to in paragraph 2 of this article. Accession shall be effected by the deposit of an instrument of accession with the Secretary-General of the United Nations.

Article 40

Territorial application clause

1. Any State may, at the time of signature, ratification or accession, declare that this Convention shall extend to all or any of the territories for the international relations of which it is responsible. Such a declaration shall take effect when the Convention enters into force for the State concerned.

2. At any time thereafter any such extension shall be made by notification addressed to the Secretary-General of the United Nations and shall take effect as from the ninetieth day after the day of receipt by the Secretary-General of the United Nations of this notification, or as from the date of entry into force of the Convention for the State concerned, whichever is the later.

3. With respect to those territories to which this Convention is not extended at the time of signature, ratification or accession, each State concerned shall consider the possibility of taking the necessary steps in order to extend the application of this Convention to such territories, subject, where necessary for constitutional reasons, to the consent of the Governments of such territories.

Article 41

Federal clause

In the case of a Federal or non-unitary State, the following provisions shall apply:

(a) With respect to those articles of this Convention that come within the legislative jurisdiction of the federal legislative authority, the obligations of the Federal Government shall to this extent be the same as those of parties which are not Federal States;

(b) With respect to those articles of this Convention that come within the legislative jurisdiction of constituent States, provinces or cantons which are not, under the constitutional system of the Federation, bound to take legislative action, the Federal Government shall bring such articles with a favourable recommendation to the notice of the appropriate authorities of States, provinces or cantons at the earliest possible moment;

(c) A Federal State Party to this Convention shall, at the request of any other Contracting State transmitted through the Secretary-General of the United Nations, supply a statement of the law and practice of the Federation and its constituent units in regard to any particular provision of the Convention showing the extent to which effect has been given to that provision by legislative or other action.

Article 42

Reservations

1. At the time of signature, ratification or accession, any State may make reservations to articles of the Convention other than to articles 1, 3, 4, 16(1), 33, 36-46 inclusive.

2. Any State making a reservation in accordance with paragraph 1 of this article may at any time withdraw the reservation by a communication to that effect addressed to the Secretary-General of the United Nations.

Article 43

Entry into force

1. This Convention shall come into force on the ninetieth day following the day of deposit of the sixth instrument of ratification or accession.

2. For each State ratifying or acceding to the Convention after the deposit of the sixth instrument of ratification or accession, the Convention shall enter into force on the ninetieth day following the date of deposit by such State of its instrument of ratification or accession.

Article 44

Denunciation

1. Any Contracting State may denounce this Convention at any time by a notification addressed to the Secretary-General of the United Nations.

2. Such denunciation shall take effect for the Contracting State concerned one year from the date upon which it is received by the Secretary-General of the United Nations.

3. Any State which has made a declaration or notification under article 40 may, at any time thereafter, by a notification to the Secretary-General of the United Nations, declare that the Convention shall cease to extend to such territory one year after the date of receipt of the notification by the Secretary-General.

Article 45

Revision

1. Any Contracting State may request revision of this Convention at any time by a notification addressed to the Secretary-General of the United Nations.

2. The General Assembly of the United Nations shall recommend the steps, if any, to be taken in respect of such request.

Article 46

Notifications by the Secretary-General of the United Nations

The Secretary-General of the United Nations shall inform all Members of the United Nations and non-member States referred to in article 39:

(a) Of declarations and notifications in accordance with section B of article 1;

(b) Of signatures, ratifications and accessions in accordance with article 39;

(c) Of declarations and notifications in accordance with article 40;

(d) Of reservations and withdrawals in accordance with article 42;

(e) Of the date on which this Convention will come into force in accordance with article 43;

(f) Of denunciations and notifications in accordance with article 44;

(g) Of requests for revision in accordance with article 45.

IN FAITH WHEREOF the undersigned, duly authorized, have signed this Convention on behalf of their respective Governments.

DONE at Geneva, this twenty-eighth day of July, one thousand nine hundred and fifty-one, in a single copy, of which the English and French texts are equally authentic and which shall remain deposited in the archives of the United Nations, and certified true copies of which shall be delivered to all Members of the United Nations and to the non-member States referred to in article 39.

PROTOCOL RELATING TO THE STATUS OF REFUGEES, 606 U.N.T.S. 267, *entered into force* Oct. 4, 1967:

The States Parties to the present Protocol,

Considering that the Convention relating to the Status of Refugees done at Geneva on 28 July 1951 (hereinafter referred to as the Convention) covers only those persons who have become refugees as a result of events occurring before I January 1951,

Considering that new refugee situations have arisen since the Convention was adopted and that the refugees concerned may therefore not fall within the scope of the Convention,

Considering that it is desirable that equal status should be enjoyed by all refugees covered by the definition in the Convention irrespective of the date-line 1 January 1951,

Have agreed as follows:

Article I

General provision

1. The States Parties to the present Protocol undertake to apply articles 2 to 34 inclusive of the Convention to refugees as hereinafter defined.

2. For the purpose of the present Protocol, the term "refugee" shall, except as regards the application of paragraph 3 of this article, mean any person within the definition of article 1 of the Convention as if the words "As a result of events occurring before 1 January 1951 and..." and the words "...as a result of such events", in article 1 A (2) were omitted.

3. The present Protocol shall be applied by the States Parties hereto without any geographic limitation, save that existing declarations made by

States already Parties to the Convention in accordance with article 1 B (I) (a) of the Convention, shall, unless extended under article 1 B (2) thereof, apply also under the present Protocol.

Article II

Co-operation of the national authorities with the United Nations

1. The States Parties to the present Protocol undertake to co-operate with the Office of the United Nations High Commissioner for Refugees, or any other agency of the United Nations which may succeed it, in the exercise of its functions, and shall in particular facilitate its duty of supervising the application of the provisions of the present Protocol.

2. In order to enable the Office of the High Commissioner or any other agency of the United Nations which may succeed it, to make reports to the competent organs of the United Nations, the States Parties to the present Protocol undertake to provide them with the information and statistical data requested, in the appropriate form, concerning:

(a) The condition of refugees;

(b) The implementation of the present Protocol;

(c) Laws, regulations and decrees which are, or may hereafter be, in force relating to refugees.

Article III

Information on national legislation

The States Parties to the present Protocol shall communicate to the Secretary-General of the United Nations the laws and regulations which they may adopt to ensure the application of the present Protocol.

Article IV

Settlement of disputes

Any dispute between States Parties to the present Protocol which relates to its interpretation or application and which cannot be settled by other means shall be referred to the International Court of Justice at the request of any one of the parties to the dispute.

Article V

Accession

The present Protocol shall be open for accession on behalf of all States Parties to the Convention and of any other State Member of the United Nations or member of any of the specialized agencies or to which an invitation to accede may have been addressed by the General Assembly of the United Nations. Accession shall be effected by the deposit of an instrument of accession with the Secretary-General of the United Nations.

Article VI

Federal clause

In the case of a Federal or non-unitary State, the following provisions shall apply:

(a) With respect to those articles of the Convention to be applied in accordance with article I, paragraph 1, of the present Protocol that come within the legislative jurisdiction of the federal legislative authority, the obligations of the Federal Government shall to this extent be the same as those of States Parties which are not Federal States;

(b) With respect to those articles of the Convention to be applied in accordance with article I, paragraph 1, of the present Protocol that come within the legislative jurisdiction of constituent States, provinces or cantons which are not, under the constitutional system of the Federation, bound to take legislative action, the Federal Government shall bring such articles with a favourable recommendation to the notice of the appropriate authorities of States, provinces or cantons at the earliest possible moment;

(c) A Federal State Party to the present Protocol shall, at the request of any other State Party hereto transmitted through the Secretary-General of the United Nations, supply a statement of the law and practice of the Federation and its constituent units in regard to any particular provision of the Convention to be applied in accordance with article I, paragraph 1, of the present Protocol, showing the extent to which effect has been given to that provision by legislative or other action.

Article VII

Reservations and declarations

1. At the time of accession, any State may make reservations in respect of article IV of the present Protocol and in respect of the application in accordance with article I of the present Protocol of any provisions of the Convention other than those contained in articles 1, 3, 4, 16(1) and 33 thereof, provided that in the case of a State Party to the Convention reservations made under this article shall not extend to refugees in respect of whom the Convention applies.

2. Reservations made by States Parties to the Convention in accordance with article 42 thereof shall, unless withdrawn, be applicable in relation to their obligations under the present Protocol.

3. Any State making a reservation in accordance with paragraph 1 of this article may at any time withdraw such reservation by a communication to that effect addressed to the Secretary-General of the United Nations.

4. Declarations made under article 40, paragraphs 1 and 2, of the Convention by a State Party thereto which accedes to the present Protocol shall be deemed to apply in respect of the present Protocol, unless upon accession a notification to the contrary is addressed by the State Party concerned to

the Secretary-General of the United Nations. The provisions of article 40, paragraphs 2 and 3, and of article 44, paragraph 3, of the Convention shall be deemed to apply *mutatis mutandis* to the present Protocol.

Article VIII

Entry into Protocol

1. The present Protocol shall come into force on the day of deposit of the sixth instrument of accession.

2. For each State acceding to the Protocol after the deposit of the sixth instrument of accession, the Protocol shall come into force on the date of deposit by such State of its instrument of accession.

Article IX

Denunciation

1. Any State Party hereto may denounce this Protocol at any time by a notification addressed to the Secretary-General of the United Nations.

2. Such denunciation shall take effect for the State Party concerned one year from the date on which it is received by the Secretary-General of the United Nations.

Article X

Notifications by the Secretary-General of the United Nations

The Secretary-General of the United Nations shall inform the States referred to in article V above of the date of entry into force, accessions, reservations and withdrawals of reservations to and denunciations of the present Protocol, and of declarations and notifications relating hereto.

Article XI

Deposit in the archives of the Secretariat of the United Nations

A copy of the present Protocol, of which the Chinese, English, French, Russian and Spanish texts are equally authentic, signed by the President of the General Assembly and by the Secretary-General of the United Nations, shall be deposited in the archives of the Secretariat of the United Nations. The Secretary-General will transmit certified copies thereof to all States Members of the United Nations and to the other States referred to in article 5 above.

VIENNA CONVENTION ON THE LAW OF TREATIES, 1155 U.N.T.S. 331, *entered into force* January 27, 1980:

The States Parties to the present Convention

Considering the fundamental role of treaties in the history of international relations,

Recognizing the ever-increasing importance of treaties as a source of international law and as a means of developing peaceful co-operation among nations, whatever their constitutional and social systems,

Noting that the principles of free consent and of good faith and the *pacta sunt servanda* rule are universally recognized,

Affirming that disputes concerning treaties, like other international disputes, should be settled by peaceful means and in conformity with the principles of justice and international law,

Recalling the determination of the peoples of the United Nations to establish conditions under which justice and respect for the obligations arising from treaties can be maintained,

Having in mind the principles of international law embodied in the Charter of the United Nations, such as the principles of the equal rights and self-determination of peoples, of the sovereign equality and independence of all States, of non-interference in the domestic affairs of States, of the prohibition of the threat or use of force and of universal respect for, and observance of, human rights and fundamental freedoms for all,

Believing that the codification and progressive development of the law of treaties achieved in the present Convention will promote the purposes of the United Nations set forth in the Charter, namely, the maintenance of international peace and security, the development of friendly relations and the achievement of co-operation among nations,

Affirming that the rules of customary international law will continue to govern questions not regulated by the provisions of the present Convention,

Have agreed as follows:

PART I—INTRODUCTION

Article 1

Scope of the present Convention

The present Convention applies to treaties between States.

Article 2

Use of terms

1. For the purposes of the present Convention:

a. 'treaty' means an international agreement concluded between States in written form and governed by international law, whether embodied in a single instrument or in two or more related instruments and whatever its particular designation;

b. 'ratification', 'acceptance', 'approval' and 'accession' mean in each case the international act so named whereby a State establishes on the international plane its consent to be bound by a treaty;

c. 'full powers' means a document emanating from the competent authority of a State designating a person or persons to represent the State for negotiating, adopting or authenticating the text of a treaty, for expressing the consent of the State to be bound by a treaty, or for accomplishing any other act with respect to a treaty;

d. 'reservation' means a unilateral statement, however phrased or named, made by a State, when signing, ratifying, accepting, approving or acceding to a treaty, whereby it purports to exclude or to modify the legal effect of certain provisions of the treaty in their application to that State;

e. 'negotiating State' means a State which took part in the drawing up and adoption of the text of the treaty;

f. 'contracting State' means a State which has consented to be bound by the treaty, whether or not the treaty has entered into force;

g. 'party' means a State which has consented to be bound by the treaty and for which the treaty is in force;

h. 'third State' means a State not a party to the treaty;

i. 'international organization' means an intergovernmental organization.

2. The provisions of paragraph 1 regarding the use of terms in the present Convention are without prejudice to the use of those terms or to the meanings which may be given to them in the internal law of any State.

Article 3

International agreements not within the scope of the present Convention

The fact that the present Convention does not apply to international agreements concluded between States and other subjects of international law or between such other subjects of international law, or to international agreements not in written form, shall not affect:

a. the legal force of such agreements;

b. the application to them of any of the rules set forth in the present Convention to which they would be subject under international law independently of the Convention;

c. the application of the Convention to the relations of States as between themselves under international agreements to which other subjects of international law are also parties.

Article 4

Non-retroactivity of the present Convention

Without prejudice to the application of any rules set forth in the present Convention to which treaties would be subject under international law independently of the Convention, the Convention applies only to treaties which are concluded by States after the entry into force of the present Convention with regard to such States.

Article 5

Treaties constituting international organizations and treaties adopted within an international organization

The present Convention applies to any treaty which is the constituent instrument of an international organization and to any treaty adopted within an international organization without prejudice to any relevant rules of the organization.

PART II—CONCLUSION AND ENTRY INTO FORCE OF TREATIES

SECTION 1. CONCLUSION OF TREATIES

Article 6

Capacity of States to conclude treaties

Every State possesses capacity to conclude treaties.

Article 7

Full powers

1. A person is considered as representing a State for the purpose of adopting or authenticating the text of a treaty or for the purpose of expressing the Consent of the State to be bound by a treaty if:

a. he produces appropriate full powers; or

b. it appears from the practice of the States concerned or from other circumstances that their intention was to consider that person as representing the State for such purposes and to dispense with full powers.

2. In virtue of their functions and without having to produce full powers, the following are considered as representing their State:

a. Heads of State, Heads of Government and Ministers for Foreign Affairs, for the purpose of performing all acts relating to the conclusion of a treaty;

b. heads of diplomatic missions, for the purpose of adopting the text of a treaty between the accrediting State and the State to which they are accredited;

c. representatives accredited by States to an international conference or to an international organization or one of its organs, for the purpose of adopting the text of a treaty in that conference, organization or organ.

Article 8

Subsequent confirmation of an act performed without authorization

An act relating to the conclusion of a treaty performed by a person who cannot be considered under article 7 as authorized to represent a State for that purpose is without legal effect unless afterwards confirmed by that State.

Article 9

Adoption of the text

1. The adoption of the text of a treaty takes place by the consent of all the States participating in its drawing up except as provided in paragraph 2.

2. The adoption of the text of a treaty at an international conference takes place by the vote of two-thirds of the States present and voting, unless by the same majority they shall decide to apply a different rule.

Article 10

Authentication of the text

The text of a treaty is established as authentic and definitive:

a. by such procedure as may be provided for in the text or agreed upon by the States participating in its drawing up; or

b. failing such procedure, by the signature, signature ad referendum or initialling by the representatives of those States of the text of the treaty or of the Final Act of a conference incorporating the text.

Article 11

Means of expressing consent to be bound by a treaty

The consent of a State to be bound by a treaty may be expressed by signature, exchange of instruments constituting a treaty, ratification, acceptance, approval or accession, or by any other means if so agreed.

Article 12

Consent to be bound by a treaty expressed by signature

1. The consent of a State to be bound by a treaty is expressed by the signature of its representative when:

a. the treaty provides that signature shall have that effect;

b. it is otherwise established that the negotiating States were agreed that signature should have that effect; or

c. the intention of the State to give that effect to the signature appears from the full powers of its representative or was expressed during the negotiation.

2. For the purposes of paragraph 1:

a. the initialling of a text constitutes a signature of the treaty when it is established that the negotiating States so agreed;

b. the signature ad referendum of a treaty by a representative, if confirmed by his State, constitutes a full signature of the treaty.

Article 13

Consent to be bound by a treaty expressed by an exchange of instruments constituting a treaty

The consent of States to be bound by a treaty constituted by instruments exchanged between them is expressed by that exchange when:

a. he instruments provide that their exchange shall have that effect; or

b. it is otherwise established that those States were agreed that the exchange of instruments should have that effect

Article 14

Consent to be bound by a treaty expressed by ratification, acceptance or approval

1. The consent of a State to be bound by a treaty is expressed by ratification when:

a. the treaty provides for such consent to be expressed by means of ratification;

b. it is otherwise established that the negotiating States were agreed that ratification should be required;

c. the representative of the State has signed the treaty subject to ratification; or

d. the intention of the State to sign the treaty subject to ratification appears from the full powers of its representative or was expressed during the negotiation.

2. The consent of a State to be bound by a treaty is expressed by acceptance or approval under conditions similar to those which apply to ratification.

Article 15

Consent to be bound by a treaty expressed by accession

The consent of a State to be bound by a treaty is expressed by accession when:

a. the treaty provides that such consent may be expressed by that State by means of accession;

b. it is otherwise established that the negotiating States were agreed that such consent may be expressed by that State by means of accession; or

c. all the parties have subsequently agreed that such consent may be expressed by that State by means of accession.

Article 16

Exchange or deposit of instruments of ratification, acceptance, approval or accession

Unless the treaty otherwise provides, instruments of ratification, acceptance, approval or accession establish the consent of a State to be bound by a treaty upon:

a. their exchange between the contracting States;

b. their deposit with the depositary; or

c. their notification to the contracting States or to the depositary, if so agreed.

Article 17

Consent to be bound by part of a treaty and choice of differing provisions

1. Without prejudice to articles 19 to 23, the consent of a State to be bound by part of a treaty is effective only if the treaty so permits or the other contracting States so agree.

2. The consent of a State to be bound by a treaty which permits a choice between differing provisions is effective only if it is made clear to which of the provisions the consent relates.

Article 18

Obligation not to defeat the object and purpose of a treaty prior to its entry into force

A State is obliged to refrain from acts which would defeat the object and purpose of a treaty when:

a. it has signed the treaty or has exchanged instruments constituting the treaty subject to ratification, acceptance or approval, until it shall have made its intention clear not to become a party to the treaty; or

b. it has expressed its consent to be bound by the treaty, pending the entry into force of the treaty and provided that such entry into force is not unduly delayed.

SECTION 2. RESERVATIONS

Article 19

Formulation of reservations

A State may, when signing, ratifying, accepting, approving or acceding to a treaty, formulate a reservation unless:

a. the reservation is prohibited by the treaty;

b. the treaty provides that only specified reservations, which do not include the reservation in question, may be made; or

c. in cases not falling under sub-paragraphs (a) and (b), the reservation is incompatible with the object and purpose of the treaty.

Article 20

Acceptance of and objection to reservations

1. A reservation expressly authorized by a treaty does not require any subsequent acceptance by the other contracting States unless the treaty so provides.

2. When it appears from the limited number of the negotiating States and the object and purpose of a treaty that the application of the treaty in its entirety between all the parties is an essential condition of the consent of each one to be bound by the treaty, a reservation requires acceptance by all the parties.

3. When a treaty is a constituent instrument of an international organization and unless it otherwise provides, a reservation requires the acceptance of the competent organ of that organization.

4. In cases not falling under the preceding paragraphs and unless the treaty otherwise provides:

a. acceptance by another contracting State of a reservation constitutes the reserving State a party to the treaty in relation to that other State if or when the treaty is in force for those States;

b. an objection by another contracting State to a reservation does not preclude the entry into force of the treaty as between the objecting and reserving States unless a contrary intention is definitely expressed by the objecting State;

c. an act expressing a State's consent to be bound by the treaty and containing a reservation is effective as soon as at least one other contracting State has accepted the reservation.

5. For the purposes of paragraphs 2 and 4 and unless the treaty otherwise provides, a reservation is considered to have been accepted by a State if it shall have raised no objection to the reservation by the end of a period of twelve months after it was notified of the reservation or by the date on which it expressed its consent to be bound by the treaty, whichever is later.

Article 21

Legal effects of reservations and of objections to reservations

1. A reservation established with regard to another party in accordance with articles 19, 20 and 23:

   a. modifies for the reserving State in its relations with that other party the provisions of the treaty to which the reservation relates to the extent of the reservation; and

   b. modifies those provisions to the same extent for that other party in its relations with the reserving State.

2. The reservation does not modify the provisions of the treaty for the other parties to the treaty inter se.

3. When a State objecting to a reservation has not opposed the entry into force of the treaty between itself and the reserving State, the provisions to which the reservation relates do not apply as between the two States to the extent of the reservation.

Article 22

Withdrawal of reservations and of objections to reservations

1. Unless the treaty otherwise provides, a reservation may be withdrawn at any time and the consent of a State which has accepted the reservation is not required for its withdrawal.

2. Unless the treaty otherwise provides, an objection to a reservation may be withdrawn at any time.

3. Unless the treaty otherwise provides, or it is otherwise agreed:

   a. the withdrawal of a reservation becomes operative in relation to another contracting State only when notice of it has been received by that State;

   b. the withdrawal of an objection to a reservation becomes operative only when notice of it has been received by the State which formulated the reservation.

Article 23

Procedure regarding reservations

1. A reservation, an express acceptance of a reservation and an objection to a reservation must be formulated in writing and communicated to the contracting States and other States entitled to become parties to the treaty.

2. If formulated when signing the treaty subject to ratification, acceptance or approval, a reservation must be formally confirmed by the reserving

State when expressing its consent to be bound by the treaty. In such a case the reservation shall be considered as having been made on the date of its confirmation.

3. An express acceptance of, or an objection to, a reservation made previously to confirmation of the reservation does not itself require confirmation.

4. The withdrawal of a reservation or of an objection to a reservation must be formulated in writing.

SECTION 3. ENTRY INTO FORCE AND PROVISIONAL APPLICATION OF TREATIES

Article 24

Entry into force

1. A treaty enters into force in such manner and upon such date as it may provide or as the negotiating States may agree.

2. Failing any such provision or agreement, a treaty enters into force as soon as consent to be bound by the treaty has been established for all the negotiating States.

3. When the consent of a State to be bound by a treaty is established on a date after the treaty has come into force, the treaty enters into force for that State on that date, unless the treaty otherwise provides.

4. The provisions of a treaty regulating the authentication of its text, the establishment of the consent of States to be bound by the treaty, the manner or date of its entry into force, reservations, the functions of the depositary and other matters arising necessarily before the entry into force of the treaty apply from the time of the adoption of its text.

Article 25

Provisional application

1. A treaty or a part of a treaty is applied provisionally pending its entry into force if:

a. the treaty itself so provides; or

b. the negotiating States have in some other manner so agreed.

2. Unless the treaty otherwise provides or the negotiating States have otherwise agreed, the provisional application of a treaty or a part of a treaty with respect to a State shall be terminated if that State notifies the other States between which the treaty is being applied provisionally of its intention not to become a party to the treaty.

PART III—OBSERVANCE, APPLICATION AND INTERPRETATION OF TREATIES

SECTION 1. OBSERVANCE OF TREATIES

Article 26

Pacta sunt servanda

Every treaty in force is binding upon the parties to it and must be performed by them in good faith.

Article 27

Internal law and observance of treaties

A party may not invoke the provisions of its internal law as justification for its failure to perform a treaty. This rule is without prejudice to article 46.

SECTION 2. APPLICATION OF TREATIES

Article 28

Non-retroactivity of treaties

Unless a different intention appears from the treaty or is otherwise established, its provisions do not bind a party in relation to any act or fact which took place or any situation which ceased to exist before the date of the entry into force of the treaty with respect to that party.

Article 29

Territorial scope of treaties

Unless a different intention appears from the treaty or is otherwise established, a treaty is binding upon each party in respect of its entire territory.

Article 30

Application of successive treaties relating to the same subject-matter

1. Subject to Article 103 of the Charter of the United Nations, the rights and obligations of States parties to successive treaties relating to the same subject-matter shall be determined in accordance with the following paragraphs.

2. When a treaty specifies that it is subject to, or that it is not to be considered as incompatible with, an earlier or later treaty, the provisions of that other treaty prevail.

3. When all the parties to the earlier treaty are parties also to the later treaty but the earlier treaty is not terminated or suspended in operation under article 59, the earlier treaty applies only to the extent that its provisions are compatible with those of the latter treaty.

4. When the parties to the later treaty do not include all the parties to the earlier one:

> a. as between States parties to both treaties the same rule applies as in paragraph 3;

> b. as between a State party to both treaties and a State party to only one of the treaties, the treaty to which both States are parties governs their mutual rights and obligations.

5. Paragraph 4 is without prejudice to article 41, or to any question of the termination or suspension of the operation of a treaty under article 60 or to any question of responsibility which may arise for a State from the conclusion or application of a treaty, the provisions of which are incompatible with its obligations towards another State under another treaty.

SECTION 3. INTERPRETATION OF TREATIES

Article 31

General rule of interpretation

1. A treaty shall be interpreted in good faith in accordance with the ordinary meaning to be given to the terms of the treaty in their context and in the light of its object and purpose.

2. The context for the purpose of the interpretation of a treaty shall comprise, in addition to the text, including its preamble and annexes:

> a. any agreement relating to the treaty which was made between all the parties in connexion with the conclusion of the treaty;

> b. any instrument which was made by one or more parties in connexion with the conclusion of the treaty and accepted by the other parties as an instrument related to the treaty.

3. There shall be taken into account, together with the context:

> a. any subsequent agreement between the parties regarding the interpretation of the treaty or the application of its provisions;

> b. any subsequent practice in the application of the treaty which establishes the agreement of the parties regarding its interpretation;

> c. any relevant rules of international law applicable in the relations between the parties.

4. A special meaning shall be given to a term if it is established that the parties so intended.

Article 32

Supplementary means of interpretation

Recourse may be had to supplementary means of interpretation, including the preparatory work of the treaty and the circumstances of its conclusion, in order to confirm the meaning resulting from the application of article 31, or to determine the meaning when the interpretation according to article 31:

    a. leaves the meaning ambiguous or obscure; or

    b. leads to a result which is manifestly absurd or unreasonable.

Article 33

Interpretation of treaties authenticated in two or more languages

1. When a treaty has been authenticated in two or more languages, the text is equally authoritative in each language, unless the treaty provides or the parties agree that, in case of divergence, a particular text shall prevail.

2. A version of the treaty in a language other than one of those in which the text was authenticated shall be considered an authentic text only if the treaty so provides or the parties so agree.

3. The terms of the treaty are presumed to have the same meaning in each authentic text.

4. Except where a particular text prevails in accordance with paragraph 1, when a comparison of the authentic texts discloses a difference of meaning which the application of articles 31 and 32 does not remove, the meaning which best reconciles the texts, having regard to the object and purpose of the treaty, shall be adopted.

SECTION 4. TREATIES AND THIRD STATES

Article 34

General rule regarding third States

A treaty does not create either obligations or rights for a third State without its consent.

Article 35

Treaties providing for obligations for third States

An obligation arises for a third State from a provision of a treaty if the parties to the treaty intend the provision to be the means of establishing the obligation and the third State expressly accepts that obligation in writing.

Article 36

Treaties providing for rights for third States

1. A right arises for a third State from a provision of a treaty if the parties to the treaty intend the provision to accord that right either to the third State, or to a group of States to which it belongs, or to all States, and the third State assents thereto. Its assent shall be presumed so long as the contrary is not indicated, unless the treaty otherwise provides.

2. A State exercising a right in accordance with paragraph 1 shall comply with the conditions for its exercise provided for in the treaty or established in conformity with the treaty.

Article 37

Revocation or modification of obligations or rights of third States

1. When an obligation has arisen for a third State in conformity with article 35, the obligation may be revoked or modified only with the consent of the parties to the treaty and of the third State, unless it is established that they had otherwise agreed.

2. When a right has arisen for a third State in conformity with article 36, the right may not be revoked or modified by the parties if it is established that the right was intended not to be revocable or subject to modification without the consent of the third State.

Article 38

Rules in a treaty becoming binding on third States through international custom

Nothing in articles 34 to 37 precludes a rule set forth in a treaty from becoming binding upon a third State as a customary rule of international law, recognized as such.

PART IV—AMENDMENT AND MODIFICATION OF TREATIES

Article 39

General rule regarding the amendment of treaties

A treaty may be amended by agreement between the parties. The rules laid down in Part II apply to such an agreement except in so far as the treaty may otherwise provide.

Article 40

Amendment of multilateral treaties

1. Unless the treaty otherwise provides, the amendment of multilateral treaties shall be governed by the following paragraphs.

2. Any proposal to amend a multilateral treaty as between all the parties must be notified to all the contracting States, each one of which shall have the right to take part in:

    a. the decision as to the action to be taken in regard to such proposal;

    b. the negotiation and conclusion of any agreement for the amendment of the treaty.

3. Every State entitled to become a party to the treaty shall also be entitled to become a party to the treaty as amended.

4. The amending agreement does not bind any State already a party to the treaty which does not become a party to the amending agreement; article 30, paragraph 4(b), applies in relation to such State.

5. Any State which becomes a party to the treaty after the entry into force of the amending agreement shall, failing an expression of a different intention by that State:

a. be considered as a party to the treaty as amended; and

b. be considered as a party to the unamended treaty in relation to any party to the treaty not bound by the amending agreement.

Article 41

Agreements to modify multilateral treaties between certain of the parties only

1. Two or more of the parties to a multilateral treaty may conclude an agreement to modify the treaty as between themselves alone if:

a. the possibility of such a modification is provided for by the treaty; or

b. the modification in question is not prohibited by the treaty and:

i. does not affect the enjoyment by the other parties of their rights under the treaty or the performance of their obligations;

ii. does not relate to a provision, derogation from which is incompatible with the effective execution of the object and purpose of the treaty as a whole.

2. Unless in a case falling under paragraph 1(a) the treaty otherwise provides, the parties in question shall notify the other parties of their intention to conclude the agreement and of the modification to the treaty for which it provides.

PART V—INVALIDITY, TERMINATION AND SUSPENSION OF THE OPERATION OF TREATIES

SECTION 1. GENERAL PROVISIONS

Article 42

Validity and continuance in force of treaties

1. The validity of a treaty or of the consent of a State to be bound by a treaty may be impeached only through the application of the present Convention.

2. The termination of a treaty, its denunciation or the withdrawal of a party, may take place only as a result of the application of the provisions of the

treaty or of the present Convention. The same rule applies to suspension of the operation of a treaty.

Article 43

Obligations imposed by international law independently of a treaty

The invalidity, termination or denunciation of a treaty, the withdrawal of a party from it, or the suspension of its operation, as a result of the application of the present Convention or of the provisions of the treaty, shall not in any way impair the duty of any State to fulfil any obligation embodied in the treaty to which it would be subject under international law independently of the treaty.

Article 44

Separability of treaty provisions

1. A right of a party, provided for in a treaty or arising under article 56, to denounce, withdraw from or suspend the operation of the treaty may be exercised only with respect to the whole treaty unless the treaty otherwise provides or the parties otherwise agree.

2. A ground for invalidating, terminating, withdrawing from or suspending the operation of a treaty recognized in the present Convention may be invoked only with respect to the whole treaty except as provided in the following paragraphs or in article 60.

3. If the ground relates solely to particular clauses, it may be invoked only with respect to those clauses where:

a. the said clauses are separable from the remainder of the treaty with regard to their application;

b. it appears from the treaty or is otherwise established that acceptance of those clauses was not an essential basis of the consent of the other party or parties to be bound by the treaty as a whole; and

c. continued performance of the remainder of the treaty would not be unjust.

4. In cases falling under articles 49 and 50 the State entitled to invoke the fraud or corruption may do so with respect either to the whole treaty or, subject to paragraph 3, to the particular clauses alone.

5. In cases falling under articles 51, 52 and 53, no separation of the provisions of the treaty is permitted.

Article 45

Loss of a right to invoke a ground for invalidating, terminating, withdrawing from or suspending the operation of a treaty

A State may no longer invoke a ground for invalidating, terminating, withdrawing from or suspending the operation of a treaty under articles 46 to 50 or articles 60 and 62 if, after becoming aware of the facts:

a. it shall have expressly agreed that the treaty is valid or remains in force or continues in operation, as the case may be; or

b. it must by reason of its conduct be considered as having acquiesced in the validity of the treaty or in its maintenance in force or in operation, as the case may be.

SECTION 2. INVALIDITY OF TREATIES

Article 46

Provisions of internal law regarding competence to conclude treaties

1. A State may not invoke the fact that its consent to be bound by a treaty has been expressed in violation of a provision of its internal law regarding competence to conclude treaties as invalidating its consent unless that violation was manifest and concerned a rule of its internal law of fundamental importance.

2. A violation is manifest if it would be objectively evident to any State conducting itself in the matter in accordance with normal practice and in good faith.

Article 47

Specific restrictions on authority to express the consent of a State

If the authority of a representative to express the consent of a State to be bound by a particular treaty has been made subject to a specific restriction, his omission to observe that restriction may not be invoked as invalidating the consent expressed by him unless the restriction was notified to the other negotiating States prior to his expressing such consent.

Article 48

Error

1. A State may invoke an error in a treaty as invalidating its consent to be bound by the treaty if the error relates to a fact or situation which was assumed by that State to exist at the time when the treaty was concluded and formed an essential basis of its consent to be bound by the treaty.

2. Paragraph 1 shall not apply if the State in question contributed by its own conduct to the error or if the circumstances were such as to put that State on notice of a possible error.

3. An error relating only to the wording of the text of a treaty does not affect its validity; article 79 then applies.

Article 49

Fraud

If a State has been induced to conclude a treaty by the fraudulent conduct of another negotiating State, the State may invoke the fraud as invalidating its consent to be bound by the treaty.

Article 50

Corruption of a representative of a State

If the expression of a State's consent to be bound by a treaty has been procured through the corruption of its representative directly or indirectly by another negotiating State, the State may invoke such corruption as invalidating its consent to be bound by the treaty.

Article 51

Coercion of a representative of a State

The expression of a State's consent to be bound by a treaty which has been procured by the coercion of its representative through acts or threats directed against him shall be without any legal effect.

Article 52

Coercion of a State by the threat or use of force

A treaty is void if its conclusion has been procured by the threat or use of force in violation of the principles of international law embodied in the Charter of the United Nations.

Article 53

Treaties conflicting with a peremptory norm of general international law (*jus cogens*)

A treaty is void if, at the time of its conclusion, it conflicts with a peremptory norm of general international law. For the purposes of the present Convention, a peremptory norm of general international law is a norm accepted and recognized by the international community of States as a whole as a norm from which no derogation is permitted and which can be modified only by a subsequent norm of general international law having the same character.

SECTION 3. TERMINATION AND SUSPENSION OF THE OPERATION OF TREATIES

Article 54

Termination of or withdrawal from a treaty under its provisions or by consent of the parties

The termination of a treaty or the withdrawal of a party may take place:

a. in conformity with the provisions of the treaty; or

b. at any time by consent of all the parties after consultation with the other contracting States.

Article 55

Reduction of the parties to a multilateral treaty below the number necessary for its entry into force

Unless the treaty otherwise provides, a multilateral treaty does not terminate by reason only of the fact that the number of the parties falls below the number necessary for its entry into force.

Article 56

Denunciation of or withdrawal from a treaty containing no provision regarding termination, denunciation or withdrawal

1. A treaty which contains no provision regarding its termination and which does not provide for denunciation or withdrawal is not subject to denunciation or withdrawal unless:

a. it is established that the parties intended to admit the possibility of denunciation or withdrawal; or

b. a right of denunciation or withdrawal may be implied by the nature of the treaty.

2. A party shall give not less than twelve months' notice of its intention to denounce or withdraw from a treaty under paragraph 1.

Article 57

Suspension of the operation of a treaty under its provisions or by consent of the parties

The operation of a treaty in regard to all the parties or to a particular party may be suspended:

a. in conformity with the provisions of the treaty; or

b. at any time by consent of all the parties after consultation with the other contracting States.

Article 58

Suspension of the operation of a multilateral treaty by agreement between certain of the parties only

1. Two or more parties to a multilateral treaty may conclude an agreement to suspend the operation of provisions of the treaty, temporarily and as between themselves alone, if:

a. the possibility of such a suspension is provided for by the treaty; or

b. the suspension in question is not prohibited by the treaty and:

i. does not affect the enjoyment by the other parties of their rights under the treaty or the performance of their obligations;

ii. is not incompatible with the object and purpose of the treaty.

2. Unless in a case falling under paragraph 1(a) the treaty otherwise provides, the parties in question shall notify the other parties of their intention to conclude the agreement and of those provisions of the treaty the operation of which they intend to suspend.

Article 59

Termination or suspension of the operation of a treaty implied by conclusion of a later treaty

1. A treaty shall be considered as terminated if all the parties to it conclude a later treaty relating to the same subject-matter and:

a. it appears from the later treaty or is otherwise established that the parties intended that the matter should be governed by that treaty; or

b. the provisions of the later treaty are so far incompatible with those of the earlier one that the two treaties are not capable of being applied at the same time.

2. The earlier treaty shall be considered as only suspended in operation if it appears from the later treaty or is otherwise established that such was the intention of the parties.

Article 60

Termination or suspension of the operation of a treaty as a consequence of its breach

1. A material breach of a bilateral treaty by one of the parties entitles the other to invoke the breach as a ground for terminating the treaty or suspending its operation in whole or in part.

2. A material breach of a multilateral treaty by one of the parties entitles:

a. the other parties by unanimous agreement to suspend the operation of the treaty in whole or in part or to terminate it either:

i. in the relations between themselves and the defaulting State, or

ii. as between all the parties;

b. a party specially affected by the breach to invoke it as a ground for suspending the operation of the treaty in whole or in part in the relations between itself and the defaulting State;

c. any party other than the defaulting State to invoke the breach as a ground for suspending the operation of the treaty in whole or in part with respect to itself if the treaty is of such a character that a material breach of its provisions by one party radically changes the position of every party with respect to the further performance of its obligations under the treaty.

3. A material breach of a treaty, for the purposes of this article, consists in:

a. a repudiation of the treaty not sanctioned by the present Convention; or

b. the violation of a provision essential to the accomplishment of the object or purpose of the treaty.

4. The foregoing paragraphs are without prejudice to any provision in the treaty applicable in the event of a breach.

5. Paragraphs 1 to 3 do not apply to provisions relating to the protection of the human person contained in treaties of a humanitarian character, in particular to provisions prohibiting any form of reprisals against persons protected by such treaties.

Article 61

Supervening impossibility of performance

1. A party may invoke the impossibility of performing a treaty as a ground for terminating or withdrawing from it if the impossibility results from the permanent disappearance or destruction of an object indispensable for the execution of the treaty. If the impossibility is temporary, it may be invoked only as a ground for suspending the operation of the treaty.

2. Impossibility of performance may not be invoked by a party as a ground for terminating, withdrawing from or suspending the operation of a treaty if the impossibility is the result of a breach by that party either of an obligation under the treaty or of any other international obligation owed to any other party to the treaty.

Article 62

Fundamental change of circumstances

1. A fundamental change of circumstances which has occurred with regard to those existing at the time of the conclusion of a treaty, and which was not foreseen by the parties, may not be invoked as a ground for terminating or withdrawing from the treaty unless:

a. the existence of those circumstances constituted an essential basis of the consent of the parties to be bound by the treaty; and

b. the effect of the change is radically to transform the extent of obligations still to be performed under the treaty.

2. A fundamental change of circumstances may not be invoked as a ground for terminating or withdrawing from a treaty:

    a. if the treaty establishes a boundary; or

    b. if the fundamental change is the result of a breach by the party invoking it either of an obligation under the treaty or of any other international obligation owed to any other party to the treaty.

3. If, under the foregoing paragraphs, a party may invoke a fundamental change of circumstances as a ground for terminating or withdrawing from a treaty it may also invoke the change as a ground for suspending the operation of the treaty.

Article 63

Severance of diplomatic or consular relations

The severance of diplomatic or consular relations between parties to a treaty does not affect the legal relations established between them by the treaty except in so far as the existence of diplomatic or consular relations is indispensable for the application of the treaty.

Article 64

Emergence of a new peremptory norm of general international law (*jus cogens*)

If a new peremptory norm of general international law emerges, any existing treaty which is in conflict with that norm becomes void and terminates.

SECTION 4. PROCEDURE

Article 65

Procedure to be followed with respect to invalidity, termination, withdrawal from or suspension of the operation of a treaty

1. A party which, under the provisions of the present Convention, invokes either a defect in its consent to be bound by a treaty or a ground for impeaching the validity of a treaty, terminating it, withdrawing from it or suspending its operation, must notify the other parties of its claim. The notification shall indicate the measure proposed to be taken with respect to the treaty and the reasons therefor.

2. If, after the expiry of a period which, except in cases of special urgency, shall not be less than three months after the receipt of the notification, no party has raised any objection, the party making the notification may carry out in the manner provided in article 67 the measure which it has proposed.

3. If, however, objection has been raised by any other party, the parties shall seek a solution through the means indicated in article 33 of the Charter of the United Nations.

4. Nothing in the foregoing paragraphs shall affect the rights or obligations of the parties under any provisions in force binding the parties with regard to the settlement of disputes.

5. Without prejudice to article 45, the fact that a State has not previously made the notification prescribed in paragraph 1 shall not prevent it from making such notification in answer to another party claiming performance of the treaty or alleging its violation.

Article 66

Procedures for judicial settlement, arbitration and conciliation

If, under paragraph 3 of article 65, no solution has been reached within a period of 12 months following the date on which the objection was raised, the following procedures shall be followed:

a. any one of the parties to a dispute concerning the application or the interpretation of articles 53 or 64 may, by a written application, submit it to the International Court of Justice for a decision unless the parties by common consent agree to submit the dispute to arbitration;

b. any one of the parties to a dispute concerning the application or the interpretation of any of the other articles in Part V of the present Convention may set in motion the procedure specified in the Annexe to the Convention by submitting a request to that effect to the Secretary-General of the United Nations.

Article 67

Instruments for declaring invalid, terminating, withdrawing from or suspending the operation of a treaty

1. The notification provided for under article 65 paragraph 1 must be made in writing.

2. Any act declaring invalid, terminating, withdrawing from or suspending the operation of a treaty pursuant to the provisions of the treaty or of paragraphs 2 or 3 of article 65 shall be carried out through an instrument communicated to the other parties. If the instrument is not signed by the Head of State, Head of Government or Minister for Foreign Affairs, the representative of the State communicating it may be called upon to produce full powers.

Article 68

Revocation of notifications and instruments provided for in articles 65 and 67

A notification or instrument provided for in articles 65 or 67 may be revoked at any time before it takes effect.

SECTION 5. CONSEQUENCES OF THE INVALIDITY, TERMINATION OR SUSPENSION OF THE OPERATION OF A TREATY

Article 69

Consequences of the invalidity of a treaty

1. A treaty the invalidity of which is established under the present Convention is void. The provisions of a void treaty have no legal force.

2. If acts have nevertheless been performed in reliance on such a treaty:

   a. each party may require any other party to establish as far as possible in their mutual relations the position that would have existed if the acts had not been performed;

   b. acts performed in good faith before the invalidity was invoked are not rendered unlawful by reason only of the invalidity of the treaty.

3. In cases falling under articles 49, 50, 51 or 52, paragraph 2 does not apply with respect to the party to which the fraud, the act of corruption or the coercion is imputable.

4. In the case of the invalidity of a particular State's consent to be bound by a multilateral treaty, the foregoing rules apply in the relations between that State and the parties to the treaty.

Article 70

Consequences of the termination of a treaty

1. Unless the treaty otherwise provides or the parties otherwise agree, the termination of a treaty under its provisions or in accordance with the present Convention:

   a. releases the parties from any obligation further to perform the treaty;

   b. does not affect any right, obligation or legal situation of the parties created through the execution of the treaty prior to its termination.

2. If a State denounces or withdraws from a multilateral treaty, paragraph 1 applies in the relations between that State and each of the other parties to the treaty from the date when such denunciation or withdrawal takes effect.

Article 71

Consequences of the invalidity of a treaty which conflicts with a peremptory norm of general international law

1. In the case of a treaty which is void under article 53 the parties shall:

   a. eliminate as far as possible the consequences of any act performed in reliance on any provision which conflicts with the peremptory norm of general international law; and

b. bring their mutual relations into conformity with the peremptory norm of general international law.

2. In the case of a treaty which becomes void and terminates under article 64, the termination of the treaty:

a. releases the parties from any obligation further to perform the treaty;

b. does not affect any right, obligation or legal situation of the parties created through the execution of the treaty prior to its termination; provided that those rights, obligations or situations may thereafter be maintained only to the extent that their maintenance is not in itself in conflict with the new peremptory norm of general international law.

Article 72

Consequences of the suspension of the operation of a treaty

1. Unless the treaty otherwise provides or the parties otherwise agree, the suspension of the operation of a treaty under its provisions or in accordance with the present Convention:

a. releases the parties between which the operation of the treaty is suspended from the obligation to perform the treaty in their mutual relations during the period of the suspension;

b. does not otherwise affect the legal relations between the parties established by the treaty.

2. During the period of the suspension the parties shall refrain from acts tending to obstruct the resumption of the operation of the treaty.

PART VI—MISCELLANEOUS PROVISIONS

Article 73

Cases of State succession, State responsibility and outbreak of hostilities

The provisions of the present Convention shall not prejudge any question that may arise in regard to a treaty from a succession of States or from the international responsibility of a State or from the outbreak of hostilities between States.

Article 74

Diplomatic and consular relations and the conclusion of treaties

The severance or absence of diplomatic or consular relations between two or more States does not prevent the conclusion of treaties between those States. The conclusion of a treaty does not in itself affect the situation in regard to diplomatic or consular relations.

Article 75

Case of an aggressor State

The provisions of the present Convention are without prejudice to any obligation in relation to a treaty which may arise for an aggressor State in consequence of measures taken in conformity with the Charter of the United Nations with reference to that State's aggression.

PART VII—DEPOSITARIES, NOTIFICATIONS, CORRECTIONS AND REGISTRATION

Article 76

Depositaries of treaties

1. The designation of the depositary of a treaty may be made by the negotiating States, either in the treaty itself or in some other manner. The depositary may be one or more States, an international organization or the chief administrative officer of the organization.

2. The functions of the depositary of a treaty are international in character and the depositary is under an obligation to act impartially in their performance. In particular, the fact that a treaty has not entered into force between certain of the parties or that a difference has appeared between a State and a depositary with regard to the performance of the latter's functions shall not affect that obligation.

Article 77

Functions of depositaries

1. The functions of a depositary, unless otherwise provided in the treaty or agreed by the contracting States, comprise in particular:

a. keeping custody of the original text of the treaty and of any full powers delivered to the depositary;

b. preparing certified copies of the original text and preparing any further text of the treaty in such additional languages as may be required by the treaty and transmitting them to the parties and to the States entitled to become parties to the treaty;

c. receiving any signatures to the treaty and receiving and keeping custody of any instruments, notifications and communications relating to it;

d. examining whether the signature or any instrument, notification or communication relating to the treaty is in due and proper form and, if need be, bringing the matter to the attention of the State in question;

e. informing the parties and the States entitled to become parties to the treaty of acts, notifications and communications relating to the treaty;

f. informing the States entitled to become parties to the treaty when the number of signatures or of instruments of ratification, acceptance, approval or accession required for the entry into force of the treaty has been received or deposited;

g. registering the treaty with the Secretariat of the United Nations;

h. performing the functions specified in other provisions of the present Convention.

2. In the event of any difference appearing between a State and the depositary as to the performance of the latter's functions, the depositary shall bring the question to the attention of the signatory States and the contracting States or, where appropriate, of the competent organ of the international organization concerned.

Article 78

Notifications and communications

Except as the treaty or the present Convention otherwise provide, any notification or communication to be made by any State under the present Convention shall:

a. if there is no depositary, be transmitted direct to the States for which it is intended, or if there is a depositary, to the latter;

b. be considered as having been made by the State in question only upon its receipt by the State to which it was transmitted or, as the case may be, upon its receipt by the depositary;

c. if transmitted to a depositary, be considered as received by the State for which it was intended only when the latter State has been informed by the depositary in accordance with article 77, paragraph 1 (e).

Article 79

Correction of errors in texts or in certified copies of treaties

1. Where, after the authentication of the text of a treaty, the signatory States and the contracting States are agreed that it contains an error, the error shall, unless they decide upon some other means of correction, be corrected:

a. by having the appropriate correction made in the text and causing the correction to be initialled by duly authorized representatives;

b. by executing or exchanging an instrument or instruments setting out the correction which it has been agreed to make; or

c. by executing a corrected text of the whole treaty by the same procedure as in the case of the original text.

2. Where the treaty is one for which there is a depositary, the latter shall notify the signatory States and the contracting States of the error and of the proposal to correct it and shall specify an appropriate time-limit within which objection to the proposed correction may be raised. If, on the expiry of the time-limit:

a. no objection has been raised, the depositary shall make and initial the correction in the text and shall execute a *procès-verbal* of the rectification of the text and communicate a copy of it to the parties and to the States entitled to become parties to the treaty;

b. an objection has been raised, the depositary shall communicate the objection to the signatory States and to the contracting States.

3. The rules in paragraphs 1 and 2 apply also where the text has been authenticated in two or more languages and it appears that there is a lack of concordance which the signatory States and the contracting States agree should be corrected.

4. The corrected text replaces the defective text *ab initio*, unless the signatory States and the contracting States otherwise decide.

5. The correction of the text of a treaty that has been registered shall be notified to the Secretariat of the United Nations.

6. Where an error is discovered in a certified copy of a treaty, the depositary shall execute a *procès-verbal* specifying the rectification and communicate a copy of it to the signatory States and to the contracting Slates.

Article 80

Registration and publication of treaties

1. Treaties shall, after their entry into force, be transmitted to the Secretariat of the United Nations for registration or filing and recording, as the case may be, and for publication.

2. The designation of a depositary shall constitute authorization for it to perform the acts specified in the preceding paragraph.

PART VIII—FINAL PROVISIONS

Article 81

Signature

The present Convention shall be open for signature by all States Members of the United Nations or of any of the specialized agencies or of the International Atomic Energy Agency or parties to the Statute of the International Court of Justice, and by any other State invited by the General Assembly of the United Nations to become a party to the Convention, as follows: until 30 November 1969, at the Federal Ministry for Foreign Affairs of the Republic of Austria, and subsequently, until 30 April 1970, at United Nations Headquarters, New York.

Article 82

Ratification

The present Convention is subject to ratification. The instruments of ratification shall be deposited with the Secretary-General of the United Nations.

Article 83

Accession

The present Convention shall remain open for accession by any State belonging to any of the categories mentioned in article 81. The instruments of accession shall be deposited with the Secretary-General of the United Nations.

Article 84

Entry into force

1. The present Convention shall enter into force on the thirtieth day following the date of deposit of the thirty-fifth instrument of ratification or accession.

2. For each State ratifying or acceding to the Convention after the deposit of the thirty-fifth instrument of ratification or accession, the Convention shall enter into force on the thirtieth day after deposit by such State of its instrument of ratification or accession.

Article 85

Authentic texts

The original of the present Convention, of which the Chinese, English, French, Russian and Spanish texts are equally authentic, shall be deposited with the Secretary-General of the United Nations.

IN WITNESS WHEREOF the undersigned Plenipotentiaries, being duly authorized thereto by their respective Governments, have signed the present Convention.

DONE at Vienna, this twenty-third day of May, one thousand nine hundred and sixty-nine. ...

Annex

1. A list of conciliators consisting of qualified jurists shall be drawn up and maintained by the Secretary-General of the United Nations. To this end, every State which is a Member of the United Nations or a party to the present Convention shall be invited to nominate two conciliators, and the names of the persons so nominated shall constitute the list. The term of a conciliator, including that of any conciliator nominated to fill a casual vacancy, shall be five years and may be renewed. A conciliator whose term expires shall continue to fulfil any function for which he shall have been chosen under the following paragraph.

2. When a request has been made to the Secretary-General under article 66, the Secretary-General shall bring the dispute before a conciliation commission constituted as follows:

The State or States constituting one of the parties to the dispute shall appoint:

a. one conciliator of the nationality of that State or of one of those States, who may or may not be chosen from the list referred to in paragraph 1; and

b. one conciliator not of the nationality of that State or of any of those States, who shall be chosen from the list.

The State or States constituting the other party to the dispute shall appoint two conciliators in the same way. The four conciliators chosen by the parties shall be appointed within sixty days following the date on which the Secretary-General receives the request.

The four conciliators shall, within sixty days following the date of the last of their own appointments, appoint a fifth conciliator chosen from the list, who shall be chairman.

If the appointment of the chairman or of any of the other conciliators has not been made within the period prescribed above for such appointment, it shall be made by the Secretary-General within sixty days following the expiry of that period. The appointment of the chairman may be made by the Secretary-General either from the list or from the membership of the International Law Commission. Any of the periods within which appointments must be made may be extended by agreement between the parties to the dispute.

Any vacancy shall be filled in the manner prescribed for the initial appointment.

3. The Conciliation Commission shall decide its own procedure. The Commission, with the consent of the parties to the dispute, may invite any party to the treaty to submit to it its views orally or in writing. Decisions and recommendations of the Commission shall be made by a majority vote of the five members.

4. The Commission may draw the attention of the parties to the dispute to any measures which might facilitate an amicable settlement.

5. The Commission shall hear the parties, examine the claims and objections, and make proposals to the parties with a view to reaching an amicable settlement of the dispute.

6. The Commission shall report within twelve months of its constitution. Its report shall be deposited with the Secretary-General and transmitted to the parties to the dispute. The report of the Commission, including any conclusions stated therein regarding the facts or questions of law, shall not be binding upon the parties and it shall have no other character than that of recommendations submitted for the consideration of the parties in order to facilitate an amicable settlement of the dispute.

7. The Secretary-General shall provide the Commission with such assistance and facilities as it may require. The expenses of the Commission shall be borne by the United Nations.

B. OTHER UNITED NATIONS INSTRUMENTS

VIENNA DECLARATION AND PROGRAMME OF ACTION, World Conference on Human Rights, Vienna, 14-25 June 1993, U.N. Doc. A/CONF.157/24 (Part I) at 20 (1993):

The World Conference on Human Rights,

Considering that the promotion and protection of human rights is a matter of priority for the international community, and that the Conference affords a unique opportunity to carry out a comprehensive analysis of the international human rights system and of the machinery for the protection of human rights, in order to enhance and thus promote a fuller observance of those rights, in a just and balanced manner,

Recognizing and affirming that all human rights derive from the dignity and worth inherent in the human person, and that the human person is the central subject of human rights and fundamental freedoms, and consequently should be the principal beneficiary and should participate actively in the realization of these rights and freedoms,

Reaffirming their commitment to the purposes and principles contained in the Charter of the United Nations and the Universal Declaration of Human Rights,

Reaffirming the commitment contained in Article 56 of the Charter of the United Nations to take joint and separate action, placing proper emphasis on developing effective international cooperation for the realization of the purposes set out in Article 55, including universal respect for, and observance of, human rights and fundamental freedoms for all,

Emphasizing the responsibilities of all States, in conformity with the Charter of the United Nations, to develop and encourage respect for human rights and fundamental freedoms for all, without distinction as to race, sex, language or religion,

Recalling the Preamble to the Charter of the United Nations, in particular the determination to reaffirm faith in fundamental human rights, in the dignity and worth of the human person, and in the equal rights of men and women and of nations large and small,

Recalling also the determination expressed in the Preamble of the Charter of the United Nations to save succeeding generations from the scourge of war, to establish conditions under which justice and respect for obligations arising from treaties and other sources of international law can be maintained, to promote social progress and better standards of life in larger freedom, to practice tolerance and good neighbourliness, and to employ international machinery for the promotion of the economic and social advancement of all peoples,

Emphasizing that the Universal Declaration of Human Rights, which constitutes a common standard of achievement for all peoples and all nations, is the source of inspiration and has been the basis for the United Nations in making advances in standard setting as contained in the existing international human rights instruments, in particular the International Covenant on Civil and Political Rights and the International Covenant on Economic, Social and Cultural Rights,

Considering the major changes taking place on the international scene and the aspirations of all the peoples for an international order based on the principles enshrined in the Charter of the United Nations, including promoting and encouraging respect for human rights and fundamental freedoms for all and respect for the principle of equal rights and self-determination of peoples, peace, democracy, justice, equality, rule of law, pluralism, development, better standards of living and solidarity,

Deeply concerned by various forms of discrimination and violence, to which women continue to be exposed all over the world,

Recognizing that the activities of the United Nations in the field of human rights should be rationalized and enhanced in order to strengthen the United Nations machinery in this field and to further the objectives of universal respect for observance of international human rights standards,

Having taken into account the Declarations adopted by the three regional meetings at Tunis, San Jose and Bangkok and the contributions made by Governments, and bearing in mind the suggestions made by intergovernmental and non-governmental organizations, as well as the studies prepared by independent experts during the preparatory process leading to the World Conference on Human Rights,

Welcoming the International Year of the World's Indigenous People 1993 as a reaffirmation of the commitment of the international community to ensure their enjoyment of all human rights and fundamental freedoms and to respect the value and diversity of their cultures and identities,

Recognizing also that the international community should devise ways and means to remove the current obstacles and meet challenges to the full realization of all human rights and to prevent the continuation of human rights violations resulting thereof throughout the world,

Invoking the spirit of our age and the realities of our time which call upon the peoples of the world and all States Members of the United Nations to rededicate themselves to the global task of promoting and protecting all human rights and fundamental freedoms so as to secure full and universal enjoyment of these rights,

Determined to take new steps forward in the commitment of the international community with a view to achieving substantial progress in human rights endeavours by an increased and sustained effort of international cooperation and solidarity,

Solemnly adopts **the Vienna Declaration and Programme of Action**.

I

1. The World Conference on Human Rights reaffirms the solemn commitment of all States to fulfil their obligations to promote universal respect for, and observance and protection of, all human rights and fundamental freedoms for all in accordance with the Charter of the United Nations, other instruments relating to human rights, and international law. The universal nature of these rights and freedoms is beyond question.

In this framework, enhancement of international cooperation in the field of human rights is essential for the full achievement of the purposes of the United Nations.

Human rights and fundamental freedoms are the birthright of all human beings; their protection and promotion is the first responsibility of Governments.

2. All peoples have the right of self-determination. By virtue of that right they freely determine their political status, and freely pursue their economic, social and cultural development.

Taking into account the particular situation of peoples under colonial or other forms of alien domination or foreign occupation, the World Conference on Human Rights recognizes the right of peoples to take any legitimate action, in accordance with the Charter of the United Nations, to realize their inalienable right of self-determination. The World Conference on Human Rights considers the denial of the right of self-determination as a violation of human rights and underlines the importance of the effective realization of this right.

In accordance with the Declaration on Principles of International Law concerning Friendly Relations and Cooperation Among States in accordance with the Charter of the United Nations, this shall not be construed as authorizing or encouraging any action which would dismember or impair, totally or in part, the territorial integrity or political unity of sovereign and independent States conducting themselves in compliance with the principle of equal rights and self-determination of peoples and thus possessed of a Government representing the whole people belonging to the territory without distinction of any kind.

3. Effective international measures to guarantee and monitor the implementation of human rights standards should be taken in respect of people under foreign occupation, and effective legal protection against the violation of their human rights should be provided, in accordance with human rights norms and international law, particularly the Geneva Convention relative to the Protection of Civilian Persons in Time of War, of 14 August 1949, and other applicable norms of humanitarian law.

4. The promotion and protection of all human rights and fundamental freedoms must be considered as a priority objective of the United Nations in accordance with its purposes and principles, in particular the purpose of international cooperation. In the framework of these purposes and principles, the promotion and protection of all human rights is a legitimate concern of the

international community. The organs and specialized agencies related to human rights should therefore further enhance the coordination of their activities based on the consistent and objective application of international human rights instruments.

5. All human rights are universal, indivisible and interdependent and interrelated. The international community must treat human rights globally in a fair and equal manner, on the same footing, and with the same emphasis. While the significance of national and regional particularities and various historical, cultural and religious backgrounds must be borne in mind, it is the duty of States, regardless of their political, economic and cultural systems, to promote and protect all human rights and fundamental freedoms.

6. The efforts of the United Nations system towards the universal respect for, and observance of, human rights and fundamental freedoms for all, contribute to the stability and well-being necessary for peaceful and friendly relations among nations, and to improved conditions for peace and security as well as social and economic development, in conformity with the Charter of the United Nations.

7. The processes of promoting and protecting human rights should be conducted in conformity with the purposes and principles of the Charter of the United Nations, and international law.

8. Democracy, development and respect for human rights and fundamental freedoms are interdependent and mutually reinforcing. Democracy is based on the freely expressed will of the people to determine their own political, economic, social and cultural systems and their full participation in all aspects of their lives. In the context of the above, the promotion and protection of human rights and fundamental freedoms at the national and international levels should be universal and conducted without conditions attached. The international community should support the strengthening and promoting of democracy, development and respect for human rights and fundamental freedoms in the entire world.

9. The World Conference on Human Rights reaffirms that least developed countries committed to the process of democratization and economic reforms, many of which are in Africa, should be supported by the international community in order to succeed in their transition to democracy and economic development.

10. The World Conference on Human Rights reaffirms the right to development, as established in the Declaration on the Right to Development, as a universal and inalienable right and an integral part of fundamental human rights.

As stated in the Declaration on the Right to Development, the human person is the central subject of development.

While development facilitates the enjoyment of all human rights, the lack of development may not be invoked to justify the abridgement of internationally recognized human rights.

States should cooperate with each other in ensuring development and eliminating obstacles to development. The international community should promote an effective international cooperation for the realization of the right to development and the elimination of obstacles to development.

Lasting progress towards the implementation of the right to development requires effective development policies at the national level, as well as equitable economic relations and a favourable economic environment at the international level.

11. The right to development should be fulfilled so as to meet equitably the developmental and environmental needs of present and future generations. The World Conference on Human Rights recognizes that illicit dumping of toxic and dangerous substances and waste potentially constitutes a serious threat to the human rights to life and health of everyone.

Consequently, the World Conference on Human Rights calls on all States to adopt and vigorously implement existing conventions relating to the dumping of toxic and dangerous products and waste and to cooperate in the prevention of illicit dumping.

Everyone has the right to enjoy the benefits of scientific progress and its applications. The World Conference on Human Rights notes that certain advances, notably in the biomedical and life sciences as well as in information technology, may have potentially adverse consequences for the integrity, dignity and human rights of the individual, and calls for international cooperation to ensure that human rights and dignity are fully respected in this area of universal concern.

12. The World Conference on Human Rights calls upon the international community to make all efforts to help alleviate the external debt burden of developing countries, in order to supplement the efforts of the Governments of such countries to attain the full realization of the economic, social and cultural rights of their people.

13. There is a need for States and international organizations, in cooperation with non-governmental organizations, to create favourable conditions at the national, regional and international levels to ensure the full and effective enjoyment of human rights. States should eliminate all violations of human rights and their causes, as well as obstacles to the enjoyment of these rights.

14. The existence of widespread extreme poverty inhibits the full and effective enjoyment of human rights; its immediate alleviation and eventual elimination must remain a high priority for the international community.

15. Respect for human rights and for fundamental freedoms without distinction of any kind is a fundamental rule of international human rights law. The speedy and comprehensive elimination of all forms of racism and racial discrimination, xenophobia and related intolerance is a priority task for the international community. Governments should take effective measures to prevent and combat them. Groups, institutions, intergovernmental and non-governmental organizations and individuals are urged to intensify their efforts in cooperating and coordinating their activities against these evils.

16. The World Conference on Human Rights welcomes the progress made in dismantling apartheid and calls upon the international community and the United Nations system to assist in this process.

The World Conference on Human Rights also deplores the continuing acts of violence aimed at undermining the quest for a peaceful dismantling of apartheid.

17. The acts, methods and practices of terrorism in all its forms and manifestations as well as linkage in some countries to drug trafficking are activities aimed at the destruction of human rights, fundamental freedoms and democracy, threatening territorial integrity, security of States and destabilizing legitimately constituted Governments. The international community should take the necessary steps to enhance cooperation to prevent and combat terrorism.

18. The human rights of women and of the girl-child are an inalienable, integral and indivisible part of universal human rights. The full and equal participation of women in political, civil, economic, social and cultural life, at the national, regional and international levels, and the eradication of all forms of discrimination on grounds of sex are priority objectives of the international community.

Gender-based violence and all forms of sexual harassment and exploitation, including those resulting from cultural prejudice and international trafficking, are incompatible with the dignity and worth of the human person, and must be eliminated. This can be achieved by legal measures and through national action and international cooperation in such fields as economic and social development, education, safe maternity and health care, and social support.

The human rights of women should form an integral part of the United Nations human rights activities, including the promotion of all human rights instruments relating to women.

The World Conference on Human Rights urges Governments, institutions, intergovernmental and non-governmental organizations to intensify their efforts for the protection and promotion of human rights of women and the girl-child.

19. Considering the importance of the promotion and protection of the rights of persons belonging to minorities and the contribution of such promotion and protection to the political and social stability of the States in which such persons live,

The World Conference on Human Rights reaffirms the obligation of States to ensure that persons belonging to minorities may exercise fully and effectively all human rights and fundamental freedoms without any discrimination and in full equality before the law in accordance with the Declaration on the Rights of Persons Belonging to National or Ethnic, Religious and Linguistic Minorities.

The persons belonging to minorities have the right to enjoy their own culture, to profess and practice their own religion and to use their own language in private and in public, freely and without interference or any form of discrimination.

20. The World Conference on Human Rights recognizes the inherent dignity and the unique contribution of indigenous people to the development and plurality of society and strongly reaffirms the commitment of the international community to their economic, social and cultural well-being and their enjoyment of the fruits of sustainable development. States should ensure the full and free participation of indigenous people in all aspects of society, in particular in matters of concern to them. Considering the importance of the promotion and protection of the rights of indigenous people, and the contribution of such promotion and protection to the political and social stability of the States in which such people live, States should, in accordance with international law, take concerted positive steps to ensure respect for all human rights and fundamental freedoms of indigenous people, on the basis of equality and non-discrimination, and recognize the value and diversity of their distinct identities, cultures and social organization.

21. The World Conference on Human Rights, welcoming the early ratification of the Convention on the Rights of the Child by a large number of States and noting the recognition of the human rights of children in the World Declaration on the Survival, Protection and Development of Children and Plan of Action adopted by the World Summit for Children, urges universal ratification of the Convention by 1995 and its effective implementation by States parties through the adoption of all the necessary legislative, administrative and other measures and the allocation to the maximum extent of the available resources. In all actions concerning children, non-discrimination and the best interest of the child should be primary considerations and the views of the child given due weight. National and international mechanisms and programmes should be strengthened for the defense and protection of children, in particular, the girl-child, abandoned children, street children, economically and sexually exploited children, including through child pornography, child prostitution or sale of organs, children victims of diseases including acquired immunodeficiency syndrome, refugee and displaced children, children in detention, children in armed conflict, as well as children victims of famine and drought and other emergencies. International cooperation and solidarity should be promoted to support the implementation of the Convention and the rights of the child should be a priority in the United Nations system-wide action on human rights.

The World Conference on Human Rights also stresses that the child for the full and harmonious development of his or her personality should grow up in a family environment which accordingly merits broader protection.

22. Special attention needs to be paid to ensuring non-discrimination, and the equal enjoyment of all human rights and fundamental freedoms by disabled persons, including their active participation in all aspects of society.

23. The World Conference on Human Rights reaffirms that everyone, without distinction of any kind, is entitled to the right to seek and to enjoy in other countries asylum from persecution, as well as the right to return to one's own country. In this respect it stresses the importance of the Universal Declaration of Human Rights, the 1951 Convention relating to the Status of Refugees, its 1967 Protocol and regional instruments. It expresses its appreciation to States that continue to admit and host large numbers of refugees in their territories, and to the Office of the United Nations High Commissioner for Refugees for its dedication to its task. It also expresses its appreciation to the United Nations Relief and Works Agency for Palestine Refugees in the Near East.

The World Conference on Human Rights recognizes that gross violations of human rights, including in armed conflicts, are among the multiple and complex factors leading to displacement of people.

The World Conference on Human Rights recognizes that, in view of the complexities of the global refugee crisis and in accordance with the Charter of the United Nations, relevant international instruments and international solidarity and in the spirit of burden-sharing, a comprehensive approach by the international community is needed in coordination and cooperation with the countries concerned and relevant organizations, bearing in mind the mandate of the United Nations High Commissioner for Refugees. This should include the development of strategies to address the root causes and effects of movements of refugees and other displaced persons, the strengthening of emergency preparedness and response mechanisms, the provision of effective protection and assistance, bearing in mind the special needs of women and children, as well as the achievement of durable solutions, primarily through the preferred solution of dignified and safe voluntary repatriation, including solutions such as those adopted by the international refugee conferences. The World Conference on Human Rights underlines the responsibilities of States, particularly as they relate to the countries of origin.

In the light of the comprehensive approach, the World Conference on Human Rights emphasizes the importance of giving special attention including through intergovernmental and humanitarian organizations and finding lasting solutions to questions related to internally displaced persons including their voluntary and safe return and rehabilitation.

In accordance with the Charter of the United Nations and the principles of humanitarian law, the World Conference on Human Rights further emphasizes the importance of and the need for humanitarian assistance to victims of all natural and man-made disasters.

24. Great importance must be given to the promotion and protection of the human rights of persons belonging to groups which have been rendered vulnerable, including migrant workers, the elimination of all forms of discrimination against them, and the strengthening and more effective implementation of existing human rights instruments. States have an obligation to create and maintain adequate measures at the national level, in particular in the

fields of education, health and social support, for the promotion and protection of the rights of persons in vulnerable sectors of their populations and to ensure the participation of those among them who are interested in finding a solution to their own problems.

25. The World Conference on Human Rights affirms that extreme poverty and social exclusion constitute a violation of human dignity and that urgent steps are necessary to achieve better knowledge of extreme poverty and its causes, including those related to the problem of development, in order to promote the human rights of the poorest, and to put an end to extreme poverty and social exclusion and to promote the enjoyment of the fruits of social progress. It is essential for States to foster participation by the poorest people in the decision-making process by the community in which they live, the promotion of human rights and efforts to combat extreme poverty.

26. The World Conference on Human Rights welcomes the progress made in the codification of human rights instruments, which is a dynamic and evolving process, and urges the universal ratification of human rights treaties. All States are encouraged to accede to these international instruments; all States are encouraged to avoid, as far as possible, the resort to reservations.

27. Every State should provide an effective framework of remedies to redress human rights grievances or violations. The administration of justice, including law enforcement and prosecutorial agencies and, especially, an independent judiciary and legal profession in full conformity with applicable standards contained in international human rights instruments, are essential to the full and non-discriminatory realization of human rights and indispensable to the processes of democracy and sustainable development. In this context, institutions concerned with the administration of justice should be properly funded, and an increased level of both technical and financial assistance should be provided by the international community. It is incumbent upon the United Nations to make use of special programmes of advisory services on a priority basis for the achievement of a strong and independent administration of justice.

28. The World Conference on Human Rights expresses its dismay at massive violations of human rights especially in the form of genocide, "ethnic cleansing" and systematic rape of women in war situations, creating mass exodus of refugees and displaced persons. While strongly condemning such abhorrent practices it reiterates the call that perpetrators of such crimes be punished and such practices immediately stopped.

29. The World Conference on Human Rights expresses grave concern about continuing human rights violations in all parts of the world in disregard of standards as contained in international human rights instruments and international humanitarian law and about the lack of sufficient and effective remedies for the victims.

The World Conference on Human Rights is deeply concerned about violations of human rights during armed conflicts, affecting the civilian population, especially women, children, the elderly and the disabled. The Conference therefore calls upon States and all parties to armed conflicts strictly to observe international humanitarian law, as set forth in the Geneva Conventions of 1949 and other rules and principles of international law, as well as minimum standards for protection of human rights, as laid down in international conventions.

The World Conference on Human Rights reaffirms the right of the victims to be assisted by humanitarian organizations, as set forth in the Geneva Conventions of 1949 and other relevant instruments of international humanitarian law, and calls for the safe and timely access for such assistance.

30. The World Conference on Human Rights also expresses its dismay and condemnation that gross and systematic violations and situations that constitute serious obstacles to the full enjoyment of all human rights continue to occur in different parts of the world. Such violations and obstacles include, as well as torture and cruel, inhuman and degrading treatment or punishment, summary and arbitrary executions, disappearances, arbitrary detentions, all forms of racism, racial discrimination and apartheid, foreign occupation and alien domination, xenophobia, poverty, hunger and other denials of economic, social and cultural rights, religious intolerance, terrorism, discrimination against women and lack of the rule of law.

31. The World Conference on Human Rights calls upon States to refrain from any unilateral measure not in accordance with international law and the Charter of the United Nations that creates obstacles to trade relations among States and impedes the full realization of the human rights set forth in the Universal Declaration of Human Rights and international human rights instruments, in particular the rights of everyone to a standard of living adequate for their health and well-being, including food and medical care, housing and the necessary social services. The World Conference on Human Rights affirms that food should not be used as a tool for political pressure.

32. The World Conference on Human Rights reaffirms the importance of ensuring the universality, objectivity and non-selectivity of the consideration of human rights issues.

33. The World Conference on Human Rights reaffirms that States are duty-bound, as stipulated in the Universal Declaration of Human Rights and the International Covenant on Economic, Social and Cultural Rights and in other international human rights instruments, to ensure that education is aimed at strengthening the respect of human rights and fundamental freedoms. The World Conference on Human Rights emphasizes the importance of incorporating the subject of human rights education programmes and calls upon States to do so. Education should promote understanding, tolerance, peace and friendly relations between the nations and all racial or religious groups and encourage the development of United Nations activities in pursuance of these objectives. Therefore, education on human rights and the dissemination of proper information, both theoretical and practical, play an important role in the promotion and respect of human rights with regard to all individuals without distinction of any kind such as race, sex, language or religion, and this should be integrated in the education policies at the national as well as

international levels. The World Conference on Human Rights notes that resource constraints and institutional inadequacies may impede the immediate realization of these objectives.

34. Increased efforts should be made to assist countries which so request to create the conditions whereby each individual can enjoy universal human rights and fundamental freedoms. Governments, the United Nations system as well as other multilateral organizations are urged to increase considerably the resources allocated to programmes aiming at the establishment and strengthening of national legislation, national institutions and related infrastructures which uphold the rule of law and democracy, electoral assistance, human rights awareness through training, teaching and education, popular participation and civil society.

The programmes of advisory services and technical cooperation under the Centre for Human Rights should be strengthened as well as made more efficient and transparent and thus become a major contribution to improving respect for human rights. States are called upon to increase their contributions to these programmes, both through promoting a larger allocation from the United Nations regular budget, and through voluntary contributions.

35. The full and effective implementation of United Nations activities to promote and protect human rights must reflect the high importance accorded to human rights by the Charter of the United Nations and the demands of the United Nations human rights activities, as mandated by Member States. To this end, United Nations human rights activities should be provided with increased resources.

36. The World Conference on Human Rights reaffirms the important and constructive role played by national institutions for the promotion and protection of human rights, in particular in their advisory capacity to the competent authorities, their role in remedying human rights violations, in the dissemination of human rights information, and education in human rights.

The World Conference on Human Rights encourages the establishment and strengthening of national institutions, having regard to the "Principles relating to the status of national institutions" and recognizing that it is the right of each State to choose the framework which is best suited to its particular needs at the national level.

37. Regional arrangements play a fundamental role in promoting and protecting human rights. They should reinforce universal human rights standards, as contained in international human rights instruments, and their protection. The World Conference on Human Rights endorses efforts under way to strengthen these arrangements and to increase their effectiveness, while at the same time stressing the importance of cooperation with the United Nations human rights activities.

The World Conference on Human Rights reiterates the need to consider the possibility of establishing regional and subregional arrangements for the promotion and protection of human rights where they do not already exist.

38. The World Conference on Human Rights recognizes the important role of non-governmental organizations in the promotion of all human rights and in humanitarian activities at national, regional and international levels. The World Conference on Human Rights appreciates their contribution to increasing public awareness of human rights issues, to the conduct of education, training and research in this field, and to the promotion and protection of all human rights and fundamental freedoms. While recognizing that the primary responsibility for standard-setting lies with States, the conference also appreciates the contribution of non-governmental organizations to this process. In this respect, the World Conference on Human Rights emphasizes the importance of continued dialogue and cooperation between Governments and non-governmental organizations. Non-governmental organizations and their members genuinely involved in the field of human rights should enjoy the rights and freedoms recognized in the Universal Declaration of Human Rights, and the protection of the national law. These rights and freedoms may not be exercised contrary to the purposes and principles of the United Nations. Non-governmental organizations should be free to carry out their human rights activities, without interference, within the framework of national law and the Universal Declaration of Human Rights.

39. Underlining the importance of objective, responsible and impartial information about human rights and humanitarian issues, the World Conference on Human Rights encourages the increased involvement of the media, for whom freedom and protection should be guaranteed within the framework of national law.

II
A. INCREASED COORDINATION ON HUMAN RIGHTS WITHIN THE UNITED NATIONS SYSTEM

1. The World Conference on Human Rights recommends increased coordination in support of human rights and fundamental freedoms within the United Nations system. To this end, the World Conference on Human Rights urges all United Nations organs, bodies and the specialized agencies whose activities deal with human rights to cooperate in order to strengthen, rationalize and streamline their activities, taking into account the need to avoid unnecessary duplication. The World Conference on Human Rights also recommends to the Secretary-General that high-level officials of relevant United Nations bodies and specialized agencies at their annual meeting, besides coordinating their activities, also assess the impact of their strategies and policies on the enjoyment of all human rights.

2. Furthermore, the World Conference on Human Rights calls on regional organizations and prominent international and regional finance and development institutions to assess also the impact of their policies and programmes on the enjoyment of human rights.

3. The World Conference on Human Rights recognizes that relevant specialized agencies and bodies and institutions of the United Nations system as

well as other relevant intergovernmental organizations whose activities deal with human rights play a vital role in the formulation, promotion and implementation of human rights standards, within their respective mandates, and should take into account the outcome of the World Conference on Human Rights within their fields of competence.

4. The World Conference on Human Rights strongly recommends that a concerted effort be made to encourage and facilitate the ratification of and accession or succession to international human rights treaties and protocols adopted within of the United Nations system with the aim of universal acceptance. The Secretary-General, in consultation with treaty bodies, should consider opening a dialogue with States not having acceded to these human rights treaties, in order to identify obstacles and to seek ways of overcoming them.

5. The World Conference on Human Rights encourages States to consider limiting the extent of any reservations they lodge to international human rights instruments, formulate any reservations as precisely and narrowly as possible, ensure that none is incompatible with the object and purpose of the relevant treaty and regularly review any reservations with a view to withdrawing them.

6. The World Conference on Human Rights, recognizing the need to maintain consistency with the high quality of existing international standards and to avoid proliferation of human rights instruments, reaffirms the guidelines relating to the elaboration of new international instruments contained in General Assembly resolution 41/120 of 4 December 1986 and calls on the United Nations human rights bodies, when considering the elaboration of new international standards, to keep those guidelines in mind, to consult with human rights treaty bodies on the necessity for drafting new standards and to request the Secretariat to carry out technical reviews of proposed new instruments.

7. The World Conference on Human Rights recommends that human rights officers be assigned if and when necessary to regional offices of the United Nations Organization with the purpose of disseminating information and offering training and other technical assistance in the field of human rights upon the request of concerned Member States. Human rights training for international civil servants who are assigned to work relating to human rights should be organized.

8. The World Conference on Human Rights welcomes the convening of emergency sessions of the Commission on Human Rights as a positive initiative and that other ways of responding to acute violations of human rights be considered by the relevant organs of the United Nations system.

Resources

9. The World Conference on Human Rights, concerned by the growing disparity between the activities of the Centre for Human Rights and the human, financial and other resources available to carry them out, and bearing in mind the resources needed for other important United Nations programmes, requests the Secretary-General and the General Assembly to take immediate

steps to increase substantially the resources for the human rights programme from within the existing and future regular budgets of the United Nations, and to take urgent steps to seek increased extra-budgetary resources.

10. Within this framework, an increased proportion of the regular budget should be allocated directly to the Centre for Human Rights to cover its costs and all other costs borne by the Centre for Human Rights, including those related to the United Nations human rights bodies. Voluntary funding of the Centre's technical cooperation activities should reinforce this enhanced budget; the World Conference on Human Rights calls for generous contributions to the existing trust funds.

11. The World Conference on Human Rights requests the Secretary-General and the General Assembly to provide sufficient human, financial and other resources to the Centre for Human Rights to enable it effectively, efficiently and expeditiously to carry out its activities.

12. The World Conference on Human Rights, noting the need to ensure that human and financial resources are available to carry out the human rights activities, as mandated by intergovernmental bodies, urges the Secretary-General, in accordance with Article 101 of the Charter of the United Nations, and Member States to adopt a coherent approach aimed at securing that resources commensurate to the increased mandates are allocated to the Secretariat. The World Conference on Human Rights invites the Secretary-General to consider whether adjustments to procedures in the programme budget cycle would be necessary or helpful to ensure the timely and effective implementation of human rights activities as mandated by Member States.

Centre for Human Rights

13. The World Conference on Human Rights stresses the importance of strengthening the United Nations Centre for Human Rights.

14. The Centre for Human Rights should play an important role in coordinating system-wide attention for human rights. The focal role of the Centre can best be realized if it is enabled to cooperate fully with other United Nations bodies and organs. The coordinating role of the Centre for Human Rights also implies that the office of the Centre for Human Rights in New York is strengthened.

15. The Centre for Human Rights should be assured adequate means for the system of thematic and country rapporteurs, experts, working groups and treaty bodies. Follow-up on recommendations should become a priority matter for consideration by the Commission on Human Rights.

16. The Centre for Human Rights should assume a larger role in the promotion of human rights. This role could be given shape through cooperation with Member States and by an enhanced programme of advisory services and technical assistance. The existing voluntary funds will have to be expanded substantially for these purposes and should be managed in a more efficient and coordinated way. All activities should follow strict and transparent project management rules and regular programme and project evaluations should be

held periodically. To this end, the results of such evaluation exercises and other relevant information should be made available regularly. The Centre should, in particular, organize at least once a year information meetings open to all Member States and organizations directly involved in these projects and programmes.

Adaptation and strengthening of the United Nations machinery for human rights, including the question of the establishment of a United Nations High Commissioner for Human Rights

17. The World Conference on Human Rights recognizes the necessity for a continuing adaptation of the United Nations human rights machinery to the current and future needs in the promotion and protection of human rights, as reflected in the present Declaration and within the framework of a balanced and sustainable development for all people. In particular, the United Nations human rights organs should improve their coordination, efficiency and effectiveness.

18. The World Conference on Human Rights recommends to the General Assembly that when examining the report of the Conference at its forty-eighth session, it begin, as a matter of priority, consideration of the question of the establishment of a High Commissioner for Human Rights for the promotion and protection of all human rights.

B. EQUALITY, DIGNITY AND TOLERANCE

1. Racism, racial discrimination, xenophobia and other forms of intolerance

19. The World Conference on Human Rights considers the elimination of racism and racial discrimination, in particular in their institutionalized forms such as apartheid or resulting from doctrines of racial superiority or exclusivity or contemporary forms and manifestations of racism, as a primary objective for the international community and a worldwide promotion programme in the field of human rights. United Nations organs and agencies should strengthen their efforts to implement such a programme of action related to the third decade to combat racism and racial discrimination as well as subsequent mandates to the same end. The World Conference on Human Rights strongly appeals to the international community to contribute generously to the Trust Fund for the Programme for the Decade for Action to Combat Racism and Racial Discrimination.

20. The World Conference on Human Rights urges all Governments to take immediate measures and to develop strong policies to prevent and combat all forms and manifestations of racism, xenophobia or related intolerance, where necessary by enactment of appropriate legislation, including penal measures, and by the establishment of national institutions to combat such phenomena.

21. The World Conference on Human Rights welcomes the decision of the Commission on Human Rights to appoint a Special Rapporteur on contemporary forms of racism, racial discrimination, xenophobia and related intolerance.

The World Conference on Human Rights also appeals to all States parties to the International Convention on the Elimination of All Forms of Racial Discrimination to consider making the declaration under article 14 of the Convention.

22. The World Conference on Human Rights calls upon all Governments to take all appropriate measures in compliance with their international obligations and with due regard to their respective legal systems to counter intolerance and related violence based on religion or belief, including practices of discrimination against women and including the desecration of religious sites, recognizing that every individual has the right to freedom of thought, conscience, expression and religion. The conference also invites all States to put into practice the revisions of the Declaration on the Elimination of All Forms of intolerance and of Discrimination Based on Religion or Belief.

23. The World Conference on Human Rights stresses that all persons who perpetrate or authorize criminal acts associated with ethnic cleansing are individually responsible and accountable for such human rights violations, and that the international community should exert every effort to bring those legally responsible for such violations to justice.

24. The World Conference on Human Rights calls on all States to take immediate measures, individually and collectively, to combat the practice of ethnic cleansing to bring it quickly to an end. Victims of the abhorrent practice of ethnic cleansing are entitled to appropriate and effective remedies.

2. Persons belonging to national or ethnic, religious and linguistic minorities

25. The World Conference on Human Rights calls on the Commission on Human Rights to examine ways and means to promote and protect effectively the rights of persons belonging to minorities as set out in the Declaration on the Rights of Persons belonging to National or Ethnic, Religious and Linguistic Minorities. In this context, the World Conference on Human Rights calls upon the Centre for Human Rights to provide, at the request of Governments concerned and as part of its programme of advisory services and technical assistance, qualified expertise on minority issues and human rights, as well as on the prevention and resolution of disputes, to assist in existing or potential situations involving minorities.

26. The World Conference on Human Rights urges States and the international community to promote and protect the rights of persons belonging to national or ethnic, religious and linguistic minorities in accordance with the Declaration on the Rights of Persons belonging to National or Ethnic, Religious and Linguistic Minorities.

27. Measures to be taken, where appropriate, should include facilitation of their full participation in all aspects of the political, economic, social, religious and cultural life of society and in the economic progress and development in their country.

Indigenous people

28. The World Conference on Human Rights calls on the Working Group on Indigenous Populations of the Sub-Commission on Prevention of Discrimination and Protection of Minorities to complete the drafting of a declaration on the rights of indigenous people at its eleventh session.

29. The World Conference on Human Rights recommends that the Commission on Human Rights consider the renewal and updating of the mandate of the Working Group on Indigenous Populations upon completion of the drafting of a declaration on the rights of indigenous people.

30. The World Conference on Human Rights also recommends that advisory services and technical assistance programmes within the United Nations system respond positively to requests by States for assistance which would be of direct benefit to indigenous people. The World Conference on Human Rights further recommends that adequate human and financial resources be made available to the Centre for Human Rights within the overall framework of strengthening the Centre's activities as envisaged by this document.

31. The World Conference on Human Rights urges States to ensure the full and free participation of indigenous people in all aspects of society, in particular in matters of concern to them.

32. The World Conference on Human Rights recommends that the General Assembly proclaim an international decade of the world's indigenous people, to begin from January 1994, including action-orientated programmes, to be decided upon in partnership with indigenous people. An appropriate voluntary trust fund should be set up for this purpose. In the framework of such a decade, the establishment of a permanent forum for indigenous people in the United Nations system should be considered.

Migrant workers

33. The World Conference on Human Rights urges all States to guarantee the protection of the human rights of all migrant workers and their families.

34. The World Conference on Human Rights considers that the creation of conditions to foster greater harmony and tolerance between migrant workers and the rest of the society of the State in which they reside is of particular importance.

35. The World Conference on Human Rights invites States to consider the possibility of signing and ratifying, at the earliest possible time, the International Convention on the Rights of All Migrant Workers and Members of Their Families.

3. The equal status and human rights of women

36. The World Conference on Human Rights urges the full and equal enjoyment by women of all human rights and that this be a priority for Governments and for the United Nations. The World Conference on Human

Rights also underlines the importance of the integration and full participation of women as both agents and beneficiaries in the development process, and reiterates the objectives established on global action for women towards sustainable and equitable development set forth in the Rio Declaration on Environment and Development and chapter 24 of Agenda 21, adopted by the United Nations Conference on Environment and Development (Rio de Janeiro, Brazil, 3-14 June 1992).

37. The equal status of women and the human rights of women should be integrated into the mainstream of United Nations system-wide activity. These issues should be regularly and systematically addressed throughout relevant United Nations bodies and mechanisms. In particular, steps should be taken to increase cooperation and promote further integration of objectives and goals between the Commission on the Status of Women, the Commission on Human Rights, the Committee for the Elimination of Discrimination against Women, the United Nations Development Fund for Women, the United Nations Development Programme and other United Nations agencies. In this context, cooperation and coordination should be strengthened between the Centre for Human Rights and the Division for the Advancement of Women.

38. In particular, the World Conference on Human Rights stresses the importance of working towards the elimination of violence against women in public and private life, the elimination of all forms of sexual harassment, exploitation and trafficking in women, the elimination of gender bias in the administration of justice and the eradication of any conflicts which may arise between the rights of women and the harmful effects of certain traditional or customary practices, cultural prejudices and religious extremism. The World Conference on Human Rights calls upon the General Assembly to adopt the draft declaration on violence against women and urges States to combat violence against women in accordance with its provisions. Violations of the human rights of women in situations of armed conflict are violations of the fundamental principles of international human rights and humanitarian law. All violations of this kind, including in particular murder, systematic rape, sexual slavery, and forced pregnancy, require a particularly effective response.

39. The World Conference on Human Rights urges the eradication of all forms of discrimination against women, both hidden and overt. The United Nations should encourage the goal of universal ratification by all States of the Convention on the Elimination of All Forms of Discrimination against Women by the year 2000. Ways and means of addressing the particularly large number of reservations to the Convention should be encouraged. Inter alia, the Committee on the Elimination of Discrimination against Women should continue its review of reservations to the Convention. States are urged to withdraw reservations that are contrary to the object and purpose of the Convention or which are otherwise incompatible with international treaty law.

40. Treaty monitoring bodies should disseminate necessary information to enable women to make more effective use of existing implementation procedures in their pursuits of full and equal enjoyment of human rights and non-discrimination. New procedures should also be adopted to strengthen implementation of

the commitment to women's equality and the human rights of women. The Commission on the Status of Women and the Committee on the Elimination of Discrimination against Women should quickly examine the possibility of introducing the right of petition through the preparation of an optional protocol to the Convention on the Elimination of All Forms of Discrimination against Women. The World Conference on Human Rights welcomes the decision of the Commission on Human Rights to consider the appointment of a special rapporteur on violence against women at its fiftieth session.

41. The World Conference on Human Rights recognizes the importance of the enjoyment by women of the highest standard of physical and mental health throughout their life span. In the context of the World Conference on Women and the Convention on the Elimination of All Forms of Discrimination against Women, as well as the Proclamation of Tehran of 1968, the World Conference on Human Rights reaffirms, on the basis of equality between women and men, a woman's right to accessible and adequate health care and the widest range of family planning services, as well as equal access to education at all levels.

42. Treaty monitoring bodies should include the status of women and the human rights of women in their deliberations and findings, making use of gender-specific data. States should be encouraged to supply information on the situation of women *de jure* and de facto in their reports to treaty monitoring bodies. The World Conference on Human Rights notes with satisfaction that the Commission on Human Rights adopted at its forty-ninth session resolution 1993/46 of 8 March 1993 stating that rapporteurs and working groups in the field of human rights should also be encouraged to do so. Steps should also be taken by the Division for the Advancement of Women in cooperation with other United Nations bodies, specifically the Centre for Human Rights, to ensure that the human rights activities of the United Nations regularly address violations of women's human rights, including gender-specific abuses. Training for United Nations human rights and humanitarian relief personnel to assist them to recognize and deal with human rights abuses particular to women and to carry out their work without gender bias should be encouraged.

43. The World Conference on Human Rights urges Governments and regional and international organizations to facilitate the access of women to decision-making posts and their greater participation in the decision-making process. It encourages further steps within the United Nations Secretariat to appoint and promote women staff members in accordance with the Charter of the United Nations, and encourages other principal and subsidiary organs of the United Nations to guarantee the participation of women under conditions of equality.

44. The World Conference on Human Rights welcomes the World Conference on Women to be held in Beijing in 1995 and urges that human rights of women should play an important role in its deliberations, in accordance with the priority themes of the World Conference on Women of equality, development and peace.

4. The rights of the child

45. The World Conference on Human Rights reiterates the principle of "First Call for Children" and, in this respect, underlines the importance of major national and international efforts, especially those of the United Nations Children's Fund, for promoting respect for the rights of the child to survival, protection, development and participation.

46. Measures should be taken to achieve universal ratification of the Convention on the Rights of the Child by 1995 and the universal signing of the World Declaration on the Survival, Protection and Development of Children and Plan of Action adopted by the World Summit for Children, as well as their effective implementation. The World Conference on Human Rights urges States to withdraw reservations to the Convention on the Rights of the Child contrary to the object and purpose of the Convention or otherwise contrary to international treaty law.

47. The World Conference on Human Rights urges all nations to undertake measures to the maximum extent of their available resources, with the support of international cooperation, to achieve the goals in the World Summit Plan of Action. The Conference calls on States to integrate the Convention on the Rights of the Child into their national action plans. By means of these national action plans and through international efforts, particular priority should be placed on reducing infant and maternal mortality rates, reducing malnutrition and illiteracy rates and providing access to safe drinking water and to basic education. Whenever so called for, national plans of action should be devised to combat devastating emergencies resulting from natural disasters and armed conflicts and the equally grave problem of children in extreme poverty.

48. The World Conference on Human Rights urges all States, with the support of international cooperation, to address the acute problem of children under especially difficult circumstances. Exploitation and abuse of children should be actively combated, including by addressing their root causes. Effective measures are required against female infanticide, harmful child labour, sale of children and organs, child prostitution, child pornography, as well as other forms of sexual abuse.

49. The World Conference on Human Rights supports all measures by the United Nations and its specialized agencies to ensure the effective protection and promotion of human rights of the girl child. The World Conference on Human Rights urges States to repeal existing laws and regulations and remove customs and practices which discriminate against and cause harm to the girl child.

50. The World Conference on Human Rights strongly supports the proposal that the Secretary-General initiate a study into means of improving the protection of children in armed conflicts. Humanitarian norms should be implemented and measures taken in order to protect and facilitate assistance to children in war zones. Measures should include protection for children against indiscriminate use of all weapons of war, especially anti-personnel mines. The

need for aftercare and rehabilitation of children traumatized by war must be addressed urgently. The Conference calls on the Committee on the Rights of the Child to study the question of raising the armed forces.

51. The World Conference on Human Rights recommends that matters relating to human rights and the situation of children be regularly reviewed and monitored by all relevant organs and mechanisms of the United Nations system and by the supervisory bodies of the specialized agencies in accordance with their mandates.

52. The World Conference on Human Rights recognizes the important role played by non-governmental organizations in the effective implementation of all human rights instruments and, in particular, the Convention on the Rights of the Child.

53. The World Conference on Human Rights recommends that the Committee on the Rights of the Child, with the assistance of the Centre for Human Rights, be enabled expeditiously and effectively to meet its mandate, especially in view of the unprecedented extent of ratification and subsequent submission of country reports.

5. Freedom from torture

54. The World Conference on Human Rights welcomes the ratification by many Member States of the Convention against Torture and Other Cruel, Inhuman or Degrading Treatment or Punishment and encourages its speedy ratification by all other Member States.

55. The World Conference on Human Rights emphasizes that one of the most atrocious violations against human dignity is the act of torture, the result of which destroys the dignity and impairs the capability of victims to continue their lives and their activities.

56. The World Conference on Human Rights reaffirms that under human rights law and international humanitarian law, freedom from torture is a right which must be protected under all circumstances, including in times of internal or international disturbance or armed conflicts.

57. The World Conference on Human Rights therefore urges all States to put an immediate end to the practice of torture and eradicate this evil forever through full implementation of the Universal Declaration of Human Rights as well as the relevant conventions and, where necessary, strengthening of existing mechanisms. The World Conference on Human Rights calls on all States to cooperate fully with the Special Rapporteur on the question of torture in the fulfillment of his mandate.

58. Special attention should be given to ensure universal respect for, and effective implementation of, the Principles of Medical Ethics relevant to the Role of Health Personnel, particularly Physicians, in the Protection of Prisoners and Detainees against Torture and other Cruel, Inhuman or Degrading Treatment or Punishment adopted by the General Assembly of the United Nations.

59. The World Conference on Human Rights stresses the importance of further concrete action within the framework of the United Nations with the view to providing assistance to victims of torture and ensure more effective remedies for their physical, psychological and social rehabilitation. Providing the necessary resources for this purpose should be given high priority, inter alia, by additional contributions to the United Nations Voluntary Fund for the Victims of Torture.

60. States should abrogate legislation leading to impunity for those responsible for grave violations of human rights such as torture and prosecute such violations, thereby providing a firm basis for the rule of law.

61. The World Conference on Human Rights reaffirms that efforts to eradicate torture should, first and foremost, be concentrated on prevention and, therefore, calls for the early adoption of an optional protocol to the Convention against Torture and Other Cruel, Inhuman and Degrading Treatment or Punishment, which is intended to establish a preventive system of regular visits to places of detention.

Enforced disappearances

62. The World Conference on Human Rights, welcoming the adoption by the General Assembly of the Declaration on the Protection of All Persons from Enforced Disappearance, calls upon all States to take effective legislative, administrative, judicial or other measures to prevent, terminate and punish acts of enforced disappearances. The World Conference on Human Rights reaffirms that it is the duty of all States, under any circumstances, to make investigations whenever there is reason to believe that an enforced disappearance has taken place on a territory under their jurisdiction and, if allegations are confirmed, to prosecute its perpetrators.

6. The rights of the disabled person

63. The World Conference on Human Rights reaffirms that all human rights and fundamental freedoms are universal and thus unreservedly include persons with disabilities. Every person is born equal and has the same rights to life and welfare, education and work, living independently and active participation in all aspects of society. Any direct discrimination or other negative discriminatory treatment of a disabled person is therefore a violation of his or her rights. The World Conference on Human Rights calls on Governments, where necessary, to adopt or adjust legislation to assure access to these and other rights for disabled persons.

64. The place of disabled persons is everywhere. Persons with disabilities should be guaranteed equal opportunity through the elimination of all socially determined barriers, be they physical, financial, social or psychological, which exclude or restrict full participation in society.

65. Recalling the World Programme of Action concerning Disabled Persons, adopted by the General Assembly at its thirty-seventh session, the World Conference on Human Rights calls upon the General Assembly and the

Economic and Social Council to adopt the draft standard rules on the equalization of opportunities for persons with disabilities, at their meetings in 1993.

C. COOPERATION, DEVELOPMENT AND STRENGTHENING OF HUMAN RIGHTS

66. The World Conference on Human Rights recommends that priority be given to national and international action to promote democracy, development and human rights.

67. Special emphasis should be given to measures to assist in the strengthening and building of institutions relating to human rights, strengthening of a pluralistic civil society and the protection of groups which have been rendered vulnerable. In this context, assistance provided upon the request of Governments for the conduct of free and fair elections, including assistance in the human rights aspects of elections and public information about elections, is of particular importance. Equally important is the assistance to be given to the strengthening of the rule of law, the promotion of freedom of expression and the administration of justice, and to the real and effective participation of the people in the decision-making processes.

68. The World Conference on Human Rights stresses the need for the implementation of strengthened advisory services and technical assistance activities by the Centre for Human Rights. The Centre should make available to States upon request assistance on specific human rights issues, including the preparation of reports under human rights treaties as well as for the implementation of coherent and comprehensive plans of action for the promotion and protection of human rights. Strengthening the institutions of human rights and democracy, the legal protection of human rights, training of officials and others, broad-based education and public information aimed at promoting respect for human rights should all be available as components of these programmes.

69. The World Conference on Human Rights strongly recommends that a comprehensive programme be established within the United Nations in order to help States in the task of building and strengthening adequate national structures which have a direct impact on the overall observance of human rights and the maintenance of the rule of law. Such a programme, to be coordinated by the Centre for Human Rights, should be able to provide, upon the request of the interested Government, technical and financial assistance to national projects in reforming penal and correctional establishments, education and training of lawyers, judges and security forces in human rights, and any other sphere of activity relevant to the good functioning of the rule of law. That programme should make available to States assistance for the implementation of plans of action for the promotion and protection of human rights.

70. The World Conference on Human Rights requests the Secretary-General of the United Nations to submit proposals to the United Nations General Assembly, containing alternatives for the establishment, structure, operational modalities and funding of the proposed programme.

71. The World Conference on Human Rights recommends that each State consider the desirability of drawing up a national action plan identifying steps whereby that State would improve the promotion and protection of human rights.

72. The World Conference on Human Rights on Human Rights reaffirms that the universal and inalienable right to development, as established in the Declaration on the Right to Development, must be implemented and realized. In this context, the World Conference on Human Rights welcomes the appointment by the Commission on Human Rights of a thematic working group on the right to development and urges that the Working Group, in consultation and cooperation with other organs and agencies of the United Nations system, promptly formulate, for early consideration by the United Nations General Assembly, comprehensive and effective measures to eliminate obstacles to the implementation and realization of the Declaration on the Right to Development and recommending ways and means towards the realization of the right to development by all States.

73. The World Conference on Human Rights recommends that non-governmental and other grass-roots organizations active in development and/or human rights should be enabled to play a major role on the national and international levels in the debate, activities and implementation relating to the right to development and, in cooperation with Governments, in all relevant aspects of development cooperation.

74. The World Conference on Human Rights appeals to Governments, competent agencies and institutions to increase considerably the resources devoted to building well-functioning legal systems able to protect human rights, and to national institutions working in this area. Actors in the field of development cooperation should bear in mind the mutually reinforcing interrelationship between development, democracy and human rights. Cooperation should be based on dialogue and transparency. The World Conference on Human Rights also calls for the establishment of comprehensive programmes, including resource banks of information and personnel with expertise relating to the strengthening of the rule of law and of democratic institutions.

75. The World Conference on Human Rights encourages the Commission on Human Rights, in cooperation with the Committee on Economic, Social and Cultural Rights, to continue the examination of optional protocols to the International Covenant on Economic, Social and Cultural Rights.

76. The World Conference on Human Rights recommends that more resources be made available for the strengthening or the establishment of regional arrangements for the promotion and protection of human rights under the programmes of advisory services and technical assistance of the Centre for Human Rights. States are encouraged to request assistance for such purposes as regional and subregional workshops, seminars and information exchanges designed to strengthen regional arrangements for the promotion and protection of human rights in accord with universal human rights standards as contained in international human rights instruments.

308 SELECTED INTERNATIONAL HUMAN RIGHTS INSTRUMENTS

77. The World Conference on Human Rights supports all measures by the United Nations and its relevant specialized agencies to ensure the effective promotion and protection of trade union rights, as stipulated in the International Covenant on Economic, Social and Cultural Rights and other relevant international instruments. It calls on all States to abide fully by their obligations in this regard contained in international instruments.

D. HUMAN RIGHTS EDUCATION

78. The World Conference on Human Rights considers human rights education, training and public information essential for the promotion and achievement of stable and harmonious relations among communities and for fostering mutual understanding, tolerance and peace.

79. States should strive to eradicate illiteracy and should direct education towards the full development of the human personality and to the strengthening of respect for human rights and fundamental freedoms. The World Conference on Human Rights calls on all States and institutions to include human rights, humanitarian law, democracy and rule of law as subjects in the curricula of all learning institutions in formal and non-formal settings.

80. Human rights education should include peace, democracy, development and social justice, as set forth in international and regional human rights instruments, in order to achieve common understanding and awareness with a view to strengthening universal commitment to human rights.

81. Taking into account the World Plan of Action on Education for Human Rights and Democracy, adopted in March 1993 by the International Congress on Education for Human Rights and Democracy of the United Nations Educational, Scientific and Cultural Organization, and other human rights instruments, the World Conference on Human Rights recommends that States develop specific programmes and strategies for ensuring the widest human rights education and the dissemination of public information, taking particular account of the human rights needs of women.

82. Governments, with the assistance of intergovernmental organizations, national institutions and non-governmental organizations, should promote an increased awareness of human rights and mutual tolerance. The World Conference on Human Rights underlines the importance of strengthening the World Public Information Campaign for Human Rights carried out by the United Nations. They should initiate and support education in human rights and undertake effective dissemination of public information in this field. The advisory services and technical assistance programmes of the United Nations system should be able to respond immediately to requests from States for educational and training activities in the field of human rights as well as for special education concerning standards as contained in international human rights instruments and in humanitarian law and their application to special groups such as military forces, law enforcement personnel, police and the health profession. The proclamation of a United Nations decade for human

rights education in order to promote, encourage and focus these educational activities should be considered.

E. IMPLEMENTATION AND MONITORING METHODS

83. The World Conference on Human Rights urges Governments to incorporate standards as contained in international human rights instruments in domestic legislation and to strengthen national structures, institutions and organs of society which play a role in promoting and safeguarding human rights.

84. The World Conference on Human Rights recommends the strengthening of United Nations activities and programmes to meet requests for assistance by States which want to establish or strengthen their own national institutions for the promotion and protection of human rights.

85. The World Conference on Human Rights also encourages the strengthening of cooperation between national institutions for the promotion and protection of human rights, particularly through exchanges of information and experience, as well as cooperation with regional organizations and the United Nations.

86. The World Conference on Human Rights strongly recommends in this regard that representatives of national institutions for the promotion and protection of human rights convene periodic meetings under the auspices of the Centre for Human Rights to examine ways and means of improving their mechanisms and sharing experiences.

87. The World Conference on Human Rights recommends to the human rights treaty bodies, to the meetings of chairpersons of the treaty bodies and to the meetings of States parties that they continue to take steps aimed at coordinating the multiple reporting requirements and guidelines for preparing State reports under the respective human rights conventions and study the suggestion that the submission of one overall report on treaty obligations undertaken by each State would make these procedures more effective and increase their impact.

88. The World Conference on Human Rights recommends that the States parties to international human rights instruments, the General Assembly and the Economic and Social Council should consider studying the existing human rights treaty bodies and the various thematic mechanisms and procedures with a view to promoting greater efficiency and effectiveness through better coordination of the various bodies, mechanisms and procedures, taking into account the need to avoid unnecessary duplication and overlapping of their mandates and tasks.

89. The World Conference on Human Rights recommends continued work on the improvement of the functioning, including the monitoring tasks, of the treaty bodies, taking into account multiple proposals made in this respect, in particular those made by the treaty bodies themselves and by the

meetings of the chairpersons of the treaty bodies. The comprehensive national approach taken by the Committee on the Rights of the Child should also be encouraged.

90. The World Conference on Human Rights recommends that States parties to human rights treaties consider accepting all the available optional communication procedures.

91. The World Conference on Human Rights views with concern the issue of impunity of perpetrators of human rights violations, and supports the efforts of the Commission on Human Rights and the Sub-Commission on Prevention of Discrimination and Protection of Minorities to examine all aspects of the issue.

92. The World Conference on Human Rights recommends that the Commission on Human Rights examine the possibility for better implementation of existing human rights instruments at the international and regional levels and encourages the International Law Commission to continue its work on an international criminal court.

93. The World Conference on Human Rights appeals to States which have not yet done so to accede to the Geneva Conventions of 12 August 1949 and the Protocols thereto, and to take all appropriate national measures, including legislative ones, for their full implementation.

94. The World Conference on Human Rights recommends the speedy completion and adoption of the draft declaration on the right and responsibility of individuals, groups and organs of society to promote and protect universally recognized human rights and fundamental freedoms.

95. The World Conference on Human Rights underlines the importance of preserving and strengthening the system of special procedures, rapporteurs, representatives, experts and working groups of the Commission on Human Rights and the Sub-Commission on the Prevention of Discrimination and Protection of Minorities, in order to enable them to carry out their mandates in all countries throughout the world, providing them with the necessary human and financial resources. The procedures and mechanisms should be enabled to harmonize and rationalize their work through periodic meetings. All States are asked to cooperate fully with these procedures and mechanisms.

96. The World Conference on Human Rights recommends that the United Nations assume a more active role in the promotion and protection of human rights in ensuring full respect for international humanitarian law in all situations of armed conflict, in accordance with the purposes and principles of the Charter of the United Nations.

97. The World Conference on Human Rights, recognizing the important role of human rights components in specific arrangements concerning some peace-keeping operations by the United Nations, recommends that the Secretary-General take into account the reporting, experience and capabilities of the Centre for Human Rights and human rights mechanisms, in conformity with the Charter of the United Nations.

98. To strengthen the enjoyment of economic, social and cultural rights, additional approaches should be examined, such as a system of indicators to measure progress in the realization of the rights set forth in the International Covenant on Economic, Social and Cultural Rights. There must be a concerted effort to ensure recognition of economic, social and cultural rights at the national, regional and international levels.

F. FOLLOW-UP TO THE WORLD CONFERENCE ON HUMAN RIGHTS

99. The World Conference on Human Rights on Human Rights recommends that the General Assembly, the Commission on Human Rights and other organs and agencies of the United Nations system related to human rights consider ways and means for the full implementation, without delay, of the recommendations contained in the present Declaration, including the possibility of proclaiming a United Nations decade for human rights. The World Conference on Human Rights further recommends that the Commission on Human Rights annually review the progress towards this end.

100. The World Conference on Human Rights requests the Secretary-General of the United Nations to invite on the occasion of the fiftieth anniversary of the Universal Declaration of Human Rights all States, all organs and agencies of the United Nations system related to human rights, to report to him on the progress made in the implementation of the present Declaration and to submit a report to the General Assembly at its fifty-third session, through the Commission on Human Rights and the Economic and Social Council. Likewise, regional and, as appropriate, national human rights institutions, as well as non-governmental organizations, may present their views to the Secretary-General on the progress made in the implementation of the present Declaration. Special attention should be paid to assessing the progress towards the goal of universal ratification of international human rights treaties and protocols adopted within the framework of the United Nations system.

DECLARATION ON THE ELIMINATION OF VIOLENCE AGAINST WOMEN, G.A. res. 48/104, 48 U.N. GAOR Supp. (No. 49) at 217, U.N. Doc. A/48/49 (1993):

The General Assembly,

Recognizing the urgent need for the universal application to women of the rights and principles with regard to equality, security, liberty, integrity and dignity of all human beings,

Noting that those rights and principles are enshrined in international instruments, including the Universal Declaration of Human Rights, the International Covenant on Civil and Political Rights, the International Covenant on Economic, Social and Cultural Rights, the Convention on the Elimination of All Forms of Discrimination against Women and the Convention against Torture and Other Cruel, Inhuman or Degrading Treatment or Punishment,

Recognizing that effective implementation of the Convention on the Elimination of All Forms of Discrimination against Women would contribute to the elimination of violence against women and that the Declaration on the Elimination of Violence against Women, set forth in the present resolution, will strengthen and complement that process,

Concerned that violence against women is an obstacle to the achievement of equality, development and peace, as recognized in the Nairobi Forward-looking Strategies for the Advancement of Women, in which a set of measures to combat violence against women was recommended, and to the full implementation of the Convention on the Elimination of All Forms of Discrimination against Women,

Affirming that violence against women constitutes a violation of the rights and fundamental freedoms of women and impairs or nullifies their enjoyment of those rights and freedoms, and concerned about the long-standing failure to protect and promote those rights and freedoms in the case of violence against women,

Recognizing that violence against women is a manifestation of historically unequal power relations between men and women, which have led to domination over and discrimination against women by men and to the prevention of the full advancement of women, and that violence against women is one of the crucial social mechanisms by which women are forced into a subordinate position compared with men,

Concerned that some groups of women, such as women belonging to minority groups, indigenous women, refugee women, migrant women, women living in rural or remote communities, destitute women, women in institutions or in detention, female children, women with disabilities, elderly women and women in situations of armed conflict, are especially vulnerable to violence,

Recalling the conclusion in paragraph 23 of the annex to Economic and Social Council resolution 1990/15 of 24 May 1990 that the recognition that violence against women in the family and society was pervasive and cut across lines of income, class and culture had to be matched by urgent and effective steps to eliminate its incidence,

Recalling also Economic and Social Council resolution 1991/18 of 30 May 1991, in which the Council recommended the development of a framework for an international instrument that would address explicitly the issue of violence against women,

Welcoming the role that women's movements are playing in drawing increasing attention to the nature, severity and magnitude of the problem of violence against women,

Alarmed that opportunities for women to achieve legal, social, political and economic equality in society are limited, inter alia, by continuing and endemic violence,

Convinced that in the light of the above there is a need for a clear and comprehensive definition of violence against women, a clear statement of the rights to be applied to ensure the elimination of violence against women in all its forms, a commitment by States in respect of their responsibilities, and a commitment by the international community at large to the elimination of violence against women,

Solemnly proclaims the following Declaration on the Elimination of Violence against Women and urges that every effort be made so that it becomes generally known and respected:

Article 1

For the purposes of this Declaration, the term "violence against women" means any act of gender-based violence that results in, or is likely to result in, physical, sexual or psychological harm or suffering to women, including threats of such acts, coercion or arbitrary deprivation of liberty, whether occurring in public or in private life.

Article 2

Violence against women shall be understood to encompass, but not be limited to, the following:

(a) Physical, sexual and psychological violence occurring in the family, including battering, sexual abuse of female children in the household, dowry-related violence, marital rape, female genital mutilation and other traditional practices harmful to women, non-spousal violence and violence related to exploitation;

(b) Physical, sexual and psychological violence occurring within the general community, including rape, sexual abuse, sexual harassment and intimidation at work, in educational institutions and elsewhere, trafficking in women and forced prostitution;

(c) Physical, sexual and psychological violence perpetrated or condoned by the State, wherever it occurs.

Article 3

Women are entitled to the equal enjoyment and protection of all human rights and fundamental freedoms in the political, economic, social, cultural, civil or any other field. These rights include, inter alia:

(a) The right to life;

(b) The right to equality;

(c) The right to liberty and security of person;

(d) The right to equal protection under the law;

(e) The right to be free from all forms of discrimination;

(f) The right to the highest standard attainable of physical and mental health;

(g) The right to just and favourable conditions of work;

(h) The right not to be subjected to torture, or other cruel, inhuman or degrading treatment or punishment.

Article 4

States should condemn violence against women and should not invoke any custom, tradition or religious consideration to avoid their obligations with respect to its elimination. States should pursue by all appropriate means and without delay a policy of eliminating violence against women and, to this end, should:

(a) Consider, where they have not yet done so, ratifying or acceding to the Convention on the Elimination of All Forms of Discrimination against Women or withdrawing reservations to that Convention;

(b) Refrain from engaging in violence against women;

(c) Exercise due diligence to prevent, investigate and, in accordance with national legislation, punish acts of violence against women, whether those acts are perpetrated by the State or by private persons;

(d) Develop penal, civil, labour and administrative sanctions in domestic legislation to punish and redress the wrongs caused to women who are subjected to violence; women who are subjected to violence should be provided with access to the mechanisms of justice and, as provided for by national legislation, to just and effective remedies for the harm that they have suffered; States should also inform women of their rights in seeking redress through such mechanisms;

(e) Consider the possibility of developing national plans of action to promote the protection of women against any form of violence, or to include provisions for that purpose in plans already existing, taking into account, as appropriate, such cooperation as can be provided by non-governmental organizations, particularly those concerned with the issue of violence against women;

(f) Develop, in a comprehensive way, preventive approaches and all those measures of a legal, political, administrative and cultural nature that promote the protection of women against any form of violence, and ensure that the revictimization of women does not occur because of laws insensitive to gender considerations, enforcement practices or other interventions;

(g) Work to ensure, to the maximum extent feasible in the light of their available resources and, where needed, within the framework of international cooperation, that women subjected to violence and, where appropriate, their children have specialized assistance, such as rehabilitation, assistance in child care and maintenance, treatment, counselling, and health and social services, facilities and programmes, as well as support structures, and should take all other appropriate measures to promote their safety and physical and psychological rehabilitation;

(h) Include in government budgets adequate resources for their activities related to the elimination of violence against women;

(i) Take measures to ensure that law enforcement officers and public officials responsible for implementing policies to prevent, investigate and punish violence against women receive training to sensitize them to the needs of women;

(j) Adopt all appropriate measures, especially in the field of education, to modify the social and cultural patterns of conduct of men and women and to eliminate prejudices, customary practices and all other practices based on the idea of the inferiority or superiority of either of the sexes and on stereotyped roles for men and women;

(k) Promote research, collect data and compile statistics, especially concerning domestic violence, relating to the prevalence of different forms of violence against women and encourage research on the causes, nature, seriousness and consequences of violence against women and on the effectiveness of measures implemented to prevent and redress violence against women; those statistics and findings of the research will be made public;

(l) Adopt measures directed towards the elimination of violence against women who are especially vulnerable to violence;

(m) Include, in submitting reports as required under relevant human rights instruments of the United Nations, information pertaining to violence against women and measures taken to implement the present Declaration;

(n) Encourage the development of appropriate guidelines to assist in the implementation of the principles set forth in the present Declaration;

(o) Recognize the important role of the women's movement and non-governmental organizations world wide in raising awareness and alleviating the problem of violence against women;

(p) Facilitate and enhance the work of the women's movement and non-governmental organizations and cooperate with them at local, national and regional levels;

(q) Encourage intergovernmental regional organizations of which they are members to include the elimination of violence against women in their programmes, as appropriate.

Article 5

The organs and specialized agencies of the United Nations system should, within their respective fields of competence, contribute to the recognition and realization of the rights and the principles set forth in the present Declaration and, to this end, should, inter alia:

(a) Foster international and regional cooperation with a view to defining regional strategies for combating violence, exchanging experiences and financing programmes relating to the elimination of violence against women;

(b) Promote meetings and seminars with the aim of creating and raising awareness among all persons of the issue of the elimination of violence against women;

(c) Foster coordination and exchange within the United Nations system between human rights treaty bodies to address the issue of violence against women effectively;

(d) Include in analyses prepared by organizations and bodies of the United Nations system of social trends and problems, such as the periodic reports on the world social situation, examination of trends in violence against women;

(e) Encourage coordination between organizations and bodies of the United Nations system to incorporate the issue of violence against women into ongoing programmes, especially with reference to groups of women particularly vulnerable to violence;

(f) Promote the formulation of guidelines or manuals relating to violence against women, taking into account the measures referred to in the present Declaration;

(g) Consider the issue of the elimination of violence against women, as appropriate, in fulfilling their mandates with respect to the implementation of human rights instruments;

(h) Cooperate with non-governmental organizations in addressing the issue of violence against women.

Article 6

Nothing in the present Declaration shall affect any provision that is more conducive to the elimination of violence against women that may be contained in the legislation of a State or in any international convention, treaty or other instrument in force in a State.

BODY OF PRINCIPLES FOR THE PROTECTION OF ALL PERSONS UNDER ANY FORM OF DETENTION OR IMPRISONMENT, G.A. res. 43/173, annex, 43 U.N. GAOR Supp. (No. 49) at 298, U.N. Doc. A/43/49 (1988):

SCOPE OF THE BODY OF PRINCIPLES

These principles apply for the protection of all persons under any form of detention or imprisonment.

USE OF TERMS

For the purposes of the Body of Principles:

(a) "Arrest" means the act of apprehending a person for the alleged commission of an offence or by the action of an authority;

(b) "Detained person" means any person deprived of personal liberty except as a result of conviction for an offence;

(c) "Imprisoned person" means any person deprived of personal liberty as a result of conviction for an offence;

(d) "Detention" means the condition of detained persons as defined above;

(e) "Imprisonment" means the condition of imprisoned persons as defined above;

(f) The words "a judicial or other authority" means a judicial or other authority under the law whose status and tenure should afford the strongest possible guarantees of competence, impartiality and independence.

Principle 1

All persons under any form of detention or imprisonment shall be treated in a humane manner and with respect for the inherent dignity of the human person.

Principle 2

Arrest, detention or imprisonment shall only be carried out strictly in accordance with the provisions of the law and by competent officials or persons authorized for that purpose.

Principle 3

There shall be no restriction upon or derogation from any of the human rights of persons under any form of detention or imprisonment recognized or existing in any State pursuant to law, conventions, regulations or custom on the pretext that this Body of Principles does not recognize such rights or that it recognizes them to a lesser extent.

Principle 4

Any form of detention or imprisonment and all measures affecting the human rights of a person under any form of detention or imprisonment shall be ordered by, or be subject to the effective control of, a judicial or other authority.

Principle 5

1. These principles shall be applied to all persons within the territory of any given State, without distinction of any kind, such as race, colour, sex, language, religion or religious belief, political or other opinion, national, ethnic or social origin, property, birth or other status.

2. Measures applied under the law and designed solely to protect the rights and special status of women, especially pregnant women and nursing mothers, children and juveniles, aged, sick or handicapped persons shall not be deemed to be discriminatory. The need for, and the application of, such measures shall always be subject to review by a judicial or other authority.

Principle 6

No person under any form of detention or imprisonment shall be subjected to torture or to cruel, inhuman or degrading treatment or punishment.*

---

*The term "cruel, inhuman or degrading treatment or punishment" should be interpreted so as to extend the widest possible protection against abuses, whether physical or mental, including the holding of a detained or imprisoned person in conditions which deprive him, temporarily or permanently, of the use of any of his natural senses, such as sight or hearing, or of his awareness of place and the passing of time.

No circumstance whatever may be invoked as a justification for torture or other cruel, inhuman or degrading treatment or punishment.

Principle 7

1. States should prohibit by law any act contrary to the rights and duties contained in these principles, make any such act subject to appropriate sanctions and conduct impartial investigations upon complaints.

2. Officials who have reason to believe that a violation of this Body of Principles has occurred or is about to occur shall report the matter to their superior authorities and, where necessary, to other appropriate authorities or organs vested with reviewing or remedial powers.

3. Any other person who has ground to believe that a violation of this Body of Principles has occurred or is about to occur shall have the right to report the matter to the superiors of the officials involved as well as to other appropriate authorities or organs vested with reviewing or remedial powers.

Principle 8

Persons in detention shall be subject to treatment appropriate to their unconvicted status. Accordingly, they shall, whenever possible, be kept separate from imprisoned persons.

Principle 9

The authorities which arrest a person, keep him under detention or investigate the case shall exercise only the powers granted to them under the law and the exercise of these powers shall be subject to recourse to a judicial or other authority.

Principle 10

Anyone who is arrested shall be informed at the time of his arrest of the reason for his arrest and shall be promptly informed of any charges against him.

Principle 11

1. A person shall not be kept in detention without being given an effective opportunity to be heard promptly by a judicial or other authority. A detained person shall have the right to defend himself or to be assisted by counsel as prescribed by law.

2. A detained person and his counsel, if any, shall receive prompt and full communication of any order of detention, together with the reasons therefor.

3. A judicial or other authority shall be empowered to review as appropriate the continuance of detention.

Principle 12

1. There shall be duly recorded:

(a) The reasons for the arrest;

(b) The time of the arrest and the taking of the arrested person to a place of custody as well as that of his first appearance before a judicial or other authority;

(c) The identity of the law enforcement officials concerned;

(d) Precise information concerning the place of custody.

2. Such records shall be communicated to the detained person, or his counsel, if any, in the form prescribed by law.

Principle 13

Any person shall, at the moment of arrest and at the commencement of detention or imprisonment, or promptly thereafter, be provided by the authority responsible for his arrest, detention or imprisonment, respectively with information on and an explanation of his rights and how to avail himself of such rights.

Principle 14

A person who does not adequately understand or speak the language used by the authorities responsible for his arrest, detention or imprisonment is entitled to receive promptly in a language which he understands the information referred to in principle 10, principle 11, paragraph 2, principle 12, paragraph 1, and principle 13 and to have the assistance, free of charge, if necessary, of an interpreter in connection with legal proceedings subsequent to his arrest.

Principle 15

Notwithstanding the exceptions contained in principle 16, paragraph 4, and principle 18, paragraph 3, communication of the detained or imprisoned person with the outside world, and in particular his family or counsel, shall not be denied for more than a matter of days.

Principle 16

1. Promptly after arrest and after each transfer from one place of detention or imprisonment to another, a detained or imprisoned person shall be entitled to notify or to require the competent authority to notify members of his family or other appropriate persons of his choice of his arrest, detention or imprisonment or of the transfer and of the place where he is kept in custody.

2. If a detained or imprisoned person is a foreigner, he shall also be promptly informed of his right to communicate by appropriate means with a consular post or the diplomatic mission of the State of which he is a national or which is otherwise entitled to receive such communication in accordance with international law or with the representative of the competent international organization, if he is a refugee or is otherwise under the protection of an intergovernmental organization.

3. If a detained or imprisoned person is a juvenile or is incapable of understanding his entitlement, the competent authority shall on its own

initiative undertake the notification referred to in the present principle. Special attention shall be given to notifying parents or guardians.

4. Any notification referred to in the present principle shall be made or permitted to be made without delay. The competent authority may however delay a notification for a reasonable period where exceptional needs of the investigation so require.

Principle 17

1. A detained person shall be entitled to have the assistance of a legal counsel. He shall be informed of his right by the competent authority promptly after arrest and shall be provided with reasonable facilities for exercising it.

2. If a detained person does not have a legal counsel of his own choice, he shall be entitled to have a legal counsel assigned to him by a judicial or other authority in all cases where the interests of justice so require and without payment by him if he does not have sufficient means to pay.

Principle 18

1. A detained or imprisoned person shall be entitled to communicate and consult with his legal counsel.

2. A detained or imprisoned person shall be allowed adequate time and facilities for consultation with his legal counsel.

3. The right of a detained or imprisoned person to be visited by and to consult and communicate, without delay or censorship and in full confidentiality, with his legal counsel may not be suspended or restricted save in exceptional circumstances, to be specified by law or lawful regulations, when it is considered indispensable by a judicial or other authority in order to maintain security and good order.

4. Interviews between a detained or imprisoned person and his legal counsel may be within sight, but not within the hearing, of a law enforcement official.

5. Communications between a detained or imprisoned person and his legal counsel mentioned in the present principle shall be inadmissible as evidence against the detained or imprisoned person unless they are connected with a continuing or contemplated crime.

Principle 19

A detained or imprisoned person shall have the right to be visited by and to correspond with, in particular, members of his family and shall be given adequate opportunity to communicate with the outside world, subject to reasonable conditions and restrictions as specified by law or lawful regulations.

Principle 20

If a detained or imprisoned person so requests, he shall if possible be kept in a place of detention or imprisonment reasonably near his usual place of residence.

Principle 21

1. It shall be prohibited to take undue advantage of the situation of a detained or imprisoned person for the purpose of compelling him to confess, to incriminate himself otherwise or to testify against any other person.

2. No detained person while being interrogated shall be subject to violence, threats or methods of interrogation which impair his capacity of decision or his judgement.

Principle 22

No detained or imprisoned person shall, even with his consent, be subjected to any medical or scientific experimentation which may be detrimental to his health.

Principle 23

1. The duration of any interrogation of a detained or imprisoned person and of the intervals between interrogations as well as the identity of the officials who conducted the interrogations and other persons present shall be recorded and certified in such form as may be prescribed by law.

2. A detained or imprisoned person, or his counsel when provided by law, shall have access to the information described in paragraph 1 of the present principle.

Principle 24

A proper medical examination shall be offered to a detained or imprisoned person as promptly as possible after his admission to the place of detention or imprisonment, and thereafter medical care and treatment shall be provided whenever necessary. This care and treatment shall be provided free of charge.

Principle 25

A detained or imprisoned person or his counsel shall, subject only to reasonable conditions to ensure security and good order in the place of detention or imprisonment, have the right to request or petition a judicial or other authority for a second medical examination or opinion.

Principle 26

The fact that a detained or imprisoned person underwent a medical examination, the name of the physician and the results of such an examination shall be duly recorded. Access to such records shall be ensured. Modalities therefore shall be in accordance with relevant rules of domestic law.

Principle 27

Non-compliance with these principles in obtaining evidence shall be taken into account in determining the admissibility of such evidence against a detained or imprisoned person.

Principle 28

A detained or imprisoned person shall have the right to obtain within the limits of available resources, if from public sources, reasonable quantities of educational, cultural and informational material, subject to reasonable conditions to ensure security and good order in the place of detention or imprisonment.

Principle 29

1. In order to supervise the strict observance of relevant laws and regulations, places of detention shall be visited regularly by qualified and experienced persons appointed by, and responsible to, a competent authority distinct from the authority directly in charge of the administration of the place of detention or imprisonment.

2. A detained or imprisoned person shall have the right to communicate freely and in full confidentiality with the persons who visit the places of detention or imprisonment in accordance with paragraph 1 of the present principle, subject to reasonable conditions to ensure security and good order in such places.

Principle 30

1. The types of conduct of the detained or imprisoned person that constitute disciplinary offences during detention or imprisonment, the description and duration of disciplinary punishment that may be inflicted and the authorities competent to impose such punishment shall be specified by law or lawful regulations and duly published.

2. A detained or imprisoned person shall have the right to be heard before disciplinary action is taken. He shall have the right to bring such action to higher authorities for review.

Principle 31

The appropriate authorities shall endeavour to ensure, according to domestic law, assistance when needed to dependent and, in particular, minor members of the families of detained or imprisoned persons and shall devote a particular measure of care to the appropriate custody of children left without supervision.

Principle 32

1. A detained person or his counsel shall be entitled at any time to take proceedings according to domestic law before a judicial or other authority to challenge the lawfulness of his detention in order to obtain his release without delay, if it is unlawful.

2. The proceedings referred to in paragraph 1 of the present principle shall be simple and expeditious and at no cost for detained persons without adequate means. The detaining authority shall produce without unreasonable delay the detained person before the reviewing authority.

Principle 33

1. A detained or imprisoned person or his counsel shall have the right to make a request or complaint regarding his treatment, in particular in case of torture or other cruel, inhuman or degrading treatment, to the authorities responsible for the administration of the place of detention and to higher authorities and, when necessary, to appropriate authorities vested with reviewing or remedial powers.

2. In those cases where neither the detained or imprisoned person nor his counsel has the possibility to exercise his rights under paragraph 1 of the present principle, a member of the family of the detained or imprisoned person or any other person who has knowledge of the case may exercise such rights.

3. Confidentiality concerning the request or complaint shall be maintained if so requested by the complainant.

4. Every request or complaint shall be promptly dealt with and replied to without undue delay. If the request or complaint is rejected or, in case of inordinate delay, the complainant shall be entitled to bring it before a judicial or other authority. Neither the detained or imprisoned person nor any complainant under paragraph 1 of the present principle shall suffer prejudice for making a request or complaint.

Principle 34

Whenever the death or disappearance of a detained or imprisoned person occurs during his detention or imprisonment, an inquiry into the cause of death or disappearance shall be held by a judicial or other authority, either on its own motion or at the instance of a member of the family of such a person or any person who has knowledge of the case. When circumstances so warrant, such an inquiry shall be held on the same procedural basis whenever the death or disappearance occurs shortly after the termination of the detention or imprisonment. The findings of such inquiry or a report thereon shall be made available upon request, unless doing so would jeopardize an ongoing criminal investigation.

Principle 35

1. Damage incurred because of acts or omissions by a public official contrary to the rights contained in these principles shall be compensated according to the applicable rules or liability provided by domestic law.

2. Information required to be recorded under these principles shall be available in accordance with procedures provided by domestic law for use in claiming compensation under the present principle.

Principle 36

1. A detained person suspected of or charged with a criminal offence shall be presumed innocent and shall be treated as such until proved guilty according to law in a public trial at which he has had all the guarantees necessary for his defence.

2. The arrest or detention of such a person pending investigation and trial shall be carried out only for the purposes of the administration of justice on grounds and under conditions and procedures specified by law. The imposition of restrictions upon such a person which are not strictly required for the purpose of the detention or to prevent hindrance to the process of investigation or the administration of justice, or for the maintenance of security and good order in the place of detention shall be forbidden.

Principle 37

A person detained on a criminal charge shall be brought before a judicial or other authority provided by law promptly after his arrest. Such authority shall decide without delay upon the lawfulness and necessity of detention. No person may be kept under detention pending investigation or trial except upon the written order of such an authority. A detained person shall, when brought before such an authority, have the right to make a statement on the treatment received by him while in custody.

Principle 38

A person detained on a criminal charge shall be entitled to trial within a reasonable time or to release pending trial.

Principle 39

Except in special cases provided for by law, a person detained on a criminal charge shall be entitled, unless a judicial or other authority decides otherwise in the interest of the administration of justice, to release pending trial subject to the conditions that may be imposed in accordance with the law. Such authority shall keep the necessity of detention under review.

General clause

Nothing in this Body of Principles shall be construed as restricting or derogating from any right defined in the International Covenant on Civil and Political Rights.

ECONOMIC AND SOCIAL COUNCIL RESOLUTION 1235 (XLII), 42 U.N. ESCOR Supp. (No. 1) at 17, U.N. Doc. E/4393 (1967):

The Economic and Social Council,

Noting resolutions 8 (XXIII) and 9 (XXIII) of the Commission on Human Rights,

1. *Welcomes* the decision of the Commission on Human Rights to give annual consideration to the item entitled "Question of the violation of human rights and fundamental freedoms, including policies of racial discrimination and segregation and of apartheid, in all countries, with particular reference to colonial and other dependent countries and territories," without prejudice to the functions and powers of organs already in existence or which may be estab-

lished within the framework of measures of implementation included in international covenants and conventions on the protection of human rights and fundamental freedoms; and concurs with the requests for assistance addressed to the Sub-Commission on Prevention of Discrimination and Protection of Minorities and to the Secretary-General;

2. *Authorizes* the Commission on Human Rights and the Sub-Commission on Prevention of Discrimination and Protection of Minorities, in conformity with the provisions of paragraph 1 of the Commission's resolution 8 (XXIII), to examine information relevant to gross violations of human rights and fundamental freedoms, as exemplified by the policy of apartheid as practised in the Republic of South Africa and in the Territory of South West Africa under the direct responsibility of the United Nations and now illegally occupied by the Government of the Republic of South Africa, and to racial discrimination as practiced notably in Southern Rhodesia, contained in the communications listed by the Secretary-General pursuant to Economic and Social Council resolution 728 F (XXVIII) of 30 July 1959;

3. *Decides* that the Commission on Human Rights may, in appropriate cases, and after careful consideration of the information thus made available to it, in conformity with the provisions of paragraph 1 above, make a thorough study of situations which reveal a consistent pattern of violations of human rights, as exemplified by the policy of apartheid as practised in the Republic of South Africa and in the Territory of South West Africa under the direct responsibility of the United Nations and now illegally occupied by the Government of the Republic of South Africa, and racial discrimination as practised notably in Southern Rhodesia, and report, with recommendations thereon, to the Economic and Social Council;

4. *Decides* to review the provisions of paragraphs 2 and 3 of the present resolution after the entry into force of the International Covenants on Human Rights;

5. *Takes note* of the fact that the Commission on Human Rights, in its resolution 6 (XXIII), has instructed an *ad hoc* study group to study in all its aspects the question of the ways and means by which the Commission might be enabled or assisted to discharge functions in relation to violations of human rights and fundamental freedoms, whilst maintaining and fulfilling its other functions;

6. *Requests* the Commission on Human Rights to report to it on the result of this study after having given consideration to the conclusions of the *ad hoc* study group referred to in paragraph 5 above.

ECONOMIC AND SOCIAL COUNCIL RESOLUTION 1503 (XLVIII), 48 U.N. ESCOR (No. 1A) at 8, U.N. Doc. E/4832/Add.1 (1970):

Procedure for dealing with communications relating to violations of human rights and fundamental freedoms

The Economic and Social Council,

Noting resolutions 7 (XXVI) and 17 (XXV) of the Commission on Human Rights and resolution 2 (XXI) of the Sub-Commission on Prevention of Discrimination and Protection of Minorities,

1. *Authorizes* the Sub-Commission on Prevention of Discrimination and Protection of Minorities to appoint a working group consisting of not more than twenty-five members, with due regard to geographical distribution, to meet once a year in private meetings for a period not exceeding ten days immediately before the sessions of the Sub-Commission to consider all communications, including replies of Governments thereon, received by the Secretary-General under Council resolution 728 F (XXVIII) of 30 July 1559 with a view to bringing to the attention of the Sub-Commission those communications, together with replies of Governments, if any, which appear to reveal a consistent pattern of gross and reliably attested violations of human rights and fundamental freedoms within the terms of reference of the Sub-Commission;

2. *Decides* that the Sub-Commission on Prevention of Discrimination and Protection of Minorities should, as the first step in the implementation of the present resolution, devise at its twenty-third session appropriate procedures for dealing with the question of admissibility of communications received by the Secretary-General under Council resolution 728 F (XXVIII) and in accordance with Council resolution 1235 (XLII) of 6 June 1967;

3. *Requests* the Secretary-General to prepare a document on the question of admissibility of communications for the Sub-Commission's consideration at its twenty-third session;

4. *Further requests* the Secretary-General:

(a) To furnish to the members of the Sub-Commission every month a list of communications prepared by him in accordance with Council resolution 728 F (XXVIII) and a brief description of them together with the text of any replies received from Governments;

(b) To make available to the members of the working group at their meetings the originals of such communications listed as they may request, having due regard to the provisions of paragraph 2(b) of Council resolution 728 F (XXVIII) concerning the divulging of the identity of the authors of communications;

(c) To circulate to the members of the Sub-Commission, in the working languages, the originals of such communications as are referred to the Sub-Commission by the working group;

5. *Requests* the Sub-Commission on Prevention of Discrimination and Protection of Minorities to consider in private meetings, in accordance with paragraph 1 above, the communications brought before it in accordance with the decision of a majority of the members of the working group and any replies of Governments relating thereto and other relevant information, with a view to determining whether to refer to the Commission on Human Rights particular situations which appear to reveal a consistent pattern of gross and

reliably attested violations of human rights requiring consideration by the Commission;

6. *Requests* the Commission on Human Rights after it has examined any situation referred to it by the Sub-Commission to determine:

(a) Whether it requires a thorough study by the Commission and a report and recommendations thereon to the Council in accordance with paragraph 3 of Council resolution 1235 (XLII);

(b) Whether it may be a subject of an investigation by an *ad hoc* committee to be appointed by the Commission which shall be undertaken only with the express consent of the State concerned and shall be conducted in constant co-operation with that State and under conditions determined by agreement with it. In any event, the investigation may be undertaken only if:

(i) All available means at the national level have been resorted to and exhausted;

(ii) The situation does not relate to a matter which is being dealt with under other procedures prescribed in the constituent instruments of, or conventions adopted by, the United Nations and the specialized agencies, or in regional conventions, or which the State concerned wishes to submit to other procedures in accordance with general or special international agreements to which it is a party.

7. *Decides* that if the Commission on Human Rights appoints an *ad hoc* committee to carry on an investigation with the consent of the State concerned:

(a) The composition of the committee shall be determined by the Commission. The members of the committee shall be independent persons whose competence and impartiality is beyond question. Their appointment shall be subject to the consent of the Government concerned;

(b) The committee shall establish its own rules of procedure. It shall be subject to the quorum rule. It shall have authority to received communications and hear witnesses, as necessary. The investigation shall be conducted in co-operation with the Government concerned;

(c) The committee's procedure shall be confidential, its proceedings shall be conducted in private meetings and its communications shall not be publicized in any way;

(d) The committee shall strive for friendly solutions before, during and even after the investigation;

(e) The committee shall report to the Commission on Human Rights with such observations and suggestions as it may deem appropriate;

8. *Decides* that all actions envisaged in the implementation of the present resolution by the Sub-Commission on Prevention of Discrimination and Protection of Minorities or the Commission on Human Rights shall remain confidential until such time as the Commission may decide to make recommendations to the Economic and Social Council;

9. *Decides* to authorize the Secretary-General to provide all facilities which may be required to carry out the present resolution, making use of the existing staff of the Division of Human Rights of the United Nations Secretariat:

10. *Decides* that the procedure set out in the present resolution for dealing with communications relating to violations of human rights and fundamental freedoms should be reviewed if any new organ entitled to deal with such communications should be established within the United Nations or by international agreement.

INSTITUTION-BUILDING OF THE UNITED NATIONS HUMAN RIGHTS COUNCIL, HRC res 5/1, U.N. Doc A/HRC/5/21 at 4 (2007)(footnotes omitted):

The Human Rights Council,

Acting in compliance with the mandate entrusted to it by the United Nations General Assembly in resolution 60/251 of 15 March 2006,

Having considered the draft text on institution-building submitted by the President of the Council,

1. *Adopts* the draft text entitled "United Nations Human Rights Council: Institution-Building", as contained in the annex to the present resolution, including its appendix(ces); .....

Annex

UNITED NATIONS HUMAN RIGHTS COUNCIL: INSTITUTION-BUILDING

I. UNIVERSAL PERIODIC REVIEW MECHANISM

A. Basis of the review

1. The basis of the review is:

(*a*) The Charter of the United Nations;

(*b*) The Universal Declaration of Human Rights;

(*c*) Human rights instruments to which a State is party;

(*d*) Voluntary pledges and commitments made by States, including those undertaken when presenting their candidatures for election to the Human Rights Council (hereinafter "the Council").

---

*The term "cruel, inhuman or degrading treatment or punishment" should be interpreted so as to extend the widest possible protection against abuses, whether physical or mental, including the holding of a detained or imprisoned person in conditions which deprive him, temporarily or permanently, of the use of any of his natural senses, such as sight or hearing, or of his awareness of place and the passing of time.

2. In addition to the above and given the complementary and mutually interrelated nature of international human rights law and international humanitarian law, the review shall take into account applicable international humanitarian law.

B. Principles and objectives

1. Principles

3. The universal periodic review should:

(*a*) Promote the universality, interdependence, indivisibility and interrelatedness of allhuman rights;

(*b*) Be a cooperative mechanism based on objective and reliable information and on interactive dialogue;

(*c*) Ensure universal coverage and equal treatment of all States;

(*d*) Be an intergovernmental process, United Nations Member-driven and action-oriented;

(*e*) Fully involve the country under review;

(*f*) Complement and not duplicate other human rights mechanisms, thus representing an added value;

(*g*) Be conducted in an objective, transparent, non-selective, constructive, non-confrontational and non-politicized manner;

(*h*) Not be overly burdensome to the concerned State or to the agenda of the Council;

(*i*) Not be overly long; it should be realistic and not absorb a disproportionate amount of time, human and financial resources;

(*j*) Not diminish the Council's capacity to respond to urgent human rights situations;

(*k*) Fully integrate a gender perspective;

(*l*) Without prejudice to the obligations contained in the elements provided for in the basis of review, take into account the level of development and specificities of countries;

(*m*) Ensure the participation of all relevant stakeholders, including non-governmental organizations and national human rights institutions, in accordance with General Assembly resolution 60/251 of 15 March 2006 and Economic and Social Council resolution 1996/31 of 25 July 1996, as well as any decisions that the Council may take in this regard.

2. Objectives

4. The objectives of the review are:

(*a*) The improvement of the human rights situation on the ground;

(*b*) The fulfilment of the State's human rights obligations and commitments and assessment of positive developments and challenges faced by the State;

(*c*) The enhancement of the State's capacity and of technical assistance, in consultation with, and with the consent of, the State concerned;

(*d*) The sharing of best practice among States and other stakeholders;

(*e*) Support for cooperation in the promotion and protection of human rights;

(*f*) The encouragement of full cooperation and engagement with the Council, other human rights bodies and the Office of the United Nations High Commissioner for Human Rights.

C. Periodicity and order of the review

5. The review begins after the adoption of the universal periodic review mechanism by the Council

6. The order of review should reflect the principles of universality and equal treatment.

7. The order of the review should be established as soon as possible in order to allow States to prepare adequately.

8. All member States of the Council shall be reviewed during their term of membership.

9. The initial members of the Council, especially those elected for one or two-year terms, should be reviewed first.

10. A mix of member and observer States of the Council should be reviewed.

11. Equitable geographic distribution should be respected in the selection of countries for review.

12. The first member and observer States to be reviewed will be chosen by the drawing of lots from each Regional Group in such a way as to ensure full respect for equitable geographic distribution. Alphabetical order will then be applied beginning with those countries thus selected, unless other countries volunteer to be reviewed.

13. The period between review cycles should be reasonable so as to take into account the capacity of States to prepare for, and the capacity of other stakeholders to respond to, the requests arising from the review.

14. The periodicity of the review for the first cycle will be of four years. This will imply the consideration of 48 States per year during three sessions of the working group of two weeks each.

D. Process and modalities of the review

1. Documentation

15. The documents on which the review would be based are:

(*a*) Information prepared by the State concerned, which can take the form of a national report, on the basis of general guidelines to be adopted by the Council at its sixth session (first session of the second cycle), and any other information considered relevant by the State concerned, which could be presented either orally or in writing, provided that the written presentation summarizing the information will not exceed 20 pages, to guarantee equal treatment to all States and not to overburden the mechanism. States are level with all relevant stakeholders; encouraged to prepare the information through a broad consultation process at the national level with all relevant stakeholders;

(*b*) Additionally a compilation prepared by the Office of the High Commissioner for Human Rights of the information contained in the reports of treaty bodies, special procedures, including observations and comments by the State concerned, and other relevant official United Nations documents, which shall not exceed 10 pages;

(*c*) Additional, credible and reliable information provided by other relevantstakeholders to the universal periodic review which should also be taken into consideration by the Council in the review. The Office of the High Commissioner for Human Rights will prepare a summary of such information which shall not exceed 10 pages.

16. The documents prepared by the Office of the High Commissioner for Human Rights should be elaborated following the structure of the general guidelines adopted by the Council regarding the information prepared by the State concerned.

17. Both the State's written presentation and the summaries prepared by the Office of the High Commissioner for Human Rights shall be ready six weeks prior to the review by the working group to ensure the distribution of documents simultaneously in the six officiallanguages of the United Nations, in accordance with General Assembly resolution 53/208 of 14 January 1999.

2. Modalities

18. The modalities of the review shall be as follows:

(*a*) The review will be conducted in one working group, chaired by the President of the Council and composed of the 47 member States of the Council. Each member State will decide on the composition of its delegation;

(*b*) Observer States may participate in the review, including in the interactive dialogue;

(*c*) Other relevant stakeholders may attend the review in the working group;

(*d*) A group of three rapporteurs, selected by the drawing of lots among the members of the Council and from different Regional Groups (*troika*) will be formed to facilitate each review, including the preparation of the report of the working group. The Office of the High Commissioner for Human Rights will provide the necessary assistance and expertise to the rapporteurs.

19. The country concerned may request that one of the rapporteurs be from its own Regional Group and may also request the substitution of a rapporteur on only one occasion.

20. A rapporteur may request to be excused from participation in a specific review process.

21. Interactive dialogue between the country under review and the Council will take place in the working group. The rapporteurs may collate issues or questions to be transmitted to the State under review to facilitate its preparation and focus the interactive dialogue, while guaranteeing fairness and transparency.

22. The duration of the review will be three hours for each country in the working group. Additional time of up to one hour will be allocated for the consideration of the outcome by the plenary of the Council.

23. Half an hour will be allocated for the adoption of the report of each country under review in the working group.

24. A reaonable time frame should be allocated between the review and the adoption of the report of each State in the working group.

25. The final outcome will be adopted by the plenary of the Council.

E. Outcome of the review

1. Format of the outcome

26. The format of the outcome of the review will be a report consisting of a summary of the proceedings of the review process; conclusions and/or recommendations, and the voluntary commitments of the State concerned.

2. Content of the outcome

27. The universal periodic review is a cooperative mechanism. Its outcome may include, inter alia:

(*a*) An assessment undertaken in an objective and transparent manner of the human rights situation in the country under review, including positive developments and the challenges faced by the country;

(*b*) Sharing of best practices;

(*c*) An emphasis on enhancing cooperation for the promotion and protection of human rights;

(*d*) The provision of technical assistance and capacity-building in consultation with, and with the consent of, the country concerned;

(*e*) Voluntary commitments and pledges made by the country under review.

3. Adoption of the outcome

28. The country under review should be fully involved in the outcome.

29. Before the adoption of the outcome by the plenary of the Council, the State concerned should be offered the opportunity to present replies to questions or issues that were not sufficiently addressed during the interactive dialogue.

30. The State concerned and the member States of the Council, as well as observer States, will be given the opportunity to express their views on the outcome of the review before the plenary takes action on it.

31. Other relevant stakeholders will have the opportunity to make general comments before the adoption of the outcome by the plenary.

32. Recommendations that enjoy the support of the State concerned will be identified as such. Other recommendations, together with the comments of the State concerned thereon, will be noted. Both will be included in the outcome report to be adopted by the Council.

F. Follow-up to the review

33. The outcome of the universal periodic review, as a cooperative mechanism, should be implemented primarily by the State concerned and, as appropriate, by other relevant stakeholders.

34. The subsequent review should focus, inter alia, on the implementation of the preceding outcome.

35. The Council should have a standing item on its agenda devoted to the universal periodic review.

36. The international community will assist in implementing the recommendations and conclusions regarding capacity-building and technical assistance, in consultation with, and with the consent of, the country concerned.

37. In considering the outcome of the universal periodic review, the Council will decide if and when any specific follow-up is necessary.

38. After exhausting all efforts to encourage a State to cooperate with the universal periodic review mechanism, the Council will address, as appropriate, cases of persistent non-cooperation with the mechanism.

II. SPECIAL PROCEDURES

A. Selection and appointment of mandate-holders

39. The following general criteria will be of paramount importance while nominating, selecting and appointing mandate-holders: (a) expertise; (b) experience in the field of the mandate; (c) independence; (d) impartiality; (e) personal integrity; and (f) objectivity.

40. Due consideration should be given to gender balance and equitable geographic representation, as well as to an appropriate representation of different legal systems.

41. Technical and objective requirements for eligible candidates for mandate -holders will be approved by the Council at its sixth session (first session of the second cycle), in order to ensure that eligible candidates are highly qualified individuals who possess established competence, relevant expertise and extensive professional experience in the field of human rights.

42. The following entities may nominate candidates as special procedures mandate-holders: (a) Governments; (b) Regional Groups operating within the United Nations human rights system; (c) international organizations or their offices (e.g. the Office of the High Commissioner for Human Rights); (d) non-governmental organizations; (e) other human rights bodies; (f) individual nominations.

43. The Office of the High Commissioner for Human Rights shall immediately prepare,maintain and periodically update a public list of eligible candidates in a standardizedformat, which shall include personal data, areas of expertise and professional experience. Upcoming vacancies of mandates shall be publicized.

44. The principle of non-accumulation of human rights functions at a time shall be respected.

45. A mandate-holder's tenure in a given function, whether a thematic or country mandate, will be no longer than six years (two terms of three years for thematic mandate-holders).

46. Individuals holding decision-making positions in Government or in any other organization or entity which may give rise to a conflict of interest with the responsibilities inherent to the mandate shall be excluded. Mandate-holders will act in their personal capacity.

47. A consultative group would be established to propose to the President, at least one month before the beginning of the session in which the Council would consider the selection of mandate-holders, a list of candidates who possess the highest qualifications for the mandates in question and meet the general criteria and particular requirements.

48. The consultative group shall also give due consideration to the exclusion of nominated candidates from the public list of eligible candidates brought to its attention.

49. At the beginning of the annual cycle of the Council, Regional Groups would be invited to appoint a member of the consultative group, who would serve in his/her personal capacity. The Group will be assisted by the Office of the High Commissioner for Human Rights.

50. The consultative group will consider candidates included in the public list; however,under exceptional circumstances and if a particular post justifies it, the Group may consider additional nominations with equal or more suitable qualifications for the post. Recommendations to the President shall be public and substantiated.

51. The consultative group should take into account, as appropriate, the views of stakeholders, including the current or outgoing mandate-holders, in determining the necessary expertise, experience, skills, and other relevant requirements for each mandate.

52. On the basis of the recommendations of the consultative group and following broad consultations, in particular through the regional coordinators, the President of the Council will identify an appropriate candidate for each vacancy. The President will present to member States and observers a list of candidates to be proposed at least two weeks prior to the beginning of the session in which the Council will consider the appointments.

53. If necessary, the President will conduct further consultations to ensure the endorsement of the proposed candidates. The appointment of the special procedures mandate-holders will be completed upon the subsequent approval of the Council. Mandate-holders shall be appointed before the end of the session.

B. Review, rationalization and improvement of mandates

54. The review, rationalization and improvement of mandates, as well as the creation of new ones, must be guided by the principles of universality, impartiality, objectivity and non-selectivity, constructive international dialogue and cooperation, with a view to enhancing the promotion and protection of all human rights, civil, political, economic, social and cultural rights, including the right to development.

55. The review, rationalization and improvement of each mandate would take place in the context of the negotiations of the relevant resolutions. An assessment of the mandate may take place in a separate segment of the interactive dialogue between the Council and special procedures mandate-holders.

56. The review, rationalization and improvement of mandates would focus on the relevance, scope and contents of the mandates, having as a framework the internationally recognized human rights standards, the system of special procedures and General Assembly resolution 60/251.

57. Any decision to streamline, merge or possibly discontinue mandates should always be guided by the need for improvement of the enjoyment and protection of human rights.

58. The Council should always strive for improvements:

(*a*) Mandates should always offer a clear prospect of an increased level of human rights protection and promotion as well as being coherent within the system of human rights;

(*b*) Equal attention should be paid to all human rights. The balance of thematic mandates should broadly reflect the accepted equal importance of civil, political, economic, social and cultural rights, including the right to development;

(*c*) Every effort should be made to avoid unnecessary duplication;

(*d*) Areas which constitute thematic gaps will be identified and addressed, including by means other than the creation of special procedures mandates, such as by expanding an existing mandate, bringing a cross-cutting issue to the attention of mandate-holders or by requesting a joint action to the relevant mandate-holders;

(*e*) Any consideration of merging mandates should have regard to the content and predominant functions of each mandate, as well as to the workload of individual mandate-holders;

(*f*) In creating or reviewing mandates, efforts should be made to identify whether the structure of the mechanism (expert, rapporteur or working group) is the most effective in terms of increasing human rights protection;

(*g*) New mandates should be as clear and specific as possible, so as to avoid ambiguity.

59. It should be considered desirable to have a uniform nomenclature of mandate-holders, titles of mandates as well as a selection and appointment process, to make the whole system more understandable.

60. Thematic mandate periods will be of three years. Country mandate periods will be of one year.

61. Mandates included in Appendix I, where applicable, will be renewed until the date on which they are considered by the Council according to the programme of work.[4]

62. Current mandate-holders may continue serving, provided they have not exceeded the six-year term limit (Appendix II). On an exceptional basis, the term of those mandate-holders who have served more than six years may be extended until the relevant mandate is considered by the Council and the selection and appointment process has concluded.

63. Decisions to create, review or discontinue country mandates should also take into account the principles of cooperation and genuine dialogue aimed at strengthening the capacity of Member States to comply with their human rights obligations.

64. In case of situations of violations of human rights or a lack of cooperation that require the Council's attention, the principles of objectivity, non-

selectivity, and the elimination of double standards and politicization should apply.

III. HUMAN RIGHTS COUNCIL ADVISORY COMMITTEE

65. The Human Rights Council Advisory Committee (hereinafter "the Advisory Committee"), composed of 18 experts serving in their personal capacity, will function as a think-tank for the Council and work at its direction. The establishment of this subsidiary body and its functioning will be executed according to the guidelines stipulated below below.

A. Nomination

66. All Member States of the United Nations may propose or endorse candidates from their own region. When selecting their candidates, States should consult their national human rights institutions and civil society organizations and, in this regard, include the names of those supporting their candidates.

67. The aim is to ensure that the best possible expertise is made available to the Council. For this purpose, technical and objective requirements for the submission of candidatures will be established and approved by the Council at its sixth session (first session of the second cycle). These should include:

(*a*) Recognized competence and experience in the field of human rights;

(*b*) High moral standing;

(*c*) Independence and impartiality.

68. Individuals holding decision-making positions in Government or in any other organization or entity which might give rise to a conflict of interest with the responsibilities inherent in the mandate shall be excluded. Elected members of the Committee will act in their personal capacity.

69. The principle of non-accumulation of human rights functions at the same time shall be respected.

B. Election

70. The Council shall elect the members of the Advisory Committee, in secret ballot, from the list of candidates whose names have been presented in accordance with the agreed requirements.

71. The list of candidates shall be closed two months prior to the election date. The Secretariat will make available the list of candidates and relevant information to member States and to the public at least one month prior to their election.

72. Due consideration should be given to gender balance and appropriate representation of different civilizations and legal systems.

73. The geographic distribution will be as follows:

- □ African States: 5
- □ Asian States: 5
- □ Eastern European States: 2
- □ Latin American and Caribbean States: 3
- □ Western European and other States: 3

74. The members of the Advisory Committee shall serve for a period of three years. They shall be eligible for re-election once. In the first term, one third of the experts will serve for one year and another third for two years. The staggering of terms of membership will be defined by the drawing of lots.

C. Functions

75. The function of the Advisory Committee is to provide expertise to the Council in the manner and form requested by the Council, focusing mainly on studies and research- based advice. Further, such expertise shall be rendered only upon the latter's request, in compliance with its resolutions and under its guidance.

76. The Advisory Committee should be implementation-oriented and the scope of its advice should be limited to thematic issues pertaining to the mandate of the Council;namely promotion and protection of all human rights.

77. The Advisory Committee shall not adopt resolutions or decisions. The Advisory Committee may propose within the scope of the work set out by the Council, for the latter's consideration and approval, suggestions for further enhancing its procedural efficiency, as well as further research proposals within the scope of the work set out by the Council.

78. The Council shall issue specific guidelines for the Advisory Committee when it requests a substantive contribution from the latter and shall review all or any portion of those guidelines if it deems necessary in the future.

D. Methods of work

79. The Advisory Committee shall convene up to two sessions for a maximum of 10 working days per year. Additional sessions may be scheduled on an ad hoc basis with prior approval of the Council.

80. The Council may request the Advisory Committee to undertake certain tasks that could be performed collectively, through a smaller team or individually. The Advisory Committee will report on such efforts to the Council.

81. Members of the Advisory Committee are encouraged to communicate between sessions, individually or in teams. However, the Advisory Committee shall not establish subsidiary bodies unless the Council authorizes it to do so.

82. In the performance of its mandate, the Advisory Committee is urged to establish interaction with States, national human rights institutions, non-

governmental organizations and other civil society entities in accordance with the modalities of the Council.

83. Member States and observers, including States that are not members of the Council, the specialized agencies, other intergovernmental organizations and national human rights institutions, as well as non-governmental organizations shall be entitled to participate in the work of the Advisory Committee based on arrangements, including Economic and Social Council resolution 1996/31 and practices observed by the Commission on Human Rights and the Council, while ensuring the most effective contribution of these entities.

84. The Council will decide at its sixth session (first session of its second cycle) on the most appropriate mechanisms to continue the work of the Working Groups on Indigenous Populations; Contemporary Forms of Slavery; Minorities; and the Social Forum.

IV. COMPLAINT PROCEDURE

A. Objective and scope

85. A complaint procedure is being established to address consistent patterns of gross and reliably attested violations of all human rights and all fundamental freedoms occurring in any part of the world and under any circumstances.

86. Economic and Social Council resolution 1503 (XLVIII) of 27 May 1970 as revised by resolution 2000/3 of 19 June 2000 served as a working basis and was improved where necessary, so as to ensure that the complaint procedure is impartial, objective, efficient, victims-oriented and conducted in a timely manner. The procedure will retain its confidential nature, with a view to enhancing cooperation with the State concerned.

B. Admissibility criteria for communications

87. A communication related to a violation of human rights and fundamental freedoms, for the purpose of this procedure, shall be admissible, provided that:

(a) It is not manifestly politically motivated and its object is consistent with the Charter of the United Nations, the Universal Declaration of Human Rights and other applicable instruments in the field of human rights law;

(b) It gives a factual description of the alleged violations, including the rights which are alleged to be violated;

(c) Its language is not abusive. However, such a communication may be considered if it meets the other criteria for admissibility after deletion of the abusive language;

(*d*) It is submitted by a person or a group of persons claiming to be the victims of violations of human rights and fundamental freedoms, or by any person or group of persons, including non-governmental organizations, acting in good faith in accordance with the principles of human rights, not resorting to politically motivated stands contrary to the provisions of the Charter of the United Nations and claiming to have direct and reliable knowledge of the violations concerned. Nonetheless, reliably attested communications shall not be inadmissible solely because the knowledge of the individual authors is second-hand, provided that they are accompanied by clear evidence;

(*e*) It is not exclusively based on reports disseminated by mass media;

(*f*) It does not refer to a case that appears to reveal a consistent pattern of gross and reliably attested violations of human rights already being dealt with by a special procedure, a treaty body or other United Nations or similar regional complaints procedure in the field of human rights;

(*g*) Domestic remedies have been exhausted, unless it appears that such remedies would be ineffective or unreasonably prolonged.

88. National human rights institutions, established and operating under the Principles Relating to the Status of National Institutions (the Paris Principles), in particular in regard to quasi-judicial competence, may serve as effective means of addressing individual human rights violations.

C. Working groups

89. Two distinct working groups shall be established with the mandate to examine the communications and to bring to the attention of the Council consistent patterns of gross and reliably attested violations of human rights and fundamental freedoms.

90. Both working groups shall, to the greatest possible extent, work on the basis of consensus. In the absence of consensus, decisions shall be taken by simple majority of the votes. They may establish their own rules of procedure.

1. Working Group on Communications: composition, mandate and powers

91. The Human Rights Council Advisory Committee shall appoint five of its members, one from each Regional Group, with due consideration to gender balance, to constitute the Working Group on Communications.

92. In case of a vacancy, the Advisory Committee shall appoint an independent and highly qualified expert of the same Regional Group from the Advisory Committee.

93. Since there is a need for independent expertise and continuity with regard to the examination and assessment of communications received, the

independent and highly qualified experts of the Working Group on Communications shall be appointed for three years. Their mandate is renewable only once.

94. The Chairperson of the Working Group on Communications is requested, together with the secretariat, to undertake an initial screening of communications received, based on the admissibility criteria, before transmitting them to the States concerned. Manifestly ill-founded or anonymous communications shall be screened out by the Chairperson and shall therefore not be transmitted to the State concerned. In a perspective of accountability and transparency, the Chairperson of the Working Group on Communications shall provide all its members with a list of all communications rejected after initial screening. This list should indicate the grounds of all decisions resulting in the rejection of a communication. All other communications, which have not been screened out, shall be transmitted to the State concerned, so as to obtain the views of the latter on the allegations of violations.

95. The members of the Working Group on Communications shall decide on the admissibility of a communication and assess the merits of the allegations of violations, including whether the communication alone or in combination with other communications appear to reveal a consistent pattern of gross and reliably attested violations of human rights and fundamental freedoms. The Working Group on Communications shall provide the Working Group on Situations with a file containing all admissible communications as well as recommendations thereon. When the Working Group on Communications requires further consideration or additional information, it may keep a case under review until its next session and request such information from the State concerned. The Working Group on Communications may decide to dismiss a case. All decisions of the Working Group on Communications shall be based on a rigorous application of the admissibility criteria and duly justified.

2. Working Group on Situations: composition, mandate and powers

96. Each Regional Group shall appoint a representative of a member State of the Council, with due consideration to gender balance, to serve on the Working Group on Situations. Members shall be appointed for one year. Their mandate may be renewed once, if the State concerned is a member of the Council.

97. Members of the Working Group on Situations shall serve in their personal capacity. In order to fill a vacancy, the respective Regional Group to which the vacancy belongs, shall appoint a representative from member States of the same Regional Group.

98. The Working Group on Situations is requested, on the basis of the information and recommendations provided by the Working Group on Communications, to present the Council with a report on consistent patterns of gross and reliably attested violations of human rights and fundamental freedoms and to make recommendations to the Council on the course of action to take, normally in the form of a draft resolution or decision with respect to the

situations referred to it. When the Working Group on Situations requires further consideration or additional information, its members may keep a case under review until its next session. The Working Group on Situations may also decide to dismiss a case.

99. All decisions of the Working Group on Situations shall be duly justified and indicate why the consideration of a situation has been discontinued or action recommended thereon. Decisions to discontinue should be taken by consensus; if that is not possible, by simple majority of the votes.

D. Working modalities and confidentiality

100. Since the complaint procedure is to be, inter alia, victims-oriented and conducted in a confidential and timely manner, both Working Groups shall meet at least twice a year for five working days each session, in order to promptly examine the communications received, including replies of States thereon, and the situations of which the Council is already seized under the complaint procedure.

101. The State concerned shall cooperate with the complaint procedure and make every effort to provide substantive replies in one of the United Nations official languages to any of the requests of the Working Groups or the Council. The State concerned shall also make every effort to provide a reply not later than three months after the request has been made. If necessary, this deadline may however be extended at the request of the State concerned.

102. The Secretariat is requested to make the confidential files available to all members of the Council, at least two weeks in advance, so as to allow sufficient time for the consideration of the files.

103. The Council shall consider consistent patterns of gross and reliably attested violations of human rights and fundamental freedoms brought to its attention by the Working Group on Situations as frequently as needed, but at least once a year.

104. The reports of the Working Group on Situations referred to the Council shall be examined in a confidential manner, unless the Council decides otherwise. When the Working Group on Situations recommends to the Council that it consider a situation in a public meeting, in particular in the case of manifest and unequivocal lack of cooperation, the Council shall consider such recommendation on a priority basis at its next session.

105. So as to ensure that the complaint procedure is victims-oriented, efficient and conducted in a timely manner, the period of time between the transmission of the complaint to the State concerned and consideration by the Council shall not, in principle, exceed 24 months.

106. The complaint procedure shall ensure that both the author of a communication and the State concerned are informed of the proceedings at the following key stages:

(a) When a communication is deemed inadmissible by the Working Group on Communications or when it is taken up for consideration by the

Working Group on Situations; or when a communication is kept pending by one of the Working Groups or by the Council;

(*b*) At the final outcome.

107. In addition, the complainant shall be informed when his/her communication is registered by the complaint procedure.

108. Should the complainant request that his/her identity be kept confidential, it will not be transmitted to the State concerned.

F. Measures

109. In accordance with established practice the action taken in respect of a particular situation should be one of the following options:

(*a*) To discontinue considering the situation when further consideration or action is not warranted;

(*b*) To keep the situation under review and request the State concerned to provide further information within a reasonable period of time;

(*c*) To keep the situation under review and appoint an independent and highly qualified expert to monitor the situation and report back to the Council;

(*d*) To discontinue reviewing the matter under the confidential complaint procedure in order to take up public consideration of the same;

(*e*) To recommend to OHCHR to provide technical cooperation, capacity-building assistance or advisory services to the State concerned.

V. AGENDA AND FRAMEWORK FOR THE PROGRAMME OF WORK

A. Principles

☐ Universality

☐ Impartiality

☐ Objectivity

☐ Non-selectiveness

☐ Constructive dialogue and cooperation

☐ Predictability

☐ Flexibility

☐ Transparency

☐ Accountability

☐ Balance

☐ Inclusive/comprehensive

☐ Gender perspective

☐ Implementation and follow-up of decisions

B. Agenda

Item 1. Organizational and procedural matters

Item 2. Annual report of the United Nations High Commissioner for Human Rights and reports of the Office of the High Commissioner and the Secretary-General

Item 3. Promotion and protection of all human rights, civil, political, economic, social and cultural rights, including the right to development

Item 4. Human rights situations that require the Council's attention

Item 5. Human rights bodies and mechanisms

Item 6. Universal Periodic Review

Item 7. Human rights situation in Palestine and other occupied Arab territories

Item 8. Follow-up and implementation of the Vienna Declaration and Programme of Action

Item 9. Racism, racial discrimination, xenophobia and related forms of intolerance, follow-up and implementation of the Durban Declaration and Programme of Action

Item 10. Technical assistance and capacity-building

C. Framework forthe programme of work

Item 1. Organizational and procedural matters

☐ Election of the Bureau

☐ Adoption of the annual programme of work

☐ Adoption of the programme of work of the session, including other business

☐ Selection and appointment of mandate-holders

☐ Election of members of the Human Rights Council Advisory Committee

☐ Adoption of the report of the session

☐ Adoption of the annual report

Item 2. Annual report of the United Nations High Commissioner for Human Rights and reports of the Office of the High Commissioner and the Secretary-General

☐ Presentation of the annual report and updates

Item 3. Promotion and protection of all human rights, civil, political, economic, social and cultural rights, including the right to development

☐ Economic, social and cultural rights

☐ Civil and political rights

☐ Rights of peoples, and specific groups and individuals

☐ Right to development

☐ Interrelation of human rights and human rights thematic issues

Item 4. Human rights situations that require the Council's attention

Item 5. Human rights bodies and mechanisms

☐ Report of the Human Rights Council Advisory Committee

☐ Report of the complaint procedure

Item 6. Universal Periodic Review

Item 7. Human rights situation in Palestine and other occupied Arab territories

☐ Human rights violations and implications of the Israeli occupation of Palestine and other occupied Arab territories

☐ Right to self-determination of the Palestinian people

Item 8. Follow-up and implementation of the Vienna Declaration and Programme of Action

Item 9. Racism, racial discrimination, xenophobia and related forms of intolerance, follow-up and implementation of the Durban Declaration and Programme of Action

Item 10. Technical assistance and capacity-building

VI. METHODS OF WORK

110. The methods of work, pursuant to General Assembly resolution 60/251 should be transparent, impartial, equitable, fair, pragmatic; lead to clarity, predictability, and inclusiveness. They may also be updated and adjusted over time.

A. Institutional arrangements

1. Briefings on prospective resolutions or decisions

111. The briefings on prospective resolutions or decisions would be informative only, whereby delegations would be apprised of resolutions and/or decisions tabled or intended to be tabled. These briefings will be organized by interested delegations.

2. President's open-ended information meetings on resolutions, decisions and other related business

112. The President's open-ended information meetings on resolutions, decisions and other related business shall provide information on the status of negotiations on draft resolutions and/or decisions so that delegations may gain a bird's eye view of the status of such drafts. The consultations shall have a purely informational function, combined with information on the extranet, and be held in a transparent and inclusive manner. They shall not serve as a negotiating forum.

3. Informal consultations on proposals convened by main sponsors

113. Informal consultations shall be the primary means for the negotiation of draft resolutions and/or decisions, and their convening shall be the responsibility of the sponsor(s). At least one informal open-ended consultation should be held on each draft resolution and/or decision before it is considered for action by the Council. Consultations should, as much as possible, be scheduled in a timely, transparent and inclusive manner that takes into account the constraints faced by delegations, particularly smaller ones.

4. Role of the Bureau

114. The Bureau shall deal with procedural and organizational matters. The Bureau shall regularly communicate the contents of its meetings through a timely summary report.

5. Other work formats may include panel debates, seminars and round tables

115. Utilization of these other work formats, including topics and modalities, would be decided by the Council on a case-by-case basis. They may serve as tools of the Council for enhancing dialogue and mutual understanding on certain issues. They should be utilized in the context of the Council's agenda and annual programme of work, and reinforce and/or complement its intergovernmental nature. They shall not be used to substitute or replace existing human rights mechanisms and established methods of work.

6. High-Level Segment

116. The High-Level Segment shall be held once a year during the main session of the Council. It shall be followed by a general segment wherein delegations that did not participate in the High-Level Segment may deliver general statements.

B. Working culture

117. There is a need for:

(a) Early notification of proposals;

(*b*) Early submission of draft resolutions and decisions, preferably by the end of the penultimate week of a session;

(*c*) Early distribution of all reports, particularly those of special procedures, to be transmitted to delegations in a timely fashion, at least 15 days in advance of their consideration by the Council, and in all official United Nations languages;

(*d*) Proposers of a country resolution to have the responsibility to secure the broadest possible support for their initiatives (preferably 15 members), before action is taken;

(*e*) Restraint in resorting to resolutions, in order to avoid proliferation of resolutions without prejudice to the right of States to decide on the periodicity of presenting their draft proposals by:

(i) Minimizing unnecessary duplication of initiatives with the General Assembly/Third Committee;

(ii) Clustering of agenda items;

(iii) Staggering the tabling of decisions and/or resolutions and consideration of action on agenda items/issues.

C. Outcomes other than resolutions and decisions

118. These may include recommendations, conclusions, summaries of discussions and President's Statement. As such outcomes would have different legal implications, they should supplement and not replace resolutions and decisions.

D. Special sessions of the Council

119. The following provisions shall complement the general framework provided by General Assembly resolution 60/251 and the rules of procedure of the Human Rights Council.

120. The rules of procedure of special sessions shall be in accordance with the rules of procedure applicable for regular sessions of the Council.

121. The request for the holding of a special session, in accordance with the requirement established in paragraph 10 of General Assembly resolution 60/251, shall be submitted to the President and to the secretariat of the Council. The request shall specify the item proposed for consideration and include any other relevant information the sponsors may wish to provide.

122. The special session shall be convened as soon as possible after the formal request is communicated, but, in principle, not earlier than two working days, and not later than five working days after the formal receipt of the request. The duration of the special session shall not exceed three days (six working sessions), unless the Council decides otherwise.

123. The secretariat of the Council shall immediately communicate the request for theholding of a special session and any additional information

provided by the sponsors in the request, as well as the date for the convening of the special session, to all United Nations Member States and make the information available to the specialized agencies, other intergovernmental intergovernmental organizations and national human rights institutions, as well as to non-governmental organizations in consultative status by the most expedient and expeditious means of communication. Special session documentation, in particular draft resolutions and decisions, should be made available in all official United Nations languages to all States in an equitable, timely and transparent manner.

124. The President of the Council should hold open-ended informative consultations before the special session on its conduct and organization. In this regard, the secretariat may also be requested to provide additional information, including, on the methods of work of previous special sessions.

125. Members of the Council, concerned States, observer States, specialized agencies, other intergovernmental organizations and national human rights institutions, as well as non-governmental organizations in consultative status may contribute to the special session in accordance with the rules of procedure of the Council.

126. If the requesting or other States intend to present draft resolutions or decisions at the special session, texts should be made available in accordance with the Council's relevant rules of procedure. Nevertheless, sponsors are urged to present such texts as early as possible.

127. The sponsors of a draft resolution or decision should hold open-ended consultations on the text of their draft resolution(s) or decision(s) with a view to achieving the widest participation in their consideration and, if possible, achieving consensus on them.

128. A special session should allow participatory debate, be results-oriented and geared to achieving practical outcomes, the implementation of which can be monitored and reported on at the following regular session of the Council for possible follow-up decision.

VII. RULES OF PROCEDURE

S.C. Res. 1325, U.N. Doc. S/RES/1325 (Oct. 13, 2000):

The Security Council,

Recalling its resolutions 1261 (1999) of 25 August 1999, 1265 (1999) of 17 September 1999, 1296 (2000) of 19 April 2000 and 1314 (2000) of 11 August 2000, as well as relevant statements of its President, and *recalling also* the statement of its President to the press on the occasion of the United Nations Day for Women's Rights and International Peace (International Women's Day) of 8 March 2000 (SC/6816), ...

1. Urges Member States to ensure increased representation of women at all decision-making levels in national, regional and international institutions and mechanisms for the prevention, management, and resolution of conflict;

2. *Encourages* the Secretary-General to implement his strategic plan of action (A/49/587) calling for an increase in the participation of women at decision making levels in conflict resolution and peace processes;

3. *Urges* the Secretary-General to appoint more women as special representatives and envoys to pursue good offices on his behalf, and in this regard *calls on* Member States to provide candidates to the Secretary-General, for inclusion in a regularly updated centralized roster;

4. *Further urges* the Secretary-General to seek to expand the role and contribution of women in United Nations field-based operations, and especially among military observers, civilian police, human rights and humanitarian personnel;

5. *Expresses* its willingness to incorporate a gender perspective into peacekeeping operations, and *urges* the Secretary-General to ensure that, where appropriate, field operations include a gender component;

6. *Requests* the Secretary-General to provide to Member States training guidelines and materials on the protection, rights and the particular needs of women, as well as on the importance of involving women in all peacekeeping and peacebuilding measures, *invites* Member States to incorporate these elements as well as HIV/AIDS awareness training into their national training programmes for military and civilian police personnel in preparation for deployment, and *further requests* the Secretary-General to ensure that civilian personnel of peacekeeping operations receive similar training;

7. *Urges* Member States to increase their voluntary financial, technical and logistical support for gender-sensitive training efforts, including those undertaken by relevant funds and programmes, inter alia, the United Nations Fund for Women and United Nations Children's Fund, and by the Office of the United Nations High Commissioner for Refugees and other relevant bodies;

8. *Calls on* all actors involved, when negotiating and implementing peace agreements, to adopt a gender perspective, including, inter alia:

(a) The special needs of women and girls during repatriation and resettlement and for rehabilitation, reintegration and post-conflict reconstruction;

(b) Measures that support local women's peace initiatives and indigenous processes for conflict resolution, and that involve women in all of the implementation mechanisms of the peace agreements;

(c) Measures that ensure the protection of and respect for human rights of women and girls, particularly as they relate to the constitution, the electoral system, the police and the judiciary;

9. *Calls upon* all parties to armed conflict to respect fully international law applicable to the rights and protection of women and girls, especially as civilians. ...

10. *Calls on* all parties to armed conflict to take special measures to protect women and girls from gender-based violence, particularly rape and other forms of sexual abuse, and all other forms of violence in situations of armed conflict;

11. *Emphasizes* the responsibility of all States to put an end to impunity and to prosecute those responsible for genocide, crimes against humanity, and war crimes including those relating to sexual and other violence against women and girls, and in this regard *stresses* the need to exclude these crimes, where feasible from amnesty provisions;

12. *Calls upon* all parties to armed conflict to respect the civilian and humanitarian character of refugee camps and settlements, and to take into account the particular needs of women and girls, including in their design, and recalls its resolutions 1208 (1998) of 19 November 1998 and 1296 (2000) of 19 April 2000;

13. *Encourages* all those involved in the planning for disarmament, demobilization and reintegration to consider the different needs of female and male ex-combatants and to take into account the needs of their dependants; ...

S.C. Res. 1371, U.N. Doc. S/RES/1371 (Sept. 28, 2001):

The Security Council,

Reaffirming its resolutions 1269 (1999) of 19 October 1999 and 1368 (2001) of 12 September 2001,

Reaffirming also its unequivocal condemnation of the terrorist attacks which took place in New York, Washington, D.C., and Pennsylvania on 11 September 2001, and expressing its determination to prevent all such acts,

Reaffirming further that such acts, like any act of international terrorism, constitute a threat to international peace and security,

Reaffirming the inherent right of individual or collective self-defence as recognized by the Charter of the United Nations as reiterated in resolution 1368 (2001), ...

Acting under Chapter VII of the Charter of the United Nations,

1. *Decides* that all States shall:

(a) Prevent and suppress the financing of terrorist acts;

(b) Criminalize the wilful provision or collection, by any means, directly or indirectly, of funds by their nationals or in their territories with the intention that the funds should be used, or in the knowledge that they are to be used, in order to carry out terrorist acts;

(c) Freeze without delay funds and other financial assets or economic resources of persons who commit, or attempt to commit, terrorist acts or participate in or facilitate the commission of terrorist acts; of entities owned or controlled directly or indirectly by such persons; and of persons and entities acting on behalf of, or at the direction of such persons and entities, including funds derived or generated from property owned or controlled directly or indirectly by such persons and associated persons and entities;

(d) Prohibit their nationals or any persons and entities within their territories from making any funds, financial assets or economic resources or financial or other related services available, directly or indirectly, for the benefit of persons who commit or attempt to commit or facilitate or participate in the commission of terrorist acts, of entities owned or controlled, directly or indirectly, by such persons and of persons and entities acting on behalf of or at the direction of such persons;

2. *Decides also* that all States shall:

(a) Refrain from providing any form of support, active or passive, to entities or persons involved in terrorist acts, including by suppressing recruitment of members of terrorist groups and eliminating the supply of weapons to terrorists;

(b) Take the necessary steps to prevent the commission of terrorist acts, including by provision of early warning to other States by exchange of information;

(c) Deny safe haven to those who finance, plan, support, or commit terrorist acts, or provide safe havens;

(d) Prevent those who finance, plan, facilitate or commit terrorist acts from using their respective territories for those purposes against other States or their citizens;

(e) Ensure that any person who participates in the financing, planning, preparation or perpetration of terrorist acts or in supporting terrorist acts is brought to justice and ensure that, in addition to any other measures against them, such terrorist acts are established as serious criminal offences in domestic laws and regulations and that the punishment duly reflects the seriousness of such terrorist acts;

(f) Afford one another the greatest measure of assistance in connection with criminal investigations or criminal proceedings relating to the financing or support of terrorist acts, including assistance in obtaining evidence in their possession necessary for the proceedings;

(g) Prevent the movement of terrorists or terrorist groups by effective border controls and controls on issuance of identity papers and travel documents, and through measures for preventing counterfeiting, forgery or fraudulent use of identity papers and travel documents; ....

C. REGIONAL INSTRUMENTS

AFRICAN [BANJUL] CHARTER ON HUMAN AND PEOPLES' RIGHTS, *adopted* **June 27, 1981, OAU Doc. CAB/LEG/67/3 rev. 5, 21 I.L.M. 58 (1982),** *entered into force* **Oct. 21, 1986:**

Preamble

The African States members of the Organization of African Unity, parties to the present convention entitled "African Charter on Human and Peoples' Rights",

Recalling Decision 115 (XVI) of the Assembly of Heads of State and Government at its Sixteenth Ordinary Session held in Monrovia, Liberia, from 17 to 20 July 1979 on the preparation of "a preliminary draft on an African Charter on Human and Peoples' Rights providing *inter alia* for the establishment of bodies to promote and protect human and peoples' rights";

Considering the Charter of the Organization of African Unity, which stipulates that "freedom, equality, justice and dignity are essential objectives for the achievement of the legitimate aspirations of the African peoples";

Reaffirming the pledge they solemnly made in Article 2 of the said Charter to eradicate all forms of colonialism from Africa, to coordinate and intensify their cooperation and efforts to achieve a better life for the peoples of Africa and to promote international cooperation having due regard to the Charter of the United Nations and the Universal Declaration of Human Rights;

Taking into consideration the virtues of their historical tradition and the values of African civilization which should inspire and characterize their reflection on the concept of human and peoples' rights;

Recognizing on the one hand, that fundamental human rights stem from the attributes of human beings, which justifies their national and international protection and on the other hand that the reality and respect of peoples' rights should necessarily guarantee human rights;

Considering that the enjoyment of rights and freedoms also implies the performance of duties on the part of everyone;

Convinced that it is henceforth essential to pay a particular attention to the right to development and that civil and political rights cannot be dissociated from economic, social and cultural rights in their conception as well as universality and that the satisfaction of economic, social and cultural rights is a guarantee for the enjoyment of civil and political rights;

Conscious of their duty to achieve the total liberation of Africa, the peoples of which are still struggling for their dignity and genuine independence, and undertaking to eliminate colonialism, neo-colonialism, apartheid, zionism and to dismantle aggressive foreign military bases and all forms of discrimination, particularly those based on race, ethnic group, color, sex, language, religion or political opinions;

Reaffirming their adherence to the principles of human and peoples' rights and freedoms contained in the declarations, conventions and other instruments adopted by the Organization of African Unity, the Movement of Non-Aligned Countries and the United Nations;

Firmly convinced of their duty to promote and protect human and peoples' rights and freedoms taking into account the importance traditionally attached to these rights and freedoms in Africa;

Have agreed as follows:

PART I—RIGHTS AND DUTIES

CHAPTER I
HUMAN AND PEOPLES' RIGHTS

Article 1

The Member States of the Organization of African Unity parties to the present Charter shall recognize the rights, duties and freedoms enshrined in this Charter and shall undertake to adopt legislative or other measures to give effect to them.

Article 2

Every individual shall be entitled to the enjoyment of the rights and freedoms recognized and guaranteed in the present Charter without distinction of any kind such as race, ethnic group, color, sex, language, religion, political or any other opinion, national and social origin, fortune, birth or other status.

Article 3

1. Every individual shall be equal before the law.

2. Every individual shall be entitled to equal protection of the law.

Article 4

Human beings are inviolable. Every human being shall be entitled to respect for his life and the integrity of his person. No one may be arbitrarily deprived of this right.

Article 5

Every individual shall have the right to the respect of the dignity inherent in a human being and to the recognition of his legal status. All forms of exploitation and degradation of man particularly slavery, slave trade, torture, cruel, inhuman or degrading punishment and treatment shall be prohibited.

Article 6

Every individual shall have the right to liberty and to the security of his person. No one may be deprived of his freedom except for reasons and conditions previously laid down by law. In particular, no one may be arbitrarily arrested or detained.

Article 7

1. Every individual shall have the right to have his cause heard. This comprises:

(a) the right to an appeal to competent national organs against acts of violating his fundamental rights as recognized and guaranteed by conventions, laws, regulations and customs in force;

(b) the right to be presumed innocent until proved guilty by a competent court or tribunal;

(c) the right to defence, including the right to be defended by counsel of his choice;

(d) the right to be tried within a reasonable time by an impartial court or tribunal.

2. No one may be condemned for an act or omission which did not constitute a legally punishable offence at the time it was committed. No penalty may be inflicted for an offence for which no provision was made at the time it was committed. Punishment is personal and can be imposed only on the offender.

Article 8

Freedom of conscience, the profession and free practice of religion shall be guaranteed. No one may, subject to law and order, be submitted to measures restricting the exercise of these freedoms.

Article 9

1. Every individual shall have the right to receive information.

2. Every individual shall have the right to express and disseminate his opinions within the law.

Article 10

1. Every individual shall have the right to free association provided that he abides by the law.

2. Subject to the obligation of solidarity provided for in Article 29 no one may be compelled to join an association.

Article 11

Every individual shall have the right to assemble freely with others. The exercise of this right shall be subject only to necessary restrictions provided for by law in particular those enacted in the interest of national security, the safety, health, ethics and rights and freedoms of others.

Article 12

1. Every individual shall have the right to freedom of movement and residence within the borders of a State provided he abides by the law.

2. Every individual shall have the right to leave any country including his own, and to return to his country. This right may only be subject to restrictions, provided for by law for the protection of national security, law and order, public health or morality.

3. Every individual shall have the right, when persecuted, to seek and obtain asylum in other countries in accordance with laws of those countries and international conventions.

4. A non-national legally admitted in a territory of a State Party to the present Charter, may only be expelled from it by virtue of a decision taken in accordance with the law.

5. The mass expulsion of non-nationals shall be prohibited. Mass expulsion shall be that which is aimed at national, racial, ethnic or religious groups.

Article 13

1. Every citizen shall have the right to participate freely in the government of his country, either directly or through freely chosen representatives in accordance with the provisions of the law.

2. Every citizen shall have the right of equal access to the public service of his country.

3. Every individual shall have the right of access to public property and services in strict equality of all persons before the law.

Article 14

The right to property shall be guaranteed. It may only be encroached upon in the interest of public need or in the general interest of the community and in accordance with the provisions of appropriate laws.

Article 15

Every individual shall have the right to work under equitable and satisfactory conditions, and shall receive equal pay for equal work.

Article 16

1. Every individual shall have the right to enjoy the best attainable state of physical and mental health.

2. States parties to the present Charter shall take the necessary measures to protect the health of their people and to ensure that they receive medical attention when they are sick.

Article 17

1. Every individual shall have the right to education.

2. Every individual may freely, take part in the cultural life of his community.

3. The promotion and protection of morals and traditional values recognized by the community shall be the duty of the State.

Article 18

1. The family shall be the natural unit and basis of society. It shall be protected by the State which shall take care of its physical health and morals.

2. The State shall have the duty to assist the family which is the custodian or morals and traditional values recognized by the community.

3. The State shall ensure the elimination of every discrimination against women and also ensure the protection of the rights of the woman and the child as stipulated in international declarations and conventions.

4. The aged and the disabled shall also have the right to special measures of protection in keeping with their physical or moral needs.

Article 19

All peoples shall be equal; they shall enjoy the same respect and shall have the same rights. Nothing shall justify the domination of a people by another.

Article 20

1. All peoples shall have the right to existence. They shall have the unquestionable and inalienable right to self-determination. They shall freely determine their political status and shall pursue their economic and social development according to the policy they have freely chosen.

2. Colonized or oppressed peoples shall have the right to free themselves from the bonds of domination by resorting to any means recognized by the international community.

3. All peoples shall have the right to the assistance of the States Parties to the present Charter in their liberation struggle against foreign domination, be it political, economic or cultural.

Article 21

1. All peoples shall freely dispose of their wealth and natural resources. This right shall be exercised in the exclusive interest of the people. In no case shall a people be deprived of it.

2. In case of spoliation the dispossessed people shall have the right to the lawful recovery of its property as well as to an adequate compensation.

3. The free disposal of wealth and natural resources shall be exercised without prejudice to the obligation of promoting international economic cooperation based on mutual respect, equitable exchange and the principles of international law.

4. States Parties to the present Charter shall individually and collectively exercise the right to free disposal of their wealth and natural resources with a view to strengthening African unity and solidarity.

5. States Parties to the present Charter shall undertake to eliminate all forms of foreign economic exploitation particularly that practiced by international monopolies so as to enable their peoples to fully benefit from the advantages derived from their national resources.

Article 22

1. All peoples shall have the right to their economic, social and cultural development with due regard to their freedom and identity and in the equal enjoyment of the common heritage of mankind.

2. States shall have the duty, individually or collectively, to ensure the exercise of the right to development.

Article 23

1. All peoples shall have the right to national and international peace and security. The principles of solidarity and friendly relations implicitly affirmed by the Charter of the United Nations and reaffirmed by that of the Organization of African Unity shall govern relations between States.

2. For the purpose of strengthening peace, solidarity and friendly relations, States Parties to the present Charter shall ensure that:

(a) any individual enjoying the right of asylum under Article 12 of the present Charter shall not engage in subversive activities against his country of origin or any other State Party to the present Charter;

(b) their territories shall not be used as bases for subversive or terrorist activities against the people of any other State Party to the present Charter.

Article 24

All peoples shall have the right to a general satisfactory environment favorable to their development.

Article 25

States Parties to the present Charter shall have the duty to promote and ensure through teaching, education and publication, the respect of the rights and freedoms contained in the present Charter and to see to it that these freedoms and rights as well as corresponding obligations and duties are understood.

Article 26

States Parties to the present Charter shall have the duty to guarantee the independence of the Courts and shall allow the establishment and improvement of appropriate national institutions entrusted with the promotion and protection of the rights and freedoms guaranteed by the present Charter.

CHAPTER II
DUTIES

Article 27

1. Every individual shall have duties towards his family and society, the State and other legally recognized communities and the international community.

2. The rights and freedoms of each individual shall be exercised with due regard to the rights of others, collective security, morality and common interest.

Article 28

Every individual shall have the duty to respect and consider his fellow beings without discrimination, and to maintain relations aimed at promoting, safeguarding and reinforcing mutual respect and tolerance.

Article 29

The individual shall also have the duty:

1. To preserve the harmonious development of the family and to work for the cohesion and respect of the family; to respect his parents at all times, to maintain them in case of need;

2. To serve his national community by placing his physical and intellectual abilities at its service;

3. Not to compromise the security of the State whose national or resident he is;

4. To preserve and strengthen social and national solidarity, particularly when the latter is threatened;

5. To preserve and strengthen the national independence and the territorial integrity of his country and to contribute to its defence in accordance with the law;

6. To work to the best of his abilities and competence, and to pay taxes imposed by law in the interest of the society;

7. To preserve and strengthen positive African cultural values in his relations with other members of the society, in the spirit of tolerance, dialogue and consultation and, in general, to contribute to the promotion of the moral well being of society;

8. To contribute to the best of his abilities, at all times and at all levels, to the promotion and achievement of African unity.

PART II—MEASURES OF SAFEGUARD

CHAPTER I
ESTABLISHMENT AND ORGANIZATION OF THE AFRICAN COMMISSION ON HUMAN AND PEOPLES' RIGHTS

Article 30

An African Commission on Human and Peoples' Rights, hereinafter called "the Commission", shall be established within the Organization of African Unity to promote human and peoples' rights and ensure their protection in Africa.

Article 31

1. The Commission shall consist of eleven members chosen from amongst African personalities of the highest reputation, known for their high morality, integrity, impartiality and competence in matters of human and peoples' rights; particular consideration being given to persons having legal experience.

2. The members of the Commission shall serve in their personal capacity.

Article 32

The Commission shall not include more than one national of the same State.

Article 33

The members of the Commission shall be elected by secret ballot by the Assembly of Heads of State and Government, from a list of persons nominated by the States Parties to the present Charter.

Article 34

Each State Party to the present Charter may not nominate more than two candidates. The candidates must have the nationality of one of the States Parties to the present Charter. When two candidates are nominated by a State, one of them may not be a national of that State.

Article 35

1. The Secretary-General of the Organization of African Unity shall invite States Parties to the present Charter at least four months before the elections to nominate candidates.

2. The Secretary-General of the Organization of African Unity shall make an alphabetical list of the persons thus nominated and communicate it to the Heads of State and Government at least one month before the elections.

Article 36

The members of the Commission shall be elected for a six year period and shall be eligible for re-election. However, the term of office of four of the members elected at the first election shall terminate after two years and the term of office of three others, at the end of four years.

Article 37

Immediately after the first election, the Chairman of the Assembly of Heads of State and Government of the Organization of African Unity shall draw lots to decide the names of those members referred to in Article 36.

Article 38

After their election, the members of the Commission shall make a solemn declaration to discharge their duties impartially and faithfully.

Article 39

1. In the case of death or resignation of a member of the Commission the Chairman of the Commission shall immediately inform the Secretary-General of the Organization of African Unity, who shall declare the seat vacant from the date of death or from the date on which the resignation takes effect.

2. If, in the unanimous opinion of other members of the Commission, a member has stopped discharging his duties for any reason other than a temporary absence, the Chairman of the Commission shall inform the Secretary-General of the Organization of African Unity, who shall then declare the seat vacant.

3. In each of the cases anticipated above, the Assembly of Heads of State and Government shall replace the member whose seat became vacant for the remaining period of his term unless the period is less than six months.

Article 40

Every member of the Commission shall be in office until the date his successor assumes office.

Article 41

The Secretary-General of the Organization of African Unity shall appoint the Secretary of the Commission. He shall also provide the staff and services necessary for the effective discharge of the duties of the Commission. The Organization of African Unity shall bear the cost of the staff and services.

Article 42

1. The Commission shall elect its Chairman and Vice-Chairman for a two-year period. They shall be eligible for re-election.

2. The Commission shall lay down its rules of procedure.

3. Seven members shall form the quorum.

4. In case of equality of votes, the Chairman shall have a casting vote.

5. The Secretary General may attend the meetings of the Commission. He shall neither participate in deliberations nor shall he be entitled to vote. The Chairman of the Commission may, however, invite him to speak.

Article 43

In discharging their duties, members of the Commission shall enjoy diplomatic privileges and immunities provided for in the General Convention on the Privileges and Immunities of the Organization of African Unity.

Article 44

Provision shall be made for the emoluments and allowances of the members of the Commission in the Regular Budget of the Organization of African Unity.

CHAPTER II
MANDATE OF THE COMMISSION

Article 45

The functions of the Commission shall be:

1. To promote Human and Peoples' Rights and in particular:

(a) to collect documents, undertake studies and researches on African problems in the field of human and peoples' rights, organize seminars, symposia and conferences, disseminate information, encourage national and local institutions concerned with human and peoples' rights, and should the case arise, give its views or make recommendations to Governments.

(b) to formulate and lay down, principles and rules aimed at solving legal problems relating to human and peoples' rights and fundamental freedoms upon which African Governments may base their legislation.

(c) co-operate with other African and international institutions concerned with the promotion and protection of human and peoples' rights.

2. Ensure the protection of human and peoples' rights under conditions laid down by the present Charter.

3. Interpret all the provisions of the present Charter at the request of a State Party, an institution of the OAU or an African Organization recognized by the OAU.

4. Perform any other tasks which may be entrusted to it by the Assembly of Heads of State and Government.

CHAPTER III
PROCEDURE OF THE COMMISSION

Article 46

The Commission may resort to any appropriate method of investigation; it may hear from the Secretary General of the Organization of African Unity or any other person capable of enlightening it.

Communication From States

Article 47

If a State Party to the present Charter has good reasons to believe that another State Party to this Charter has violated the provisions of the Charter, it may draw, by written communication, the attention of that State to the matter. This communication shall also be addressed to the Secretary General of the OAU and to the Chairman of the Commission. Within three months of the receipt of the communication, the State to which the communication is addressed shall give the enquiring State, written explanation or statement elucidating the matter. This should include as much as possible relevant information relating to the laws and rules of procedure applied and applicable, and the redress already given or course of action available.

Article 48

If within three months from the date on which the original communication is received by the State to which it is addressed, the issue is not settled to the satisfaction of the two States involved through bilateral negotiation or by any other peaceful procedure, either State shall have the right to submit the matter to the Commission through the Chairman and shall notify the other States involved.

Article 49

Notwithstanding the provisions of Article 47, if a State Party to the present Charter considers that another State Party has violated the provisions of the Charter, it may refer the matter directly to the Commission by addressing a communication to the Chairman, to the Secretary General of the Organization of African Unity and the State concerned.

Article 50

The Commission can only deal with a matter submitted to it after making sure that all local remedies, if they exist, have been exhausted, unless it is obvious to the Commission that the procedure of achieving these remedies would be unduly prolonged.

Article 51

1. The Commission may ask the States concerned to provide it with all relevant information.

2. When the Commission is considering the matter, States concerned may be represented before it and submit written or oral representation.

Article 52

After having obtained from the States concerned and from other sources all the information it deems necessary and after having tried all appropriate means to reach an amicable solution based on the respect of Human and Peoples' Rights, the Commission shall prepare, within a reasonable period of time from the notification referred to in Article 48, a report stating the facts and its findings. This report shall be sent to the States concerned and communicated to the Assembly of Heads of State and Government.

Article 53

While transmitting its report, the Commission may make to the Assembly of Heads of State and Government such recommendations as it deems useful.

Article 54

The Commission shall submit to each ordinary Session of the Assembly of Heads of State and Government a report on its activities.

Other Communications

Article 55

1. Before each Session, the Secretary of the Commission shall make a list of the communications other than those of States Parties to the present Charter and transmit them to the members of the Commission, who shall indicate which communications should be considered by the Commission.

2. A communication shall be considered by the Commission if a simple majority of its members so decide.

Article 56

Communications relating to human and peoples' rights referred to in Article 55 received by the Commission, shall be considered if they:

1. Indicate their authors even if the latter request anonymity,

2. Are compatible with the Charter of the Organization of African Unity or with the present Charter,

3. Are not written in disparaging or insulting language directed against the State concerned and its institutions or to the Organization of African Unity,

4. Are not based exclusively on news [disseminated] through the mass media,

5. Are sent after exhausting local remedies, if any, unless it is obvious that this procedure is unduly prolonged,

6. Are submitted within a reasonable period from the time local remedies are exhausted or from the date the Commission is seized of the matter, and

7. Do not deal with cases which have been settled by these States involved in accordance with the principles of the Charter of the United Nations, or the Charter of the Organization of African Unity or the provisions of the present Charter.

Article 57

Prior to any substantive consideration, all communications shall be brought to the knowledge of the State concerned by the Chairman of the Commission.

Article 58

1. When it appears after deliberations of the Commission that one or more communications apparently relate to special cases which reveal the existence of a series of serious or massive violations of human and peoples' rights, the Commission shall draw the attention of the Assembly of Heads of State and Government to these special cases.

2. The Assembly of Heads of State and Government may then request the Commission to undertake an in-depth study of these cases and make a factual report, accompanied by its findings and recommendations.

3. A case of emergency duly noticed by the Commission shall be submitted by the latter to the Chairman of the Assembly of Heads of State and Government who may request an in-depth study.

Article 59

1. All measures taken within the provisions of the present Chapter shall remain confidential until such a time as the Assembly of Heads of State and Government shall otherwise declare.

2. However, the report shall be published by the Chairman of the Commission upon the decision of the Assembly of Heads of State and Government.

3. The report on the activities of the Commission shall be published by its Chairman after it has been considered by the Assembly of Heads of State and Government.

CHAPTER IV
APPLICABLE PRINCIPLES

Article 60

The Commission shall draw inspiration from international law on human and peoples' rights, particularly from the provisions of various African instruments on human and peoples' rights, the Charter of the United Nations, the Charter of the Organization of African Unity, the Universal Declaration of Human Rights, other instruments adopted by the United Nations and by African countries in the field of human and peoples' rights as well as from the provisions of various instruments adopted within the Specialized Agencies of the United Nations of which the parties to the present Charter are members.

Article 61

The Commission shall also take into consideration, as subsidiary measures to determine the principles of law, other general or special international conventions, laying down rules expressly recognized by member States of the Organization of African Unity, African practices consistent with international norms on human and peoples' rights, customs generally accepted as law, general principles of law recognized by African States as well as legal precedents and doctrine.

Article 62

Each State Party shall undertake to submit every two years, from the date the present Charter comes into force, a report on the legislative or other measures taken with a view to giving effect to the rights and freedoms recognized and guaranteed by the present Charter.

Article 63

1. The present Charter shall be open to signature, ratification or adherence of the member states of the Organization of African Unity.

2. The instruments of ratification or adherence to the present Charter shall be deposited with the Secretary-General of the Organization of African Unity.

3. The present Charter shall come into force three months after the reception by the Secretary General of the instruments of ratification or adherence of a simple majority of the member states of the Organization of African Unity.

PART III—GENERAL PROVISIONS

Article 64

1. After the coming into force of the present Charter, members of the Commission shall be elected in accordance with the relevant Articles of the present Charter.

2. The Secretary-General of the Organization of African Unity shall convene the first meeting of the Commission at the Headquarters of the Organization within three months of the constitution of the Commission. Thereafter, the Commission shall be convened by its Chairman whenever necessary but at least once a year.

Article 65

For each of the States that will ratify or adhere to the present Charter after its coming into force, the Charter shall take effect three months after the date of the deposit by that State of its instrument of ratification or adherence.

Article 66

Special protocols or agreements may, if necessary, supplement the provisions of the present Charter.

Article 67

The Secretary General of the Organization of African Unity shall inform member States of the Organization of the deposit of each instrument of ratification or adherence.

Article 68

The present Charter may be amended if a State Party makes a written request to that effect to the Secretary General of the Organization of African Unity. The Assembly of Heads of State and Government may only consider the draft amendment after all the States parties have been duly informed of it and the Commission has given its opinion on it at the request of the sponsoring State. The amendment shall be approved by a simple majority of the States parties. It shall come into force for each State which has accepted it in accordance with its constitutional procedure three months after the Secretary-General has received notice of the acceptance.

ADOPTED BY THE EIGHTEENTH ASSEMBLY OF HEADS OF STATE AND GOVERNMENT, JUNE 1981, NAIROBI, KENYA

PROTOCOL TO THE AFRICAN CHARTER ON HUMAN AND PEOPLES' RIGHTS ON THE RIGHTS OF WOMEN IN AFRICA, *adopted* **Sept. 13, 2000, OAU Doc. CAB/LEG/66.6,** *reprinted in* **1 Afr. Hum. Rts. L.J. 40,** *entered into force* **Nov. 25, 2005:**

The States Parties to this Protocol,

Considering that Article 66 of the African Charter on Human and Peoples' Rights provides for special protocols or agreements, if necessary, to supplement the provisions of the African Charter, and that the Assembly of Heads of State and Government of the Organization of African Unity meeting in its Thirty-first Ordinary Session in Addis Ababa, Ethiopia, in June 1995, endorsed by resolution AHG/Res.240 (XXXI) the recommendation of the African Commission on Human and Peoples' Rights to elaborate a Protocol on the Rights of Women in Africa;

Considering that Article 2 of the African Charter on Human and Peoples' Rights enshrines the principle of non-discrimination on the grounds of race, ethnic group, colour, sex, language, religion, political or any other opinion, national and social origin, fortune, birth or other status;

Further Considering that Article 18 of the African Charter on Human and Peoples' Rights calls on all States Parties to eliminate every discrimination against women and to ensure the protection of the rights of women as stipulated in international declarations and conventions;

Noting that Articles 60 and 61 of the African Charter on Human and Peoples' Rights recognise regional and international human rights instruments and African practices consistent with international norms on human and peoples' rights as being important reference points for the application and interpretation of the African Charter;

Recalling that women's rights have been recognised and guaranteed in all international human rights instruments, notably the Universal Declaration of Human Rights, the International Covenant on Civil and Political Rights, the International Covenant on Economic, Social and Cultural Rights, the Convention on the Elimination of All Forms of Discrimination Against Women and its Optional Protocol, the African Charter on the Rights and Welfare of the Child, and all other international and regional conventions and covenants relating to the rights of women as being inalienable, interdependent and indivisible human rights;

Noting that women's rights and women's essential role in development, have been reaffirmed in the United Nations Plans of Action on the Environment and Development in 1992, on Human Rights in 1993, on Population and Development in 1994 and on Social Development in 1995;

Recalling also United Nations Security Council's Resolution 1325 (2000) on the role of Women in promoting peace and security;

Reaffirming the principle of promoting gender equality as enshrined in the Constitutive Act of the African Union as well as the New Partnership for

Africa's Development, relevant Declarations, Resolutions and Decisions, which underline the commitment of the African States to ensure the full participation of African women as equal partners in Africa's development;

Further Noting that the African Platform for Action and the Dakar Declaration of 1994 and the Beijing Platform for Action of 1995 call on all Member States of the United Nations, which have made a solemn commitment to implement them, to take concrete steps to give greater attention to the human rights of women in order to eliminate all forms of discrimination and of gender-based violence against women;

Recognizing the crucial role of women in the preservation of African values based on the principles of equality, peace, freedom, dignity, justice, solidarity and democracy;

Bearing in Mind related Resolutions, Declarations, Recommendations, Decisions, Conventions and other Regional and Sub-Regional Instruments aimed at eliminating all forms of discrimination and at promoting equality between women and men;

Concerned that despite the ratification of the African Charter on Human and Peoples' Rights and other international human rights instruments by the majority of States Parties, and their solemn commitment to eliminate all forms of discrimination and harmful practices against women, women in Africa still continue to be victims of discrimination and harmful practices;

Firmly Convinced that any practice that hinders or endangers the normal growth and affects the physical and psychological development of women and girls should be condemned and eliminated;

Determined to ensure that the rights of women are promoted, realised and protected in order to enable them to enjoy fully all their human rights;

HAVE AGREED AS FOLLOWS:

Article 1

Definitions

For the purpose of the present Protocol:

a) "African Charter" means the African Charter on Human and Peoples' Rights;

b) "African Commission" means the African Commission on Human and Peoples' Rights;

c) "Assembly" means the Assembly of Heads of State and Government of the African Union;

d) "AU" means the African Union;

e) "Constitutive Act" means the Constitutive Act of the African Union;

f) "Discrimination against women" means any distinction, exclusion or restriction or any differential treatment based on sex and whose objectives or effects compromise or destroy the recognition, enjoyment or the exercise by women, regardless of their marital status, of human rights and fundamental freedoms in all spheres of life;

g) "Harmful Practices" means all behaviour, attitudes and/or practices which negatively affect the fundamental rights of women and girls, such as their right to life, health, dignity, education and physical integrity;

h) "NEPAD" means the New Partnership for Africa's Development established by the Assembly;

i) "States Parties" means the States Parties to this Protocol;

j) "Violence against women" means all acts perpetrated against women which cause or could cause them physical, sexual, psychological, and economic harm, including the threat to take such acts; or to undertake the imposition of arbitrary restrictions on or deprivation of fundamental freedoms in private or public life in peace time and during situations of armed conflicts or of war;

k) "Women" means persons of female gender, including girls;

Article 2

Elimination of Discrimination Against Women

1. States Parties shall combat all forms of discrimination against women through appropriate legislative, institutional and other measures. In this regard they shall:

a) include in their national constitutions and other legislative instruments, if not already done, the principle of equality between women and men and ensure its effective application;

b) enact and effectively implement appropriate legislative or regulatory measures, including those prohibiting and curbing all forms of discrimination particularly those harmful practices which endanger the health and general well-being of women;

c) integrate a gender perspective in their policy decisions, legislation, development plans, programmes and activities and in all other spheres of life;

d) take corrective and positive action in those areas where discrimination against women in law and in fact continues to exist;

e) support the local, national, regional and continental initiatives directed at eradicating all forms of discrimination against women.

2. States Parties shall commit themselves to modify the social and cultural patterns of conduct of women and men through public education, information, education and communication strategies, with a view to achieving the elimination of harmful cultural and traditional practices and all other practices which are based on the idea of the inferiority or the superiority of either of the sexes, or on stereotyped roles for women and men.

Article 3

Right to Dignity

1. Every woman shall have the right to dignity inherent in a human being and to the recognition and protection of her human and legal rights;

2. Every woman shall have the right to respect as a person and to the free development of her personality;

3. States Parties shall adopt and implement appropriate measures to prohibit any exploitation or degradation of women;

4. States Parties shall adopt and implement appropriate measures to ensure the protection of every woman's right to respect for her dignity and protection of women from all forms of violence, particularly sexual and verbal violence.

Article 4

The Rights to Life, Integrity and Security of the Person

1. Every woman shall be entitled to respect for her life and the integrity and security of her person. All forms of exploitation, cruel, inhuman or degrading punishment and treatment shall be prohibited.

2. States Parties shall take appropriate and effective measures to:

a) enact and enforce laws to prohibit all forms of violence against women including unwanted or forced sex whether the violence takes place in private or public;

b) adopt such other legislative, administrative, social and economic measures as may be necessary to ensure the prevention, punishment and eradication of all forms of violence against women;

c) identify the causes and consequences of violence against women and take appropriate measures to prevent and eliminate such violence;

d) actively promote peace education through curricula and social communication in order to eradicate elements in traditional and cultural beliefs, practices and stereotypes which legitimise and exacerbate the persistence and tolerance of violence against women;

e) punish the perpetrators of violence against women and implement programmes for the rehabilitation of women victims;

f) establish mechanisms and accessible services for effective information, rehabilitation and reparation for victims of violence against women;

g) prevent and condemn trafficking in women, prosecute the perpetrators of such trafficking and protect those women most at risk;

h) prohibit all medical or scientific experiments on women without their informed consent;

i) provide adequate budgetary and other resources for the implementation and monitoring of actions aimed at preventing and eradicating violence against women;

j) ensure that, in those countries where the death penalty still exists, not to carry out death sentences on pregnant or nursing women.

k) ensure that women and men enjoy equal rights in terms of access to refugee status, determination procedures and that women refugees are accorded the full protection and benefits guaranteed under international refugee law, including their own identity and other documents;

Article 5

Elimination of Harmful Practices

States Parties shall prohibit and condemn all forms of harmful practices which negatively affect the human rights of women and which are contrary to recognised international standards. States Parties shall take all necessary legislative and other measures to eliminate such practices, including:

a) creation of public awareness in all sectors of society regarding harmful practices through information, formal and informal education and outreach programmes;

b) prohibition, through legislative measures backed by sanctions, of all forms of female genital mutilation, scarification, medicalisation and para-medicalisation of female genital mutilation and all other practices in order to eradicate them;

c) provision of necessary support to victims of harmful practices through basic services such as health services, legal and judicial support, emotional and psychological counselling as well as vocational training to make them self-supporting;

d) protection of women who are at risk of being subjected to harmful practices or all other forms of violence, abuse and intolerance.

Article 6

Marriage

States Parties shall ensure that women and men enjoy equal rights and are regarded as equal partners in marriage. They shall enact appropriate national legislative measures to guarantee that:

a) no marriage shall take place without the free and full consent of both parties;

b) the minimum age of marriage for women shall be 18 years;

c) monogamy is encouraged as the preferred form of marriage and that the rights of women in marriage and family, including in polygamous marital relationships are promoted and protected;

d) every marriage shall be recorded in writing and registered in accordance with national laws, in order to be legally recognised;

e) the husband and wife shall, by mutual agreement, choose their matrimonial regime and place of residence;

f) a married woman shall have the right to retain her maiden name, to use it as she pleases, jointly or separately with her husband's surname;

g) a woman shall have the right to retain her nationality or to acquire the nationality of her husband;

h) a woman and a man shall have equal rights, with respect to the nationality of their children except where this is contrary to a provision in national legislation or is contrary to national security interests;

i) a woman and a man shall jointly contribute to safeguarding the interests of the family, protecting and educating their children;

j) during her marriage, a woman shall have the right to acquire her own property and to administer and manage it freely.

Article 7

Separation, Divorce and Annulment of Marriage

States Parties shall enact appropriate legislation to ensure that women and men enjoy the same rights in case of separation, divorce or annulment of marriage. In this regard, they shall ensure that:

a) separation, divorce or annulment of a marriage shall be effected by judicial order;

b) women and men shall have the same rights to seek separation, divorce or annulment of a marriage;

c) in case of separation, divorce or annulment of marriage, women and men shall have reciprocal rights and responsibilities towards their children. In any case, the interests of the children shall be given paramount importance;

d) in case of separation, divorce or annulment of marriage, women and men shall have the right to an equitable sharing of the joint property deriving from the marriage.

Article 8

Access to Justice and Equal Protection before the Law

Women and men are equal before the law and shall have the right to equal protection and benefit of the law. States Parties shall take all appropriate measures to ensure:

a) effective access by women to judicial and legal services, including legal aid;

b) support to local, national, regional and continental initiatives directed at providing women access to legal services, including legal aid;

c) the establishment of adequate educational and other appropriate structures with particular attention to women and to sensitise everyone to the rights of women;

d) that law enforcement organs at all levels are equipped to effectively interpret and enforce gender equality rights;

e) that women are represented equally in the judiciary and law enforcement organs;

f) reform of existing discriminatory laws and practices in order to promote and protect the rights of women.

Article 9

Right to Participation in the Political and Decision-Making Process

1. States Parties shall take specific positive action to promote participative governance and the equal participation of women in the political life of their countries through affirmative action, enabling national legislation and other measures to ensure that:

a) women participate without any discrimination in all elections;

b) women are represented equally at all levels with men in all electoral processes;

c) women are equal partners with men at all levels of development and implementation of State policies and development programmes.

2. States Parties shall ensure increased and effective representation and participation of women at all levels of decision-making.

Article 10

Right to Peace

1. Women have the right to a peaceful existence and the right to participate in the promotion and maintenance of peace.

2. States Parties shall take all appropriate measures to ensure the increased participation of women:

a) in programmes of education for peace and a culture of peace;

b) in the structures and processes for conflict prevention, management and resolution at local, national, regional, continental and international levels;

c) in the local, national, regional, continental and international decision making structures to ensure physical, psychological, social and legal protection of asylum seekers, refugees, returnees and displaced persons, in particular women;

d) in all levels of the structures established for the management of camps and settlements for asylum seekers, refugees, returnees and displaced persons, in particular, women;

e) in all aspects of planning, formulation and implementation of post conflict reconstruction and rehabilitation.

3. States Parties shall take the necessary measures to reduce military expenditure significantly in favour of spending on social development in general, and the promotion of women in particular.

Article 11

Protection of Women in Armed Conflicts

1. States Parties undertake to respect and ensure respect for the rules of international humanitarian law applicable in armed conflict situations which affect the population, particularly women.

2. States Parties shall, in accordance with the obligations incumbent upon them under the international humanitarian law, protect civilians including women, irrespective of the population to which they belong, in the event of armed conflict.

3. States Parties undertake to protect asylum seeking women, refugees, returnees and internally displaced persons, against all forms of violence, rape and other forms of sexual exploitation, and to ensure that such acts are considered war crimes, genocide and/or crimes against humanity and that their perpetrators are brought to justice before a competent criminal jurisdiction.

4. States Parties shall take all necessary measures to ensure that no child, especially girls under 18 years of age, take a direct part in hostilities and that no child is recruited as a soldier.

Article 12

Right to Education and Training

1. States Parties shall take all appropriate measures to:

a) eliminate all forms of discrimination against women and guarantee equal opportunity and access in the sphere of education and training;

b) eliminate all stereotypes in textbooks, syllabuses and the media, that perpetuate such discrimination;

c) protect women, especially the girl-child from all forms of abuse, including sexual harassment in schools and other educational institutions and provide for sanctions against the perpetrators of such practices;

d) provide access to counselling and rehabilitation services to women who suffer abuses and sexual harassment;

e) integrate gender sensitisation and human rights education at all levels of education curricula including teacher training.

2. States Parties shall take specific positive action to:

a) promote literacy among women;

b) promote education and training for women at all levels and in all disciplines, particularly in the fields of science and technology;

c) promote the enrolment and retention of girls in schools and other training institutions and the organisation of programmes for women who leave school prematurely.

Article 13

Economic and Social Welfare Rights

States Parties shall adopt and enforce legislative and other measures to guarantee women equal opportunities in work and career advancement and other economic opportunities. In this respect, they shall:

a) promote equality of access to employment;

b) promote the right to equal remuneration for jobs of equal value for women and men;

c) ensure transparency in recruitment, promotion and dismissal of women and combat and punish sexual harassment in the workplace;

d) guarantee women the freedom to choose their occupation, and protect them from exploitation by their employers violating and exploiting their fundamental rights as recognised and guaranteed by conventions, laws and regulations in force;

e) create conditions to promote and support the occupations and economic activities of women, in particular, within the informal sector;

f) establish a system of protection and social insurance for women working in the informal sector and sensitise them to adhere to it;

g) introduce a minimum age for work and prohibit the employment of children below that age, and prohibit, combat and punish all forms of exploitation of children, especially the girl-child;

h) take the necessary measures to recognise the economic value of the work of women in the home;

i) guarantee adequate and paid pre and post-natal maternity leave in both the private and public sectors;

j) ensure the equal application of taxation laws to women and men;

k) recognise and enforce the right of salaried women to the same allowances and entitlements as those granted to salaried men for their spouses and children;

l) recognise that both parents bear the primary responsibility for the upbringing and development of children and that this is a social function for which the State and the private sector have secondary responsibility;

m) take effective legislative and administrative measures to prevent the exploitation and abuse of women in advertising and pornography.

Article 14

Health and Reproductive Rights

1. States Parties shall ensure that the right to health of women, including sexual and reproductive health is respected and promoted. This includes:

a) the right to control their fertility;

b) the right to decide whether to have children, the number of children and the spacing of children;

c) the right to choose any method of contraception;

d) the right to self protection and to be protected against sexually transmitted infections, including HIV/AIDS;

e) the right to be informed on one's health status and on the health status of one's partner, particularly if affected with sexually transmitted infections, including HIV/AIDS, in accordance with internationally recognised standards and best practices;

[f)] g) the right to have family planning education.

2. States Parties shall take all appropriate measures to:

a) provide adequate, affordable and accessible health services, including information, education and communication programmes to women especially those in rural areas;

b) establish and strengthen existing pre-natal, delivery and post-natal health and nutritional services for women during pregnancy and while they are breast-feeding;

c) protect the reproductive rights of women by authorising medical abortion in cases of sexual assault, rape, incest, and where the continued pregnancy endangers the mental and physical health of the mother or the life of the mother or the foetus.

Article 15

Right to Food Security

States Parties shall ensure that women have the right to nutritious and adequate food. In this regard, they shall take appropriate measures to:

a) provide women with access to clean drinking water, sources of domestic fuel, land, and the means of producing nutritious food;

b) establish adequate systems of supply and storage to ensure food security.

Article 16

Right to Adequate Housing

Women shall have the right to equal access to housing and to acceptable living conditions in a healthy environment. To ensure this right, States Parties shall grant to women, whatever their marital status, access to adequate housing.

Article 17

Right to Positive Cultural Context

1. Women shall have the right to live in a positive cultural context and to participate at all levels in the determination of cultural policies.

2. States Parties shall take all appropriate measures to enhance the participation of women in the formulation of cultural policies at all levels.

Article 18

Right to a Healthy and Sustainable Environment

1. Women shall have the right to live in a healthy and sustainable environment.

2. States Parties shall take all appropriate measures to:

   a) ensure greater participation of women in the planning, management and preservation of the environment and the sustainable use of natural resources at all levels;

   b) promote research and investment in new and renewable energy sources and appropriate technologies, including information technologies and facilitate women's access to, and participation in their control;

   c) protect and enable the development of women's indigenous knowledge systems;

   [d)] c) regulate the management, processing, storage and disposal of domestic waste;

   [e)] d) ensure that proper standards are followed for the storage, transportation and disposal of toxic waste.

Article 19

Right to Sustainable Development

Women shall have the right to fully enjoy their right to sustainable development. In this connection, the States Parties shall take all appropriate measures to:

   a) introduce the gender perspective in the national development planning procedures;

   b) ensure participation of women at all levels in the conceptualisation, decision-making, implementation and evaluation of development policies and programmes;

c) promote women's access to and control over productive resources such as land and guarantee their right to property;

d) promote women's access to credit, training, skills development and extension services at rural and urban levels in order to provide women with a higher quality of life and reduce the level of poverty among women;

e) take into account indicators of human development specifically relating to women in the elaboration of development policies and programmes; and

f) ensure that the negative effects of globalisation and any adverse effects of the implementation of trade and economic policies and programmes are reduced to the minimum for women.

Article 20

Widows' Rights

States Parties shall take appropriate legal measures to ensure that widows enjoy all human rights through the implementation of the following provisions:

a) that widows are not subjected to inhuman, humiliating or degrading treatment;

b) a widow shall automatically become the guardian and custodian of her children, after the death of her husband, unless this is contrary to the interests and the welfare of the children;

c) a widow shall have the right to remarry, and in that event, to marry the person of her choice.

Article 21

Right to Inheritance

1. A widow shall have the right to an equitable share in the inheritance of the property of her husband. A widow shall have the right to continue to live in the matrimonial house. In case of remarriage, she shall retain this right if the house belongs to her or she has inherited it.

2. Women and men shall have the right to inherit, in equitable shares, their parents' properties.

Article 22

Special Protection of Elderly Women

The States Parties undertake to:

a) provide protection to elderly women and take specific measures commensurate with their physical, economic and social needs as well as their access to employment and professional training;

b) ensure the right of elderly women to freedom from violence, including sexual abuse, discrimination based on age and the right to be treated with dignity.

Article 23

Special Protection of Women with Disabilities

The States Parties undertake to:

a) ensure the protection of women with disabilities and take specific measures commensurate with their physical, economic and social needs to facilitate their access to employment, professional and vocational training as well as their participation in decision-making;

b) ensure the right of women with disabilities to freedom from violence, including sexual abuse, discrimination based on disability and the right to be treated with dignity.

Article 24

Special Protection of Women in Distress

The States Parties undertake to:

a) ensure the protection of poor women and women heads of families including women from marginalized population groups and provide the an environment suitable to their condition and their special physical, economic and social needs;

b) ensure the right of pregnant or nursing women or women in detention by providing them with an environment which is suitable to their condition and the right to be treated with dignity.

Article 25

Remedies

States Parties shall undertake to:

a) provide for appropriate remedies to any woman whose rights or freedoms, as herein recognised, have been violated;

b) ensure that such remedies are determined by competent judicial, administrative or legislative authorities, or by any other competent authority provided for by law.

Article 26

Implementation and Monitoring

1. States Parties shall ensure the implementation of this Protocol at national level, and in their periodic reports submitted in accordance with Article 62 of the African Charter, indicate the legislative and other measures undertaken for the full realisation of the rights herein recognised.

2. States Parties undertake to adopt all necessary measures and in particular shall provide budgetary and other resources for the full and effective implementation of the rights herein recognised.

Article 27

Interpretation

The African Court on Human and Peoples' Rights shall be seized with matters of interpretation arising from the application or implementation of this Protocol.

Article 28

Signature, Ratification and Accession

1. This Protocol shall be open for signature, ratification and accession by the States Parties, in accordance with their respective constitutional procedures.

2. The instruments of ratification or accession shall be deposited with the Chairperson of the Commission of the AU.

Article 29

Entry into Force

1. This Protocol shall enter into force thirty (30) days after the deposit of the fifteenth (15) instrument of ratification.

2. For each State Party that accedes to this Protocol after its coming into force, the Protocol shall come into force on the date of deposit of the instrument of accession.

3. The Chairperson of the Commission of the AU shall notify all Member States of the coming into force of this Protocol.

Article 30

Amendment and Revision

1. Any State Party may submit proposals for the amendment or revision of this Protocol.

2. Proposals for amendment or revision shall be submitted, in writing, to the Chairperson of the Commission of the AU who shall transmit the same to the States Parties within thirty (30) days of receipt thereof.

3. The Assembly, upon advice of the African Commission, shall examine these proposals within a period of one (1) year following notification of States Parties, in accordance with the provisions of paragraph 2 of this article.

4. Amendments or revision shall be adopted by the Assembly by a simple majority.

5. The amendment shall come into force for each State Party, which has accepted it thirty (30) days after the Chairperson of the Commission of the AU has received notice of the acceptance.

Article 31

Status of the Present Protocol

None of the provisions of the present Protocol shall affect more favourable provisions for the realisation of the rights of women contained in the national legislation of States Parties or in any other regional, continental or international conventions, treaties or agreements applicable in these States Parties.

Article 32

Transitional Provisions

Pending the establishment of the African Court on Human and Peoples' Rights, the African Commission on Human and Peoples' Rights shall be the seized with matters of interpretation arising from the application and implementation of this Protocol.

Adopted by the 2nd Ordinary Session
of the Assembly of the Union

Maputo, 11 July 2003

AMERICAN CONVENTION ON HUMAN RIGHTS, Nov. 22, 1969, O.A.S. Treaty Series No. 36, at 1, OEA/Ser. L./V/II.23 doc. rev. 2, *entered into force* **July 18, 1978:**

PREAMBLE

The American states signatory to the present Convention,

Reaffirming their intention to consolidate in this hemisphere, within the framework of democratic institutions, a system of personal liberty and social justice based on respect for the essential rights of man;

Recognizing that the essential rights of man are not derived from one's being a national of a certain state, but are based upon attributes of the human personality, and that they therefore justify international protection in the form of a convention reinforcing or complementing the protection provided by the domestic law of the American states;

Considering that these principles have been set forth in the Charter of the Organization of American States, in the American Declaration of the Rights and Duties of Man, and in the Universal Declaration of Human Rights, and that they have been reaffirmed and refined in other international instruments, worldwide as well as regional in scope;

Reiterating that, in accordance with the Universal Declaration of Human Rights, the ideal of free men enjoying freedom from fear and want can be achieved only if conditions are created whereby everyone may enjoy his economic, social, and cultural rights, as well as his civil and political rights; and

Considering that the Third Special Inter-American Conference (Buenos Aires, 1967) approved the incorporation into the Charter of the Organization itself of broader standards with respect to economic, social, and educational rights and resolved that an inter-American convention on human rights should determine the structure, competence, and procedure of the organs responsible for these matters,

Have agreed upon the following:

PART I—STATE OBLIGATIONS AND RIGHTS PROTECTED

CHAPTER I
GENERAL OBLIGATIONS

ARTICLE 1

Obligation to Respect Rights

1. The States Parties to this Convention undertake to respect the rights and freedoms recognized herein and to ensure to all persons subject to their jurisdiction the free and full exercise of those rights and freedoms, without any discrimination for reasons of race, color, sex, language, religion, political or other opinion, national or social origin, economic status, birth, or any other social condition.

2. For the purposes of this Convention, "person" means every human being.

ARTICLE 2

Domestic Legal Effects

Where the exercise of any of the rights or freedoms referred to in Article 1 is not already ensured by legislative or other provisions, the States Parties undertake to adopt, in accordance with their constitutional processes and the provisions of this Convention, such legislative or other measures as may be necessary to give effect to those rights or freedoms.

CHAPTER II
CIVIL AND POLITICAL RIGHTS

ARTICLE 3

Right to Juridical Personality

Every person has the right to recognition as a person before the law.

ARTICLE 4

Right to Life

1. Every person has the right to have his life respected. This right shall be protected by law and, in general, from the moment of conception. No one shall be arbitrarily deprived of his life.

2. In countries that have not abolished the death penalty, it may be imposed only for the most serious crimes and pursuant to a final judgment rendered by a competent court and in accordance with a law establishing such punishment, enacted prior to the commission of the crime. The application of such punishment shall not be extended to crimes to which it does not presently apply.

3. The death penalty shall not be reestablished in states that have abolished it.

4. In no case shall capital punishment be inflicted for political offenses or related common crimes.

5. Capital punishment shall not be imposed upon persons who, at the time the crime was committed, were under 18 years of age or over 70 years of age; nor shall it be applied to pregnant women.

6. Every person condemned to death shall have the right to apply for amnesty, pardon, or commutation of sentence, which may be granted in all cases. Capital punishment shall not be imposed while such a petition is pending decision by the competent authority.

ARTICLE 5

Right to Humane Treatment

1. Every person has the right to have his physical, mental, and moral integrity respected.

2. No one shall be subjected to torture or to cruel, inhuman, or degrading punishment or treatment. All persons deprived of their liberty shall be treated with respect for the inherent dignity of the human person.

3. Punishment shall not be extended to any person other than the criminal.

4. Accused persons shall, save in exceptional circumstances, be segregated from convicted persons, and shall be subject to separate treatment appropriate to their status as unconvicted persons.

5. Minors while subject to criminal proceedings shall be separated from adults and brought before specialized tribunals, as speedily as possible, so that they may be treated in accordance with their status as minors.

6. Punishments consisting of deprivation of liberty shall have as an essential aim the reform and social readaptation of the prisoners.

ARTICLE 6

Freedom from Slavery

1. No one shall be subject to slavery or to involuntary servitude, which are prohibited in all their forms, as are the slave trade and traffic in women.

2. No one shall be required to perform forced or compulsory labor. This provision shall not be interpreted to mean that, in those countries in which the penalty established for certain crimes is deprivation of liberty at forced labor, the carrying out of such a sentence imposed by a competent court is prohibited. Forced labor shall not adversely affect the dignity or the physical or intellectual capacity of the prisoner.

3. For the purposes of this article, the following do not constitute forced or compulsory labor:

a) work or service normally required of a person imprisoned in execution of a sentence or formal decision passed by the competent judicial authority. Such work or service shall be carried out under the supervision and control of public authorities, and any persons performing such work or service shall not be placed at the disposal of any private party, company, or juridical person;

b) military service and, in countries in which conscientious objectors are recognized, national service that the law may provide for in lieu of military service;

c) service exacted in time of danger or calamity that threatens the existence or the well-being of the community; or

d) work or service that forms part of normal civic obligations.

ARTICLE 7

Right to Personal Liberty

1. Every person has the right to personal liberty and security.

2. No one shall be deprived of his physical liberty except for the reasons and under the conditions established beforehand by the constitution of the State Party concerned or by a law established pursuant thereto.

3. No one shall be subject to arbitrary arrest or imprisonment.

4. Anyone who is detained shall be informed of the reasons for his detention and shall be promptly notified of the charge or charges against him.

5. Any person detained shall be brought promptly before a judge or other officer authorized by law to exercise judicial power and shall be entitled to trial within a reasonable time or to be released without prejudice to the continuation of the proceedings. His release may be subject to guarantees to assure his appearance for trial.

6. Anyone who is deprived of his liberty shall be entitled to recourse to a competent court, in order that the court may decide without delay on the lawfulness of his arrest or detention and order his release if the arrest or detention is unlawful. In States Parties whose laws provide that anyone who believes himself to be threatened with deprivation of his liberty is entitled to recourse to a competent court in order that it may decide on the lawfulness of such threat, this remedy may not be restricted or abolished. The interested party or another person in his behalf is entitled to seek these remedies.

7. No one shall be detained for debt. This principle shall not limit the orders of a competent judicial authority issued for nonfulfillment of duties of support.

ARTICLE 8

Right to a Fair Trial

1. Every person has the right to a hearing, with due guarantees and within a reasonable time, by a competent, independent, and impartial tribunal, previously established by law, in the substantiation of any accusation of a criminal nature made against him or for the determination of his rights and obligations of a civil, labor, fiscal, or any other nature.

2. Every person accused of a criminal offense has the right to be presumed innocent so long as his guilt has not been proven according to law. During the proceedings, every person is entitled, with full equality, to the following minimum guarantees:

a) the right of the accused to be assisted without charge by a translator or interpreter, if he does not understand or does not speak the language of the tribunal or court;

b) prior notification in detail to the accused of the charges against him;

c) adequate time and means for the preparation of his defense;

d) the right of the accused to defend himself personally or to be assisted by legal counsel of his own choosing, and to communicate freely and privately with his counsel;

e) the inalienable right to be assisted by counsel provided by the state, paid or not as the domestic law provides, if the accused does not defend himself personally or engage his own counsel within the time period established by law;

f) the right of the defense to examine witnesses present in the court and to obtain the appearance, as witnesses, of experts or other persons who may throw light on the facts;

g) the right not to be compelled to be a witness against himself or to plead guilty; and

h) the right to appeal the judgment to a higher court.

3. A confession of guilt by the accused shall be valid only if it is made without coercion of any kind.

4. An accused person acquitted by a nonappealable judgment shall not be subjected to a new trial for the same cause.

5. Criminal proceedings shall be public, except insofar as may be necessary to protect the interests of justice.

ARTICLE 9

Freedom from Ex Post Facto Laws

No one shall be convicted of any act or omission that did not constitute a criminal offense, under the applicable law, at the time it was committed. A heavier penalty shall not be imposed than the one that was applicable at the time the criminal offense was committed. If subsequent to the commission of the offense the law provides for the imposition of a lighter punishment, the guilty person shall benefit therefrom.

ARTICLE 10

Right to Compensation

Every person has the right to be compensated in accordance with the law in the event he has been sentenced by a final judgment through a miscarriage of justice.

ARTICLE 11

Right to Privacy

1. Everyone has the right to have his honor respected and his dignity recognized.

2. No one may be the object of arbitrary or abusive interference with his private life, his family, his home, or his correspondence, or of unlawful attacks on his honor or reputation.

3. Everyone has the right to the protection of the law against such interference or attacks.

ARTICLE 12

Freedom of Conscience and Religion

1. Everyone has the right to freedom of conscience and of religion. This right includes freedom to maintain or to change one's religion or beliefs, and freedom to profess or disseminate one's religion or beliefs, either individually or together with others, in public or in private.

2. No one shall be subject to restrictions that might impair his freedom to maintain or to change his religion or beliefs.

3. Freedom to manifest one's religion and beliefs may be subject only to the limitations prescribed by law that are necessary to protect public safety, order, health, or morals, or the rights or freedoms of others.

4. Parents or guardians, as the case may be, have the right to provide for the religious and moral education of their children or wards that is in accord with their own convictions.

ARTICLE 13

Freedom of Thought and Expression

1. Everyone has the right to freedom of thought and expression. This right includes freedom to seek, receive, and impart information and ideas of all kinds, regardless of frontiers, either orally, in writing, in print, in the form of art, or through any other medium of one's choice.

2. The exercise of the right provided for in the foregoing paragraph shall not be subject to prior censorship but shall be subject to subsequent imposition of liability, which shall be expressly established by law to the extent necessary to ensure:

   a) respect for the rights or reputations of others; or

   b) the protection of national security, public order, or public health or morals.

3. The right of expression may not be restricted by indirect methods or means, such as the abuse of government or private controls over newsprint, radio broadcasting frequencies, or equipment used in the dissemination of information, or by any other means tending to impede the communication and circulation of ideas and opinions.

4. Notwithstanding the provisions of paragraph 2 above, public entertainments may be subject by law to prior censorship for the sole purpose of regulating access to them for the moral protection of childhood and adolescence.

5. Any propaganda for war and any advocacy of national, racial, or religious hatred that constitute incitements to lawless violence or to any other similar action against any person or group of persons on any grounds including those of race, color, religion, language, or national origin shall be considered as offenses punishable by law.

ARTICLE 14

Right of Reply

1. Anyone injured by inaccurate or offensive statements or ideas disseminated to the public in general by a legally regulated medium of communication has the right to reply or to make a correction using the same communications outlet, under such conditions as the law may establish.

2. The correction or reply shall not in any case remit other legal liabilities that may have been incurred.

3. For the effective protection of honor and reputation, every publisher, and every newspaper, motion picture, radio, and television company, shall have a person responsible who is not protected by immunities or special privileges.

ARTICLE 15

Right of Assembly

The right of peaceful assembly, without arms, is recognized. No restrictions may be placed on the exercise of this right other than those imposed in conformity with the law and necessary in a democratic society in the interest of national security, public safety or public order, or to protect public health or morals or the rights or freedom of others.

ARTICLE 16

Freedom of Association

1. Everyone has the right to associate freely for ideological, religious, political, economic, labor, social, cultural, sports, or other purposes.

2. The exercise of this right shall be subject only to such restrictions established by law as may be necessary in a democratic society, in the interest of national security, public safety or public order, or to protect public health or morals or the rights and freedoms of others.

3. The provisions of this article do not bar the imposition of legal restrictions, including even deprivation of the exercise of the right of association, on members of the armed forces and the police.

ARTICLE 17

Rights of the Family

1. The family is the natural and fundamental group unit of society and is entitled to protection by society and the state.

2. The right of men and women of marriageable age to marry and to raise a family shall be recognized, if they meet the conditions required by domestic laws, insofar as such conditions do not affect the principle of nondiscrimination established in this Convention.

3. No marriage shall be entered into without the free and full consent of the intending spouses.

4. The States Parties shall take appropriate steps to ensure the equality of rights and the adequate balancing of responsibilities of the spouses as to marriage, during marriage, and in the event of its dissolution. In case of dissolution, provision shall be made for the necessary protection of any children solely on the basis of their own best interests.

5. The law shall recognize equal rights for children born out of wedlock and those born in wedlock.

ARTICLE 18

Right to a Name

Every person has the right to a given name and to the surnames of his parents or that of one of them. The law shall regulate the manner in which this right shall be ensured for all, by the use of assumed names if necessary.

ARTICLE 19

Rights of the Child

Every minor child has the right to the measures of protection required by his condition as a minor on the part of his family, society, and the state.

ARTICLE 20

Right to Nationality

1. Every person has the right to a nationality.

2. Every person has the right to the nationality of the state in whose territory he was born if he does not have the right to any other nationality.

3. No one shall be arbitrarily deprived of his nationality or of the right to change it.

ARTICLE 21

Right to Property

1. Everyone has the right to the use and enjoyment of his property. The law may subordinate such use and enjoyment to the interest of society.

2. No one shall be deprived of his property except upon payment of just compensation, for reasons of public utility or social interest, and in the cases and

3. Usury and any other form of exploitation of man by man shall be prohibited by law.

ARTICLE 22

Freedom of Movement and Residence

1. Every person lawfully in the territory of a State Party has the right to move about in it, and to reside in it subject to the provisions of the law.

2. Every person has the right lo leave any country freely, including his own.

3. The exercise of the foregoing rights may be restricted only pursuant to a law to the extent necessary in a democratic society to prevent crime or to protect national security, public safety, public order, public morals, public health, or the rights or freedoms of others.

4. The exercise of the rights recognized in paragraph 1 may also be restricted by law in designated zones for reasons of public interest.

5. No one can be expelled from the territory of the state of which he is a national or be deprived of the right to enter it.

6. An alien lawfully in the territory of a State Party to this Convention may be expelled from it only pursuant to a decision reached in accordance with law.

7. Every person has the right to seek and be granted asylum in a foreign territory, in accordance with the legislation of the state and international

conventions, in the event he is being pursued for political offenses or related common crimes.

8. In no case may an alien be deported or returned to a country, regardless of whether or not it is his country of origin, if in that country his right to life or personal freedom is in danger of being violated because of his race, nationality, religion, social status, or political opinions.

9. The collective expulsion of aliens is prohibited.

ARTICLE 23

Right to Participate in Government

1. Every citizen shall enjoy the following rights and opportunities:

a) to take part in the conduct of public affairs, directly or through freely chosen representatives;

b) to vote and to be elected in genuine periodic elections, which shall be by universal and equal suffrage and by secret ballot that guarantees the free expression of the will of the voters; and

c) to have access, under general conditions of equality, to the public service of his country.

2. The law may regulate the exercise of the rights and opportunities referred to in the preceding paragraph only on the basis of age, nationality, residence, language, education, civil and mental capacity, or sentencing by a competent court in criminal proceedings.

ARTICLE 24

Right to Equal Protection

All persons are equal before the law. Consequently, they are entitled, without discrimination, to equal protection of the law.

ARTICLE 25

Right to Judicial Protection

1. Everyone has the right to simple and prompt recourse, or any other effective recourse, to a competent court or tribunal for protection against acts that violate his fundamental rights recognized by the constitution or laws of the state concerned or by this Convention, even though such violation may have been committed by persons acting in the course of their official duties.

2. The States Parties undertake:

a) to ensure that any person claiming such remedy shall have his rights determined by the competent authority provided for by the legal system of the state;

b) to develop the possibilities of judicial remedy; and

c) to ensure that the competent authorities shall enforce such remedies when granted.

CHAPTER III
ECONOMIC, SOCIAL, AND CULTURAL RIGHTS

ARTICLE 26

Progressive Development

The States Parties undertake to adopt measures, both internally and through international cooperation, especially those of an economic and technical nature, with a view to achieving progressively, by legislation or other appropriate means, the full realization of the rights implicit in the economic, social, educational, scientific, and cultural standards set forth in the Charter of the Organization of American States as amended by the Protocol of Buenos Aires.

CHAPTER IV
SUSPENSION OF GUARANTEES,
INTERPRETATION, AND APPLICATION

ARTICLE 27

Suspension of Guarantees

1. In time of war, public danger, or other emergency that threatens the independence or security of a State Party, it may take measures derogating from its obligations under the present Convention to the extent and for the period of time strictly required by the exigencies of the situation, provided that such measures are not inconsistent with its other obligations under international law and do not involve discrimination on the ground of race, color, sex, language, religion, or social origin.

2. The foregoing provision does not authorize any suspension of the following articles: Article 3 (Right to Juridical Personality), Article 4 (Right to Life), Article 5 (Right to Humane Treatment), Article 6 (Freedom from Slavery), Article 9 (Freedom from *Ex Post Facto* Laws), Article 12 (Freedom of Conscience and Religion), Article 17 (Rights of the Family), Article 18 (Right to a Name), Article 19 (Rights of the Child), Article 20 (Right to Nationality), and Article 23 (Right to Participate in Government), or of the judicial guarantees essential for the protection of such rights.

3. Any State Party availing itself of the right of suspension shall immediately inform the other States Parties, through the Secretary General of the Organization of American States, of the provisions the application of which it has suspended, the reasons that gave rise to the suspension, and the date set for the termination of such suspension.

ARTICLE 28

Federal Clause

1. Where a State Party is constituted as a federal state, the national government of such State Party shall implement all the provisions of the

Convention over whose subject matter it exercises legislative and judicial jurisdiction.

2. With respect to the provisions over whose subject matter the constituent units of the federal state have jurisdiction, the national government shall immediately take suitable measures, in accordance with its constitution and its laws, to the end that the competent authorities of the constituent units may adopt appropriate provisions for the fulfillment of this Convention.

3. Whenever two or more States Parties agree to form a federation or other type of association, they shall take care that the resulting federal or other compact contains the provisions necessary for continuing and rendering effective the standards of this Convention in the new state that is organized.

ARTICLE 29

Restrictions Regarding Interpretation

No provision of this Convention shall be interpreted as:

a) permitting any State Party, group, or person to suppress the enjoyment or exercise of the rights and freedoms recognized in this Convention or to restrict them to a greater extent than is provided for herein;

b) restricting the enjoyment or exercise of any right or freedom recognized by virtue of the laws of any State Party or by virtue of another convention to which one of the said states is a party;

c) precluding other rights or guarantees that are inherent in the human personality or derived from representative democracy as a form of government; or

d) excluding or limiting the effect that the American Declaration of the Rights and Duties of Man and other international acts of the same nature may have.

ARTICLE 30

Scope of Restrictions

The restrictions that, pursuant to this Convention, may be placed on the enjoyment or exercise of the rights or freedoms recognized herein may not be applied except in accordance with laws enacted for reasons of general interest and in accordance with the purpose for which such restrictions have been established.

ARTICLE 31

Recognition of Other Rights

Other rights and freedoms recognized in accordance with the procedures established in Articles 76 and 77 may be included in the system of protection of this Convention.

CHAPTER V
PERSONAL RESPONSIBILITIES

ARTICLE 32

Relationship between Duties and Rights

1. Every person has responsibilities to his family, his community, and mankind.

2. The rights of each person are limited by the rights of others, by the security of all, and by the just demands of the general welfare, in a democratic society.

PART II—MEANS OF PROTECTION

CHAPTER VI
COMPETENT ORGANS

ARTICLE 33

The following organs shall have competence with respect to matters relating to the fulfillment of the commitments made by the States Parties to this Convention:

a) the Inter-American Commission on Human Rights, referred to as "The Commission"; and

b) the Inter-American Court of Human Rights, referred to as "The Court".

CHAPTER VII
INTER-AMERICAN COMMISSION ON HUMAN RIGHTS

Section 1. Organization

ARTICLE 34

The Inter-American Commission on Human Rights shall be composed of seven members, who shall be persons of high moral character and recognized competence in the field of human rights.

ARTICLE 35

The Commission shall represent all the member countries of the Organization of American States.

ARTICLE 36

1. The members of the Commission shall be elected in a personal capacity by the General Assembly of the Organization from a list of candidates proposed by the governments of the member states.

2. Each of those governments may propose up to three candidates, who may be nationals of the states proposing them or of any other member state of the Organization of American States. When a slate of three is proposed, at least one of the candidates shall be a national of a state other than the one proposing the slate.

ARTICLE 37

1. The members of the Commission shall be elected for a term of four years and may be reelected only once, but the terms of three of the members chosen in the first election shall expire at the end of two years. Immediately following that election the General Assembly shall determine the names of those three members by lot.

2. No two nationals of the same state may be members of the Commission.

ARTICLE 38

Vacancies that may occur on the Commission for reasons other than the normal expiration of a term shall be filled by the Permanent Council of the Organization in accordance with the provisions of the Statute of the Commission.

ARTICLE 39

The Commission shall prepare its Statute, which it shall submit to the General Assembly for approval. It shall establish its own Regulations.

ARTICLE 40

Secretariat services for the Commission shall be furnished by the appropriate specialized unit of the General Secretariat of the Organization. This unit shall be provided with the resources required to accomplish the tasks assigned to it by the Commission.

Section 2. Functions

ARTICLE 41

The main function of the Commission shall be to promote respect for and defense of human rights. In the exercise of its mandate, it shall have the following functions and powers:

a) to develop an awareness of human rights among the peoples of America;

b) to make recommendations to the governments of the member states, when it considers such action advisable, for the adoption of progressive measures in favor of human rights within the framework of their domestic law and constitutional provisions as well as appropriate measures to further the observance of those rights;

c) to prepare such studies or reports as it considers advisable in the performance of its duties;

d) to request the governments of the member states to supply it with information on the measures adopted by them in matters of human rights;

e) to respond, through the General Secretariat of the Organization of American States, to inquiries made by the member states on matters related to human rights and, within the limits of its possibilities, to provide those states with the advisory services they request;

f) to take action on petitions and other communications pursuant to its authority under the provisions of Articles 44 through 51 of this Convention; and

g) to submit an annual report to the General Assembly of the Organization of American States.

ARTICLE 42

The States Parties shall transmit to the Commission a copy of each of the reports and studies that they submit annually to the Executive Committees of the Inter-American Economic and Social Council and the Inter-American Council for Education, Science, and Culture, in their respective fields, so that the Commission may watch over the promotion of the rights implicit in the economic, social, educational, scientific, and cultural standards set forth in the Charter of the Organization of American States as amended by the Protocol of Buenos Aires.

ARTICLE 43

The States Parties undertake to provide the Commission with such information as it may request of them as to the manner in which their domestic law ensures the effective application of any provisions of this Convention.

Section 3. Competence

ARTICLE 44

Any person or group of persons, or any nongovernmental entity legally recognized in one or more member states of the Organization, may lodge petitions with the Commission containing denunciations or complaints of violation of this Convention by a State Party.

ARTICLE 45

1. Any State Party may, when it deposits its instrument of ratification of or adherence to this Convention, or at any later time, declare that it recognizes the competence of the Commission to receive and examine communications in which a State Party alleges that another State Party has committed a violation of a human right set forth in this Convention.

2. Communications presented by virtue of this article may be admitted and examined only if they are presented by a State Party that has made a declaration recognizing the aforementioned competence of the Commission. The Commission shall not admit any communication against a State Party that has not made such a declaration.

3. A declaration concerning recognition of competence may be made to be valid for an indefinite time, for a specified period, or for a specific case.

4. Declarations shall be deposited with the General Secretariat of the Organization of American States, which shall transmit copies thereof to the member states of that Organization.

ARTICLE 46

1. Admission by the Commission of a petition or communication lodged in accordance with Articles 44 or 45 shall be subject to the following requirements:

 a) that the remedies under domestic law have been pursued and exhausted in accordance with generally recognized principles of international law;

 b) that the petition or communication is lodged within a period of six months from the date on which the party alleging violation of his rights was notified of the final judgment;

 c) that the subject of the petition or communication is not pending in another international proceeding for settlement; and

 d) that, in the case of Article 44, the petition contains the name, nationality, profession, domicile, and signature of the person or persons or of the legal representative of the entity lodging the petition.

2. The provisions of paragraphs 1.a and 1.b of this article shall not be applicable when:

 a) the domestic legislation of the state concerned does not afford due process of law for the protection of the right or rights that have allegedly been violated;

 b) the party alleging violation of his rights has been denied access to the remedies under domestic law or has been prevented from exhausting them; or

 c) there has been unwarranted delay in rendering a final judgment under the aforementioned remedies.

ARTICLE 47

The Commission shall consider inadmissible any petition or communication submitted under Articles 44 or 45 if:

a) any of the requirements indicated in Article 46 has not been met;

b) the petition or communication does not state facts that tend to establish a violation of the rights guaranteed by this Convention;

c) the statements of the petitioner or of the state indicate that the petition or communication is manifestly groundless or obviously out of order; or

d) the petition or communication is substantially the same as one previously studied by the Commission or by another international organization.

Section 4. Procedure

ARTICLE 48

1. When the Commission receives a petition or communication alleging violation of any of the rights protected by this Convention, it shall proceed as follows:

a) If it considers the petition or communication admissible, it shall request information from the government of the state indicated as being responsible for the alleged violations and shall furnish that government a transcript of the pertinent portions of the petition or communication. This information shall be submitted within a reasonable period to be determined by the Commission in accordance with the circumstances of each case.

b) After the information has been received, or after the period established has elapsed and the information has not been received, the Commission shall ascertain whether the grounds for the petition or communication still exist. If they do not, the Commission shall order the record to be closed.

c) The Commission may also declare the petition or communication inadmissible or out of order on the basis of information or evidence subsequently received.

d) If the record has not been closed, the Commission shall, with the knowledge of the parties, examine the matter set forth in the petition or communication in order to verify the facts. If necessary and advisable, the Commission shall carry out an investigation, for the effective conduct of which it shall request, and the states concerned shall furnish to it, all necessary facilities.

e) The Commission may request the states concerned to furnish any pertinent information and, if so requested, shall hear oral statements or receive written statements from the parties concerned.

f) The Commission shall place itself at the disposal of the parties concerned with a view to reaching a friendly settlement of the matter on the basis of respect for the human rights recognized in this Convention.

2. However, in serious and urgent cases, only the presentation of a petition or communication that fulfills all the formal requirements of admissibility shall be necessary in order for the Commission to conduct an investigation with the prior consent of the state in whose territory a violation has allegedly been committed.

ARTICLE 49

If a friendly settlement has been reached in accordance with paragraph 1.f of Article 48, the Commission shall draw up a report, which shall be transmitted to the petitioner and to the States Parties to this Convention, and shall then be communicated to the Secretary General of the Organization of American

States for publication. This report shall contain a brief statement of the facts and of the solution reached. If any party in the case so requests, the fullest possible information shall be provided to it.

ARTICLE 50

1. If a settlement is not reached, the Commission shall, within the time limit established by its Statute, draw up a report setting forth the facts and stating its conclusions. If the report, in whole or in part, does not represent the unanimous agreement of the members of the Commission, any member may attach to it a separate opinion. The written and oral statements made by the parties in accordance with paragraph 1.e of Article 48 shall also be attached to the report.

2. The report shall be transmitted to the states concerned, which shall not be at liberty to publish it.

3. In transmitting the report, the Commission may make such proposals and recommendations as it sees fit.

ARTICLE 51

1. If, within a period of three months from the date of the transmittal of the report of the Commission to the states concerned, the matter has not either been settled or submitted by the Commission or by the state concerned to the Court and its jurisdiction accepted, the Commission may, by the vote of an absolute majority of its members, set forth its opinion and conclusions concerning the question submitted for its consideration.

2. Where appropriate, the Commission shall make pertinent recommendations and shall prescribe a period within which the state is to take the measures that are incumbent upon it to remedy the situation examined.

3. When the prescribed period has expired, the Commission shall decide by the vote of an absolute majority of its members whether the state has taken adequate measures and whether to publish its report.

CHAPTER VIII
INTER-AMERICAN COURT OF HUMAN RIGHTS

Section 1. Organization

ARTICLE 52

1. The Court shall consist of seven judges, nationals of the member states of the Organization, elected in an individual capacity from among jurists of the highest moral authority and of recognized competence in the field of human rights, who possess the qualifications required for the exercise of the highest judicial functions in conformity with the law of the state of which they are nationals or of the state that proposes them as candidates.

2. No two judges may be nationals of the same state.

ARTICLE 53

1. The judges of the Court shall be elected by secret ballot by an absolute majority vote of the States Parties to the Convention, in the General Assembly of the Organization, from a panel of candidates proposed by those states.

2. Each of the States Parties may propose up to three candidates, nationals of the state that proposes them or of any other member state of the Organization of American States. When a slate of three is proposed, at least one of the candidates shall be a national of a state other than the one proposing the slate.

ARTICLE 54

1. The judges of the Court shall be elected for a term of six years and may be reelected only once. The term of three of the judges chosen in the first election shall expire at the end of three years. Immediately after the election, the names of the three judges shall be determined by lot in the General Assembly.

2. A judge elected to replace a judge whose term has not expired shall complete the term of the latter.

3. The judges shall continue in office until the expiration of their term. However, they shall continue to serve with regard to cases that they have begun to hear and that are still pending, for which purposes they shall not be replaced by the newly elected judges.

ARTICLE 55

1. If a judge is a national of any of the States Parties to a case submitted to the Court, he shall retain his right to hear that case.

2. If one of the judges called upon to hear a case should be a national of one of the States Parties to the case, any other State Party in the case may appoint a person of its choice to serve on the Court as an ad hoc judge.

3. If among the judges called upon to hear a case none is a national of any of the States Parties to the case, each of the latter may appoint an ad hoc judge.

4. An ad hoc judge shall possess the qualifications indicated in Article 52.

5. If several States Parties to the Convention should have the same interest in a case, they shall be considered as a single party for purposes of the above provisions. In case of doubt, the Court shall decide.

ARTICLE 56

Five judges shall constitute a quorum for the transaction of business by the Court.

ARTICLE 57

The Commission shall appear in all cases before the Court.

ARTICLE 58

1. The Court shall have its seat at the place determined by the States Parties to the Convention in the General Assembly of the Organization; however, it may convene in the territory of any member state of the Organization of American States when a majority of the Court considers it desirable, and with the prior consent of the state concerned. The seat of the Court may be changed by the States Parties to the Convention in the General Assembly by a two-thirds vote.

2. The Court shall appoint its own Secretary.

3. The Secretary shall have his office at the place where the Court has its seat and shall attend the meetings that the Court may hold away from its seat.

ARTICLE 59

The Court shall establish its Secretariat, which shall function under the direction of the Secretary of the Court, in accordance with the administrative standards of the General Secretariat of the Organization in all respects not incompatible with the independence of the Court. The staff of the Court's Secretariat shall be appointed by the Secretary General of the Organization, in consultation with the Secretary of the Court.

ARTICLE 60

The Court shall draw up its Statute which it shall submit to the General Assembly for approval. It shall adopt its own Rules of Procedure.

Section 2. Jurisdiction and Functions

ARTICLE 61

1. Only the States Parties and the Commission shall have the right to submit a case to the Court.

2. In order for the Court to hear a case, it is necessary that the procedures set forth in Articles 48 and 50 shall have been completed.

ARTICLE 62

1. A State Party may, upon depositing its instrument of ratification or adherence to this Convention, or at any subsequent time, declare that it recognizes as binding, *ipso facto*, and not requiring special agreement, the jurisdiction of the Court on all matters relating to the interpretation or application of this Convention.

2. Such declaration may be made unconditionally, on the condition of reciprocity, for a specified period, or for specific cases. It shall be presented to the Secretary General of the Organization, who shall transmit copies thereof to the other member states of the Organization and to the Secretary of the Court.

3. The jurisdiction of the Court shall comprise all cases concerning the interpretation and application of the provisions of this Convention that are submitted to it, provided that the States Parties to the case recognize or have recognized such jurisdiction, whether by special declaration pursuant to the preceding paragraphs, or by a special agreement.

ARTICLE 63

1. If the Court finds that there has been a violation of a right or freedom protected by this Convention, the Court shall rule that the injured party be ensured the enjoyment of his right or freedom that was violated. It shall also rule, if appropriate, that the consequences of the measure or situation that constituted the breach of such right or freedom be remedied and that fair compensation be paid to the injured party.

2. In cases of extreme gravity and urgency, and when necessary to avoid irreparable damage to persons, the Court shall adopt such provisional measures as it deems pertinent in matters it has under consideration. With respect to a case not yet submitted to the Court, it may act at the request of the Commission.

ARTICLE 64

1. The member states of the Organization may consult the Court regarding the interpretation of this Convention or of other treaties concerning the protection of human rights in the American states. Within their spheres of competence, the organs listed in Chapter X of the Charter of the Organization of American States, as amended by the Protocol of Buenos Aires, may in like manner consult the Court.

2. The Court, at the request of a member state of the Organization, may provide that state with opinions regarding the compatibility of any of its domestic laws with the aforesaid international instruments.

ARTICLE 65

To each regular session of the General Assembly of the Organization of American States the Court shall submit, for the Assembly's consideration, a report on its work during the previous year. It shall specify, in particular, the cases in which a state has not complied with its judgments, making any pertinent recommendations.

Section 3. Procedure

ARTICLE 66

1. Reasons shall be given for the judgment of the Court.

2. If the judgment does not represent in whole or in part the unanimous opinion of the judges, any judge shall be entitled to have his dissenting or separate opinion attached to the judgment.

ARTICLE 67

The judgment of the Court shall be final and not subject to appeal. In case of disagreement as to the meaning or scope of the judgment, the Court shall interpret it at the request of any of the parties, provided the request is made within ninety days from the date of notification of the judgment.

ARTICLE 68

1. The States Parties to the Convention undertake to comply with the judgment of the Court in any case to which they are parties.

2. That part of a judgment that stipulates compensatory damages may be executed in the country concerned in accordance with domestic procedure governing the execution of judgments against the state.

ARTICLE 69

The parties to the case shall be notified of the judgment of the Court and it shall be transmitted to the States Parties to the Convention.

CHAPTER IX
COMMON PROVISIONS

ARTICLE 70

1. The judges of the Court and the members of the Commission shall enjoy, from the moment of their election and throughout their term of office, the immunities extended to diplomatic agents in accordance with international law. During the exercise of their official function they shall, in addition, enjoy the diplomatic privileges necessary for the performance of their duties.

2. At no time shall the judges of the Court or the members of the Commission be held liable for any decisions or opinions issued in the exercise of their functions.

ARTICLE 71

The position of judge of the Court or member of the Commission is incompatible with any other activity that might affect the independence or impartiality of such judge or member, as determined in the respective statutes.

ARTICLE 72

The judges of the Court and the members of the Commission shall receive emoluments and travel allowances in the form and under the conditions set forth in their statutes, with due regard for the importance and independence of their office. Such emoluments and travel allowances shall be determined in the budget of the Organization of American States, which shall also include the expenses of the Court and its Secretariat. To this end, the Court shall draw up its own budget and submit it for approval to the General Assembly through the General Secretariat. The latter may not introduce any changes in it.

ARTICLE 73

The General Assembly may, only at the request of the Commission or the Court, as the case may be, determine sanctions to be applied against members of the Commission or judges of the Court when there are justifiable grounds for such action as set forth in the respective statutes. A vote of a two-thirds majority of the member states of the Organization shall be required for a decision in the case of members of the Commission and, in the case of judges of the Court, a two-thirds majority vote of the States Parties to the Convention shall also be required.

PART III—GENERAL AND TRANSITORY PROVISIONS

CHAPTER X
SIGNATURE, RATIFICATION, RESERVATIONS, AMENDMENTS, PROTOCOLS, AND DENUNCIATION

ARTICLE 74

1. This Convention shall be open for signature and ratification by or adherence of any member state of the Organization of American States.

2. Ratification of or adherence to this Convention shall be made by the deposit of an instrument of ratification or adherence with the General Secretariat of the Organization of American States. As soon as eleven states have deposited their instruments of ratification or adherence, the Convention shall enter into force. With respect to any state that ratifies or adheres thereafter, the Convention shall enter into force on the date of the deposit of its instrument of ratification or adherence.

3. The Secretary General shall inform all member states of the Organization of the entry into force of the Convention.

ARTICLE 75

This Convention shall be subject to reservations only in conformity with the provisions of the Vienna Convention on the Law of Treaties signed on May 23, 1969.

ARTICLE 76

1. Proposals to amend this Convention may be submitted to the General Assembly for the action it deems appropriate by any State Party directly, and by the Commission or the Court through the Secretary General.

2. Amendments shall enter into force for the States ratifying them on the date when two-thirds of the States Parties to this Convention have deposited their respective instruments of ratification. With respect to the other States Parties, the amendments shall enter into force on the dates on which they deposit their respective instruments of ratification.

ARTICLE 77

1. In accordance with Article 31, any State Party and the Commission may submit proposed protocols to this Convention for consideration by the States Parties at the General Assembly with a view to gradually including other rights and freedoms within its system of protection.

2. Each protocol shall determine the manner of its entry into force and shall be applied only among the States Parties to it.

ARTICLE 78

1. The States Parties may denounce this Convention at the expiration of a five-year period from the date of its entry into force and by means of notice given one year in advance. Notice of the denunciation shall be addressed to the Secretary General of the Organization, who shall inform the other States Parties.

2. Such a denunciation shall not have the effect of releasing the State Party concerned from the obligations contained in this Convention with respect to any act that may constitute a violation of those obligations and that has been taken by that state prior to the effective date of denunciation.

CHAPTER XI
TRANSITORY PROVISIONS

Section 1. Inter-American Commission on Human Rights

ARTICLE 79

Upon the entry into force of this Convention, the Secretary General shall, in writing, request each member state of the Organization to present, within ninety days, its candidates for membership on the Inter-American Commission on Human Rights. The Secretary General shall prepare a list in alphabetical order of the candidates presented, and transmit it to the member states of the Organization at least thirty days prior to the next session of the General Assembly.

ARTICLE 80

The members of the Commission shall be elected by secret ballot of the General Assembly from the list of candidates referred to in Article 79. The candidates who obtain the largest number of votes and an absolute majority of the votes of the representatives of the member states shall be declared elected. Should it become necessary to have several ballots in order to elect all the members of the Commission, the candidates who receive the smallest number of votes shall be eliminated successively, in the manner determined by the General Assembly.

Section 2. Inter-American Court of Human Rights

ARTICLE 81

Upon the entry into force of this Convention, the Secretary General shall, in writing, request each State Party to present, within ninety days, its candidates for membership on the Inter-American Court of Human Rights. The Secretary General shall prepare a list in alphabetical order of the candidates presented and transmit it to the States Parties at least thirty days prior to the next session of the General Assembly.

ARTICLE 82

The judges of the Court shall be elected from the list of candidates referred to in Article 81, by secret ballot of the States Parties to the Convention in the General Assembly. The candidates who obtain the largest number of votes and an absolute majority of the votes of the representatives of the States Parties shall be declared elected. Should it become necessary to have several ballots in order to elect all the judges of the Court, the candidates who receive the smallest number of votes shall be eliminated successively, in the manner determined by the States Parties.

AMERICAN DECLARATION OF THE RIGHTS AND DUTIES OF MAN, O.A.S. res. XXX, *adopted by* **the Ninth International Conference of American States, Bogota (1948): Novena Conferencia Internacional Americana, 6** *Actas y Documentos* **297-302 (1953):**

WHEREAS:

The American peoples have acknowledged the dignity of the individual, and their national constitutions recognize that juridical and political institutions, which regulate life in human society, have as their principal aim the protection of the essential rights of man and the creation of circumstances that will permit him to achieve spiritual and material progress and attain happiness;

The American states have on repeated occasions recognized that the essential rights of man are not derived from the fact that he is a national of certain state, but are based upon attributes of his human personality;

The international protection of the rights of man should be the principal guide of an evolving American law;

The affirmation of essential human rights by the American states together with the guarantees given by the internal regimes of the states established the initial system of protection considered by the American states as being suited to the present social and juridical conditions not without a recognition on their part that they should increasingly strengthen that system in the international field as conditions become more favorable.

The Ninth International Conference of American States

AGREES:

To adopt the following

AMERICAN DECLARATION OF THE RIGHTS AND DUTIES OF MAN

Preamble

All men are born free and equal, in dignity and in rights, and, being endowed by nature with reason and conscience, they should conduct themselves as brothers one to another.

The fulfillment of duty by each individual is a prerequisite to the rights of all. Rights and duties are interrelated in every social and political activity of man. While rights exalt individual liberty, duties express the dignity of that liberty.

Duties of a juridical nature presuppose others of a moral nature which support them in principle and constitute their basis.

Inasmuch as spiritual development is the supreme end of human existence and the highest expression thereof, it is the duty of man to serve that end with all his strength and resources.

Since culture is the highest social and historical expression of that spiritual development, it is the duty of man to preserve, practice and foster culture by every means within his power.

And, since moral conduct constitutes the noblest flowering of culture, it is the duty of every man always to hold it in high respect.

CHAPTER ONE

Rights

ARTICLE I. Every human being has the right to life, liberty and the security of his person.

ARTICLE II. All persons are equal before the law and have the rights and duties established in this declaration, without distinction as to race, sex, language, creed or any other factor.

ARTICLE III. Every person has the right freely to profess a religious faith, and to manifest and practice it both in public and in private.

ARTICLE IV. Every person has the right to freedom of investigation, of opinion, and of the expression and dissemination of ideas, by any medium whatsoever.

ARTICLE V. Every person has the right to the protection of the law against abusive attacks upon his honor, his reputation, and his private and family life.

ARTICLE VI. Every person has the right to establish a family, the basic element of society, and to receive protection therefor.

ARTICLE VII. All women, during pregnancy and the nursing period, and all children have the right to special protection, care and aid.

ARTICLE VIII. Every person has the right to fix his residence within the territory of the state of which he is a national, to move about freely within such territory, and not to leave it except by his own will.

ARTICLE IX. Every person has the right to the inviolability of his home.

ARTICLE X. Every person has the right to the inviolability and transmission of his correspondence.

ARTICLE XI. Every person has the right to the preservation of his health through sanitary and social measures relating to food, clothing, housing and medical care, to the extent permitted by public and community resources.

ARTICLE XII. Every person has the right to an education, which should be based on the principles of liberty, morality and human solidarity.

Likewise every person has the right to an education that will prepare him to attain a decent life, to raise his standard of living and to be a useful member of society.

The right to an education includes the right to equality of opportunity in every case, in accordance with natural talents, merit and the desire to utilize the resources that the state or the community is in a position to provide.

Every person has the right to receive, free, at least a primary education.

ARTICLE XIII. Every person has the right to take part in the cultural life of the community, to enjoy the arts, and to participate in the benefits that result from intellectual progress, especially scientific discoveries.

He likewise has the right to the protection of his moral and material interests as regards his inventions or any literary, scientific or artistic works of which he is the author.

ARTICLE XIV. Every person has the right to work, under proper conditions and to follow his vocation freely, in so far as existing conditions of employment permit.

Every person who works has the right to receive such remuneration as will, in proportion to this capacity and skill, assure him a standard of living suitable for himself and for his family.

ARTICLE XV. Every person has the right to leisure time, to wholesome recreation and to the opportunity for advantageous use of his free time to his spiritual, cultural and physical benefit.

ARTICLE XVI. Every person has the right to social security which will protect him from the consequences of unemployment, old age, and disabilities arising from causes beyond his control that make it physically or mentally impossible for him to earn a living.

ARTICLE XVII. Every person has the right to be recognized everywhere as a person having rights and obligations, and to enjoy the basic civil rights.

ARTICLE XVIII. Every person may resort to the courts to ensure respect for his legal rights. There should likewise be available to him a simple, brief procedure whereby the courts will protect him from acts of authority that, to his prejudice, violate any fundamental constitutional rights.

ARTICLE XIX. Every person has the right to the nationality to which he is entitled by law and to change it, if he so wishes, for the nationality of any other country that is willing to grant it to him.

ARTICLE XX. Every person having legal capacity is entitled to participate in the government of his country, directly or through his representatives, and to take part in popular elections, which shall be by secret ballot, and shall be honest, periodic and free.

ARTICLE XXI. Every person has the right to assemble peaceably with others in a formal public meeting or an informal gathering, in connection with matters of common interest of any nature.

ARTICLE XXII. Every person has the right to associate with others to promote, exercise and protect his legitimate interests of a political, economic, religious, social, cultural, professional, labor union or other nature.

ARTICLE XXIII. Every person has a right to own such private property as meets the essential needs of decent living and helps to maintain the dignity of the individual and of the home.

ARTICLE XXIV. Every person has the right to submit respectful petitions to any competent authority, for reasons of either general or private interest, and the right to obtain a prompt decision thereon.

ARTICLE XXV. No person may be deprived of his liberty except in the cases and according to the procedures established by preexisting law.

No person may be deprived of liberty for nonfulfillment of obligations of a purely civil character.

Every individual who has been deprived of his liberty has the right to have the legality of his detention ascertained without delay by a court, and the right to be tried without undue delay, or, otherwise, to be released. He also has the right to humane treatment during the time he is in custody.

ARTICLE XXVI. Every accused person is presumed to be innocent until proved guilty.

Every person accused of an offense has the right to be given an impartial and public hearing, and to be tried by courts previously established in accordance with preexisting laws, and not to receive cruel, infamous or unusual punishment.

ARTICLE XXVII. Every person has the right, in case of pursuit not resulting from ordinary crimes, to seek and receive asylum in foreign territory, in accordance with the laws of each country and with international agreements.

ARTICLE XXVIII. The rights of man are limited by the rights of others, by the security of all, and by the just demands of the general welfare and the advancement of democracy.

CHAPTER TWO

Rights

ARTICLE XXIX. It is the duty of the individual so to conduct himself in relation to others that each and every one may fully form and develop his personality.

ARTICLE XXX. It is the duty of every person to aid, support, educate and protect his minor children, and it is the duty of children to honor their parents always and to aid, support and protect them when they need it.

ARTICLE XXXI. It is the duty of every person to acquire at least an elementary education.

ARTICLE XXXII. It is the duty of every person to vote in the popular elections of the country to which he is a national, when he is legally capable of doing so.

ARTICLE XXXIII. It is the duty of every person to obey the law and other legitimate commands of the authorities of his country and those of the country in which he may be.

ARTICLE XXXIV. It is the duty of every able-bodied person to render whatever civil and military service his country may require for its defense and preservation, and, in case of public disaster, to render such services as may be in his power.

It is likewise his duty to hold any public office to which he may be elected by popular vote in the state of which he is a national.

ARTICLE XXXV. It is the duty of every person to cooperate with the state and the community with respect to social security and welfare, in accordance with his ability and with existing circumstances.

ARTICLE XXXVI. It is the duty of every person to pay the taxes established by law for the support of public services.

ARTICLE XXXVII. It is the duty of every person to work, as far as his capacity and possibilities permit, in order to obtain the means of livelihood or to benefit his community.

ARTICLE XXXVIII. It is the duty of every person to refrain from taking part in political activities that, according to law, are reserved exclusively to the citizens of the state in which he is an alien.

ADDITIONAL PROTOCOL TO THE AMERICAN CONVENTION ON HUMAN RIGHTS IN THE AREA OF ECONOMIC, SOCIAL AND CULTURAL RIGHTS "PROTOCOL OF SAN SALVADOR," O.A.S. Treaty Series No. 69 (1988), *entered into force* **November 16, 1999,** *reprinted in* **Basic Documents Pertaining to Human Rights in the Inter-American System, OEA/Ser.L.V/II.82 doc.6 rev.1 at 67 (1992):**

Preamble

The States Parties to the American Convention on Human Rights "Pact San José, Costa Rica,"

Reaffirming their intention to consolidate in this hemisphere, within the framework of democratic institutions, a system of personal liberty and social justice based on respect for the essential rights of man;

Recognizing that the essential rights of man are not derived from one's being a national of a certain State, but are based upon attributes of the human person, for which reason they merit international protection in the form of a convention reinforcing or complementing the protection provided by the domestic law of the American States;

Considering the close relationship that exists between economic, social and cultural rights, and civil and political rights, in that the different categories of rights constitute an indivisible whole based on the recognition of the dignity of the human person, for which reason both require permanent protection and promotion if they are to be fully realized, and the violation of some rights in favor of the realization of others can never be justified;

Recognizing the benefits that stem from the promotion and development of cooperation among States and international relations;

Recalling that, in accordance with the Universal Declaration of Human Rights and the American Convention on Human Rights, the ideal of free human beings enjoying freedom from fear and want can only be achieved if conditions are created whereby everyone may enjoy his economic, social and cultural rights as well as his civil and political rights;

Bearing in mind that, although fundamental economic, social and cultural rights have been recognized in earlier international instruments of both world and regional scope, it is essential that those rights be reaffirmed, developed, perfected and protected in order to consolidate in America, on the basis of full respect for the rights of the individual, the democratic representative form of government as well as the right of its peoples to development, self-determination, and the free disposal of their wealth and natural resources; and

Considering that the American Convention on Human Rights provides that draft additional protocols to that Convention may be submitted for consideration to the States Parties, meeting together on the occasion of the General Assembly of the Organization of American States, for the purpose of gradually incorporating other rights and freedoms into the protective system thereof,

Have agreed upon the following Additional Protocol to the American Convention on Human Rights "Protocol of San Salvador:"

Article 1

Obligation to Adopt Measures

The States Parties to this Additional Protocol to the American Convention on Human Rights undertake to adopt the necessary measures, both domestically and through international cooperation, especially economic and technical, to the extent allowed by their available resources, and taking into account their degree of development, for the purpose of achieving progressively and pursuant to their internal legislations, the full observance of the rights recognized in this Protocol.

Article 2

Obligation to Enact Domestic Legislation

If the exercise of the rights set forth in this Protocol is not already guaranteed by legislative or other provisions, the States Parties undertake to adopt, in accordance with their constitutional processes and the provisions of this Protocol, such legislative or other measures as may be necessary for making those rights a reality.

Article 3

Obligation of nondiscrimination

The State Parties to this Protocol undertake to guarantee the exercise of the rights set forth herein without discrimination of any kind for reasons related to race, color, sex, language, religion, political or other opinions, national or social origin, economic status, birth or any other social condition.

Article 4

Inadmissibility of Restrictions

A right which is recognized or in effect in a State by virtue of its internal legislation or international conventions may not be restricted or curtailed on the pretext that this Protocol does not recognize the right or recognizes it to a lesser degree.

Article 5

Scope of Restrictions and Limitations

The State Parties may establish restrictions and limitations on the enjoyment and exercise of the rights established herein by means of laws promulgated for the purpose of preserving the general welfare in a democratic society only to the extent that they are not incompatible with the purpose and reason underlying those rights.

Article 6

Right to Work

1. Everyone has the right to work, which includes the opportunity to secure the means for living a dignified and decent existence by performing a freely elected or accepted lawful activity.

2. The State Parties undertake to adopt measures that will make the right to work fully effective, especially with regard to the achievement of full employment, vocational guidance, and the development of technical and vocational training projects, in particular those directed to the disabled. The States Parties also undertake to implement and strengthen programs that help to ensure suitable family care, so that women may enjoy a real opportunity to exercise the right to work.

Article 7

Just, Equitable, and Satisfactory Conditions of Work

The States Parties to this Protocol recognize that the right to work to which the foregoing article refers presupposes that everyone shall enjoy that right under just, equitable, and satisfactory conditions, which the States Parties undertake to guarantee in their internal legislation, particularly with respect to:

a. Remuneration which guarantees, as a minimum, to all workers dignified and decent living conditions for them and their families and fair and equal wages for equal work, without distinction;

b. The right of every worker to follow his vocation and to devote himself to the activity that best fulfills his expectations and to change employment in accordance with the pertinent national regulations;

c. The right of every worker to promotion or upward mobility in his employment, for which purpose account shall be taken of his qualifications, competence, integrity and seniority;

d. Stability of employment, subject to the nature of each industry and occupation and the causes for just separation. In cases of unjustified dismissal, the worker shall have the right to indemnity or to reinstatement on the job or any other benefits provided by domestic legislation;

e. Safety and hygiene at work;

f. The prohibition of night work or unhealthy or dangerous working conditions and, in general, of all work which jeopardizes health, safety, or morals, for persons under 18 years of age. As regards minors under the age of 16, the work day shall be subordinated to the provisions regarding compulsory education and in no case shall work constitute an impediment to school attendance or a limitation on benefiting from education received;

g. A reasonable limitation of working hours, both daily and weekly. The days shall be shorter in the case of dangerous or unhealthy work or of night work;

h. Rest, leisure and paid vacations as well as remuneration for national holidays.

Article 8

Trade Union Rights

1. The States Parties shall ensure:

a. The right of workers to organize trade unions and to join the union of their choice for the purpose of protecting and promoting their interests. As an extension of that right, the States Parties shall permit trade unions to establish national federations or confederations, or to affiliate with those that already exist, as well as to form international trade union organizations and to affiliate with that of their choice. The States Parties shall also permit trade unions, federations and confederations to function freely;

b. The right to strike.

2. The exercise of the rights set forth above may be subject only to restrictions established by law, provided that such restrictions are characteristic of a democratic society and necessary for safeguarding public order or for protecting public health or morals or the rights and freedoms of others. Members of the armed forces and the police and of other essential public services shall be subject to limitations and restrictions established by law.

3. No one may be compelled to belong to a trade union.

Article 9

Right to Social Security

1. Everyone shall have the right to social security protecting him from the consequences of old age and of disability which prevents him, physically or mentally, from securing the means for a dignified and decent existence. In the event of the death of a beneficiary, social security benefits shall be applied to his dependents.

2. In the case of persons who are employed, the right to social security shall cover at least medical care and an allowance or retirement benefit in the case of work accidents or occupational disease and, in the case of women, paid maternity leave before and after childbirth.

Article 10

Right to Health

1. Everyone shall have the right to health, understood to mean the enjoyment of the highest level of physical, mental and social well-being.

2. In order to ensure the exercise of the right to health, the States Parties agree to recognize health as a public good and, particularly, to adopt the following measures to ensure that right:

a. Primary health care, that is, essential health care made available to all individuals and families in the community;

b. Extension of the benefits of health services to all individuals subject to the State's jurisdiction;

c. Universal immunization against the principal infectious diseases;

d. Prevention and treatment of endemic, occupational and other diseases;

e. Education of the population on the prevention and treatment of health problems, and

f. Satisfaction of the health needs of the highest risk groups and of those whose poverty makes them the most vulnerable.

Article 11

Right to a Healthy Environment

1. Everyone shall have the right to live in a healthy environment and to have access to basic public services.

2. The States Parties shall promote the protection, preservation, and improvement of the environment.

Article 12

Right to Food

1. Everyone has the right to adequate nutrition which guarantees the possibility of enjoying the highest level of physical, emotional and intellectual development.

2. In order to promote the exercise of this right and eradicate malnutrition, the States Parties undertake to improve methods of production, supply and distribution of food, and to this end, agree to promote greater international cooperation in support of the relevant national policies.

Article 13

Right to Education

1. Everyone has the right to education.

2. The States Parties to this Protocol agree that education should be directed towards the full development of the human personality and human dignity and should strengthen respect for human rights, ideological pluralism, fundamental freedoms, justice and peace. They further agree that education ought to enable everyone to participate effectively in a democratic and pluralistic society and achieve a decent existence and should foster

understanding, tolerance and friendship among all nations and all racial, ethnic or religious groups and promote activities for the maintenance of peace.

3. The States Parties to this Protocol recognize that in order to achieve the full exercise of the right to education:

a. Primary education should be compulsory and accessible to all without cost;

b. Secondary education in its different forms, including technical and vocational secondary education, should be made generally available and accessible to all by every appropriate means, and in particular, by the progressive introduction of free education;

c. Higher education should be made equally accessible to all, on the basis of individual capacity, by every appropriate means, and in particular, by the progressive introduction of free education;

d. Basic education should be encouraged or intensified as far as possible for those persons who have not received or completed the whole cycle of primary instruction;

e. Programs of special education should be established for the handicapped, so as to provide special instruction and training to persons with physical disabilities or mental deficiencies.

4. In conformity with the domestic legislation of the States Parties, parents should have the right to select the type of education to be given to their children, provided that it conforms to the principles set forth above.

5. Nothing in this Protocol shall be interpreted as a restriction of the freedom of individuals and entities to establish and direct educational institutions in accordance with the domestic legislation of the States Parties.

Article 14

Right to the Benefits of Culture

1. The States Parties to this Protocol recognize the right of everyone:

a. To take part in the cultural and artistic life of the community;

b. To enjoy the benefits of scientific and technological progress;

c. To benefit from the protection of moral and material interests deriving from any scientific, literary or artistic production of which he is the author.

2. The steps to be taken by the States Parties to this Protocol to ensure the full exercise of this right shall include those necessary for the conservation, development and dissemination of science, culture and art.

3. The States Parties to this Protocol undertake to respect the freedom indispensable for scientific research and creative activity.

4. The States Parties to this Protocol recognize the benefits to be derived from the encouragement and development of international cooperation and relations in the fields of science, arts and culture, and accordingly agree to foster greater international cooperation in these fields.

Article 15

Right to the Formation and the Protection of Families

1. The family is the natural and fundamental element of society and ought to be protected by the State, which should see to the improvement of its spiritual and material conditions.

2. Everyone has the right to form a family, which shall be exercised in accordance with the provisions of the pertinent domestic legislation.

3. The States Parties hereby undertake to accord adequate protection to the family unit and in particular:

a. To provide special care and assistance to mothers during a reasonable period before and after childbirth;

b. To guarantee adequate nutrition for children at the nursing stage and during school attendance years;

c. To adopt special measures for the protection of adolescents in order to ensure the full development of their physical, intellectual and moral capacities;

d. To undertake special programs of family training so as to help create a stable and positive environment in which children will receive and develop the values of understanding, solidarity, respect and responsibility.

Article 16

Rights of Children

Every child, whatever his parentage, has the right to the protection that his status as a minor requires from his family, society and the State. Every child has the right to grow under the protection and responsibility of his parents; save in exceptional, judicially-recognized circumstances, a child of young age ought not to be separated from his mother. Every child has the right to free and compulsory education, at least in the elementary phase, and to continue his training at higher levels of the educational system.

Article 17

Protection of the Elderly

Everyone has the right to special protection in old age. With this in view the States Parties agree to take progressively the necessary steps to make this right a reality and, particularly, to:

a. Provide suitable facilities, as well as food and specialized medical care, for elderly individuals who lack them and are unable to provide them for themselves;

b. Undertake work programs specifically designed to give the elderly the opportunity to engage in a productive activity suited to their abilities and consistent with their vocations or desires;

c. Foster the establishment of social organizations aimed at improving the quality of life for the elderly.

Article 18

Protection of the Handicapped

Everyone affected by a diminution of his physical or mental capacities is entitled to receive special attention designed to help him achieve the greatest possible development of his personality. The States Parties agree to adopt such measures as may be necessary for this purpose and, especially, to:

a. Undertake programs specifically aimed at providing the handicapped with the resources and environment needed for attaining this goal, including work programs consistent with their possibilities and freely accepted by them or their legal representatives, as the case may be;

b. Provide special training to the families of the handicapped in order to help them solve the problems of coexistence and convert them into active agents in the physical, mental and emotional development of the latter;

c. Include the consideration of solutions to specific requirements arising from needs of this group as a priority component of their urban development plans;

d. Encourage the establishment of social groups in which the handicapped can be helped to enjoy a fuller life.

Article 19

Means of Protection

1. Pursuant to the provisions of this article and the corresponding rules to be formulated for this purpose by the General Assembly of the Organization of American States, the States Parties to this Protocol undertake to submit periodic reports on the progressive measures they have taken to ensure due respect for the rights set forth in this Protocol.

2. All reports shall be submitted to the Secretary General of the OAS, who shall transmit them to the Inter-American Economic and Social Council and the Inter-American Council for Education, Science and Culture so that they may examine them in accordance with the provisions of this article. The Secretary General shall send a copy of such reports to the Inter-American Commission on Human Rights.

3. The Secretary General of the Organization of American States shall also transmit to the specialized organizations of the inter-American system of which the States Parties to the present Protocol are members, copies or pertinent portions of the reports submitted, insofar as they relate to matters within the purview of those organizations, as established by their constituent instruments.

4. The specialized organizations of the inter-American system may submit reports to the Inter-American Economic and Social Council and the Inter-American Council for Education, Science and Culture relative to compliance with the provisions of the present Protocol in their fields of activity.

5. The annual reports submitted to the General Assembly by the Inter-American Economic and Social Council and the Inter-American Council for Education, Science and Culture shall contain a summary of the information received from the States Parties to the present Protocol and the specialized organizations concerning the progressive measures adopted in order to ensure respect for the rights acknowledged in the Protocol itself and the general recommendations they consider to be appropriate in this respect.

6. Any instance in which the rights established in paragraph a) of Article 8 and in Article 13 are violated by action directly attributable to a State Party to this Protocol may give rise, through participation of the Inter-American Commission on Human Rights and, when applicable, of the Inter-American Court of Human Rights, to application of the system of individual petitions governed by Article 44 through 51 and 61 through 69 of the American Convention on Human Rights.

7. Without prejudice to the provisions of the preceding paragraph, the Inter-American Commission on Human Rights may formulate such observations and recommendations as it deems pertinent concerning the status of the economic, social and cultural rights established in the present Protocol in all or some of the States Parties, which it may include in its Annual Report to the General Assembly or in a special report, whichever it considers more appropriate.

8. The Councils and the Inter-American Commission on Human Rights, in discharging the functions conferred upon them in this article, shall take into account the progressive nature of the observance of the rights subject to protection by this Protocol. Article 20 ReservationsThe States Parties may, at the time of approval, signature, ratification or accession, make reservations to one or more specific provisions of this Protocol, provided that such reservations are not incompatible with the object and purpose of the Protocol.

Article 21

Signature, Ratification or Accession. Entry into Effect

1. This Protocol shall remain open to signature and ratification or accession by any State Party to the American Convention on Human Rights.

2. Ratification of or accession to this Protocol shall be effected by depositing an instrument of ratification or accession with the General Secretariat of the Organization of American States.

3. The Protocol shall enter into effect when eleven States have deposited their respective instruments of ratification or accession.

4. The Secretary General shall notify all the member states of the Organization of American States of the entry of the Protocol into effect.

Article 22

Inclusion of other Rights and Expansion of those Recognized

1. Any State Party and the Inter-American Commission on Human Rights may submit for the consideration of the States Parties meeting on the occasion of the General Assembly proposed amendments to include the recognition of other rights or freedoms or to extend or expand rights or freedoms recognized in this Protocol.

2. Such amendments shall enter into effect for the States that ratify them on the date of deposit of the instrument of ratification corresponding to the number representing two thirds of the States Parties to this Protocol. For all other States Parties they shall enter into effect on the date on which they deposit their respective instrument of ratification.

INTER-AMERICAN CONVENTION TO PREVENT AND PUNISH TORTURE, O.A.S. Treaty Series No. 67, *entered into force* **Feb. 28, 1987,** *reprinted in* **Basic Documents Pertaining to Human Rights in the Inter-American System, OEA/Ser.L.V/II.82 doc.6 rev.1 at 83 (1992):**

The American States signatory to the present Convention,

Aware of the provision of the American Convention on Human Rights that no one shall be subjected to torture or to cruel, inhuman, or degrading punishment or treatment;

Reaffirming that all acts of torture or any other cruel, inhuman, or degrading treatment or punishment constitute an offense against human dignity and a denial of the principles set forth in the Charter of the Organization of American States and in the Charter of the United Nations and are violations of the fundamental human rights and freedoms proclaimed in the American Declaration of the Rights and Duties of Man and the Universal Declaration of Human Rights;

Noting that, in order for the pertinent rules contained in the aforementioned global and regional instruments to take effect, it is necessary to draft an Inter-American Convention that prevents and punishes torture;

Reaffirming their purpose of consolidating in this hemisphere the conditions that make for recognition of and respect for the inherent dignity of man, and ensure the full exercise of his fundamental rights and freedoms,

Have agreed upon the following:

Article 1

The State Parties undertake to prevent and punish torture in accordance with the terms of this Convention.

Article 2

For the purposes of this Convention, torture shall be understood to be any act intentionally performed whereby physical or mental pain or suffering is inflicted on a person for purposes of criminal investigation, as a means of intimidation, as personal punishment, as a preventive measure, as a penalty, or for any other purpose. Torture shall also be understood to be the use of methods upon a person intended to obliterate the personality of the victim or to diminish his physical or mental capacities, even if they do not cause physical pain or mental anguish.

The concept of torture shall not include physical or mental pain or suffering that is inherent in or solely the consequence of lawful measures, provided that they do not include the performance of the acts or use of the methods referred to in this article.

Article 3

The following shall be held guilty of the crime of torture:

a. A public servant or employee who acting in that capacity orders, instigates or induces the use of torture, or who directly commits it or who, being able to prevent it, fails to do so.

b. A person who at the instigation of a public servant or employee mentioned in subparagraph (a) orders, instigates or induces the use of torture, directly commits it or is an accomplice thereto.

Article 4

The fact of having acted under orders of a superior shall not provide exemption from the corresponding criminal liability.

Article 5

The existence of circumstances such as a state of war, threat of war, state of siege or of emergency, domestic disturbance or strife, suspension of constitutional guarantees, domestic political instability, or other public emergencies or disasters shall not be invoked or admitted as justification for the crime of torture.

Neither the dangerous character of the detainee or prisoner, nor the lack of security of the prison establishment or penitentiary shall justify torture.

Article 6

In accordance with the terms of Article 1, the States Parties shall take effective measures to prevent and punish torture within their jurisdiction.

The States Parties shall ensure that all acts of torture and attempts to commit torture are offenses under their criminal law and shall make such acts punishable by severe penalties that take into account their serious nature.

The States Parties likewise shall take effective measures to prevent and punish other cruel, inhuman, or degrading treatment or punishment within their jurisdiction.

Article 7

The States Parties shall take measures so that, in the training of police officers and other public officials responsible for the custody of persons temporarily or definitively deprived of their freedom, special emphasis shall be put on the prohibition of the use of torture in interrogation, detention, or arrest.

The States Parties likewise shall take similar measures to prevent other cruel, inhuman, or degrading treatment or punishment.

Article 8

The States Parties shall guarantee that any person making an accusation of having been subjected to torture within their jurisdiction shall have the right to an impartial examination of his case.

Likewise, if there is an accusation or well-grounded reason to believe that an act of torture has been committed within their jurisdiction, the States Parties shall guarantee that their respective authorities will proceed properly and immediately to conduct an investigation into the case and to initiate, whenever appropriate, the corresponding criminal process.

After all the domestic legal procedures of the respective State and the corresponding appeals have been exhausted, the case may be submitted to the international fora whose competence has been recognized by that State.

Article 9

The States Parties undertake to incorporate into their national laws regulations guaranteeing suitable compensation for victims of torture.

None of the provisions of this article shall affect the right to receive compensation that the victim or other persons may have by virtue of existing national legislation.

Article 10

No statement that is verified as having been obtained through torture shall be admissible as evidence in a legal proceeding, except in a legal action taken against a person or persons accused of having elicited it through acts of torture, and only as evidence that the accused obtained such statement by such means.

Article 11

The States Parties shall take the necessary steps to extradite anyone accused of having committed the crime of torture or sentenced for commission of that crime, in accordance with their respective national laws on extradition and their international commitments on this matter.

Article 12

Every State Party shall take the necessary measures to establish its jurisdiction over the crime described in this Convention in the following cases:

a. When torture has been committed within its jurisdiction;

b. When the alleged criminal is a national of that State; or

c. When the victim is a national of that State and it so deems appropriate.

Every State Party shall also take the necessary measures to establish its jurisdiction over the crime described in this Convention when the alleged criminal is within the area under its jurisdiction and it is not appropriate to extradite him in accordance with Article 11.

This Convention does not exclude criminal jurisdiction exercised in accordance with domestic law.

Article 13

The crime referred to in Article 2 shall be deemed to be included among the extraditable crimes in every extradition treaty entered into between States Parties. The States Parties undertake to include the crime of torture as an extraditable offence in every extradition treaty to be concluded between them.

Every State Party that makes extradition conditional on the existence of a treaty may, if it receives a request for extradition from another State Party with which it has no extradition treaty, consider this Convention as the legal basis for extradition in respect of the crime of torture. Extradition shall be subject to the other conditions that may be required by the law of the requested State.

States Parties which do not make extradition conditional on the existence of a treaty shall recognize such crimes as extraditable offences between themselves, subject to the conditions required by the law of the requested State.

Extradition shall not be granted nor shall the person sought be returned when there are grounds to believe that his life is in danger, that he will be subjected to torture or to cruel, inhuman or degrading treatment, or that he will be tried by special or ad hoc courts in the requesting State.

Article 14

When a State Party does not grant the extradition, the case shall be submitted to its competent authorities as if the crime had been committed within its jurisdiction, for the purposes of investigation, and when appropriate, for criminal action, in accordance with its national law. Any decision adopted by these authorities shall be communicated to the State that has requested the extradition.

Article 15

No provision of this Convention may be interpreted as limiting the right of asylum, when appropriate, nor as altering the obligations of the States Parties in the matter of extradition.

Article 16

This Convention shall not limit the provisions of the American Convention on Human Rights, other conventions on the subject, or the Statutes of the Inter-American Commission on Human Rights, with respect to the crime of torture.

Article 17

The States Parties undertake to inform the Inter-American Commission on Human Rights of any legislative, judicial, administrative, or other measures they adopt in application of this Convention.

In keeping with its duties and responsibilities, the Inter-American Commission on Human Rights will endeavor in its annual report to analyze the existing situation in the member states of the Organization of American States in regard to the prevention and elimination of torture.

Article 18

This Convention is open to signature by the member states of the Organization of American States.

Article 19

This Convention is subject to ratification. The instruments of ratification shall be deposited with the General Secretariat of the Organization of American States.

Article 20

This Convention is open to accession by any other American state. The instruments of accession shall be deposited with the General Secretariat of the Organization of American States.

Article 21

The States Parties may, at the time of approval, signature, ratification, or accession, make reservations to this Convention, provided that such reservations are not incompatible with the object and purpose of the Convention and concern one or more specific provisions.

Article 22

This Convention shall enter into force on the thirtieth day following the date on which the second instrument of ratification is deposited. For each State ratifying or acceding to the Convention after the second instrument of ratification has been deposited, the Convention shall enter into force on the thirtieth day following the date on which that State deposits its instrument of ratification or accession.

Article 23

This Convention shall remain in force indefinitely, but may be denounced by any State Party. The instrument of denunciation shall be deposited with the General Secretariat of the Organization of American States. After one year from the date of deposit of the instrument of denunciation, this Convention shall cease to be in effect for the denouncing State but shall remain in force for the remaining States Parties.

Article 24

The original instrument of this Convention, the English, French, Portuguese, and Spanish texts of which are equally authentic, shall be deposited with the General Secretariat of the Organization of American States, which shall send a certified copy to the Secretariat of the United Nations for registration and publication, in accordance with the provisions of Article 102 of the United Nations Charter. The General Secretariat of the Organization of American

States shall notify the member states of the Organization and the States that have acceded to the Convention of signatures and of deposits of instruments of ratification, accession, and denunciation, as well as reservations, if any.

INTER-AMERICAN CONVENTION ON THE PREVENTION, PUNISHMENT AND ERADICATION OF VIOLENCE AGAINST WOMEN, 33 I.L.M. 1534 (1994), *entered into force* March 5, 1995:

PREAMBLE

THE STATES PARTIES TO THIS CONVENTION,

RECOGNIZING that full respect for human rights has been enshrined in the American Declaration of the Rights and Duties of Man and the Universal Declaration of Human Rights, and reaffirmed in other international and regional instruments;

AFFIRMING that violence against women constitutes a violation of their human rights and fundamental freedoms, and impairs or nullifies the observance, enjoyment and exercise of such rights and freedoms;

CONCERNED that violence against women is an offense against human dignity and a manifestation of the historically unequal power relations between women and men;

RECALLING the Declaration on the Elimination of Violence against Women, adopted by the Twenty-fifth Assembly of Delegates of the Inter-American Commission of Women, and affirming that violence against women pervades every sector of society regardless of class, race or ethnic group, income, culture, level of education, age or religion and strikes at its very foundations;

CONVINCED that the elimination of violence against women is essential for their individual and social development and their full and equal participation in all walks of life; and

CONVINCED that the adoption of a convention on the prevention, punishment and eradication of all forms of violence against women within the framework of the Organization of American States is a positive contribution to protecting the rights of women and eliminating violence against them,

HAVE AGREED to the following:

CHAPTER I
DEFINITION AND SCOPE OF APPLICATION

Article 1

For the purposes of this Convention, violence against women shall be understood as any act or conduct, based on gender, which causes death or physical, sexual or psychological harm or suffering to women, whether in the public or the private sphere.

Article 2

Violence against women shall be understood to include physical, sexual and psychological violence:

a. that occurs within the family or domestic unit or within any other interpersonal relationship, whether or not the perpetrator shares or has shared the same residence with the woman, including, among others, rape, battery and sexual abuse;

b. that occurs in the community and is perpetrated by any person, including, among others, rape, sexual abuse, torture, trafficking in persons, forced prostitution, kidnapping and sexual harassment in the workplace, as well as in educational institutions, health facilities or any other place; and

c. that is perpetrated or condoned by the state or its agents regardless of where it occurs.

CHAPTER II
RIGHTS PROTECTED

Article 3

Every woman has the right to be free from violence in both the public and private spheres.

Article 4

Every woman has the right to the recognition, enjoyment, exercise and protection of all human rights and freedoms embodied in regional and international human rights instruments. These rights include, among others:

a. The right to have her life respected;

b. The right to have her physical, mental and moral integrity respected;

c. The right to personal liberty and security;

d. The right not to be subjected to torture;

e. The right to have the inherent dignity of her person respected and her family protected;

f. The right to equal protection before the law and of the law;

g. The right to simple and prompt recourse to a competent court for protection against acts that violate her rights;

h. The right to associate freely;

i. The right of freedom to profess her religion and beliefs within the law; and

j. The right to have equal access to the public service of her country and to take part in the conduct of public affairs, including decision-making.

Article 5

Every woman is entitled to the free and full exercise of her civil, political, economic, social and cultural rights, and may rely on the full protection of those rights as embodied in regional and international instruments on human rights. The States Parties recognize that violence against women prevents and nullifies the exercise of these rights.

Article 6

The right of every woman to be free from violence includes, among others:

a. The right of women to be free from all forms of discrimination; and

b. The right of women to be valued and educated free of stereotyped patterns of behavior and social and cultural practices based on concepts of inferiority or subordination.

CHAPTER III
DUTIES OF THE STATES

Article 7

The States Parties condemn all forms of violence against women and agree to pursue, by all appropriate means and without delay, policies to prevent, punish and eradicate such violence and undertake to:

a. refrain from engaging in any act or practice of violence against women and to ensure that their authorities, officials, personnel, agents, and institutions act in conformity with this obligation;

b. apply due diligence to prevent, investigate and impose penalties for violence against women;

c. include in their domestic legislation penal, civil, administrative and any other type of provisions that may be needed to prevent, punish and eradicate violence against women and to adopt appropriate administrative measures where necessary;

d. adopt legal measures to require the perpetrator to refrain from harassing, intimidating or threatening the woman or using any method that harms or endangers her life or integrity, or damages her property;

e. take all appropriate measures, including legislative measures, to amend or repeal existing laws and regulations or to modify legal or customary practices which sustain the persistence and tolerance of violence against women;

f. establish fair and effective legal procedures for women who have been subjected to violence which include, among others, protective measures, a timely hearing and effective access to such procedures;

g. establish the necessary legal and administrative mechanisms to ensure that women subjected to violence have effective access to restitution, reparations or other just and effective remedies; and

h. adopt such legislative or other measures as may be necessary to give effect to this Convention.

Article 8

The States Parties agree to undertake progressively specific measures, including programs:

a. to promote awareness and observance of the right of women to be free from violence, and the right of women to have their human rights respected and protected;

b. to modify social and cultural patterns of conduct of men and women, including the development of formal and informal educational programs appropriate to every level of the educational process, to counteract prejudices, customs and all other practices which are based on the idea of the inferiority or superiority of either of the sexes or on the stereotyped roles for men and women which legitimize or exacerbate violence against women;

c. to promote the education and training of all those involved in the administration of justice, police and other law enforcement officers as well as other personnel responsible for implementing policies for the prevention, punishment and eradication of violence against women;

d. to provide appropriate specialized services for women who have been subjected to violence, through public and private sector agencies, including shelters, counseling services for ail family members where appropriate, and care and custody of the affected children;

e. to promote and support governmental and private sector education designed to raise the awareness of the public with respect to the problems of and remedies for violence against women;

f. to provide women who are subjected to violence access to effective readjustment and training programs to enable them to fully participate in public, private and social life;

g. to encourage the communications media to develop appropriate media guidelines in order to contribute to the eradication of violence against women in all its forms, and to enhance respect for the dignity of women;

h. to ensure research and the gathering of statistics and other relevant information relating to the causes, consequences and frequency of violence against women, in order to assess the effectiveness of measures to prevent, punish and eradicate violence against women and to formulate and implement the necessary changes; and

i. to foster international cooperation for the exchange of ideas and experiences and the execution of programs aimed at protecting women who are subjected to violence.

Article 9

With respect to the adoption of the measures in this Chapter, the States Parties shall take special account of the vulnerability of women to violence by reason of, among others, their race or ethnic background or their status as migrants, refugees or displaced persons. Similar consideration shall be given to women subjected to violence while pregnant or who are disabled, of minor age, elderly, socioeconomically disadvantaged, affected by armed conflict or deprived of their freedom.

CHAPTER IV
INTER-AMERICAN MECHANISMS OF PROTECTION

Article 10

In order to protect the right of every woman to be free from violence, the States Parties shall include in their national reports to the Inter-American Commission of Women information on measures adopted to prevent and prohibit violence against women, and to assist women affected by violence, as well as on any difficulties they observe in applying those measures, and the factors that contribute to violence against women.

Article 11

The States Parties to this Convention and the Inter-American Commission of Women may request of the Inter-American Court of Human Rights advisory opinions on the interpretation of this Convention.

Article 12

Any person or group of persons, or any nongovernmental entity legally recognized in one or more member states of the Organization, may lodge petitions with the Inter-American Commission on Human Rights containing denunciations or complaints of violations of Article 7 of this Convention by a State Party, and the Commission shall consider such claims in accordance with the norms and procedures established by the American Convention on Human Rights and the Statutes and Regulations of the Inter-American Commission on Human Rights for lodging and considering petitions.

CHAPTER V
GENERAL PROVISIONS

Article 13

No part of this Convention shall be understood to restrict or limit the domestic law of any State Party that affords equal or greater protection and guarantees of the rights of women and appropriate safeguards to prevent and eradicate violence against women.

Article 14

No part of this Convention shall be understood to restrict or limit the American Convention on Human Rights or any other international convention on the subject that provides for equal or greater protection in this area.

Article 15

This Convention is open to signature by all the member States of the Organization of American States.

Article 16

This Convention is subject to ratification. The instruments of ratification shall be deposited with the General Secretariat of the Organization of American States.

Article 17

This Convention is open to accession by any other state. Instruments of accession shall be deposited with the General Secretariat of the Organization of American States.

Article 18

Any State may, at the time of approval, signature, ratification, or accession, make reservations to this Convention provided that such reservations are:

a. not incompatible with the object and purpose of the Convention, and

b. not of a general nature and relate to one or more specific provisions.

Article 19

Any State Party may submit to the General Assembly, through the Inter-American Commission of Women, proposals for the amendment of this Convention.

Amendments shall enter into force for the states ratifying them on the date when two-thirds of the States Parties to this Convention have deposited their respective instruments of ratification. With respect to the other States Parties, the amendments shall enter into force on the dates on which they deposit their respective instruments of ratification.

Article 20

If a State Party has two or more territorial units in which the matters dealt with in this Convention are governed by different systems of law, it may, at the time of signature, ratification or accession, declare that this Convention shall extend to all its territorial units or to only one or more of them.

Such a declaration may be amended at any time by subsequent declarations, which shall expressly specify the territorial unit or units to which this Convention applies. Such subsequent declarations shall be transmitted to the General Secretariat of the Organization of American

States, and shall enter into force thirty days after the date of their receipt.

Article 21

This Convention shall enter into force on the thirtieth day after the date of deposit of the second instrument of ratification. For each State that ratifies or accedes to the Convention after the second instrument of ratification is deposited, it shall enter into force thirty days after the date on which that State deposited its instrument of ratification or accession.

Article 22

The Secretary General shall inform all member states of the Organization of American States of the entry into force of this Convention.

Article 23

The Secretary General of the Organization of American States shall present an annual report to the member states of the Organization on the status of this Convention, including the signatures, deposits of instruments of ratification and accession, and declarations, and any reservations that may have been presented by the States Parties, accompanied by a report thereon if needed.

Article 24

This Convention shall remain in force indefinitely, but any of the States Parties may denounce it by depositing an instrument to that effect with the General Secretariat of the Organization of American States. One year after the date of deposit of the instrument of denunciation, this Convention shall cease to be in effect for the denouncing State but shall remain in force for the remaining States Parties.

Article 25

The original instrument of this Convention, the English, French, Portuguese and Spanish texts of which are equally authentic, shall be deposited with the General Secretariat of the Organization of American States, which shall send a certified copy to the Secretariat of the United Nations for registration and publication in accordance with the provisions of Article 102 of the United Nations Charter.

IN WITNESS WHEREOF the undersigned Plenipotentiaries, being duly authorized thereto by their respective governments, have signed this Convention, which shall be called the Inter-American Convention on the Prevention, Punishment and Eradication of Violence against Women Convention of Belém do Pará.

DONE IN THE CITY OF BELÉM DO PARÁ, BRAZIL, the ninth of June in the year one thousand nine hundred ninety-four.

INTER-AMERICAN CONVENTION ON FORCED DISAPPEARANCE OF PERSONS, 33 I.L.M.1429 (1994), *entered into force* March 28, 1996:

PREAMBLE

The member states of the Organization of American States signatory to the present Convention,

DISTURBED by the persistence of the forced disappearance of persons;

REAFFIRMING that the true meaning of American solidarity and good neighborliness can be none other than that of consolidating in this Hemisphere, in the framework of democratic institutions, a system of individual freedom and social justice based on respect for essential human rights;

CONSIDERING that the forced disappearance of persons in an affront to the conscience of the Hemisphere and a grave and abominable offense against the inherent dignity of the human being, and one that contradicts the principles and purposes enshrined in the Charter of the Organization of American States;

CONSIDERING that the forced disappearance of persons of persons violates numerous non-derogable and essential human rights enshrined in the American Convention on Human Rights, in the American Declaration of the Rights and Duties of Man, and in the Universal Declaration of Human Rights;

RECALLING that the international protection of human rights is in the form of a convention reinforcing or complementing the protection provided by domestic law and is based upon the attributes of the human personality;

REAFFIRMING that the systematic practice of the forced disappearance of persons constitutes a crime against humanity;

HOPING that this Convention may help to prevent, punish, and eliminate the forced disappearance of persons in the Hemisphere and make a decisive contribution to the protection of human rights and the rule of law,

RESOLVE to adopt the following Inter-American Convention on Forced Disappearance of Persons:

Article I

The States Parties to this Convention undertake:

a. Not to practice, permit, or tolerate the forced disappearance of persons, even in states of emergency or suspension of individual guarantees;

b. To punish within their jurisdictions, those persons who commit or attempt to commit the crime of forced disappearance of persons and their accomplices and accessories;

c. To cooperate with one another in helping to prevent, punish, and eliminate the forced disappearance of persons;

d. To take legislative, administrative, judicial, and any other measures necessary to comply with the commitments undertaken in this Convention.

Article II

For the purposes of this Convention, forced disappearance is considered to be the act of depriving a person or persons of his or their freedom, in whatever way, perpetrated by agents of the state or by persons or groups of persons acting with the authorization, support, or acquiescence of the state, followed by an absence of information or a refusal to acknowledge that deprivation of freedom or to give information on the whereabouts of that person, thereby impeding his or her recourse to the applicable legal remedies and procedural guarantees.

Article III

The States Parties undertake to adopt, in accordance with their constitutional procedures, the legislative measures that may be needed to define the forced disappearance of persons as an offense and to impose an appropriate punishment commensurate with its extreme gravity. This offense shall be deemed continuous or permanent as long as the fate or whereabouts of the victim has not been determined.

The States Parties may establish mitigating circumstances for persons who have participated in acts constituting forced disappearance when they help to cause the victim to reappear alive or provide information that sheds light on the forced disappearance of a person.

Article IV

The acts constituting the forced disappearance of persons shall be considered offenses in every State Party. Consequently, each State Party shall take measures to establish its jurisdiction over such cases in the following instances:

a. When the forced disappearance of persons or any act constituting such offense was committed within its jurisdiction;

b. When the accused is a national of that state;

c. When the victim is a national of that state and that state sees fit to do so. Every State Party shall, moreover, take the necessary measures to establish its jurisdiction over the crime described in this Convention when the alleged criminal is within its territory and it does not proceed to extradite him.

This Convention does not authorize any State Party to undertake, in the territory of another State Party, the exercise of jurisdiction or the performance of functions that are placed within the exclusive purview of the authorities of that other Party by its domestic law.

Article V

The forced disappearance of persons shall not be considered a political offense for purposes of extradition.

The forced disappearance of persons shall be deemed to be included among the extraditable offenses in every extradition treaty entered into between States Parties.

The States Parties undertake to include the offense of forced disappearance as one which is extraditable in every extradition treaty to be concluded between them in the future.

Every State Party that makes extradition conditional on the existence of a treaty and receives a request for extradition from another State Party with which it has no extradition treaty may consider this Convention as the necessary legal basis for extradition with respect to the offense of forced disappearance.

States Parties which do not make extradition conditional on the existence of a treaty shall recognize such offense as extraditable, subject to the conditions imposed by the law of the requested state.

Extradition shall be subject to the provisions set forth in the constitution and other laws of the request state.

Article VI

When a State Party does not grant the extradition, the case shall be submitted to its competent authorities as if the offense had been committed within its jurisdiction, for the purposes of investigation and when appropriate, for criminal action, in accordance with its national law. Any decision adopted by these authorities shall be communicated to the state that has requested the extradition.

Article VII

Criminal prosecution for the forced disappearance of persons and the penalty judicially imposed on its perpetrator shall not be subject to statutes of limitations.

However, if there should be a norm of a fundamental character preventing application of the stipulation contained in the previous paragraph, the period of limitation shall be equal to that which applies to the gravest crime in the domestic laws of the corresponding State Party.

Article VIII

The defense of due obedience to superior orders or instructions that stipulate, authorize, or encourage forced disappearance shall not be admitted. All persons who receive such orders have the right and duty not to obey them.

The States Parties shall ensure that the training of public law-enforcement personnel or officials includes the necessary education on the offense of forced disappearance of persons.

Article IX

Persons alleged to be responsible for the acts constituting the offense of forced disappearance of persons may be tried only in the competent jurisdictions of ordinary law in each state, to the exclusion of all other special jurisdictions, particularly military jurisdictions.

The acts constituting forced disappearance shall not be deemed to have been committed in the course of military duties.

Privileges, immunities, or special dispensations shall not be admitted in such trials, without prejudice to the provisions set forth in the Vienna Convention on Diplomatic Relations.

Article X

In no case may exceptional circumstances such as a state of war, the threat of war, internal political instability, or any other public emergency be invoked to justify the forced disappearance of persons. In such cases, the right to expeditious and effective judicial procedures and recourse shall be retained as a means of determining the whereabouts or state of health of a person who has been deprived of freedom, or of identifying the official who ordered or carried out such deprivation of freedom.

In pursuing such procedures or recourse, and in keeping with applicable domestic law, the competent judicial authorities shall have free and immediate access to all detention centers and to each of their units, and to all places where there is reason to believe the disappeared person might be found including places that are subject to military jurisdiction.

Article XI

Every person deprived of liberty shall be held in an officially recognized place of detention and be brought before a competent judicial authority without delay, in accordance with applicable domestic law.

The States Parties shall establish and maintain official up-to-date registries of their detainees and, in accordance with their domestic law, shall make them available to relatives, judges, attorneys, any other person having a legitimate interest, and other authorities.

Article XII

The States Parties shall give each other mutual assistance in the search for, identification, location, and return of minors who have been removed to another state or detained therein as a consequence of the forced disappearance of their parents or guardians.

Article XIII

For the purposes of this Convention, the processing of petitions or communications presented to the Inter-American Commission on Human Rights alleging the forced disappearance of persons shall be subject to the procedures established in the American Convention on Human Rights and to the Statue and Regulations of the Inter-American Commission on Human Rights and to the Statute and Rules of Procedure of the Inter-American Court of Human Rights, including the provisions on precautionary measures.

Article XIV

Without prejudice to the provisions of the preceding article, when the Inter-American Commission on Human Rights receives a petition or communication regarding an alleged forced disappearance, its Executive Secretariat shall urgently and confidentially address the respective government, and shall request that government to provide as soon as possible information as to the whereabouts of the allegedly disappeared person together with any other information it considers pertinent, and such request shall be without prejudice as to the admissibility of the petition.

Article XV

None of the provisions of this Convention shall be interpreted as limiting other bilateral or multilateral treaties or other agreements signed by the Parties.

This Convention shall not apply to the international armed conflicts governed by the 1949 Geneva Conventions and their Protocols, concerning protection of wounded, sick, and shipwrecked members of the armed forces; and prisoners of war and civilians in time of war.

Article XVI

This Convention is open for signature by the member states of the Organization of American States.

Article XVII

This Convention is subject to ratification. The instruments of ratification shall be deposited with the General Secretariat of the Organization of American States.

Article XVIII

This Convention shall be open to accession by any other state. The instruments of accession shall be deposited with the General Secretariat of the Organization of American States.

Article XIX

The states may express reservations with respect to this Convention when adopting, signing, ratifying or acceding to it, unless such reservations are incompatible with the object and purpose of the Convention and as long as they refer to one or more specific provisions.

Article XX

This Convention shall enter into force for the ratifying states on the thirtieth day from the date of deposit of the second instrument of ratification.

For each state ratifying or acceding to the Convention after the second instrument of ratification has been deposited, the Convention shall enter into force on the thirtieth day from the date on which that state deposited its instrument of ratification or accession.

Article XXI

This Convention shall remain in force indefinitely, buy may be denounced by any State Party. The instrument of denunciation shall be deposited with the General Secretariat of the Organization of American States. The Convention shall cease to be in effect for the denouncing state and shall remain in force for the other States Parties one year from the date of deposit of the instrument of denunciation.

Article XXII

The original instrument of this Convention, the Spanish, English, Portuguese, and French texts of which are equally authentic, shall be deposited with the General Secretariat of the Organization of American States, which shall forward certified copies thereof to the United Nations Secretariat, for registration and publication, in accordance with Article 102 of the Charter of the United Nations. The General Secretariat of the Organization of American States shall notify member states of the Organization and states acceding to the Convention of the signatures and deposit of instruments of ratification, accession or denunciation, as well as of any reservations that may be expressed.

[EUROPEAN] CONVENTION FOR THE PROTECTION OF HUMAN RIGHTS AND FUNDAMENTAL FREEDOMS, 213 U.N.T.S. 222, *entered into force* Sept. 3, 1953, as amended by Protocols Nos 3, 5, 8, and 11 *which entered into force* on 21 September 1970, 20 December 1971, 1 January 1990, and 1 November 1998 *respectively*:

The Governments signatory hereto, being Members of the Council of Europe,

Considering the Universal Declaration of Human Rights proclaimed by the General Assembly of the United Nations on 10th December 1948;

Considering that this Declaration aims at securing the universal and effective recognition and observance of the Rights therein declared;

Considering that the aim of the Council of Europe is the achievement of greater unity between its Members and that one of the methods by which that aim is to be pursued is the maintenance and further realization of Human Rights and Fundamental Freedoms;

Reaffirming their profound belief in those Fundamental Freedoms which are the foundation of justice and peace in the world and are best maintained on the one hand by an effective political democracy and on the other by a common understanding and observance of the Human Rights upon which they depend;

Being resolved, as the Governments of European countries which are like-minded and have a common heritage of political traditions, ideals, freedom and the rule of law, to take the first steps for the collective enforcement of certain of the Rights stated in the Universal Declaration;

Have agreed as follows:

Article 1

The High Contracting Parties shall secure to everyone within their jurisdiction the rights and freedoms defined in Section I of this Convention.

SECTION I

Article 2

1. Everyone's right to life shall be protected by law. No one shall be deprived of his life intentionally save in the execution of a sentence of a court following his conviction of a crime for which this penalty is provided by law.

2. Deprivation of life shall not be regarded as inflicted in contravention of this Article when it results from the use of force which is no more than absolutely necessary:

    a. in defence of any person from unlawful violence;

    b. in order to effect a lawful arrest or to prevent the escape of a person lawfully detained;

    c. in action lawfully taken for the purpose of quelling a riot or insurrection.

Article 3

No one shall be subjected to torture or to inhuman or degrading treatment or punishment.

Article 4

1. No one shall be held in slavery or servitude.

2. No one shall be required to perform forced or compulsory labour.

3. For the purpose of this Article the term "forced or compulsory labour" shall not include

   a. any work required to be done in the ordinary course of detention imposed according to the provisions of Article 5 of this Convention or during conditional release from such detention;

   b. any service of a military character or, in case of conscientious objectors in countries where they are recognised, service exacted instead of compulsory military service;

   c. any service exacted in case of an emergency or calamity threatening the life or well-being of the community;

   d. any work or service which forms part of normal civil obligations.

Article 5

1. Everyone has the right to liberty and security of person. No one shall be deprived of his liberty save in the following cases and in accordance with the procedure prescribed by law:

   a. the lawful detention of a person after conviction by a competent court;

   b. the lawful arrest or detention of a person for non-compliance with the lawful order of a court or in order to secure the fulfillment of any obligation prescribed by law;

   c. the lawful arrest or detention of a person effected for the purpose of bringing him before the competent legal authority on reasonable suspicion of having committed an offence or when it is reasonably considered necessary to prevent his committing an offence or fleeing after having done so;

   d. the detention of a minor by lawful order for the purpose of educational supervision or his lawful detention for the purpose of bringing him before the competent legal authority;

   e. the lawful detention of persons for the prevention of the spreading of infectious diseases, of persons of unsound mind, alcoholics or drug addicts or vagrants;

   f. the lawful arrest or detention of a person to prevent his effecting an unauthorised entry into the country or of a person against whom action is being taken with a view to deportation or extradition.

2. Everyone who is arrested shall be informed promptly, in a language which he understands, of the reasons for his arrest and of any charge against him.

3. Everyone arrested or detained in accordance with the provisions of paragraph 1(c) of this Article shall be brought promptly before a judge or other officer authorised by law to exercise judicial power and shall be entitled to trial within a reasonable time or to release pending trial. Release may be conditioned by guarantees to appear for trial.

4. Everyone who is deprived of his liberty by arrest or detention shall be entitled to take proceedings by which the lawfulness of his detention shall be decided speedily by a court and his release ordered if the detention is not lawful.

5. Everyone who has been the victim of arrest or detention in contravention of the provisions of this Article shall have an enforceable right to compensation.

Article 6

1. In the determination of his civil rights and obligations or of any criminal charge against him, everyone is entitled to a fair and public hearing within a reasonable time by an independent and impartial tribunal established by law. Judgment shall be pronounced publicly but the press and public may be excluded from all or part of the trial in the interests of morals, public order or national security in a democratic society, where the interests of juveniles or the protection of the private life of the parties so require, or to the extent strictly necessary in the opinion of the court in special circumstances where publicity would prejudice the interests of justice.

2. Everyone charged with a criminal offence shall be presumed innocent until proved guilty according to law.

3. Everyone charged with a criminal offence has the following minimum rights:

a. to be informed promptly, in a language which he understands and in detail, of the nature and cause of the accusation against him;

b. to have adequate time and facilities for the preparation of his defence;

c. to defend himself in person or through legal assistance of his own choosing or, if he has not sufficient means to pay for legal assistance, to be given it free when the interests of justice so require;

d. to examine or have examined witnesses against him and to obtain the attendance and examination of witnesses on his behalf under the same conditions as witnesses against him;

e. to have the free assistance of an interpreter if he cannot understand or speak the language used in court.

Article 7

1. No one shall be held guilty of any criminal offence on account of any act or omission which did not constitute a criminal offence under national or international law at the time when it was committed. Nor shall a heavier penalty be imposed than the one that was applicable at the time the criminal offence was committed.

2. This Article shall not prejudice the trial and punishment of any person for any act or omission which, at the time when it was committed, was criminal according to the general principles of law recognised by civilised nations.

Article 8

1. Everyone has the right to respect for his private and family life, his home and his correspondence.

2. There shall be no interference by a public authority with the exercise of this right except such as is in accordance with the law and is necessary in a democratic society in the interests of national security, public safety or the economic well-being of the country, for the prevention of disorder or crime, for the protection of health or morals, or for the protection of the rights and freedoms of others.

Article 9

1. Everyone has the right to freedom of thought, conscience and religion; this right includes freedom to change his religion or belief and freedom, either alone or in community with others and in public or private, to manifest his religion or belief, in worship, teaching, practice and observance.

2. Freedom to manifest one's religion or beliefs shall be subject only to such limitations as are prescribed by law and are necessary in a democratic society in the interests of public safety, for the protection of public order, health or morals, or for the protection of the rights and freedoms of others.

Article 10

1. Everyone has the right to freedom of expression. This right shall include freedom to hold opinions and to receive and impart information and ideas without interference by public authority and regardless of frontiers. This Article shall not prevent States from requiring the licensing of broadcasting, television or cinema enterprises.

2. The exercise of these freedoms, since it carries with it duties and responsibilities, may be subject to such formalities, conditions, restrictions or penalties as are prescribed by law and are necessary in a democratic society, in the interests of national security, territorial integrity or public safety, for the prevention of disorder or crime, for the protection of health or morals, for the protection of the reputation or rights of others, for preventing the disclosure of information received in confidence, or for maintaining the authority and impartiality of the judiciary.

Article 11

1. Everyone has the right to freedom of peaceful assembly and to freedom of association with others, including the right to form and to join trade unions for the protection of his interests.

2. No restrictions shall be placed on the exercise of these rights other than such as are prescribed by law and are necessary in a democratic society in the interests of national security or public safety, for the prevention of disorder or crime, for the protection of health or morals or for the protection of the rights and freedoms of others. This Article shall not prevent the imposition of lawful restrictions on the exercise of these rights by members of the armed forces, of the police or of the administration of the State.

Article 12

Men and women of marriageable age have the right to marry and to found a family, according to the national laws governing the exercise of this right.

Article 13

Everyone whose rights and freedoms as set forth in this Convention are violated shall have an effective remedy before a national authority notwithstanding that the violation has been committed by persons acting in an official capacity.

Article 14

The enjoyment of the rights and freedoms set forth in this Convention shall be secured without discrimination on any ground such as sex, race, colour, language, religion, political or other opinion, national or social origin, association with a national minority, property, birth or other status.

Article 15

1. In time of war or other public emergency threatening the life of the nation any High Contracting Party may take measures derogating from its obligations under this Convention to the extent strictly required by the exigencies of the situation, provided that such measures are not inconsistent with its other obligations under international law.

2. No derogation from Article 2, except in respect of deaths resulting from lawful acts of war, or from Articles 3, 4 (paragraph 1) and 7 shall be made under this provision.

3. Any High Contracting Party availing itself of this right of derogation shall keep the Secretary-General of the Council of Europe fully informed of the measures which it has taken and the reasons therefor. It shall also inform the Secretary-General of the Council of Europe when such measures have ceased to operate and the provisions of the Convention are again being fully executed.

Article 16

Nothing in Articles 10, 11 and 14 shall be regarded as preventing the High Contracting Parties from imposing restrictions on the political activity of aliens.

Article 17

Nothing in this Convention may be interpreted as implying for any State, group or person any right to engage in any activity or perform any act aimed at the destruction of any of the rights and freedoms set forth herein or at their limitation to a greater extent than is provided for in the Convention.

Article 18

The restrictions permitted under this Convention to the said rights and freedoms shall not be applied for any purpose other than those for which they have been prescribed.

SECTION II

Article 19

To ensure the observance of the engagements undertaken by the High Contracting Parties in the Convention and the protocols thereto, there shall be set up a European Court of Human Rights, hereinafter referred to as "the Court". It shall function on a permanent basis.

Article 20

The Court shall consist of a number of judges equal to that of the High Contracting Parties.

Article 21

1. The judges shall be of high moral character and must either possess the qualifications required for appointment to high judicial office or be juris-consults of recognised competence.

2. The judges shall sit on the Court in their individual capacity.

3. During their term of office the judges shall not engage in any activity which is incompatible with their independence, impartiality or with the demands of a full-time office; all questions arising from the application of this paragraph shall be decided by the Court.

Article 22

1. The judges shall be elected by the Parliamentary Assembly with respect to each High Contracting Party by a majority of votes cast from a list of three candidates nominated by the High Contracting Party.

2. The same procedure shall be followed to complete the Court in the event of the accession of new High Contracting Parties and in filling casual vacancies.

Article 23

1. The judges shall be elected for a period of six years. They may be re-elected. However, the terms of office of one-half of the judges elected at the first election shall expire at the end of three years.

2. The judges whose terms of office are to expire at the end of the initial period of three years shall be chosen by lot by the Secretary General of the Council of Europe immediately after their election.

3. In order to ensure that, as far as possible, the terms of office of one-half of the judges are renewed every three years, the Parliamentary Assembly may decide, before proceeding to any subsequent election, that the term or terms of office of one or more judges to be elected shall be for a period other than six years but not more than nine and not less than three years.

4. In cases where more than one term of office is involved and where the Parliamentary Assembly applies the preceding paragraph, the allocation of the terms of office shall be effected by a drawing of lots by the Secretary General of the Council of Europe immediately after the election.

5. A judge elected to replace a judge whose term of office has not expired shall hold office for the remainder of his predecessor's term.

6. The terms of office of judges shall expire when they reach the age of 70.

7. The judges shall hold office until replaced. They shall, however, continue to deal with such cases as they already have under consideration.

Article 24

No judge may be dismissed from his office unless the other judges decide by a majority of two-thirds that he has ceased to fulfil the required conditions.

Article 25

The Court shall have a registry, the functions and organisation of which shall be laid down in the rules of the Court. The Court shall be assisted by legal secretaries.

Article 26

The plenary Court shall

a. elect its President and one or two Vice-Presidents for a period of three years; they may be re-elected;

b. set up Chambers, constituted for a fixed period of time;

c. elect the Presidents of the Chambers of the Court; they may be re-elected;

d. adopt the rules of the Court; and

e. elect the Registrar and one or more Deputy Registrars.

Article 27

1. To consider cases brought before it, the Court shall sit in committees of three judges, in Chambers of seven judges and in a Grand Chamber of seventeen judges. The Court's Chambers shall set up committees for a fixed period of time.

2. There shall sit as an ex officio member of the Chamber and the Grand Chamber the judge elected in respect of the State Party concerned or, if there is none or if he is unable to sit, a person of its choice who shall sit in the capacity of judge.

3. The Grand Chamber shall also include the President of the Court, the Vice-Presidents, the Presidents of the Chambers and other judges chosen in accordance with the rules of the Court. When a case is referred to the Grand Chamber under Article 43, no judge from the Chamber which rendered the judgment shall sit in the Grand Chamber, with the exception of the President of the Chamber and the judge who sat in respect of the State Party concerned.

Article 28

A committee may, by a unanimous vote, declare inadmissible or strike out of its list of cases an individual application submitted under Article 34 where such a decision can be taken without further examination. The decision shall be final.

Article 29

1. If no decision is taken under Article 28, a Chamber shall decide on the admissibility and merits of individual applications submitted under Article 34.

2. A Chamber shall decide on the admissibility and merits of inter-State applications submitted under Article 33.

3. The decision on admissibility shall be taken separately unless the Court, in exceptional cases, decides otherwise.

Article 30

Where a case pending before a Chamber raises a serious question affecting the interpretation of the Convention r the protocols thereto, or where the resolution of a question before the Chamber might have a result inconsistent with a judgment previously delivered by the Court, the Chamber may, at any time before it has rendered its judgment, relinquish jurisdiction in favour of the Grand Chamber, unless one of the parties to the case objects.

Article 31

The Grand Chamber shall

a. determine applications submitted either under Article 33 or Article 34 when a Chamber has relinquished jurisdiction under Article 30 or when the case has been referred to it under Article 43; and

b. consider requests for advisory opinions submitted under Article 47.

Article 32

1. The jurisdiction of the Court shall extend to all matters concerning the interpretation and application of the Convention and the protocols thereto which are referred to it as provided in Articles 33, 34 and 47.

2. In the event of dispute as to whether the Court has jurisdiction, the Court shall decide.

Article 33

Any High Contracting Party may refer to the Court any alleged breach of the provisions of the Convention and the protocols thereto by another High Contracting Party.

Article 34

The Court may receive applications from any person, non-governmental organisation or group of individuals claiming to be the victim of a violation by one of the High Contracting Parties of the rights set forth in the Convention or the protocols thereto. The High Contracting Parties undertake not to hinder in any way the effective exercise of this right.

Article 35

1. The Court may only deal with the matter after all domestic remedies have been exhausted, according to the generally recognised rules of international law, and within a period of six months from the date on which the final decision was taken.

2. The Court shall not deal with any individual application submitted under Article 34 that

   a. is anonymous; or

   b. is substantially the same as a matter that has already been examined by the Court or has already been submitted to another procedure of international investigation or settlement and contains no relevant new information.

3. The Court shall declare inadmissible any individual application submitted under Article 34 which it considers incompatible with the provisions of the Convention or the protocols thereto, manifestly ill-founded, or an abuse of the right of application.

4. The Court shall reject any application which it considers inadmissible under this Article. It may do so at any stage of the proceedings.

Article 36

1. In all cases before a Chamber or the Grand Chamber, a High Contracting Party one of whose nationals is an applicant shall have the right to submit written comments and to take part in hearings.

2. The President of the Court may, in the interest of the proper administration of justice, invite any High Contracting Party which is not a party to the proceedings or any person concerned who is not the applicant to submit written comments or take part in hearings.

Article 37

1. The Court may at any stage of the proceedings decide to strike an application out of its list of cases where the circumstances lead to the conclusion that

a. the applicant does not intend to pursue his application; or

b. the matter has been resolved; or

c. for any other reason established by the Court, it is no longer justified to continue the examination of the application.

However, the Court shall continue the examination of the application if respect for human rights as defined in the Convention and the protocols thereto so requires.

2. The Court may decide to restore an application to its list of cases if it considers that the circumstances justify such a course.

Article 38

1. If the Court declares the application admissible, it shall

a. pursue the examination of the case, together with the representatives of the parties, and if need be, undertake an investigation, for the effective conduct of which the States concerned shall furnish all necessary facilities;

b. place itself at the disposal of the parties concerned with a view to securing a friendly settlement of the matter on the basis of respect for human rights as defined in the Convention and the protocols thereto.

2. Proceedings conducted under paragraph 1.b shall be confidential.

Article 39

If a friendly settlement is effected, the Court shall strike the case out of its list by means of a decision which shall be confined to a brief statement of the facts and of the solution reached.

Article 40

1. Hearings shall be public unless the Court in exceptional circumstances decides otherwise.

2. Documents deposited with the Registrar shall be accessible to the public unless the President of the Court decides otherwise.

Article 41

If the Court finds that there has been a violation of the Convention or the protocols thereto, and if the internal law of the High Contracting Party concerned allows only partial reparation to be made, the Court shall, if necessary, afford just satisfaction to the injured party.

Article 42

Judgments of Chambers shall become final in accordance with the provisions of Article 44, paragraph 2.

Article 43

1. Within a period of three months from the date of the judgment of the Chamber, any party to the case may, in exceptional cases, request that the case be referred to the Grand Chamber.

2. A panel of five judges of the Grand Chamber shall accept the request if the case raises a serious question affecting the interpretation or application of the Convention or the protocols thereto, or a serious issue of general importance.

3. If the panel accepts the request, the Grand Chamber shall decide the case by means of a judgment.

Article 44

1. The judgment of the Grand Chamber shall be final.

2. The judgment of a Chamber shall become final

    a. when the parties declare that they will not request that the case be referred to the Grand Chamber; or

    b. three months after the date of the judgment, if reference of the case to the Grand Chamber has not been requested; or

    c. when the panel of the Grand Chamber rejects the request to refer under Article 43.

3. The final judgment shall be published.

Article 45

1. Reasons shall be given for judgments as well as for decisions declaring applications admissible or inadmissible.

2. If a judgment does not represent, in whole or in part, the unanimous opinion of the judges, any judge shall be entitled to deliver a separate opinion.

Article 46

1. The High Contracting Parties undertake to abide by the final judgment of the Court in any case to which they are parties.

2. The final judgment of the Court shall be transmitted to the Committee of Ministers, which shall supervise its execution.

Article 47

1. The Court may, at the request of the Committee of Ministers, give advisory opinions on legal questions concerning the interpretation of the Convention and the protocols thereto.

2. Such opinions shall not deal with any question relating to the content or scope of the rights or freedoms defined in Section I of the Convention and the

protocols thereto, or with any other question which the Court or the Committee of Ministers might have to consider in consequence of any such proceedings as could be instituted in accordance with the Convention.

3. Decisions of the Committee of Ministers to request an advisory opinion of the Court shall require a majority vote of the representatives entitled to sit on the Committee.

Article 48

The Court shall decide whether a request for an advisory opinion submitted by the Committee of Ministers is within its competence as defined in Article 47.

Article 49

1. Reasons shall be given for advisory opinions of the Court.

2. If the advisory opinion does not represent, in whole or in part, the unanimous opinion of the judges, any judge shall be entitled to deliver a separate opinion.

3. Advisory opinions of the Court shall be communicated to the Committee of Ministers.

Article 50

The expenditure on the Court shall be borne by the Council of Europe.

Article 51

The judges shall be entitled, during the exercise of their functions, to the privileges and immunities provided for in Article 40 of the Statute of the Council of Europe and in the agreements made thereunder.

SECTION III

Article 52

On receipt of a request from the Secretary General of the Council of Europe any High Contracting Party shall furnish an explanation of the manner in which its internal law ensures the effective implementation of any of the provisions of the Convention.

Article 53

Nothing in this Convention shall be construed as limiting or derogating from any of the human rights and fundamental freedoms which may be ensured under the laws of any High Contracting Party or under any other agreement to which it is a Party.

Article 54

Nothing in this Convention shall prejudice the powers conferred on the Committee of Ministers by the Statute of the Council of Europe.

Article 55

The High Contracting Parties agree that, except by special agreement, they will not avail themselves of treaties, conventions or declarations in force between them for the purpose of submitting, by way of petition, a dispute arising out of the interpretation or application of this Convention to a means of settlement other than those provided for in this Convention.

Article 56

1. Any State may at the time of its ratification or at any time thereafter declare by notification addressed to the Secretary General of the Council of Europe that the present Convention shall, subject to paragraph 4 of this Article, extend to all or any of the territories for whose international relations it is responsible.

2. The Convention shall extend to the territory or territories named in the notification as from the thirtieth day after the receipt of this notification by the Secretary General of the Council of Europe.

3. The provisions of this Convention shall be applied in such territories with due regard, however, to local requirements.

4. Any State which has made a declaration in accordance with paragraph 1 of this article may at any time thereafter declare on behalf of one or more of the territories to which the declaration relates that it accepts the competence of the Court to receive applications from individuals, non-governmental organisations or groups of individuals as provided by Article 34 of the Convention.

Article 57

1. Any State may, when signing this Convention or when depositing its instrument of ratification, make a reservation in respect of any particular provision of the Convention to the extent that any law then in force in its territory is not in conformity with the provision. Reservations of a general character shall not be permitted under this article.

2. Any reservation made under this article shall contain a brief statement of the law concerned.

Article 58

1. A High Contracting Party may denounce the present Convention only after the expiry of five years from the date on which it became a party to it and after six months' notice contained in a notification addressed to the Secretary General of the Council of Europe, who shall inform the other High Contracting Parties.

2. Such a denunciation shall not have the effect of releasing the High Contracting Party concerned from its obligations under this Convention in respect of any act which, being capable of constituting a violation of such obligations, may have been performed by it before the date at which the denunciation became effective.

3. Any High Contracting Party which shall cease to be a member of the Council of Europe shall cease to be a Party to this Convention under the same conditions.

4. The Convention may be denounced in accordance with the provisions of the preceding paragraphs in respect of any territory to which it has been declared to extend under the terms of Article 56.

Article 59

1. This Convention shall be open to the signature of the members of the Council of Europe. It shall be ratified. Ratifications shall be deposited with the Secretary General of the Council of Europe.

2. The present Convention shall come into force after the deposit of ten instruments of ratification.

3. As regards any signatory ratifying subsequently, the Convention shall come into force at the date of the deposit of its instrument of ratification.

4. The Secretary General of the Council of Europe shall notify all the members of the Council of Europe of the entry into force of the Convention, the names of the High Contracting Parties who have ratified it, and the deposit of all instruments of ratification which may be effected subsequently.

DONE AT ROME this 4th day of November 1950 in English and French, both texts being equally authentic, in a single copy which shall remain deposited in the archives of the Council of Europe. The Secretary-General shall transmit certified copies to each of the signatories.

PROTOCOL NO. 1 TO THE [EUROPEAN] CONVENTION ON THE PROTECTION OF HUMAN RIGHTS AND FUNDAMENTAL FREEDOMS, E.T.S. 9, 213 U.N.T.S. 262, *entered into force* May 18, 1954:

The Governments signatory hereto, being Members of the Council of Europe,

Being resolved to take steps to ensure the collective enforcement of certain rights and freedoms other than those already included in Section I of the Convention for the Protection of Human Rights and Fundamental Freedoms signed at Rome on 4th November, 1950 (hereinafter referred to as 'the Convention'),

Have agreed as follows:

Article 1

Every natural or legal person is entitled to the peaceful enjoyment of his possessions. No one shall be deprived of his possessions except in the public interest and subject to the conditions provided for by law and by the general principles of international law.

The preceding provisions shall not, however, in any way impair the right of a State to enforce such laws as it deems necessary to control the use of property in accordance with the general interest or to secure the payment of taxes or other contributions or penalties.

Article 2

No person shall be denied the right to education. In the exercise of any functions which it assumes in relation to education and to teaching, the State shall respect the right of parents to ensure such education and teaching in conformity with their own religious and philosophical convictions.

Article 3

The High Contracting Parties undertake to hold free elections at reasonable intervals by secret ballot, under conditions which will ensure the free expression of the opinion of the people in the choice of the legislature.

Article 4

Any High Contracting Party may at the time of signature or ratification or at any time thereafter communicate to the Secretary-General of the Council of Europe a declaration stating the extent to which it undertakes that the provisions of the present Protocol shall apply to such of the territories for the international relations of which it is responsible as are named therein.

Any High Contracting Party which has communicated a declaration in virtue of the preceding paragraph may from time to time communicate a further declaration modifying the terms of any former declaration or terminating the application of the provisions of this Protocol in respect of any territory.

A declaration made in accordance with this article shall be deemed to have been made in accordance with paragraph 1 of Article 63 of the Convention.

Article 5

As between the High Contracting Parties the provisions of Articles 1, 2, 3 and 4 of this Protocol shall be regarded as additional articles to the convention and all the provisions of the Convention shall apply accordingly.

Article 6

This Protocol shall be open for signature by the Members of the Council of Europe, who are the signatories of the Convention; it shall be ratified at the same time as or after the ratification of the Convention. It shall enter into force after the deposit of ten instruments of ratification. As regards any signatory ratifying subsequently, the Protocol shall enter into force at the date of the deposit of its instrument of ratification.

The instruments of ratification shall be deposited with the Secretary-General of the Council of Europe, who will notify all the Members of the names of those who have ratified.

DONE at Paris on the 20th day of March 1952, In English and French, both text being equally authentic, in a single copy which shall remain deposited in the archives of the Council of Europe. The Secretary-General shall transmit certified copies to each of the signatory Governments.

PROTOCOL NO. 4 TO THE [EUROPEAN] CONVENTION FOR THE PROTECTION OF HUMAN RIGHTS AND FUNDAMENTAL FREEDOMS, E.T.S. 46, *entered into force* May 2, 1968:

The Governments signatory hereto, being Members of the Council of Europe,

Being resolved to take steps to ensure the collective enforcement of certain rights and freedoms other than those already included in Section I of the Convention for the Protection of Human Rights and Fundamental Freedoms signed at Rome on 4th November 1950 (hereinafter referred to as "the Convention") and in Articles 1 to 3 of the First Protocol to the Convention, signed at Paris on 20th March 1952,

Have agreed as follows:

Article 1

No one shall be deprived of his liberty merely on the ground of inability to fulfil a contractual obligation.

Article 2

1. Everyone lawfully within the territory of a State shall, within that territory, have the right to liberty of movement and freedom to choose his residence.

2. Everyone shall be free to leave any country, including his own.

3. No restrictions shall be placed on the exercise of these rights other than such as are in accordance with law and are necessary in a democratic society in the interests of national security or public safety, for the maintenance of "*ordre public*", for the prevention of crime, for the protection of health or morals, or for the protection of the rights and freedoms of others.

4. The rights set forth in paragraph 1 may also be subject, in particular areas, to restrictions imposed in accordance with law and justified by the public interests in a democratic society.

Article 3

1. No one shall be expelled, by means either of an individual or of a collective measure, from the territory of the State of which he is a national.

2. No one shall be deprived of the right to enter the territory of the State of which he is a national.

Article 4

Collective expulsion of aliens is prohibited.

Article 5

1. Any High Contracting Party may, at the time of signature or ratification of this Protocol, or at any time thereafter, communicate to the Secretary-General of the Council of Europe a declaration stating the extent to which it

undertakes that the provisions of this Protocol shall apply to such of the territories for the international relations of which it is responsible as are named therein.

2. Any High Contracting Party which has communicated a declaration in virtue of the preceding paragraph may, from time to time, communicate a further declaration modifying the terms of any former declaration or terminating the application of the provisions of this Protocol in respect of any territory.

3. A declaration made in accordance with this Article shall be deemed to have been made in accordance with paragraph 1 of Article 63 of the Convention.

4. The territory of any State to which this Protocol applies by virtue of ratification or acceptance by that State, and each territory to which this Protocol is applied by virtue of a declaration by that State under this Article, shall be treated as separate territories for the purpose of the references in Articles 2 and 3 to the territory of a State.

Article 6

1. As between the High Contracting Parties the provisions of Articles 1 to 5 of this Protocol shall be regarded as additional Articles to the Convention, and all the provisions of the Convention shall apply be accordingly.

2. Nevertheless, the right of individual recourse recognised by a declaration made under Article 25 of the Convention, or the acceptance of the compulsory jurisdiction of the Court by a declaration made under Article 46 of the Convention, shall not be effective in relation to this Protocol unless the High Contracting Party concerned has made a statement recognizing such right, or accepting such jurisdiction, in respect of all or any of Articles 1 to 4 of the Protocol.

Article 7

1. This Protocol shall be open for signature by the Members of the Council of Europe who are the signatories of the Convention; it shall be ratified at the same time as or after the ratification of the Convention. It shall enter into force after the deposit of five instruments of ratification. As regards any signatory ratifying subsequently, the Protocol shall enter into force at the date of the deposit of its instrument of ratification.

2. The instruments of ratification shall be deposited with the Secretary-General of the Council of Europe, who will notify all Members of the names of those who have ratified.

IN WITNESS WHEREOF, the undersigned, being duly authorised thereto, have signed this Protocol.

DONE at Strasbourg this 16th day of September 1963, in English and in French, both texts being equally authoritative, in a single copy which shall remain deposited in the archives of the Council of Europe. The Secretary-General shall transmit certified copies to each of the signatory States.

PROTOCOL NO. 6 TO THE [EUROPEAN] CONVENTION FOR THE PROTECTION OF HUMAN RIGHTS AND FUNDAMENTAL FREEDOMS, E.T.S. 114, *entered into force* **March 1, 1985:**

The member States of the Council of Europe, signatory to this Protocol to the Convention for the Protection of Human Rights and Fundamental Freedoms, signed at Rome on 4 November 1950 (hereinafter referred to as "the Convention"),

Considering that the evolution that has occurred in several member States of the Council of Europe expresses a general tendency in favour of abolition of the death penalty.

Have agreed as follows:

Article 1

The death penalty shall be abolished. No one shall be condemned to such penalty or executed.

Article 2

A State may make provision in its law for the death penalty in respect of acts committed in time of war or of imminent threat of war; such penalty shall be applied only in the instances laid down in the law and in accordance with its provisions. The State shall communicate to the Secretary General of the Council of Europe the relevant provisions of that law.

Article 3

No derogation from the provisions of this Protocol shall be made under Article 15 of the Convention (3).

Article 4

No reservation may be made under Article 64 of the Convention in respect of the provisions of this Protocol (4).

Article 5

1. Any State may at the time of signature or when depositing its instrument of ratification, acceptance or approval, specify the territory or territories to which this Protocol shall apply.

2. Any State may at any later date, by a declaration addressed to the Secretary General of the Council of Europe, extend the application of this Protocol to any other territory specified in the declaration. In respect of such territory the Protocol shall enter into force on the first day of the month following the date of receipt of such a declaration by the Secretary General.

3. Any declaration made under the two preceding paragraphs may, in respect of any territory specified in such declaration, be withdrawn by a notification addressed to the Secretary General. The withdrawal shall become effective on the first day of the month following the date of receipt of such notification by the Secretary General.

Article 6

As between the State Parties the provisions of Articles 1 to 5 of this Protocol shall be regarded as additional articles to the Convention and all the provisions of the Convention shall apply accordingly.

Article 7

This Protocol shall be open for signature by the member States of the Council of Europe, signatories to the Convention. It shall be subject to ratification, acceptance or approval. A member State of the Council of Europe may not ratify, accept or approve this Protocol unless it has, simultaneously or previously, ratified the Convention. Instruments of ratification, acceptance or approval shall be deposited with the Secretary General of the Council of Europe.

Article 8

1. This Protocol shall enter into force on the first day of the month following the date on which five member States of the Council of Europe have expressed their consent to be bound by the Protocol in accordance with the provisions of Article 7.

2. In respect of any member State which subsequently expresses its consent to be bound by it, the Protocol shall enter into force on the first day of the month following the date of the deposit of the instrument of ratification, acceptance or approval.

Article 9

The Secretary General of the Council of Europe shall notify the member States of the Council of:

a. any signature;

b. the deposit of any instrument of ratification, acceptance or approval;

c. any date of entry into force of this Protocol in accordance with Articles 5 and 8;

d. any other act, notification or communication relating to this Protocol.

In witness whereof the undersigned, being duly authorised thereto, have signed this Protocol.

DONE at Strasbourg, the twenty-eight April one thousand nine hundred and eighty-three, in English and French, both texts being equally authentic, in a single copy which shall be deposited in the archives of the Council of Europe. The Secretary General of the Council of Europe shall transmit certified copies to each member State of the Council of Europe.

PROTOCOL NO. 7 TO THE [EUROPEAN] CONVENTION FOR THE PROTECTION OF HUMAN RIGHTS AND FUNDAMENTAL FREEDOMS, E.T.S. 117, *entered into force* Nov. 1, 1988:

The member States of the Council of Europe signatory hereto,

Being resolved to take further steps to ensure the collective enforcement of certain rights and freedoms by means of the Convention for the Protection of Human Rights and Fundamental Freedoms signed at Rome on 4 November 1950 (hereinafter referred to as "The Convention");

Have agreed as follows:

Article 1

1. An alien lawfully resident in the territory of a State shall not be expelled therefrom except in pursuance of a decision reached in accordance with law and shall be allowed:

   a. to submit reasons against his expulsion,

   b. to have his case reviewed, and

   c. to be represented for these purposes before the competent authority or a person or persons designated by that authority. An alien may be expelled before the exercise of his rights under paragraph 1(a), (b) and (c) of this Article, when such expulsion is necessary in the interests of public order or is grounded on reasons of national security.

Article 2

1. Everyone convicted of a criminal offence by a tribunal shall have the right to have conviction or sentence reviewed by a higher tribunal. The exercise of this right, including the grounds on which it may be exercised, shall be governed by law.

2. This right may be subject to exceptions in regard to offences of a minor character, as prescribed by law, or in cases in which the person concerned was tried in the first instance by the highest tribunal or was convicted following an appeal against acquittal.

Article 3

When a person has by a final decision been convicted of a criminal offence and when subsequently his conviction has been reversed, or he has been pardoned, on the ground that a new or newly discovered fact shows conclusively that there has been a miscarriage of justice, the person who has suffered punishment as a result of such conviction shall be compensated according to the law or the practice of that State concerned, unless it is proved that the non-disclosure of the unknown fact in time is wholly or partly attributable to him.

Article 4

1. No one shall be liable to be tried or punished again in criminal proceedings under the jurisdiction of the same State for an offence for which he has already been finally acquitted or convicted in accordance with the law and penal procedure of the State.

2. The provisions of the preceding paragraph shall not prevent the re-opening of the case in accordance with the law and penal procedure of the State concerned, if there is evidence of new or newly discovered facts, or if there has

been a fundamental defect in the previous proceedings, which could affect the outcome of the case.

3. No derogation from this Article shall be made under Article 15 of the Convention.

Article 5

Spouses shall enjoy equality of rights and responsibilities of a private law character between them, and in their relations with their children, as to marriage, during marriage and in the event of its dissolution. This Article shall not prevent States from taking such measures as are necessary in the interests of the children.

Article 6

1. Any State may at the time of signature or when depositing its instrument of ratification, acceptance or approval, specify the territory or territories to which this Protocol shall apply and state the extent to which it undertakes that the provisions of this Protocol shall apply to this or these territories.

2. Any State may at any later date, by a declaration addressed to the Secretary-General of the Council of Europe, extend the application of this Protocol to any other territory specified in the declaration. In respect of such territory the Protocol shall enter into force on the first day of the month following the expiration of a period of two months after the date of receipt by the Secretary General of such declaration.

3. Any declaration made under the two preceding paragraphs may, in respect of any territory specified in such declaration, be withdrawn or modified by a notification addressed to the Secretary General. The withdrawal or modification shall become effective on the first day of the month following the expiration of a period of two months after the date of receipt of such notification by the Secretary General.

4. A declaration made in accordance with this Article shall be deemed to have been made in accordance with paragraph 1 of Article 63 of the Convention.

5. The territory of any State to which this Protocol applies by virtue of ratification, acceptance or approval by that State, and each territory to which this Protocol is applied by virtue of a declaration by that State under this Article, may be treated as separate territories for the purpose of the reference in Article 1 to the territory of a State.

Article 7

1. As between the State Parties, the provisions of Articles 1 to 6 of this Protocol shall be regarded as additional Articles to the Convention, and all the provisions of the Convention shall apply accordingly.

2. Nevertheless, the right of individual recourse recognised by a declaration made under Article 25 of the Convention, or the acceptance of the compulsory jurisdiction of the Court by a declaration made under Article 46 of the

Convention, shall not be effective in relation to this Protocol unless the State concerned has made a statement recognising such right, or accepting such jurisdiction in respect of Articles 1 to 5 of this Protocol.

Article 8

This Protocol shall be open for signature by member States of the Council of Europe which have signed the Convention. It is subject to ratification, acceptance or approval. A member State of the Council of Europe may not ratify, accept or approve this Protocol without previously or simultaneously ratifying the Convention. Instruments of ratification, acceptance or approval shall be deposited with the Secretary General of the Council of Europe.

Article 9

1. This Protocol shall enter into force on the first day of the month following the expiration of a period of two months after the date on which seven member States of the Council of Europe have expressed their consent to be bound by the Protocol in accordance with the provisions of Article 8.

2. In respect to any member State which subsequently expresses its consent to be bound by it, the Protocol shall enter into force on the first day of the month following the expiration of a period of two months after the date of the deposit of the instrument of ratification, acceptance or approval.

Article 10

The Secretary General of the Council of Europe shall notify all the member States of the Council of:

a. any signature;

b. the deposit of any instrument of ratification, acceptance or approval;

c. any date of entry into force of this Protocol in accordance with Articles 6 and 9;

d. any other act, notification or declaration relating to this Protocol.

In witness whereof the undersigned, being duly authorised thereto, have signed this Protocol.

PROTOCOL NO. 12 TO THE [EUROPEAN] CONVENTION FOR THE PROTECTION OF HUMAN RIGHTS AND FUNDAMENTAL FREEDOMS, E.T.S. 177, *opened for signature* Nov. 4, 2000:

The member States of the Council of Europe signatory hereto,

Having regard to the fundamental principle according to which all persons are equal before the law and are entitled to the equal protection of the law;

Being resolved to take further steps to promote the equality of all persons through the collective enforcement of a general prohibition of discrimination by means of the Convention for the Protection of Human Rights and

Fundamental Freedoms signed at Rome on 4 November 1950 (hereinafter referred to as "the Convention");

Reaffirming that the principle of non-discrimination does not prevent States Parties from taking measures in order to promote full and effective equality, provided that there is an objective and reasonable justification for those measures,

Have agreed as follows:

Article 1

General prohibition of discrimination

1. The enjoyment of any right set forth by law shall be secured without discrimination on any ground such as sex, race, colour, language, religion, political or other opinion, national or social origin, association with a national minority, property, birth or other status.

2. No one shall be discriminated against by any public authority on any ground such as those mentioned in paragraph 1.

Article 2

Territorial application

1. Any State may, at the time of signature or when depositing its instrument of ratification, acceptance or approval, specify the territory or territories to which this Protocol shall apply.

2. Any State may at any later date, by a declaration addressed to the Secretary General of the Council of Europe, extend the application of this Protocol to any other territory specified in the declaration. In respect of such territory the Protocol shall enter into force on the first day of the month following the expiration of a period of three months after the date of receipt by the Secretary General of such declaration.

3. Any declaration made under the two preceding paragraphs may, in respect of any territory specified in such declaration, be withdrawn or modified by a notification addressed to the Secretary General of the Council of Europe. The withdrawal or modification shall become effective on the first day of the month following the expiration of a period of three months after the date of receipt of such notification by the Secretary General.

4. A declaration made in accordance with this article shall be deemed to have been made in accordance with paragraph 1 of Article 56 of the Convention.

5. Any State which has made a declaration in accordance with paragraph 1 or 2 of this article may at any time thereafter declare on behalf of one or more of the territories to which the declaration relates that it accepts the competence of the Court to receive applications from individuals, non-governmental organisations or groups of individuals as provided by Article 34 of the Convention in respect of Article 1 of this Protocol.

Article 3

Relationship to the Convention

As between the States Parties, the provisions of Articles 1 and 2 of this Protocol shall be regarded as additional articles to the Convention, and all the provisions of the Convention shall apply accordingly.

Article 4

Signature and ratification

This Protocol shall be open for signature by member States of the Council of Europe which have signed the Convention. It is subject to ratification, acceptance or approval. A member State of the Council of Europe may not ratify, accept or approve this Protocol without previously or simultaneously ratifying the Convention. Instruments of ratification, acceptance or approval shall be deposited with the Secretary General of the Council of Europe.

Article 5

Entry into force

1. This Protocol shall enter into force on the first day of the month following the expiration of a period of three months after the date on which ten member States of the Council of Europe have expressed their consent to be bound by the Protocol in accordance with the provisions of Article 4.

2. In respect of any member State which subsequently expresses its consent to be bound by it, the Protocol shall enter into force on the first day of the month following the expiration of a period of three months after the date of the deposit of the instrument of ratification, acceptance or approval.

Article 6

Depositary functions

The Secretary General of the Council of Europe shall notify all the member States of the Council of Europe of:

a. any signature;

b. the deposit of any instrument of ratification, acceptance or approval;

c. any date of entry into force of this Protocol in accordance with Articles 2 and 5;

d. any other act, notification or communication relating to this Protocol.

In witness whereof the undersigned, being duly authorised thereto, have signed this Protocol.

DONE at Rome, this 4th day of November 2000, in English and in French, both texts being equally authentic, in a single copy which shall be deposited in the archives of the Council of Europe. The Secretary General of the Council of Europe shall transmit certified copies to each member State of the Council of Europe.

PROTOCOL NO. 14 TO THE [EUROPEAN] CONVENTION FOR THE PROTECTION OF HUMAN RIGHTS AND FUNDAMENTAL FREEDOMS, E.T.S. 194, *not entered into force*:

Preamble

The member States of the Council of Europe, signatories to this Protocol to the Convention for the Protection of Human Rights and Fundamental Freedoms, signed at Rome on 4 November 1950 (hereinafter referred to as "the Convention"),

Having regard to Resolution No. 1 and the Declaration adopted at the European Ministerial Conference on Human Rights, held in Rome on 3 and 4 November 2000;

Having regard to the Declarations adopted by the Committee of Ministers on 8 November 2001, 7 November 2002 and 15 May 2003, at their 109th, 111th and 112th Sessions, respectively;

Having regard to Opinion No. 251 (2004) adopted by the Parliamentary Assembly of the Council of Europe on 28 April 2004;

Considering the urgent need to amend certain provisions of the Convention in order to maintain and improve the efficiency of the control system for the long term, mainly in the light of the continuing increase in the workload of the European Court of Human Rights and the Committee of Ministers of the Council of Europe;

Considering, in particular, the need to ensure that the Court can continue to play its pre-eminent role in protecting human rights in Europe,

Have agreed as follows:

Article 1

Paragraph 2 of Article 22 of the Convention shall be deleted.

Article 2

Article 23 of the Convention shall be amended to read as follows:

"Article 23 – Terms of office and dismissal

1. The judges shall be elected for a period of nine years. They may not be re-elected.

2. The terms of office of judges shall expire when they reach the age of 70.

3. The judges shall hold office until replaced. They shall, however, continue to deal with such cases as they already have under consideration.

4. No judge may be dismissed from office unless the other judges decide by a majority of two-thirds that that judge has ceased to fulfil the required conditions."

Article 3

Article 24 of the Convention shall be deleted.

Article 4

Article 25 of the Convention shall become Article 24 and its text shall be amended to read as follows:

"Article 24 – Registry and rapporteurs

1. The Court shall have a registry, the functions and organisation of which shall be laid down in the rules of the Court.

2. When sitting in a single-judge formation, the Court shall be assisted by rapporteurs who shall function under the authority of the President of the Court. They shall form part of the Court's registry."

Article 5

Article 26 of the Convention shall become Article 25 ("Plenary Court") and its text shall be amended as follows:

1. At the end of paragraph d, the comma shall be replaced by a semi-colon and the word "and" shall be deleted.

2. At the end of paragraph e, the full stop shall be replaced by a semi-colon.

3. A new paragraph f shall be added which shall read as follows: "f. make any request under Article 26, paragraph 2."

Article 6

Article 27 of the Convention shall become Article 26 and its text shall be amended to read as follows:

"Article 26 – Single-judge formation, committees, Chambers and Grand Chamber

1. To consider cases brought before it, the Court shall sit in a single-judge formation, in committees of three judges, in Chambers of seven judges and in a Grand Chamber of seventeen judges. The Court's Chambers shall set up committees for a fixed period of time.

2. At the request of the plenary Court, the Committee of Ministers may, by a unanimous decision and for a fixed period, reduce to five the number of judges of the Chambers.

3. When sitting as a single judge, a judge shall not examine any application against the High Contracting Party in respect of which that judge has been elected.

4. There shall sit as an ex officio member of the Chamber and the Grand Chamber the judge elected in respect of the High Contracting Party concerned. If there is none or if that judge is unable to sit, a person chosen by the President of the Court from a list submitted in advance by that Party shall sit in the capacity of judge.

5. The Grand Chamber shall also include the President of the Court, the Vice-Presidents, the Presidents of the Chambers and other judges chosen in

accordance with the rules of the Court. When a case is referred to the Grand Chamber under Article 43, no judge from the Chamber which rendered the judgment shall sit in the Grand Chamber, with the exception of the President of the Chamber and the judge who sat in respect of the High Contracting Party concerned."

Article 7

After the new Article 26, a new Article 27 shall be inserted into the Convention, which shall read as follows:

"Article 27 – Competence of single judges

1. A single judge may declare inadmissible or strike out of the Court's list of cases an application submitted under Article 34, where such a decision can be taken without further examination.

2. The decision shall be final.

3. If the single judge does not declare an application inadmissible or strike it out, that judge shall forward it to a committee or to a Chamber for further examination."

Article 8

Article 28 of the Convention shall be amended to read as follows:

"Article 28 – Competence of committees

1. In respect of an application submitted under Article 34, a committee may, by a unanimous vote,

    a. declare it inadmissible or strike it out of its list of cases, where such decision can be taken without further examination; or

    b. declare it admissible and render at the same time a judgment on the merits, if the underlying question in the case, concerning the interpretation or the application of the Convention or the Protocols thereto, is already the subject of well-established case-law of the Court.

2. Decisions and judgments under paragraph 1 shall be final.

3. If the judge elected in respect of the High Contracting Party concerned is not a member of the committee, the committee may at any stage of the proceedings invite that judge to take the place of one of the members of the committee, having regard to all relevant factors, including whether that Party has contested the application of the procedure under paragraph 1.b."

Article 9

Article 29 of the Convention shall be amended as follows:

1. Paragraph 1 shall be amended to read as follows:"If no decision is taken under Article 27 or 28, or no judgment rendered under Article 28, a Chamber shall decide on the admissibility and merits of individual applications submitted under Article 34. The decision on admissibility may be taken separately."

2. At the end of paragraph 2 a new sentence shall be added which shall read as follows: "The decision on admissibility shall be taken separately unless the Court, in exceptional cases, decides otherwise."

3. Paragraph 3 shall be deleted.

Article 10

Article 31 of the Convention shall be amended as follows:

1. At the end of paragraph a, the word "and" shall be deleted.

2. Paragraph b shall become paragraph c and a new paragraph b shall be inserted and shall read as follows: "b. decide on issues referred to the Court by the Committee of Ministers in accordance with Article 46, paragraph 4; and".

Article 11

Article 32 of the Convention shall be amended as follows:

At the end of paragraph 1, a comma and the number 46 shall be inserted after the number 34.

Article 12

Paragraph 3 of Article 35 of the Convention shall be amended to read as follows:

"3. The Court shall declare inadmissible any individual application submitted under Article 34 if it considers that :

a. the application is incompatible with the provisions of the Convention or the Protocols thereto, manifestly ill-founded, or an abuse of the right of individual application; or

b. the applicant has not suffered a significant disadvantage, unless respect for human rights as defined in the Convention and the Protocols thereto requires an examination of the application on the merits and provided that no case may be rejected on this ground which has not been duly considered by a domestic tribunal."

Article 13

A new paragraph 3 shall be added at the end of Article 36 of the Convention, which shall read as follows:

"3. In all cases before a Chamber or the Grand Chamber, the Council of Europe Commissioner for Human Rights may submit written comments and take part in hearings."

Article 14

Article 38 of the Convention shall be amended to read as follows:

"Article 38 – Examination of the case

The Court shall examine the case together with the representatives of the parties and, if need be, undertake an investigation, for the effective conduct of which the High Contracting Parties concerned shall furnish all necessary facilities."

Article 15

Article 39 of the Convention shall be amended to read as follows:

"Article 39 – Friendly settlements

1. At any stage of the proceedings, the Court may place itself at the disposal of the parties concerned with a view to securing a friendly settlement of the matter on the basis of respect for human rights as defined in the Convention and the Protocols thereto.

2. Proceedings conducted under paragraph 1 shall be confidential.

3. If a friendly settlement is effected, the Court shall strike the case out of its list by means of a decision which shall be confined to a brief statement of the facts and of the solution reached.

4. This decision shall be transmitted to the Committee of Ministers, which shall supervise the execution of the terms of the friendly settlement as set out in the decision."

Article 16

Article 46 of the Convention shall be amended to read as follows:

"Article 46 – Binding force and execution of judgments

1. The High Contracting Parties undertake to abide by the final judgment of the Court in any case to which they are parties.

2. The final judgment of the Court shall be transmitted to the Committee of Ministers, which shall supervise its execution.

3. If the Committee of Ministers considers that the supervision of the execution of a final judgment is hindered by a problem of interpretation of the judgment, it may refer the matter to the Court for a ruling on the question of interpretation. A referral decision shall require a majority vote of two thirds of the representatives entitled to sit on the Committee.

4. If the Committee of Ministers considers that a High Contracting Party refuses to abide by a final judgment in a case to which it is a party, it may, after serving formal notice on that Party and by decision adopted by a majority vote of two thirds of the representatives entitled to sit on the Committee, refer to the Court the question whether that Party has failed to fulfil its obligation under paragraph 1.

5. If the Court finds a violation of paragraph 1, it shall refer the case to the Committee of Ministers for consideration of the measures to be taken. If the Court finds no violation of paragraph 1, it shall refer the case to the Committee of Ministers, which shall close its examination of the case."

Article 17

Article 59 of the Convention shall be amended as follows:

1. A new paragraph 2 shall be inserted which shall read as follows:
"2. The European Union may accede to this Convention."

2. Paragraphs 2, 3 and 4 shall become paragraphs 3, 4 and 5 respectively.

Final and transitional provisions

Article 18

1. This Protocol shall be open for signature by member States of the Council of Europe signatories to the Convention, which may express their consent to be bound by

a. signature without reservation as to ratification, acceptance or approval; or

b. signature subject to ratification, acceptance or approval, followed by ratification, acceptance or approval.

2. The instruments of ratification, acceptance or approval shall be deposited with the Secretary General of the Council of Europe.

Article 19

This Protocol shall enter into force on the first day of the month following the expiration of a period of three months after the date on which all Parties to the Convention have expressed their consent to be bound by the Protocol, in accordance with the provisions of Article 18.

Article 20

1. From the date of the entry into force of this Protocol, its provisions shall apply to all applications pending before the Court as well as to all judgments whose execution is under supervision by the Committee of Ministers.

2. The new admissibility criterion inserted by Article 12 of this Protocol in Article 35, paragraph 3.b of the Convention, shall not apply to applications declared admissible before the entry into force of the Protocol. In the two years following the entry into force of this Protocol, the new admissibility criterion may only be applied by Chambers and the Grand Chamber of the Court.

Article 21

The term of office of judges serving their first term of office on the date of entry into force of this Protocol shall be extended ipso jure so as to amount to a total period of nine years. The other judges shall complete their term of office, which shall be extended ipso jure by two years.

Article 22

The Secretary General of the Council of Europe shall notify the member States of the Council of Europe of:

a. any signature;

b. the deposit of any instrument of ratification, acceptance or approval;

c. the date of entry into force of this Protocol in accordance with Article 19; and

d. any other act, notification or communication relating to this Protocol.

In witness whereof, the undersigned, being duly authorised thereto, have signed this Protocol.

Done at Strasbourg, this 13th day of May 2004, in English and in French, both texts being equally authentic, in a single copy which shall be deposited in the archives of the Council of Europe. The Secretary General of the Council of Europe shall transmit certified copies to each member State of the Council of Europe.

EUROPEAN SOCIAL CHARTER (REVISED), E.T.S. No. 163, *entered into force* January 7, 1999 (excerpts):...

Preamble

Recognising the advantage of embodying in a Revised Charter, designed progressively to take the place of the European Social Charter, the rights guaranteed by the Charter as amended, the rights guaranteed by the Additional Protocol of 1988 and to add new rights,

Have agreed as follows:

The Parties accept as the aim of their policy, to be pursued by all appropriate means both national and international in character, the attainment of conditions in which the following rights and principles may be effectively realised:

PART I

1. Everyone shall have the opportunity to earn his living in an occupation freely entered upon ... .

2. All workers have the right to just conditions of work ... .

3. All workers have the right to safe and healthy working conditions ... .

4. All workers have the right to a fair remuneration sufficient for a decent standard of living for themselves and their families ... .

5. All workers and employers have the right to freedom of association in national or international organisations for the protection of their economic and social interests ... .

6. All workers and employers have the right to bargain collectively. ...

7. Children and young persons have the right to a special protection against the physical and moral hazards to which they are exposed. ...

8. Employed women, in case of maternity, have the right to a special protection. ...

PART II

Article 1 – The right to work...

Article 2 – The right to just conditions of work...

Article 3 – The right to safe and healthy working conditions...

Article 4 – The right to a fair remuneration...

Article 5 – The right to organise...

Article 6 – The right to bargain collectively...

Article 7 – The right of children and young persons to protection...

Article 8 – The right of employed women to protection of maternity...

Article 9 – The right to vocational guidance...

Article 10 – The right to vocational training...

Article 11 – The right to protection of health...

Article 12 – The right to social security...

Article 13 – The right to social and medical assistance...

Article 14 – The right to benefit from social welfare services...

Article 15 – The right of persons with disabilities to independence, social...

Article 16 – The right of the family to social, legal and economic protection...

Article 17 – The right of children and young persons to social, legal and economic protection...

Article 18 – The right to engage in a gainful occupation in the territory of other Parties...

Article 19 – The right of migrant workers and their families to protection and assistance...

Article 20 – The right to equal opportunities and equal treatment in matters...

Article 21 – The right to information and consultation...

Article 22 – The right to take part in the determination and improvement of the working conditions and working environment...

Article 23 – The right of elderly persons to social protection...

Article 24 – The right to protection in cases of termination of employment...

Article 25 – The right of workers to the protection of their claims in the event...

Article 26 – The right to dignity at work...

Article 27 – The right of workers with family responsibilities to equal opportunities and equal treatment...

Article 28 – The right of workers' representatives to protection in the undertaking and facilities to be accorded to them...

Article 29 – The right to information and consultation in collective redundancy procedures...

Article 30 – The right to protection against poverty and social exclusion...

Article 31 – The right to housing...

PART III

Article A – Undertaking

1. Subject to the provisions of Article B below, each of the Parties undertakes:

    a. to consider Part I of this Charter as a declaration of the aims which it will pursue by all appropriate means, as stated in the introductory paragraph of that part;

    b. to consider itself bound by at least six of the following nine articles of Part II of this Charter: Articles 1, 5, 6, 7, 12, 13, 16, 19 and 20;

    c. to consider itself bound by an additional number of articles or numbered paragraphs of Part II of the Charter which it may select, provided that the total number of articles or numbered paragraphs by which it is bound is not less than sixteen articles or sixty-three numbered paragraphs.

2. The articles or paragraphs selected in accordance with sub-paragraphs b and c of paragraph 1 of this article shall be notified to the Secretary General of the Council of Europe at the time when the instrument of ratification, acceptance or approval is deposited.

3. Any Party may, at a later date, declare by notification addressed to the Secretary General that it considers itself bound by any articles or any numbered paragraphs of Part II of the Charter which it has not already accepted under the terms of paragraph 1 of this article. Such undertakings subsequently given shall be deemed to be an integral part of the ratification, acceptance or approval and shall have the same effect as from the first day of the month following the expiration of a period of one month after the date of the notification.

468 SELECTED INTERNATIONAL HUMAN RIGHTS INSTRUMENTS

4. Each Party shall maintain a system of labour inspection appropriate to national conditions.

Article B – Links with the European Social Charter and the 1988 Additional Protocol...

PART IV

Article C – Supervision of the implementation of the undertakings contained in this Charter

The implementation of the legal obligations contained in this Charter shall be submitted to the same supervision as the European Social Charter.

Article D – Collective complaints

1. The provisions of the Additional Protocol to the European Social Charter providing for a system of collective complaints shall apply to the undertakings given in this Charter for the States which have ratified the said Protocol.

2. Any State which is not bound by the Additional Protocol to the European Social Charter providing for a system of collective complaints may when depositing its instrument of ratification, acceptance or approval of this Charter or at any time thereafter, declare by notification addressed to the Secretary General of the Council of Europe, that it accepts the supervision of its obligations under this Charter following the procedure provided for in the said Protocol.

Article E – Non-discrimination

Article F – Derogations in time of war or public emergency

1. In time of war or other public emergency threatening the life of the nation any Party may take measures derogating from its obligations under this Charter to the extent strictly required by the exigencies of the situation, provided that such measures are not inconsistent with its other obligations under international law. ...

Article H – Relations between the Charter and domestic law or international agreements

The provisions of this Charter shall not prejudice the provisions of domestic law or of any bilateral or multilateral treaties, conventions or agreements which are already in force, or may come into force, under which more favourable treatment would be accorded to the persons protected.

Article I – Implementation of the undertakings given

1. Without prejudice to the methods of implementation foreseen in these articles the relevant provisions of Articles 1 to 31 of Part II of this Charter shall be implemented by:

    a. laws or regulations;

    b. agreements between employers or employers' organisations and workers' organisations;

c. a combination of those two methods;

d. other appropriate means....

ADDITIONAL PROTOCOL TO THE EUROPEAN SOCIAL CHARTER PROVIDING FOR A SYSTEM OF COLLECTIVE COMPLAINTS (E.T.S. No. 158), *entered into force* January 7, 1998:

Preamble

The member States of the Council of Europe, signatories to this Protocol to the European Social Charter, opened for signature in Turin on 18 October 1961 (hereinafter referred to as "the Charter"),

Resolved to take new measures to improve the effective enforcement of the social rights guaranteed by the Charter;

Considering that this aim could be achieved in particular by the establishment of a collective complaints procedure, which, inter alia, would strengthen the participation of management and labour and of non-governmental organisations,

Have agreed as follows:

Article 1

The Contracting Parties to this Protocol recognise the right of the following organisations to submit complaints alleging unsatisfactory application of the Charter:

a. international organisations of employers and trade unions referred to in paragraph 2 of Article 27 of the Charter;

b. other international non-governmental organisations which have consultative status with the Council of Europe and have been put on a list established for this purpose by the Governmental Committee;

c. representative national organisations of employers and trade unions within the jurisdiction of the Contracting Party against which they have lodged a complaint.

Article 2

1. Any Contracting State may also, when it expresses its consent to be bound by this Protocol, in accordance with the provisions of Article 13, or at any moment thereafter, declare that it recognises the right of any other representative national non-governmental organisation within its jurisdiction which has particular competence in the matters governed by the Charter, to lodge complaints against it.

2. Such declarations may be made for a specific period.

3. The declarations shall be deposited with the Secretary General of the Council of Europe who shall transmit copies thereof to the Contracting Parties and publish them.

Article 3

The international non-governmental organisations and the national non-governmental organisations referred to in Article 1.b and Article 2 respectively may submit complaints in accordance with the procedure prescribed by the aforesaid provisions only in respect of those matters regarding which they have been recognised as having particular competence.

Article 4

The complaint shall be lodged in writing, relate to a provision of the Charter accepted by the Contracting Party concerned and indicate in what respect the latter has not ensured the satisfactory application of this provision.

Article 5

Any complaint shall be addressed to the Secretary General who shall acknowledge receipt of it, notify it to the Contracting Party concerned and immediately transmit it to the Committee of Independent Experts.

Article 6

The Committee of Independent Experts may request the Contracting Party concerned and the organisation which lodged the complaint to submit written information and observations on the admissibility of the complaint within such time-limit as it shall prescribe.

Article 7

1. If it decides that a complaint is admissible, the Committee of Independent Experts shall notify the Contracting Parties to the Charter through the Secretary General. It shall request the Contracting Party concerned and the organisation which lodged the complaint to submit, within such time-limit as it shall prescribe, all relevant written explanations or information, and the other Contracting Parties to this Protocol, the comments they wish to submit, within the same time-limit.

2. If the complaint has been lodged by a national organisation of employers or a national trade union or by another national or international non-governmental organisation, the Committee of Independent Experts shall notify the international organisations of employers or trade unions referred to in paragraph 2 of Article 27 of the Charter, through the Secretary General, and invite them to submit observations within such time-limit as it shall prescribe.

3. On the basis of the explanations, information or observations submitted under paragraphs 1 and 2 above, the Contracting Party concerned and the organisation which lodged the complaint may submit any additional written information or observations within such time- limit as the Committee of Independent Experts shall prescribe.

4. In the course of the examination of the complaint, the Committee of Independent Experts may organise a hearing with the representatives of the parties.

Article 8

1. The Committee of Independent Experts shall draw up a report in which it shall describe the steps taken by it to examine the complaint and present its conclusions as to whether or not the Contracting Party concerned has ensured the satisfactory application of the provision of the Charter referred to in the complaint.

2. The report shall be transmitted to the Committee of Ministers. It shall also be transmitted to the organisation that lodged the complaint and to the Contracting Parties to the Charter, which shall not be at liberty to publish it. It shall be transmitted to the Parliamentary Assembly and made public at the same time as the resolution referred to in Article 9 or no later than four months after it has been transmitted to the Committee of Ministers.

Article 9

1. On the basis of the report of the Committee of Independent Experts, the Committee of Ministers shall adopt a resolution by a majority of those voting. If the Committee of Independent Experts finds that the Charter has not been applied in a satisfactory manner, the Committee of Ministers shall adopt, by a majority of two-thirds of those voting, a recommendation addressed to the Contracting Party concerned. In both cases, entitlement to voting shall be limited to the Contracting Parties to the Charter.

2. At the request of the Contracting Party concerned, the Committee of Ministers may decide, where the report of the Committee of Independent Experts raises new issues, by a two-thirds majority of the Contracting Parties to the Charter, to consult the Governmental Committee.

Article 10

The Contracting Party concerned shall provide information on the measures it has taken to give effect to the Committee of Ministers' recommendation, in the next report which it submits to the Secretary General under Article 21 of the Charter.

Article 11

Articles 1 to 10 of this Protocol shall apply also to the articles of Part II of the first Additional Protocol to the Charter in respect of the States Parties to that Protocol, to the extent that these articles have been accepted.

Article 12

The States Parties to this Protocol consider that the first paragraph of the appendix to the Charter, relating to Part III, reads as follows: "It is understood that the Charter contains legal obligations of an international character, the application of which is submitted solely to the supervision provided for in Part IV thereof and in the provisions of this Protocol."

Article 13

1. This Protocol shall be open for signature by member States of the Council of Europe signatories to the Charter, which may express their consent to be bound by:

> a. signature without reservation as to ratification, acceptance or approval; or

> b. signature subject to ratification, acceptance or approval, followed by ratification, acceptance or approval.

2. A member State of the Council of Europe may not express its consent to be bound by this Protocol without previously or simultaneously ratifying the Charter.

3. Instruments of ratification, acceptance or approval shall be deposited with the Secretary General of the Council of Europe.

Article 14

1. This Protocol shall enter into force on the first day of the month following the expiration of a period of one month after the date on which five member States of the Council of Europe have expressed their consent to be bound by the Protocol in accordance with the provisions of Article 13.

2. In respect of any member State which subsequently expresses its consent to be bound by it, the Protocol shall enter into force on the first day of the month following the expiration of a period of one month after the date of the deposit of the instrument of ratification, acceptance or approval.

Article 15

1. Any Party may at any time denounce this Protocol by means of a notification addressed to the Secretary General of the Council of Europe.

2. Such denunciation shall become effective on the first day of the month following the expiration of a period of twelve months after the date of receipt of such notification by the Secretary General.

Article 16

The Secretary General of the Council of Europe shall notify all the member States of the Council of:

a. any signature;

b. the deposit of any instrument of ratification, acceptance or approval;

c. the date of entry into force of this Protocol in accordance with Article 14;

d. any other act, notification or declaration relating to this Protocol.

In witness whereof the undersigned, being duly authorised thereto, have signed this Protocol.

Done at Strasbourg, this 9th day of November 1995, in English and French, both texts being equally authentic, in a single copy which shall be deposited in the archives of the Council of Europe. The Secretary General of the Council of Europe shall transmit certified copies to each member State of the Council of Europe.

CHARTER OF FUNDAMENTAL RIGHTS OF THE EUROPEAN UNION, 2000 O.J. (C 364) 1, *entered into force* Dec. 7, 2000:

SOLEMN PROCLAMATION

The European Parliament, the Council and the Commission solemnly proclaim the text below as the Charter of fundamental rights of the European Union.

Done at Nice on the seventh day of December in the year two thousand.

For the European Parliament

For the Council of the European Union

For the European Commission

PREAMBLE

The peoples of Europe, in creating an ever closer union among them, are resolved to share a peaceful future based on common values.

Conscious of its spiritual and moral heritage, the Union is founded on the indivisible, universal values of human dignity, freedom, equality and solidarity; it is based on the principles of democracy and the rule of law. It places the individual at the heart of its activities, by establishing the citizenship of the Union and by creating an area of freedom, security and justice.

The Union contributes to the preservation and to the development of these common values while respecting the diversity of the cultures and traditions of the peoples of Europe as well as the national identities of the Member States and the organisation of their public authorities at national, regional and local levels; it seeks to promote balanced and sustainable development and ensures free movement of persons, goods, services and capital, and the freedom of establishment.

To this end, it is necessary to strengthen the protection of fundamental rights in the light of changes in society, social progress and scientific and technological developments by making those rights more visible in a Charter.

This Charter reaffirms, with due regard for the powers and tasks of the Community and the Union and the principle of subsidiarity, the rights as they result, in particular, from the constitutional traditions and international obligations common to the Member States, the Treaty on European Union, the Community Treaties, the European Convention for the Protection of Human Rights and Fundamental Freedoms, the Social Charters adopted by the Community and by the Council of Europe and the case-law of the Court of Justice of the European Communities and of the European Court of Human Rights.

Enjoyment of these rights entails responsibilities and duties with regard to other persons, to the human community and to future generations.

The Union therefore recognises the rights, freedoms and principles set out hereafter.

CHAPTER I
DIGNITY

Article 1

Human dignity

Human dignity is inviolable. It must be respected and protected.

Article 2

Right to life

1. Everyone has the right to life.

2. No one shall be condemned to the death penalty, or executed.

Article 3

Right to the integrity of the person

1. Everyone has the right to respect for his or her physical and mental integrity.

2. In the fields of medicine and biology, the following must be respected in particular:

– the free and informed consent of the person concerned, according to the procedures laid down by law,

– the prohibition of eugenic practices, in particular those aiming at the selection of persons,

– the prohibition on making the human body and its parts as such a source of financial gain,

– the prohibition of the reproductive cloning of human beings.

Article 4

Prohibition of torture and inhuman or degrading treatment or punishment

No one shall be subjected to torture or to inhuman or degrading treatment or punishment.

Article 5

Prohibition of slavery and forced labour

1. No one shall be held in slavery or servitude.

2. No one shall be required to perform forced or compulsory labour.

3. Trafficking in human beings is prohibited.

Article 6

Right to liberty and security

Everyone has the right to liberty and security of person.

Article 7

Respect for private and family life

Everyone has the right to respect for his or her private and family life, home and communications.

Article 8

Protection of personal data

1. Everyone has the right to the protection of personal data concerning him or her.

2. Such data must be processed fairly for specified purposes and on the basis of the consent of the person concerned or some other legitimate basis laid down by law. Everyone has the right of access to data which has been collected concerning him or her, and the right to have it rectified.

3. Compliance with these rules shall be subject to control by an independent authority.

Article 9

Right to marry and right to found a family

The right to marry and the right to found a family shall be guaranteed in accordance with the national laws governing the exercise of these rights.

Article 10

Freedom of thought, conscience and religion

1. Everyone has the right to freedom of thought, conscience and religion. This right includes freedom to change religion or belief and freedom, either alone or in community with others and in public or in private, to manifest religion or belief, in worship, teaching, practice and observance.

2. The right to conscientious objection is recognised, in accordance with the national laws governing the exercise of this right.

Article 11

Freedom of expression and information

1. Everyone has the right to freedom of expression. This right shall include freedom to hold opinions and to receive and impart information and ideas without interference by public authority and regardless of frontiers.

2. The freedom and pluralism of the media shall be respected.

Article 12

Freedom of assembly and of association

1. Everyone has the right to freedom of peaceful assembly and to freedom of association at all levels, in particular in political, trade union and civic matters, which implies the right of everyone to form and to join trade unions for the protection of his or her interests.

2. Political parties at Union level contribute to expressing the political will of the citizens of the Union.

Article 13

Freedom of the arts and sciences

The arts and scientific research shall be free of constraint. Academic freedom shall be respected.

Article 14

Right to education

1. Everyone has the right to education and to have access to vocational and continuing training.

2. This right includes the possibility to receive free compulsory education.

3. The freedom to found educational establishments with due respect for democratic principles and the right of parents to ensure the education and teaching of their children in conformity with their religious, philosophical and pedagogical convictions shall be respected, in accordance with the national laws governing the exercise of such freedom and right.

Article 15

Freedom to choose an occupation and right to engage in work

1. Everyone has the right to engage in work and to pursue a freely chosen or accepted occupation.

2. Every citizen of the Union has the freedom to seek employment, to work, to exercise the right of establishment and to provide services in any Member State.

3. Nationals of third countries who are authorised to work in the territories of the Member States are entitled to working conditions equivalent to those of citizens of the Union.

Article 16

Freedom to conduct a business

The freedom to conduct a business in accordance with Community law and national laws and practices is recognised.

Article 17

Right to property

1. Everyone has the right to own, use, dispose of and bequeath his or her lawfully acquired possessions. No one may be deprived of his or her possessions, except in the public interest and in the cases and under the conditions provided for by law, subject to fair compensation being paid in good time for their loss. The use of property may be regulated by law in so far as is necessary for the general interest.

2. Intellectual property shall be protected.

Article 18

Right to asylum

The right to asylum shall be guaranteed with due respect for the rules of the Geneva Convention of 28 July 1951 and the Protocol of 31 January 1967 relating to the status of refugees and in accordance with the Treaty establishing the European Community.

Article 19

Protection in the event of removal, expulsion or extradition

1. Collective expulsions are prohibited.

2. No one may be removed, expelled or extradited to a State where there is a serious risk that he or she would be subjected to the death penalty, torture or other inhuman or degrading treatment or punishment.

CHAPTER III
EQUALITY

Article 20

Equality before the law

Everyone is equal before the law.

Article 21

Non-discrimination

1. Any discrimination based on any ground such as sex, race, colour, ethnic or social origin, genetic features, language, religion or belief, political or any other opinion, membership of a national minority, property, birth, disability, age or sexual orientation shall be prohibited.

2. Within the scope of application of the Treaty establishing the European Community and of the Treaty on European Union, and without prejudice to the special provisions of those Treaties, any discrimination on grounds of nationality shall be prohibited.

Article 22

Cultural, religious and linguistic diversity

The Union shall respect cultural, religious and linguistic diversity.

Article 23

Equality between men and women

Equality between men and women must be ensured in all areas, including employment, work and pay. The principle of equality shall not prevent the maintenance or adoption of measures providing for specific advantages in favour of the under-represented sex.

Article 24

The rights of the child

1. Children shall have the right to such protection and care as is necessary for their well-being. They may express their views freely. Such views shall be taken into consideration on matters which concern them in accordance with their age and maturity.

2. In all actions relating to children, whether taken by public authorities or private institutions, the child's best interests must be a primary consideration. Every child shall have the right to maintain on a regular basis a personal relationship and direct contact with both his or her parents, unless that is contrary to his or her interests.

Article 25

The rights of the elderly

The Union recognises and respects the rights of the elderly to lead a life of dignity and independence and to participate in social and cultural life.

Article 26

Integration of persons with disabilities

The Union recognises and respects the right of persons with disabilities to benefit from measures

designed to ensure their independence, social and occupational integration and participation in the life of the community.

CHAPTER IV
SOLIDARITY

Article 27

Workers' right to information and consultation within the undertaking

Workers or their representatives must, at the appropriate levels, be guaranteed information and consultation in good time in the cases and under the conditions provided for by Community law and national laws and practices.

Article 28

Right of collective bargaining and action

Workers and employers, or their respective organisations, have, in accordance with Community law and national laws and practices, the right to negotiate and conclude collective agreements at the appropriate levels and, in cases of conflicts of interest, to take collective action to defend their interests, including strike action.

Article 29

Right of access to placement services

Everyone has the right of access to a free placement service.

Article 30

Protection in the event of unjustified dismissal

Every worker has the right to protection against unjustified dismissal, in accordance with Community law and national laws and practices.

Article 31

Fair and just working conditions

1. Every worker has the right to working conditions which respect his or her health, safety and dignity.

2. Every worker has the right to limitation of maximum working hours, to daily and weekly rest periods and to an annual period of paid leave.

Article 32

Prohibition of child labour and protection of young people at work

The employment of children is prohibited. The minimum age of admission to employment may not be lower than the minimum school-leaving age, without prejudice to such rules as may be more favourable to young people and except for limited derogations. Young people admitted to work must have working conditions appropriate to their age and be protected against economic exploitation and any work likely to harm their safety, health or physical, mental, moral or social development or to interfere with their education.

Article 33

Family and professional life

1. The family shall enjoy legal, economic and social protection.

2. To reconcile family and professional life, everyone shall have the right to protection from dismissal for a reason connected with maternity and the right to paid maternity leave and to parental leave following the birth or adoption of a child.

Article 34

Social security and social assistance

1. The Union recognises and respects the entitlement to social security benefits and social services providing protection in cases such as maternity, illness, industrial accidents, dependency or old age, and in the case of loss of employment, in accordance with the rules laid down by Community law and national laws and practices.

2. Everyone residing and moving legally within the European Union is entitled to social security benefits and social advantages in accordance with Community law and national laws and practices.

3. In order to combat social exclusion and poverty, the Union recognises and respects the right to social and housing assistance so as to ensure a decent existence for all those who lack sufficient resources, in accordance with the rules laid down by Community law and national laws and practices.

Article 35

Health care

Everyone has the right of access to preventive health care and the right to benefit from medical treatment under the conditions established by national laws and practices. A high level of human health protection shall be ensured in the definition and implementation of all Union policies and activities.

Article 36

Access to services of general economic interest

The Union recognises and respects access to services of general economic interest as provided for in national laws and practices, in accordance with the Treaty establishing the European Community, in order to promote the social and territorial cohesion of the Union.

Article 37

Environmental protection

A high level of environmental protection and the improvement of the quality of the environment must be integrated into the policies of the Union and ensured in accordance with the principle of sustainable development.

Article 38

Consumer protection

Union policies shall ensure a high level of consumer protection.

CHAPTER V
CITIZENS' RIGHTS

Article 39

Right to vote and to stand as a candidate at elections to the European Parliament

1. Every citizen of the Union has the right to vote and to stand as a candidate at elections to the European Parliament in the Member State in which he or she resides, under the same conditions as nationals of that State.

2. Members of the European Parliament shall be elected by direct universal suffrage in a free and secret ballot.

Article 40

Right to vote and to stand as a candidate at municipal elections

Every citizen of the Union has the right to vote and to stand as a candidate at municipal elections in the Member State in which he or she resides under the same conditions as nationals of that State.

Article 41

Right to good administration

1. Every person has the right to have his or her affairs handled impartially, fairly and within a reasonable time by the institutions and bodies of the Union.

2. This right includes:

– the right of every person to be heard, before any individual measure which would affect him or her adversely is taken;

– the right of every person to have access to his or her file, while respecting the legitimate interests of confidentiality and of professional and business secrecy;

– the obligation of the administration to give reasons for its decisions.

3. Every person has the right to have the Community make good any damage caused by its institutions or by its servants in the performance of their duties, in accordance with the general principles common to the laws of the Member States.

4. Every person may write to the institutions of the Union in one of the languages of the Treaties and must have an answer in the same language.

Article 42

Right of access to documents

Any citizen of the Union, and any natural or legal person residing or having its registered office in a Member State, has a right of access to European Parliament, Council and Commission documents.

Article 43

Ombudsman

Any citizen of the Union and any natural or legal person residing or having its registered office in a Member State has the right to refer to the Ombudsman of the Union cases of maladministration in the activities of the Community institutions or bodies, with the exception of the Court of Justice and the Court of First Instance acting in their judicial role.

Article 44

Right to petition

Any citizen of the Union and any natural or legal person residing or having its registered office in a Member State has the right to petition the European Parliament.

Article 45

Freedom of movement and of residence

1. Every citizen of the Union has the right to move and reside freely within the territory of the Member States.

2. Freedom of movement and residence may be granted, in accordance with the Treaty establishing the European Community, to nationals of third countries legally resident in the territory of a Member State.

Article 46

Diplomatic and consular protection

Every citizen of the Union shall, in the territory of a third country in which the Member State of which he or she is a national is not represented, be entitled to protection by the diplomatic or consular authorities of any Member State, on the same conditions as the nationals of that Member State.

CHAPTER VI
JUSTICE

Article 47

Right to an effective remedy and to a fair trial

Everyone whose rights and freedoms guaranteed by the law of the Union are violated has the right to an effective remedy before a tribunal in compliance with the conditions laid down in this Article. Everyone is entitled to a fair and public hearing within a reasonable time by an independent and impartial tribunal previously established by law. Everyone shall have the possibility of being advised, defended and represented. Legal aid shall be made available to those who lack sufficient resources in so far as such aid is necessary to ensure effective access to justice.

Article 48

Presumption of innocence and right of defence

1. Everyone who has been charged shall be presumed innocent until proved guilty according to law.

2. Respect for the rights of the defence of anyone who has been charged shall be guaranteed.

Article 49

Principles of legality and proportionality of criminal offences and penalties

1. No one shall be held guilty of any criminal offence on account of any act or omission which did not constitute a criminal offence under national law or international law at the time when it was committed. Nor shall a heavier penalty be imposed than that which was applicable at the time the criminal offence was committed. If, subsequent to the commission of a criminal offence, the law provides for a lighter penalty, that penalty shall be applicable.

2. This Article shall not prejudice the trial and punishment of any person for any act or omission which, at the time when it was committed, was criminal according to the general principles recognised by the community of nations.

3. The severity of penalties must not be disproportionate to the criminal offence.

Article 50

Right not to be tried or punished twice in criminal proceedings for the same criminal offence

No one shall be liable to be tried or punished again in criminal proceedings for an offence for which he or she has already been finally acquitted or convicted within the Union in accordance with the law.

CHAPTER VII
GENERAL PROVISIONS

Article 51

Scope

1. The provisions of this Charter are addressed to the institutions and bodies of the Union with due regard for the principle of subsidiarity and to the

Member States only when they are implementing Union law. They shall therefore respect the rights, observe the principles and promote the application thereof in accordance with their respective powers.

2. This Charter does not establish any new power or task for the Community or the Union, or modify powers and tasks defined by the Treaties.

Article 52

Scope of guaranteed rights

1. Any limitation on the exercise of the rights and freedoms recognised by this Charter must be provided for by law and respect the essence of those rights and freedoms. Subject to the principle of proportionality, limitations may be made only if they are necessary and genuinely meet objectives of general interest recognised by the Union or the need to protect the rights and freedoms of others.

2. Rights recognised by this Charter which are based on the Community Treaties or the Treaty on European Union shall be exercised under the conditions and within the limits defined by those Treaties.

3. In so far as this Charter contains rights which correspond to rights guaranteed by the Convention for the Protection of Human Rights and Fundamental Freedoms, the meaning and scope of those rights shall be the same as those laid down by the said Convention. This provision shall not prevent Union law providing more extensive protection.

Article 53

Level of protection

Nothing in this Charter shall be interpreted as restricting or adversely affecting human rights and fundamental freedoms as recognised, in their respective fields of application, by Union law and international law and by international agreements to which the Union, the Community or all the Member States are party, including the European Convention for the Protection of Human Rights and Fundamental Freedoms, and by the Member States' constitutions.

Article 54

Prohibition of abuse of rights

Nothing in this Charter shall be interpreted as implying any right to engage in any activity or to perform any act aimed at the destruction of any of the rights and freedoms recognised in this Charter or at their limitation to a greater extent than is provided for herein.

D. U.S. RESERVATIONS, DECLARATIONS, AND UNDERSTANDINGS

INTERNATIONAL CONVENTION ON THE PREVENTION AND PUNISHMENT OF THE CRIME OF GENOCIDE, Cong. Rec. S1355-01 (daily ed., Feb. 19, 1986):

I. The Senate's advice and consent is subject to the following reservations:

(1) That with reference to Article IX of the Convention, before any dispute to which the United States is a party may be submitted to the jurisdiction of the International Court of Justice under this article, the specific consent of the United States is required in each case.

(2) That nothing in the Convention requires or authorizes legislation or other action by the United States of America prohibited by the Constitution of the United States as interpreted by the United States.

II. The Senate's advice and consent is subject to the following understandings, which shall apply to the obligations of the United States under this Convention:

(1) That the term "intent to destroy, in whole or in part, a national, ethnical, racial, or religious group as such" appearing in Article II means the specific intent to destroy, in whole or in substantial part, a national ethnical, racial or religious group as such by the facts specified in Article II.

(2) That the term "mental harm" in Article II(b) means permanent impairment of mental faculties through drugs, torture or similar techniques.

(3) That the pledge to grant extradition in accordance with a state's laws and treaties in force found in Article VII extends only to acts which are criminal under the laws of both the requesting and the requested state and nothing in Article VI affects the right of any state to bring to trial before its own tribunals any of its nationals for acts committed outside a state.

(4) That acts in the course of armed conflicts committed without the specific intent required by Article II are not sufficient to constitute genocide as defined by this Convention.

(5) That with regard to the reference to an international penal tribunal in Article VI of the Convention, the United States declares that it reserves the right to effect its participation in any such tribunal only by a treaty entered into specifically for that purpose with the advice and consent of the Senate.

III. The Senate's advice and consent is subject to the following declaration:That the President will not deposit the instrument of ratification until after the implementing legislation referred to in Article V has been enacted.

CONVENTION AGAINST TORTURE AND OTHER CRUEL, INHUMAN OR DEGRADING TREATMENT OR PUNISHMENT, Cong. Rec. S17486-01 (daily ed., Oct. 27, 1990):

I. The Senate's advice and consent is subject to the following reservations:

(1) That the United States considers itself bound by the obligation under Article 16 to prevent "cruel, inhuman or degrading treatment or punishment," only insofar as the term "cruel, inhuman or degrading treatment or punishment" means the cruel, unusual and inhumane treatment or punishment prohibited by the Fifth, Eighth, and/or Fourteenth Amendments to the Constitution of the United States.

(2) That pursuant to Article 30(2) the United States declares that it does not consider itself bound by Article 30(1), but reserves the right specifically to agree to follow this or any other procedure for arbitration in a particular case.

II. The Senate's advice and consent is subject to the following understandings, which shall apply to the obligations of the United States under this Convention:

(1) (a) That with reference to Article 1, the United States understands that, in order to constitute torture, an act must be specifically intended to inflict severe physical or mental pain or suffering and that mental pain or suffering refers to prolonged mental harm caused by or resulting from: (1) the intentional infliction or threatened infliction of severe physical pain or suffering; (2) the administration or application, or threatened administration or application, of mind altering substances or other procedures calculated to disrupt profoundly the senses or the personality; (3) the threat of imminent death; (4) or the threat that another person will imminently be subjected to death, severe physical pain or suffering, or the administration or application of mind altering substances or other procedures calculated to disrupt profoundly the senses or personality.

(b) That the United States understands that the definition of torture in Article 1 is intended to apply only to acts directed against persons in the offender's custody or physical control.

(c) That with reference to Article 1 of the Convention, the United States understands that "sanctions" includes judicially imposed sanctions and other enforcement actions authorized by United States law or by judicial interpretation of such law. Nonetheless, the United States understands that a State Party could not through its domestic sanctions defeat the object and purpose of the Convention to prohibit torture.

(d) That with reference to Article 1 of the Convention, the United States understands that the term "acquiescence" requires that the public official, prior to the activity constituting torture, have awareness of such activity and thereafter breach his legal responsibility to intervene to prevent such activity.

(e) That with reference to Article 1 of the Convention, the United States understands that noncompliance with applicable legal procedural standards does not *per se* constitute torture.

(2) That the United States understands the phrase, "where there are substantial grounds for believing that he would be in danger of being subjected to torture," as used in Article 3 of the Convention, to mean "if it is more likely than not that he would be tortured."

(3) That it is the understanding of the United States that Article 14 requires a State Party to provide a private right of action for damages only for acts of torture committed in territory under the jurisdiction of that State Party.

(4) That the United States understands that international law does not prohibit the death penalty, and does not consider this Convention to restrict or prohibit the United States from applying the death penalty consistent with the Fifth, Eighth and/or Fourteenth Amendments to the Constitution of the United States, including any constitutional period of confinement prior to the imposition of the death penalty.

(5) That the United States understands that this Convention shall be implemented by the United States Government to the extent that it exercises legislative and judicial jurisdiction over the matters covered by the Convention and otherwise by the state and local governments. Accordingly, in implementing Articles 10-14 and 16, the United States Government shall take measures appropriate to the Federal system to the end that the competent authorities of the constituent units of the United States of America may take appropriate measures for the fulfillment of the Convention.

III. The Senate's advice and consent is subject to the following declarations:

(1) That the United States declares that the provisions of Articles 1 through 16 of the Convention are not self-executing.

(2) That the United States declares, pursuant to Article 21, paragraph 1, of the Convention, that it recognizes the competence of the Committee against Torture to receive and consider communications to the effect that a State Party claims that another State Party is not fulfilling its obligations under the Convention. It is the understanding of the United States that, pursuant to the above mentioned article, such communications shall be accepted and processed only if they come from a State Party which has made a similar declaration.

IV. The Senate's advice and consent is subject to the following proviso, which shall not be included in the instrument of ratification to be deposited by the President:

The President of the United States shall not deposit the instrument of ratification until such time as he has notified all present and prospective ratifying parties to this Convention that nothing in this Convention requires or authorizes legislation, or other action, by the United States of America prohibited by the Constitution of the United States as interpreted by the United States.

INTERNATIONAL COVENANT ON CIVIL AND POLITICAL RIGHTS, 138 Cong. Rec. S4781-01 (daily ed., April 2, 1992):

I. The Senate's advice and consent is subject to the following reservations:

(1) That Article 20 does not authorize or require legislation or other action by the United States that would restrict the right of free speech and association protected by the Constitution and laws of the United States.

(2) That the United States reserves the right, subject to its Constitutional constraints, to impose capital punishment on any person (other than a pregnant woman) duly convicted under existing or future laws permitting the imposition of capital punishment, including such punishment for crimes committed by persons below eighteen years of age.

(3) That the United States considers itself bound by Article 7 to the extent that "cruel, inhuman or degrading treatment or punishment" means the cruel and unusual treatment or punishment prohibited by the Fifth, Eighth and/or Fourteenth Amendments to the Constitution of the United States.

(4) That because U.S. law generally applies to an offender the penalty in force at the time the offense was committed, the United States does not adhere to the third clause of paragraph 1 of Article 15.

(5) That the policy and practice of the United States are generally in compliance with and supportive of the Covenant's provisions regarding treatment of juveniles in the criminal justice system. Nevertheless, the United States reserves the right, in exceptional circumstances, to treat juveniles as adults, notwithstanding paragraphs 2(b) and 3 of Article 10 and paragraph 4 of Article 14. The United States further reserves to these provisions with respect to individuals who volunteer for military service prior to age 18.

II. The Senate's advice and consent is subject to the following understandings, which shall apply to the obligations of the United States under this Covenant:

(1) That the Constitution and laws of the United States guarantee all persons equal protection of the law and provide extensive protections against discrimination. The United States understands distinctions based upon race, color, sex, language, religion, political or other opinion, national or social origin, property, birth or any other status - as those terms are used in Article 2, paragraph 1 and Article 26 - to be permitted when such distinctions are, at minimum, rationally related to a legitimate govern-

mental objective. The United States further understands the prohibition in paragraph 1 of Article 4 upon discrimination, in time of public emergency, based "solely" on the status of race, color, sex, language, religion or social origin not to bar distinctions that may have a disproportionate effect upon persons of a particular status.

(2) That the United States understands the right to compensation referred to in Articles 9(5) and 14(6) to require the provision of effective and enforceable mechanisms by which a victim of an unlawful arrest or detention or a miscarriage of justice may seek and, where justified, obtain compensation from either the responsible individual or the appropriate governmental entity. Entitlement to compensation may be subject of the reasonable requirements of domestic law.

(3) That the United States understands the reference to "exceptional circumstance" in paragraph 2(a) of Article 10 to permit the imprisonment of an accused person with convicted persons where appropriate in light of an individual's overall dangerousness, and to permit accused persons to waive their right to segregation from convicted persons. The United States further understands that paragraph 3 of Article 10 does not diminish the goals of punishment, deterrence, and incapacitation as additional legitimate purposes for a penitentiary system.

(4) That the United States understands that subparagraphs 3(b) and (d) of Article 14 do not require the provision of a criminal defendant's counsel of choice when the defendant is provided with court-appointed counsel on grounds of indigence, when the defendant is financially able to retain alternative counsel, or when imprisonment is not imposed. The United States further understands that paragraph 3(e) does not prohibit a requirement that the defendant make a showing that any witness whose attendance he seeks to compel is necessary for his defense. The United States understands the prohibition upon double jeopardy in paragraph 7 to apply only when the judgment of acquittal has been rendered by a court of the same governmental unit, whether the Federal Government or a constituent unit, is seeking a new trial for the same cause.

(5) That the United States understands that this Covenant shall be implemented by the Federal Government to the extent that it exercises legislative and judicial jurisdiction over the matters covered therein, and otherwise by the state and local governments; to the extent that state and local governments exercise jurisdiction over such matters, the Federal Government shall take measures appropriate to the Federal system to the end that the competent authorities of the state or local governments may take appropriate measures for the fulfillment of the Covenant.

III. The Senate's advice and consent is subject to the following declarations:

(1) That the United States declares that the provisions of Articles 1 through 27 of the Covenant are not self-executing.

(2) That it is the view of the United States that States Party to the Covenant should wherever possible refrain from imposing any restrictions or limitations on the exercise of the rights recognized and protected by the Covenant, even when such restrictions and limitations are permissible under the terms of the Covenant. For the United States, Article 5, paragraph 2, which provides that fundamental human rights existing in any State Party may not be diminished on the pretext that the Covenant recognizes them to a lesser extent, has particular relevance to Article 19, paragraph 3, which would permit certain restrictions on the freedom of expression. The United States declares that it will continue to adhere to the requirements and constraints of its Constitution in respect to all such restrictions and limitations.

(3) That the United States declares that it accepts the competence of the Human Rights Committee to receive and consider communications under Article 41 in which a State Party claims that another State Party is not fulfilling its obligations under the Covenant.

(4) That the United States declares that the right referred to in Article 47 may be exercised only in accordance with international law.

IV. The Senate's advice and consent is subject to the following proviso, which shall not be included in the instrument of ratification to be deposited by the President:

Nothing in this Covenant requires or authorizes legislation, or other action, by the United Sates of America prohibited by the Constitution of the United States as interpreted by the United States.

INTERNATIONAL CONVENTION ON THE ELIMINATION OF ALL FORMS OF RACIAL DISCRIMINATION, 140 Cong. Rec. S7634-02 (daily ed., June 24, 1994):

I. The Senate's advice and consent is subject to the following reservations:

(1) That the Constitution and laws of the United States contain extensive protections of individual freedom of speech, expression and association. Accordingly, the United States does not accept any obligation under this Convention, in particular under Articles 4 and 7, to restrict those rights, through the adoption of legislation or any other measures, to the extent that they are protected by the Constitution and laws of the United States.

(2) That the Constitution and the laws of the United States establish extensive protections against discrimination, reaching significant areas of non-governmental activity. Individual privacy and freedom from governmental interference in private conduct, however, are also recognized as among the fundamental values which shape our free and democratic society. The United States understands that the identification of the rights protected under the Convention by reference in

Article 1 to the fields of "public life" reflects a similar distinction between spheres of public conduct that are customarily the subject of governmental regulation, and spheres of private conduct that are not. To the extent, however, that the Convention calls for a broader regulation of private conduct, the United States does not accept any obligation under this Convention to enact legislation or take other measures under paragraph (1) of Article 2, subparagraphs (1)(c) and (d) of Article 2, Article 3 and Article 5 with respect to private conduct except as mandated by the Constitution and laws of the United States.

(3) That with reference to Article 22 of the Convention, before any dispute to which the United States is a party may be submitted to the jurisdiction of the International Court of Justice under this article, the specific consent of the United States is required in each case.

II. The Senate's advice and consent is subject to the following understanding, which shall apply to the obligations of the United States under this Convention:

That the United States understands that this Convention shall be implemented by the Federal Government to the extent that it exercises jurisdiction over the matters covered therein, and otherwise by the state and local governments. To the extent that state and local governments exercise jurisdiction over such matters, the Federal Government shall, as necessary, take appropriate measures to ensure the fulfillment of this Convention.

III. The Senate's advice and consent is subject to the following declaration:

That the United States declares that the provisions of the Convention are not self-executing.

IV. The Senate's advice and consent is subject to the following proviso, which shall not be included in the instrument of ratification to be deposited by the President:

Nothing in this Convention requires or authorizes legislation, or other action, by the Untied States of America prohibited by the Constitution of the Untied States as interpreted by the United States.

E. U.S. LEGISLATION

HUMAN RIGHTS AND DEVELOPMENT ASSISTANCE, 22 U.S.C. 2151n (2000 & Supp. V 2005):

(a) Violations barring assistance; assistance for needy people.

No assistance may be provided under this part to the government of any country which engages in a consistent pattern of gross violations of internationally recognized human rights, including torture or cruel, inhuman, or degrading treatment or punishment, prolonged detention without charges, causing the disappearance of persons by the abduction and clandestine detention of those persons, or other flagrant denial of the right to life, liberty, and the security of person, unless such assistance will directly benefit the needy people in such country.

(b) Information to Congressional Committees for realization of assistance for needy people; concurrent resolution terminating assistance.

In determining whether this standard is being met with regard to funds allocated under this part, the Committee on Foreign Relations of the Senate or the Committee on Foreign Affairs of the House of Representatives may require the Administrator primarily responsible for administering part I of this Act to submit in writing information demonstrating that such assistance will directly benefit the needy people in such country, together with a detailed explanation of the assistance to be provided (including the dollar amounts of such assistance) and an explanation of how such assistance will directly benefit the needy people in such country. If either committee or either House of Congress disagrees with the Administrator's justification it may initiate action to terminate assistance to any country by a concurrent resolution under section 617 of this Act [22 USCS § 2367].

(c) Protection of children from exploitation.

No assistance may be provided to any government failing to take appropriate and adequate measures, within their means, to protect children from exploitation, abuse or forced conscription into military or paramilitary services.

(d) Factors considered.

In determining whether or not a government falls within the provisions of subsection (a) and in formulating development assistance programs under this part, the Administrator shall consider, in consultation with the Assistant Secretary of State for Democracy, Human Rights, and Labor and in consultation with the Ambassador at Large for International Religious Freedom--

(1) the extent of cooperation of such government in permitting an unimpeded investigation of alleged violations of internationally recognized human rights by appropriate international organizations, including the International Committee of the Red Cross, or groups or persons acting under the authority of the United Nations or of the Organization of American States;

(2) specific actions which have been taken by the President or the Congress relating to multilateral or security assistance to a less developed country because of the human rights practices or policies of such country; and

(3) whether the government--

(A) has engaged in or tolerated particularly severe violations of religious freedom, as defined in section 3 of the International Religious Freedom Act of 1998 [22 USCS § 6402]; or

(B) has failed to undertake serious and sustained efforts to combat particularly severe violations of religious freedom (as defined in section 3 of the International Religious Freedom Act of 1998 [22 USCS § 6402]), when such efforts could have been reasonably undertaken.

(e) Report to Speaker of House and Committee on Foreign Relations of the Senate.

The Secretary of State shall transmit to the Speaker of the House of Representatives and the Committee on Foreign Relations of the Senate, by February 25 of each year, a full and complete report regarding--

(1) the status of internationally recognized human rights, within the meaning of subsection (a)--

(A) in countries that receive assistance under this part, and

(B) in all other foreign countries which are members of the United Nations and which are not otherwise the subject of a human rights report under this Act;

(2) wherever applicable, practices regarding coercion in population control, including coerced abortion and involuntary sterilization;

(3) the status of child labor practices in each country, including--

(A) whether such country has adopted policies to protect children from exploitation in the workplace, including a prohibition of forced and bonded labor and policies regarding acceptable working conditions; and

(B) the extent to which each country enforces such policies, including the adequacy of the resources and oversight dedicated to such policies;

(4) the votes of each member of the United Nations Commission on Human Rights on all country-specific and thematic resolutions voted on at the Commission's annual session during the period covered during the preceding year;

(5) the extent to which each country has extended protection to refugees, including the provision of first asylum and resettlement;

(6) the steps the Administrator has taken to alter United States programs under this part in any country because of human rights considerations;

(7) wherever applicable, violations of religious freedom, including particularly severe violations of religious freedom (as defined in section 3 of the International Religious Freedom Act of 1998 [22 USCS § 6402]);[;]

(8) wherever applicable, a description of the nature and extent of acts of anti-Semitism and anti-Semitic incitement that occur during the preceding year, including descriptions of--

(A) acts of physical violence against, or harassment of Jewish people, and acts of violence against, or vandalism of Jewish community institutions, including schools,

(B) instances of propaganda in government and nongovernment media that attempt to justify or promote racial hatred or incite acts of violence against Jewish people;

(C) the actions, if any, taken by the government of the country to respond to such violence and attacks or to eliminate such propaganda or incitement;

(D) the actions taken by such government to enact and enforce laws relating to the protection of the right to religious freedom of Jewish people; and

(E) the efforts of such government to promote anti-bias and tolerance education;

(9) wherever applicable, consolidated information regarding the commission of war crimes, crimes against humanity, and evidence of acts that may constitute genocide (as defined in article 2 of the Convention on the Prevention and Punishment of the Crime of Genocide and modified by the United States instrument of ratification to that convention and section 2(a) of);

(10) for each country with respect to which the report indicates that extrajudicial killings, torture, or other serious violations of human rights have occurred in the country, the extent to which the United States has taken or will take action to encourage an end to such practices in the country; and

(11) (A) wherever applicable, a description of the nature and extent–

(i) of the compulsory recruitment and conscription of individuals under the age of 18 by armed forces of the government of the country, government-supported paramilitaries, or other armed groups, and the participation of such individuals in such groups; and

(ii) that such individuals take a direct part in hostilities;

(B) what steps, if any, taken by the government of the country to eliminate such practices; and

(C) such other information related to the use by such government of individuals under the age of 18 as soldiers, as determined to be appropriate by the Secretary.

(f) Promotion of civil and political rights; grants to nongovernmental organizations in South Africa; priority, etc.

The President is authorized and encouraged to use not less than $ 3,000,000 of the funds made available under this chapter, chapter 10 of this part [22 USCS §§ 2293 et seq.], and chapter 4 of part II for each fiscal year for studies to identify, and for openly carrying out, programs and activities which will encourage or promote increased adherence to civil and political rights, including the right to free religious belief and practice, as set forth in the Universal Declaration of Human Rights, in countries eligible for assistance under this chapter or under chapter 10 of this part [22 USCS §§ 2293 et seq.], except that funds made available under chapter 10 of this part [22 USCS §§ 2293 et seq.] may only be used under this subsection with respect to countries in sub-Saharan Africa. None of these funds may be used, directly or indirectly, to influence the outcome of any election in any country.

(g) Country reports regarding severe forms of trafficking in persons.

(1) The report required by subsection (d) shall include the following:

(A) A description of the nature and extent of severe forms of trafficking in persons, as defined in section 103 of the Trafficking Victims Protection Act of 2000 [22 USCS § 7102], in each foreign country.

(B) With respect to each country that is a country of origin, transit, or destination for victims of severe forms of trafficking in persons, an assessment of the efforts by the government of that country to combat such trafficking. The assessment shall address the following:

(i) Whether government authorities in that country participate in, facilitate, or condone such trafficking.

(ii) Which government authorities in that country are involved in activities to combat such trafficking.

(iii) What steps the government of that country has taken to prohibit government officials from participating in, facilitating, or condoning such trafficking, including the investigation, prosecution, and conviction of such officials.

(iv) What steps the government of that country has taken to prohibit other individuals from participating in such trafficking, including the investigation, prosecution, and conviction of individuals involved in severe forms of trafficking in persons, the criminal and civil penalties for such trafficking, and the efficacy of those penalties in eliminating or reducing such trafficking.

(v) What steps the government of that country has taken to assist victims of such trafficking, including efforts to prevent victims from being further victimized by traffickers, government officials, or others, grants of relief from deportation, and provision of humanitarian relief, including provision of mental and physical health care and shelter.

(vi) Whether the government of that country is cooperating with governments of other countries to extradite traffickers when requested, or, to the extent that such cooperation would be inconsistent with the laws of such country or with extradition treaties to which such country is a party, whether the government of that country is taking all appropriate measures to modify or replace such laws and treaties so as to permit such cooperation.

(vii) Whether the government of that country is assisting in international investigations of transnational trafficking networks and in other cooperative efforts to combat severe forms of trafficking in persons.

(viii) Whether the government of that country refrains from prosecuting victims of severe forms of trafficking in persons due to such victims having been trafficked, and refrains from other discriminatory treatment of such victims.

(ix) Whether the government of that country recognizes the rights of victims of severe forms of trafficking in persons and ensures their access to justice.

(C) Such other information relating to trafficking in persons as the Secretary of State considers appropriate.

(2) In compiling data and making assessments for the purposes of paragraph (1), United States diplomatic mission personnel shall consult with human rights organizations and other appropriate nongovernmental organizations.

HUMAN RIGHTS AND SECURITY ASSISTANCE, 22 U.S.C. § 2304 (2000 & Supp. V 2005):

(a) Observance of human rights as principal goal of foreign policy; implementation requirements.

(1) The United States shall, in accordance with its international obligations as set forth in the Charter of the United Nations and in keeping with the constitutional heritage and traditions of the United States, promote and encourage increased respect for human rights and fundamental freedoms throughout the world without distinction as to race, sex, language, or religion. Accordingly, a principal goal of the foreign policy of the United States shall be to promote the increased observance of internationally recognized human rights by all countries.

(2) Except under circumstances specified in this section, no security assistance may be provided to any country the government of which engages in a consistent pattern of gross violations of internationally recognized human rights. Security assistance may not be provided to the police, domestic intelligence, or similar law enforcement forces of a country, and licenses may not be issued under the Export Administration Act of 1979 [50 USCS Appx §§ 2401 et seq.] for the export of crime control and detection instruments and equipment to a country, the government of which engages in a consistent pattern of gross violations of internationally recognized human rights unless the President certifies in writing to the Speaker of the House of Representatives and the chairman of the Committee on Foreign Relations of the Senate and the chairman of the Committee on Banking, Housing, and Urban Affairs of the Senate (when licenses are to be issued pursuant to the Export Administration Act of 1979 [50 USCS Appx §§ 2401 et seq.])[.] that extraordinary circumstances exist warranting provision of such assistance and issuance of such licenses. Assistance may not be provided under chapter 5 of this part [22 USCS §§ 2347 et seq.] to a country the government of which engages in a consistent pattern of gross violations of internationally recognized human rights unless the President certifies in writing to the Speaker of the House of Representatives and the chairman of the Committee on Foreign Relations of the Senate that extraordinary circumstances exist warranting provision of such assistance.

(3) In furtherance of paragraphs (1) and (2), the President is directed to formulate and conduct international security assistance programs of the United States in a manner which will promote and advance human rights and

avoid identification of the United States, through such programs, with governments which deny to their people internationally recognized human rights and fundamental freedoms, in violation of international law or in contravention of the policy of the United States as expressed in this section or otherwise.

(4) In determining whether the government of a country engages in a consistent pattern of gross violations of internationally recognized human rights, the President shall give particular consideration to whether the government—

(A) has engaged in or tolerated particularly severe violations of religious freedom, as defined in section 3 of the International Religious Freedom Act of 1998 [22 USCS § 6402]; or

(B) has failed to undertake serious and sustained efforts to combat particularly severe violations of religious freedom when such efforts could have been reasonably undertaken.

(b) Report by Secretary of State on practices of proposed recipient countries; considerations.

The Secretary of State shall transmit to the Congress, as part of the presentation materials for security assistance programs proposed for each fiscal year, a full and complete report, prepared with the assistance of the Assistant Secretary of State for Democracy, Human Rights, and Labor and with the assistance of the Ambassador at Large for International Religious Freedom, with respect to practices regarding the observance of and respect for internationally recognized human rights in each country proposed as a recipient of security assistance. Wherever applicable, such report shall include consolidated information regarding the commission of war crimes, crimes against humanity, and evidence of acts that may constitute genocide (as defined in article 2 of the Convention on the Prevention and Punishment of the Crime of Genocide and modified by the United States instrument of ratification to that convention and section 2(a) of the Genocide Convention Implementation Act of 1987 [18 USCS § 1091]). Wherever applicable, such report shall include information on practices regarding coercion in population control, including coerced abortion and involuntary sterilization. Such report shall also include, wherever applicable, information on violations of religious freedom, including particularly severe violations of religious freedom (as defined in section 3 of the International Religious Freedom Act of 1998 [22 USCS § 6402]). Wherever applicable, [such report shall also include] a description of the nature and extent of acts of anti-Semitism and anti-Semitic incitement that occur, including the descriptions of such acts required under section 116(d)(8) [22 USCS § 2151n(d)(8)]. Such report shall also include, for each country with respect to which the report indicates that extrajudicial killings, torture, or other serious violations of human rights have occurred in the country, the extent to which the United States has taken or will take action to encourage an end to such practices in the country. Each report under this section shall list the votes of each member of the United Nations Commission on Human Rights on all country-specific and thematic resolutions voted on at the Commission's annual session during the period covered during the preceding year. Each report under this section shall also include (i) wherever applicable, a description of the nature and extent of the compulsory recruitment and conscription of individuals under the age of 18 by armed forces of the government of the country, government-supported paramilitaries, or other armed groups, the participation of such individuals in such groups, and the nature and extent that such individuals take a direct part in hostilities, (ii) what steps, if any, taken by the government of the country to eliminate such practices, and (iii) such other information related to the use by such government of individuals under the age of 18 as soldiers, as determined to be appropriate by the Secretary of State. Each report under this section shall describe the extent to which each country has extended protection to refugees, including the provision of first asylum and resettlement. In determining whether a government falls within the provisions of subsection (a)(3) and in the preparation of any report or statement required under this section, consideration shall be given to—

(1) the relevant findings of appropriate international organizations, including nongovernmental organizations, such as the International Committee of the Red Cross; and

(2) the extent of cooperation by such government in permitting an unimpeded investigation by any such organization of alleged violations of internationally recognized human rights.

(c) Congressional request for information; information required; 30 day period; failure to supply information; termination or restriction of assistance.

(1) Upon the request of the Senate or the House of Representatives by resolution of either such House, or upon the request of the Committee on Foreign Relations of the Senate or the Committee on Foreign Affairs of the House of Representatives, the Secretary of State shall, within thirty days after receipt of such request, transmit to both such committees a statement, prepared with the assistance of the Assistant Secretary of State for Democracy, Human Rights, and Labor, with respect to the country designated in such request, setting forth—

(A) all the available information about observance of and respect for human rights and fundamental freedom in that country, and a detailed description of practices by the recipient government with respect thereto;

(B) the steps the United States has taken to—

(i) promote respect for and observance of human rights in that country and discourage any practices which are inimical to internationally recognized human rights, and

(ii) publicly or privately call attention to, and disassociate the United States and any security assistance provided for such country from, such practices;

(C) whether, in the opinion of the Secretary of State, notwithstanding any such practices—

(i) extraordinary circumstances exist which necessitate a continuation of security assistance for such country, and, if so, a description of such circumstances and the extent to which such assistance should be continued (subject to such conditions as Congress may impose under this section), and

(ii) on all the facts it is in the national interest of the United States to provide such assistance; and

(D) such other information as such committee or such House may request.

(2) (A) A resolution of request under paragraph (1) of this subsection shall be considered in the Senate in accordance with the provisions of section 601(b) of the International Security Assistance and Arms Export Control Act of 1976 [unclassified].

(B) The term "certification", as used in section 601 of such Act [unclassified], means, for the purposes of this subsection, a resolution of request of the Senate under paragraph (1) of this subsection.

(3) In the event a statement with respect to a country is requested pursuant to paragraph (1) of this subsection but is not transmitted in accordance therewith within thirty days after receipt of such request, no security assistance shall be delivered to such country except as may thereafter be specifically authorized by law from such country unless and until such statement is transmitted.

(4) (A) In the event a statement with respect to a country is transmitted under paragraph (1) of this subsection, the Congress may at any time thereafter adopt a joint resolution terminating, restricting, or continuing security assistance for such country. In the event such a joint resolution is adopted, such assistance shall be so terminated, so restricted, or so continued, as the case may be.

(B) Any such resolution shall be considered in the Senate in accordance with the provisions of section 601(b) of the International Security Assistance and Arms Export Control Act of 1976 [unclassified].

(C) The term "certification", as used in section 601 of such Act [unclassified], means, for the purposes of this paragraph, a statement transmitted under paragraph (1) of this subsection.

(d) Definitions.

For the purposes of this section–

(1) the term "gross violations of internationally recognized human rights" includes torture or cruel, inhuman, or degrading treatment or punishment, prolonged detention without charges and trial, causing the disappearance of persons by the abduction and clandestine detention of those persons, and other flagrant denial of the right to life, liberty, or the security of person; and

(2) the term "security assistance" means–

(A) assistance under chapter 2 [22 USCS §§ 2311 et seq.] (military assistance) or chapter 4 [22 USCS §§ 2346 et seq.] (economic support fund) or chapter 5 [22 USCS §§ 2347 et seq.] (military education and training) or chapter 6 [22 USCS §§ 2348 et seq.] (peacekeeping operations) or chapter 8 [22 USCS §§ 2349aa et seq.] (antiterrorism assistance) of this part;

(B) sales of defense articles or services, extensions of credits (including participations in credits, and guaranties of loans under the Arms Export Control Act; or

(C) any license in effect with respect to the export of defense articles or defense services to or for the armed forces, police, intelligence, or other internal security forces of a foreign country under section 38 of the Arms Export Control Act [22 USCS § 2778].

(e) Removal of prohibition on assistance.

Notwithstanding any other provision of law, funds authorized to be appropriated under part I of this Act may be made available for the furnishing of assistance to any country with respect to which the President finds that such a significant improvement in its human rights record has occurred as to warrant lifting the prohibition on furnishing such assistance in the national interest of the United States.

(f) Allocations concerned with performance record of recipient countries without contravention of other provisions.

In allocating the funds authorized to be appropriated by this Act and the Arms Export Control Act, the President shall take into account significant improvements in the human rights records of recipient countries, except that such allocations may not contravene any other provision of law.

(g) Report to Congress on use of certain authorities relating to human rights conditions.

Whenever the provisions of subsection (e) or (f) of this section are applied, the President shall report to the Congress before making any funds available pursuant to those subsections. The report shall specify the country involved, the amount and kinds of assistance to be provided, and the justification for providing the assistance, including a description of the significant improvements which have occurred in the country's human rights record.

(h) Country reports regarding severe forms of trafficking in persons.

(1) The report required by subsection (b) shall include the following:

(A) A description of the nature and extent of severe forms of trafficking in persons, as defined in section 103 of the Trafficking Victims Protection Act of 2000 [22 USCS § 7102], in each foreign country.

(B) With respect to each country that is a country of origin, transit, or destination for victims of severe forms of trafficking in persons, an assessment of the efforts by the government of that country to combat such trafficking. The assessment shall address the following:

(i) Whether government authorities in that country participate in, facilitate, or condone such trafficking.

(ii) Which government authorities in that country are involved in activities to combat such trafficking.

(iii) What steps the government of that country has taken to prohibit government officials from participating in, facilitating, or condoning such trafficking, including the investigation, prosecution, and conviction of such officials.

(iv) What steps the government of that country has taken to prohibit other individuals from participating in such trafficking, including the investigation, prosecution, and conviction of individuals involved in severe forms of trafficking in persons, the criminal and civil penalties for such trafficking, and the efficacy of those penalties in eliminating or reducing such trafficking.

(v) What steps the government of that country has taken to assist victims of such trafficking, including efforts to prevent victims from being further victimized by traffickers, government officials, or others, grants of relief from deportation, and provision of humanitarian relief, including provision of mental and physical health care and shelter.

(vi) Whether the government of that country is cooperating with governments of other countries to extradite traffickers when requested, or, to the extent that such cooperation would be inconsistent with the laws of such country or with extradition treaties to which such country is a party, whether the government of that country is taking all appropriate measures to modify or replace such laws and treaties so as to permit such cooperation.

(vii) Whether the government of that country is assisting in international investigations of transnational trafficking networks and in other cooperative efforts to combat severe forms of trafficking in persons.

(viii) Whether the government of that country refrains from prosecuting victims of severe forms of trafficking in persons due to such victims having been trafficked, and refrains from other discriminatory treatment of such victims.

(ix) Whether the government of that country recognizes the rights of victims of severe forms of trafficking in persons and ensures their access to justice.

(C) Such other information relating to trafficking in persons as the Secretary of State considers appropriate.

(2) In compiling data and making assessments for the purposes of paragraph (1), United States diplomatic mission personnel shall consult with human rights organizations and other appropriate nongovernmental organizations.

HUMAN RIGHTS AND UNITED STATES ASSISTANCE POLICIES WITH INTERNATIONAL FINANCIAL INSTITUTIONS, 22 U.S.C. § 262d (1994 & Supp. V 1999), *amended by* **Pub. L. 106-569, 114 Stat. 2944 (2000):**

(a) Policy goals

The United States Government, in connection with its voice and vote in the International Bank for Reconstruction and Development, the International Development Association, the International Finance Corporation, the Inter-American Development Bank, the African Development Fund, the Asian Development Bank, and the African Development Bank, the European Bank for Reconstruction and Development, and the International Monetary Fund, shall advance the cause of human rights, including by seeking to channel assistance toward countries other than those whose governments engage in -

(1) a pattern of gross violations of internationally recognized human rights, such as torture or cruel, inhumane, or degrading treatment or punishment, prolonged detention without charges, or other flagrant denial to life, liberty, and the security of person; or

(2) provide refuge to individuals committing acts of international terrorism by hijacking aircraft.

(b) Policy considerations for Executive Directors of institutions in implementation of duties

Further, the Secretary of the Treasury shall instruct each Executive Director of the above institutions to consider in carrying out his duties:

(1) specific actions by either the executive branch or the Congress as a whole on individual bilateral assistance programs because of human rights considerations;

(2) the extent to which the economic assistance provided by the above institutions directly benefit the needy people in the recipient country;

(3) whether the recipient country -

(A) is seeking to acquire unsafeguarded special nuclear material (as defined in section 6305 (8) of this title) or a nuclear explosive device (as defined in section 6305 (4) of this title);

(B) is not a State Party to the Treaty on the Non-Proliferation of Nuclear Weapons; or

(C) has detonated a nuclear explosive device; and

(4) in relation to assistance for the Socialist Republic of Vietnam, the People's Democratic Republic of Laos, Russia and the other independent states of the former Soviet Union (as defined in section 5801 of this title), and Democratic Kampuchea (Cambodia), the responsiveness of the governments of such countries in providing a more substantial accounting of Americans missing in action.

(c) Reporting requirements

(1) Not later than 30 days after the end of each calendar quarter, the Secretary of the Treasury shall report quarterly on all loans considered by the Boards of Executive Directors of the institutions listed in subsection (a) of this section to the Chairman and ranking minority member of the Committee on Banking, Finance and Urban Affairs of the House of Representatives, or the designees of such Chairman and ranking minority member, and the Chairman and ranking minority member of the Committee on Foreign Relations of the Senate.

(2) Each report required by paragraph (1) shall--

(A) include a list of all loans considered by the Board of Executive Directors of the institutions listed in subsection (a) of this section and shall specify with respect to each such loan--

(i) the institution involved;

(ii) the date of final action;

(iii) the borrower;

(iv) the amount;

(v) the project or program;

(vi) the vote of the United States Government;

(vii) the reason for United States Government opposition, if any;

(viii) the final disposition of the loan; and

(ix) if the United States Government opposed the loan, whether the loan meets basic human needs.

(B) indicate whether the United States has opposed any loan, financial assistance, or technical assistance to a country on human rights grounds;

(C) indicate whether the United States has voted in favor of a loan, financial assistance, or technical assistance to a country with respect to which the United States had, in the preceding 2 years, opposed a loan, financial assistance, or technical assistance on human rights grounds; and

(D) in cases where the United States changed its voting position from opposition to support or from support to opposition, on human rights grounds–

(i) indicate the policy considerations that were taken into account in the development of the United States voting position;

(ii) describe human rights conditions in the country involved;

(iii) indicate how the United States voted on all other loans, financial assistance, and technical assistance to such country during the preceding 2 years; and

(iv) contain information as to how the United States voting position relates to the overall United States Government policy on human rights in such country.

(d) Requirements of United States assistance through institutions for projects in recipient countries

The United States Government, in connection with its voice and vote in the institutions listed in subsection (a) of this section, shall seek to channel assistance to projects which address basic human needs of the people of the recipient country.

(e) Criteria for determination of gross violations of internationally recognized human rights standards

In determining whether a country is in gross violation of internationally recognized human rights standards, as defined by the provisions of subsection (a) of this section, the United States Government shall give consideration to the extent of cooperation of such country in permitting an unimpeded investigation of alleged violations of internationally recognized human rights by appropriate international organizations including, but not limited to, the International Committee of the Red Cross, Amnesty International, the International Commission of Jurists, and groups or persons acting under the authority of the United Nations or the Organization of American States.

(f) Opposition by United States Executive Directors of institutions to financial or technical assistance to violating countries

The United States Executive Directors of the institutions listed in subsection (a) of this section are authorized and instructed to oppose any loan, any extension of financial assistance, or any technical assistance to any country described in subsection (a)(1) or (2), unless such assistance is directed specifically to programs which serve the basic human needs of the citizens of such country.

(g) Consultative and additional reporting requirements

The Secretary of the Treasury or his delegate shall consult frequently and in a timely manner with the chairmen and ranking minority members of the Committee on Banking, Finance and Urban Affairs of the House of Representatives and of the Committee on Foreign Relations of the Senate to inform them regarding any prospective changes in policy direction toward countries which have or recently have had poor human rights records.

(g) **Violations of religious freedom

In determining whether the government of a country engages in a pattern of gross violations of internationally recognized human rights, as described in subsection (a) of this section, the President shall give particular consideration to whether a foreign government -

(1) has engaged in or tolerated particularly severe violations of religious freedom, as defined in section 6402 of this title; or

---

[**Ed. note: The statute enacted by Congress contains two consecutive subsections denoted (g).]

(2) has failed to undertake serious and sustained efforts to combat particularly severe violations of religious freedom when such efforts could have been reasonably undertaken.

FOREIGN SOVEREIGN IMMUNITIES ACT OF 1976, 28 U.S.C. §§ 1602 et seq. (1994 & Supp 1999):...

Sec. 1604. Immunity of a foreign state from jurisdiction

Subject to existing international agreements to which the United States is a party at the time of enactment of this Act a foreign state shall be immune from the jurisdiction of the courts of the United States and of the States except as provided in sections 1605 to 1607 of this chapter... .

Sec. 1605. General exceptions to the jurisdictional immunity of a foreign state

(a) A foreign state shall not be immune from the jurisdiction of courts of the United States or of the States in any case -

(1) in which the foreign state has waived its immunity either explicitly or by implication, notwithstanding any withdrawal of the waiver which the foreign state may purport to effect except in accordance with the terms of the waiver;

(2) in which the action is based upon a commercial activity carried on in the United States by the foreign state; or upon an act performed in the United States in connection with a commercial activity of the foreign state elsewhere; or upon an act outside the territory of the United States in connection with a commercial activity of the foreign state elsewhere and that act causes a direct effect in the United States;

(3) in which rights in property taken in violation of international law are in issue and that property or any property exchanged for such property is present in the United States in connection with a commercial activity carried on in the United States by the foreign state; or that property or any property exchanged for such property is owned or operated by an agency or instrumentality of the foreign state and that agency or instrumentality is engaged in a commercial activity in the United States;

(4) in which rights in property in the United States acquired by succession or gift or rights in immovable property situated in the United States are in issue;

(5) not otherwise encompassed in paragraph (2) above, in which money damages are sought against a foreign state for personal injury or death, or damage to or loss of property, occurring in the United States and caused by the tortious act or omission of that foreign state or of any official or employee of that foreign state while acting within the scope of his office or employment; except this paragraph shall not apply to -

(A) any claim based upon the exercise or performance or the failure to exercise or perform a discretionary function regardless of whether the discretion be abused, or

(B) any claim arising out of malicious prosecution, abuse of process, libel, slander, misrepresentation, deceit, or interference with contract rights;

(6) in which the action is brought, either to enforce an agreement made by the foreign state with or for the benefit of a private party to submit to arbitration all or any differences which have arisen or which may arise between the parties with respect to a defined legal relationship, whether contractual or not, concerning a subject matter capable of settlement by arbitration under the laws of the United States, or to confirm an award made pursuant to such an agreement to arbitrate, if (A) the arbitration takes place or is intended to take place in the United States, (B) the agreement or award is or may be governed by a treaty or other international agreement in force for the United States calling for the recognition and enforcement of arbitral awards, (C) the underlying claim, save for the agreement to arbitrate, could have been brought in a United States court under this section or section 1607, or (D) paragraph (1) of this subsection is otherwise applicable; or (7) not otherwise covered by paragraph (2), in which money damages are sought against a foreign state for personal injury or death that was caused by an act of torture, extrajudicial killing, aircraft sabotage, hostage taking, or the provision of material support or resources (as defined in section 2339A of title 18) for such an act if such act or provision of material support is engaged in by an official, employee, or agent of such foreign state while acting within the scope of his or her office, employment, or agency, except that the court shall decline to hear a claim under this paragraph -

(A) if the foreign state was not designated as a state sponsor of terrorism under section 6(j) of the Export Administration Act of 1979 (50 U.S.C. App. 2405(j)) or section 620A of the Foreign Assistance Act of 1961 (22 U.S.C. 2371) at the time the act occurred, unless later so designated as a result of such act; and

(B) even if the foreign state is or was so designated, if -

(i) the act occurred in the foreign state against which the claim has been brought and the claimant has not afforded the foreign state a reasonable opportunity to arbitrate the claim in accordance with accepted international rules of arbitration; or

(ii) neither the claimant nor the victim was a national of the United States (as that term is defined in section 101(a)(22) of the Immigration and Nationality Act) when the act upon which the claim is based occurred.

(b) A foreign state shall not be immune from the jurisdiction of the courts of the United States in any case in which a suit in admiralty is brought to enforce a maritime lien against a vessel or cargo of the foreign state, which maritime lien is based upon a commercial activity of the foreign state: Provided, That -

(1) notice of the suit is given by delivery of a copy of the summons and of the complaint to the person, or his agent, having possession of the vessel or cargo against which the maritime lien is asserted; and if the vessel or cargo is arrested pursuant to process obtained on behalf of the party bringing the suit, the service of process of arrest shall be deemed to constitute valid delivery of such notice, but the party bringing the suit shall be liable for any damages sustained by the foreign state as a result of the arrest if the party bringing the suit had actual or constructive knowledge that the vessel or cargo of a foreign state was involved; and

(2) notice to the foreign state of the commencement of suit as provided in section 1608 of this title is initiated within ten days either of the delivery of notice as provided in paragraph (1) of this subsection or, in the case of a party who was unaware that the vessel or cargo of a foreign state was involved, of the date such party determined the existence of the foreign state's interest.

(c) Whenever notice is delivered under subsection (b)(1), the suit to enforce a maritime lien shall thereafter proceed and shall be heard and determined according to the principles of law and rules of practice of suits in rem whenever it appears that, had the vessel been privately owned and possessed, a suit in rem might have been maintained. A decree against the foreign state may include costs of the suit and, if the decree is for a money judgment, interest as ordered by the court, except that the court may not award judgment against the foreign state in an amount greater than the value of the vessel or cargo upon which the maritime lien arose. Such value shall be determined as of the time notice is served under subsection (b)(1). Decrees shall be subject to appeal and revision as provided in other cases of admiralty and maritime jurisdiction. Nothing shall preclude the plaintiff in any proper case from seeking relief in personam in the same action brought to enforce a maritime lien as provided in this section.

(d) A foreign state shall not be immune from the jurisdiction of the courts of the United States in any action brought to foreclose a preferred mortgage, as defined in the Ship Mortgage Act, 1920 (46 U.S.C. 911 and following). Such action shall be brought, heard, and determined in accordance with the provisions of that Act and in accordance with the principles of law and rules of practice of suits in rem, whenever it appears that had the vessel been privately owned and possessed a suit in rem might have been maintained.

(e) For purposes of paragraph (7) of subsection (a) -

(1) the terms "torture" and "extrajudicial killing" have the meaning given those terms in section 3 of the Torture Victim Protection Act of 1991;

(2) the term "hostage taking" has the meaning given that term in Article 1 of the International Convention Against the Taking of Hostages; and

(3) the term "aircraft sabotage" has the meaning given that term in Article 1 of the Convention for the Suppression of Unlawful Acts Against the Safety of Civil Aviation.

(f) No action shall be maintained under subsection (a)(7) unless the action is commenced not later than 10 years after the date on which the cause of action arose. All principles of equitable tolling, including the period during which the foreign state was immune from suit, shall apply in calculating this limitation period … .

(g) Limitation on Discovery … .

F. OTHER DOCUMENTS

CHARTER OF THE INTERNATIONAL MILITARY TRIBUNAL (IMT), Agreement for the Prosecution and Punishment of the Major War Criminals of the European Axis (London Agreement), August 8, 1945, 58 Stat. 1544, E.A.S. No. 472, 82 U.N.T.S.280:

The following acts, or any of them, are crimes coming within the jurisdiction of the Tribunal for which there shall be individual responsibility:

(a) Crimes against Peace: namely, planning, preparation, initiation or waging of a war of aggression, or a war in violation of international treaties, agreements or assurances, or participation in a common plan or conspiracy for the accomplishment of any of the foregoing:

(b) War Crimes: namely, violations of the laws or customs of war. Such violations include, but not be limited to, murder, ill-treatment or deportation to slave labor or for any other purpose of civilian population of or in occupied territory, murder or ill-treatment of prisoners of war or persons on the seas, killing of hostages, plunder of public or private property, wanton destruction of cities, towns or villages, or devastation not justified by military necessity:

(c) Crimes against Humanity: namely, murder, extermination, enslavement, deportation, and other inhumane acts committed against any civilian population, before or during the war, or persecutions on political, racial or religious grounds in execution of or in connection with any crime within the jurisdiction of the Tribunal, whether or not in violation of the domestic law of the country where perpetrated … .

CONTROL COUNCIL LAW NO. 10, Punishment of Persons Guilty of War Crimes, Crimes Against Peace and Against Humanity, December 20, 1945, 3 Official Gazette Control Council for Germany 50-55 (1946):

In order to give effect to the terms of the Moscow Declaration of 30 October 1943 and the London Agreement of 8 August 1945, and the Charter issued pursuant thereto and in order to establish a uniform legal basis in Germany for the prosecution of war criminals and other similar offenders, other than those dealt with by the International Military Tribunal, the Control Council enacts as follows:

Article I

The Moscow Declaration of 30 October 1943 "Concerning Responsibility of Hitlerites for Committed Atrocities" and the London Agreement of 8 August 1945 "Concerning Prosecution and Punishment of Major War Criminals of the European Axis" are made integral parts of this Law. Adherence to the provisions of the London Agreement by any of the United Nations, as provided for in Article V of that Agreement, shall not entitle such Nation to participate or interfere in the operation of this Law within the Control Council area of authority in Germany.

Article II

1. Each of the following acts is recognized as a crime:

a) *Crimes against Peace*. Initiation of invasions of other countries and wars of aggression in violation of international laws and treaties, including but not limited to planning, preparation, initiation or waging a war of aggression, or a war in violation of international treaties, agreements, or assurances, or participation in a common plan or conspiracy for the accomplishment of any of the foregoing.

b) *War Crimes*. Atrocities or offences against persons or property, constituting violations of the laws or customs of war, including but not limited to, murder, ill treatment or deportation to slave labour or for any other purpose of civilian population from occupied territory, murder or ill treatment of prisoners of war or persons on the seas, killing of hostages, plunder of public or private property, wanton destruction of cities, towns or villages, or devastation not justified by military necessity.

c) *Crimes against Humanity*. Atrocities and offences, including but not limited to murder, extermination, enslavement, deportation, imprisonment, torture, rape, or other inhumane acts committed against any civilian population, or persecutions on political, racial or religious grounds whether or not in violation of the domestic laws of the country where perpetrated.

d) Membership in categories of a criminal group or organization declared criminal by the International Military Tribunal.

2. Any person without regard to nationality or the capacity in which he acted, is deemed to have committed a crime as defined in paragraph 1 of this Article, if he was (a) a principal or (b) was an accessory to the commission of any such crime or ordered or abetted the same or (c) took a consenting part therein or (d) was connected with plans or enterprises involving its commission or (e) was a member of any organization or group connected with the commission of any such crime or (f) with reference to paragraph 1 (a), if he held a high political, civil or military (including General Staff) position in Germany or in one of its Allies, co-belligerents or satellites or held high position in the financial, industrial or economic life of any such country.

3. Any person found guilty of any of the Crimes above mentioned may upon conviction be punished as shall be determined by the tribunal to be just. Such punishment may consist of one or more of the following:

a) Death.

b) Imprisonment for life or a term of years, with or without hard labour.

c) Fine, and imprisonment with or without hard labour, in lieu thereof.

d) Forfeiture of property.

e) Restitution of property wrongfully acquired.

f) Deprivation of some or all civil rights. Any property declared to be forfeited or the restitution of which is ordered by the Tribunal shall be delivered to the Control Council for Germany, which shall decide on its disposal.

4. a) The official position of any person, whether as Head of State or as a responsible official in a Government Department, does not free him from responsibility for a crime or entitle him to mitigation of punishment.

b) The fact that any person acted pursuant to the order of his Government or of a superior does not free him from responsibility for a crime, but may be considered in mitigation.

5. In any trial or prosecution for a crime herein referred to, the accused shall not be entitled to the benefits of any statute of limitation in respect to the period from 30 January 1933 to 1 July 1945, nor shall any immunity, pardon or amnesty granted under the Nazi regime be admitted as a bar to trial or punishment.

Article III

1. Each occupying authority, within its Zone of occupation,

a) shall have the right to cause persons within such Zone suspected of having committed a crime, including those charged with crime by one of the United Nations, to be arrested and shall take under control the property, real and personal, owned or controlled by the said persons, pending decisions as to its eventual disposition.

b) shall report to the Legal Directorate the names of all suspected criminals, the reasons for and the places of their detention, if they are detained, and the names and location of witnesses.

c) shall take appropriate measures to see that witnesses and evidence will be available when required.

d) shall have the right to cause all persons so arrested and charged, and not delivered to another authority as herein provided, or released, to be brought to trial before an appropriate tribunal. Such tribunal may, in the case of crimes committed by persons of German citizenship or nationality against other persons of German citizenship or nationality, or stateless persons, be a German Court, if authorized by the occupying authorities.

2. The tribunal by which persons charged with offences hereunder shall be tried and the rules and procedure thereof shall be determined or designated by each Zone Commander for his respective Zone. Nothing herein is intended to, or shall impair or limit the jurisdiction or power of any court or tribunal now or hereafter established in any Zone by the Commander thereof, or of the International Military Tribunal established by the London Agreement of 8 August 1945.

3. Persons wanted for trial by an International Military Tribunal will not be tried without the consent of the Committee of Chief Prosecutors. Each Zone Commander will deliver such persons who are within his Zone to that committee upon request and will make witnesses and evidence available to it.

4. Persons known to be wanted for trial in another Zone or outside Germany will not be tried prior to decision under Article IV unless the fact of their apprehension has been reported in accordance with Section 1(b) of this Article, three months have elapsed thereafter, and no request for delivery of the type contemplated by Article IV has been received by the Zone Commander concerned.

5. The execution of death sentences may be deferred by not to exceed one month after the sentence has become final when the Zone Commander concerned has reason to believe that the testimony of those under sentence would be of value in the investigation and trial of crimes within or without his Zone.

6. Each Zone Commander will cause such effect to be given to the judgments of courts of competent jurisdiction, with respect to the property taken under his control pursuant hereto, as he may deem proper in the interest of justice.

Article IV

1. When any person in a Zone in Germany is alleged to have committed a crime, as defined in Article II, in a country other than Germany or in another Zone, the government of that nation or the Commander of the latter Zone, as the case may be, may request the Commander of the Zone in which the person is located for his arrest and delivery for trial to the country or Zone in which the crime was committed. Such request for delivery shall be granted by the Commander receiving it unless he believes such person is wanted for trial or as a witness by an International Military Tribunal, or in Germany, or in a nation other than the one making the request, or the Commander is not satisfied that delivery should be made, in any of which cases he shall have the right to forward the said request to the Legal Directorate of the Allied Control Authority. A similar procedure shall apply to witnesses, material exhibits and other forms of evidence.

2. The Legal Directorate shall consider all requests referred to it, and shall determine the same in accordance with the following principles, its determination to be communicated to the Zone Commander.

a) A person wanted for trial or as a witness by an International Military Tribunal shall not be delivered for trial or required to give evidence outside Germany, as the case may be, except upon approval of the Committee of Chief Prosecutors acting under the London Agreement of 8 August 1945.

b) A person wanted for trial by several authorities (other than an International Military Tribunal) shall be disposed of in accordance with the following priorities:

1) If wanted for trial in the Zone in which he is, he should not be delivered unless arrangements are made for his return after trial elsewhere;

2) If wanted for trial in a Zone other than that in which he is, he should be delivered to that Zone in preference to delivery outside Germany unless arrangements are made for his return to that Zone after trial elsewhere;

3) If wanted for trial outside Germany by two or more of the United Nations, of one of which he is a citizen, that one should have priority;

4) If wanted for trial outside Germany by several countries, not all of which are United Nations, United Nations should have priority;

5) If wanted for trial outside Germany by two or more of the United Nations, then, subject to Article IV 2(b)(3) above, that which has the most serious charges against him, which are moreover supported by evidence, should have priority.

Article V

The delivery, under Article IV of this Law, of persons for trial shall be made on demands of the Governments or Zone Commanders in such a manner that the delivery of criminals to one jurisdiction will not become the means of defeating or unnecessarily delaying the carrying out of justice in another place. If within six months the delivered person has not been convicted by the Court of the zone or country to which he has been delivered, then such person shall be returned upon demand of the Commander of the Zone where the person was located prior to delivery.

STATUTE OF THE INTERNATIONAL TRIBUNAL FOR THE PROSECUTION OF PERSONS RESPONSIBLE FOR SERIOUS VIOLATIONS OF INTERNATIONAL HUMANITARIAN LAW COMMITTED IN THE TERRITORY OF THE FORMER YUGOSLAVIA SINCE 1991, U.N. Doc. S/25704 at 36, annex (1993) and S/25704/Add.1 (1993), *adopted by* **Security Council on 25 May 1993, U.N. Doc. S/RES/827 (1993):**

Having been established by the Security Council acting under Chapter VII of the Charter of the United Nations, the International Tribunal for the Prosecution of Persons Responsible for Serious Violations of International

Humanitarian Law Committed in the Territory of the Former Yugoslavia since 1991 (hereinafter referred to as "the International Tribunal") shall function in accordance with the provisions of the present Statute.

Article 1

Competence of the International Tribunal

The International Tribunal shall have the power to prosecute persons responsible for serious violations of international humanitarian law committed in the territory of the former Yugoslavia since 1991 in accordance with the provisions of the present Statute.

Article 2

Grave breaches of the Geneva Conventions of 1949

The International Tribunal shall have the power to prosecute persons committing or ordering to be committed grave breaches of the Geneva Conventions of 12 August 1949, namely the following acts against persons or property protected under the provisions of the relevant Geneva Convention:

(a) wilful killing; (b) torture or inhuman treatment, including biological experiments; (c) wilfully causing great suffering or serious injury to body or health; (d) extensive destruction and appropriation of property, not justified by military necessity and carried out unlawfully and wantonly; (e) compelling a prisoner of war or a civilian to serve in the forces of a hostile power; (f) wilfully depriving a prisoner of war or a civilian of the rights of fair and regular trial; (g) unlawful deportation or transfer or unlawful confinement of a civilian; (h) taking civilians as hostages.

Article 3

Violations of the laws or customs of war

The International Tribunal shall have the power to prosecute persons violating the laws or customs of war. Such violations shall include, but not be limited to:

(a) employment of poisonous weapons or other weapons calculated to cause unnecessary suffering; (b) wanton destruction of cities, towns or villages, or devastation not justified by military necessity; (c) attack, or bombardment, by whatever means, of undefended towns, villages, dwellings, or buildings; (d) seizure of, destruction or wilful damage done to institutions dedicated to religion, charity and education, the arts and sciences, historic monuments and works of art and science; (e) plunder of public or private property.

Article 4

Genocide

1. The International Tribunal shall have the power to prosecute persons committing genocide as defined in paragraph 2 of this article or of committing any of the other acts enumerated in paragraph 3 of this article.

2. Genocide means any of the following acts committed with intent to destroy, in whole or in part, a national, ethnical, racial or religious group, as such:

(a) killing members of the group; (b) causing serious bodily or mental harm to members of the group; (c) deliberately inflicting on the group conditions of life calculated to bring about its physical destruction in whole or in part; (d) imposing measures intended to prevent births within the group; (e) forcibly transferring children of the group to another group.

3. The following acts shall be punishable:

(a) genocide; (b) conspiracy to commit genocide; (c) direct and public incitement to commit genocide; (d) attempt to commit genocide; (e) complicity in genocide.

Article 5

Crimes against humanity

The International Tribunal shall have the power to prosecute persons responsible for the following crimes when committed in armed conflict, whether international or internal in character, and directed against any civilian population:

(a) murder; (b) extermination; (c) enslavement; (d) deportation; (e) imprisonment; (f) torture; (g) rape; (h) persecutions on political, racial and religious grounds; (i) other inhumane acts.

STATUTE OF THE INTERNATIONAL TRIBUNAL FOR THE PROSECUTION OF PERSONS RESPONSIBLE FOR SERIOUS VIOLATIONS OF INTERNATIONAL HUMANITARIAN LAW COMMITTED IN THE TERRITORY OF THE RWANDA, adopted by S.C. Res. 955, U.N. SCOR, 49th Sess., 3453d mtg. at 3, U.N. Doc. S/RES/955 (1994):

The Security Council, Reaffirming all its previous resolutions on the situation in Rwanda,

Having considered the reports of the Secretary-General pursuant to paragraph 3 of resolution 935 (1994)1 July 1994 (S/1994/879 and S/1994/906), ...

Acting under Chapter VII of the Charter of the United Nations, ...

Statute of the International Tribunal for Rwanda

Having been established by the Security Council acting under Chapter VII of the Charter of the United Nations, the International Criminal Tribunal for the Prosecution of Persons Responsible for Genocide and Other Serious Violations of International Humanitarian Law Committed in the Territory of Rwanda and Rwandan Citizens responsible for genocide and other such violations committed in the territory of neighbouring States, between 1 January 1994 and 31 December 1994 (hereinafter referred to as "The International Tribunal for Rwanda") shall function in accordance with the provisions of the present Statute.

Article 1

Competence of the International Tribunal for Rwanda

The International Tribunal for Rwanda shall have the power to prosecute persons responsible for serious violations of international humanitarian law committed in the territory of Rwanda and Rwandan citizens responsible for such violations committed in the territory of neighbouring States between 1 January 1994 and 31 December 1994, in accordance with the provisions of the present Statute.

Article 2

Genocide

1. The International Tribunal for Rwanda shall have the power to prosecute persons committing genocide as defined in paragraph 2 of this article or of committing any of the other acts enumerated in paragraph 3 of this article

2. Genocide means any of the following acts committed with intent to destroy, in whole or in part, a national, ethnical, racial or religious group, as such:

a) Killing members of the group;

b) Causing serious bodily or mental harm to members of the group;

c) Deliberately inflicting on the group conditions of life calculated to bring about its physical destruction in whole or in part;

d) Imposing measures intended to prevent births within the group;

e) Forcibly transferring children of the group to another group.

3. The following acts shall be punishable:

a) Genocide;

b) Conspiracy to commit genocide;

c) Direct and public incitement to commit genocide;

d) Attempt to commit genocide;

e) Complicity in genocide.

Article 3

Crimes against Humanity

The International Tribunal for Rwanda shall have the power to prosecute persons responsible for the following crimes when committed as part of a widespread or systematic attack against any civilian population on national, political, ethnic, racial or religious grounds:

a) Murder;

b) Extermination;

c) Enslavement;

d) Deportation;

e) Imprisonment;

f) Torture;

g) Rape;

h) Persecutions on political, racial and religious grounds;

i) Other inhumane acts.

Article 4

Violations of Article 3 common to the Geneva Conventions and of Additional Protocol II

The International Tribunal for Rwanda shall have the power to prosecute persons committing or ordering to be committed serious violations of Article 3 common to the Geneva Conventions of 12 August 1949 for the Protection of War Victims, and of Additional Protocol II thereto of 8 June 1977. These violations shall include, but shall not be limited to:

a) Violence to life, health and physical or mental well-being of persons, in particular murder as well as cruel treatment such as torture, mutilation or any form of corporal punishment;

b) Collective punishments;

c) Taking of hostages;

d) Acts of terrorism;

e) Outrages upon personal dignity, in particular humiliating and degrading treatment, rape, enforced prostitution and any form of indecent assault;

f) Pillage;

g) The passing of sentences and the carrying out of executions without previous judgement pronounced by a regularly constituted court, affording all the judicial guarantees which are recognised as indispensable by civilised peoples;

h) Threats to commit any of the foregoing acts.

ROME STATUTE OF THE INTERNATIONAL CRIMINAL COURT, U.N. Doc. A/CONF.183/9, *adopted* July 17, 1998, *as corrected by the procés-verbaux of* November 10, 1998, July 12, 1999, and May 8, 2000 (excerpts):

Article 1

The Court

An International Criminal Court ("the Court") is hereby established. It shall be a permanent institution and shall have the power to exercise its jurisdiction over persons for the most serious crimes of international concern, as referred to in this Statute, and shall be complementary to national criminal jurisdictions. The jurisdiction and functioning of the Court shall be governed by the provisions of this Statute ... .

Article 5

Crimes within the jurisdiction of the Court

1. The jurisdiction of the Court shall be limited to the most serious crimes of concern to the international community as a whole. The Court has jurisdiction in accordance with this Statute with respect to the following crimes:

(a) The crime of genocide;

(b) Crimes against humanity;

(c) War crimes;

(d) The crime of aggression.

2. The Court shall exercise jurisdiction over the crime of aggression once a provision is adopted in accordance with articles 121 and 123 defining the crime and setting out the conditions under which the Court shall exercise jurisdiction with respect to this crime. Such a provision shall be consistent with the relevant provisions of the Charter of the United Nations.

Article 6

Genocide

For the purpose of this Statute, "genocide" means any of the following acts committed with intent to destroy, in whole or in part, a national, ethnical, racial or religious group, as such:

(a) Killing members of the group;

(b) Causing serious bodily or mental harm to members of the group;

(c) Deliberately inflicting on the group conditions of life calculated to bring about its physical destruction in whole or in part;

(d) Imposing measures intended to prevent births within the group;

(e) Forcibly transferring children of the group to another group.

Article 7

Crimes against humanity

1. For the purpose of this Statute, "crime against humanity" means any of the following acts when committed as part of a widespread or systematic attack directed against any civilian population, with knowledge of the attack:

(a) Murder;

(b) Extermination;

(c) Enslavement;

(d) Deportation or forcible transfer of population;

(e) Imprisonment or other severe deprivation of physical liberty in violation of fundamental rules of international law;

(f) Torture;

(g) Rape, sexual slavery, enforced prostitution, forced pregnancy, enforced sterilization, or any other form of sexual violence of comparable gravity;

(h) Persecution against any identifiable group or collectivity on political, racial, national, ethnic, cultural, religious, gender as defined in paragraph3, or other grounds that are universally recognized as impermissible under international law, in connection with any act referred to in this paragraph or any crime within the jurisdiction of the Court;

(i) Enforced disappearance of persons;

(j) The crime of apartheid;

(k) Other inhumane acts of a similar character intentionally causing great suffering, or serious injury to body or to mental or physical health.

2. For the purpose of paragraph 1:

(a) "Attack directed against any civilian population" means a courseof conduct involving the multiple commission of acts referred to in paragraph 1 against any civilian population, pursuant to or in furtherance ofa State or organizational policy to commit such attack;

(b) "Extermination" includes the intentional infliction of conditions of life, interalia the deprivation of access to food and medicine, calculated to bring about the destruction of part of a population;

(c) "Enslavement" means the exercise of any or all of the powers attaching to the right of ownership over a person and includes the exercise of such power in the course of trafficking in persons, in particular women and children;

(d) "Deportation or forcible transfer of population" means forced displacement of the persons concerned by expulsion or other coercive acts from the area in which they are lawfully present, without grounds permitted under international law;

(e) "Torture" means the intentional infliction of severe pain or suffering, whether physical or mental, upon a person in the custody or under the control of the accused; except that torture shall not include pain or suffering arising only from, inherent in or incidental to, lawful sanctions;

(f) "Forced pregnancy" means the unlawful confinement of a woman forcibly made pregnant, with the intent of affecting the ethnic composition of any population or carrying out other grave violations of international law. This definition shall not in any way be interpreted as affecting national laws relating to pregnancy;

(g) "Persecution" means the intentional and severe deprivation of fundamental rights contrary to international law by reason of the identity of the group or collectivity;

(h) "The crime of apartheid" means inhumane acts of a character similar to those referred to in paragraph 1, committed in the context of an institutionalized regime of systematic oppression and domination by one racial group over any other racial group or groups and committed with the intention of maintaining that regime;

(i) "Enforced disappearance of persons" means the arrest, detention or abduction of persons by, or with the authorization, support or acquiescence of, a State or a political organization, followed by a refusal to acknowledge that deprivation of freedom or to give information on the fate or whereabouts of those persons, with the intention of removing them from the protection of the law for a prolonged period of time.

3. For the purpose of this Statute, it is understood that the term "gender" refers to the two sexes, male and female, within the context of society. The term "gender" does not indicate any meaning different from the above.

Article 8

War crimes

1. The Court shall have jurisdiction in respect of war crimes in particular when committed as part of a plan or policy or as part of a large-scale commission of such crimes.

2. For the purpose of this Statute, "war crimes" means:

(a) Grave breaches of the Geneva Conventions of 12 August 1949, namely, any of the following acts against persons or property protected under the provisions of the relevant Geneva Convention:

(i) Wilful killing;

(ii) Torture or inhuman treatment, including biological experiments;

(iii) Wilfully causing great suffering, or serious injury to body or health;

(iv) Extensive destruction and appropriation of property, not justified by military necessity and carried out unlawfully and wantonly;

(v) Compelling a prisoner of war or other protected person to serve in the forces of a hostile Power;

(vi) Wilfully depriving a prisoner of war or other protected person of the rights of fair and regular trial;

(vii) Unlawful deportation or transfer or unlawful confinement;

(viii) Taking of hostages.

(b) Other serious violations of the laws and customs applicable in international armed conflict, within the established framework of international law, namely, any of the following acts:

(i) Intentionally directing attacks against the civilian population as such or against individual civilians not taking direct part in hostilities;

(ii) Intentionally directing attacks against civilian objects, that is, objects which are not military objectives;

(iii) Intentionally directing attacks against personnel, installations, material, units or vehicles involved in a humanitarian assistance or peacekeeping mission in accordance with the Charter of the United Nations, as long as they are entitled to the protection given to civilians or civilian objects under the international law of armed conflict;

(iv) Intentionally launching an attack in the knowledge that such attack will cause incidental loss of life or injury to civilians or damage to civilian objects or widespread, long-term and severe damage to the natural environment which would be clearly excessive in relation to the concrete and direct overall military advantage anticipated;

(v) Attacking or bombarding, by whatever means, towns, villages, dwellings or buildings which are undefended and which are not military objectives;

(vi) Killing or wounding a combatant who, having laid down his arms or having no longer means of defence, has surrendered at discretion;

(vii) Making improper use of a flag of truce, of the flag or of the military insignia and uniform of the enemy or of the United Nations, as well as of the distinctive emblems of the Geneva Conventions, resulting in death or serious personal injury;

(viii) The transfer, directly or indirectly, by the Occupying Power of parts of its own civilian population into the territory it occupies, or the deportation or transfer of all or parts of the population of the occupied territory within or outside this territory;

(ix) Intentionally directing attacks against buildings dedicated to religion, education, art, science or charitable purposes, historic monuments, hospitals and places where the sick and wounded are collected, provided they are not military objectives;

(x) Subjecting persons who are in the power of an adverse party to physical mutilation or to medical or scientific experiments of any kind which are neither justified by the medical, dental or hospital treatment of the person concerned nor carried out in his or her interest, and which cause death to or seriously endanger the health of such person or persons;

(xi) Killing or wounding treacherously individuals belonging to the hostile nation or army;

(xii) Declaring that no quarter will be given;

(xiii) Destroying or seizing the enemy's property unless such destruction or seizure be imperatively demanded by the necessities of war;

(xiv) Declaring abolished, suspended or inadmissible in a court of law the rights and actions of the nationals of the hostile party;

(xv) Compelling the nationals of the hostile party to take part in the operations of war directed against their own country, even if they were in the belligerent's service before the commencement of the war;

(xvi) Pillaging a town or place, even when taken by assault;

(xvii) Employing poison or poisoned weapons;

(xviii) Employing asphyxiating, poisonous or other gases, and all analogous liquids, materials or devices;

(xix) Employing bullets which expand or flatten easily in the human body, such as bullets with a hard envelope which does not entirely cover the core or is pierced with incisions;

(xx) Employing weapons, projectiles and material and methods of warfare which are of a nature to cause superfluous injury or unnecessary suffering or which are inherently indiscriminate in violation of the international law of armed conflict, provided that such weapons, projectiles and material and methods of warfare are the subject of a comprehensive prohibition and are included in an annex to this Statute, by an amendment in accordance with the relevant provisions set forth in articles 121 and 123;

(xxi) Committing outrages upon personal dignity, in particular humiliating and degrading treatment;

(xxii) Committing rape, sexual slavery, enforced prostitution, forced pregnancy,as defined in article 7, paragraph2(f), enforced sterilization, or any other form of sexual violence also constituting a grave breach of the Geneva Conventions;

(xxiii) Utilizing the presence of a civilian or other protected person to render certain points, areas or military forces immune from military operations;

(xxiv) Intentionally directing attacks against buildings, material, medical units and transport, and personnel using the distinctive emblems of the Geneva Conventions in conformity with international law;

(xxv) Intentionally using starvation of civilians as a method of warfare by depriving them of objects indispensable to their survival, including wilfully impeding relief supplies as provided for under the Geneva Conventions;

(xxvi) Conscripting or enlisting children under the age of fifteen years into the national armed forces or using them to participate actively in hostilities.

(c) In the case of an armed conflict not of an international character, serious violations of article 3 common to the four Geneva Conventions of 12August 1949, namely, any of the following acts committed against persons taking no active part in the hostilities, including members of armed forces who have laid down their arms and those placed hors de combat by sickness, wounds, detention or any other cause:

(i) Violence to life and person, in particular murder of all kinds, mutilation, cruel treatment and torture;

(ii) Committing outrages upon personal dignity, in particular humiliating and degrading treatment;

(iii) Taking of hostages;

(iv) The passing of sentences and the carrying out of executions without previous judgement pronounced by a regularly constituted court, affording all judicial guarantees which are generally recognized as indispensable.

(d) Paragraph 2 (c) applies to armed conflicts not of an international character and thus does not apply to situations of internal disturbances and tensions, such as riots, isolated and sporadic acts of violence or other acts of a similar nature.

(e) Other serious violations of the laws and customs applicable in armed conflicts not of an international character, within the established framework of international law, namely, any of the following acts:

(i) Intentionally directing attacks against the civilian population as such or against individual civilians not taking direct part in hostilities;

(ii) Intentionally directing attacks against buildings, material, medical units and transport, and personnel using the distinctive emblems of the Geneva Conventions in conformity with international law;

(iii) Intentionally directing attacks against personnel, installations, material, units or vehicles involved in a humanitarian assistance or peacekeeping mission in accordance with the Charter of the United Nations, as long as they are entitled to the protection given to civilians or civilian objects under the international law of armed conflict;

(iv) Intentionally directing attacks against buildings dedicated to religion, education, art, science or charitable purposes, historic monuments, hospitals and places where the sick and wounded are collected, provided they are not military objectives;

(v) Pillaging a town or place, even when taken by assault;

(vi) Committing rape, sexual slavery, enforced prostitution, forced pregnancy, as defined in article 7, paragraph 2(f), enforced sterilization, and any other form of sexual violence also constituting a serious violation of article3 common to the four Geneva Conventions;

(vii) Conscripting or enlisting children under the age of fifteen years into armed forces or groups or using them to participate actively in hostilities;

(viii) Ordering the displacement of the civilian population for reasons related to the conflict, unless the security of the civilians involved or imperative military reasons so demand;

(ix) Killing or wounding treacherously a combatant adversary;

(x) Declaring that no quarter will be given;

(xi) Subjecting persons who are in the power of another party to the conflict to physical mutilation or to medical or scientific experiments of any kind which are neither justified by the medical, dental or hospital treatment of the person concerned nor carried out in his or her interest, and which cause death to or seriously endanger the health of such person or persons;

(xii) Destroying or seizing the property of an adversary unless such destruction or seizure be imperatively demanded by the necessities of the conflict;

(f) Paragraph 2 (e) applies to armed conflicts not of an international character and thus does not apply to situations of internal disturbances and tensions, such as riots, isolated and sporadic acts of violence or other acts of a similar nature. It applies to armed conflicts that take place in the territory of a State when there is protracted armed conflict between governmental authorities and organized armed groups or between such groups.

3. Nothing in paragraph 2 (c) and (e) shall affect the responsibility of a Government to maintain or re-establish law and order in the State or to defend the unity and territorial integrity of the State, by all legitimate means ... .

Article 12

Preconditions to the exercise of jurisdiction

1. A State which becomes a Party to this Statute thereby accepts the jurisdiction of the Court with respect to the crimes referred to in article 5.

2. In the case of article 13, paragraph (a) or (c), the Court may exercise its jurisdiction if one or more of the following States are Parties to this Statute or have accepted the jurisdiction of the Court in accordance with paragraph 3:

(a) The State on the territory of which the conduct in question occurred or, if the crime was committed on board a vessel or aircraft, the State of registration of that vessel or aircraft;

(b) The State of which the person accused of the crime is a national.

3. If the acceptance of a State which is not a Party to this Statute is required under paragraph2, that State may, by declaration lodged with the Registrar, accept the exercise of jurisdiction by the Court with respect to the crime in question. The accepting State shall cooperate with the Court without any delay or exception in accordance with Part 9.

Article 13

Exercise of jurisdiction

The Court may exercise its jurisdiction with respect to a crime referred to in article 5 in accordance with the provisions of this Statute if:

(a) A situation in which one or more of such crimes appears to have been committed is referred to the Prosecutor by a State Party in accordance with article 14;

(b) A situation in which one or more of such crimes appears to have been committed is referred to the Prosecutor by the Security Council acting under Chapter VII of the Charter of the United Nations; or

(c) The Prosecutor has initiated an investigation in respect of such a crime in accordance with article 15 .... .

Article 15

Prosecutor

1. The Prosecutor may initiate investigations *proprio motu* on the basis of information on crimes within the jurisdiction of the Court.

2. The Prosecutor shall analyse the seriousness of the information received. For this purpose, he or she may seek additional information from States, organs of the United Nations, intergovernmental or non-governmental organizations, or other reliable sources that he or she deems appropriate, and may receive written or oral testimony at the seat of the Court.

3. If the Prosecutor concludes that there is a reasonable basis to proceed with an investigation, he or she shall submit to the Pre-Trial Chamber a request for authorization of an investigation, together with any supporting material collected. Victims may make representations to the Pre-Trial Chamber, in accordance with the Rules of Procedure and Evidence.

4. If the Pre-Trial Chamber, upon examination of the request and the supporting material, considers that there is a reasonable basis to proceed with an investigation, and that the case appears to fall within the jurisdiction of the Court, it shall authorize the commencement of the investigation, without prejudice to subsequent determinations by the Court with regard to the jurisdiction and admissibility of a case.

5. The refusal of the Pre-Trial Chamber to authorize the investigation shall not preclude the presentation of a subsequent request by the Prosecutor based on new facts or evidence regarding the same situation.

6. If, after the preliminary examination referred to in paragraphs 1 and 2, the Prosecutor concludes that the information provided does not constitute a reasonable basis for an investigation, he or she shall inform those who provided the information. This shall not preclude the Prosecutor from considering further information submitted to him or her regarding the same situation in the light of new facts or evidence.

Article 16

Deferral of investigation or prosecution

No investigation or prosecution may be commenced or proceeded with under this Statute for a period of 12 months after the Security Council, in a resolution adopted under Chapter VII of the Charter of the UnitedNations, has requested the Court to that effect; that request may be renewed by the Council under the same conditions.

Article 17

Issues of admissibility

1. Having regard to paragraph 10 of the Preamble and article 1, the Court shall determine that a case is inadmissible where:

(a) The case is being investigated or prosecuted by a State which has jurisdiction over it, unless the State is unwilling or unable genuinely to carry out the investigation or prosecution;

(b) The case has been investigated by a State which has jurisdiction over it and the State has decided not to prosecute the person concerned, unless the decision resulted from the unwillingness or inability of the State genuinely to prosecute;

(c) The person concerned has already been tried for conduct which is the subject of the complaint, and a trial by the Court is not permitted under article 20, paragraph 3;

(d) The case is not of sufficient gravity to justify further action by the Court.

2. In order to determine unwillingness in a particular case, the Court shall consider, having regard to the principles of due process recognized by international law, whether one or more of the following exist, as applicable:

(a) The proceedings were or are being undertaken or the national decision was made for the purpose of shielding the person concerned from criminal responsibility for crimes within the jurisdiction of the Court referred to in article 5;

(b) There has been an unjustified delay in the proceedings which in the circumstances is inconsistent with an intent to bring the person concerned to justice;

(c) The proceedings were not or are not being conducted independently or impartially, and they were or are being conducted in a manner which, in the circumstances, is inconsistent with an intent to bring the person concerned to justice.

3. In order to determine inability in a particular case, the Court shall consider whether, due to a total or substantial collapse or unavailability of its national judicial system, the State is unable to obtain the accused or the necessary evidence and testimony or otherwise unable to carry out its proceedings .... .

Article 28

Responsibility of commanders and other superiors

In addition to other grounds of criminal responsibility under this Statute for crimes within the jurisdiction of the Court:

(a) A military commander or person effectively acting as a military commander shall be criminally responsible for crimes within the jurisdiction of the Court committed by forces under his or her effective command and control, or effective authority and control as the case may be, as a result of his or her failure to exercise control properly over such forces, where:

(i) That military commander or person either knew or, owing to the circumstances at the time, should have known that the forces were committing or about to commit such crimes; and

(ii) That military commander or person failed to take all necessary and reasonable measures within his or her power to prevent or repress their commission or to submit the matter to the competent authorities for investigation and prosecution.

(b) With respect to superior and subordinate relationships not described in paragraph (a), a superior shall be criminally responsible for crimes within the jurisdiction of the Court committed by subordinates under his or her effective authority and control, as a result of his or her failure to exercise control properly over such subordinates, where:

(i) The superior either knew, or consciously disregarded information which clearly indicated, that the subordinates were committing or about to commit such crimes;

(ii) The crimes concerned activities that were within the effective responsibility and control of the superior; and

(iii) The superior failed to take all necessary and reasonable measures within his or her power to prevent or repress their commission or to submit the matter to the competent authorities for investigation and prosecution.

BIBLIOGRAPHY FOR RESEARCH ON INTERNATIONAL HUMAN RIGHTS LAW

David Weissbrodt, Fionnuala Ní Aoláin, Mary Rumsey, Marci Hoffman, and Joan Fitzpatrick[1]

---

[1]The authors also wish to thank Lyonette Louis-Jacques for her work in creating the original version of the bibliography.

A. Compilations of Human Rights Instruments

§ 1.   United Nations (U.N.)

FRANCIS M. DENG, COMPILATION AND ANALYSIS OF LEGAL NORMS, REPORT OF THE REPRESENTATIVE OF THE SECRETARY-GENERAL ON INTERNALLY DISPLACED PERSONS, U.N. DOC. E/CN.4/1996/52/ADD. 2 (1995) AND PART II, LEGAL ASPECTS RELATING TO PROTECTION AGAINST ARBITRARY DISPLACEMENT, U.N. DOC. E/CN4/1998/53/ADD.1 (1998).

[New York; Geneva: U.N., 175 pp., Guiding Principles on Internal Displacement, E/CN.4/1998/53/Add.2, http://www.unhchr.ch/Huridocda/Huridoca. nsf/TestFrame/d2e008c61b70263ec125661e0036f36e?Opendocument; Compilation and Analysis of Legal Norms, Part II: Legal Aspects Relating to the Protection against Arbitrary Displacement, E/CN.4/1998/53/Add.1, http://www. unhchr.ch/Huridocda/Huridoca.nsf/TestFrame/49dc663a776b2cc2c125661e002d 5588?Opendocument.]

INTERNATIONAL INSTRUMENTS OF THE UNITED NATIONS: A COMPILATION OF: AGREEMENTS, CHARTERS, CONVENTIONS, DECLARATIONS, PRINCIPLES, PROCLAMATIONS, PROTOCOLS, TREATIES, ADOPTED BY THE GENERAL ASSEMBLY OF THE UNITED NATIONS, 1945-1995 (Irving Sarnoff comp. and ed., 1997).

[New York: United Nations, 461 pp.]

OFFICE OF THE UNHCHR, HUMAN RIGHTS: A COMPILATION OF INTERNATIONAL INSTRUMENTS, U.N. DOC. ST/HR/1/Rev…[issued irregularly; latest revision, 2002].[New York: U.N. Includes texts of human rights instruments principally adopted by the U.N., the ILO, and UNESCO; dates of their entry into force; and a list of instruments in chronological order of adoption. Includes universal and regional instruments.]

Office of the High Commissioner of Human Rights, International Human Rights Instruments, http://www2.ohchr.org/english/law.

[Contains the full text of many international human rights instruments.]

U.N., United Nations Treaty Collection, http://untreaty.un.org.

[Contains over 40,000 treaties from the UNITED NATIONS TREATY SERIES. Images of the documents are available as well as a search device. This Web site is free.]

U.N. High Commissioner for Human Rights, *The Right to Human Rights Education: A Compilation of Provisions of International and Regional Instruments Dealing with Human Rights Education*, U.N. Doc. HR/PUB/ DECADE/1999/2 (1999).

[New York: United Nations. United Nations Decade for Human Rights Education, no. 3.]

§ 2.   International Labour Organization (ILO)

INTERNATIONAL LABOUR OFFICE, INTERNATIONAL LABOUR CONVENTIONS AND RECOMMENDATIONS, 1919-1991 (1992).

[Geneva: International Labour Office, 1481 pp., 2 vols.]

International Labour Organization, ILOLEX, http://www.ilo.org/ilolex/english.

[This Web site is the ILO's database on International Labour Standards, including the full text of all ILO conventions.]

INTERNATIONAL LABOUR ORGANISATION, CONSTITUTION OF THE INTERNATIONAL LABOUR ORGANISATION AND STANDING ORDERS OF THE INTERNATIONAL LABOUR CONFERENCE (1998).

[Geneva: International Labour Office, 100 pp. ILO constitution, rules, and information on practice/procedure. Updated periodically.]

§ 3.   UNESCO

UNESCO, *Executive Board, Decisions Adopted By the Executive Board at Its 104th Session*, 104 EX/Decision 3.3 (1978).

[Paris: UNESCO, 6 pp. Sets forth UNESCO procedures in human rights cases.]

UNESCO, Human Rights of Women: A Collection of International and Regional Normative Instruments (Janusz Symonides & Vladimir Volodin eds., 1999).

[Paris: UNESCO, 435 pp., http://unesdoc.unesco.org/images/0011/001191/119140eo.pdf.]

UNESCO, THE STRUGGLE AGAINST DISCRIMINATION: A COLLECTION OF INTERNATIONAL INSTRUMENTS ADOPTED BY THE UNITED NATIONS SYSTEM (Janusz Symonides ed., 1996).

[Paris: UNESCO, 313 pp., http://unesdoc.unesco.org/images/0010/001060/106049e.pdf.]

UNESCO, UNESCO AND HUMAN RIGHTS: STANDARD-SETTING INSTRUMENTS, MAJOR MEETINGS, PUBLICATIONS (Janusz Symonides & Vladimir Volodin eds., 2d ed. 1999).

[Paris: UNESCO, 537 pp., http://unesdoc.unesco.org/images/0011/001183/118311eo.pdf.]

UNESCO, UNESCO's STANDARD-SETTING INSTRUMENTS (1981- 1994).

[Paris: UNESCO, looseleaf. Includes the full text of the standard-setting instruments.]

§ 4.   UNCHR

BASIC DOCUMENTS ON INTERNATIONAL MIGRATION LAW (Richard Plender ed., 3d rev. ed. 2007).

[Leiden; Boston: Martinus Nijhoff Publishers, 850 pp. Brings together the principal international conventions, declarations, and instruments governing international migration. Text of materials and information on current state ratification of each instrument.]

BENJAMIN MULAMBA MBUYI, REFUGEES AND INTERNATIONAL LAW (1993).

[Scarborough, Ontario: Carswell Thompson Canada Limited, 677 pp. Text in English and French. Contains texts of instruments concerning refugees, bibliographical references, and index.]

OFFICE OF THE UNHCR, COLLECTION OF INTERNATIONAL INSTRUMENTS AND OTHER LEGAL TEXTS CONCERNING REFUGEES AND DISPLACED PERSONS, U.N. Doc. HCR/IP/1/Rev.1, U.N. Sales No. GV.96.0.2 (Jean-Pierre Colombey ed., 1995).

[New York; Geneva: Division of International Protection of the Office of the United Nations

High Commissioner for Refugees. Revision of: Collection of international instruments concerning refugees. Includes indexes. Contents: v. 1, Universal instruments; v. 2, Regional instruments.]

Office of the UNHCR, *Conclusions on the International Protection of Refugees Adopted by the Executive Committee of the UNHCR Programme* (2004).

[Geneva: UNHCR, 280 pp. http://www.unhcr.org/publ/PUBL/41b041534.pdf.]

OFFICE OF THE UNHCR, HANDBOOK ON PROCEDURES AND CRITERIA FOR DETERMINING REFUGEE STATUS UNDER THE 1951 CONVENTION AND THE 1967 PROTOCOL RELATING TO THE STATUS OF REFUGEES (rev. ed. 1992).

[Geneva: UNHCR, 93 pp. Revision of the 1979 edition. Explains terms and procedures for determining refugee status. Annexes contain full texts or excerpts of international instruments related to refugees. http://www.unhcr.org/home/PUBL/3d58e13b4.pdf.]

Office of the UNHCR, *United Nations Resolutions and Decisions Relating to the Office of the United Nations High Commissioner for Refugees*, U.N. Doc. HCR/INF.49 (1984-1993).

[Geneva: UNHCR, looseleaf, 185 pp. Contains texts of resolutions and decisions of the General Assembly and the Economic and Social Council relating to the Office of the UNHCR. Updated by addenda through 1993.]

UNHCR, Legal Information [formerly REFWORLD], http://www.unhcr.org/cgi-bin/texis/vtx/template?page=research&src=/static/legal.html.

[Contains the full-text of many instruments related to refugees, asylum, detention, statelessness, etc. The site is updated daily. The REFWORLD CD-ROM contains more information and is updated on a quarterly basis.]

§ 5.   Council of Europe

J.C. ALDERSON, HUMAN RIGHTS AND THE POLICE (1984).

[Strasbourg: Council of Europe, Directorate of Human Rights, 207 pp. Contains Council of Europe guidelines for police.]

APPLYING AND SUPERVISING THE ECHR: GUARANTEEING THE EFFECTIVENESS OF THE EUROPEAN CONVENTION ON HUMAN RIGHTS - COLLECTED TEXTS (2004).

[Strasbourg: Council of Europe, Directorate General of Human Rights, 110 pp.]

RALPH BEDDARD, HUMAN RIGHTS AND EUROPE 241-70 (3d ed. 1993).

[Cambridge: Grotius Publications Ltd., 278 pp. Annex contains the texts of the European Convention on Human Rights and Protocols 1, 2, 4, 6, 7, 9, and 10.]

COUNCIL OF EUROPE, COLLECTION OF RECOMMENDATIONS, RESOLUTIONS AND DECLARATIONS OF THE COMMITTEE OF MINISTERS CONCERNING HUMAN RIGHTS, 1949-87 (1989).

[Strasbourg: Council of Europe, 214 pp.]

Council of Europe, Conventions, http://conventions.coe.int.

[Includes conventions and draft treaties.]

COUNCIL OF EUROPE, HUMAN RIGHTS TODAY: EUROPEAN LEGAL TEXTS (1999).

[Strasbourg: Council of Europe Pub. 209 pp. Contains texts of the European Convention on Human Rights and its Protocols; rules of procedure of the European Commission, the Court of Human Rights, and the Committee of Ministers; and various human rights instruments from other organs of the Council of Europe. Includes signatures, ratifications, declarations, and reservations concerning the European Convention and its Protocols.]

Council of Europe, *European Convention on Human Rights: Collected Texts*, 33A Yearbook of the European Convention on Human Rights 274-83 (1994).

[The Hague: Martinus Nijhoff Pub., 283 pp. Includes the text of Protocol No. 11 in English and French (in appendix one).]

COUNCIL OF EUROPE, HUMAN RIGHTS IN INTERNATIONAL LAW: BASIC TEXTS (2d ed. 2000).

[Strasbourg: Council of Europe Press, 538 pp.]

EUROPEAN CONVENTION ON HUMAN RIGHTS: TEXTS AND DOCUMENTS (Herbert Miehsler & Herbert Petzold eds., 1982).

[Koln: Carl Heymanns Verlag, 2 vols., collection in the official languages. Volume one contains texts of European Convention on Human Rights and other European treaties, including U.N. documents. Volume two includes documents of the Council of Europe and the European Community.]

FRAMEWORK CONVENTION FOR THE PROTECTION OF NATIONAL MINORITIES: COLLECTED TEXTS (2005).

[Strasbourg: Council of Europe Pub., 83 pp. Covers the European Convention on Human Rights, the European Convention for the Prevention of Torture and Inhuman or Degrading Treatment or Punishment, and the Framework Convention for the Protection of National Minorities. The three conventions are accompanied by their Protocols, explanatory reports, and the rules adopted by different organs of the conventions: the European Court of Human Rights, the European Committee for the Prevention of Torture, and the Committee of Ministers of the Council of Europe.]

Protocol No. 11 to the Convention for the Protection of Human Rights and Fundamental Freedoms, restructuring the control machinery established thereby, 15 HUM. RTS. L.J. 86 (1994).

[Kehl; Arlington, VA: N.P. Engel, 29 July 1994. Article includes the text of Protocol No. 11, explanatory report, and speeches made for the signing ceremony.]

J.G. MERRILLS & A.H. ROBERTSON, HUMAN RIGHTS IN EUROPE: A STUDY OF THE EUROPEAN CONVENTION ON HUMAN RIGHTS (4th ed. 2001).

[Manchester: Manchester University Press, 362 pp. Appendix provides the texts of the convention and its protocols.]

YEARBOOK OF THE EUROPEAN CONVENTION ON HUMAN RIGHTS (1955/1957-).

[The Hague: Martinus Nijhoff Pub., annual, v. 1- . Volume one contains the text of the convention; later volumes contain the protocols as promulgated. Includes status, ratifications, signatures, and reservations information.]

§ 6.   African Union (AU)

The African Charter on Human and Peoples' Rights, OAU Doc. CAB/LEG/67/3/Rev.5 (1981), *reprinted in* 21 I.L.M. 58 (1982), *entered into force* Oct. 21, 1986.

AFRICAN UNION, COMPENDIUM OF KEY HUMAN RIGHTS DOCUMENTS OF THE AFRICAN UNION (C. H. Heyns & Magnus Killander eds., 2005).

[Pretoria: Pretoria University Law Press, 267 pp.]

DOCUMENTS OF THE ORGANIZATION OF AFRICAN UNITY (Gino J. Naldi ed., 1992).

[London; New York: Mansell, 246 pp. Contains several important human rights documents including the 1969 OAU Convention Governing the Specific Aspects of Refugee Problems in Africa, 1982 African Charter on Human and Peoples' Rights, 1988 Rules of Procedure of the African Commission on Human and Peoples' Rights, and 1990 African Charter on the Rights and Welfare of the Child.]

MUNYONZWE HAMALENGWA ET AL., THE INTERNATIONAL LAW OF HUMAN RIGHTS IN AFRICA: BASIC DOCUMENTS AND ANNOTATED BIBLIOGRAPHY (1988).

[Dordrecht; Boston: Martinus Nijhoff Pub., 427 pp.]

HUMAN RIGHTS AND DEVELOPMENT IN AFRICA 317-39 (Claude E. Welch, Jr. & Ronald I. Meltzer eds., 1984).

[Albany: State University of New York Press, 349 pp. Includes African Charter on Human and Peoples' Rights; concordance of basic human rights in the Banjul Charter and other major human rights treaties; and major African conferences on human rights, 1961-1981 (locations, dates, and sources).]

DOCUMENTS OF THE AFRICAN COMMISSION ON HUMAN AND PEOPLES' RIGHTS: 1987-1998 (Rachel Murray & Malcolm D. Evans eds., 2001).

[Oxford; Portland, OR.: Hart Pub., 828 pp.]

Documents of the African Commission on Human and Peoples' Rights, 1999-2005 (Rachel Murray & Malcolm D. Evans eds., 2007).

[Oxford; Portland, OR: Hart Pub., 522 pp.]

The Participation of NGOs in the Work of the African Commission on Human and Peoples' Rights: A Compilation of Basic Documents (1996).

[Geneva, Switzerland: International Commission of Jurists, 259 pp. Part 1 publishes basic documents on conclusions and recommendations of workshops; Part 2 discusses the main actions taken by the ACHPR; and Part 3 addresses the main actions taken by the Assembly of Heads of State and Government of the OAU.]

Rules of Procedure of the African Commission on Human and Peoples' Rights, Adopted on 6 October 1995, http://www.achpr.org/english/_info/rules_en.html.

U.N. Centre for Human Rights, *The African Charter on Human and Peoples' Rights*, U.N. Doc. HR/PUB/09/1 (1990).

[New York: U.N. Centre for Hum. Rts., 51 pp. Contains the Charter and Rules of Procedure of the African Commission on Human and Peoples' Rights. An annex contains a list of countries that have signed, ratified, or acceded to the Charter.]

§ 7.   Organization of American States (OAS)

Basic Documents Pertaining to Human Rights in the Inter-American System, OAS Doc. No. OAS/Ser.L/V/I.4 rev.10 (2004).

[Washington: General Secretariat of the Organization of American States. Available on the OAS Web site, http://www.cidh.oas.org/Basicos/English/Basic.TOC.htm.]

Scott J. Davidson, The Inter-American System of Human Rights (1997).

[Aldershot, Hants, Brookfield, VT: Dartmouth, 385 pp.]

Los Derechos Humanos en el Sistema Interamericano: Compilación de Instrumentos (3d ed. 2001).

[San José, Costa Rica: CEJIL (Centro por la Justicia y el Derecho International), 221 pp.]

Human Rights: The Inter-American System (Thomas Buergenthal & Robert E. Norris eds., 1982-1993).

[Dobbs Ferry, NY: Oceana Publications, Inc., looseleaf. Contains texts of basic documents: OAS Charter, American Convention on Human Rights and its legislative history, related Inter-American conventions, statutes, rules, decisions, advisory opinions and resolutions of the Inter-American Commission and Court of Human Rights, OAS General Assembly resolutions, selected findings of country reports, and annual reports. Includes status information for instruments, bibliographies, and indexes by case number, country, right, article of instrument, topic, and victim's name.]

THE INTER-AMERICAN SYSTEM OF HUMAN RIGHTS (David J. Harris & Stephen Livingstone eds., 1998).

[Oxford: Clarendon Press; New York: Oxford Univ. Press, 588 pp. Collection of essays includes a section of relevant laws and regulations.]

INTER-AMERICAN YEARBOOK ON HUMAN RIGHTS (1968-).

[Washington: General Secretariat of the Organization of American States.]

JO M. PASQUALUCCI, THE PRACTICE AND PROCEDURE OF THE INTER-AMERICAN COURT OF HUMAN RIGHTS (2003).

[Cambridge; New York: Cambridge University Press, 533 pp. Appendices include basic documents, including rules of procedure.]

DANIEL ZOVATTO, LOS DERECHOS HUMANOS EN EL SISTEMA INTERAMERICANO: RECOMPILACION DE INSTRUMENTOS BASICOS (1987).

[San José, Costa Rica: Instituto Interamericano de Derechos Humanos, 357 pp. Spanish compilation of declarations, regulations, statutes, and treaties of Inter-American bodies. Includes a list of OAS resolutions concerning human rights and chronological index.]

§ 8.   Humanitarian Law

CUSTOMARY INTERNATIONAL HUMANITARIAN LAW (Jean-Marie Henckaerts & Louise Doswald-Beck eds., 2006)

[Cambridge: Cambridge University Press, 3 vols.]

DOCUMENTS ON THE LAWS OF WAR (Adam Roberts & Richard Guelff eds., 3d ed. 2000).

[Oxford; New York: Oxford Univ. Press, 765 pp.]

HUMANITARIAN LAW IN ARMED CONFLICTS: MANUAL (The Federal Ministry of Defense of the Federal Republic of Germany ed., 1992).

[Bonn: German Ministry of Defense, 154 pp. English version of the German tri-service manual (issued August 1992), ZDv 15/2 Humanitaeres Voelkerrecht in bewaffneten Konflikten: Handbuch.]

INTERNATIONAL COMMITTEE OF THE RED CROSS, INTERNATIONAL HUMANITARIAN LAW – TREATIES & DOCUMENTS, http://www.icrc.org/ihl.

INTERNATIONAL COMMITTEE OF THE RED CROSS, INTERNATIONAL LAW CONCERNING THE CONDUCT OF HOSTILITIES: COLLECTION OF HAGUE CONVENTIONS AND SOME OTHER INTERNATIONAL INSTRUMENTS (rev. ed. 1996).

[Geneva: ICRC, 214 pp.]

INTERNATIONAL COMMITTEE OF THE RED CROSS, INTERNATIONAL RED CROSS HANDBOOK (13th ed. 1994).

[Geneva: ICRC, 961 pp. Paperback.]

INTERNATIONAL COMMITTEE OF THE RED CROSS, PROTOCOLS ADDITIONAL TO THE GENEVA CONVENTIONS OF 12 AUGUST 1949 (1977).

[Geneva: ICRC, 134 pp. Includes texts of Protocols, resolutions of the Diplomatic Conference, and extracts from the Final Act of the Diplomatic Conference.]

INTERNATIONAL COMMITTEE OF THE RED CROSS, SUMMARY OF THE GENEVA CONVENTIONS OF AUGUST 12, 1949 AND THEIR ADDITIONAL PROTOCOLS (1983).

[Geneva: ICRC, 22 pp. In small booklet form.]

THE LAWS OF ARMED CONFLICTS: A COLLECTION OF CONVENTIONS, RESOLUTIONS AND OTHER DOCUMENTS (Dietrich Schindler & Jiri Toman 4th rev. ed. 2004).

[Dordrecht; Boston: Martinus Nijhoff Pub., 1493 pp. Scientific Collection of the Henri Dunant Institute.]

U.N. CENTRE FOR HUMAN RIGHTS, HUMAN RIGHTS: A COMPILATION OF INTERNATIONAL INSTRUMENTS, U.N. Doc. ST/HR/1/Rev.5, U.N. Sales No. E.94.XIV.1 (1994).

[New York: U.N., 950 pp., 2 vols. Volume I, Part 2 contains texts of instruments pertaining to humanitarian law. 2003 version http://www2.unog.ch/intinstr/uninstr.exe?language=en.]

§ 9.   Organization for Security and Co-Operation in Europe (OSCE)

Amnesty International, *Conference on Security and Cooperation in Europe (CSCE): The Road to Helsinki II* (1992).

[London: AI, 25 pp. AI Index: IOR 52/01/92. Appendix 2 contains: Extracts from the Document of the Moscow Meeting of the Conference on the Human Dimension of the CSCE adopted October 3, 1991.]

GIOVANNI BARBERINI, CODICE DELLA CONFERENZA SULLA SICUREZZA E LA COOPERAZIONE IN EUROPA/C.S.C.E. DOCUMENTS (1990).

[Napoli: Edizion Scientifiche Italiane, 853 pp. Bilingual in Italian and English. Contains the texts of basic documents: Final Act, concluding documents of the Belgrade, Madrid, and Vienna conferences, rules of procedure of the CSCE, various meeting reports, and major U.N. human rights instruments (appendix).]

THE CHALLENGES OF CHANGE: THE HELSINKI SUMMIT OF THE CSCE AND ITS AFTERMATH, 385-446 (Arie Bloed ed., 1994).

[Dordrecht; Boston: Martinus Nijhoff Pub., 463 pp. Annex contains the text of CSCE Helsinki Document 1992: The Challenges of Change (Helsinki Declaration) and Helsinki Decisions.]

COLLECTION OF HUMAN RIGHTS DOCUMENTS OF THE EUROPEAN COMMUNITY AND ITS MEMBER STATES (1992).

[Netherlands: Ministry of Foreign Affairs, 193 pp.]

The Conference on Security and Co-operation in Europe: Analysis and Basic Documents, 1972-1993 (Arie Bloed ed., 2d ed. 1993).

[Dordrecht; Boston: Martinus Nijhoff Pub., 1337 pp. Revised edition of From Helsinki to Vienna (1990).]

Conference on Security and Cooperation in Europe: Final Act, 73 Dep't St. Bull. 323-50; 14 I.L.M. 1292-1325 (1975).

Alexis Heraclides, Helsinki-II and its Aftermath: The Making of the CSCE into an International Organization 209-64 (1993).

[London; New York: Pinter Publishers, 274 pp.]

Human Rights, European Politics, and the Helsinki Accord: The Documentary Evolution of the Conference on Security and Cooperation in Europe, 1973-75 (Igor I. Kavass et al. eds., 1981).

[Buffalo, NY: W.S. Hein, 6 vols.]

Organization for Security and Co-Operation in Europe (OSCE) Web site, http://www.osce.org/documents.

[This library contains documents, journals, and decisions issued by various CSCE/OSCE negotiating bodies during different events and meetings, which took place between 1973 and the present.]

U.S. Congress, Commission on Security and Cooperation in Europe, Document of the Copenhagen Meeting of the Conference on the Human Dimension of the CSCE (1990).

[Washington, DC: U.S. Government Printing Office, 24 pp.]

§ 10.   United States

Note: For texts of many recently ratified treaties, see also International Legal Materials (I.L.M.), listed in the HUMAN RIGHTS CASE LAW/OTHER section of this bibliography. If the text of a treaty cannot be found in the following sources, contact the Assistant Legal Adviser for Treaty Affairs, U.S. Department of State, 2201 C Street N.W., Washington, DC 20520.

Human Rights Documents: Compilation of Documents Pertaining to Human Rights (1983).

[Washington, D.C.: U.S. Government Printing Office, 774 pp. (98th Cong., 1st Sess., Committee Print.) Includes U.S. laws containing human rights provisions. For an update of this compilation, see U.S. Legislation Relating Human Rights to U.S. Foreign Policy, listed below.]

International Human Rights Instruments: A Compilation of Treaties, Agreements and Declarations of Especial Interest to the United States (Richard B. Lillich ed., 2d ed. 1990-).

[Buffalo, NY: W.S. Hein, looseleaf. Texts of over 40 key human rights treaties and agreements concluded through the U.N., OAS, ILO, and other international bodies. Includes related reservations, declarations, U.S. action, bibliographies, and citations to U.S. cases in which the instruments have been invoked.]

INTERNATIONAL HUMAN RIGHTS LAW GROUP, U.S. LEGISLATION RELATING HUMAN RIGHTS TO U.S. FOREIGN POLICY (4th ed. 1991-).

[Buffalo, NY: W.S. Hein, 186 pp.]

U.S. DEPT. OF STATE, TREATIES IN FORCE: A LIST OF TREATIES AND OTHER INTERNATIONAL AGREEMENTS OF THE UNITED STATES IN FORCE ON JANUARY 1, [DATE] (1929-).

[Washington, DC: U.S. Government Printing Office. This official annual publication addresses bilateral agreements (Part I) and multilateral treaties (Part II). Part I arranges bilateral agreements by country and subject, while Part II arranges multilateral treaties by subject and includes lists of States parties. An electronic version is available on the State Department's Web site, http://www.state.gov/s/l/treaty/treaties/2007/index.htm. Note that the electronic version is usually more current than the print.]

§ 11. Other Collections

GUDMUNDUR ALFREDSSON & KATARINA TOMASEVSKI, A THEMATIC GUIDE TO DOCUMENTS ON HEALTH AND HUMAN RIGHTS: GLOBAL AND REGIONAL STANDARDS ADOPTED BY INTERGOVERNMENTAL ORGANIZATIONS, INTERNATIONAL NON-GOVERNMENTAL ORGANIZATIONS AND PROFESSIONAL ASSOCIATIONS (1998).

[The Hague; Boston: Martinus Nijhoff Publishers, 629 pp.]

AMNESTY INTERNATIONAL, ETHICAL CODES AND DECLARATIONS RELEVANT TO THE HEALTH PROFESSIONS (4th rev. ed. 2000).

[London: AI, 174 pp. AI Index: ACT 75/01/94. On the Web http://www. amnesty.org/en/library/info/ACT75/005/2000.]

APCDOC: Documents from the World Conference on Human Rights (WCHR) (1993).

[Hannover, Germany: APC/Comlink. Set of computer diskettes containing documents from the Second World Conference on Human Rights in Vienna (1993), including the Universal Declaration of Human Rights, Convention on the Rights of the Child, and other major documents from the conference.]

BASIC DOCUMENTS ON HUMAN RIGHTS (Ian Brownlie & Guy S. Goodwin-Gill, 5th ed. 2006).

[Oxford; New York: Oxford Univ. Press, 1274 pp.]

BLACKSTONE'S INTERNATIONAL HUMAN RIGHTS DOCUMENTS (P.R. Ghandhi ed., 5th ed. 2006).

[Oxford; New York: Oxford Univ. Press, 514 pp.]

CENTER FOR THE STUDY OF HUMAN RIGHTS, TWENTY-FIVE+ HUMAN RIGHTS DOCUMENTS (2001).

[New York: Columbia University. Replaces Twenty-Five Human Rights Documents (1994).]

COMMON RIGHTS & EXPECTATIONS: PRIMARY INTERNATIONAL TREATIES PROTECTING THE RIGHTS OF ALL PEOPLE: UNITED NATIONS TEXTS, PARTICIPATING NATIONS, CURRENT NORTH AMERICAN RESERVATIONS AND DECLARATIONS (1996).

[Ottawa: Gerald and Maas, enl. ed. of: The Crime of Genocide & Bill of Human Rights (1989); 101 pp. Includes texts of: Convention on the Prevention and Punishment of the Crime of Genocide, Universal Declaration of Human Rights, International Covenant on Economic, Social and Cultural Rights, International Covenant on Civil and Political Rights, First Optional Protocol, Second Optional Protocol, Convention Relating to the Status of Refugees, 1967 Protocol.]

RALPH CRAWSHAW & LEIF HOLMSTRÖM, ESSENTIAL TEXTS ON HUMAN RIGHTS FOR THE POLICE: A COMPILATION OF INTERNATIONAL INSTRUMENTS (2001).

[The Hague; Boston: Kluwer Law International, 330 pp.]

MUNYONZWE HAMALENGWA ET AL., THE INTERNATIONAL LAW OF HUMAN RIGHTS IN AFRICA: BASIC DOCUMENTS AND ANNOTATED BIBLIOGRAPHY (1988).

[Dordrecht; Boston: Martinus Nijhoff Pub., 427 pp.]

HEALTH AND HUMAN RIGHTS: BASIC INTERNATIONAL DOCUMENTS (Stephen P. Marks ed., 2d 2006).

[Cambridge, MA: Harvard University, Francois-Xavier Bagnoud Center for Health and Human Rights, 392 pp.]

LOUIS HENKIN ET AL., HUMAN RIGHTS: DOCUMENTARY SUPPLEMENT (2001).

[New York: Foundation Press, 1099 pp.]

HUMAN RIGHTS SOURCEBOOK (Albert P. Blaustein et al. eds., 1987).

[New York: Paragon House Publishers, 970 pp. Contains texts of major human rights instruments and related documents such as procedural rules for enforcement, national constitutional provisions, statutes, and cases.]

INTERNATIONAL HUMAN RIGHTS AND COMPARATIVE MENTAL DISABILITY LAW: DOCUMENTS SUPPLEMENT (Michael L. Perlin ed. 2006).

[Durham, N.C.: Carolina Academic Press, 422 pp. Includes the Disability Convention, other international instruments, and selected national laws.]

INTERNATIONAL HUMAN RIGHTS. DOCUMENTARY SUPPLEMENT (Richard B. Lillich ed., 2006

[New York, NY: Aspen Publishers, 260 pp. Supplement to International Human Rights, Problems of Law, Policy, and Practice, 4th ed. Includes major U.N. human rights treaties, the three regional human rights treaties, several other international human rights instruments, two U.S. statutes concerning foreign assistance and human rights, and a model communication.]

FRANCISCO FORREST MARTIN ET AL., INTERNATIONAL HUMAN RIGHTS LAW AND PRACTICE: CASES, TREATIES, AND MATERIALS, DOCUMENTARY SUPPLEMENT (1997).

[The Hague; Boston: Kluwer, 1063 pp. Includes basic U.N., EU, OAS, OAU instruments, as well as documents pertaining to international criminal tribunals and humanitarian treaties.]

INTERNATIONAL COMMISSION OF JURISTS, THE RIGHT TO REPARATION FOR VICTIMS OF HUMAN RIGHTS VIOLATIONS: A COMPILATION OF ESSENTIAL DOCUMENTS (1998).

[Geneva, Switzerland: The Commission, 43 pp.]

INTERNATIONAL DOCUMENTS ON CHILDREN (Geraldine Van Bueren ed., 2d rev. ed. 1998).

[The Hague; Boston: M. Nijhoff, 532 pp.]

INTERNATIONAL LAW, HUMAN RIGHTS (Pieter van Dijk et al. ed., 4th rev. ed. 2002).

[Lelystad: Koninklijke Vermande, 471 pp. Includes various global and regional conventions, declarations, and other instruments.]

SCOTT LECKIE & ANNE GALLAGHER, ECONOMIC, SOCIAL, AND CULTURAL RIGHTS: A LEGAL RESOURCE GUIDE (2006).

[Philadelphia, Pa.: University of Pennsylvania Press, 776 pp. Contains key treaties, declarations, general comments, interpretive texts, and charters.]

RADU MARES, BUSINESS AND HUMAN RIGHTS: A COMPILATION OF DOCUMENTS (2004).

[Leiden; Boston: Nijhoff; Herndon, VA: Distributed in Canada, USA and Mexico by Brill Academic Publishers, 654 pp.]

GÖRAN MELANDER, GUDMUNDUR ALFREDSSON & LEIF HOLMSTRÖM, THE RAOUL WALLENBERG INSTITUTE COMPILATION OF HUMAN RIGHTS INSTRUMENTS (2d rev. ed. 2004).

[Leiden; Boston: M. Nijhoff Publishers, 684 pp. Compilation of international and regional human rights instruments covering civil, cultural, economic, political, social, and solidarity rights.]

DANIEL O'DONNELL, PROTECCION INTERNACIONAL DE LOS DERECHOS HUMANOS (2d ed. 1989).

[Lima, Peru: Comision Andina De Juristas, 752 pp. See "Anexos" for a compilation of human rights instruments in Spanish.]

THE PROTECTION OF HUMAN RIGHTS IN THE ADMINISTRATION OF CRIMINAL JUSTICE: A COMPENDIUM OF UNITED NATIONS NORMS AND STANDARDS (M. Cherif Bassiouni ed., 1994).

[Irvington, NY: Transnational Publishers, 500 pp. Contains relevant procedural norms and standards applicable to national, regional, and international criminal processes.]

THE RIGHTS OF THE CHILD: INTERNATIONAL INSTRUMENTS (Maria Rita Saulle ed., 1995).

[Irvington-on-Hudson, N.Y.: Transnational Publishers, 779 pp. Includes nearly 100 international and regional instruments, all of which ultimately contributed to the United Nations Convention on the Rights of the Child. Contains virtually all modern international legal initiatives on the abduction, repatriation, adoption, and civil registry of minors, as well as conventions on crimes committed by minors, the legal capacity of minors, and humanitarian law with regard to minors. In addition to the text of the convention itself, this volume includes the final deliberations in their entirety of the United Nations Working Group that drafted the convention.]

JEREMY ROSENBLATT, INTERNATIONAL CONVENTIONS AFFECTING CHILDREN (2000).

[Dordrecht: Kluwer Law International, 265 pp. Text and commentary on all international conventions that bear directly on the rights of the child. The legal issues covered include, among others, the child and immigration, inter-country adoption, international child abduction, human rights, and armed conflict.]

HENRY J. STEINER & PHILIP ALSTON, INTERNATIONAL HUMAN RIGHTS IN CONTEXT: LAW, POLITICS, MORALS: TEXT AND MATERIALS 1147-1228 (2d ed. 2000).

[Oxford: Clarendon Press, New York: Oxford Univ. Press, 1532 pp. The Annex on Documents includes basic global and regional instruments.]

ERIC SUY, CORPUS IURIS GENTIUM: A COLLECTION OF BASIC TEXTS ON MODERN INTERSTATE RELATIONS, 2d rev. ed (1996).

[Leuven: Acco, 1996, 666 pp. Includes a section on human rights.]

MAXIME E. TARDU, HUMAN RIGHTS: THE INTERNATIONAL PETITION SYSTEM (1979-1985).

[Dobbs Ferry, NY: Oceana Publications, Inc., looseleaf, 3 vols.]

United Nations, *Compendium of United Nations Standards and Norms in Crime Prevention and Criminal Justice*, U.N. Doc. ST/CSDHA/16 (1992).

[New York: U.N., 278 pp.]

WOMEN AND HUMAN RIGHTS: THE BASIC DOCUMENTS (1996).

[New York, NY: Columbia University; Center for the Study of Human Rights, 251 pp.]

B. Status of Human Rights Instruments

The principal compilations of human rights instruments listed above often include the ratification status of the instruments. Listed below are the two major sources on the status of U.N. human rights instruments only. The other sources provide information on the status of several international human rights conventions and instruments as well as reservations and declarations.

§ 1.   Sources on the Status of U.N. Human Rights Instruments

U.N., MULTILATERAL TREATIES DEPOSITED WITH THE SECRETARY-GENERAL: STATUS AS AT [date], U.N. Doc. ST/LEG/Ser.E/18 (Vol. I) and U.N. Doc. ST/LEG/Ser.E/18 (Vol. II), U.N. Sales No. E.00.V.2.

[New York: U.N., 924 pp. (Vol. I) and 628 pp. (Vol. II) (1982-). Published annually. Includes the texts of declarations and reservations made by States parties. Addresses U.N. and League of Nations treaties. This publication is also available on the World Wide Web, United Nations Treaty Collection, http://untreaty.un.org. The electronic version is updated much more frequently than the print.]

U.N., HUMAN RIGHTS. INTERNATIONAL INSTRUMENTS. CHART OF RATIFICATIONS AS AT [date], U.N. Doc. ST/HR/4/Rev.17, Sales No. 87.XIV.2 (1993-). Updated annually.

[New York: U.N. This chart lists 25 major U.N. human rights instruments horizontally, at the top, and countries in alphabetical order along the vertical margin. Various symbols indicate the status of the instruments for each state. For each instrument the total number of States parties and the number of signatures not followed by ratification are listed. This source updates the chart of ratifications included with *Human Rights: Status of International Instruments* (1987), listed below, and does not contain texts of declarations and reservations. This information is also available from the OHCHR Web site, Ratifications and Reservations, http://www2.ohchr.org/english/bodies/ratification/index.htm. This database is updated more frequently than the print information.]

U.N. High Commissioner for Human Rights, Ratifications and Reservations, http://www2.ohchr.org/english/bodies/ratification/index.htm.

[Information on the status of ratifications is available as well as the full text of many international human rights instruments.]

§ 2.   Other Sources

Commission on Human Rights, *Status of the International Covenants on Human Rights*, U.N. Doc. E/CN.4/1998/83 (1998).

[Geneva: U.N., 16 pp. For updated information, see U.N. High Commissioner for Human Rights, Ratifications and Reservations, http://www2.ohchr.org/english/bodies/ratification/index.htm.]

Committee Against Torture, *Status of the Convention Against Torture and Other Cruel, Inhuman or Degrading Treatment or Punishment, and Reservations, Declarations and Objections Under the Convention*, U.N. Doc. CAT/C/2/Rev.5 (1998).

[Geneva: U.N., 45 pp. For updated information, see U.N. High Commissioner for Human Rights, http://www2.ohchr.org/english/bodies/ratification/9.htm.]

Committee on Economic, Social and Cultural Rights, *Status of the International Covenant on Economic, Social and Cultural Rights and Reservations, Withdrawals, Declarations and Objections Under the Covenant*, U.N. Doc. E/C.12/1993/3/Rev.5 (2001).

[Geneva: U.N., 39 pp. For updated information, see U.N. High Commissioner for Human Rights, http://www2.ohchr.org/english/bodies/ratification/3.htm.]

Committee on the Elimination of Discrimination Against Women, *Other Matters. Declarations, Reservations, Objections and Notifications of Withdrawal of Reservations Relating to the Convention on the Elimination of All Forms of Discrimination Against Women*, U.N. Doc. CEDAW/SP/2000/2 (2000).

[Geneva: U.N. For updated information, see U.N. High Commissioner for Human Rights, http://www2.ohchr.org/english/bodies/ratification/8.htm.]

Committee on the Elimination of Racial Discrimination, *Declarations, Reservations, Withdrawals of Reservations and Objections to Reservations and Declarations Relating to the International Convention on the Elimination of All Forms of Racial Discrimination*, U.N. Doc. CERD/C/60/Rev.3 (1999).

[Geneva: U.N., 62 pp. For updated information, see U.N. High Commissioner for Human Rights, http://www2.ohchr.org/english/bodies/ratification/2.htm.]

Committee on the Rights of the Child, *Reservations, Declarations and Objections Relating to the Convention on the Rights of the Child*, U.N. Doc. CRC/C/2/Rev.8 (1999).

[Geneva: U.N., 102 pp. For updated information, see U.N. High Commissioner for Human Rights, http://www2.ohchr.org/english/bodies/ratification/11.htm.]

Committee on the Rights of the Child, *States Parties to the Convention on the Rights of the Child and Status of the Submission of Reports Under Article 44 of the Convention*, U.N. Doc. CRC/C/127 (2003).

[Geneva: U.N., 30 pp. For updated information, see Office of the High Commissioner for Human Rights, http://www2.ohchr.org/english/bodies/ratification/11.htm [does not contain information on status of submission of reports.]

COUNCIL OF EUROPE, THE STATUS OF INTERNATIONAL TREATIES ON HUMAN RIGHTS (2006)

[Strasbourg: Council of Europe Pub., 225 pp.]

Council of Europe, Treaty Office Web Site, http://conventions.coe.int/treaty/EN/cadreprincipal.htm.

[The Council of Europe's Web site provides updated status information, signatures, and ratifications, as well as declarations and reservations.]

Human Rights Committee, *Reservations, Declarations, Notifications and Objections Relating to the International Covenant on Civil and Political Rights and the Optional Protocols Thereto*, U.N. Doc. CCPR/C/2/Rev.4 (1994).

[Geneva: U.N., 139 pp. For updated information, see U.N. High Commissioner for Human Rights, http://www.ohchr.org/english/countries/ratification/4_1.htm [Civil and Political Covenant], http://www2.ohchr.org/english/bodies/ratification/5.htm [First Optional Protocol], http://www2.ohchr.org/english/bodies/ratification/12.htm [Second Optional Protocol].]

Inter-American Commission on Human Rights, *Basic Documents Pertaining to Human Rights in the Inter-American System*, OAS/Ser.L/V/I.4 Rev.7 (2000).

[Washington, DC: IACHR Court, General Secretariat, Organization of American States, 1988- . Also available on the Web from the Inter-American Commission on Human Rights, http://www.cidh.oas.org/Basicos/English/Basic. TOC.htm. Check annual reports for status information.]

International Committee of the Red Cross, *State Parties to the Following International Humanitarian Law and Other Related Treaties as of* [date], http://www.icrc.org/IHL.nsf/(SPF)/party_main_treaties/$File/IHL_and_other_related_Treaties.pdf. Updated constantly.

[Further information is available from the International Humanitarian Law Database on the Web, http://www.icrc.org/ihl. Also available on the ICRC International Humanitarian Law CD-ROM.]

International Labour Office, *Lists of Ratifications by Convention and by Country (as at 31 December 2002)* (2003).

[Geneva: International Labour Office, Report III (Part 2) of the 87th Session of the International Labour Conference; Third Item on the Agenda; Information and Reports on the Application of Conventions and Recommendations, 245 pp. Part one contains a list of ratifications by convention with dates of entry into force, names of States parties, and dates of registration of ratification (with notes on conditional ratification or denunciation of conventions). Part two lists ratified conventions and conventions in force by country, noting each country's date of ILO membership. Also lists, by session, conventions adopted and the total number of ratifications to date. Current information available on the Web from ILOLEX: The ILO's database on International Labour Standards, http://www.ilo.org/ilolex/english/newratframeE.htm, and on CD-ROM.]

Jean-Bernard Marie, *International Instruments Relating to Human Rights: Classification and Status of Ratifications as of 1 January 2000*, 21 HUM. RTS. L.J. 91 (2000).

[Covers the principal international human rights conventions.]

Netherlands Institute of Human Rights (SIM), Human Rights Treaties Web Site, http://sim.law.uu.nl/SIM/Library/RATIF.nsf/Country?OpenView.

[Provides information on signatures and ratifications for most primary treaties and instruments.]

U.N. CENTRE FOR HUMAN RIGHTS, HUMAN RIGHTS: STATUS OF INTERNATIONAL INSTRUMENTS, U.N. Doc. ST/HR/5, U.N. Sales No. E.87.XIV.2 (1987).

[New York: U.N., 336 pp. Lists 22 major U.N. human rights instruments and includes the ratification status, declarations, reservations, objections by States parties, and notes for each instrument. It is updated by Human Rights. International Instruments. *Chart of Ratifications as at 30 June 1998*, U.N. Doc. ST/HR/4/Rev.17 (New York: U.N., 12 pp.). This periodic update includes

25 major U.N. human rights instruments and indicates the status of the instruments for each state. Neither publication includes the full text of the treaties.]

UNESCO, THE DIVISION OF HUMAN RIGHTS AND PEACE, HUMAN RIGHTS: MAJOR INTERNATIONAL INSTRUMENTS, STATUS AS OF 31 MAY 2000 (2000).

[New York: UNESCO, 36 pp.]

OHCHR, Ratifications and Reservations, http://www2.ohchr.org/english/.

[Provides status of ratification information for the major human rights instruments and protocols. Access is available by country at http://www2.ohchr.org/english; click through the map to select a country. Ratifications are available by treaty at http://www2.ohchr.org/english.]

UNHCR, *International Instruments: States Parties to the 1951 Convention Relating to the Status of Refugees and the 1967 Protocol*, 19 REFUGEE SURVEY Q. 145 (2000).

[Geneva: UNHCR, status as of May 3, 2000. Current information is also available on the UNHCR Web site, http://www.unhcr.org/protect/PROTECTION/3b73b0d63.pdf.]

Robin C.A. White, *State of Ratifications of Human Rights Instruments*, 27 EUR. L. REV. 63 (2002).

Robin C.A. White, *State of Ratification of Human Rights Instruments*, 25 EUR. L. REV. 70 (2000).

Robin C.A. White, *State of Ratifications of Human Rights Instruments*, 26 EUR. L. REV. 103 (2001).

C. Legislative History of Human Rights Instruments

ANGELA BENNETT, THE GENEVA CONVENTION: THE HIDDEN ORIGINS OF THE RED CROSS (2005).

[Stroud, Gloucestershire: Sutton, 236 pp.]

MARC J. BOSSUYT, GUIDE TO THE "TRAVAUX PREPARATOIRES" OF THE INTERNATIONAL COVENANT ON CIVIL AND POLITICAL RIGHTS (1987).

[Dordrecht; Boston: Martinus Nijhoff Pub., 851 pp.]

CHARTER OF THE UNITED NATIONS: A COMMENTARY (Bruno Simma et al. eds., 2d ed. 2002).

[Oxford; New York: Oxford Univ. Press, 2 vols.]

COLLECTED EDITION OF THE "TRAVAUX PREPARATOIRES" OF THE EUROPEAN CONVENTION ON HUMAN RIGHTS=RECUEIL DES TRAVAUX PREPARATOIRES DE LA CONVENTION EUROPEENNE DES DROITS DE L'HOMME (1975-1985).

[The Hague: Martinus Nijhoff Pub., 8 vols.]

THE COLLECTED TRAVAUX PREPARATOIRES OF THE 1951 GENEVA CONVENTION RELATING TO THE STATUS OF REFUGEES (Alex Takkenberg & Christopher C. Tahbaz eds., 1990).

[Amsterdam: Dutch Refugee Council, 3 vols.]

MANFRED NOWAK ET AL., THE UNITED NATIONS CONVENTION AGAINST TORTURE: A COMMENTARY (2008).

[Oxford; New York: Oxford Univ. Press, 1680 pp. Not the complete travaux, but containing references to travaux documents.]

INTERNATIONAL COMMITTEE OF THE RED CROSS, COMMENTARY ON THE GENEVA CONVENTIONS OF 12 AUGUST, 1949 SERIES (Jean S. Pictet ed., 1952-).

[Geneva: ICRC, 4 vols. Titles include: I Geneva Convention for the Amelioration of the Condition of the Wounded and Sick in Armed Forces in the Field (1952); II Geneva Convention for the Amelioration of the Condition of Wounded, Sick and Shipwrecked Members of Armed Forces at Sea (1960); III Geneva Convention Relative to the Treatment of Prisoners of War (1960); and IV Geneva Convention Relative to the Protection of Civilian Persons in Time of War (1958).]

M. GLEN JOHNSON AND JANUSZ SYMONIDES, THE UNIVERSAL DECLARATION OF HUMAN RIGHTS: A HISTORY OF ITS CREATION AND IMPLEMENTATION, 1948-1998 (1998).

[Paris: UNESCO Pub., 166 pp.]

JOHANNES MORSINK, THE UNIVERSAL DECLARATION OF HUMAN RIGHTS: ORIGINS, DRAFTING, AND INTENT (1999).

[Philadelphia: University of Pennsylvania Press, 378 pp.]

LARS A. REHOF, GUIDE TO THE TRAVAUX PREPARATOIRES OF THE UNITED NATIONS CONVENTION ON THE ELIMINATION OF ALL FORMS OF DISCRIMINATION AGAINST WOMEN (1993).

[Dordrecht; Boston: Martinus Nijhoff Pub., 385 pp.]

NEHEMIAH ROBINSON, CONVENTION RELATING TO THE STATUS OF REFUGEES: ITS HISTORY, CONTENTS AND INTERPRETATION (1953).

[New York: Institute of Jewish Affairs, 238 pp.]

THE UNITED NATIONS CONVENTION ON THE RIGHTS OF THE CHILD: A GUIDE TO THE TRAVAUX PREPARATOIRES (Sharon Detrick comp. & ed., 1992).

[Dordrecht; Boston: Martinus Nijhoff Pub., 712 pp.]

ALBERT VERDOODT, NAISSANCE ET SIGNIFICATION DE LA DECLARATION UNIVERSELLE DES DROITS DE L'HOMME (1964).

[Louvain-Paris: Editions Nauwelaerts, 356 pp.]

PAUL WEIS, THE REFUGEES CONVENTION, 1951: THE TRAVAUX PREPARATOIRES ANALYSED (1995).

[Cambridge; New York: Grotius Publications, 383 pp. Volume seven of the CAMBRIDGE INTERNATIONAL DOCUMENT SERIES. Published under the auspices of the Refugee Studies Programme, University of Oxford. Travaux preparatoires documents are also UNHCR, http://www.unhcr.org/doclist/protect/3bc44e424.html.]

D. Human Rights Case Law, Jurisprudence, Decisions, and Digests

§ 1.   U.N.

SHIV R.S. BEDI, THE DEVELOPMENT OF HUMAN RIGHTS LAW BY THE JUDGES OF THE INTERNATIONAL COURT OF JUSTICE (2007).

[Oxford; Portland, OR.: Hart, 488 pp.]

Commission on Human Rights, *Report on the ... Session*, U.N. Doc. E/CN.4/ [year of the session]/[#].

[New York: U.N. Covers the Commission's resolutions and decisions (*e.g.*, Commission on Human Rights, Report on the Fifty-First Session, U.N. Doc. E/ CN.4/1995/176 (1995)). Another significant document is the Annotated Agenda, issued several weeks before each session, listing issues and documents to be considered; ordinarily identified by the symbol: U.N. Doc. E/CN.4/[year of the session]/1/Add.1.] In 2006 the Commission was replaced by the Human Rights Council. G.A. res. 60/251, U.N. Doc. A/RES/60/251 (March 15, 2006).

Committee Against Torture, *Consideration of Reports Submitted by the States Parties*, U.N. Doc. CAT/C/[#] ([year]).

[Concluding observations of the Committee for each report submitted by States parties. The U.N. symbol will vary depending on the country (*e.g.*, for Mauritius: U.N. Doc. CAT/C/24/Add.3 (1995)).]

Committee Against Torture, *Decisions*, U.N. Doc. CAT/C/[#]/D/[#]/[year of communication] ([year]).

[Decisions are determinations on the admissibility or merits of individual complaints (*e.g.*, Communication No. 22/1995, U.N. Doc. CAT/C/14/D/22/1995 (1995)).]

Committee Against Torture, *Report of the Committee Against Torture*, U.N. Doc. [session no.] U.N. GAOR Supp. (No. 44), U.N. Doc. A/[session no.]/44 ([year]).

[New York: U.N. (Note: the supplement number for the forty-third, forty-fourth, and forty-sixth sessions is not 44, but 46.) Annual report of the Committee to the General Assembly. Contains conclusions and recommendations adopted by the Committee, reports by States parties, parties ratified, an overview of activities of the Committee, as well as several annexes including a list of states and status of submission of reports (*e.g.*, Report of the Committee Against Torture, 49 U.N. GAOR Supp. (No. 44), U.N. Doc. A/49/44 (1994)).]

Committee on the Elimination of All Forms of Racial Discrimination, *Report of the Committee on the Elimination of Racial Discrimination*, U.N. Doc. [session no.] U.N. GAOR Supp. (No. 18), U.N. Doc. A/[session no.]/18 ([year]).

[New York: U.N. Annual report of the Committee to the General Assembly. Contains consideration of reports, decisions, opinions, status information, and summary of the activities of the Committee (*e.g.*, Report of the Committee on the Elimination of Racial Discrimination, 49 U.N. GAOR Supp. (No. 18), U.N. Doc. A/49/18 (1995)).]

Committee on the Elimination of All Forms of Racial Discrimination, *Consideration of Reports Submitted by the States Parties*, U.N. Doc. CERD/C/[#] ([year]).

[Concluding observations of the Committee for each report submitted by the States parties. The U.N. symbol will vary depending on the country (*e.g.*, for Sri Lanka: U.N. Doc. CERD/C/234/Add.1 (1994)).]

Committee on the Elimination of All Forms of Racial Discrimination, *Decisions*, U.N. Doc. CERD/C/[#]/D/[#]/[year of initial submission] ([year]).

[Decisions are admissibility determinations of individual complaints (*e.g.*, Communication No. 5/1994, U.N. Doc. CERD/C/46/D/5/1994 (1995)).]

Committee on the Elimination of All Forms of Racial Discrimination, *Opinions*, U.N. Doc. CERD/C/[#]/D/[#]/[year of submission] ([year]).

[Opinions are determinations by the Committee on the merits of individual complaints(*e.g.*,Communication No.3/1991,U.N.Doc.CERD/C/44/D/3/1991 (1994)).]

Committee on the Elimination of Discrimination Against Women, *Report of the Committee on the Elimination of Discrimination Against Women*, U.N. Doc. [session no.] U.N. GAOR Supp. (No. 38), U.N. Doc. A/[session no.]/38 ([year]).

[New York: U.N. Annual report of the Committee to the General Assembly. Contains conclusions and recommendations adopted by the Committee, reports of States parties, parties ratified, overview of the activities of the Committee, as well as several annexes including a list of ratifications and status of submission of reports (*e.g.*,Report of the Committee on the Elimination of Discrimination Against Women, 50 U.N. GAOR Supp. (No. 38), U.N. Doc. A/50/38 (1995)).]

COMMITTEE ON THE ELIMINATION OF DISCRIMINATION AGAINST WOMEN, THE WORK OF CEDAW: REPORTS OF THE COMMITTEE ON THE ELIMINATION OF DISCRIMINATION AGAINST WOMEN *(CEDAW)*, Vol. 1, 1982-1985, Vol. 2, 1986-1987, U.N. Doc. ST/CSDHA/5 (1989), U.N. Sales No. E.89.IV.4.

[New York: U.N., 752 pp. Contains reports of the Committee and the summary records.]

Committee on the Elimination of Discrimination Against Women, *Consideration of Reports Submitted by the States Parties*, U.N. Doc. CEDAW/C/[country abbrev.]/SP.1 ([year]).

[Concluding observation of the Committee for each report submitted by States parties. The U.N. symbol will vary depending on the country (*e.g.*, for Croatia: U.N. Doc. CEDAW/C/CRO/SP.1 (1994)).]

Committee on the Elimination of Discrimination Against Women, WomenWatch Web Site, http://www.un.org/womenwatch/daw/cedaw.

[Provides access to general recommendations, reports, and other documents submitted to the Committee. Covers the 13th session through the current session.]

Committee on Economic, Social and Cultural Rights, *Consideration of Reports Submitted by the States Parties Under Articles 16 and 17 of the Covenant*, U.N. Doc. E/C.12/[year]/[#] ([year]).

[Concluding observations of the Committee for each report submitted by States parties. The U.N. symbol will vary depending on the country (*e.g.*, for Uruguay: U.N. Doc. E/C.12/1994/3 (1994)).]

Committee on Economic, *Social and Cultural Rights, Report of the Committee on Economic, Social and Cultural Rights*, U.N. Doc. E/[year]/[#] and E/C.12/[year]/[#] ([year]).

[New York: U.N. Contains draft decisions recommended for adoption, submission, and consideration of reports by States parties, and several annexes (*e.g.*, Report of the Committee on Economic, Social and Cultural Rights, U.N. Doc. E/1994/23 and E/C.12/1993/19 (1994)).]

Committee on the Rights of the Child, *Compilation of the Conclusions and Recommendations Adopted by the Committee on the Rights of the Child*, U.N. Doc. CRC/C/19/Rev.10 (2002).

[Provides the text of the conclusions and recommendations adopted by the Committee. Includes information about activities and relations with other U.N. organs and human rights treaty bodies.]

Committee on the Rights of the Child, *Consideration of Reports Submitted by the States Parties*, U.N. Doc. CRC/C/[#] ([year]).

[Concluding observations of the Committee for each report submitted by States parties. The U.N. symbol will vary depending on the country (*e.g.*, for Colombia: CRC/C/15/Add.30 (1995).]

Committee on the Rights of the Child, *Report of the Committee on the Rights of the Child*, U.N. Doc. [session no.] U.N. GAOR Supp. (No. 41), U.N. Doc. A/[session no.]/41 ([year]).

[New York: U.N. Annual report of the Committee to the General Assembly. Contains conclusions and recommendations adopted by the Committee, reports by States parties, ratifications, an overview of the activities of the Committee, as well as several annexes including a list of States parties and status of submission of reports (*e.g.*, Report of the Committee on the Rights of the Child, 49 U.N. GAOR Supp. (No. 41), U.N. Doc. A/49/41 (1994)).]

General Assembly, *Resolutions and Decisions Adopted by the General Assembly during the First Part of Its...Session.*

[New York: U.N. A massive press release of each mid-January containing resolutions and decisions of the General Assembly for the session just concluded in December. The press release is not an official U.N. record, but it is the most comprehensive hard-copy account of the General Assembly's actions published until the official records are issued many months later. One volume of the official records contains the resolutions and decisions. That volume ordinarily has the same title as indicated above with the following document symbol: A/[session no.]/[supplement no.] (*e.g.*, General Assembly, Resolutions and Decisions Adopted by the General Assembly During the First Part of its Forty-Eighth Session, Volume I: 21 September - 23 December 1993, 48 U.N. GAOR Supp. (No. 49), U.N. Doc. A/48/49 (1994)). Full text of General Assembly Resolutions and Decisions are available on the Web, http://www.un.org, under "General Assembly."]

Human Rights Committee, *Consideration of Reports Submitted by States Parties under Article 40 of the Covenant*, U.N. Doc. CCPR/C/[#]/Add.[#] ([year]).

[Concluding observations of the Committee for each report submitted by States parties. The U.N. symbol will vary depending on the country (*e.g.*, for the United States: U.N. Doc. CCPR/C/79/Add.50 (1995)).]

Human Rights Committee, *Decisions*, U.N. Doc. CCPR/C/[#]/D/[#]/[year of submission] ([year]).

[Decisions are admissibility determinations of individual complaints (*e.g.*, Communication No. 525/1993, U.N. Doc. CCPR/C/53/D/525/1993 (1995)).]

Human Rights Committee, *General Comments Adopted by the Human Rights Committee Under Article 40, Paragraph 4 of the International Covenant on Civil and Political Rights (up to April 1989)*, U.N. Doc. CCPR/C/21/Rev.1 (1989), and CCPR/C/21/Rev.1/Add.1 through CCPR/C/21/Rev.1/Add.10 (2000).

[New York: U.N. The 1989 document is a 25-page compilation of comments by the Human Rights Committee to assist States parties in fulfilling their reporting obligations pursuant to the articles of the Covenant. Subsequent addenda update that compilation.]

Human Rights Committee, *Report of the Human Rights Committee*, U.N. Doc. [session no.] U.N. GAOR Supp. (No. 40), U.N. Doc. A/[session no.]/40 ([year]).

[New York: U.N. Annual report of the Committee to the General Assembly. Decisions of the Human Rights Committee on cases submitted under the Optional Protocol to the Civil and Political Covenant. Also includes the general comments of the Committee on the meaning of various Covenant provisions, communications, decisions, and views (*e.g.*, Report of the Human Rights Committee, 49 U.N. GAOR Supp. (No. 40), U.N. Doc. A/49/40 (1994)).]

Human Rights Committee, *Selected Decisions Under the Optional Protocol (Second to Sixteenth Sessions)*, U.N. Doc. CCPR/C/OP/1 (1985).

[New York: U.N., 1985, 167 pp. Reprint of selected decisions and views. Includes an index by article of the Covenant and the Optional Protocol.]

Human Rights Committee, *Selected Decisions Under the Optional Protocol (Seventeenth to Thirty-Second Sessions)*, U.N. Doc. CCPR/C/OP/2 (1990).

[New York: U.N., 1990, 246 pp., second compilation. Reprint of selected decisions and views. Includes an index by articles of the Covenant and Optional Protocol, author, and victim.]

Human Rights Committee, *Views*, U.N. Doc. CCPR/C/[#]/D/[#]/[year of submission] ([year]).

[Views are determinations by the Committee on the merits of individual complaints (*e.g.*, Communication No. 514/1992, U.N. Doc. CCPR/C/53/D/514/1992 (1995)).]

Human Rights Committee, *Yearbook of the Human Rights Committee*, U.N. Doc. CCPR/6.

[New York: U.N., 1977- . Published in two volumes with about a seven-year time lag. Volume I contains summary records and volume II contains States' periodic reports and the annual report of the Committee.]

Human Rights Council, *Report on the . . . Session*, U.N. Doc. A/HRC/[[#] of the session]/[#].

[Geneva: U.N. Covers the Council's resolutions and decisions (*e.g.*, Human Rights Council res. 5/1, Institution Building of the United Nations Human Rights Council (June 18, 2007), U.N. Doc. A/HRC/RES/5/1, http://www2.ohchr.org/english/bodies/hrcouncil.

International Human Rights Instruments, *Compilation of General Comments and General Recommendations Adopted by Human Rights Bodies*, U.N. Doc. HRI/GEN/1/Rev.4 (2000).

[214 pp., Feb. 7, 2000. Compilation of the general comments adopted by the Human Rights Committee, the general comments adopted by the Committee on Economic, Social and Cultural Rights, the general recommendations adopted by the Committee on the Elimination of Discrimination Against Women, and the general recommendations adopted by the Committee on Elimination of All Forms of Racial Discrimination.]

UNHCR, REFWORLD CD-ROM.

[Contains over 800 abstracts and over 1600 full texts of precedent-setting judicial decisions from 23 countries and international/regional bodies.]

Sub-Commission on Prevention of Discrimination and Protection of Minorities, *Report of the Sub-Commission on Prevention of Discrimination and Protection of Minorities on its . . . Session* (1946- 2005).

[Geneva: U.N. E/CN.4/[year]/[#] and E/CN.4/Sub.2/[year]/[#]. Reports of the Sub-Commission's resolutions and decisions (*e.g.*, Sub-Commission on Prevention of Discrimination and Protection of Minorities, Report of the Sub-Commission on Prevention of Discrimination and Protection of Minorities on its Forty-Sixth Session, U.N. Doc. E/CN.4/1995/2, E/CN.4/Sub.2/1994/56 (1995)). In 1999 the name of this U.N. body changed to Sub-Commission on the

Promotion and Protection of Human Rights. Another significant document is the Annotated Agenda, issued several weeks before each session listing issues and documents to be considered; ordinarily identified by the symbol: E/CN.4/Sub.2/[year of the session]/1/Add.1.] In 2006 the Sub-Commission concluded its sessions and in 2008 it was replaced by the Human Rights Council Advisory Committee.

U.N., *Yearbook on Human Rights* (1946-1988). [New York: U.N. (annual 1946-72, biennial 1973-1988).

[Extracts of selected reports on national human rights developments, texts of relevant decisions, and descriptions of human rights activities including the specialized agencies of the U.N.: Food and Agriculture Organization (FAO), ILO, UNESCO, and World Health Organization (WHO).]

U.N High Commissioner for Human Rights, Treaty Bodies Database, http://www.unhchr.ch/tbs/doc.nsf.

[Contains the full-text of States reports, concluding observations, decisions, views, etc. for major treaty bodies. Coverage and language varies.]

University of Minnesota Human Rights Library, Other Treaty-Based Committees, http://www1.umn.edu/humanrts/un-orgs.htm#cmte.

[Contains selected decisions, general comments, and other documents for major human rights instruments.]

§ 2.   ILO

INTERNATIONAL LABOUR OFFICE, FREEDOM OF ASSOCIATION: A WORKERS' EDUCATION MANUAL (2d rev. ed. 1987).

[Geneva: International Labour Office, 149 pp. Revises Freedom of Association: Digest of Decisions and Principles of the Freedom of Association Committee of the Governing Body of the ILO (1985).]

INTERNATIONAL LABOUR OFFICE, GENERAL REPORT OF THE COMMITTEE OF EXPERTS ON THE APPLICATION OF CONVENTIONS AND RECOMMENDATIONS (1936-).

[Geneva: International Labour Office. Published annually as Report III (Part 4A) Third item on the agenda: Information and reports on the application of Conventions and Recommendations. Provides observations on reports submitted by governments indicating their compliance with ILO conventions and recommendations.]

International Labour Organization, ILOLEX, Digest of Decisions of the Freedom of Association Committee, http://www.ilo.org/wcmsp5/groups/public/---ed_norm/---normes/documents/publication/wcms_090632.pdf.

[This digest contains decisions and principles covering most aspects of freedom of association and the protection of trade union rights.]

INTERNATIONAL LABOUR OFFICE, OFFICIAL BULLETIN (1919-).

[Geneva: International Labour Office. Published three times a year. Contains Committee on Freedom of Association Reports (cases and recommendations).]

International Labour Organization, TRIBLEX, http://www.ilo.org/dyn/triblex/triblex_browse.home.

[Thematic analysis of the case law of the ILO Administrative Tribunal, which hears complaints from serving and former officials of the ILO, or of one of the thirty-odd international organizations that recognize its jurisdiction, about breach of the terms of their appointment or staff rules or regulations. Available in French and English.]

§ 3.   Council of Europe and European Union

1 VINCENT BERGER, THE CASE LAW OF THE EUROPEAN COURT OF HUMAN RIGHTS: 1960-1987 (1989).

[Sarasota, FL: UNIFO Pub., 478 pp. Summarizes cases and includes brief bibliographies and notes on domestic changes influenced by the cases. Appendices include a bibliography, text of the European Convention on Human Rights, and ratification information.]

2 VINCENT BERGER, THE CASE LAW OF THE EUROPEAN COURT OF HUMAN RIGHTS: 1988-1990 (1992).

[Sarasota, FL: UNIFO Pub., 310 pp.]

3 VINCENT BERGER, THE CASE LAW OF THE EUROPEAN COURT OF HUMAN RIGHTS: 1990-1993 (1995).

[Dublin: Round Hall Press, 454 pp.]

BRITISH INSTITUTE OF HUMAN RIGHTS, HUMAN RIGHTS CASE DIGEST (1990-).

[London: Sweet & Maxwell (now published by Brill).]

COLLECTION OF RECOMMENDATIONS, RESOLUTIONS AND DECLARATIONS OF THE COMMITTEE OF MINISTERS CONCERNING HUMAN RIGHTS, 1949-87 (1989).

[Strasbourg: Council of Europe, 214 pp.]

COLLECTION OF RESOLUTIONS ADOPTED BY THE COMMITTEE OF MINISTERS IN APPLICATION OF ARTICLES 32 AND 54 OF THE EUROPEAN CONVENTION FOR THE PROTECTION OF HUMAN RIGHTS AND FUNDAMENTAL FREEDOMS, 1959-1983 (1984).

[Strasbourg: Council of Europe, 149 pp. Provides a list of resolutions under Article 32 (on pages 7-9) and a list of decisions under Article 54 (on page 10). Updated by supplements.]

COUNCIL OF EUROPE, YEARBOOK OF THE EUROPEAN CONVENTION ON HUMAN RIGHTS (1955/57-).

[The Hague: Martinus Nijhoff Pub. (vol. 1-). Part One provides texts of protocols to the European Convention, instruments, ratifications, reservations, procedures of the Commission and Court of Human Rights, and descriptions of related activities of the Council of Europe. Part Two contains texts of European Commission decisions, statistical charts, summaries of judgments of the Court, and related resolutions of the Committee of Ministers. Part Three covers measures implementing the convention by governments, the Council of Europe, and the European Communities.]

DIGEST OF STRASBOURG CASE-LAW RELATING TO THE EUROPEAN CONVENTION ON HUMAN RIGHTS (1984-).

[Koln: Carl Heymanns Verlag, 6 vols. Updated by volumes containing looseleaf supplements.]

CHRISTIANE DUPARC, THE EUROPEAN COMMUNITY AND HUMAN RIGHTS (1993).

[Luxembourg: Office for Official Publications of the European Communities, 61 pp. Provides a brief introduction to the European Community's efforts to protect human rights and discusses human rights provisions in the treaties establishing the European Communities, and human rights in the Community's external policy. An annex includes texts containing commitments made by the Community, and its Member States.]

ESSENTIAL HUMAN RIGHTS CASES (Susan Nash & Mark Furse eds., 2002).

[Bristol: Jordan Publishing Limited, 420 pp.]

EUROPEAN COMMISSION OF HUMAN RIGHTS, DECISIONS AND REPORTS=DECISIONS ET RAPPORTS (1975-).

[Strasbourg: European Commission of Human Rights. Continues COLLECTION OF DECISIONS WITH INDICES, but lags several years behind; 1994 volume covers 1989.]

EUROPEAN COMMISSION OF HUMAN RIGHTS, STOCK-TAKING ON THE EUROPEAN CONVENTION ON HUMAN RIGHTS: A PERIODIC NOTE ON THE CONCRETE RESULTS ACHIEVED UNDER THE CONVENTION: THE FIRST THIRTY YEARS: 1954 UNTIL 1984 (1984).

[Strasbourg: European Commission of Human Rights, 333 pp. Updated by yearly supplements through 1988. Briefly presents information on the procedures of the European Commission and Court of Human Rights and the Committee of Ministers, a summary of decisions of those bodies between 1954 and 1984 relating to construction of the European Human Rights Convention, statistics on the disposition of cases, and an index by principal Convention article with a listing of cases.]

EUROPEAN COURT OF HUMAN RIGHTS, PUBLICATIONS OF THE EUROPEAN COURT OF HUMAN RIGHTS=PUBLICATIONS DE LA COUR EUROPEENNE DES DROITS DE L'HOMME.

[Strasbourg: Council of Europe. Series A (1974-1996) contains the official texts of judgments and decisions of the European Court of Human Rights; each decision is numbered and separately published, but with no index. Series B (1965-) contains oral arguments, pleadings, and documents. The Yearbook of the European Convention on Human Rights, listed below, often includes summaries of decisions of the Court of Human Rights. A bi-monthly unofficial periodical,

European Law Review, also contains summaries of European Court of Human Rights decisions. The HUDOC database provides access to the jurisprudence of the European Convention on Human Rights, http://echr.coe.int/echr/en/hudoc.]

EUROPEAN COURT OF HUMAN RIGHTS, RECUEIL DES ARR···TS ET DÉCISIONS (1996-).

[Köln: Carl Heymanns Verlag, (no.1-). Continues PUBLICATIONS DE LA COUR EUROPÉENNE DES DROITS DE L'HOMME. SÉRIE A, ARR···TS ET DÉCISIONS. The HUDOC database provides access to the jurisprudence of the European Convention on Human Rights, http://echr.coe.int/echr/en/hudoc.]

EUROPEAN LAW CENTER, EUROPEAN HUMAN RIGHTS REPORTS [EHRR] (1979-) (unofficial).

[London: Sweet & Maxwell. Decisions of the European Court of Human Rights (1960-), selected decisions of the Commission of Human Rights, and resolutions of the Committee of Ministers. As of volume five, part 18, provides summaries and extracts of resolutions of the Committee of Ministers and decisions of the Commission with headnotes and cross-references to European Commission cases. Also includes decisions of the Inter-American Court of Human Rights (OAS). The Reports are available on LEXIS and WESTLAW.]

LEADING CASES OF THE EUROPEAN COURT OF HUMAN RIGHTS (Rick Lawson & Henry G. Schermers eds., 2d ed. 1999).

[Nijmegen: Ars Aequi Libri, 798 pp.]

REPORTS OF CASES BEFORE THE COURT OF JUSTICE AND THE COURT OF FIRST INSTANCE (1990-).

[Luxembourg: Court of Justice of the European Communities. From 1959 to 1989, published as Reports of Cases Before the Court. Available on LEXIS and on WESTLAW. Recent case law of the Court of Justice and the Court of First Instance is available on the Web, http://curia.europa.eu.]

STRASBOURG CASE LAW: LEADING CASES FROM THE EUROPEAN HUMAN RIGHTS REPORTS (Richard Gordon et al. ed., 2000).

[London: Sweet & Maxwell, 750 pp. A one-volume digest of key cases from the European Court of Human Rights, arranged by Convention article. Includes extracts from key judgments.]

A SYSTEMATIC GUIDE TO THE CASE-LAW OF THE EUROPEAN COURT OF HUMAN RIGHTS, 1960-2000 (Peter Kempees ed., 1996-2000).

[The Hague, Boston, Mass.: M. Nijhoff, 4 v. Designed to assist decision-makers at the national level and members of the legal profession.]

§ 4.   OAS

INTER-AMERICAN COMMISSION ON HUMAN RIGHTS, ANNUAL REPORT OF THE INTER-AMERICAN COMMISSION ON HUMAN RIGHTS (1975-).

[Washington, D.C.: General Secretariat, OAS. Covers activities of the Commission, resolutions on the cases decided by the Commission during the year, updates on human rights situations in several countries, and new instruments in the Inter-American human rights system (*e.g.*, OAS Doc. No. OEA/Ser.L/V/II.88 Doc. 9 rev. (1995), 344 pp.). The Annual Reports from 1979-1980 through the present are available on the Commission's Web site, http://www.cidh.oas.org/annual.eng.htm. Some of the earlier reports on the Web are only available in Spanish.]

HUMAN RIGHTS: THE INTER-AMERICAN SYSTEM (Thomas Buergenthal & Robert Norris eds., 1984-1993).

[Dobbs Ferry, NY: Oceana Publications, Inc., 6 vol. looseleaf.]

INTER-AMERICAN COMMISSION ON HUMAN RIGHTS, TEN YEARS OF ACTIVITIES, 1971-1981 (1982).

[Washington, D.C.: OAS, 403 pp. Collection of decisions and activities of the Inter-American Commission providing easy access to older jurisprudence of the Commission.]

INTER-AMERICAN COURT OF HUMAN RIGHTS, ANNUAL REPORT OF THE INTER-AMERICAN COURT OF HUMAN RIGHTS (1979-).

[Washington, D.C.: Inter-American Court of Human Rights (*e.g.*, OAS Doc. OEA/Ser.L/V/III.31 Doc. 9 (1994).) The Annual Reports from 1980 through the present are available on the Court's Web site, http://www.corteidh.or.cr/informes.cfm. Some of the earlier reports on the Web are only available in Spanish.]

INTER-AMERICAN COURT OF HUMAN RIGHTS, SERIES A: JUDGMENTS AND OPINIONS (1982-); SERIES B: PLEADINGS, ORAL ARGUMENTS AND DOCUMENTS (1983-); AND SERIES C: DECISIONS AND JUDGMENTS (1987-).

[San José, Costa Rica: Court Secretariat. Separate paperback pamphlets in English and Spanish. Selected jurisprudence is available on the Court's Web site, http://www.corteidh.or.cr/index.cfm (under "Jurisprudence".]

INTER-AMERICAN YEARBOOK ON HUMAN RIGHTS=ANUARIO INTER-AMERICANO DE DERECHOS HUMANOS (1968-).

[Washington, D.C.: General Secretariat, OAS (1968-84); Dordrecht; Boston: Martinus Nijhoff Pub. (1985-). Provides background information on the Inter-American system for the protection of human rights, bodies involved, and key instruments. Includes texts of instruments, status information, statutes, procedural rules, relevant resolutions, and discussion of human rights practices in selected OAS countries.]

INTERNATIONAL HUMAN RIGHTS REPORTS [IHRR] (1994-).

[Nottingham, U.K.: University of Nottingham (vol. 1- , no. 1- , 1994-), published three times a year. Covers judgments and opinions of the Inter-American Court of Human Rights.]

Richard J. Wilson, *Researching the Jurisprudence of the Inter-American Commission on Human Rights: A Litigator's Perspective; Inter-American Commission on Human Rights: Individual Case Resolutions*, 10 AM. U. J. INT'L L. & POL'Y 1-331 (1994).

[An introduction and comprehensive index to case reports of the Inter-American Commission on Human Rights.]

Center for Human Rights and Humanitarian Law, Washington College of Law, American University, Inter-American Human Rights Database, http://www.wcl.american.edu/humright/digest.

[Contains selected Annual Reports and Special Reports adopted by the Inter-American Commission, available in both English and Spanish. Good for older documents, but not up-to-date.]

University of Minnesota, Human Rights Library, Inter-American System, http://www1.umn.edu/humanrts/inter-americansystem.htm.

[Selected case law from the Court, http://www1.umn.edu/humanrts/iachr/iachr.html and Annual Reports from the Commission from 1991 to present, http://www1.umn.edu/humanrts/cases/commissn.htm.]

§ 5.   International Criminal Tribunals

ANNOTATED LEADING CASES OF INTERNATIONAL CRIMINAL TRIBUNALS (Andre Klip & Goran Sluiter eds., 1999-).

[Antwerpen; Oxford: Intersentia; Hart. Vol. 1 covers 1993-1998 (720 pp.) and includes the leading cases of the Tribunal's first five years. Decisions are reprinted with annotations by scholars in international criminal law.]

GLOBAL WAR CRIMES TRIBUNAL COLLECTION (1997-).

[Nijmegen, the Netherlands: Global Law Association; several volumes.]

International Criminal Court (ICC) Web site, http://www.icc-cpi.int.

INTERNATIONAL CRIMINAL TRIBUNAL FOR RWANDA, REPORTS OF ORDERS, DECISIONS AND JUDGEMENTS 1995-1997 (2000).

[Bruxelles: Bruylant, 834 pp.]

International Criminal Tribunal for Rwanda Web site, http://www.ictr.org.

[Provides information and documentation on the Court as well as the case law.]

INTERNATIONAL CRIMINAL TRIBUNAL FOR THE FORMER YUGOSLAVIA, JUDICIAL REPORTS= RECUEILS JUDICIAIRES (1999-).

[The Hague; Boston: Kluwer Law International, 2 v. Publishes all public indictments, as well as decisions and judgements issued in a given year.]

International Criminal Tribunal for the Former Yugoslavia, Annual Reports, http://www.un.org/icty/publications-e/index.htm.

[Summaries of significant decisions and judgments.]

International Criminal Tribunal for the Former Yugoslavia Web site, http://www.un.org/icty/index.html.

[Provides information and documents related to the Court as well as judgments and decisions.]

Web site of the Rome Statute of the International Criminal Court, http://www.un.org/law/icc/index.html.

[This Web site contains a good deal of the documentation establishing the Court, but is not updated after Dec. 19, 2003.]

§ 6. Other

Note: Researchers should also consult references in chapters 13 and 14 of the principal book for U.S. cases relating to international human rights.

AFRICAN HUMAN RIGHTS LAW REPORTS (2000-).

[Lansdowne, South Africa: Juta Law (vol. 1-). Selected decisions from African courts and of the African Commission on Human and Peoples' Rights, and of the United Nations treaty bodies, dealing with African countries.]

BUTTERWORTHS HUMAN RIGHTS CASES [BHRC] (1996-).

[London: Butterworths (vol. 1-). Provides the full-text of cases from a wide range of jurisdictions.]

COMMONWEALTH HUMAN RIGHTS LAW DIGEST (1996-).

[London: Interights (vol. 1-). Reports on human rights and related cases from national courts in Commonwealth jurisdictions. See also the Commonwealth Human Rights Case Law Database, which provides summaries of recent decisions from national courts in Commonwealth jurisdictions, http://www.interights.org/database-search/index.htm. Many of the cases are unpublished decisions which are not readily available in other jurisdictions.]

HUMAN RIGHTS LAW JOURNAL [HRLJ] (1980-).

[Kehl am Rhein [West Germany]; Arlington [Va.]: N.P. Engel (vol. 1-). Provides the full-text of decisions and reports from U.N. treaty bodies, Inter-American Commission and Court, the European Court of Human Rights, and other international courts and tribunals.]

INTERNATIONAL HUMAN RIGHTS REPORTS [IHRR] (1994-).

[Nottingham, U.K.: Human Rights Law Centre, Dept. of Law, University of Nottingham (vol. 1-). Contains materials from a variety of international human rights bodies: U.N., Council of Europe, Inter-American Commission, etc.]

INTERNATIONAL LAW REPORTS (1919/22-).

[London: Butterworths & Co. Vols. 1-16 published under the title Annual Digest and Reports of Public International Law Cases. Contains decisions of international law tribunals and municipal courts.]

INTERNATIONAL LEGAL MATERIALS [ILM] (1962-).

[Washington, D.C.: American Society of International Law (vol.1-). Reports significant decisions and instruments on many issues, including human rights, with annual indices; indexed by LEGALTRAC; and also available on LEXIS (1975-) and WESTLAW (1980-).]

INTERNATIONAL COURT OF JUSTICE, RECUEIL DE ARRETS, AVIS CONSULTATIFS ET ORDONNANCES = REPORTS OF JUDGMENTS, ADVISORY OPINIONS AND ORDERS (1947-).

[The Hague: International Court of Justice. Published in both French and English. Judgments are available on WESTLAW. See also the ICJ Web site, http://www.icj-cij.org.]

INTERNATIONAL COURT OF JUSTICE, YEARBOOK (1947-).

[The Hague: International Court of Justice. Contains summaries of judgments, advisory opinions, and orders of the court as well as summaries of the court's work and biographies of the judges.]

INTERIGHTS, International Law Reports, part of INTERIGHTS Bulletin, searchable at http://www.interights.org/database-search/index.htm.

[These reports highlight recent decisions of tribunals applying international human rights law. Copies of all decisions reported in this database are available from the organization.]

Netherlands Institute of Human Rights (SIM), Case Law Database, available from http://sim.law.uu.nl/SIM/Dochome.nsf?Open.

[Provides access to databases containing summaries of the case law of the Human Rights Committee, the Committee Against Torture, and the Committee on the Elimination of Racial Discrimination. There is also a database containing information on judgments of the European Court of Human Rights and the concluding comments of the United Nations treaty bodies. Coverage varies. Users must register to use the databases, but there is no fee for access.]

B.G. RAMCHARAN, THE PRINCIPLE OF LEGALITY IN INTERNATIONAL HUMAN RIGHTS INSTITUTIONS: SELECTED LEGAL OPINIONS (1997).

[The Hague, The Netherlands; Boston: Martinus Nijhoff, 393 pp.]

E. Rules of Procedure and Guidelines

Committee Against Torture, *General Guidelines Regarding the Form and Contents of Periodic Reports to Be Submitted by States Parties under Article 19, Paragraph 1*, U.N. Doc. CAT/C/14/Rev.1 (1998).

[Geneva: U.N., 2 pp. Revised as of 18 May 1998, http://www.unhchr.ch/tbs/doc.nsf/(Symbol)/CAT.C.14.Rev.1.En?OpenDocument.]

Committee Against Torture, *Rules of Procedure*, U.N. Doc. CAT/C/3/Rev.4 (2002).

[Geneva: U.N., 43 pp., http://www.unhchr.ch/tbs/doc.nsf/(Symbol)/CAT.C.3. Rev.4.En?OpenDocument.]

Committee on Economic, Social and Cultural Rights, *Revised General Guidelines Regarding the Form and Contents of Reports to be Submitted by*

States Parties Under Article 16 and 17 of the International Covenant on Economic, Social and Cultural Rights, U.N. Doc. E/C.12/1991/1 (1991).

[Geneva: U.N., 22 pp., http://www.unhchr.ch/tbs/doc.nsf/(Symbol)/903e9a1 332660f74c12563ef004ea4b0?Opendocument.]

Committee on Economic, Social and Cultural Rights, *Rules of Procedure of the Committee*, U.N. Doc. E/C.12/1990/4/Rev.1 (1993).

[Geneva: U.N., 16 pp., http://daccessdds.un.org/doc/UNDOC/GEN/G93/183/ 98/PDF/G9318398.pdf?OpenElement.]

Committee on the Elimination of Discrimination Against Women, *Revised Draft Rules of Procedure of the Committee on the Elimination of Discrimination Against Women*, U.N. Doc. CEDAW/C/2001/I/WG.1/WP.1 (2000).

[Geneva: U.N., 17 pp., http://www.un.org/womenwatch/daw/cedaw/states-meeting/rulesandprocedure/SP%20meeting%20-%20rules%20of%20proce-dure.pdf.]

Committee on the Elimination of Discrimination Against Women, *Guidelines for Preparation of Reports by States Parties*, U.N. Doc. HRI/GEN/2/ Rev.1/Add.2 (2003).

[Geneva: U.N., 7 pp., http://daccessdds.un.org/doc/UNDOC/GEN/G03/417/ 51/PDF/G0341751.pdf?OpenElement.]

Committee on the Elimination of Racial Discrimination, *General Guidelines Regarding the Form and Contents of Reports to Be Submitted by States Parties under Article 9, Paragraph 1, of the Convention*, U.N. Doc. CERD/C/70/Rev.5 (2000).

[Geneva: U.N., 10 pp., http://www.unhchr.ch/tbs/doc.nsf/(Symbol)/CERD. C.70.Rev.5.En?Opendocument.]

Committee on the Elimination of Racial Discrimination, *Rules of Procedure of the Committee on the Elimination of Racial Discrimination*, U.N. Doc. CERD/C/35/Rev.3 (1989).

[New York: U.N., 46 pp., http://www.unhchr.ch/tbs/doc.nsf/(Symbol)/cb35d cd69a1b52a3802564ed0054a104?Opendocument.]

Committee on the Rights of the Child, *General Guidelines Regarding the Form and Contents of Periodic Reports to Be Submitted by States Parties under Article 44 of the Convention*, U.N. Doc. C/CRC/58 (1996).

[Geneva: U.N., 49 pp., http://www2.ohchr.org/english/bodies/crc/index. htm, under "Reporting to the Committee".]

Committee on the Rights of the Child, *Provisional Rules of Procedure*, U.N. Doc. CRC/C/4/Rev.1 (2005).

[Geneva: U.N., 22 pp., http://www.unhchr.ch/tbs/doc.nsf/(Symbol)/CRC. C.4.Rev.1.En?OpenDocument.]

Economic and Social Council, *Rules of Procedure of the Economic and Social Council*, U.N. Doc. E/5975/Rev. 2 (1992).

[New York: U.N., 19 pp., http://www.un.org/docs/ecosoc/ECOSOC%20rules.pdf.]

European Commission of Human Rights, *Rules of Procedure*, as in force at 28 June 1993, http://www.hrcr.org/docs/Eur_Commission/commrules.html.

[As of 1999, the European Commission of Human Rights merged into the European Court of Human Rights; however, as of 2008 the rules are still on the Web.]

Executive Committee of the High Commissioner's Programme, *Rules of Procedure*, Thirty-seventh session, U.N. Doc. A/AC.96/187/Rev.3 (1986).

[Geneva: U.N., 24 pp.]

International Criminal Court, *Rules of Procedure and Evidence*, ICC-ASP/1/3 (2005).

[New York: U.N., 101 pp., http://www.icc-cpi.int/library/about/officialjournal/Rules_of_Proc_and_Evid_070704-EN.pdf.]

General Assembly, *Rules of Procedure of the General Assembly*, U.N. Doc. A/520/Rev.15 (1984).

[New York: U.N. 106 pp. Embodies amendments and additions adopted by the General Assembly up to 31 December 1984, http://www.un.org/ga/59/ga_rules.html.]

General Assembly Rules of Procedure (1985), U.N. Doc. A/520/Rev.15, http://www2.ohchr.org/english/bodies/hrcouncil/docs/gaA.520.Rev.15_En.pdf. [Human Rights Council rules of procedure.]

Amendments to the Annexes of the Rules of Procedure of the General Assembly (Aug. 21, 1991), U.N. Doc. A/520/Rev.15/Amend. 1.

Amendments to the Annexes of the Rules of Procedure of the General Assembly (Oct. 8, 1993), U.N. Doc. A/520/Rev.15/Amend. 2.

G.A. Res. 57/301, Amendment to Rule 1 of the Rules of Procedure of the General Assembly and Opening Date and Duration of the General Debate (Mar. 17, 2003).

Code of Conduct for Special Procedures Mandate-Holders of the Human Rights Council, Human Rights Council Res. 5/2, Annex, U.N. Doc. A/HRC/5/21, at 40 (Aug. 7, 2007).

Human Rights Council, Decision 6/102, Follow-up to Human Rights Council Resolution 5/1 (establishing "General Guidelines for the Preparation of Information under the Universal Periodic Review") (Sept. 27, 2007), http://ap.ohchr.org/documents/E/HRC/decisions/A_HRC_DEC_6_102.pdf.

Human Rights Council, Information and Guidelines for Relevant Stakeholders on the Universal Periodic Review Mechanism [as of July 2008], http://www.ohchr.org/EN/HRBodies/UPR/Documents/TechnicalGuideEN.pdf.

Human Rights Committee, *Consolidated Guidelines for State Reports under the International Covenant on Civil and Political Rights*, U.N. Doc.

CCPR/C/66/GUI/Rev. 2 (2001).[Geneva: U.N., 4 pp., http://www.unhchr.ch/tbs/doc.nsf/(Symbol)/CCPR.C.66.GUI.Rev.2.En?Opendocument.]

Human Rights Committee, *International Covenant on Civil and Political Rights, Rules of Procedure of the Human Rights Committee*, U.N. Doc. CCPR/C/3/Rev. 8 (2005).[Geneva: U.N., 27 pp., http://www.unhchr.ch/tbs/doc.nsf/(Symbol)/CCPR.C.3.Rev.8.En?Opendocument.]

International Criminal Tribunal for the Former Yugoslavia, Basic Documents, http://www.un.org/icty/legaldoc-e/index.htm.

[The Hague: International Tribunal for the Former Yugoslavia. Contains the Statute of the Tribunal, Rules of Procedure and Evidence, and other basic texts including Code of Professional Conduct, Directive on Assignment of Defence Counsel, Rules of Detention, Practice Directions, and several others.]

Rules of Procedure of the African Commission on Human and Peoples' Rights, 9 HUM. RTS L.J. 326 (1988).

International Criminal Tribunal for Rwanda, *Rules of Procedure and Evidence, entered into force* 29 June 1995, http://69.94.11.53/ENGLISH/rules/080314/080314.pdf.

[At the ICTR Web site, rules are under "Basic Legal Texts" and include amendments adopted through Mar. 14, 2008.]

International Labour Office, *Handbook of Procedures Relating to International Labour Conventions and Recommendations*, Doc. No. D.31.1965 (Rev.2006).

[Geneva: ILO, 77 pp., http://www.ilo.org/wcmsp5/groups/public/---ed_norm/---normes/documents/publication/wcms_087791.pdf.]

International Tribunal for the Prosecution of Persons Responsible for Serious Violations of International Humanitarian Law Committed in the Territory of the Former Yugoslavia Since 1991, *Rules of Procedure and Evidence*, U.N. Doc. IT/32 (1994), as amended, http://www.un.org/icty/legaldoc-e/basic/rpe/IT032Rev41eb.pdf (2008).

[New York: U.N. Latest revision is IT/32/REV.41, Feb. 28, 2008.]

Rules of Procedure of the African Commission on Human and Peoples' Rights, Adopted on Oct. 6, 1995, http://www.achpr.org/english/_info/rules_en.html.

Rules of Procedure of the Inter-American Commission on Human Rights (2006), http://www.cidh.org/Basicos/English/Basic18.Rules%20of%20Procedure%20of%20the%20Commission.htm.

Rules of Procedure of the Inter-American Court of Human Rights, approved Nov. 25, 2003, http://www.cidh.org/Basicos/English/Basic20.Rules%20of%20Procedure%20of%20the%20Court.htm.

F. Research Guides on Major Human Rights Instruments

§ 1.   International Covenant on Civil and Political Rights and Optional Protocols

International Covenant on Civil and Political Rights, G.A. res. 2200A (XXI), December 16, 1966, 21 U.N. GAOR Supp. (No.16) at 52, U.N. Doc. A/6316 (1966), 999 U.N.T.S. 171, *entered into force* March 23, 1976.

[For electronic version, see the OHCHR Web site, http://www.unhchr.ch/ html/menu3/b/a_ccpr.htm or the University of Minnesota Human Rights Library, http://www1.umn.edu/humanrts/instree/b3ccpr.htm.]

Optional Protocol to the International Covenant on Civil and Political Rights, G.A. res. 2200A (XXI), December 16, 1966, 21 U.N. GAOR Supp. (No. 16) at 59, U.N. Doc. A/6316 (1966), 999 U.N.T.S. 302, *entered into force* March 23, 1976.

[For electronic version, see the OHCHR Web site, http://www.unhchr.ch/ html/menu3/b/a_opt.htm or the University of Minnesota Human Rights Library, http://www1.umn.edu/humanrts/instree/b4ccprp1.htm.]

Second Optional Protocol to the International Covenant on Civil and Political Rights Aiming at the Abolition of the Death Penalty, G.A. res. 44/128, Annex, 44 U.N. GAOR Supp. (No. 49) at 207, U.N. Doc. A/44/49 (1989), *entered into force* July 11, 1991.

[For electronic version, see the OHCHR Web site, http://www.unhchr.ch/ html/menu3/b/a_opt2.htm or the University of Minnesota Human Rights Library, http://www1.umn.edu/humanrts/instree/b5ccprp2.htm.]

a.   Status

Office of the High Commissioner for Human Rights, Ratifications and Reservations, http://www2.ohchr.org/english/bodies/ratification/index.htm.

[Provides the most current status information for the main treaties and relevant protocols.]

U.N. CENTRE FOR HUMAN RIGHTS, HUMAN RIGHTS: STATUS OF INTERNATIONAL INSTRUMENTS, U.N. Doc. ST/HR/5, U.N. Sales No. E.87.XIV.2 (1987).

[New York: U.N., 336 pp. Lists 22 major U.N. human rights instruments and includes the ratification status, declarations, reservations, objections by States parties, and notes for each instrument. It is updated by Human Rights. International Instruments. *Chart of Ratifications as at 31 December 1997*, U.N. Doc. ST/HR/4/Rev.16, (New York: U.N., 11 pp.). This periodic update includes 25 major U.N. human rights instruments and indicates the status of the instruments for each state. Neither publication includes the full text of the treaties. This information is also available from the OHCHR Web site, http://www.ohchr.org/english/countries/ratification/index.htm. This database is updated more frequently than the print information.]

U. N., MULTILATERAL TREATIES DEPOSITED WITH THE SECRETARY-GENERAL: STATUS AS AT 31 DECEMBER 1999, U.N. Doc. ST/LEG/Ser.E/18 (Vol. I) and U.N. Doc. ST/LEG/Ser.E/18 (Vol. II), U.N. Sales No. E.00.V.2.

[New York: U.N., 703 pp. (Vol. I) and 485 pp. (Vol. II) (1982-). Published annually. Includes the texts of declarations and reservations made by States parties. Addresses U.N. and League of Nations treaties. This publication is also available on the Web by subscription, United Nations Treaty Collection, http://www.untreaty.un.org. The electronic version is updated more frequently than the print.]

b.   Reservations, Declarations, and Objections

Human Rights Committee, *Reservations, Declarations, Notifications and Objections Relating to the International Covenant on Civil and Political Rights and the Optional Protocol Thereto*, U.N. Doc. CCPR/C/2/Rev.4 (1994).

[139 pp., August 24, 1994. Lists the States that have signed, ratified, or acceded to the convention; provides the full text of the declarations, reservations, and objections; and provides notification of withdrawals of reservations, and objections to reservations and declarations. Declarations and Reservations are available on the Web, United Nations Treaty Collection, http://www.untreaty.un.org. See also the OHCHR Web site, http://www.ohchr.org/english/countries/ratification/4.htm, http://www.ohchr.org/english/countries/ratification/5.htm (Optional Protocol), and http://www.ohchr.org/english/countries/ratification/12.htm (Second Optional Protocol).]

c.   Status of Reports

International Human Rights Instruments, *Status of the International Human Rights Instruments and the General Situation of Overdue Reports*, U.N. Doc. HRI/MC/2000/2 (2000).

[7 pp., March 29, 2000. Information on the status of six instruments including the International Covenant on Civil and Political Rights; the International Covenant on Economic, Social and Cultural Rights; the International Convention on the Elimination of All Forms of Racial Discrimination; the Convention on the Elimination of All Forms of Discrimination Against Women; the Convention Against Torture and Other Cruel, Inhuman or Degrading Treatment; and the Convention on the Rights of the Child. Also includes the general situation of overdue reports. Updated information on reporting status from non-State parties and State parties is available from the OHCHR Web site, Treaty Bodies Database, http://www.unhchr.ch/tbs/doc.nsf.]

d.   Decisions, Jurisprudence, and Reports

i.   Comments

Human Rights Committee, *General Comments Adopted by the Human Rights Committee Under Article 40, Paragraph 4 of the International Covenant on Civil and Political Rights* (up to April 1989), U.N. Doc. CCPR/C/21/Rev.1 (1989) and CCPR/C/21/Rev.1/Add.1, 2, and 3.

[25 pp., May 19, 1989 (plus addenda). Compilation of comments by the Human Rights Committee to assist States parties in fulfilling their reporting obligations pursuant to the articles of the Covenant. Updated collection http://www.ohchr.org/english/bodies/hrc/comments.htm.]

International Human Rights Instruments, *Compilation of General Comments and General Recommendations Adopted by Human Rights Bodies*, U.N. Doc. HRI/GEN/1/Rev. 7 (2004).

[353 pp., May 12, 2004. Compilation of the general comments adopted by the various human rights body committees, http://www.unhchr.ch/tbs/doc.nsf/0/ca12c3a4ea8d6c53c1256d500056e56f?Opendocument.]

Human Rights Committee, *Consideration of Reports Submitted by States Parties under Article 40 of the Covenant*, U.N. Doc. CCPR/C/[#]/Add.[#] ([year]).

[Concluding observations of the Committee for each report submitted by States parties. The U.N. symbol will vary depending on the country (*e.g.*, for the United States: U.N. Doc. CCPR/C/79/Add.50 (1995)).]

U.N. High Commissioner for Human Rights, Treaty Bodies Database, http://www.unhchr.ch/tbs/doc.nsf.

[The treaty bodies database contains all documents issued since 1992 by the committees established to monitor the implementation of the principal international human rights treaties. The treaty bodies include the Human Rights Committee; the Committee on Economic, Social and Cultural Rights; the Committee Against Torture; the Committee on the Elimination of Racial Discrimination; the Committee on the Elimination of Discrimination against Women; and the Committee on the Rights of the Child.]

U.N. High Commissioner for Human Rights, Full-text of the Covenant with links to the General Comments by Article, http://www.unhchr.ch/html/menu3/b/a_ccpr.htm.

ii.   Decisions under First Optional Protocol
Human Rights Committee, *Selected Decisions Under the Optional Protocol (Second to Sixteenth Sessions)*, U.N. Doc. CCPR/C/OP/1 (1985).

[New York: U.N., 1985, 167 pp. Reprint of selected decisions and views. Includes an index by article of the Covenant and the Optional Protocol.]

Human Rights Committee, *Selected Decisions Under the Optional Protocol (Seventeenth to Thirty-Second Sessions)*, U.N. Doc. CCPR/C/OP/2 (1990).

[New York: U.N., 1990, 246 pp., second volume. Reprint of selected decisions and views. Includes an index by article of the Covenant, the Optional Protocol, author, and victim.]

Human Rights Committee, Selected Decisions of the Human Rights Committee under the Optional Protocol (Sixty-Sixth to Seventy-Fourth sessions), U.N. Doc. CCPR/C/OP/7 (2006).

[New York: U.N., 2006, 174 pp.]

Human Rights Committee, *Decisions*, U.N. Doc. CCPR/C/[#]/D/[#]/[year of submission] ([year]).

[Decisions are admissibility determinations of individual complaints (*e.g.*, Communication No. 525/1993, U.N. Doc. CCPR/C/53/D/525/1993)(1995)).]

Human Rights Committee, *Views*, U.N. Doc. CCPR/C/[#]/D/[#]/[year of submission] ([year]).

[Views are determinations by the Committee on the merits of individual complaints (*e.g.*, Communication No. 514/1992, U.N. Doc., CCPR/C/53/D/514/1992 (1995)).]

Human Rights Committee, *Report of the Human Rights Committee*, [session no.] U.N. GAOR Supp. (No. 40), U.N. Doc. A/[session no.]/40 ([year]).

[New York: U.N. Annual report of the Committee to the General Assembly. Decisions and views of the Human Rights Committee on cases submitted under the Optional Protocol to the Civil and Political Covenant. Also includes the general comments of the Committee on the meaning of various Covenant provisions and communications (*e.g.*, Report of the Human Rights Committee, 49 U.N. GAOR Supp. (No. 40), U.N. Doc. A/49/40 (1994)).]

Human Rights Committee, *Yearbook of the Human Rights Committee*, U.N. Doc. CCPR/6.

[New York: U.N., 1977- . Published in two volumes with about a seven-year time lag. Volume 1 contains summary records and volume II contains States' periodic reports and the annual report of the Committee.]

U.N High Commissioner for Human Rights, Treaty Bodies Database, http://www.unhchr.ch/tbs/doc.nsf.

[Contains the full text of States reports, concluding observations, decisions, views, etc. for six major treaty bodies. Coverage and language varies.]

University of Minnesota Human Rights Library, Other Treaty-Based Committees, http://www1.umn.edu/humanrts/un-orgs.htm#othertreatybased.

[Contains selected decisions, general comments, and other documents for major human rights instruments.]

e.   Legislative History ("Travaux Preparatoires")

MARC J. BOSSUYT, GUIDE TO THE "TRAVAUX PREPARATOIRES" OF THE INTERNATIONAL COVENANT ON CIVIL AND POLITICAL RIGHTS (1987).

[Dordrecht; Boston: Martinus Nijhoff Pub., 851 pp.].

f.   Rules of Procedure and Guidelines

Human Rights Committee, *International Covenant on Civil and Political Rights, Rules of Procedure of the Human Rights Committee*, U.N. Doc. CCPR/C/3/Rev. 8 (2005).

[Geneva: U.N., 27 pp., http://www.unhchr.ch/tbs/doc.nsf/(Symbol)/CCPR.C.3. Rev.8.En?Opendocument. Contains information on the Committee sessions; distribution of reports, and other official documents; the conduct of business; and functions of the Committee.]

Human Rights Committee, *Consolidated Guidelines for State reports under the International Covenant on Civil and Political Rights*, U.N. Doc. CCPR/C/66/GUI/Rev. 2 (2001).

[Geneva: U.N., 4 pp. Guidelines to be followed by States parties in preparation of the initial reports.]

g.   Commentaries

i.   Books

ACCESS TO JUSTICE AS A HUMAN RIGHT (Francesco Francioni ed., 2007).

[New York: Oxford Univ. Press, 244 pp. Analyzes present status of access to justice: its development in customary international law, the stress put on it in times of emergency, its problematic exercise in the case of violations of the law of war, its application to torture victims, its development in the case law of the U.N. Human Rights Committee and of the European Court of Human Rights, its application to the emerging field of environmental justice, and access to justice as part of fundamental rights in European law.]

JOHANN BAIR, THE INTERNATIONAL COVENANT ON CIVIL AND POLITICAL RIGHTS AND ITS (FIRST) OPTIONAL PROTOCOL: A SHORT COMMENTARY BASED ON VIEWS, GENERAL COMMENTS, AND CONCLUDING OBSERVATIONS BY THE HUMAN RIGHTS COMMITTEE (2006).

[Frankfurt am Main; New York: P. Lang, 212 pp.]

THE FUTURE OF UN HUMAN RIGHTS TREATY MONITORING (Henry J. Steiner, "Individual claims in a world of massive violations: What role for the Human Rights Committee?," chapter 2) (Philip Alston and James Crawford eds., 2000).

[Cambridge, U.K.; New York: Cambridge University Press, 563 pp.]

P.R. GHANDHI, THE HUMAN RIGHTS COMMITTEE AND THE RIGHT OF INDIVIDUAL COMMUNICATION: LAW AND PRACTICE (1998).

[Aldershot, Hants; Brookfield, Vt.: Ashgate, Dartmouth, 522 pp.]

THE INTERNATIONAL BILL OF RIGHTS: THE COVENANT ON CIVIL AND POLITICAL RIGHTS (Louis Henkin ed., 1981).

[New York: Columbia University Press, 523 pp.]

SARAH JOSEPH ET AL., THE INTERNATIONAL COVENANT ON CIVIL AND POLITICAL RIGHTS: CASES, MATERIALS, AND COMMENTARY (2d ed. 2004).

[New York: Oxford Univ. Press, 985 pp.]

LIESBETH LIJNZAAD, RESERVATIONS TO UN HUMAN RIGHTS TREATIES: RATIFY AND RUIN? (1995).

[Dordrecht; Boston: Martinus Nijhoff, 448 pp.]

DOMINIC MCGOLDRICK, THE HUMAN RIGHTS COMMITTEE: ITS ROLE IN THE DEVELOPMENT OF THE INTERNATIONAL COVENANT ON CIVIL AND POLITICAL RIGHTS (1994).

[Oxford: Clarendon; New York: Oxford Univ. Press, 576 pp.]

MANFRED NOWAK, U.N. COVENANT ON CIVIL AND POLITICAL RIGHTS: CCPR COMMENTARY (2d rev. ed. 2005).

[Kehl; Arlington, Va.: N.P. Engel, 1277 pp. Key commentary on the Civil and Political Covenant.]

THE UNITED NATIONS AND HUMAN RIGHTS: A CRITICAL APPRAISAL (Thomas Buergenthal, "The Human Rights Committee," chapter 9) (Philip Alston & Frederic Megret eds., 2d ed. 2002).

[Oxford: Clarendon, 600 pp.]

THE UN HUMAN RIGHTS TREATY SYSTEM IN THE 21ST CENTURY (Anne F. Bayefsky ed., 2000).

[The Hague: Kluwer Law International, 1116 pp. This volume compiles the papers presented at a conference held at York University, Canada, in 1997, "Enforcing International Human Rights Law: The Treaty System in the Twenty-First Century."]

DAVID WEISSBRODT, THE RIGHT TO A FAIR TRIAL UNDER THE UNIVERSAL DECLARATION OF HUMAN RIGHTS AND THE INTERNATIONAL COVENANT ON CIVIL AND POLITICAL RIGHTS: BACKGROUND, DEVELOPMENT, AND INTERPRETATIONS (2001).

[The Hague, Netherlands: Martinus Nijhoff, 167 pp.]

DAVID S. WEISSBRODT, THE HUMAN RIGHTS OF NON-CITIZENS (2008).

[Oxford; New York: Oxford Univ. Press, 257 pp. Comprehensive analysis of the rights of non-citizens, including asylum seekers, rejected asylum seekers, immigrants, non-immigrants, migrant workers, refugees, stateless persons, and trafficked persons.]

ii.   Articles

Elena A. Baylis, *General Comment 24: Confronting the Problem of Reservations to Human Rights Treaties,* 17 BERKELEY J. INT'L L. 277 (1999).

Thomas Buergenthal, *The Evolving International Human Rights System*, 100 AM. J. INT'L L. 783 (2006).

Andrew S. Butler, *Legal Aid Before Human Rights Treaty Monitoring Bodies,* 49 I.C.L.Q. 360 (2000).

Lee A. Bygrave, *Data Protection Pursuant to the Right to Privacy in Human Rights Treaties,* 6 INT'L. J.L. & INFO. TECH. 247 (1998).

Kristen D.A. Carpenter, *The International Covenant on Civil and Political Rights: A Toothless Tiger?*, 26 N.C. J. INT'L L. & COM. REG. 1 (2000).

Hilary Charlesworth, *The Human Rights Committee: Its Role in the Development of the International Covenant on Civil and Political Rights*, 13 AUSTL. Y.B. INT'L. L. 177 (1993).

Hilary Charlesworth, *The First Optional Protocol (to the International Covenant on Civil and Political Rights)*, 65 LAW INST. J. 1018 (1991).

J. S. Davison, *Intention and Effect: The Legal Status of the Final Views of the Human Rights Committee*, 2001 NEW ZEALAND L. REV. 125 (2001).

Douglas Donoho, *Human Rights Enforcement in the Twenty-first Century*, 35 GA. J. INT'L & COMP. L. 1 (2006).

Dana D. Fischer, *Reporting Under the Covenant on Civil and Political Rights: The First Five Years of the Human Rights Committee*, 76 AM. J. INT'L. L. 142 (1982).

P.R. Ghandhi, *The Human Rights Committee and Reservations to the Optional Protocol*, 8 CANTERBURY L. REV. 13 (2001).

Susan J. Gibb, *Communications Under the Optional Protocol; Not as Simple as They Look,* 34 LAW SOC'Y J. 62 (1996).

Shotaro Hamamoto, *An Undemocratic Guardian of Democracy - International Human Rights Complaint Procedures*, 28 U. WELLINGTON L. REV. 199 (2007).

Joanna Harrington, *The Absent Dialogue: Extradition and the International Covenant on Civil and Political Rights*, 32 QUEEN'S L.J. 82 (2006).

Rosalyn Higgins, *Admissibility under the Optional Protocol to the International Covenant on Civil and Political Rights,* 1991 CAN. HUM. RTS. Y.B. 57 (1991).

Sarah Joseph, *United Nations Human Rights Committee: Recent Cases,* 6 HUM. RTS. L. REV. 361 (2006).

Sarah Joseph, *United Nations Human Rights Committee: Recent Cases,* 5 HUM. RTS. L. REV. 105 (2005).

Sarah Joseph, *United Nations Human Rights Committee: Recent Cases,* 4 HUM. RTS. L. REV. 277 (2004).

Don MacKay, *The UN Covenants and the Human Rights Committee* (Special Issue: Anniversary of the Universal Declaration of Human Rights), 29 VICT. U. WELLINGTON L. REV. 11 (1999).

Michael Kearney, *The Prohibition of Propaganda for War in the International Covenant on Civil and Political Rights*, 23 NETH. Q. HUM. RTS. 551 (2005).

Konstantin Korkelia, *New Challenges to the Regime of Reservations under the International Covenant on Civil and Political Rights*, 13 EUR. J. INT'L L. 437 (2002).

Sutton Meagher, *When Personal Computers Are Transformed into Ballot Boxes: How Internet Elections in Estonia Comply with the United Nations*

International Covenant on Civil and Political Rights, 23 Am. U. Int'l L. Rev. 349 (2008).

Makau wa Mutua, *Looking Past the Human Rights Committee: An Argument for De-Marginalizing Enforcement,* 4 Buff. Hum. Rts. L. Rev. 211 (1998).

Ved P. Nanda, *The United States Reservation to the Ban on the Death Penalty for Juvenile Offenders: An Appraisal Under the International Covenant on Civil and Political Rights*, 42 DePaul L. Rev. 1311 (1993).

[Symposium: The Ratification of the International Covenant on Civil and Political Rights]

Aryeh Neier, *Political Consequences of the United States Ratification of the International Covenant on Civil and Political Rights*, 42 DePaul L. Rev. 1209 (1993).

[Symposium: The Ratification of the International Covenant on Civil and Political Rights]

Frank C. Newman, *United Nations Human Rights Covenants and the United States Government: Diluted Promises, Foreseeable Futures*, 42 DePaul L. Rev. 1241 (1993).

[Symposium: The Ratification of the International Covenant on Civil and Political Rights]

Michael O'Flaherty, *The Reporting Obligations Under Article 40 of the International Covenant on Civil and Political Rights: Lessons to be Learned from Consideration by the Human Rights Committee of Ireland's First Report,* 16 Hum. Rts. Q. 515 (1994).

Clementine Olivier, *Revisiting General Comment No.29 of the United Nations Human Rights Committee: About Fair Trial Rights and Derogations in Times of Public Emergency*, 17 Leiden J. Int'l L. 405 (2004).

Torkel Opsahl, *The Coexistence Between Geneva and Strasbourg Inter-Relationship of the International Covenant on Civil and Political Rights and the European Convention on Human Rights and Their Respective Organs of Implementation*, 1991 Can. Hum. Rts. Y.B. 151 (1991).

Monica Pinto, *Fragmentation or Unification among International Institutions: Human Rights Tribunals,* 31 N.Y.U. J. Int'l L. & Pol. 833 (1999).

Michael H. Posner & Peter J. Spiro, *Adding Teeth to United States Ratification of the Covenant on Civil and Political Rights: The International Human Rights Conformity Act of 1993*, 42 DePaul L. Rev. 1209 (1993).

[Symposium: The Ratification of the International Covenant on Civil and Political Rights]

John Quigley, *The International Covenant on Civil and Political Rights and the Supremacy Clause,* 42 DePaul L. Rev. 1287 (1993).

[Symposium: The Ratification of the International Covenant on Civil and Political Rights]

John Quigley, *Criminal Law and Human Rights: Implications of the United States Ratification of the International Covenant on Civil and Political Rights*, 6 HARV. HUM. RTS. J. 59 (1993).

Catherine J. Redgwell, *Reservations to Treaties and Human Rights Committee General Comment No. 24(52),* 46 INT'L & COMP. L. Q. (1997).

Markus G. Schmidt, *The U.N. Human Rights Committee: Process and Progress*, 5 HUM. RTS. F. 31 (1995).

Markus G. Schmidt, *Universality of Human Rights and the Death Penalty-The Approach of the Human Rights Committee,* 3 ILSA J. INT'L & COMP. L. 477 (1997).

David P. Stewart, *United States Ratification of the Covenant on Civil and Political Rights: The Significance of the Reservations, Understandings, and Declarations*, 42 DEPAUL L. REV. 1183 (1993).

[Symposium: The Ratification of the International Covenant on Civil and Political Rights]

Nadine Strossen, *United States Ratification of the International Bill of Rights: A Fitting Celebration of the Bicentennial of the U.S. Bill of Rights*, 24 U. TOL. L. REV. 203 (1992).

Alfred M. de Zayas, *The Follow-Up Procedure of the UN Human Rights Committee*, 1991 INT'L. COMMISSION JURISTS REV. 28 (1991).

David Weissbrodt, *United States Ratification of the Human Rights Covenants*, 63 MINN. L. REV. 35 (1978).

h.   Practice Guides

Australian Human Rights Centre, *A Guide to the Optional Protocol to the International Covenant on Civil and Political Rights*, http://www.austlii.edu.au/au/other/ahric/booklet/index.html.

INEKE BOEREFIJN, THE REPORTING PROCEDURE UNDER THE COVENANT ON CIVIL AND POLITICAL RIGHTS: PRACTICE AND PROCEDURES OF THE HUMAN RIGHTS COMMITTEE (1999).

[Antwerpen: Intersentia; Oxford: Hart Pub., 417 pp.]

P.R. GHANDHI, THE HUMAN RIGHTS COMMITTEE AND THE RIGHT OF INDIVIDUAL COMMUNICATION: LAW AND PRACTICE (1998).

[Aldershot, Hants; Brookfield, Vt: Ashgate, Dartmouth, 522 pp.]

ANETTE FAYE JACOBSEN, HUMAN RIGHTS MONITORING: A FIELD MISSION MANUAL (2008).

[Leiden; Boston: Martinus Nijhoff Publishers, 628 pp. Covers basic monitoring techniques for a full range of human rights issues.]

LAWYERS COMMITTEE FOR HUMAN RIGHTS, THE HUMAN RIGHTS COMMITTEE: A GUIDE FOR NGOS (1997).

[New York: Lawyers Committee for Human Rights, 19 pp.]

U.N. CENTRE FOR HUMAN RIGHTS, UNITED NATIONS ACTION IN THE FIELD OF HUMAN RIGHTS, U.N. Doc. ST/HR/2/Rev.4 at 25, 45, 69, and 314; U.N. Sales No. E.94.XIV.11 (1994).

[New York: U.N., 417 pp.]

U.N. Centre for Human Rights, *Civil and Political Rights: The Human Rights Committee* (1991).

[Geneva; New York: Centre for Human Rights, 36 pp ., Human Rights Fact Sheet No. 15.]

UNITED NATIONS INSTITUTE FOR TRAINING AND RESEARCH, MANUAL ON HUMAN RIGHTS REPORTING: UNDER SIX MAJOR INTERNATIONAL HUMAN RIGHTS INSTRUMENTS (1997).

[Geneva: United Nations, 537 pp.]

LEO ZWAAK, INTERNATIONAL HUMAN RIGHTS PROCEDURES: PETITIONING THE ECHR, CCPR AND CERD (1991).

[Nijmegan; Netherlands: Ars Aequi Libri, 168 pp.]

i.   Materials Available Through Electronic Formats

i.   Specific Web Sites

Office of the High Commissioner for Human Rights, http://www.ohchr. org/english.

Provides the text of many human rights treaties, including major human rights instruments. The Treaty Bodies Database, http://www.unhchr.ch/tbs/doc.nsf, includes the primary documents issued by and to the monitoring committees. Coverage and dates vary by committee. Access is available by type of document, by reporting status, and by status of ratification for each of the major instruments.

U.N. High Commissioner for Human Rights, Human Rights Committee, http://www.ohchr.org/english/bodies/hrc/index.htm.

Provides information about the Human Rights Committee, sessions, individual complaints, and official records.

University of Minnesota Human Rights Library, Human Rights Committee, http://www1.umn.edu/humanrts/hrcommittee/hrc-page.html.

This page of the Library is focused on the Human Rights Committee. It contains the text of the instruments, links to ratification information, case law, and other documents.

ii.   General Human Rights Web Sites

Amnesty International, http://www.amnesty.org.This official Internet site for AI contains the most up-to-date information: alerts, new documents, publications from AI (including the annual country reports), and links to other sites.

Annual Review of Population Law, http://annualreview.law.harvard.edu/ annual_review.htm.This database contains summaries and excerpts of legislation, constitutions, court decisions, and other official government documents from every country in the world relating to population policies, reproductive health, women's rights, and related topics.

ASIL Guide to Electronic Resources for International Law, Human Rights,http://www.asil.org/resource/humrts1.htm.This guide contains many links to human rights Web sites, along with site descriptions. It also includes information on approaches to human rights research on the web.

Council of Europe, Human Rights Web,http://www.coe.int/T/E/Human_ rights.This site contains an information bulletin and articles, as well as a case law search engine and links to the European Court of Human Rights and the Directorate General of Human Rights.

Derechos - Human Rights, http://www.derechos.org.This Web site offers a variety of human rights information including reports on human rights violations, actions, links and documents. Information is organized by country and by issue; an index and a search engine allow for easy finding of materials.

Human Rights First [formerly Lawyers Committee for Human Rights], http://www.humanrightsfirst.org/index.asp.The Web site of the nongovernmental organization contains information about the work of the organization, its publications, and breaking news.

Human Rights Internet, http://www.hri.ca.Human Rights Internet is an international network of human rights organizations, documentation centre, and publishing house. This site contains a lot of everything including U.N. documents, education materials, resource guides, and lists of links.

Netherlands Institute of Human Rights (SIM), Human Rights Treaties, http://www.uu.nl/uupublish/homerechtsgeleer/onderzoek/onderzoekscholen/ sim/english/18199main.html.

SIM's Web site provides the text of many important human rights instruments and documents, a case law database, and other information.

Research/Evaluation (UNHCR) [formerly REFWORLD], http://www. unhcr.org/research/3ebf8ef14.html.Contains authoritative information on refugees, including current country reports, legal and policy-related documents and literature. Organizes information under "Country of Origin and Legal Information" and "Evaluation and Policy Analysis."

University of Minnesota Human Rights Library, http://www1.umn.edu/ humanrts.Provides the full text of the International Covenant on Civil and Political Rights as well as other international instruments, links to related Internet sites, general comments of the Human Rights Committee, views and decisions of the Committee, and other human rights information. See also the large collection of links to other human rights and related sites, http://www1. umn.edu/humanrts/links/links.htm.

U.N. Treaty Collection, http://untreaty.un.org.

The U.N. Treaty Collection is a fee-based service consisting of two major sections: (1) *The Multilateral Treaties Deposited with the Secretary-General* which contains the detailed status of over 470 multilateral treaties deposited with the Secretary-General, and (2) UNITED NATIONS TREATY SERIES which consists of over 40,000 treaties registered with the Secretariat.

iii.   General Human Rights Discussion Lists and Blogs

HR-Headlines, http://www.hrea.org/lists/hr-headlines/markup/maillist.php.

Human Rights Watch Electronic Discussion lists, http://www.hrw.org/act/subscribe-mlists/subscribe.htm.

Amnesty International's Urgent Action blog, http://blogs.amnestyusa.org/urgentaction.

Derechos Human Rights, The Human Rights Blog, http://www.human-rightsblog.org.

§ 2.   International Covenant on Economic, Social and Cultural Rights

International Covenant on Economic, Social and Cultural Rights, G.A. res. 2200A (XXI), 21 U.N. GAOR Supp. (No. 16) at 49, U.N. Doc. A/6316 (1966), 993 U.N.T.S. 3, *entered into force* Jan. 3, 1976.

[For electronic version, see the OHCHR Web site, http://www.unhchr.ch/html/menu3/b/a_cescr.htm or the University of Minnesota Human Rights Library, http://www1.umn.edu/humanrts/instree/b2esc.htm.]

a.   Status

See U.N. High Commissioner for Human Rights, http://www.ohchr.org/english/countries/ratification/3.htm.

b.   Reservations, Declarations, and Objections

Committee on Economic, Social and Cultural Rights, *Status of the International Covenant on Economic, Social and Cultural Rights and Reservations, Withdrawals, Declarations and Objections Under the Covenant,* U.N. Doc. E/C.12/1993/3/Rev.4 (1999).

[35 pp., Aug. 5, 1999. Lists the states that have signed, ratified, or acceded to the convention; provides the full text of the declarations, reservations, and objections; and provides notification of withdrawals of reservations, and objections to reservations and declarations. Declarations and Reservations are available on the Web, United Nations Treaty Collection, http://www.untreaty.un.org. Updated information at the OHCHR Web site, http://www.ohchr.org/english/countries/ratification/3.htm.]

c.   Status of Reports

See the International Covenant on Civil and Political Rights, section c.

d.   Decisions, Jurisprudence, and Reports

Committee on Economic, Social and Cultural Rights, *Report of the Committee on Economic, Social and Cultural Rights*, U.N. Doc. E/[year]/[#] and E/C.12/[year]/[#] ([year]).

[New York: U.N. Contains draft decisions recommended for adoption, submission, and consideration of reports by States parties, and several annexes (*e.g.*, Report of the Committee on Economic, Social and Cultural Rights, U.N. Doc. E/1994/23 and E/C.12/1993/19 (1994)).]

International Human Rights Instruments, *Compilation of General Comments and General Recommendations Adopted by Human Rights Bodies*, U.N. Doc. HRI/GEN/1/Rev. 7 (2004).

[353 pp., May 12, 2004. Compilation of the general comments adopted by the various human rights body committees, http://www.unhchr.ch/tbs/doc.nsf/0/ca12c3a4ea8d6c53c1256d500056e56f?Opendocument.]

Committee on Economic, Social and Cultural Rights, *Consideration of Reports Submitted by the States Parties Under Articles 16 and 17 of the Covenant*, U.N. Doc. E/C.12/[year]/[#] ([year]).

[Concluding observations of the Committee for each report submitted by the States parties. The U.N. symbol will vary depending on the country (*e.g.*, for Uruguay: U.N. Doc. E/C.12/1994/3 (1994)).]

U.N. High Commissioner for Human Rights, Treaty Bodies Database, http://www.unhchr.ch/tbs/doc.nsf.

[Contains the full text of States reports, concluding observations, decisions, views, etc. for the major treaty bodies. Coverage and language vary.]

University of Minnesota Human Rights Library, Other Treaty-Based Committees, http://www1.umn.edu/humanrts/un-orgs.htm#othertreatybased.

[Contains selected decisions, general comments, and other documents for the major human rights instruments.]

e.   Rules of Procedure and Guidelines

Committee on Economic, Social and Cultural Rights, *Revised General Guidelines Regarding the Form and Contents of Reports to be Submitted by States Parties Under Article 16 and 17 of the International Covenant on Economic, Social and Cultural Rights*, U.N. Doc. E/C.12/1991/1 (1991).

[Geneva: U.N., 22 pp., http://www.unhchr.ch/tbs/doc.nsf/(Symbol)/E.C.12.1991.1.En?Opendocument.]

Committee on Economic, Social and Cultural Rights, *Rules of Procedure of the Committee*, U.N. Doc. E/C.12/1990/4/Rev.1 (1994).

[Geneva: U.N., 16 pp., http://daccessdds.un.org/doc/UNDOC/GEN/G93/183/98/PDF/G9318398.pdf?OpenElement.]

Committee on Economic, Social and Cultural Rights, *Outline for Drafting General Comments on Specific Rights of the ICESC*, http://www.unhchr.ch/html/menu2/6/cescrnote.htm#outline.

f.   Commentaries

i.   Books

PHILIP ALSTON, MAKING AND BREAKING HUMAN RIGHTS: THE UN'S SPECIALIZED AGENCIES AND IMPLEMENTATION OF THE INTERNATIONAL COVENANT ON ECONOMIC, SOCIAL AND CULTURAL RIGHTS (1979).

[London: Anti-Slavery Society; La Crosse, Wis: National Association of Interdisciplinary Ethnic Studies, 44 pp.]

KITTY ARAMBULO, STRENGTHENING THE SUPERVISION OF THE INTERNATIONAL COVENANT ON ECONOMIC, SOCIAL AND CULTURAL RIGHTS: THEORETICAL AND PROCEDURAL ASPECTS (1999).

[Antwerpen: Intersentia/Hart, 449 pp.]

GINA BEKKER, A COMPILATION OF ESSENTIAL DOCUMENTS ON ECONOMIC, SOCIAL AND CULTURAL RIGHTS (1999).

[Pretoria: Center for Human Rights, University of Pretoria, 160 pp.]

THE COMMITTEE ON ECONOMIC, SOCIAL AND CULTURAL RIGHTS (1996).

[Geneva, Switzerland; New York, New York: Centre for Human Rights, United Nations, 54 pp.]

MATTHEW C.R. CRAVEN, THE INTERNATIONAL COVENANT ON ECONOMIC, SOCIAL, AND CULTURAL RIGHTS: A PERSPECTIVE ON ITS DEVELOPMENT (1998).

[Oxford: Clarendon Press; NY: Oxford Univ. Press, 413 pp. Reprint, with corrections and new introduction. Originally published in 1995.]

CULTURAL HUMAN RIGHTS (Francesco Francioni & Martin Scheinin eds., 2008).

[Leiden ; Boston: Martinus Nijhoff Publishers, 372 pp. Explores the meaning of cultural human rights in international law.]

DEVELOPMENT AS A HUMAN RIGHT: LEGAL, POLITICAL, AND ECONOMIC DIMENSIONS (Bård-Anders Andreassen & Stephen P. Marks eds., 2006).

[Boston: Harvard School of Public Health, François-Xavier Bagnoud Center for Health and Human Rights, 318 pp.]

MARY DOWELL-JONES, CONTEXTUALISING THE INTERNATIONAL COVENANT ON ECONOMIC, SOCIAL AND CULTURAL RIGHTS: ASSESSING THE ECONOMIC DEFICIT (2004).

[Leiden; Boston: Martinus Nijhoff Publishers, 214 pp.]

ECONOMIC AND SOCIAL RIGHTS AND THE RIGHTS TO HEALTH: AN INTERDISCIPLINARY DISCUSSION HELD AT HARVARD LAW SCHOOL IN SEPTEMBER, 1993 (1995).

[Cambridge, MA: Harvard Law School Human Rights Program, 56 pp.]

ECONOMIC, SOCIAL, AND CULTURAL RIGHTS: A TEXTBOOK (Asbjørn Eide et al. eds., 2d rev. ed. 2001).

[Dordrecht; Boston: Martinus Nijhoff Pub., 506 pp. Contains bibliography, table of treaties, and subject index.]

THE FUTURE OF UN HUMAN RIGHTS TREATY MONITORING (Scott Leckie, "The Committee on Economic, Social and Cultural Rights: Catalyst for change in a system needing reform," chapter 6) (Philip Alston and James Crawford eds., 2000).

[Cambridge, U.K.; New York: Cambridge University Press, 563 pp.]

GUIDE TO INTERPRETATION OF THE INTERNATIONAL COVENANT ON ECONOMIC, SOCIAL, AND CULTURAL RIGHTS (Louis B. Sohn ed., 1993).

[Irvington, NY: Transnational, 2 vols.]

HEALTH AND HUMAN RIGHTS (Rebecca J. Cook & Charles G. Ngwena eds., 2007).

[Aldershot; Hants.; Burlington, VT: Ashgate, 605 pp. Includes essays on how courts have applied rights to improve access to health services.]

HEALTH AND HUMAN RIGHTS: A READER (Jonathan M. Mann et al. eds., 1999).

[New York: Routledge, 505 pp.]

SHAREEN HERTEL & LANSE MINKLER, ECONOMIC RIGHTS: CONCEPTUAL, MEASUREMENT, AND POLICY ISSUES (2007).

[Cambridge; New York: Cambridge University Press, 420 pp. Explains how economic rights evolved historically, how they are measured, and how they can be implemented internationally.]

HUMAN DEVELOPMENT REPORT (1990-).

[New York: Oxford Univ. Press, annual. Ten years of the report are available on CD-ROM (1990-2000). Some of the reports are also available on the UNDP Web site, http://www.undp.org/hdro.]

PAUL HUNT, RECLAIMING SOCIAL RIGHTS: INTERNATIONAL AND COMPARATIVE PERSPECTIVES (1996).

[Aldershot, Hants; Brookfield, VT: Dartmouth, 313 pp.]

GEORGE KENT, FREEDOM FROM WANT: THE HUMAN RIGHT TO ADEQUATE FOOD (2005).

[Washington, D.C.: Georgetown University Press, 271 pp.]

SCOTT LECKIE, TOWARDS AN INTERNATIONAL CONVENTION ON HOUSING RIGHTS: OPTIONS AT HABITAT II (1994).

[Washington, DC: American Society of International Law, 112 pp.]

SCOTT LECKIE, WHEN PUSH COMES TO SHOVE: FORCED EVICTIONS AND HUMAN RIGHTS (1995).

[Mexico; Utrecht, Netherlands: Habitat International Coalition, 139 pp.]

STEPHEN P. MARKS, THE RIGHT TO HEALTH IN COMPARATIVE PERSPECTIVE (2008).

[Cambridge, Mass.: Harvard School of Public Health, 215 pp. Comparative law approach to implementation of right to health.]

IAN MARTIN, THE NEW WORLD ORDER: OPPORTUNITY OR THREAT FOR HUMAN RIGHTS (1993).

[Cambridge, MA: Harvard Law School Human Rights Program, 24 pp.]

ROBERT MCCORQUODALE & MASHOOD A. BADERIN, ECONOMIC, SOCIAL AND CULTURAL RIGHTS IN ACTION (2006).

[Oxford: Oxford Univ. Press, 528 pp. Examines concepts and application of economic, social and cultural rights.]

GLENN A. MOWER, INTERNATIONAL COOPERATION FOR SOCIAL JUSTICE: GLOBAL AND REGIONAL PROTECTION OF ECONOMIC/SOCIAL RIGHTS (1985).

[Westport, Conn: Greenwood Pr., 271 pp.]

EIBE H. RIEDEL, SOCIAL SECURITY AS A HUMAN RIGHT: DRAFTING A GENERAL COMMENT ON ARTICLE 9 ICESCR-SOME CHALLENGES (2007).

[Berlin; New York: Springer, 187 pp. Describes implementation issues in realizing social security as a human right.]

THE RIGHT TO FOOD (Philip Alston et al. eds., 1984).

[Boston: Martinus Nijhoff Pub.; SIM Netherlands Institute of Human Rights, 228 pp.]

BERNARD ROBERTSON, ECONOMIC, SOCIAL AND CULTURAL RIGHTS: TIME FOR A REAPPRAISAL: A STUDY (1997).

[Wellington, New Zealand: The Roundtable, 65 pp.]

M. MAGDALENA SEPÚLVEDA, THE NATURE OF THE OBLIGATIONS UNDER THE INTERNATIONAL COVENANT ON ECONOMIC, SOCIAL AND CULTURAL RIGHTS (2003).

[Antwerpen; New York: Intersentia, 477 pp.].

LOUIS B. SOHN, THE HUMAN RIGHTS MOVEMENT: FROM ROOSEVELT'S FOUR FREEDOMS TO THE INTERDEPENDENCE OF PEACE, DEVELOPMENT AND HUMAN RIGHTS (1995).

[Cambridge, MA: Harvard Law School Human Rights Program, 31 pp.]

ELSA STAMATOPOULOU, CULTURAL RIGHTS IN INTERNATIONAL LAW: ARTICLE 27 OF THE UNIVERSAL DECLARATION OF HUMAN RIGHTS AND BEYOND (2007).

[Leiden; Boston: Martinus Nijhoff, 333 pp. Defines and explores concepts of cultural rights under the ICESCR and other instruments.]

LISA STEARNS, DOMESTIC IMPLEMENTATION OF OBLIGATIONS UNDER THE U.N. COVENANT ON ECONOMIC, SOCIAL AND CULTURAL RIGHTS: A JOINT SEMINAR BETWEEN

THE NORWEGIAN INSTITUTE FOR HUMAN RIGHTS AND THE CHINESE ACADEMY OF SOCIAL SCIENCES, OSLO, 11-13 NOVEMBER 1997 (1999).

[Oslo, Norway: Norwegian Institute of Human Rights, 183 pp.]

THE UNITED NATIONS AND HUMAN RIGHTS: A CRITICAL APPRAISAL (Philip Alston, "Committee on Economic, Social and Cultural Rights," chapter 11) (Philip Alston 2d ed., 2002).

[Oxford: Clarendon Press, 600 pp.]

U.N. CENTRE FOR HUMAN RIGHTS, RIGHT TO ADEQUATE FOOD AS A HUMAN RIGHT (1989).

[New York: United Nations, 73 pp., HUMAN RIGHTS STUDY SERIES No. 1, U.N. Sales No. E.89.XIV.2.]

DAVID S. WEISSBRODT, THE HUMAN RIGHTS OF NON-CITIZENS (2008).

[Oxford; New York: Oxford Univ. Press, 257 pp. Comprehensive analysis of the rights of non-citizens, including asylum seekers, rejected asylum seekers, immigrants, non-immigrants, migrant workers, refugees, stateless persons, and trafficked persons.]

ii.   Articles and Documents

Philip Alston and Gerard Quinn, *The Nature and Scope of States Parties' Obligations under the International Covenant on Economic, Social and Cultural Rights*, 9 HUM. RTS. Q. 156 (1987).

Philip Alston, *The United Nations' Specialized Agencies and Implementation of the International Covenant on Economic, Social and Cultural Rights*, 18 COL. J. TRANS. L. 79 (1979).

Philip Alston, *U.S. Ratification of the Covenant on Economic, Social and Cultural Rights: The Need for an Entirely New Strategy*, 84 AM. J. INT'L. L. 365 (1990).

Robert L. Bard, *The Right to Food*, 70 IOWA L. REV. 1279 (1985).

[Symposium: International Law and World Hunger]

Sherri Burr, *Health, Human Rights and International Law*, 82 AM. SOC'Y INT'L L. PROC. 122 (1988).

Audrey R. Chapman, *Monitoring Women's Right to Health under the International Covenant on Economic, Social and Cultural Rights*, 44 AM. L. REV. 1157 (1995).

Katherine E. Cox, *Should Amnesty International Expand its Mandate to Cover Economic, Social, and Cultural Rights?*, 16 ARIZ. J. INT'L & COMP. L. 261 (1999).

Asbjørn Eide, *Realization of Social and Economic Rights and the Minimum Threshold Approach*, 10 HUM. RTS. L.J. 35 (1989).

Emilie Filmer-Wilson, *The Human Rights-Based Approach to Development: The Right to Water*, 23 NETH. Q. HUM. RTS. 213 (2005).

Manouchehr Ganji, Special Rapporteur of the Commission on Human Rights, *The Realization of Economic, Social and Cultural Rights: Problems, Policies, Progress*, U.N. Doc. E/CN.4/1131/Rev.1 (1975).

Krysti Justine Guest, *Exploitation under Erasure: Economic, Social and Cultural Rights Engage Economic Globalisation*, 19 ADEL. L REV 73 (1997).

Wenonah Hauter, *The Limits of International Human Rights Law and the Role of Food Sovereignty in Protecting People from Further Trade Liberalization under the Doha Round Negotiations*, 40 VAND. J. TRANSNAT'L. L. 1071 (2007).

Noel A. Kinsella, *Can Canada Afford a Charter of Social and Economic Rights? Toward a Canadian Social Charter*, 71 SASKATCHEWAN L. REV. 7 (2008).

Scott Leckie, *An Overview and Appraisal of the Fifth Session of the UN Committee on Economic, Social and Cultural Rights*, 13 HUM. RTS. Q. 545 (1991).

Limburg Principles on the Implementation of the International Covenant of Economic, Social and Cultural Rights, 9 HUM. RTS. Q. 122 (1987).

[Symposium: The Implementation of the International Covenant on Economic, Social and Cultural Rights]

Beth Lyon, *Discourse in Development: A Post-Colonial "Agenda" for the United Nations Committee on Economic, Social and Cultural Rights through the Post-Colonial Lens*, 10 AM. U. J. GENDER SOC. POL'Y & L. 535 (2002).

Dennis McElwee, *Human Rights and Access to Health Care: Comparison of Domestic and International Law and Systems Implications for New Medical Technologies in Time of Crisis*, 20 DEV. J. INT'L. L. & POL'Y 167 (1991).

Benjamin Mason Meier, *Employing Health Rights for Global Justice: The Promise of Public Health in Response to the Insalubrious Ramifications of Globalization*, 39 CORNELL INT'L L.J. 711 (2006).

Jacqueline Mowbray, *The Right to Food and the International Economic System: An Assessment of the Rights-Based Approach to the Problem of World Hunger*, 20 LEIDEN J. INT'L L. 545 (2007).

Winston P. Nagan, *The Politics of Ratification: The Potential for United States Adoption and Enforcement of the Convention against Torture, the Covenants on Civil and Political Rights and Economic, Social and Cultural Rights*, 20 GA. J. INT'L. & COMP. L. 311 (1990).

Smita Narula, *The Right to Food: Holding Global Actors Accountable under International Law*, 44 COLUM. J. TRANSNAT'L L. 691 (2006).

Laura Niada, *Hunger and International Law: The Far-Reaching Scope of the Human Right to Food*, 22 CONN. J. INT'L L. 131 (2006).

Roger O'Keefe, *The 'Right to Take Part in Cultural Life' under Article 15 of the ICESCR*, 47 INT'L COMP. L.Q. 904 (1998).

Joseph Oloka-Onyango, *Beyond the Rhetoric: Reinventing the Struggle for Economic and Social Rights in Africa*, 27 CAL. W. INT'L. L.J. 1 (1995).

Dianne Otto, *"Gender Comment": Why Does the UN Committee on Economic, Social and Cultural Rights Need a General Comment on Women?*, 14 CAN. J. WOMEN & L. 1 (2002).

Penny Overby, *The Right to Food (Issues in International Human Rights)*, 54 SASK. L. REV. 19 (1990).

James C.N. Paul, *The Relationship of Political Human Rights to the Hunger Problem (World Food Day and Law Conference: "The Legal Faces of the Hunger Problem")*, 30 HOW. L.J. 413 (1987).

Robert E. Robinson, *Measuring State Compliance with the Obligation to Devote the 'Maximum Available Resources' to Realizing Economic, Social and Cultural Rights*, 16 HUM. RTS. Q. 693 (1994).

Jennifer Prah, T*oward a Theory of a Right to Health: Capability and Incompletely Theorized Agreements*, 18 YALE J. L. & HUM. 273 (2006).

Rajindar Sachar, Special Rapporteur on the Rights to Adequate Housing, *The Realization of Economic, Social and Cultural Rights: The Right to Housing*, U.N. Doc. E/CN.4/Sub.2/1995/12 (1995).

Martin Scheinin, *The Proposed Optional Protocol to the Covenant on Economic, Social and Cultural Rights: A Blueprint for UN Human Rights Treaty Body Reform-Without Amending the Existing Treaties*, 6 HUM. RTS. L. REV. 131 (2006).

Barbara Starke, *Urban Despair and Nietzsche's 'Eternal Return': From the Municipal Rhetoric of Economic Justice to the International Law of Economic Rights*, 28 VAND. J. TRANSNAT'L L. 185 (1995).

David P. Stewart & Michael J. Dennis, *Justiciability of Economic, Social, and Cultural Rights: Should There Be an International Complaints Mechanism to Adjudicate the Rights to Food, Water, Housing, and Health?*, 98 AM. J. INT'L L. 462 (2004).

Rajesh Swaminathan, *Regulating Development: Structural Adjustment and the Case for National Enforcement of Economic and Social Rights*, 37 COLUM. J. TRANSNAT'L L. 161 (1998).

Katarina Toma·evski, *Has the Right to Education a Future within the United Nations? A Behind-the-Scenes Account by the Special Rapporteur on the Right to Education 1998-2004*, 5 HUM. RTS. L. REV. 205 (2005).

Katarina Toma·evski, *Human Rights: The Right to Food*, 70 IOWA L. REV. 1321 (1985).[Symposium: International Law and World Hunger]

Stephen Tully, *A Human Right to Access Water? A Critique of General Comment No. 15*, 23 NETH. Q. HUM. RTS. 35 (2005).

Danilo Türk, Special Rapporteur of the Sub-Commission on the Prevention of Discrimination and Protection of Minorities, *The Realization of Economic, Social and Cultural Rights, Final Report*, U.N. Doc. E/CN.4/Sub.2/1992/16 (1992).

Alfred P. Van Huyck, *Shelter in Developing Countries (Confronting the Challenge of Realizing Human Rights Now)*, 34 How. L.J. 65 (1991).

Connie de la Vega, *Protecting Economic, Social and Cultural Rights*, 15 WHITTIER L. REV. 471 (1994).

David Weissbrodt, *Business and Human Rights*, 74 U. CIN. L. REV. 55 (2005).

David Weissbrodt, *UN Perspectives on "Business and Humanitarian and Human Rights Obligations,"* 100 AM. SOC'Y INT'L L. PROC. 135 (2006).

David Weissbrodt, *United States Ratification of the Human Rights Covenants*, 63 MINN. L. REV. 35 (1978).

Ellen Wiles, *Aspirational Principles or Enforceable Rights? The Future for Socio-economic Rights in National Law*, 22 AM. UNIV. INT'L L. REV. 35 (2006).

Willard Wirtz, *Human Rights and Responsibilities at the Workplace*, 28 SAN DIEGO L. REV. 159 (1991).

Katharine G. Young, *The Minimum Core of Economic and Social Rights: A Concept in Search of Content*, 33 YALE J. INT'L L. 113 (2008).

g. Practice Guides

CIRCLE OF RIGHTS - ECONOMIC, SOCIAL AND CULTURAL RIGHTS ACTIVISM: A TRAINING RESOURCE (2000).

[Washington, D.C.: 660 pp. International Human Rights Internship Program. Part I includes information about the substance of economic, social and cultural rights, and about strategies and tools that can be used to protect and promote them. The shorter Part II includes some suggestions for training methods that may be used to convey the material in Part I.]

U.N. CENTRE FOR HUMAN RIGHTS, THE COMMITTEE ON ECONOMIC, SOCIAL AND CULTURAL RIGHTS (1996).

[Geneva; New York: Centre for Human Rights, 50 pp., Human Rights Fact Sheet No. 16 (rev. 1).]

STEPHEN A. HANSEN, THESAURUS OF ECONOMIC, SOCIAL, AND CULTURAL RIGHTS: TERMINOLOGY AND POTENTIAL VIOLATIONS (2000).

[Washington, DC: American Association for the Advancement of Science, 282 pp.]

ALLAN MCCHESNEY, PROMOTING AND DEFENDING ECONOMIC, SOCIAL AND CULTURAL RIGHTS: A HANDBOOK (2000).

[Washington, DC: American Association for the Advancement of Science, 198 pp.]

U.N. CENTRE FOR HUMAN RIGHTS, THE COMMITTEE ON ECONOMIC, SOCIAL AND CULTURAL RIGHTS (1991).

[Geneva; New York: Centre for Human Rights, 21 pp., Human Rights Fact Sheet No. 16, Rev. 1. Also available on the OHCHR Web site, http://www.unhchr.ch/html/menu6/2/fs16.htm.]

U.N. CENTRE FOR HUMAN RIGHTS, THE HUMAN RIGHT TO ADEQUATE HOUSING (1993).

[Geneva; New York: Centre for Human Rights, 51 pp., Human Rights No. 21. Also available on the OHCHR Web site, http://www.unhchr.ch/html/menu6/2/fs21.htm.]

U.N. CENTRE FOR HUMAN RIGHTS, UNITED NATIONS ACTION IN THE FIELD OF HUMAN RIGHTS, U.N. Doc. ST/HR/2/Rev.4 at 25, 44, and 131; U.N. Sales No. E.94. XIV.11 (1994).

[New York: U.N., 417 pp.]

U.N. Centre for Human Rights/UNITAR, MANUAL ON HUMAN RIGHTS REPORTING UNDER SIX MAJOR INTERNATIONAL HUMAN RIGHTS INSTRUMENTS, U.N. Doc. HR/PUB/91/1 at 39, U.N. Sales No. E.91.XIV.1 (1991).

[New York: U.N., 203 pp.]

h.   Materials Available Through Electronic Formats

i.   Related Materials through Web Sites

International Labour Organization (ILO) Web Site, ILOLEX: ILO's Database on International Labour Standards, http://www.ilo.org/ilolex/english/.

Provides the complete text of each ILO agreement, ratification information, and other information related to the ILO's standards.

International Labour Organization (ILO) Web Site, NATLEX: Bibliographic Database Featuring National Laws on Labour, Social Security and Related Human Rights, http://www.ilo.org/dyn/natlex/natlex_browse.home.

Provides the basic information for many national laws related to labor, social security, and issues related to human rights. Some full-text documents are also included.

U.N. High Commissioner for Human Rights, Committee on Economic, Social and Cultural Rights, http://www.unhchr.ch/html/menu2/6/cescr.htm.

Provides information about the Committee on Economic, Social and Cultural Rights, sessions, guidelines, press releases, other information, and documents.

United Nations Development Programme, http://www.undp.org.

This U.N. organization focuses on development advice, advocacy, and grant support. The Web site provides information on its offices and programs around the world, the *Human Development Report*, and other documents and resources.

University of Minnesota Human Rights Library, Committee on Economic, Social and Cultural Rights, http://www1.umn.edu/humanrts/esc/esc-page.htm.

This page of the Library is focuses on the Committee on Economic, Social and Cultural Rights. It contains the text of the instruments, links to ratification information, case law, and other documents.

University of Minnesota Human Rights Library, Links related to Business and Human Rights, http://www1.umn.edu/humanrts/links/business.html.

World Bank Home Page, http://www.worldbank.org.

Contains press releases, current events, bank news, country/project information, publications, research studies, and more.

ii.   Related CD-ROM Products
ILOLEX (ILO). Trilingual database (English, French, and Spanish) includes ILO conventions, ILO recommendations, the Annual Report of the Conference Committee on the Application of Standards (1987-present), Comments of the Committee of Experts on the Application of Conventions and Recommendations (1987-present), the Triennial Report of the Committee on Freedom of Association (1985-present), ratification lists by convention and by country, the ILO Constitution, and the reports of committees and commissions established under Constitution Articles 24 and 26 to investigate complaints and representations.

iii.   General Human Rights Web Sites
University of Minnesota Human Rights Library, http://www1.umn.edu/humanrts.

Provides the full text of the International Covenant on Economic, Social and Cultural Rights as well as other international instruments, links to related Internet sites, general comments by the Committee on Economic, Social and Cultural Rights, and other human rights information.

See the International Covenant on Civil and Political Rights, section i.(ii).

iv.   General Human Rights Discussion Lists and Blogs
See the International Covenant on Civil and Political Rights, section i.(iii).

§ 3.   International Convention on the Elimination of All Forms of Racial Discrimination

International Convention on the Elimination of All Forms of Racial Discrimination, G.A. res. 2106 (XX), Annex, 20 U.N. GAOR Supp. (No.14) at 47, U.N. Doc. A/6014 (1966), 660 U.N.T.S. 195, *entered into force* Jan.4, 1969.

[For electronic version, see the OHCHR Web site, http://www.unhchr.ch/html/menu3/b/d_icerd.htm or the University of Minnesota Human Rights Library, http://www1.umn.edu/humanrts/instree/d1cerd.htm.]

a.   Status
See the International Covenant on Civil and Political Rights, section a.

Office of the High Commissioner for Human Rights, http://www2.ohchr.org/english/bodies/ratification/2.htm.

U.N., *Elimination of Racism and Racial Discrimination. Status of the International Convention on the Elimination of All Forms of Racial Discrimination*, U.N. Doc. A/55/203 (2000).

[9 pp., July 19, 2000. Contains list of States parties, entry into force dates, and states that have made declarations under Art. 14, paragraph 1.]

b.   Reservations, Declarations, and Objections

Committee on the Elimination of Racial Discrimination, *Declarations, Reservations, Withdrawals of Reservations and Objections to Reservations and Declarations Relating to the International Convention on the Elimination of All Forms of Racial Discrimination*, U.N. Doc. CERD/C/60/Rev.3 (1999).

[62 pp., Feb. 12, 1999. Lists the states that have signed, ratified, or acceded to the convention; provides the full text of the declarations, reservations, and objections; and provides notification of withdrawals of reservations, and objections to reservations and declarations. Declarations and Reservations are available on the Web, United Nations Treaty Collection, http://www.untreaty. un.org. See also the OHCHR Web site, http://www2.ohchr.org/english/bodies/ ratification/2.htm#reservations.]

c.   Status of Reports

U.N. High Commissioner for Human Rights, All Reports by Convention, http://www.unhchr.ch/tbs/doc.nsf/RepStatfrset?OpenFrameSet.

d.   Decisions, Jurisprudence, and Reports

Committee on the Elimination of Racial Discrimination, *Report of the Committee on the Elimination of All Forms of Racial Discrimination*, [session no.] U.N. GAOR Supp. (No. 18), U.N. Doc. A/[session no.]/18 ([year)).

[New York: U.N. Annual report of the Committee to the General Assembly. Contains consideration of reports, decisions, opinions, status information, and summary of activities of the Committee (*e.g.*, Report of the Committee on the Elimination of All Forms of Racial Discrimination, 49 U.N. GAOR Supp. (No. 18), U.N. Doc. A/49/18 (1995).]

International Human Rights Instruments, *Compilation of General Comments and General Recommendations Adopted by Human Rights Bodies*, U.N. Doc. HRI/GEN/1/Rev. 7 (2004).

[353 pp., May 12, 2004. Compilation of the general comments adopted by the various human rights body committees, http://www.unhchr.ch/tbs/doc.nsf/0/ ca12c3a4ea8d6c53c1256d500056e56f?Opendocument.]

Committee on the Elimination of Racial Discrimination, *Consideration of Reports Submitted by the States Parties*, U.N. Doc. CERD/C/[#] ([year]).

[Concluding observations of the Committee for each report submitted by the States parties. The U.N. symbol will vary depending on the country (*e.g.*, for Sri Lanka: U.N. Doc. CERD/C/234/Add.1 (1994), 13 pp., September 13, 1994).]

Committee on the Elimination of Racial Discrimination, *Opinions*, U.N. Doc. CERD/C/[#]/D/[#]/[year of initial submission] ([year]).

[Opinions are determinations by the Committee on the admissibility or the merits of individual complaints (*e.g.*, Communication No. 3/1991, U.N. Doc. CERD/C/44/D/3/1991 (1994)).]

U.N High Commissioner for Human Rights, Treaty Bodies Database, http://www.unhchr.ch/tbs/doc.nsf.

[Contains the full text of States reports, concluding observations, decisions, views, etc. for the major treaty bodies. Coverage and language vary.]

University of Minnesota Human Rights Library, Other Treaty-Based Committees, http://www1.umn.edu/humanrts/un-orgs.htm#othertreatybased.

[Contains selected decisions, general comments, and other documents for the major human rights instruments.]

e.   Rules of Procedure and Guidelines

Committee on the Elimination of Racial Discrimination, *Rules of Procedure of the Committee on the Elimination of All Forms of Racial Discrimination*, U.N. Doc. CERD/C/35/Rev.3 (1986).

[New York: U.N., 1986, 219 pp. Contains information on the Committee sessions, distribution of reports and other official documents, the conduct of business, and functions of the Committee.]

Committee on the Elimination of Racial Discrimination, *General Guidelines Regarding the Form and Contents of Reports to Be Submitted by States Parties under Article 9, Paragraph 1, of the Convention*, U.N. Doc. CERD/C/70/Rev.5 (2000).

[Geneva: U.N., 10 pp., http://www.unhchr.ch/tbs/doc.nsf/(Symbol)/CERD. C.70.Rev.5.En?Opendocument.]

f.   Commentaries

i.   Books

Michael P. Banton, International Action Against Racial Discrimination (1996).

[Oxford: Clarendon Press; New York, NY: Oxford Univ. Press, 362 pp.]

Th. C. van Boven, Human Rights from Exclusion to Inclusion; Principles and Practice: an Anthology from the Work of Theo Van Boven (chapters 12 and 14) (2000).

[The Hague; Boston, MA: Kluwer Law International, 503 pp.]

The Future of UN Human Rights Treaty Monitoring (Michael Banton, "Decision-taking in the Committee on the Elimination of Racial Discrimination," chapter 3) (Philip Alston and James Crawford eds., 2000).

[Cambridge, U.K.; New York: Cambridge University Press, 563 pp.]

Natan Lerner, The U.N. Convention on the Elimination of All Forms of Racial Discrimination. A Commentary (2d ed. 1980).

[Leiden, Sijthoff, 259 pp.]

Liesbeth Lijnzaad, Reservations to UN-Human Rights Treaties: Ratify and Ruin? (1995).

[Dordrecht; Boston: M. Nijhoff, 448 pp.]

REFLECTIONS ON INTERNATIONAL LAW FROM THE LOW COUNTRIES: IN HONOUR OF PAUL DE WAART (Theo van Boven, "Prevention, Early-warning and Urgent Procedures; a New Approach by the Committee on the Elimination of Racial Discrimination," chapter 10) (Erik Denters and Nico Schrijver eds., 1998).

[The Hague; Boston: M. Nijhoff Publishers, 507 pp.]

THE ROLE OF THE NATION-STATE IN THE 21ST CENTURY : HUMAN RIGHTS, INTERNATIONAL ORGANISATIONS, AND FOREIGN POLICY : ESSAYS IN HONOUR OF PETER BAEHR (P.R. Baehr et al. eds., 1998).

[The Hague; Boston: Kluwer Law International, 504 pp.]

THE UNITED NATIONS AND HUMAN RIGHTS: A CRITICAL APPRAISAL. (Patrick Thornberry, "The Committee on the Elimination of Racial Discrimination," chapter 8) (Philip Alston ed., 2d 2002).

[Oxford: Clarendon, 600 p.]

ii.   Articles

Thomas Buergenthal, *Implementing the UN Racial Convention*, 12 TEX. INT'L. L. J. 187 (1977).

Claire Charters & Andrew Erueti, *Report from the Inside: The CERD Committee's Review of the Foreshore and Seabed Act 2004*, 36 VICT. U. WELLINGTON L. REV. 257 (2006).

Lisa A. Crooms, *Indivisible Rights and Intersectional Identities or, 'What do Women's Human Rights Have to Do With the Race Convention?'*, 40 HOW. L.J. 619 (1997).

[Symposium: The International Convention on the Elimination of All Forms of Racial Discrimination]

Michael B. de Leeuw et al., *The Current State of Residential Segregation and Housing Discrimination: The United States' Obligations under the International Convention on the Elimination of All Forms of Racial Discrimination*, 13 MICH. J. RACE & L. 337 (2008).

Stephanie Farrior, *The Neglected Pillar: The "Teaching Tolerance" Provision of the International Convention on the Elimination of All Forms of Racial Discrimination*, 5 ILSA J. INT'L & COMP. L. 291 (1999).

[Symposium: The Transition of International Law: Reflections on Trends Past, Present and Future]

James Jennings, *The International Convention on the Elimination of All Forms of Racial Discrimination: Implications for Challenging Racial Hierarchy*, 40 HOW. L.J. 597 (1997).

[Symposium: The International Convention on the Elimination of All Forms of Racial Discrimination]

Michael A.G. Korengold, *Lessons Confronting Racist Speech: Good Intentions, Bad Results, and Article 4(a) of the Convention on the Elimination of All Forms of Racial Discrimination*, 77 MINN. L. REV. 719 (1993).

Drew Mahalic & Joan Gambee Mahalic, *The Limitation Provisions of the International Convention on the Elimination of All Forms of Racial Discrimination*, 9 HUM. RTS. Q. 74 (1987).

Gay J. McDougall, *Toward a Meaningful International Regime: The Domestic Relevance of International Efforts to Eliminate All Forms of Racial Discrimination*, 40 HOW. L.J. 571 (1997).

[Symposium: The International Convention on the Elimination of All Forms of Racial Discrimination]

Theodor Meron, *The Meaning and Reach of the International Convention on the Elimination of All Forms of Racial Discrimination*, 79 AM. J. INT'L. L. 283 (1985).

Nkechi Taifa, *Codification or Castration? The Applicability of the International Convention to Eliminate All Forms of Racial Discrimination to the U.S. Criminal Justice System* (Symposium: The International Convention on the Elimination of All Forms of Racial Discrimination), 40 HOW. L.J. 641 (1997).

Patrick Thornberry, *Confronting Racial Discrimination: A CERD Perspective*, 5 HUM. RTS. L. REV. 239 (2005).

g.   Practice Guides

U.N. CENTRE FOR HUMAN RIGHTS, THE COMMITTEE ON THE ELIMINATION OF RACIAL DISCRIMINATION (1991).

[Geneva; New York: Centre for Human Rights, 31 pp., Human Rights Fact Sheet No. 12. Also available on the OHCHR Web site, http://www.unhchr.ch/html/menu6/2/fs12.htm.]

U.N. CENTRE FOR HUMAN RIGHTS, UNITED NATIONS ACTION IN THE FIELD OF HUMAN RIGHTS, U.N. Doc. ST/HR/2/Rev.4 at 24, 47, 152, and 317; U.N. Sales No. E.94.XIV.11 (1994).

[New York: U.N., 417 pp.]

U.N. CENTRE FOR HUMAN RIGHTS/UNITAR, MANUAL ON HUMAN RIGHTS REPORTING UNDER SIX MAJOR INTERNATIONAL HUMAN RIGHTS INSTRUMENTS, U.N. Doc. HR/PUB/91/1 at 127, U.N. Sales No. E.91.XIV.1 (1991).

[New York: U.N., 203 pp.]

LEO ZWAAK, INTERNATIONAL HUMAN RIGHTS PROCEDURES: PETITIONING THE ECHR, CCPR AND CERD (1991).[Nijmagan, Netherlands: Ars Aequi Libri, 168 pp.]

h.   Materials Available Through Electronic Formats

i.   Specific Web Sites

Human Rights Watch, Race and Human Rights,

http://www.hrw.org/campaigns/race.

This site contains preparation and background information for the 2001 World Conference against Racism, Racial Discrimination, Xenophobia and Related Intolerance in South Africa. It also contains a general search engine of the Human Rights Watch Web site.

U.N. High Commissioner for Human Rights, Committee on the Elimination of Racial Discrimination,

http://www2.ohchr.org/english/bodies/cerd/index.htm.

Provides information about the Committee on the Elimination of Racial Discrimination, sessions, individual complaints, and official records.

University of Minnesota Human Rights Library, Committee on the Elimination of Racial Discrimination,

http://www1.umn.edu/humanrts/country/cerd-page.html.

This page of the Library is focuses on the Committee on the Elimination of Racial Discrimination. It contains the text of the instruments, links to ratification information, case law, and other documents.

ii.   General Human Rights Web Sites

University of Minnesota Human Rights Library, http://www1.umn.edu/humanrts.

Provides the full text of the International Convention on the Elimination of All Forms of Racial Discrimination as well as other international instruments, general recommendations of the Committee on the Elimination of Racial Discrimination, links to related Internet sites, and other human rights information.

See the International Covenant on Civil and Political Rights, section i.(ii).

iii.   General Human Rights Discussion Lists and Blogs

See the International Covenant on Civil and Political Rights, section i.(iii).

§ 4.   Convention on the Elimination of All Forms of Discrimination Against Women

Convention on the Elimination of All Forms of Discrimination Against Women, G.A. res. 34/180, 34 U.N. GAOR Supp. (No. 46) at 193, U.N. Doc. A/34/46 (1979), 1249 U.N.T.S. 13, *entered into force* Sept. 3, 1981.

[For electronic version, see the OHCHR Web site, http://www.unhchr.ch/html/menu3/b/e1cedaw.htm or the University of Minnesota Human Rights Library, http://www1.umn.edu/humanrts/instree/e1cedaw.htm.]

Optional Protocol to the Convention on the Elimination of Discrimination Against Women, G.A. res. 54/4, annex, 54 U.N. GAOR Supp. (No. 49) at 5, U.N. Doc. A/54/49 (Vol. I) (2000), *entered into force* Dec. 22, 2000.

[For electronic version, see the OHCHR Web site, http://www.unhchr.ch/html/menu3/b/opt_cedaw.htm or the University of Minnesota Human Rights Library, http://www1.umn.edu/humanrts/instree/cedawopprot-2000.html.]

a. Status

See the International Covenant on Civil and Political Rights, section a.

U.N., Division for the Advancement of Women, Signatures to and Ratifications of the Optional Protocol, *at* WomenWatch Web site, http://www. un.org/womenwatch/daw/cedaw/sigop.htm.

[Provides current status information for the Optional Protocol.]

b. Reservations, Declarations, and Objections

Committee on the Elimination of Discrimination against Women, *Declarations, Reservations, Objections and Notifications of Withdrawal of Reservations Relating to the Convention on the Elimination of All Forms of Discrimination Against Women*, U.N. Doc. CEDAW/SP/2000/2 (2000).

[102 pp., July 20, 2000. Contains list of states which have signed, ratified, or acceded to the convention, full text of declarations and reservations, withdrawal of reservations, and objections to reservations and declarations. Declarations and Reservations are available on the Web, United Nations Treaty Collection, http://www.untreaty.un.org. See also the OHCHR Web site, http:// www.ohchr.org/english/countries/ratification/8_1.htm.]

c. Status of Reports

U.N. High Commissioner for Human Rights, All Reports by Convention, http://www.unhchr.ch/tbs/doc.nsf/RepStatfrset?OpenFrameSet.

d. Decisions, Jurisprudence, and Reports

Committee on the Elimination of Discrimination Against Women, *Report of the Committee on the Elimination of Discrimination Against Women*, [session no.] GAOR Supp. (No. 38), U.N. Doc. A/[session no.]/38 ([year]).

[New York: U.N. Annual report of the Committee to the General Assembly. Contains conclusions and recommendations adopted by the Committee, reports by States parties, parties ratified, overview of the activities of the Committee, as well as several annexes including a list of ratifications and status of submission of reports (*e.g.*, Report of the Committee on the Elimination of Discrimination Against Women, 50 GAOR Supp. (No.38), U.N. Doc. A/50/38 (1995)).]

COMMITTEE ON THE ELIMINATION OF DISCRIMINATION AGAINST WOMEN, THE WORK OF CEDAW: REPORTS OF THE COMMITTEE ON THE ELIMINATION OF DISCRIMINATION AGAINST WOMEN (CEDAW), Vol. 1, 1982-1985, Vol.2 1986-1987, U.N. Doc. ST/ CSDHA/5 (1989), U.N. Sales No. E.89.IV.4.

[New York: U.N., 752 pp. Contains reports of the Committee and the summary records.]

Committee on the Elimination of Discrimination Against Women, *Consideration of Reports Submitted by the States Parties*, U.N. Doc. CEDAW/C/ [country abbrev.]/SP.1 ([year]).

[Concluding observations of the Committee for each report submitted by the States parties. The U.N. symbol will vary depending on the country (*e.g.*, for Croatia: U.N. Doc. CEDAW/C/CRO/SP.1 (1994)).]

International Human Rights Instruments, *Compilation of General Comments and General Recommendations Adopted by Human Rights Bodies*, U.N. Doc. HRI/GEN/1/Rev. 7 (2004).

[353 pp., May 12, 2004. Compilation of the general comments adopted by the various human rights body committees, http://www.unhchr.ch/tbs/doc.nsf/0/ca12c3a4ea8d6c53c1256d500056e56f?Opendocument.

Compilation of the general recommendations adopted by the Committee on the Elimination of Discrimination Against Women. General recommendations 1-25 are also available on the U.N. Womenwatch Web site, http://www.un.org/womenwatch/daw/cedaw/recomm.htm.]

U.N High Commissioner for Human Rights, Treaty Bodies Database, http://www.unhchr.ch/tbs/doc.nsf.

[Contains the full text of States reports, concluding observations, decisions, views, etc. for the major treaty bodies. Coverage and language vary.]

University of Minnesota Human Rights Library, Other Treaty-Based Committees, http://www1.umn.edu/humanrts/un-orgs.htm#othertreatybased.

[Contains selected decisions, general comments, and other documents for the major human rights instruments.]

e.   Legislative History ("Travaux Preparatoires")

LARS ADAM REHOF, GUIDE TO THE "TRAVAUX PREPARATOIRES" OF THE UNITED NATIONS CONVENTION ON THE ELIMINATION OF ALL FORMS OF DISCRIMINATION AGAINST WOMEN (1993).

[Dordrecht; Boston: Martinus Nijhoff Pub., 385 pp.]

f.   Rules of Procedure and Guidelines

Committee on the Elimination of Discrimination Against Women, *Revised Draft Rules of Procedure of the Committee on the Elimination of Discrimination Against Women*, U.N. Doc. CEDAW/C/2001/I/WG.1/WP.1 (2000).

[17 pp., Dec. 12, 2000. Contains information on the Committee sessions, distribution of reports and other official documents, the conduct of business, and functions of the Committee.]

Committee on the Elimination of Discrimination Against Women, *Guidelines for Preparation of Reports by States Parties*, U.N. Doc. HRI/GEN/2/Rev.1/Add.2 (2003).

[Geneva: U.N., 7 pp., http://daccessdds.un.org/doc/UNDOC/GEN/G03/417/51/PDF/G0341751.pdf?OpenElement.]

g.   Commentaries

i.   Books and Serials

ADVANCING THE HUMAN RIGHTS OF WOMEN: USING INTERNATIONAL HUMAN RIGHTS STANDARDS IN DOMESTIC LITIGATION (Andrew Byrnes et al., eds.) (1997).

[London: Commonwealth Secretariat, 192 pp.]

FAREDA BANDA, WOMEN, LAW AND HUMAN RIGHTS: AN AFRICAN PERSPECTIVE (2005).

[Oxford: Hart Publishing, 320 pp.]

INEKE BOEREFIJN, TEMPORARY SPECIAL MEASURES: ACCELERATING DE FACTO EQUALITY OF WOMEN UNDER ARTICLE 4(1) UN CONVENTION ON THE ELIMINATION OF ALL FORMS OF DISCRIMINATION AGAINST WOMEN (2003).

[Antwerpen; New York: Intersentia, 258 pp.]

CEDAW REPORTS (1987-).

[Minneapolis, MN: International Women's Rights Action Watch, University of Minnesota. Some reports are available on the IWRAW Web site, http://www1. umn.edu/humanrts/iwraw/publications/countries/shadowreports.html.]

THE CONVENTION ON THE ELIMINATION OF ALL FORMS OF DISCRIMINATION AGAINST WOMEN AND ITS OPTIONAL PROTOCOL: HANDBOOK FOR PARLIAMENTARIANS (2003).

[Geneva, Switzerland: Inter-Parliamentary Union, 121 pp.]

REBECCA J. COOK, WOMEN'S HEALTH AND HUMAN RIGHTS: THE PROMOTION AND PROTECTION OF WOMEN'S HEALTH THROUGH INTERNATIONAL HUMAN RIGHTS LAW (1994).

[Geneva: World Health Organization, 62 pp.]

MARSHA A. FREEMAN, HUMAN RIGHTS IN THE FAMILY: ISSUES AND RECOMMENDA-TION FOR IMPLEMENTATION; ARTICLES 9, 15 AND 16 OF THE CONVENTION ON THE ELIMINATION OF ALL FORMS DISCRIMINATION AGAINST WOMEN (1993).

[Minneapolis, MN: International Women's Rights Action Watch, Humphrey Institute of Public Affairs, 25 pp.]

THE FUTURE OF UN HUMAN RIGHTS TREATY MONITORING (Mara R. Bustelo, "The Committee on the Elimination of Discrimination against Women at the Crossroads," chapter 4) (Philip Alston and James Crawford eds., 2000).

[Cambridge, U.K.; New York: Cambridge University Press, 563 pp.]

HUMAN RIGHTS OF WOMEN: NATIONAL AND INTERNATIONAL PERSPECTIVES (Rebecca J. Cook, ed., 1994).

[Philadelphia: University of Pennsylvania Press, 634 pp.]

HUMAN RIGHTS WATCH WOMEN'S RIGHTS PROJECT, THE HUMAN RIGHTS WATCH GLOBAL REPORT ON WOMEN'S HUMAN RIGHTS (2000).

[New Delhi; New York: Oxford Univ. Press, 458 pp.]

THE INTERNATIONAL HUMAN RIGHTS OF WOMEN: INSTRUMENTS OF CHANGE (Carol Elizabeth Lockwood ed., 1998).

[Washington, D.C.: American Bar Association, Section of International Law and Practice, 607 pp.]

MARILOU MCPHEDRAN, THE FIRST CEDAW IMPACT STUDY: FINAL REPORT (2000).

[Toronto: Centre for Feminist Research, York University, 232 pp.]

SALLY ENGLE MERRY, HUMAN RIGHTS AND GENDER VIOLENCE: TRANSLATING INTERNATIONAL LAW INTO LOCAL JUSTICE (2006).

[Chicago: University of Chicago Press, 269 pp.]

ANDREA PARROT & NINA CUMMINGS, FORSAKEN FEMALES: THE GLOBAL BRUTALIZATION OF WOMEN (2006).

[Lanham, Md.: Rowman & Littlefield Publishers, 253 pp.]

ESCHEL M. RHOODIE, DISCRIMINATION AGAINST WOMEN: A GLOBAL SURVEY OF THE ECONOMIC, EDUCATIONAL, SOCIAL AND POLITICAL STATUS OF WOMEN (1989).

[Jefferson, NC: McFarland, 618 pp.]

RIGHTS OF WOMEN: A GUIDE TO THE IMPORTANT UNITED NATIONS TREATIES FOR WOMEN'S RIGHTS (1998).

[New York: International Women's Tribune Centre, 148 pp.]

A THEMATIC GUIDE TO DOCUMENTS ON THE HUMAN RIGHTS OF WOMEN (Gudmundur Alfredsson & Katarina Tomaevski eds., 1995).

[The Hague; Boston; London: Martinus Nijhoff Pub., 434 pp. The Raoul Wallenberg Institute Human Rights Guides, vol. 1.]

THE UNITED NATIONS AND HUMAN RIGHTS: A CRITICAL APPRAISAL

(Andrew Byrnes, "The Committee on the Elimination of Discrimination against Women," chapter 10) (Philip Alston ed., 2d ed. 2002).

[Oxford: Clarendon, 600 p.]

THE UNITED NATIONS AND THE ADVANCEMENT OF WOMEN, 1945-1995 (1995).

[New York: Department of Public Information, United Nations, 689 pp.]

WHERE HUMAN RIGHTS BEGIN: HEALTH, SEXUALITY, AND WOMEN, TEN YEARS AFTER VIENNA, CAIRO, AND BEIJING (Wendy Chavkin & Ellen Chesler eds., 2006).

[New Brunswick, N.J: Rutgers University Press, 309 pp. Essays on several issues concerning women's reproductive rights.]

WOMEN AND HUMAN RIGHTS: THE BASIC DOCUMENTS (1996).

[New York, NY: Columbia University Center for the Study of Human Rights, 251 pp.]

WOMEN AND INTERNATIONAL HUMAN RIGHTS LAW (Kelly D. Askin and Dorean M. Koenig eds., 1999).

[Ardsley, NY: Transnational, 3 vols.]

WOMEN, LAW & DEVELOPMENT INTERNATIONAL AND HUMAN RIGHTS WATCH WOMEN'S RIGHTS PROJECT, WOMEN'S HUMAN RIGHTS STEP BY STEP: A PRACTICAL GUIDE TO USING INTERNATIONAL HUMAN RIGHTS LAW AND MECHANISMS TO DEFEND WOMEN'S HUMAN RIGHTS (2003).

[Washington, D.C.: Women, Law & Development International, 197 pp.]

THE WOMEN'S WATCH (1987-2000).

[Minneapolis, MN: International Women's Rights Action Watch, University of Minnesota Affairs. Back issues are available on the IWRAW Web site from June 1995 to 2000, http://www1.umn.edu/humanrts/iwraw/reports.html.]

ii. Articles

Ladan Askari, *Girls' Rights Under International Law: An Argument for Establishing Gender Equality as a Jus Cogens,* 8 S. CAL. REV. L. & WOMEN'S STUD. 3 (1998).

Mireille G.E. Bijnsdorp, *The Strength of the Optional Protocol to the United Nations Women's Convention*, 18 N.Q.H.R. 329 (2000).

Kristin Bumiller, *Freedom from Violence as a Human Right: Toward a Feminist Politics of Nonviolence,* 28 THOS. JEFFERSON L. REV. 327 (2006).

Andrew C. Byrnes, *The 'Other' Human Rights Treaty Body: The Work of the Committee on the Elimination of Discrimination Against Women*, 14 YALE J. INT'L. L. 1 (1989).

Andrew C. Byrnes, *Slow and Steady Wins the Race? The Development of an Optional Protocol to the Women's Convention*, 91 AM. SOC'Y INT'L L. PROC. 383 (1997).

Andrew Byrnes and Jane Connors, *Enforcing the Human Rights of Women: A Complaints Procedure for the Women's Convention?,* 21 BROOK. J. INT'L L. 679 (1996).

Silvia Cartwright, *Rights and Remedies: The Drafting of an Optional Protocol to the Convention on the Elimination of All Forms of Discrimination against Women,* 9 OTAGO L. REV. 239 (1998).

Hilary Charlesworth, *Not Waving but Drowning: Gender Mainstreaming and Human Rights in the United Nations,* 18 HARV. HUM. RTS. J. 1 (2005).

Mai Chen, *Protective Laws and the Convention on the Elimination of All Forms of Discrimination against Women*, 15 WOMEN'S RIGHTS LAW REPORTER, 2 (1993).

Michael J. Cobera, *The Women's Convention and the Equal Protection Clause,* 26 ST. MARY'S L.J. 755 (1995).

Rebecca J. Cook, *International Protection of Women's Reproductive Rights,* 24 N.Y.U. J. INT'L. L. & POL. 645 (1992).

Rebecca J. Cook, *Reservations to the Convention on the Elimination of All Forms of Discrimination against Women*, 30 VA. J. INT'L. L. 643 (1990).

Lisa A. Crooms, *Using a Multi-Tiered Analysis to Reconceptualize Gender-Based Violence Against Women as a Matter of International Human Rights,* 33 NEW ENG. L. REV. 881 (1999).

Draft Optional Protocol to the Convention on the Elimination of All Forms of Discrimination against Women (Conference on the International Protection of Reproductive Rights), 44 AM. U. L. REV. 1419 (1995).

Elizabeth Evatt, *Finding a Voice for Women's Rights: The Early Days of CEDAW*, 34 GEO. WASH. INT'L L. REV. 515 (2002).

Marsha A. Freeman, *The Human Rights of Women under the CEDAW Convention: Complexities and Opportunities of Compliance*, 91 AM. SOC'Y INT'L L. PROC. 378 (1997).

Alan Goldfarb, *A Kenyan Wife's Right to Bury Her Husband: Applying the Convention on the Elimination of All Forms of Discrimination Against Women*, 14 ILSA J. INT'L. L. 1 (1990).

Malvina Halberstam, *The United States Ratification of the Convention on the Elimination of All Forms of Discrimination Against Women*, 31 GEO. WASH. J. INT'L L. & ECON. 49 (1997).

Sarah A. Huff, *The Abortion Crisis in Peru: Finding a Woman's Right to Obtain Safe and Legal Abortions in the Convention on the Elimination of All Forms of Discrimination against Women*, 30 B.C. INT'L & COMP. L. REV. 237 (2007).

Leslie Kurshan, *Rethinking Property Rights as Human Rights: Acquiring Equal Property Rights for Women Using International Human Rights Treaties*, 8 AM. U.J. GENDER SOC. POL'Y & L. 353 (2000).

Ann Elizabeth Mayer, *Reflections on the Proposed United States Reservations to CEDAW: Should the Constitution be an Obstacle to Human Rights?* (Convention on the Elimination of All Forms of Discrimination against Women), 23 HASTINGS CONST. L.Q. 727 (1996).

Jessica Neuwirth, *Inequality before the Law: Holding States Accountable for Sex Discriminatory Laws under the Convention on the Elimination of All Forms of Discrimination against Women and through the Beijing Platform for Action*, 18 HARV. HUM. RTS. J. 19 (2005).

Joseph Oloka-Onyango and Sylvia Tamale, *The Personal is Political, or Why Women's Rights are Indeed Human Rights: An African Perspective on International Feminism*, 17 HUM. RTS. Q. 691 (1995).

Jennifer Riddle, *Making CEDAW Universal: A Critique of CEDAW's Reservation Regime under Article 28 and the Effectiveness of the Reporting Process*, 34 GEO. WASH. INT'L L. REV. 605 (2002).

Jo Lynn Southard, *Protection of Women's Human Rights Under the Convention on the Elimination of All Forms of Discrimination against Women*, 8 PACE INT'L L. REV. 1 (1996).

Lisa C. Stratton, *The Right to Have Rights: Gender Discrimination in Nationality Laws*, 77 MINN. L. REV. 195 (1992).

Amanda Ulrich, *Can the World's Poorest Women Be Saved?: A Critical Third World Feminist Analysis of the CEDAW's Rural Women's Economic Rights and Alternative Approaches to Women's Economic Empowerment*, 45 ALBERTA L. REV. 477 (2007).

Jennifer L. Ulrich, *Confronting Gender-Based Violence with International Instruments: Is a Soluton to the Pandemic Within Reach?*, 7 IND. J. GLOBAL LEGAL STUD. 629 (2000).

Women's Rights are Human Rights: Selected Articles Dedicated to Women in the International Human Rights Arena, 21 BROOK. J. INT'L L. 599 (1996).

A. Wörgetter, *The Draft Optional Protocol to the Law on the Elimination of All Forms of Discrimination Against Women*, 2 AUSTRIAN REV. INT'L & EUR. L. 261 (1997).

Sarah C. Zearfoss, *The Convention for the Elimination of All Forms of Racial Discrimination Against Women: Radical, Reasonable, or Reactionary?*, 12 MICH. J. INT'L. L. 903 (1991).

h.   Practice Guides

INTERNATIONAL WOMEN'S RIGHTS ACTION WATCH, PRODUCING NGO SHADOW REPORTS TO CEDAW: A PROCEDURAL GUIDE (1998).

[Minneapolis, MN: University of Minnesota, 8 pp. Also available on the IWRAW Web site, http://www1.umn.edu/humanrts/iwraw/shadow.htm.]

STEPHEN L. ISAACS, ASSESSING THE STATUS OF WOMEN: A GUIDE TO REPORTING USING THE CONVENTION ON THE ELIMINATION OF ALL FORMS OF DISCRIMINATION AGAINST WOMEN (1988).

[New York: International Women's Rights Action Watch, 107 pp.]

U.N. CENTRE FOR HUMAN RIGHTS, DISCRIMINATION AGAINST WOMEN: THE CONVENTION AND THE COMMITTEE (1994).

[Geneva; New York: Centre for Human Rights, 71 pp., Human Rights Fact Sheet No. 22. Also available on the OHCHR Web site, http://www.unhchr.ch/html/menu6/2/fs22.htm.]

U.N. CENTRE FOR HUMAN RIGHTS, UNITED NATIONS ACTION IN THE FIELD OF HUMAN RIGHTS, U.N. Doc. ST/HR/2/Rev.4 at 25, 52, 198; U.N. Sales No. E.94.XIV.11 (1994).

[New York: U.N., 417 pp.]

U.N. Centre for Human Rights/UNITAR, *Manual on Human Rights Reporting Under Six Major International Human Rights Instruments*, U.N. Doc. HR/PUB/91/1 at 153; U.N. Sales No. E.91.XIV.1 (1991).

[New York: United Nations, 203 pp.]

WOMEN'S RIGHTS IN THE UN: A MANUAL ON HOW THE UN HUMAN RIGHTS MECHANISMS CAN PROTECT WOMEN'S RIGHTS (1995).

[Geneva: International Service for Human Rights, 69 pp.]

i.   Bibliographies and Research Guides

Rebecca J. Cook, *Women's International Human Rights: A Bibliography*, 24 N.Y.U. J. INT'L. L. & POL. 857 (1992).

Rebecca J. Cook & Valarie L. Oosterveld, *A Select Bibliography of Women's Rights*, 44 AM. U. L. REV. 1429 (1995).

UNHCR, Selected Bibliography on Refugee Women - 1990 - June 2005, http://www.unhcr.org/research/RESEARCH/42cd4afb2.pdf.

Women's Human Rights Resources Group, *Women's Human Rights Resources, Research Guides and Bibliographies,* http://www.law-lib.utoronto.ca/Diana/rg.htm.

j.   Materials Available Through Electronic Formats

i.   Specific Web Sites

U.N. High Commissioner for Human Rights, Committee on the Elimination of Discrimination against Women, http://www.ohchr.org/english/bodies/cedaw/.

This page on the Office of the High Commissioner for Human Rights Web site provides convenient links to a variety of essential information on CEDAW, including a fact sheet on the Convention and the Committee, sessions of the Committee (State party reports and concluding observations), individual complaints procedure, press releases, and the Treaty Body Database.

International Center for Research on Women, http://www.icrw.org.

This site provides information on the ICRW and its programs, and also provides contact information for the organization and its members.

International Women's Rights Action Watch, http://www1.umn.edu/humanrts/iwraw/index.htm.

Provides information on IWRAW and CEDAW. It also provides contact information for IWRAW, a list of related links, and links to publications.

U.N. Division for the Advancement of Women, Women Watch, http://www.un.org/womenwatch.

Contains many full-text documents and information related to the Convention and the Optional Protocol, http://www.un.org/womenwatch/daw/cedaw/index.html.

University of Minnesota Human Rights Library, Committee on the Elimination of Discrimination against Women, http://www1.umn.edu/humanrts/cedaw/cedaw-page.htm.

This page of the Library is focused on the Committe on the Elimination of Discrimination against Women. It contains the text of the instruments, links to ratification information, case law, and other documents.

University of Minnesota Human Rights Library, Links related to Women and Human Rights, http://www1.umn.edu/humanrts/links/women.html.

Women's Human Rights Resources, http://www.law-lib.utoronto.ca/Diana.

This site focuses on women's human rights by providing links, documents, and relevant scholarly articles.

ii.   Specific Discussion Lists and Blogs

Women's Human Rights, http://www.hrea.org/lists/women-rights/markup/maillist.php.

Human Rights Watch Women's Rights list, http://www.hrw.org/act/subscribe-mlists/subscribe.htm#women.

iii.   General Human Rights Web Sites

University of Minnesota Human Rights Library,

http://www1.umn.edu/humanrts.

Provides the full text of the Convention on the Elimination of All Forms of Discrimination against Women as well as other international instruments, general recommendations of the Committee on the Elimination of Discrimination Against Women, links to related Internet sites, and other human rights information.

See the International Covenant on Civil and Political Rights, section i. (ii).

iv.   General Human Rights Discussion Lists

See the International Covenant on Civil and Political Rights, section i. (iii).

§ 5.   Convention Against Torture and Other Cruel, Inhuman or Degrading Treatment or Punishment

Convention Against Torture and Other Cruel, Inhuman or Degrading Treatment or Punishment, G.A. res. 39/46, Annex, 39 U.N. GAOR Supp. (No. 51) at 197, U.N. Doc. A/39/51 (1984), *entered into force* June 26, 1987.

[For electronic version, see OHCHR Web site, http://www.unhchr.ch/html/menu3/b/h_cat39.htm or the University of Minnesota Human Rights Library, http://www1.umn.edu/humanrts/instree/h2catoc.htm.]

a.   Status

For updated information, see U.N. High Commissioner for Human Rights, http://www.ohchr.org/english/countries/ratification/9.htm.

b.   Reservations, Declarations, and Objections

Committee Against Torture, *Status of the Convention Against Torture and Other Cruel, Inhuman or Degrading Treatment or Punishment and Reservations, Declarations and Objections Under the Convention*, U.N. Doc. CAT/C/2/Rev.5 (1998).

[45 pp. Jan. 22, 1998. Contains list of states which have signed, ratified, or acceded; full text of declarations and reservations, withdrawal of reservations; and objections to reservations and declarations. Declarations and reservations are available on the Web, United Nations Treaty Collection, http://www.untreaty.un.org. See also U.N. High Commissioner for Human Rights, http://www.ohchr.org/english/countries/ratification/9.htm.]

c.   Status of Reports

Updated information on reporting status from non-State parties and State parties is available from the OHCHR Web site, Treaty Bodies Database, http://www.unhchr.ch/tbs/doc.nsf.]

d.   Decisions, Jurisprudence, and Reports

Committee Against Torture, *Report of the Committee Against Torture*, [session no.] U.N. GAOR Supp. (No.44), U.N. Doc. A/[session no.]/44 ([year]).

[New York: U.N. Annual report of the Committee to the General Assembly. Contains conclusions and recommendations adopted by the Committee, reports by States parties, parties ratified, overview of the activities of the Committee, as well as several annexes including a list of States and status of submission of reports (*e.g.*, Report of the Committee Against Torture, 49 U.N. GAOR Supp. (No.44), U.N. Doc. A/49/44 (1994)).]

Committee Against Torture, *Consideration of Reports Submitted by the States Parties*, U.N. Doc. CAT/C/[#] ([year]).

[Contains concluding observations of the Committee for each report submitted by the States parties. The U.N. symbol will vary depending on the country (*e.g.*, for Mauritius: U.N. Doc. CAT/C/24/Add.3 (1995)).]

Committee Against Torture, *Decisions*, U.N. Doc. CAT/C/[#]/D/[#]/[year of communication] ([year]).

[Decisions are determinations on the admissibility or merits of individual complaints (*e.g.*, Communication No. 22/1995, U.N. Doc. CAT/C/14/D/22/1995 (1995)).]

U.N High Commissioner for Human Rights, Treaty Bodies Database, http://www.unhchr.ch/tbs/doc.nsf.

[Contains the full text of States reports, concluding observations, decisions, views, etc. for the major treaty bodies. Coverage and language vary.]

University of Minnesota Human Rights Library, Other Treaty-Based Committees, http://www1.umn.edu/humanrts/un-orgs.htm#othertreatybased.

[Contains selected decisions, general comments, and other documents for the major human rights instruments. Also available on the Web, http://www1.umn.edu/humanrts/instree/guidelines.htm.]

e.   Rules of Procedure and Guidelines

Committee Against Torture, *General Guidelines Regarding the Form and Contents of Periodic Reports to Be Submitted by States Parties under Article 19*, Paragraph 1, U.N. Doc. CAT/C/14/Rev.1 (1998).

[Geneva: U.N., 2 pp. Revised as of 18 May 1998, http://www1.umn.edu/humanrts/instree/guidelines.htm.]

Committee Against Torture, *Rules of Procedure*, U.N. Doc. CAT/C/3/Rev.4 (2002).

[Geneva:U.N.,43pp.,http://www.unhchr.ch/tbs/doc.nsf/MasterFrameView/93128d14c8d9a4b88025645900548912?Opendocument.]

f.   Legislative History ("Travaux Preparatoires")

Matthew Lippman, *The Development and Drafting of the United Nations Convention Against Torture and Other Cruel, Inhuman or Degrading Treatment or Punishment*, 17 B.C. INT'L. & COMP. L. REV. 275 (1994).

g.   Commentaries

i.   Books

AHCENE BOULESBAA, THE U.N. CONVENTION ON TORTURE AND THE PROSPECTS FOR ENFORCEMENT (1999).

[The Hague; Boston: Martinus Nijhoff Publishers, 366 pp.]

AN END TO TORTURE: STRATEGIES FOR ITS ERADICATION (Bertil Dunér, ed., 1998).

[London; New York: Zed Books, 266 pp.]

J. HERMAN BURGERS AND HANS DANELIUS, THE UNITED NATIONS CONVENTION AGAINST TORTURE: A HANDBOOK ON THE CONVENTION AGAINST TORTURE AND OTHER CRUEL, INHUMAN, OR DEGRADING TREATMENT OR PUNISHMENT (1988).

[Dordrecht; Boston: Martinus Nijhoff Pub., 271 pp.]

CHILDHOOD ABUSED: PROTECTING CHILDREN AGAINST TORTURE, CRUEL, INHUMAN AND DEGRADING TREATMENT AND PUNISHMENT (Geraldine Van Bueren ed., 1998).

[Brookfield, VT: Ashgate/Dartmouth, 308 pp.]

CONCLUSIONS AND RECOMMENDATIONS OF THE U.N. COMMITTEE AGAINST TORTURE: ELEVENTH TO TWENTY-SECOND SESSION (1993-1999) (Leif Holmstrom ed., 2000).

[The Hague; Boston: Martinus Nijhoff Publishers, 304 pp.]

THE FUTURE OF UN HUMAN RIGHTS TREATY MONITORING (Roland Bank, "Country-oriented Procedures under the Convention against Torture: Towards a new dynamism," chapter 7) (Philip Alston and James Crawford eds., 2000).

[Cambridge, U.K.; New York: Cambridge University Press, 563 pp.]

THE TORTURE DEBATE IN AMERICA (Karen J. Greenberg ed., 2006).

[Cambridge; New York: Cambridge University Press, 432 pp. Summarizes arguments on use of torture.]

STEVEN R. RATNER, ACCOUNTABILITY FOR HUMAN RIGHTS ATROCITIES IN INTERNATIONAL LAW: BEYOND THE NUREMBERG LEGACY (2001).

[Oxford: Clarendon; New York: Oxford Univ. Press, 435 pp.]

NIGEL S. RODLEY, THE TREATMENT OF PRISONERS UNDER INTERNATIONAL LAW (2d ed., 1999).

[Oxford: Clarendon Press; New York: Oxford Univ. Press, 479 pp.]

PHILIPPE SANDS, TORTURE TEAM: RUMSFELD'S MEMO AND THE BETRAYAL OF AMERICAN VALUES (2008).

[New York, NY: Palgrave Macmillan, 272 pp. Describes origin of recent US policy on use of torture.] [This one is more descriptive than international-law oriented—might want to delete it]

WILLIAM SCHABAS, THE DEATH PENALTY AS CRUEL TREATMENT AND TORTURE: CAPITAL PUNISHMENT CHALLENGED IN THE WORLD'S COURTS (1996).

[Boston: Northeastern University Press, 288 pp.]

THE PHENOMENON OF TORTURE: READINGS AND COMMENTARY (William F. Schulz ed., 2007).

[Philadelphia: University of Pennsylvania Press, 424 pp. Comprehensive, historical examination of torture and efforts to eliminate it.]

TORTURE: A COLLECTION (Sanford Levinson ed., 2004).

[New York: Oxford Univ. Press, 328 pp. Includes essay on CAT.]

THE TORTURE PAPERS: THE ROAD TO ABU GHRAIB (Karen J. Greenberg & Joshua L. Dratel eds., 2005).

[Cambridge: Cambridge University Press, 1284 pp. Documents Bush administration's actions regarding use of torture.]

THE UNITED NATIONS AND HUMAN RIGHTS: A CRITICAL APPRAISAL (Andrew Byrnes, "The Committee Against Torture, chapter 13) (Philip Alston ed., 1992).

[Oxford: Clarendon Press, 765 pp.]

ii.   Articles

Patricia A. Broussard, *Female Genital Mutilation: Exploring Strategies for Ending Ritualized Torture; Shaming, Blaming, and Utilizing the Convention against Torture*, 15 DUKE J. GENDER L. & POL'Y 19 (2008).

Peter Burns and Obiora Okafor, *The United Nations Convention Against Torture and Other Cruel, Inhuman or Degrading Treatment or Punishment or How it is Still Better to Light a Candle than to Curse the Darkness*, 9 OTAGO L. REV. 299 (1998).

Barbara Cochrane Alexander, *Convention Against Torture: A Viable Alternative Legal Remedy for Domestic Violence Victims*, 15 AM. U. INT'L L. REV. 895 (2000).

John Alan Cohan, *Torture and the Necessity Doctrine*, 41 VAL. U. L. REV. 1587 (2007).

Richard Garnett, *The Defence of State Immunity for Acts of Torture*, 18 AUSTL. Y.B. INT'L L. 97 (1997).

Brian Gorlick, *The Convention and Committee Against Torture: A Complementary Protection Regime for Refugees,* 11 INT'L J. REFUGEE L. 479 (1999).

Christopher Keith Hall, *The Duty of States Parties to the Convention against Torture to Provide Procedures Permitting Victims to Recover Reparations for Torture Committed Abroad*, 18 EUR. J. INT'L L. 921 (2007).

Tracy Hresko, *In the Cellars of the Hollow Men: Use of Solitary Confinement in U.S. Prisons and Its Implications under International Laws against Torture*, 18 PACE INT'L L. REV. 1 (2006).

Jane C. Kim, *Nonrefoulement under the Convention Against Torture: How U.S. Allowances for Diplomatic Assurances Contravene Treaty Obligations and Federal Law*, 32 BROOK. J. INT'L L. 1227 (2007).

Julie Lantrip, *Torture and Cruel, Inhumane and Degrading Treatment in the Jurisprudence of the Inter-American Court of Human Rights,* 5 ILSA J. INT'L & COMP. L. 551 (1999).

Kyu Chang Lee, *Protection of North Korean Defectors in China and the Convention against Torture*, 6 REGENT J. INT'L L. 139 (2008).

Isaac A. Linnartz, *The Siren Song of Interrogational Torture: Evaluating the U.S. Implementation of the U.N. Convention Against Torture*, 57 DUKE L.J. 1485 (2008).

Jonathan H. Marks, *Doctors as Pawns? Law and Medical Ethics at Guantanamo Bay*, 37 SETON HALL L. REV. 711 (2007).

Jamie Mayerfeld, *Playing by Our Own Rules: How U.S. Marginalization of International Human Rights Law Led to Torture*, 20 HARV. HUM. RTS. J. 89 (2007).

Winston P. Nagan & Lucie Atkins, *The International Law of Torture: From Universal Proscription to Effective Application and Enforcement*, 14 HARV. HUM. RTS. J. 87 (2001).

Manfred Nowak, *Challenges to the Absolute Nature of the Prohibition of Torture and Ill-Treatment*, 23 NETH. Q. HUM. RTS. 674 (2005).

Edwin Odhiambo-Abuya, *Reinforcing Refugee Protection in the Wake of the War on Terror*, 30 B.C. INT'L & COMP. L. REV. 277 (2007).

Tania Penovic, *Mental Harm as an Instrument of Public Policy*, 15 Psychiatry Psych. & L. 140 (2008).

Prospects for U.S. Ratification of the Convention Against Torture, 1989 AM. SOC. INT'L. L. PROC. 529 (1989).

Kate Riggs et al., *Prolonged Mental Harm: The Torturous Reasoning behind a New Standard for Psychological Abuse*, 20 HARV. HUM. RTS. J. 263 (2007).

Nigel S. Rodley, *The Definition(s) of Torture in International Law*, 55 CURRENT LEGAL PROBS. 467 (2002).

Nigel S. Rodley, *The Prohibition of Torture: Absolute Means Absolute*, 34 DENV. J. INT'L L. & POL'Y 145 (2006).

Ilana A. Schoenbach, *No Statutory Exceptions: The Case of Maher Arar and a Call to End Extraordinary Renditions*, 14 Sw. J. L. & TRADE AMER. 119 (2007).

David P. Stewart, *The Torture Convention and the Reception of International Criminal Law Within the United States*, 15 NOVA L. REV. 449 (1991).

David Weissbrodt and Isabel Hortreiter, *The Principle of Non-Refoulement: Article 3 of the Convention Against Torture and Other Cruel, Inhuman or Degrading Treatment or Punishment in Comparison with the Non-Refoulement Provisions of other International Human Rights Treaties*, 5 BUFF. HUM. RTS. L. REV. 1 (1999).

h.   Practice Guides

AMNESTY INTERNATIONAL, COMBATING TORTURE: A MANUAL FOR ACTION (2003), http://www.amnesty.org/resources/pdf/combating_torture/combating_torture.pdf.

[Oxford: The Alden Press, 335 pp.]

LAURENCE BOISSON DE CHAZOURNES, ET AL., PRACTICAL GUIDE TO THE INTERNATIONAL PROCEDURES RELATIVE TO COMPLAINT AND APPEALS AGAINST ACTS OF TORTURE, DISAPPEARANCES, AND OTHER INHUMAN OR DEGRADING TREATMENT (1988).

[Geneva: World Organization Against Torture/S.O.S. Torture, 92 pp.]

CAMILLE GIFFARD, THE TORTURE REPORTING HANDBOOK: HOW TO DOCUMENT AND RESPOND TO ALLEGATIONS OF TORTURE WITHIN THE INTERNATIONAL SYSTEM FOR THE PROTECTION OF HUMAN RIGHTS (2000).

[Colchester, U.K.: Human Rights Centre, University of Essex, 158 pp. Available on the Human Rights Centre, University of Essex Web site, http://www.essex.ac.uk/torturehandbook.]

SARAH JOSEPH, SEEKING REMEDIES FOR TORTURE VICTIMS: A HANDBOOK ON THE INDIVIDUAL COMPLAINTS PROCEDURES OF THE UN TREATY BODIES (2006).

[Geneva: World Organisation Against Torture (OMCT), 514 pp. Provides overview of mandate and functions of Human Rights Committee, Committee against Torture, and Committee on the Elimination of Discrimination against Women, describing individual complaints procedures and providing strategic advice on litigating torture cases.]

U.N. CENTRE FOR HUMAN RIGHTS, THE COMMITTEE ON TORTURE (1992).

[Geneva; New York: Centre for Human Rights, 38 pp., Human Rights Fact Sheet No. 17. Also available on the OHCHR Web site, http://www.unhchr.ch/html/menu6/2/fs17.htm.]

U.N. Centre for Human Rights, Methods of Combating Torture (1989).

[Geneva; New York: Centre for Human Rights, 27 pp., Human Rights Fact Sheet No. 4. Also available on the OHCHR Web site, http://www.unhchr.ch/html/menu6/2/fs4.htm.]

U.N. Centre for Human Rights, United Nations Action in the Field of Human Rights, U.N. Doc. ST/HR/2/Rev.4 at 25, 53, and 317; U.N. Sales No. E.94.XIV.11 (1994).

[New York: U.N., 417 pp.]

U.N. Centre for Human Rights/UNITAR, *Manual on Human Rights Reporting Under Six Major International Human Rights Instruments*, U.N. Doc. HR/PUB/91/1 at 177, U.N. Sales No. E.91.XIV.1 (1991).

[New York: U.N., 203 pp.]

Lene Wendland, A Handbook on State Obligations under the UN Convention against Torture (2002), http://www.isn.ethz.ch/pubs/ph/details.cfm?lng=en&id=16024.

[Geneva: Association for the Prevention of Torture, 94 pp.]

i.   Materials Available Through Electronic Formats

i.   Specific Web Sites
Amnesty International, http://www.amnesty.org.

Amnesty International's official Web site provides links to news releases, articles, and other relevant sites. It also includes information on Amnesty International's current campaigns and petitions.

Association for the Prevention of Torture Online, http://www.apt.ch.

This site contains a newsletter and articles (.pdf formatted), as well as region-specific information. Also available in French and Spanish.

Council of Europe, European Committee for the Prevention of Torture and Inhuman or Degrading Treatment or Punishment, http://www.cpt.coe.int/en.

Contains news releases, contact information, member information, and publications. Also available in French.

U.N. High Commissioner for Human Rights, Committee Against Torture, http://www2.ohchr.org/english/bodies/cat/index.htm.

This site provides information on individual sessions, complaints and press releases. It includes links to documents and instruments.

University of Minnesota Human Rights Library, Committee Against Torture,

http://www1.umn.edu/humanrts/cat/cat-page.html.

Documents and links related to the Committee Against Torture.

University of Minnesota Human Rights Library, Links related to Torture, http://www1.umn.edu/humanrts/links/torture.html.

University of Minnesota Human Rights Library, Links to Centers for the Rehabilitation of Torture Survivors, http://www1.umn.edu/humanrts/links/tortcenters.html.

ii.   General Human Rights Web Sites
University of Minnesota Human Rights Library, http://www1.umn.edu/humanrts.

Provides the full text of the Convention Against Torture as well as other international instruments, links to related Internet sites, and other human rights information.

See the International Covenant on Civil and Political Rights, section i. (ii).

iii.   General Human Rights Discussion Lists and Blogs
See the International Covenant on Civil and Political Rights, section i. (iii).

Amnesty International's Denounce Torture blog, http://blogs.amnestyusa.org/denounce-torture.

§ 6.   Convention on the Rights of the Child

Convention on the Rights of the Child, G.A. res. 44/25, Annex, 44 U.N. GAOR Supp. (No. 49) at 167, U.N. Doc. A/44/49 (1989), *entered into force* Sept. 2, 1990.

[For electronic version, see the OHCHR Web site, http://www.unhchr.ch/html/menu3/b/k2crc.htm or the University of Minnesota Human Rights Library, http://www1.umn.edu/humanrts/instree/k2crc.htm.]

Optional Protocol to the Convention on the Rights of the Child on the involvement of children in armed conflicts, G.A. Res. 54/263, Annex I, 54 U.N. GAOR Supp. (No. 49) at 7, U.N. Doc. A/54/49, Vol. III (2000), entered into force February 12, 2002.

[For electronic version, see the OHCHR Web site, http://www.unhchr.ch/html/menu2/6/protocolchild.htm or the University of Minnesota Human Rights Library, http://www1.umn.edu/humanrts/instree/childprotarmed.html.]

Optional Protocol to the Convention on the Rights of the Child on the Sale of Children, Child Prostitution and Child Pornography, G.A. res. 54/263, Annex II, 54 U.N. GAOR Supp. (No. 49), U.N. Doc. A/54/49 (2000), *entered into force*, Jan. 18, 2002.

[For electronic version, see the OHCHR Web site, http://www.unhchr.ch/html/menu2/dopchild.htm or the University of Minnesota Human Rights Library, http://www1.umn.edu/humanrts/instree/childprotsale.html.]

a. Status

Committee on the Rights of the Child, *Reservations, Declarations and Objections Relating to the Convention on the Rights of the Child*, U.N. Doc. CRC/C/2/Rev.8 (1999).

[Geneva: U.N., 102 pp. For updated information, see U.N. High Commissioner for Human Rights, http://www.ohchr.org/english/countries/ratification/11.htm.]

b. Reservations, Declarations, and Objections

Committee on the Rights of the Child, *Reservations, Declarations and Objections Relating to the Convention on the Rights of the Child*, U.N. Doc. CRC/C/2/Rev.8 (1999).

[102 pp., Dec. 7, 1999. Lists the States that have signed, ratified, or acceded to the convention; provides the full text of the declarations, reservations, and objections; and provides withdrawals of reservations and objections to reservations and declarations. Declarations and reservations are available on the Web, United Nations Treaty Collection, http://www.untreaty.un.org. For updated information, see U.N. High Commissioner for Human Rights, http://www.ohchr.org/english/countries/ratification/11.htm.]

c. Status of Reports

Updated information on reporting status from non-State parties and State parties is available from the OHCHR Web site, Treaty Bodies Database, http://www.unhchr.ch/tbs/doc.nsf.

d. Decisions and Jurisprudence

Committee on the Rights of the Child, *Consideration of Reports Submitted by the States Parties*, U.N. Doc. CRC/C/[#].

[Concluding observations of the Committee for each report submitted by the States parties. The U.N. symbol will vary depending on the country (*e.g.*, for Colombia: U.N. Doc. CRC/C/15/Add.30 (1995)).]

Committee on the Rights of the Child, *Report of the Committee on the Rights of the Child*, [session no.] U.N. GAOR Supp. (No. 41), U.N. Doc. A/[session no]/41 ([year]).

[New York: U.N. Annual report of the Committee to the General Assembly. Contains conclusions and recommendations adopted by the Committee, reports by States parties, ratifications, overview of the activities of the Committee, as well as several annexes including a list of States parties and status of submission of reports (*e.g.*, Report of the Committee on the Rights of the Child, 49 U.N. GAOR Supp. (No. 41), U.N. Doc. A/49/41 (1994)).]

U.N High Commissioner for Human Rights, Treaty Bodies Database, http://www.unhchr.ch/tbs/doc.nsf.

[Contains the full text of States reports, concluding observations, decisions, views, etc. for the major treaty bodies. Coverage and language vary.]

University of Minnesota Human Rights Library, Other Treaty-Based Committees, http://www1.umn.edu/humanrts/un-orgs.htm#othertreatybased.

[Contains selected decisions, general comments, and other documents for the major human rights instruments.]

e. Conclusions and Recommendations of the Committee

Committee on the Rights of the Child, *Compilation of the Conclusions and Recommendations Adopted by the Committee on the Rights of the Child*, CRC/C/19/Rev.109 (2002).

[37 pp. Provides the text of the conclusions and recommendations adopted by the Committee. Includes information about activities and relations with other U.N. organs and human rights treaty bodies.]

f. Legislative History ("Travaux Preparatoires")

THE UNITED NATIONS CONVENTION ON THE RIGHTS OF THE CHILD: A GUIDE TO THE "TRAVAUX PREPARATOIRES" (Sharon Detrick comp. & ed., 1992).

[Dordrecht; Boston: Martinus Nijhoff Pub., 712 pp.]

g. Rules of Procedure and Guidelines

Committee on the Rights of the Child, *General Guidelines Regarding the Form and Contents of Periodic Reports to Be Submitted by States Parties under Article 44 of the Convention*, U.N. Doc. C/CRC/58 (1996).

[Geneva: U.N., 49 pp., http://www.unhchr.ch/tbs/doc.nsf/(Symbol)/CRC.C.58.En?Opendocument.]

Committee on the Rights of the Child, *Provisional Rules of Procedure*, U.N. Doc. CRC/C/4/Rev.1 (2005).

[Geneva: U.N., 22 pp., http://www.unhchr.ch/tbs/doc.nsf/898586b1dc7b4043c1256a450044f331/76d829e588309e4ec1256ff8004e4e63/$FILE/G0541216.pdf.]

h. Commentaries

i. Books

PHILIP ALSTON, CHILDREN, RIGHTS AND THE LAW (1992).

[Oxford: Clarendon Press; New York: Oxford Univ. Press, 268 pp.]

THE BEST INTERESTS OF THE CHILD: RECONCILING CULTURE AND HUMAN RIGHTS (Philip Alston ed., 1994).

[Oxford: Clarendon; New York: Oxford Univ. Press, 297 pp.]

KAY CASTELLE, IN THE CHILD'S BEST INTEREST: A PRIMER ON THE U.N. CONVENTION ON THE RIGHTS OF THE CHILD (3d ed. 1990).

[East Greenwich, RI: Foster Parents Plan International; New York, NY: Defense for Children International-USA, 46 pp.]

CHILDHOOD ABUSED: PROTECTING CHILDREN AGAINST TORTURE, CRUEL, INHUMAN AND DEGRADING TREATMENT AND PUNISHMENT (Geraldine Van Bueren ed., 1998).

[Brookfield, Vermont: Ashgate, 308 pp.]

CHILDREN'S RIGHTS: CRISIS AND CHALLENGE (Dennis Nurkse et al. eds., 1990).

[New York: Defense for Children International, 262 pp.]

CHILDREN'S RIGHTS: A COMPARATIVE PERSPECTIVE (Michael Freeman ed., 1996).

[Brookfield, Vermont: Dartmouth Pub. Co., 248 pp.]

CHILDREN'S RIGHTS IN AMERICA: U.N. CONVENTION ON THE RIGHTS OF THE CHILD COMPARED WITH UNITED STATES LAW (Cynthia Price Cohen et al. eds., 1990).

[Chicago: American Bar Association Center on Children and the Law, 344 pp.]

A COMMENTARY ON THE UNITED NATIONS CONVENTION ON THE RIGHTS OF THE CHILD [series] (2005-).

[Leiden; Boston: Martinus Nijhoff Publishers. This article-by-article series provides detailed commentary on the Convention; *e.g.*, MANFRED NOWAK, ARTICLE 6: THE RIGHT TO LIFE, SURVIVAL, AND DEVELOPMENT (2005)].

CONCLUDING OBSERVATIONS OF THE U.N. COMMITTEE ON THE RIGHTS OF THE CHILD: THIRD TO SEVENTEENTH SESSION (1993-1998) (Leif Holmstrom ed., 2000).

[The Hague; London: Martinus Nijhoff Publishers, 583 pp.]

CONVENTION ON THE RIGHTS OF THE CHILD (1994).

[New York: Amnesty International, 20 pp.]

SHARON DETRICK, A COMMENTARY ON THE UNITED NATIONS CONVENTION ON THE RIGHTS OF THE CHILD (1999).

[The Hague; Boston: Martinus Nijhoff Publishers, 790 pp.]

THE FUTURE OF UN HUMAN RIGHTS TREATY MONITORING (Gerison Lansdown, "The Reporting Process under the Convention on the Rights of the Child," chapter 5) (Philip Alston and James Crawford eds., 2000).

[Cambridge, U.K.; New York: Cambridge University Press, 563 pp.]

GENDER EQUALITY AND THE JUDICIARY: USING INTERNATIONAL STANDARDS TO PROMOTE THE HUMAN RIGHTS OF WOMEN AND THE GIRL CHILD (Kristine Adams & Andrew Byrnes eds., 1999).

[London: Commonwealth Secretariat, 289 pp.]

THE IDEOLOGIES OF CHILDREN'S RIGHTS (Michael Freeman and Philip Veerman eds., 1992).

[Dordrecht; Boston: Marinus Nijhoff Pub., 369 pp.]

IMPLEMENTING THE U.N. CONVENTION ON THE RIGHTS OF THE CHILD: A STANDARD OF LIVING ADEQUATE FOR DEVELOPMENT (Arlene Bowers Andrews and Natalie Hevener Kaufman eds., 1999).

[Westport, Connecticut: Praeger, 254 pp.]

IMPLEMENTING THE CONVENTION ON THE RIGHTS OF THE CHILD: RESOURCE MOBILIZATION IN LOW-INCOME COUNTRIES (James R. Himes ed., 1995).

[The Hague; Boston: Martinus Nijhoff Pub., 262 pp.]

INDEPENDENT COMMENTARY: UNITED NATIONS CONVENTION ON THE RIGHTS OF THE CHILD (Cynthia Price Cohen ed., 1988).

[New York, NY: Defense for Children International-USA, 99 pp.]

INTERNATIONAL CHILD LABOR PROBLEMS (1993).

[Washington, D.C.: U.S. Dept. of Labor, Bureau of International Labor Affairs, 26 pp.]

THE INTERNATIONAL LAW OF YOUTH RIGHTS: SOURCE DOCUMENTS AND COMMENTARY (William D. Angel ed., 1995).

[Dordrecht; Boston: Martinus Nijhoff Publishers, 1143 pp.]

LAWRENCE J. LEBLANC, CONVENTION ON THE RIGHTS OF THE CHILD: UNITED NATIONS LAWMAKING ON HUMAN RIGHTS (1995).

[Lincoln: University of Nebraska Press, 337 pp.]

A. GLENN MOWER, JR., THE CONVENTION ON THE RIGHTS OF THE CHILD: INTERNATIONAL LAW SUPPORT FOR CHILDREN (1997).

[Westport, Connecticut: Greenwood Press, 185 pp.]

MONITORING CHILDREN'S RIGHTS (Eugeen Verhellen ed., 1996).

[The Hague; Boston: Martinus Nijhoff, 940 pp.]

RELIGIOUS DIMENSIONS OF CHILD AND FAMILY LIFE: REFLECTIONS ON THE U.N. CONVENTION ON THE RIGHTS OF THE CHILD (Harold Coward and Philip Cook, eds., 1996).

[Victoria, B.C.: University of Victoria, Centre for Studies in Religion and Society, 203 pp.]

REVISITING CHILDREN'S RIGHTS: 10 YEARS OF THE U.N. CONVENTION ON THE RIGHTS OF THE CHILD (Deirdre Fottrell ed., 2000).

[The Hague, Boston: Kluwer Law International, 208 pp.]

THE RIGHTS OF THE CHILD (1996).

[Geneva, Switzerland: Centre for Human Rights, 53 pp.]

THE RIGHTS OF THE CHILD: INTERNATIONAL INSTRUMENTS (Maria Rita Saulle and Flaminia Kojanec eds., 1995).

[Irvington-on-Hudson, New York: Transnational Publishers, 779 pp.]

GERALDINE VAN BUEREN, THE INTERNATIONAL LAW ON THE RIGHTS OF THE CHILD (1995).

[Dordrecht; Boston: Martinus Nijhoff Pub., 435 pp.]

EUGEEN VERHELLEN, CONVENTION ON THE RIGHTS OF THE CHILD: BACKGROUND, MOTIVATION, STRATEGIES, MAIN THEMES (3d rev. ed. 2000).

[Leuven, Belgium: Garant, 193 pp.]

BURNS H. WESTON, CHILD LABOR AND HUMAN RIGHTS: MAKING CHILDREN MATTER (2005).

[Boulder, Colo.: Lynne Rienner Publishers, 539 pp.]

ii.   Articles

Philip Alston, *The Best Interests Principle: Towards a Reconciliation of Culture and Human Rights*, 8 INT'L. J. L. & FAM. 1 (1994).

Philip Alston, *The Unborn Child and Abortion Under the Draft Convention on the Rights of the Child*, 12 HUM. RTS. Q. 156 (1990).

[Symposium: U.N. Convention on Children's Rights]

Abdullahi An-Na'Im, *Cultural Transformation and Normative Consensus on the Best Interests of the Child*, 8 INT'L. J. L. & FAM. 62 (1994).

Kirsten M. Backstrom, *The International Human Rights of the Child: Do They Protect the Female Child?*, 30 GEO. WASH. J. INT'L L. & ECON. 541 (1996).

David A. Balton, *The Convention on the Rights of the Child: Prospects for International Enforcement*, 12 HUM. RTS. Q. 120 (1990).

[Symposium: U.N. Convention on Children's Rights]

Patrick McKinley Brennan, *The "Right" of Religious Liberty of the Child: Its Meaning, Measure, and Justification*, 20 EMORY INT'L L. REV. 129 (2006).

Don S. Browning, *The United Nations Convention on the Rights of the Child: Should It Be Ratified and Why?*, 20 EMORY INT'L L. REV. 157 (2006).

Elizabeth M. Calciano, *United Nations Convention on the Rights of the Child: Will It Help Children in the United States?*, 15 HASTINGS INT'L. & COMP. L. REV. 515 (1992).

Cynthia Price Cohen, *An Introduction to the Developing Jurisprudence of the Rights of the Child*, 3 ILSA J. INT'L & COMP. L. 659 (1997).

Cynthia Price Cohen, *The Role of the Nongovernmental Organizations in the Drafting of the Convention on the Rights of the Child*, 12 HUM. RTS. Q. 137 (1990).

[Symposium: U.N. Convention on Children's Rights]

Cynthia Price Cohen and Susan Kilbourne, *Jurisprudence of the Committee on the Rights of the Child: A Guide for Research and Analysis,* 19 MICH. J. INT'L L. 633 (1998).

Cynthia Price Cohen, et al., *Monitoring the United Nations Convention on the Rights of the Child: The Challenge of Information Management*, 18 HUM. RTS. Q. 439 (1996).

Jaap E. Doek, *The Eighteenth Birthday of the Convention of Rights of the Child: Achievements and Challenges*, 41 U. MICH. J. L. REF. 61 (2007).

Paula Donnolo and Kim Azzarelli, *Ignoring the Human Rights of Children: A Perspective on America's Failure to Ratify the United Nations Convention on the Rights of the Child* , 5 J.L. & POL'Y 203 (1996).

[Symposium: Youth, Family and the Law; Defining Rights and Establishing Recognition]

Timothy John Fitzgibbon, *The United Nations Convention on the Rights of the Child: Are Children Really Protected?*, 20 LOY. L.A. INT'L & COMP. L.J. 325 (1998).

Michael Jupp, *The United Nations Convention on the Rights of the Child: An Opportunity for Advocates* (Confronting the Challenge of Realizing Human Rights Now), 34 HOW. L. J. 15 (1991).

Per Miljeteig-Olssen, *Advocacy of Children's Rights-The Convention as More than a Legal Document*, 12 HUM. RTS. Q. 148 (1990).

[Symposium: U.N. Convention on Children's Rights]

Daniel O'Donnell, *Resettlement or Repatriation: Screened-Out Vietnamese Child Asylum Seekers and the Convention on the Rights of the Child*, 1994 INT'L. COMM'N JURISTS REV. 16 (1994).

Margaret Otlawski & Martin B, Tsamenyi, *Parental Authority and the United Nations Convention on the Rights of the Child: Are the Fears Justified?*, 6 AUST. J. FAM. L. 137 (1992).

Jay S. Ovsiovitch, *Reporting Infant and Child Mortality under the United Nations Human Rights Conventions,* 46 BUFF. L. REV. 543 (1998).

Marta Santos Pais, *The Committee on the Rights of the Child*, 1991 INT'L. COMM'N JURISTS REV. 36 (1991).

The Protection of Children's Rights under International Law [Symposium], 22 ST. L. U. PUB. L. REV., no. 2 (2003).

Alison Dundes Renteln, *Who's Afraid of the CRC: Objections to the Convention on the Rights of the Child*, 3 ILSA J. INT'L & COMP. L. 629 (1997).

Lainie Rutkow & Joshua T. Lozman, *Suffer the Children?: A Call for United States Ratification of the United Nations Convention on the Rights of the Child*, 19 HARV. HUMAN RTS. J. 161 (2006).

Kevin Mark Smith, *The United Nations Convention on the Rights of the Child: The Sacrifice of American Children on the Altar of Third-World Activism,* 38 WASHBURN L.J. 111 (1998).

David M. Smolin, *Overcoming Religious Objections to the Convention on the Rights of the Child*, 81 EMORY INT'L L. REV. 81 (2006).

Rebecca M. Stahl, *"Don't Forget about Me": Implementing Article 12 of the United Nations Convention on the Rights of the Child*, 24 ARIZ. J. INT'L & COMP. L. 803 (2007).

George Stewart, *Interpreting the Child's Right to Identity in the U.N. Convention on the Rights of the Child*, 26 FAM. L. Q. 221 (1992).

Jonathan Todres, *Emerging Limitations on the Rights of the Child: The U.N. Convention on the Rights of the Child and Its Early Case Law,* 30 COLUM. HUM. RTS. L. REV. 159 (1998).

Nsongurua J. Udombana, *War Is Not Child's Play! International Law and the Prohibition of Children's Involvement in Armed Conflicts*, 20 TEMPLE INT'L & COMP. L.J. 57 (2006).

Kathy Vandergrift, *Challenges in Implementing and Enforcing Children's Rights*, 37 CORNELL INT'L. L.J. 547 (2004).

Geraldine Van Bueren, *The United Nations Convention on the Rights of the Child: The Necessity of Incorporation into United Kingdom Law*, 22 FAM. L. 373 (1992).

i. Practice Guides

A GUIDE FOR NON-GOVERNMENTAL ORGANIZATIONS REPORTING TO THE COMMITTEE ON THE RIGHTS OF THE CHILD (rev. 1998), http://www.crin.org/docs/resources/publications/NGOCRC/NGOCRC-Guide-en.doc.

[Geneva, Switzerland: NGO Group for the Convention on the Rights of the Child, 16 pp.]

UNITED NATIONS CENTRE FOR HUMAN RIGHTS, THE RIGHTS OF THE CHILD (rev. 1 1996)

[Geneva; New York: Centre for Human Rights, 53 pp., Human Rights Fact Sheet No. 10. Also available on OHCHR Web site, http://www.unhchr.ch/html/menu6/2/fs10.htm.]

U.N. CENTRE FOR HUMAN RIGHTS, UNITED NATIONS ACTION IN THE FIELD OF HUMAN RIGHTS, U.N. Doc. ST/HR/2/Rev.4 at 26, 54, and 232; U.N. Sales No. E.94. XIV.11 (1994).

[New York: U.N., 417 pp.]

j. Materials Available Through Electronic Formats

i. Specific Web Sites

UNICEF, http://www.unicef.org.

This site contains links to publications, speeches, and statistics, as well as press releases and information on UNICEF's programs.

U.N. High Commissioner for Human Rights, Committee on the Rights of the Child, http://www2.ohchr.org/english/bodies/crc/index.htm.

This page contains session information, notes on sessions, and press releases. It also includes links to documents and instruments.

University of Minnesota Human Rights Library, Committee on the Rights of the Child,

http://www1.umn.edu/humanrts/crc/crc-page.html.

Documents and links to sites related to the Committee on the Rights of the Child.

University of Minnesota Human Rights Library, Links related to Children and Human Rights,

http://www1.umn.edu/humanrts/links/children.html.

ii.   Specific Discussion Lists and Blogs
Children's Rights, http://www.hrea.org/lists/child-rights/markup/maillist.php.

Human Rights Watch Children's Rights Action Network, http://www.hrw.org/act/subscribe-mlists/subscribe.htm#cran.

iii.   General Human Rights Web Sites
University of Minnesota Human Rights Library, http://www1.umn.edu/humanrts.

Provides the full text of the Convention on the Rights of the Child as well as other international instruments, the recommendations of the Committee on the Rights of the Child, links to related Internet sites, and other human rights information.

See the International Covenant on Civil and Political Rights, section i.(ii).

iii.   General Human Rights Discussion Lists
See the International Covenant on Civil and Political Rights, section i.(iii).

§ 7.   Convention on Migrants and their Families

International Convention on the Protection of the Rights of All Migrant Workers and Members of their Families, New York, Dec. 18, 1990, 2220 U.N.T.S. 93, 30 I.L.M. 1517, *entered into force* July 1, 2003 (1991).

International Convention on the Protection of the Rights of All Migrant Workers and Members of Their Families, G.A. Res. 45/158, at 261, U.N. GAOR, 45th Sess., Supp. No. 49, U.N. Doc. A/45/49 (Dec. 18, 1990).

a.   Status

Office of the High Commissioner for Human Rights, Ratifications and Reservations, http://www2.ohchr.org/english/bodies/ratification/index.htm.

[Provides the most current status information for the main treaties and relevant protocols.]

Office of the High Commissioner for Human Rights, http://www2.ohchr.org/english/bodies/ratification/13.htm.

b. Reservations, Declarations, and Objections

High Commissioner for Human Rights, Committee on Migrant Workers, http://www.ohchr.org/english/countries/ratification/13.htm#reservations.

c. Status of Reports

States parties' reports are http://tb.ohchr.org/default.aspx, and http://www.unhchr.ch/tbs/doc.nsf/RepStatfrset?OpenFrameSet.

d. Decisions, Jurisprudence, and Reports

i. Comments

As of August 2008, the CMW had not issued any General Comments. Once issued, General Comments will become the CMW web page, http://www2.ohchr.org/english/bodies/cmw/index.htm.

Concluding Observations/Comments on States Parties Reports are http://tb.ohchr.org/default.aspx.

e. Legislative History ("Travaux Préparatoires")

A brief summary of the drafting history of the Migrant Workers Convention appears in The International Convention on Migrant Workers and its Committee, Fact Sheet No. 24, (Rev.1) (2005), http://www.ohchr.org/Documents/Publications/FactSheet24rev.1en.pdf.

No comprehensive collection of travaux préparatoires exists for the Migrants Convention, but two partial summaries are:

Luca Bicocchi, Rights of All Migrant Workers (Part III of the Convention), Travaux Préparatoires, http://www2.ohchr.org/english/issues/migration/task-force/docs/draftinghistoryrev1.doc.

Juhani Lonnroth, *The International Convention on the Rights of All Migrant Workers and Members of Their Families in the Context of International Migration Policies: An Analysis of Ten Years of Negotiation*, 25 INT'L MIGRATION REV. 710 (1991).

f. Rules of Procedure

Committee on Migrant Workers, Provisional Rules of Procedure of the Committee on the Protection of the Rights of All Migrant Workers and Members of Their Families, *in* Compilation of Rules of Procedure Adopted by Human Rights Treaty Bodies, Addendum, U.N. Doc. HRI/GEN/3/Rev.1/Add.1 (May 7, 2004), http://daccess-ods.un.org/TMP/3775325.html.

Initial reports: Committee on Migrant Workers, Provisional Guidelines Regarding the Form and Contents of Initial Reports to Be Submitted by States Parties under article 73 of the International Convention on the Protection of the Rights of All Migrant Workers and Members of their Families, *in* Compilation of Guidelines on the Form and Content of Reports to Be Submitted by States Parties to the International Human Rights Treaties, Addendum, HRI/GEN/2/

Rev.2/Add.1 (May 6, 2005), http://www2.ohchr.org/english/bodies/cmw/docs/reporting-guidelines.pdf.

Periodic reports: Committee on Migrant Workers, Guidelines for the Periodic Reports to Be Submitted by States Parties under Article 73 of the Convention, U.N. Doc. CMW/C/2008/1 (May 22, 2008), http://www2.ohchr.org/english/bodies/cmw/docs/CMW.C.2008.1_en.pdf.

g.   Commentaries

i.   Books

SYED REFAAT AHMED, FORLORN MIGRANTS: AN INTERNATIONAL LEGAL REGIME FOR UNDOCUMENTED MIGRANT WORKERS (2000).

[Dhaka: University Press, 267 pp. Analyzes sources and scope of international law on migrant workers.]

AMNESTY INTERNATIONAL, LIVING IN THE SHADOWS: A PRIMER ON THE HUMAN RIGHTS OF MIGRANTS (2006).

[London, U.K.: Amnesty International, International Secretariat, 61 pp. http://www.amnesty.org/en/library/asset/POL33/006/2006/en/dom-POL330062006en.pdf]

Ryszard Cholewinski, *International Convention on the Protection of the Rights of All Migrant Workers and Members of Their Families, in* MIGRANT WORKERS IN INTERNATIONAL HUMAN RIGHTS LAW: THEIR PROTECTION IN COUNTRIES OF EMPLOYMENT 137 (Oxford: OUP, 1997).

RYSZARD I. CHOLEWINSKI, THE LEGAL STATUS OF MIGRANTS ADMITTED FOR EMPLOYMENT: A COMPARATIVE STUDY OF LAW AND PRACTICE IN SELECTED EUROPEAN STATES (2004).

[Strasbourg: Council of Europe Pub., 92 pp. Focuses on the rules relating to the legal status of the main categories of migrant workers admitted for employment in some Council of Europe member states.]

OPHELIA FIELD ET AL., STEMMING THE FLOW: ABUSES AGAINST MIGRANTS, ASYLUM SEEKERS AND REFUGEES (2006).

[New York: Human Rights Watch, 135 pp. http://www.hrw.org/reports/2006/libya0906/index.htm.]

INTERNATIONAL LABOUR ORGANIZATION, TOWARDS A FAIR DEAL FOR MIGRANT WORKERS IN THE GLOBAL ECONOMY (2004).

[Geneva: International Labour Office, 210 pp. http://www.ilo.org/wcmsp5/groups/public/—dgreports/—dcomm/documents/meetingdocument/kd00096.pdf.]

MIGRATION AND INTERNATIONAL LEGAL NORMS (T. Alexander Aleinikoff & Vincent Chetail eds., 2003).

[The Hague: T.M.C. Asser, 353 pp. Articulates international legal norms on migration.]

MIGRANT WOMEN AND WORK (Anuja Agrawal ed., 2006).

[New Delhi; Thousand Oaks, Calif.; London: Sage Publications, 226 pp. Focuses on migrant women in Asia.]

PETER J. VAN KRIEKEN, HEALTH, MIGRATION, AND RETURN: A HANDBOOK FOR A MULTIDISCIPLINARY APPROACH (2001).

[The Hague: T.M.C. Asser Press, 437 pp. Discusses various legal bases for the right to health, then focuses on migrants' issues in relation to the right to health.]

DAVID S. WEISSBRODT, THE HUMAN RIGHTS OF NON-CITIZENS (2008).

[Oxford; New York: Oxford Univ. Press, 257 pp. Comprehensive analysis of the rights of non-citizens, including asylum seekers, rejected asylum seekers, immigrants, non-immigrants, migrant workers, refugees, stateless persons, and trafficked persons.]

ii. Articles

Ryszard Cholewinski, *The Human and Labor Rights of Migrants: Visions of Equality*, 22 GEO. IMMIG. L.J. 177 (2008).

Connie de la Vega & Conchita Lozano-Batista, *Advocates Should Use Applicable International Standards to Address Violations of Undocumented Migrant Workers' Rights in the United States*, 3 HASTINGS RACE & POVERTY L. J. 35 (2005).

Carla Edelenbos, *The International Convention on the Protection of the Rights of All Migrant Workers and Members of Their Families*, 24 REFUGEE SURV. Q. 93 (2005).

Michael Hasenau, *ILO Standards on Migrant Workers: The Fundamentals of the UN Convention and Their Genesis*, 25 INT'L MIGRATION REV. 687 (1991).

Arthur C. Helton & Eliana Jacobs, *What Is Forced Migration?*, 13 GEO. IMMIGR. L.J. 521 (1999).

Shirley Hune, *Migrant Women in the Context of the International Convention on the Protection of the Rights of All Migrant Workers and Members of Their Families*, 25 INT'L MIGRATION REV. 800 (1991).

Rieko Karatani, *How History Separated Refugee and Migrant Regimes: In Search of Their Institutional Origins*, 17 INT'L J. REFUGEE L. 517 (2005).

Beth Lyon, *The Inter-American Court of Human Rights Defines Unauthorized Migrant Workers' Rights for the Hemisphere: A Comment on Advisory Opinion 18*, 28 N.Y.U. REV. L. & SOC. CHANGE 547 (2004).

James A. R. Nafziger & Barry C. Bartel, *The Migrant Workers Convention: Its Place in Human Rights Law*, 25 INT'L MIGRATION REV. 771 (1991).

Jan Niessen & Patrick A. Taran, *Using the New Migrant Workers' Rights Convention*, 25 INT'L MIGRATION REV. 859 (1991).

Kathleen Newland & Demetrios G. Papademetriou, *Managing International Migration: Tracking The Emergence of a New International Regime*, 3 UCLA J. INT'L L. & FOREIGN AFF. 637 (1998-1999).

Chris Nwachukwu Okeke & James A.R. Nafziger, *United States Migration Law: Essentials for Comparison*, 54 AM. J. COMP. L. 531 (2006).

Antoine Pecoud & Paul de Guchteneire, *Migration, Human Rights and the United Nations: An Investigation into the Obstacles to the UN Convention on Migrant Workers' Rights*, 24 WINDSOR Y.B. ACCESS J. 241 (2006).

Margaret L. Satterthwaite, *Crossing Borders, Claiming Rights: Using Human Rights Law To Empower Women Migrant Workers*, 8 YALE HUM. RTS. & DEV. L.J. 1 (2005).

Sandesh Sivakumaran, *The Rights of Migrant Workers One Year On: Transformation Or Consolidation?*, 36 GEO. J. INT'L L. 113 (2004).

Special Issue, *U.N. International Convention on the Protection of the Rights of All Migrant Workers and Members of Their Families*, 25 INT'L MIGRATION REV. 685 (1991).

Patrick A. Taran, *Status and Prospects for the UN Convention on Migrants' Rights*, 2 EUR. J. MIGRATION & L. 85 (2000).

Dirk Vanheule et al., *The Significance of the UN Migrant Workers' Convention of 18 December 1990 in the Event of Ratification by Belgium*, 6 EUR. J. MIGRATION & L. 285 (2004).

David Weissbrodt, The Rights of Non-Citizens, Working Paper Submitted in Accordance with Sub-Commission Decision 1998/103, Addendum, Issues Relating to Migrants, U.N. Doc. E/CN.4/Sub.2/1999/7/Add.1 (1999),

http://www.unhchr.ch/Huridocda/Huridoca.nsf/TestFrame/760aa9e939c5 3069802567a8005891bf?Opendocument.

h.   Practice guides

Yao Agbetse/Franciscans International, Understanding Instruments for the Protection of the Rights of Migrant Workers: Handbook on Migrant Workers (2004), http://www.franciscansinternational.org/resources/migration/inglese.pdf.

i.   Materials Available Through Electronic Formats

i.   Specific Web Sites

Committee on Migrant Workers (CMW), http://www2.ohchr.org/english/ bodies/cmw/index.htm. This High Commissioner for Human Rights web site has the text of the Convention, information on status and reservations, rules of procedure, states parties' reports, and other documents from the CMW.

December 18, International Advocacy and Resource Centre on the Human Rights of Migrant Workers, http://www.december18.net/web/general/start.php. December 18 advocates for the rights of migrants and of migrant workers in particular. Its web site offers news, articles, documents, and links relating to migrant issues.

International Organization for Migration (IOM), http://www.iom.int/jahia/jsp/index.jsp. The IOM is an inter-governmental organization focusing on migration. Its web site offers many resources on international migration, including the Migration Law Database, comprising international, regional, and national instruments on migration.

The Global Campaign for Ratification of the Convention on Rights of Migrants, http://www.migrantsrights.org. This organization coordinates the efforts of numerous NGOs working for the ratification of the Migrants Convention. The site is hosted by International Organization for Migration (IOM), and includes news stories and other documents about the ratification campaign.

ii. General Human Rights Web Sites

See the International Covenant on Civil and Political Rights, section i.(ii).

iii. General Human Rights Discussion Lists and Blogs

See the International Covenant on Civil and Political Rights, section i.(ii).

§ 8. Convention on the Rights of Persons with Disabilities and Its Optional Protocol

International Convention on the Protection and Promotion of the Rights and Dignity of Persons with Disabilities, G.A. Res. 61/106, Annex I, U.N. GAOR, 61st Sess., Supp. No. 49, at 65, U.N. Doc. A/61/49 (2006), 46 I.L.M. 443, *entered into force* May 3, 2008.

First Optional Protocol to the International Convention on the Protection and Promotion of the Rights and Dignity of Persons with Disabilities, G.A. Res. 61/106, Annex II, U.N. GAOR, 61st Sess., Supp. No. 49, at 80, U.N. Doc. A/61/49 (2006), 46 I.L.M. 443, 463 (2007), *entered into force* May 3, 2008.

Electronic versions:

Convention: http://www2.ohchr.org/english/law/disabilities-convention.htm; http://www1.umn.edu/humanrts/instree/disability-convention2006.html.

Protocol: http://www2.ohchr.org/english/law/disabilities-op.htm; http://www1.umn.edu/humanrts/instree/OptProt-disabilityconvention.html.

a. Status

Convention: Office of the High Commissioner for Human Rights, http://www2.ohchr.org/english/bodies/ratification/15.htm.

Optional Protocol: Office of the High Commissioner for Human Rights, http://www2.ohchr.org/english/bodies/ratification/15a.htm.

b. Reservations, Declarations, and Objections

Convention: Office of the High Commissioner for Human Rights, http://www2.ohchr.org/english/bodies/ratification/15.htm.

Optional Protocol: Office of the High Commissioner for Human Rights, http://www2.ohchr.org/english/bodies/ratification/15a.htm.

c.   Status of Reports

As of August 2008, no states had reported. States parties' reports will be the Committee on the Rights of Persons with Disabilities website, http://www2.ohchr.org/english/bodies/crpd/index.htm, and http://www.unhchr.ch/tbs/doc.nsf/RepStatfrset?OpenFrameSet.

d.   Decisions, Jurisprudence, and Reports

i.   Comments

As of August 2008, the CRPD had not issued any Comments. Once issued, Comments will become the CRPD web page, http://www2.ohchr.org/english/bodies/crpd/index.htm.

ii.   Decisions under Optional Protocol

As of August 2008, the CRPD had not issued any Decisions. Once issued, Decisions will become the CRPD web page, http://www2.ohchr.org/english/bodies/crpd/index.htm.

e.   Legislative History ("Travaux Preparatoires")

UN Enable, Ad Hoc Committee on a Comprehensive and Integral International Convention on the Protection and Promotion of the Rights and Dignity of Persons with Disabilities, http://www.un.org/esa/socdev/enable/rights/adhoccom.htm.

Provides links to the negotiating sessions for the Disabilities Convention, including documents generated at these sessions.

f.   Rules of Procedure and Guidelines

As of August 2008, the Committee on the Rights of Persons with Disabilities had not issued Rules of Procedure or reporting guidelines.

g.   Commentaries

i.   Books

PETER BARTLETT ET AL., MENTAL DISABILITY AND THE EUROPEAN CONVENTION ON HUMAN RIGHTS (2007).

[Leiden, Boston: Martinus Nijhoff Publishers, 377 pp.]

DISABLED PEOPLE AND THE RIGHT TO LIFE: THE PROTECTION AND VIOLATION OF DISABLED PEOPLE'S MOST BASIC HUMAN RIGHTS (L. J. Clements & Janet Read eds., 2008).

[London; New York: Routledge, 272 pp. Comparative approach to rights of disabled under national laws.]

DISABILITY, DIVERS-ABILITY, AND LEGAL CHANGE (Melinda Jones & Lee Ann Basser Marks eds., 1999).

[The Hague; Boston: M. Nijhoff Publishers, 400 pp. Comparative legal and sociological approach.]

DISABILITY RIGHTS (Peter David Blanck et al. ed., 2005).

[Burlington, VT: Ashgate Pub.]

[Contains chapters "The globalization of disability rights law" by Arelene S. Kanter; "Next steps - towards a United Nations Treaty on the rights of persons with disabilities," by Gerard Quinn.]

DISABILITY RIGHTS IN EUROPE: FROM THEORY TO PRACTICE (Anna Lawson & Caroline Gooding eds., 2005).

[Oxford; Portland, OR.: Hart Pub. 323 pp. Comprehensive assessment of the state of disability rights in Europe.]

HUMAN RIGHTS AND DISABLED PERSONS: ESSAYS AND RELEVANT HUMAN RIGHTS INSTRUMENTS (Theresia Degener & Yolan Koster-Dreese eds., 1995).

[Dordrecht; Boston: M. Nijhoff, 757 pp. Compiles international and regional instruments that preceded the Disabilities Convention; analyzes need for rights protection.]

THE HUMAN RIGHTS OF PERSONS WITH INTELLECTUAL DISABILITIES: DIFFERENT BUT EQUAL (Stanley S. Herr, Lawrence O. Gostin & Harold Hongju Koh eds., 2003).

[Oxford; New York: Oxford Univ. Press, 551 pp. Addresses international human rights standards and other sources of legal protection, nondiscrimination laws and the economics of equality, etc.]

LAW LIBRARY OF CONGRESS ET AL., INTERNATIONAL DISABILITY RIGHTS: AN OVERVIEW AND COMPARATIVE ANALYSIS OF INTERNATIONAL AND NATIONAL INITIATIVES TO PROMOTE AND PROTECT THE RIGHTS OF PERSONS WITH DISABILITIES (2005).

[Washington, D.C.: Law Library of Congress. http://www.ideanet.org/cir/uploads/File/Law_Library_of_Congress.pdf. Analyzes national legislation of 16 countries.]

BENGT LINDQVIST ET AL., MOVING FORWARD: PROGRESS IN GLOBAL DISABILITY RIGHTS MONITORING (2007).

[Toronto: Disability Rights Promotion International, http://www.yorku.ca/drpi/files/MovingForwardFINAL.pdf, 73 pp. Describes tools for monitoring disability rights.]

MARC MAUDINET, ACCESS TO SOCIAL RIGHTS FOR PEOPLE WITH DISABILITIES IN EUROPE (2003).

[Strasbourg: Council of Europe, 150 pp. Describes state of disability rights within COE member states.]

MICHAEL L. PERLIN, INTERNATIONAL HUMAN RIGHTS AND COMPARATIVE MENTAL DISABILITY LAW (2006).

[Durham, NC: Carolina Academic Press, 1021 pp. Casebook gives overview of international human rights law, regional human rights tribunals, U.S. constitutional mental disability law, mental disability law in an international human rights context, comparative mental disability law, and related issues.]

GERARD QUINN ET AL., HUMAN RIGHTS AND DISABILITY: THE CURRENT USE AND FUTURE POTENTIAL OF UNITED NATIONS HUMAN RIGHTS INSTRUMENTS IN THE CONTEXT OF DISABILITY (2002).

[New York: United Nations, 184 pp. Covers legal instruments preceding the Disability Convention.]

TOWARDS INTERNATIONAL INSTRUMENTS FOR DISABILITY RIGHTS: THE SPECIAL CASE OF DISABLED CHILDREN (2005).

[Strasbourg: Council of Europe, 258 pp.; proceedings of a COE conference.]

UNDERSTANDING THE ROLE OF AN INTERNATIONAL CONVENTION ON THE HUMAN RIGHTS OF PEOPLE WITH DISABILITIES: AN ANALYSIS OF THE LEGAL, SOCIAL, AND PRACTICAL IMPLICATIONS FOR POLICY MAKERS AND DISABILITY AND HUMAN RIGHTS ADVOCATES IN THE UNITED STATES: A WHITE PAPER (2002).

[Washington, DC: National Council on Disability, 102 pp., http://purl.access.gpo.gov/GPO/LPS22821. Describes case for international convention on disability rights.]

ii.   Articles

Heiner Bielefeldt, *New Inspiration for the Human Rights Debate: The Convention on the Rights of Persons with Disabilities*, 25 NETH. Q. HUM. RTS. 397 (2007).

Sally Chaffin, *Challenging the United States Position on a United Nations Convention on Disability*, 15 TEMP. POL. & CIV. RTS. L. REV. 121 (2005).

Aaron A. Dhir, *Human Rights Treaty Drafting through the Lens of Mental Disability: The Proposed International Convention on Protection and Promotion of the Rights and Dignity of Persons with Disabilities*, 41 STAN. J. INT'L L. 181 (2005).

Kris Gledhill, *Human Rights Instruments and Mental Health Law: The English Experience of the Incorporation of the European Convention on Human Rights*, 34 SYRACUSE J. INT'L. L. & COM. 359 (2007).

Lawrence O. Gostin & Lance Gable, *The Human Rights of Persons with Mental Disabilities: A Global Perspective on the Application of Human Rights Principles to Mental Health*, 63 MD. L. REV. 20 (2004).

Vanessa Torres Hernandez, *Making Good on the Promise of International Law: The Convention on the Rights of Persons with Disabilities and Inclusive Education in China and India*, 17 PAC. RIM. L. & POL'Y 497 (2008).

Melinda Jones, *Can International Law Improve Mental Health? Some Thoughts on the Proposed Convention on the Rights of People with Disabilities*, 28 INT'L J. L. & PSYCH. 183 (2005).

Tracy R. Justesen & Troy R. Justesen, *An Analysis of the Development and Adoption of the United Nations Convention Recognizing the Rights of Individuals with Disabilities: Why the United States Refuses to Sign This UN Convention*, HUM. RTS. BRIEF, Winter 2007, at 36.

Arlene S. Kanter, *The Promise and Challenge of the United Nations Convention on the Rights of Persons with Disabilities*, 34 SYRACUSE J. INT'L. L. & COM. 287 (2007).

Rosemary Kayess & Phillip French, *Out of Darkness into Light? Introducing the Convention on the Rights of Persons with Disabilities*, 8 HUM. RTS. L. REV. 1 (2008).

Rosemary Kayess & Ben Fogarty, *The Rights and Dignity of Persons with Disabilities: A United Nations Convention*, ALTERN. L.J., Mar. 2007, at 22.

Harold Hongju Koh, *Different But Equal: The Human Rights of Persons with Intellectual Disabilities*, 63 MD. L. REV. 1 (2004).

Anna Lawson, *The United Nations Convention on the Rights of Persons with Disabilities: New Era or False Dawn?*, 34 SYRACUSE J. INT'L L. & COM. 563 (2007).

Janet E. Lord, *NGO Participation in Human Rights Law and Process: Latest Developments in the Effort to Develop an International Treaty on the Rights of People with Disabilities*, 10 ILSA J. INT'L & COMP. L. 311 (2004).

Don MacKay, *The United Nations Convention on the Rights of Persons with Disabilities*, 34 SYRACUSE J. INT'L. L. & COM. 323 (2007).

Frederic Megret, *The Disabilities Convention: Human Rights of Persons with Disabilities, or Disability Rights?*, 30 HUM. RTS. Q. 494 (2008).

Tara J. Melish, *The UN Disability Convention: Historic Process, Strong Prospects, and Why the U.S. Should Ratify*, HUM. RTS. BRIEF, Winter 2007, at 37.

Tina Minkowitz, *The United Nations Convention on the Rights of Persons with Disabilities and the Right to be Free from Nonconsensual Psychiatric Interventions*, 34 SYRACUSE J. INT'L L. & COM. 405 (2007).

Michael Schwartz, *Deafness in Vietnam: Will the United Nations Convention on the Rights of Persons with Disabilities Make a Difference?*, 34 SYRACUSE J. INT'L L. & COM. 483 (2007).

Michael Ashley Stein, *A Quick Overview of the United Nations Convention on the Rights of Persons with Disabilities and Its Implications for Americans with Disabilities*, 31 MENTAL & PHYS. DISAB. L. REP. 679 (2007).

Michael Ashley Stein, *Disability Human Rights*, 95 CAL. L. REV. 75 (2007).

h.   Practice Guides

No practice guide is available as of August 2008.

i.   Materials Available Through Electronic Formats

i.   Specific Web Sites

UN Enable, http://www.un.org/disabilities. The Convention on the Rights of Persons with Disabilities and its Optional Protocol are served by a joint Secretariat, consisting of staff of both the United Nations Department of Economic and Social Affairs (DESA), based in New York, and the Office of the High Commissioner for Human Rights (OHCHR) in Geneva. DESA supports the Conference of States Parties to be convened in New York. OHCHR supports the Committee on the Rights of Persons with Disabilities.

ii.   General Human Rights Web Sites

See the International Covenant on Civil and Political Rights, section i.(ii).

iii.   General Human Rights Discussion Lists and Blogs

See the International Covenant on Civil and Political Rights, section i.(ii).

§ 9.   Convention on Disappearances

International Convention for the Protection of All Persons from Enforced Disappearance, G.A. res. A/61/177 (2006), *reprinted in* 14 INT'L. HUM. RTS. REP. 582 (2007).

Office of the High Commissioner for Human Rights, http://www2.ohchr.org/english/law/disappearance-convention.htm.

a.   Status

Office of the High Commissioner for Human Rights, http://www2.ohchr.org/english/bodies/ratification/16.htm.

b.   Reservations, Declarations, and Objections

Office of the High Commissioner for Human Rights, http://www2.ohchr.org/english/bodies/ratification/16.htm.

c.   Status of Reports

The Convention is not in force as of August 2008; thus, no parties have reported.

d.   Decisions, Jurisprudence, and Reports

i.   Comments

Working Group on Enforced or Involuntary Disappearances, Compilation of General Comments on the Declaration on the Protection of All Persons from Enforced Disappearance (2006), http://www2.ohchr.org/english/issues/disappear/docs/GeneralCommentsCompilationMay06.pdf.

The Working Group on Enforced or Involuntary Disappearances, General Comment on the Definition of Enforced Disappearance, http://www2.ohchr.org/english/issues/disappear/docs/disappearance_gc.doc.

ii. Reports

Working Group on Enforced or Involuntary Disappearances, Reports to the Commission on Human Rights, http://www2.ohchr.org/english/issues/disappear/annual.htm.

e. Legislative History ("Travaux Preparatoires")

UN COMMISSION ON HUMAN RIGHTS, REPORT OF THE INTERSESSIONAL OPEN-ENDED WORKING GROUP TO ELABORATE A DRAFT LEGALLY BINDING NORMATIVE INSTRUMENT FOR THE PROTECTION OF ALL PERSONS FROM ENFORCED DISAPPEARANCE (Geneva: U.N. 2005).

f. Rules of Procedure and Guidelines

As the convention is not yet in force, there are no rules of procedure under the Convention itself. The Working Group on Enforced or Involuntary Disappearances has issued procedures: Working Group on Enforced or Involuntary Disappearances, The WGEID Procedures, http://www2.ohchr.org/english/issues/disappear/procedures.htm.

g. Commentaries

i. Books

JAN EGELAND, HUMANITARIAN INITIATIVE AGAINST POLITICAL "DISAPPEARANCES": A STUDY OF THE STATUS AND POTENTIAL OF INTERNATIONAL HUMANITARIAN AND HUMAN RIGHTS INSTRUMENTS, AND THE ROLE OF THE INTERNATIONAL COMMITTEE OF THE RED CROSS, IN PROTECTING AGAINST THE PRACTICE OF ENFORCED OR INVOLUNTARY "DISAPPEARANCES" (1982).

[Geneva: Henry Dunant Institute, 59 pp.]

MARÍA FERNANDA PÉREZ SOLLA, ENFORCED DISAPPEARANCES IN INTERNATIONAL HUMAN RIGHTS (2006).

[Jefferson, N.C.: McFarland & Company, Inc., 247 pp. In-depth analysis of the problem of enforced disappearances in international law.]

TULLIO SCOVAZZI & GABRIELLA CITRONI, THE STRUGGLE AGAINST ENFORCED DISAPPEARANCE AND THE 2007 UNITED NATIONS CONVENTION (2007).

[Leiden; Boston: Martinus Nijhoff Publishers, 432 pp. Analyzes history of enforced disappearances and international law's response.]

ii. Articles

Amnesty International, Disappearances, http://web.amnesty.org/library/eng-344/index [index to Amnesty International's reports and documents on enforced disappearances].

Kirsten Anderson, *How Effective Is the International Convention for the Protection of All Persons from Enforced Disappearance Likely to Be in Holding Individuals Criminally Responsible for Acts of Enforced Disappearance?*, 7 MELB. J. INT'L L. 245 (2006).

High Commissioner for Human Rights, Fact Sheet No.6 (Rev.2), Enforced Or Involuntary Disappearances, http://www.unhchr.ch/html/menu6/2/fs6.htm.

Human Rights Watch, "It Was Like Suddenly My Son No Longer Existed" - Enforced Disappearances in Thailand's Southern Border Provinces (2007), http://hrw.org/reports/2007/thailand0307/index.htm [includes Part IV. International Legal Standards and Norms Relating to "Disappearances"].

International Committee of the Red Cross, Missing Persons and International Humanitarian Law, http://www.icrc.org/web/eng/siteeng0.nsf/iwpList2/Humanitarian_law:Missing_persons.

Susan McCrory, *The International Convention for the Protection of All Persons from Enforced Disappearance*, 7 HUM. RTS. L. REV. 545 (2007).

Report Submitted by the Independent Expert Charged with Examining the Existing International Criminal and Human Rights Framework for the Protection of Persons from Enforced Or Involuntary Disappearances, U.N. Doc. E/CN.4/2002/71 (2002), http://www.unhchr.ch/Huridocda/Huridoca.nsf/0/3e140ed64e7c6a83c1256b9700513970/$FILE/G0210026.pdf (submitted by Manfred Nowak).

h.   Practice Guides

No practice guide is available. See, however, Working Group on Enforced or Involuntary Disappearances, The WGEID Procedures, http://www2.ohchr.org/english/issues/disappear/procedures.htm.

i.   Materials Available Through Electronic Formats

i.   Specific Web Sites

International Coalition against Enforced Disappearances, http://www.icaed.org/home.

ii.   General Human Rights Web Sites

See the International Covenant on Civil and Political Rights, section i.(ii).

iii.   General Human Rights Discussion Lists and Blogs

See the International Covenant on Civil and Political Rights, section i.(iii).

G. Refugee Law

AMNESTY INTERNATIONAL, INTERNATIONAL SERVICE FOR HUMAN RIGHTS, THE UN AND REFUGEES' HUMAN RIGHTS: A MANUAL ON HOW UN HUMAN RIGHTS MECHANISMS CAN PROTECT THE RIGHTS OF REFUGEES (1997).

[London; Geneva: Amnesty International, International Service for Human Rights, 90 pp.]

AMNESTY INTERNATIONAL, IN SEARCH OF SAFETY: THE FORCIBLY DISPLACED AND HUMAN RIGHTS IN AFRICA (1997).

[New York, NY: Amnesty International USA, 33 pp.]

DEBORAH ANKER, THE LAW OF ASYLUM IN THE UNITED STATES (3d ed. 1999).

[Washington, DC: American Immigration Law Foundation, 616 pp.]

THE ANNOTATED REFUGEE CONVENTION (1994). [Scarborough, Ont.: Carswell, 158 pp. Series: STATUTES OF CANADA ANNOTATED. 1951 Convention Relating to the Status of Refugees.]

SIMON BAGSHAW, DEVELOPING A NORMATIVE FRAMEWORK FOR THE PROTECTION OF INTERNALLY DISPLACED PERSONS (2005).

[Ardsley, N.Y.: Transnational Publishers, 226 pp.]

HUMAN RIGHTS AND FORCED DISPLACEMENT (Anne F. Bayefsky & Joan Fitzpatrick eds., 2000).

[The Hague; Boston: M. Nijhoff Publishers, 320 pp.]

LAURA BLACK, GENDER ASYLUM LAW IN DIFFERENT COUNTRIES: DECISIONS AND GUIDELINES (1999).

[Boston, MA: Refugee Law Center, 682 pp.]

ROSEMARY BYRNE & GERGOR NOLL, NEW ASYLUM COUNTRIES? MIGRATION CONTROL AND REFUGEE PROTECTION IN AN ENLARGED EUROPEAN UNION (2002).

[The Hague; New York: Kluwer Law International, 463 pp.]

JEAN-YVES CARLIER, WHO IS A REFUGEE?: A COMPARATIVE CASE LAW STUDY (1997).

[The Hague; London: Kluwer Law International, 794 pp.]

B.S. CHIMNI, GLOBALISATION, HUMANITARIANISM AND THE EROSION OF REFUGEE PROTECTION (2000).

[Oxford: Refugee Studies Centre, 23 pp.]

ROBERTA COHEN & JACQUES CUENOD, IMPROVING INSTITUTIONAL ARRANGEMENTS FOR THE INTERNALLY DISPLACED (1995).

[Washington, D.C.: Brookings Institution and Refugee Policy Group, 100 pp. The Brookings Institution - Refugee Policy Group Project on Internal Displacement.]

ROBERTA COHEN & FRANCIS M. DENG, MASSES IN FLIGHT: THE GLOBAL CRISIS OF INTERNAL DISPLACEMENT (1998).

[Washington, D.C.: Brookings Institution Press, 414 pp.]

SARAH COLLINSON, GLOBALISATION AND THE DYNAMICS OF INTERNATIONAL MIGRATION: IMPLICATIONS FOR THE REFUGEE REGIME (1999).

[Geneva: Centre for Documentation and Research, United Nations High Commissioner for Refugees. Series: NEW ISSUES IN REFUGEE RESEARCH, No. 1, 30 pp. http://www.jha.ac/articles/u001.pdf.]

JESSICA B. COOPER, ENVIRONMENTAL REFUGEES: MEETING THE REQUIREMENTS OF THE REFUGEE DEFINITION (1998).

[New York, N.Y.: NEW YORK UNIVERSITY ENVIRONMENTAL LAW JOURNAL, 49 pp. Reprint. Originally issued as part of 6 NEW YORK UNIVERSITY ENVIRONMENTAL LAW JOURNAL no. 2 (1998).]

CREATING SURPLUS POPULATIONS: THE EFFECTS OF MILITARY AND CORPORATE POLICIES ON INDIGENOUS PEOPLES (Lenora Foerstel ed., 1996).

[Washington, D.C.: Maisonneuve Press. Compiled from papers on a conference. Dialogue on Refugee and Displaced Women in Times of Conflict.]

WENDY DAVIES, RIGHTS HAVE NO BORDERS: INTERNAL DISPLACEMENT WORLDWIDE (1998).

[Oslo, Norway: Norwegian Refugee Council; Geneva: Global IDP Survey/ NRC, 123 pp. Contains revised and edited papers from a conference held in 1997.]

ANN VIBEKE EGGLI, MASS REFUGEE INFLUX AND THE LIMITS OF PUBLIC INTERNATIONAL LAW (2002).

[The Hague; New York: Nijhoff; Norwell, MA, 319 pp.]

ERIKA FELLER & VOLKER TÜRK, REFUGEE PROTECTION IN INTERNATIONAL LAW: UNHCR's GLOBAL CONSULTATIONS ON INTERNATIONAL PROTECTION (2003).

[Cambridge; New York: Cambridge University Press, 717 pp.]

JOAN FITZPATRICK, HUMAN RIGHTS PROTECTION FOR REFUGEES, ASYLUM-SEEKERS, AND INTERNALLY DISPLACED PERSONS: A GUIDE TO INTERNATIONAL MECHANISMS AND PROCEDURES (2002).

[Ardsley, NY: Transnational Publishers, 665 pp.]

CONOR FOLEY & SUE SHUTTER, THE LAST RESORT: VIOLATIONS OF THE HUMAN RIGHTS OF MIGRANTS, REFUGEES, AND ASYLUM SEEKERS (1995).

[London: National Council for Civil Liberties, 72 pp. Series: HUMAN RIGHTS CONVENTION; rept. 9.]

FORCED MIGRATION, HUMAN RIGHTS AND SECURITY (Jane McAdam ed., 2008).

[Oxford; Portland, OR.: Hart, 302 pp. Assesses current challenges in refugee protection.]

MICHELLE FOSTER, INTERNATIONAL REFUGEE LAW AND SOCIO-ECONOMIC RIGHTS: REFUGE FROM DEPRIVATION (2007).

[Cambridge, U.K.; New York: Cambridge University Press, 387 pp. Challenges traditional distinctions between "economic migrants" and "political refugees." Argues for including claims based on socio-economic deprivation within the Refugee Convention.]

BIMAL GHOSH, HUDDLED MASSES AND UNCERTAIN SHORES: INSIGHTS INTO IRREGULAR MIGRATION (1998).

[The Hague; Boston: Martinus Nijhoff Publishers, 201 pp. Series: REFUGEES AND HUMAN RIGHTS; v. 2; "IOM, International Organization for Migration." Analyzes irregular migration in its different dimensions and the inadequacies of existing policies and measures.]

GUY S. GOODWIN-GILL & JANE MCADAM, THE REFUGEE IN INTERNATIONAL LAW (3d ed. 2007).

[Oxford: Oxford Univ. Press, 848 pp. Describes the foundations and the framework of international refugee law by concentrating on the definition of refugees, asylum for refugees, and protection of refugees.]

BRIAN GORLICK, HUMAN RIGHTS AND REFUGEES: ENHANCING PROTECTION THROUGH INTERNATIONAL HUMAN RIGHTS LAW (2000).

[Stockholm, Sweden: UNHCR. http://www.unhcr.org/research/RESEARCH/ 3ae6a0cf4.pdf.]

ATLE GRAHL-MADSEN, THE STATUS OF REFUGEES IN INTERNATIONAL LAW (1966, 1972).

[Leiden, The Netherlands: A.W. Sijthoff, 981 pp. 2 vols.]

JAMES C. HATHAWAY, THE LAW OF REFUGEE STATUS (2005).

[Cambridge; New York: Cambridge University Press, 1184 pp.]

JAMES C. HATHAWAY, TOWARD THE REFORMULATION OF INTERNATIONAL REFUGEE LAW: RESEARCH REPORT, 1992-1997 (1997).

[Toronto, Canada: York University, Centre for Refugee Studies, 196 pp. Bound with "Making international refugee law relevant again: a proposal for collectivized and solution-oriented protection," *reprinted from* 10 HARV. HUMAN RIGHTS J. 115 (1997). A project of the Refugee Law Research Unit, Centre for Refugee Studies, York University, Toronto, Canada.]

JAMES C. HATHAWAY & JOHN A. DENT, REFUGEE RIGHTS: REPORT ON A COMPARATIVE SURVEY (1995).

[Toronto: York Lanes Press, 82 pp.]

Human Rights and Mass Exoduses: Report of the Secretary-General, U.N. Doc. E/CN.4/1996/42 (1996).

[Geneva: United Nations, Commission on Human Rights, 26 pp.]

*Human Rights and Mass Exoduses: Report of the High Commissioner for Human Rights, in Commission on Human Rights: Report on the 53*rd *Session*, U.N. ESCOR, Supp. no. 3 at 250, U.N. Doc. E/1997/23, E/CN.4/1997/150 (1997).

[Geneva: United Nations, 32 pp.]

ANNE F. BAYEFSKY ET AL, HUMAN RIGHTS AND REFUGEES, INTERNALLY DISPLACED PERSONS, AND MIGRANT WORKERS: ESSAYS IN MEMORY OF JOAN FITZPATRICK AND ARTHUR HELTON (2006).

[Leiden; Boston: M. Nijhoff, 598 pp.]

HUMAN RIGHTS PROTECTION FOR REFUGEES, ASYLUM-SEEKERS, AND INTERNALLY DISPLACED PERSONS: GUIDE TO INTERNATIONAL MECHANISMS AND PROCEDURES (Joan Fitzpatrick ed., 2002).

[Ardsley, NY: Transnational Publishers, 665 pp.]

WALTER KÄLIN, GUIDING PRINCIPLES ON INTERNAL DISPLACEMENT: ANNOTATIONS (2000).

[Washington, D.C.: The American Society of International Law, 276 pp.]

SUSAN KNEEBONE, THE REFUGEES CONVENTION 50 YEARS ON: GLOBALISATION AND INTERNATIONAL LAW (2003).

[Aldershot, Hants; Burlington, VT: Ashgate, 338 pp.]

PIRKKO KOURULA, BROADENING THE EDGES: REFUGEE DEFINITION AND INTERNATIONAL PROTECTION REVISITED (1997).

[The Hague; Boston: Cambridge, Mass. Martinus Nijhoff Publishers, 407 pp. Volume 1 of a new series: REFUGEES AND HUMAN RIGHTS REFUGEES AND HUMAN RIGHTS.]

HELENE LAMBERT, SEEKING ASYLUM: COMPARATIVE LAW AND PRACTICE IN SELECTED EUROPEAN COUNTRIES (1995).

[Dordrecht; Boston: M. Nijhoff, 220 pp. Series: INTERNATIONAL STUDIES IN HUMAN RIGHTS; v. 37. A comparative study of the relevant law and practice of six European states.]

LAWYERS COMMITTEE FOR HUMAN RIGHTS, THE UNHCR AT 40: REFUGEE PROTECTION AT THE CROSSROADS (1991).

[New York: Lawyers Committee, 156 pp. A report of the LCHR (now Human Rights First).]

LAW AND MIGRATION (Selina Goulbourne ed., 1998).

[Cheltenham; Northampton, MA: E. Elgar Pub., 465 pp. Series: THE INTERNATIONAL LIBRARY OF STUDIES ON MIGRATION; 6; An Elgar Reference Collection; covers wide range of topics.]

LAW LIBRARY OF CONGRESS (U.S.), LAW OF REFUGEES IN SELECTED COUNTRIES: REPORT FOR CONGRESS (1998).

[Washington, D.C.: Law Library, Library of Congress, 184 pp.]

SCOTT LECKIE, RETURNING HOME: HOUSING AND PROPERTY RESTITUTION RIGHTS OF REFUGEES AND DISPLACED PERSONS (2003).

[Ardsley, NY: Transnational Publishers, 433 pp.]

THE LIVING LAW OF NATIONS: ESSAYS ON REFUGEES, MINORITIES, INDIGENOUS PEOPLES, AND THE HUMAN RIGHTS OF OTHER VULNERABLE GROUPS: IN MEMORY OF ATLE GRAHL-MADSEN (Gudmundur Alfredsson & Peter Macalister-Smith eds., 1996).

[Kehl, Arlington, Va.: N.P. Engel, 467 pp.]

NUALA MOLE, PROBLEMS RAISED BY CERTAIN ASPECTS OF THE PRESENT SITUATION OF REFUGEES FROM THE STANDPOINT OF THE EUROPEAN CONVENTION ON HUMAN RIGHTS (1997).

[Strasbourg: Council of Europe Pub, 66 pp.]

NGO MANUAL ON INTERNATIONAL AND REGIONAL INSTRUMENTS CONCERNING REFUGEES AND HUMAN RIGHTS (1998).

[Geneva, Switzerland: UNHCR Regional Bureau for Europe, 370 pp. EUROPEAN SERIES; v. 4, no. 2 (July 1998).]

NIRAJ NATHWANI, RETHINKING REFUGEE LAW (2003).

[The Hague; New York: Martinus Nijhoff Publishers, 168 pp.]

Office of the UNHCR, *Note on International Protection*, U.N. Doc. A/AC.96/ [#] (1959-).

[New York: U.N. Annual summaries of the major challenges facing the UNHCR, as well as recommendations to improve refugee protection.]

CATHERINE PHUONG, THE INTERNATIONAL PROTECTION OF INTERNALLY DISPLACED PERSONS (2004).

[Cambridge; New York: Cambridge University Press, 293 pp.]

POWER, ETHICS, AND HUMAN RIGHTS: ANTHROPOLOGICAL STUDIES OF REFUGEE RESEARCH AND ACTION (Ruth M. Krulfeld & Jeffery L. MacDonald eds., 1998).

[Lanham, MD: Rowman & Littlefield Publishers, 203 pp.]

THE PROBLEM OF REFUGEES IN THE LIGHT OF CONTEMPORARY INTERNATIONAL LAW ISSUES (Vera Gowlland-Debbas ed., 1996).

[The Hague; Boston: Cambridge, MA M. Nijhoff, 179 pp. Papers presented at the colloquium organized by the Graduate Institute of International Studies in collaboration with the Office of the United Nations High Commissioner for Refugees, Geneva, 26 and 27 May, 1994.]

RECONCEIVING INTERNATIONAL REFUGEE LAW (James C. Hathaway ed., 1997).

[The Hague; Cambridge, MA: M. Nijhoff Pub., 171 pp. Addresses the challenge of reconceiving refugee protection in a way that is reconcilable with the concerns of modern states, yet which does not sacrifice the rights of at-risk people to seek asylum.]

KAREN MUSALO ET AL., REFUGEE LAW AND POLICY: A COMPARATIVE AND INTERNATIONAL APPROACH (3d ed. 2007).

Durham, N.C.: Carolina Academic Press, 1196 pp. Analyzes refugee law including substance and procedure.]

REFUGEES: HUMAN RIGHTS HAVE NO BORDERS (1997).

[London: Amnesty International Publications, 137 pp.]

REFUGEES - THE TRAUMA OF EXILE: THE HUMANITARIAN ROLE OF RED CROSS AND RED CRESCENT (Diana Miserez ed., 1988).

[Dordrecht; Boston: Martinus Nijhoff Pub., 340 pp.]

SECRETARIAT, INTER-GOVERNMENTAL CONSULTATIONS ON ASYLUM, REFUGEE, AND MIGRATION POLICIES IN EUROPE, NORTH AMERICA, AND AUSTRALIA, REPORT ON TEMPORARY PROTECTION IN STATES IN EUROPE, NORTH AMERICA, AND AUSTRALIA (1995).

[Geneva: The Secretariat, various pagings.]

NICHOLAS SITAROPOULOS, JUDICIAL INTERPRETATION OF REFUGEE STATUS: IN SEARCH OF A PRINCIPLED METHODOLOGY BASED ON A CRITICAL COMPARATIVE ANALYSIS, WITH SPECIAL REFERENCE TO CONTEMPORARY BRITISH, FRENCH, AND GERMAN JURISPRUDENCE (1999).

[Athens; Baden-Baden: Nomos, 521 pp.]

THOMAS SPIJKERBOER, GENDER AND REFUGEE STATUS (2000).

[Brookfield, VT: Ashgate, 286 pp. Socio-legal study of interrelation between gender and the law of refugee status, including an examination of case law and critique of the current legal doctrine.]

NIKLAUS STEINER & MARK GIBNEY, PROBLEMS OF PROTECTION: THE UNHCR, REFUGEES, AND HUMAN RIGHTS (2003).

[New York: Routledge, 350 pp.]

Symposium on Refugees and the Problems of Forced Population Displacements in Africa, 7 INT'L J. REFUGEE L. 1 (1995).

[Special issue Summer 1995; 332 pp.]

PATRICIA TUITT, FALSE IMAGES: LAW'S CONSTRUCTION OF THE REFUGEE (1996).

[London: Pluto Press, 187 pp.]

UNHCR Symposium on Gender-Based Persecution, 1997 INT'L J. REFUGEE L. 1 (1997).

[Special issue Autumn 1997; 251 pp.]

UNCHR, THE STATE OF THE WORLD'S REFUGEES (1993-).

[Oxford; New York: Oxford Univ. Press. These annual reports are available on the Web, http://www.unhcr.org. Each report has a distinctive title.]

PETER W. VAN ARSDALE, FORCED TO FLEE: HUMAN RIGHTS AND HUMAN WRONGS IN REFUGEE HOMELANDS (2006).

[Lanham, Md.: Lexington Books, 225 pp. Uses case studies of refugee populations to examine human rights issues.]

MYRON WEINER, THE GLOBAL MIGRATION CRISIS: CHALLENGE TO STATES AND TO HUMAN RIGHTS (1995).

[New York: HarperCollins College Publishers, 253 pp.]

PIA ZAMBELLI, ANNOTATED REFUGEE CONVENTION: FIFTY YEARS OF NORTH AMERICAN JURISPRUDENCE (2004).

[Toronto: Thomson/Carswell, 865 pp.]

MARJOLEINE ZIECK, UNHCR AND VOLUNTARY REPATRIATION OF REFUGEES: A LEGAL ANALYSIS (1997).

[The Hague; Boston: Martinus Nijhoff, 494 pp.]

H. Economic Issues

§ 1.   Books

PHILIP ALSTON, LABOUR RIGHTS AS HUMAN RIGHTS (2005).

[Oxford; New York: Oxford Univ. Press, 253 pp.]

PHILIP ALSTON & MARY ROBINSON, HUMAN RIGHTS AND DEVELOPMENT: TOWARDS MUTUAL REINFORCEMENT (2005).

[Oxford; New York: Oxford Univ. Press, 551 pp.]

AMNESTY INTERNATIONAL, HUMAN RIGHTS FOR HUMAN DIGNITY: A PRIMER ON ECONOMIC, SOCIAL AND CULTURAL RIGHTS (2005).

[London: Amnesty International, 80 pp.]

AMNESTY INTERNATIONAL, HUMAN RIGHTS, TRADE AND INVESTMENT MATTERS (2006).

[London: Amnesty International UK; New York: Amnesty International USA, 54 pp. Addresses current human rights challenges for IMF, corporations, foreign investment, etc.]

SUBHABRATA BOBBY BANERJEE, CORPORATE SOCIAL RESPONSIBILITY: THE GOOD, THE BAD AND THE UGLY (2007).

[Cheltenham, Glos.; Northampton, MA: Edward Elgar, 211 pp. Critiques current trends in corporate social responsibility.]

BÅRD-ANDERS ANDREASSEN & STEPHEN P. MARKS, DEVELOPMENT AS A HUMAN RIGHT: LEGAL, POLITICAL, AND ECONOMIC DIMENSIONS (2006).

[Boston: Harvard School of Public Health, François-Xavier Bagnoud Center for Health and Human Rights; Cambridge: Distributed by Harvard University Press, 318 pp. Analyzes various dimensions of right to development.]

WOLFGANG BENEDEK & K. DE FEYTER, ECONOMIC GLOBALISATION AND HUMAN RIGHTS (2007).

[Cambridge; New York: Cambridge University Press, 329 pp.]

ROGER BLANPAIN & RUTH BEN-ISRAEL, LABOUR LAW, HUMAN RIGHTS AND SOCIAL JUSTICE (2001).

[The Hague: Kluwer Law International, 300 pp.]

W. R. BÖHNING, LABOUR RIGHTS IN CRISIS: MEASURING THE ACHIEVEMENT OF HUMAN RIGHTS IN THE WORLD OF WORK (2005).

[Basingstoke; New York: Palgrave Macmillan, 229 pp.]

ALISON BRYSK, GLOBALIZATION AND HUMAN RIGHTS (2002).

[Berkeley: University of California Press, 311 pp.]

BUREAU OF INTERNATIONAL LABOR AFFAIRS, U.S. DEPARTMENT OF LABOR, INTERNATIONAL LABOR STANDARDS AND GLOBAL ECONOMIC INTEGRATION: PROCEEDINGS OF A SYMPOSIUM (1994).

[Washington, D.C.: Dept. of Labor, 84 pp.]

BUSINESS ETHICS IN THE GLOBAL MARKET (Tibor R. Machan ed., 1999).

[Stanford, CA: Hoover Institution Press, 142 pp.]

BY THE SWEAT AND TOIL OF CHILDREN: A REPORT TO THE COMMITTEES ON APPROPRIATIONS (1995).

[Washington, D.C.: Bureau of International Labor Affairs, U.S. Department of Labor. 2 vols.]

GUY CAIRE, FREEDOM OF ASSOCIATION AND ECONOMIC DEVELOPMENT (1977).

[Geneva: International Labour Office, 159 pp.]

JOHN CAVANAGH, TRADE'S HIDDEN COSTS: WORKER RIGHTS IN A CHANGING WORLD ECONOMY (1988).

[Washington, D.C.: International Labor Rights Education and Research Fund, 66 pp.]

STEVE CHARNOVITZ, TRADE LAW AND GLOBAL GOVERNANCE (2002).

[London: Cameron May, 539 pp.]

RYSZARD I. CHOLEWINSKI, THE LEGAL STATUS OF MIGRANTS ADMITTED FOR EMPLOYMENT: A COMPARATIVE STUDY OF LAW AND PRACTICE IN SELECTED EUROPEAN STATES (2004).

[Strasbourg: Council of Europe Pub., 92 pp.]

RYSZARD I. CHOLEWINSKI, MIGRANT WORKERS IN INTERNATIONAL HUMAN RIGHTS LAW: THEIR PROTECTION IN COUNTRIES OF EMPLOYMENT (1997).

[Oxford: Clarendon Press, 465 pp.]

CIRCLE OF RIGHTS - ECONOMIC, SOCIAL AND CULTURAL RIGHTS ACTIVISM: A TRAINING RESOURCE (2000).

[Washington, D.C.: International Human Rights Internship Program and Asian Forum for Human Rights and Development, 660 pp. International Human Rights Internship Program. Part I includes information about the substance of economic, social and cultural rights, and about strategies and tools that can be used to protect and promote them. The shorter Part II includes some suggestions for training methods that may be used to convey the material in Part I.]

COMBATING CHILD LABOUR (Assefa Bequele & Jo Boyden eds., 1988).

[Geneva: International Labour Office, 226 pp.]

CONDITIONS OF EMPLOYMENT GUARANTEED UNDER THE EUROPEAN SOCIAL CHARTER/STUDY COMPILED ON THE BASIS OF THE CASE LAW OF THE COMMITTEE OF INDEPENDENT EXPERTS (1997).

[Strasbourg: Council of Europe, 171 pp.]

HECTOR BARTOLOMEI DE LA CRUZ, ET. AL., THE INTERNATIONAL LABOR ORGANIZATION: THE INTERNATIONAL STANDARDS SYSTEM AND BASIC HUMAN RIGHTS (1996).

[Boulder, CO: Westview Press, 296 pp.]

MAC DARROW, BETWEEN LIGHT AND SHADOW: THE WORLD BANK, THE INTERNATIONAL MONETARY FUND AND INTERNATIONAL HUMAN RIGHTS LAW (2003).

[Oxford; Portland, OR.: Hart Pub., 353 pp.]

TRANSNATIONAL CORPORATIONS AND HUMAN RIGHTS (Olivier de Schutter ed., 2006).

[Oxford; Portland, OR.: Hart Pub., 430 pp. Analyzes several approaches to eliciting human rights compliance from transnational corporations.]

JANET DINE, COMPANIES, INTERNATIONAL TRADE, AND HUMAN RIGHTS (2005).

[Cambridge; New York: Cambridge University Press, 319 pp.]

ECONOMIC, SOCIAL, AND CULTURAL RIGHTS: A LEGAL RESOURCE GUIDE (Scott Leckie & Anne Gallagher eds., 2006).

[Philadelphia, Pa.: University of Pennsylvania Press, 744 pp.]

JEDRZEJ GEORGE FRYNAS & SCOTT PEGG, TRANSNATIONAL CORPORATIONS AND HUMAN RIGHTS (2003).

[Houndmills, Basingstoke, Hampshire; New York: Palgrave, 223 pp.]

TIMOTHY A. GELATT, GETTING DOWN TO BUSINESS: THE HUMAN RIGHTS RESPONSIBILITIES OF CHINA'S INVESTORS AND TRADE PARTNERS (1992).

[New York, NY: International League for Human Rights, 50 pp.]

WILLEM J. M. VAN GENUGTEN, ET AL., WORLD BANK, IMF AND HUMAN RIGHTS: INCLUDING THE TILBURG GUIDING PRINCIPLES ON WORLD BANK, IMF AND HUMAN RIGHTS (2003).

[Nijmegen, The Netherlands: Wolf Legal Publishers, 2003.]

BAHRAM GHAZI, THE IMF, THE WORLD BANK GROUP, AND THE QUESTION OF HUMAN RIGHTS (2005).

[Ardsley, NY: Transnational Publishers, 445 pp.]

GLOBAL GOVERNANCE: ETHICS AND ECONOMICS OF THE WORLD ORDER (Meghnad Desai & Paul Redfern eds., 1995).

[London; New York: Pinter, 230 pp.]

GLOBAL RESPONSIBILITIES: WHO MUST DELIVER ON HUMAN RIGHTS? (Andrew Kuper ed., 2005).

[New York: Routledge, 283 pp.]

S.B.O. Gutto, *Violation of Human Rights in the Third World: Responsibility of States and Transnational Corporations, in* THIRD WORLD ATTITUDES TOWARD INTERNATIONAL LAW: AN INTRODUCTION (Frederick E. Snyder & Surakiart Sathirathai eds., 1987).

[Dordrecht; Boston: M. Nijhoff Pubs., 850 pp.]

JAMES HARRISON, THE HUMAN RIGHTS IMPACT OF THE WORLD TRADE ORGANISATION (2007).

[Portland, OR.: Hart, 276 pp. Assesses WTO's impact on human rights and argues for inclusion of human rights norms within WTO framework.]

BERTA ESPERANZA HERNÁNDEZ-TRUYOL & STEPHEN J. POWELL, JUST TRADE: A NEW COVENANT LINKING TRADE AND HUMAN RIGHTS (2008).

[New York: New York University Press, 416 pp. Describes potential integration of human rights norms with trade framework.]

HOLGER P. HESTERMEYER, HUMAN RIGHTS IN THE WTO: THE CASE OF TRIPS AND ACCESS TO MEDICATION (2007).

[Oxford: Oxford Univ. Press, 300 pp.]

ROBERT HOWSE & MAKAU MUTUA, PROTECTING HUMAN RIGHTS IN A GLOBAL ECONOMY: CHALLENGES FOR THE WORLD TRADE ORGANIZATION (2000).

[Montréal: Rights & Democracy, International Centre for Human Rights and Democratic Development, 25 pp.]

HUMAN DEVELOPMENT REPORT (1990-).

[New York: Oxford Univ. Press, annual. Ten years of the report are available on CD-ROM (1990-2000). Some of the reports are also available on the UNDP Web site, http://hdr.undp.org/en.]

HUMAN RIGHTS AND CORPORATIONS (David Kinley ed., 2009).

[Aldershot, Hants; Burlington, VT: Ashgate Pub. Co. Collects key essays on relationship of transnational corporations and human rights.]

HUMAN RIGHTS AND LABOUR LAWS: ESSAYS FOR PAUL O'HIGGINS (K.D. Ewing et al. eds., 1994).

[New York, NY: Mansell, 367 pp.]

HUMAN RIGHTS AND INTERNATIONAL TRADE (Thomas Cottier et al. eds, 2005).

[Oxford; New York: Oxford Univ. Press, 522 pp.]

HUMAN RIGHTS, LABOR RIGHTS, AND INTERNATIONAL TRADE: LAW AND POLICY PERSPECTIVES

(Lance A. Compa & Stephen F. Diamond eds., 1996).

[Philadelphia: University of Pennsylvania, 311 pp.]

INTERNATIONAL LABOR STANDARDS AND GLOBAL ECONOMIC INTEGRATION: PROCEEDINGS OF A SYMPOSIUM, BUREAU OF INTERNATIONAL LABOR AFFAIRS, U.S. DEPARTMENT OF LABOR (1994).

[Washington, DC: Dept. of Labor, 84 pp.]

INTERNATIONAL LABOUR OFFICE, ILO LAW ON FREEDOM OF ASSOCIATION: STANDARDS AND PROCEDURES (1995).

[Geneva: International Labour Office, 170 pp.]

INTERNATIONAL LABOUR OFFICE, FREEDOM OF ASSOCIATION COMMITTEE, FREEDOM OF ASSOCIATION: DIGEST OF DECISIONS AND PRINCIPLES OF THE FREEDOM OF ASSOCIATION COMMITTEE OF THE GOVERNING BODY OF THE ILO (4th ed. 1996).

[Geneva: International Labour Office, 238 pp.]

INTERNATIONAL MIGRATION, REFUGEE FLOWS AND HUMAN RIGHTS IN NORTH AMERICA: THE IMPACT OF TRADE AND RESTRUCTURING (Alan B. Simmons ed., 1996).

[New York: Center for Migration Studies, 335 pp.]

INTERNATIONAL TRADE AND HUMAN RIGHTS: FOUNDATIONS AND CONCEPTUAL ISSUES (Frederick M. Abbott et al. eds., 2006).

[Ann Arbor, Mich.: University of Michigan Press, 384 pp.]

NICOLA M. C. P. JÄGERS, CORPORATE HUMAN RIGHTS OBLIGATIONS: IN SEARCH OF ACCOUNTABILITY (2002).

[Antwerpen; New York: Intersentia, 309 pp.]

C. WILFRED JENKS, HUMAN RIGHTS AND INTERNATIONAL LABOUR STANDARDS (1960).

[London: Stevens; New York: Praeger, 159 pp.]

JUSTICE DENIED!: HUMAN RIGHTS AND THE INTERNATIONAL FINANCIAL INSTITUTIONS (1994).

[Geneva: Women's International League for Peace and Freedom; Kathmandu: International Institute for Human Rights, Environment, and Development, 185 pp.]

LABOUR RIGHTS AS HUMAN RIGHTS (Philip Alston ed., 2005).

[Oxford; New York: Oxford Univ. Press, 253 pp.]

LAWYERS COMMITTEE FOR HUMAN RIGHTS, WORKER RIGHTS UNDER THE U.S. TRADE LAWS (1989).

[New York: Lawyers Committee for Human Rights, 77pp.]

Virginia A. Leary, *Labor, in* UNITED NATIONS LEGAL ORDER (Oscar Schachter & Christopher C. Joyner eds., 1995).

[Cambridge; New York: Cambridge University Press, 2 vols.]

Virginia A. Leary, *Lessons from the Experience of the International Labour Organization, in* THE UNITED NATIONS AND HUMAN RIGHTS: A CRITICAL APPRAISAL (Philip Alston ed., 1992).

[Oxford: Clarendon Press; New York: Oxford Univ. Press, 765 pp.]

Virginia A. Leary, *Workers' Rights and International Trade: The Social Clause (GATT, ILO, NAFTA, U.S. Laws), in* FAIR TRADE AND HARMONIZATION: PREREQUISITES FOR FREE TRADE (Jagdish Bhagwati & Robert E. Hudec eds., 1996).

[Cambridge, MA; London: MIT Press, 2 vols.]

VIRGINIA A. LEARY & DANIEL WARNER, SOCIAL ISSUES, GLOBALISATION AND INTERNATIONAL INSTITUTIONS: LABOUR RIGHTS AND THE EU, ILO, OECD AND WTO (2006).

[Leiden; Boston: M. Nijhoff, 418 pp. Analyzes how and to what extent international labor issues have become issues within the EU, ILO, OECD, and WTO.]

LEGAL PROBLEMS AND CODES OF CONDUCT FOR MULTINATIONAL ENTERPRISES (Norbert Horn ed., 1980).

[Deventer, the Netherlands; Boston: Kluwer, 509 pp.]

FIONA MACMILLAN, THE WORLD TRADE ORGANIZATION AND HUMAN RIGHTS (2005).

[Oxford: Hart, 344 pp.]

RADU MARES, THE DYNAMICS OF CORPORATE SOCIAL RESPONSIBILITIES (2008).

[Boston: Martinus Nijhoff Publishers, 370 pp. Explores limitations of voluntary and legally-mandated CSR; recommends policies.]

JOSETTE MURPHY, GENDER ISSUES IN WORLD BANK LENDING (1995).

[Washington, D.C.: World Bank, 131 pp.]

NON-STATE ACTORS AND HUMAN RIGHTS (Philip Alston ed., 2005).

[Oxford; New York: Oxford Univ. Press, 387 pp.]

PATRICK J. O'MAHONEY, MULTINATIONALS AND HUMAN RIGHTS (1980).

[Great Wakering: Mayhew-McCrimmon, 318 pp.]

JOEL E. OESTREICH, POWER AND PRINCIPLE: HUMAN RIGHTS PROGRAMMING IN INTERNATIONAL ORGANIZATIONS (2007).

[Washington, D.C.: Georgetown University Press, 240 pp.]

CHERYL PAYER, THE DEBT TRAP: THE INTERNATIONAL MONETARY FUND AND THE THIRD WORLD (1974).

[New York: Monthly Review Press, 251 pp.]

THE PEOPLE VS GLOBAL CAPITAL: THE G-7, TNC'S, SAP'S AND HUMAN RIGHTS: REPORT OF THE INTERNATIONAL PEOPLE'S TRIBUNAL TO JUDGE THE G-7, TOKYO, JULY 1993 (1994).

[Tokyo: Pacific Asia Resource Center, 163 pp.]

PERPETUATING POVERTY: THE WORLD BANK, THE IMF, AND THE DEVELOPING WORLD (Doug Bandow & Ian Vásquez eds., 1994).

[Washington, D.C.: Cato Institute, 362 pp.]

RICHARD L. SIEGEL, EMPLOYMENT AND HUMAN RIGHTS: THE INTERNATIONAL DIMENSION (1994).

[Philadelphia: University of Pennsylvania Press, 272 pp.]

SIGRUN SKOGLY, THE HUMAN RIGHTS OBLIGATIONS OF THE WORLD BANK AND THE INTERNATIONAL MONETARY FUND (2001).

[London: Cavendish Pub., 225 pp.]

SOCIAL RIGHTS AS HUMAN RIGHTS: A EUROPEAN CHALLENGE (Krzysztof Drzewicki et al. eds., 1994).

[Åbo, Finland: Institute for Human Rights, Åbo Akademi University, 319 pp.]

KATARINA TOMAŜEVSKI, DEVELOPMENT AID AND HUMAN RIGHTS REVISITED (1993).

[London: Pinter, 223 pp.]

THE URUGUAY ROUND AND BEYOND: ESSAYS IN HONOR OF ARTHUR DUNKEL (Jagdish Bhagwati & Mathias Hirsch eds., 1998).

[Ann Arbor, MI: University of Michigan Press, 314 pp.]

GERALDO VON POTOBSKY ET AL., THE INTERNATIONAL LABOR ORGANIZATION: THE INTERNATIONAL STANDARDS SYSTEM AND BASIC HUMAN RIGHTS (1996).

[Boulder, CO: Westview Press, 296 pp.]

Francis Wolf, *Human Rights and the International Labour Organisation*, *in* HUMAN RIGHTS IN INTERNATIONAL LAW: LEGAL AND POLICY ISSUES (Theodor Meron ed., 1984).

[Oxford: Clarendon Press, 2 vols.]

THE WORLD BANK: GOVERNANCE AND HUMAN RIGHTS (rev. and updated, 1995).

[New York, NY: Lawyers Committee for Human Rights, 127 pp.]

WORLD BANK, ADVANCING SOCIAL DEVELOPMENT: A WORLD BANK CONTRIBUTION TO THE SOCIAL SUMMIT (1995).

[Washington, D.C.: World Bank, 60 pp.]

§ 2.   Articles

Michael K. Addo, *Human Rights Perspectives of Corporate Groups*, 37 CONN. L. REV. 667 (2005).

Daniel S. Ahrenberg, *The Labor Link: Applying the International Trading System to Enforce Violations of Forced and Child Labor*, 20 Yale J. Int'l L. 361 (1995).

Philip Alston, *International Trade as an Instrument of Positive Human Rights Policy*, 4 Hum. Rts. Q. 155 (1982).

Philip Alston, *Labor Provisions in US Trade Law: 'Aggressive Unilateralism'?*, 15 Hum. Rts. Q. 1 (1993).

Philip Alston, *Linking Trade and Human Rights*, 23 German Y.B. Int'l L. 126 (1980).

Philip Alston, *Resisting the Merger and Acquisition of Human Rights by Trade Law: A Reply to Petersmann*, 13 Eur. J. Int'l L. 621 (2002).

Theresa Amato, *Labor Rights Conditionality: United States Trade Legislation and the International Trade Order*, 65 N.Y.U. L. Rev. 79 (1990).

Robert D. Anderson & Hannu Wager, *Human Rights, Development, and the WTO: The Cases of Intellectual Property and Competition Policy*, 9 J. Int'l Econ. L. 707 (2006).

Anthony Anghie, *Time Present and Time Past: Globalization, International Financial Institutions, and the Third World*, 32 N.Y.U. J. Int'l L. & Pol. 243 (2000).

Robert Ansell & Wendy Archer, *The Universal Declaration of Human Rights and Multinational Corporations in the Third World*, 47 U.N.B.L.J. 133 (1998).

Lena Ayoub, *Nike Just Does It - and Why the United States Shouldn't: The United States' International Obligation to Hold MNCs Accountable for Their Labor Rights Violations Abroad*, 11 DePaul Bus. L.J. 395 (1999).

[Symposium: The Introduction of the Euro and its Implications for U.S. Lawyers]

Arthur A. Baer, *Latino Human Rights and the Global Economic Order*, 18 Chicano-Latino L. Rev. 80 (1996).

Mark B. Baker, *Private Codes of Corporate Conduct: Should the Fox Guard the Henhouse?*, 24 U. Miami Inter-Am. L. Rev. 399 (1993).

Lisa G. Baltazar, *Government Sanctions and Private Initiatives: Striking a New Balance for U.S. Enforcement of Internationally-Recognized Workers' Rights*, 29 Colum. Hum. Rts. L. Rev. 687 (1998).

Janice R. Bellace, *ILO Fundamental Rights at Work and Freedom of Association*, 50 Lab. L.J. 191 (1999).

Alejandro Alvarez Bejar, *Industrial Restructuring and the Role of Mexican Labor in NAFTA*, 27 U.C. Davis L. Rev. 897 (1994).

[Symposium: Free Trade and Democratic Values: NAFTA's Effect on Human Rights]

Laurel A. Beutler, *The ILO and IMF: Permissibility and Desirability of a Proposal to Meet the Contemporary Realities of the International Protection of Labor Rights*, 14 SYR. J. INT'L L. & COM. 455 (1987).

Simon Billenness, *Beyond South Africa: New Frontiers in Corporate Responsibility*, 1993 BUS. & SOC'Y REV. 28 (1993).

Jonathan L. Black-Branch, *Closing the Door on Closed-Shop Agreements: Labor Law, Trade Unionism, and the Right to Freedom of Assembly and Freedom of Association under the European Convention on Human Rights*, 27 J. COLLECTIVE NEGOTIATIONS PUB. SECTOR 307 (1998).

Adelle Blackett, *Whither Social Clause? Human Rights, Trade Theory and Treaty*, 31 COLUM. HUM. RTS. L. REV. 1 (1999).

Jennifer Bol, *Using the Inter-American System to Pursue International Labour Rights: A Case Study of the Guatemalan Maquiladoras*, 55 U. TORONTO FAC. L. REV. 351 (1997).

Leonard B. Boudin, *Economic Sanctions and Individual Rights*, 19 N.Y.U. J. INT'L L. & POL. 803 (1987).

Daniel D. Bradlow, *Human Rights, Public Finance and the Development Process: A Critical Introduction*, 8 AM. U. J. INT'L L. & POL'Y 1 (1992).

Daniel D. Bradlow, *The World Bank, the IMF, and Human Rights*, 6 TRANSNAT'L L. & CONTEMP. PROBS. 47 (1996).

[Symposium: Social Justice and Development: Critical Issues Facing the Bretton Woods System]

George Brenkert, *Can We Afford International Human Rights?*, 11 J. BUS. ETHICS 515 (1992).

Isabella D. Bunn, *The Right to Development: Implications for International Economic Law*, 15 AM. U. INT'L L. REV. 1425 (2000).

Jonathan Cahn, *Challenging the New Imperial Authority: The World Bank and the Democratization of Development*, 6 HARV. HUM. RTS. J. 159 (1993).

Julie Campagna, *United Nations Norms on the Responsibilities of Transnational Corporations and Other Business Enterprises with regard to Human Rights: The International Community Asserts Binding Law on the Global Rule Makers*, 37 JOHN MARSHALL L. REV. 1205 (2004).

Enrique R. Carrasco & M. Ayhan Kose, *Income Distribution and the Bretton Woods Institutions: Promoting an Enabling Environment for Social Development*, 6 TRANSNAT'L L. & CONTEMP. PROBS. 1 (1996).

[Symposium: Social Justice and Development: Critical Issues Facing the Bretton Woods System]

Douglass Cassel, *Corporate Initiatives: A Second Human Rights Revolution?*, 19 FORDHAM INT'L L.J. 1963 (1996).

Jonathan I. Charney, *Transnational Corporations and Developing Public International Law*, 1983 DUKE L.J. 749 (1983).

Steve Charnovitz, *Fair Labour Standards and International Trade*, 20 J. WORLD TRADE L. 61 (1986).

Steve Charnovitz, *The Globalization of Economic Human Rights*, 25 BROOK. J. INT'L L. 113 (1999).

[Symposium: The Universal Declaration of Human Rights at 50 and the Challenge of Global Markets]

Steve Charnovitz, *The Influence of International Labour Standards on the World Trading Regime*, 126 INT'L LAB. REV. 565 (1987).

Steve Charnovitz, *The World Trade Organization and Social Issues*, 28 J. WORLD TRADE 17 (1994).

Ryszard Cholewinski, *Economic and Social Rights of Refugees and Asylum Seekers in Europe*, 14 GEO. IMMIGR. L.J. 709 (2000).

David J. Christie, *Bringing Rights to the Workplace?*, 2000 JURID. REV. 73 (2000).

John D. Ciorciari, *A Prospective Enlargement of the Roles of the Bretton Woods Financial Institutions in International Peace Operations*, 22 FORDHAM INT'L L.J. 292 (1998).

Brian J.F. Clark, *United States Labor Practices in South Africa: Will a Mandatory Fair Employment Code Succeed Where the Sullivan Principles Have Failed?*, 7 FORDHAM INT'L L.J. 358 (1984).

Gracia Clark, *The Roots of Cultural Backlash in Contemporary Processes of Globalization*, 7 IND. J. GLOBAL LEGAL STUD. 257 (1999).

Lance Compa, *And the Twain Shall Meet? A North-South Controversy over Labor Rights and Trade*, 23 LAB. RES. REV. 51 (1995).

Lance Compa, *Going Multilateral: The Evolution of U.S. Hemispheric Labor Rights Policy Under GSP and NAFTA*, 10 CONN. J. INT'L L. 337 (1995).

Lance Compa, *International Labor Rights and the Sovereignty Question: NAFTA and Guatemala, Two Case Studies*, 9 AM. U. J. INT'L L. & POL. 117 (1994).

Lance Compa, *International Labor Standards and Instruments of Recourse for Working Women*, 17 YALE J. INT'L L. 151 (1992).

Lance Compa, *Labor Rights and Labor Standards in International Trade*, 25 LAW & POL'Y INT'L BUS. 165 (1993).

Margaret Conklin and Daphne Davidson, *The I.M.F. and Economic and Social Human Rights: A Case Study of Argentina, 1958-1985*, 8 HUM. RTS. Q. 227 (1986).

Sean Cooney, *Testing Times for the ILO: Institutional Reform for the New International Political Economy*, 20 COMP. LAB. L. & POL'Y J. 365 (1999).

Katherine E. Cox, *The Inevitability of Nimble Fingers? Law, Development, and Child*, 32 VAND. J. TRANSNAT'L L. 115 (1999).

Katherine E. Cox, *Should Amnesty International Expand its Mandate to Cover Economic, Social, and Cultural Rights?*, 16 ARIZ. J. INT'L & COMP. L. 261 (1999).

Marise Cremona, *Human Rights and Democracy Clauses in the EC's Trade Agreements*, 1995 LAW & JUST. 105 (1995).

H.T. Dao, *ILO Standards for the Protection of Children*, 58 NORDIC J. INT'L L. 54 (1989).

Simon Deakin & Frank Wilkinson, *Rights vs. Efficiency? The Economic Case for Transnational Labour Standards*, 23 INDUS. L.J. 289 (1994).

Armand L. C. De Mestral, *Reconciling Human Rights and International Trade Law*, 3 CAN. INT'L LAW. 71 (1998).

Janelle M. Diller & David A. Levy, *Child Labor, Trade and Investment: Toward the Harmonization of International Law*, 91 AM. J. INT'L L. 663 (1997).

Robert M. Dow, *Linking Trade Policy to Free Emigration: The Jackson-Vanik Amendment*, 4 HARV. HUM. RTS. J. 128 (1991).

Tim Dunne, *The Spectre of Globalization*, 7 IND. J. GLOBAL LEGAL STUD. 17 (1999).

Jeffrey L. Dunoff, *Does Globalization Advance Human Rights?*, 25 BROOK. J. INT'L L. 125 (1999).

[Symposium: The Universal Declaration of Human Rights at 50 and the Challenge of Global Markets]

Eejima, Nina M., *Sustainable Development and the Search for a Better Environment, A Better World: A Work in Progress*, 18 UCLA J. ENVTL. L. & POL'Y 99 (1999/2000).

Maryam Elahi, *The Impact of Financial Institutions on the Realization of Human Rights: Case Study of the International Monetary Fund in Chile*, 6 B.C. THIRD WORLD L. J. 143 (1986).

Daniel J. Elazar, *The State System + Globalization (Economic Plus Human Rights) = Federalism (State Federations Plus Regional Confederations)*, 40 S. TEX. L. REV. 555 (2000).

Peter L. Fitzgerald, *"If Property Rights Were Treated Like Human Rights, They Could Never Get Away with This": Blacklisting and Due Process in U.S. Economic Sanctions Programs*, 51 HASTINGS L.J. 73 (1999).

M. Forde, *The European Convention on Human Rights and Labor Law*, 31 AM. J. COMP. L. 301 (1983).

John W. Foster, *Meeting the Challenges: Renewing the Progress of Economic and Social Rights* (Celebrating 50 Years of the Universal Declaration of Human Rights), 47 U.N.B.L.J. 197 (1998).

Barbara A. Frey, *The Legal and Ethical Responsibilities of Transnational Corporations in the Protection of International Human Rights*, 6 MINN. J. GLOBAL TRADE 153 (1996).

Frank García, *The Global Market and Human Rights: Trading Away the Human Rights Principle*, 25 BROOK. J. INT'L L. 51 (1999).

[Symposium: The Universal Declaration of Human Rights at 50 and the Challenge of Global Markets]

Frank J. García, *Trade and Inequality: Economic Justice and the Developing World*, 21 MICH. J. INT'L L. 975 (2000).

Andrea Giampetro-Meyer et al., *The Exploitation of Child Labor: An Intractable International Problem?*, 16 LOY. L.A. INT'L & COMP. L.J. 657 (1994).

Konrad Ginther, *Participation and Accountability: Two Aspects of the Internal and International Dimension of the Right to Development*, 1992 THIRD WORLD LEGAL STUD. 55 (1992).

W.B. Gould, *The Rights of Wage Earners: Of Human Rights and International Labor Standards*, 3 INDUS. REL. L.J. 489 (1979).

Randall Green, *Human Rights and Most-Favored-Nation Tariff Rates for Products from the People's Republic of China*, 17 U. PUGET SOUND L. REV. 611 (1994).

Kimberly Gregalis Granatino, *Corporate Responsibility Now: Profit at the Expense of Human Rights with Exemption from Liability*, 23 SUFFOLK TRANSNAT'L L. REV. 191 (1999).

David L. Gregory, et. al., *Child Labor and Exploitation*, 14 ST. JOHN'S J. LEGAL COMMENT. 377 (2000).

[Symposium: Legal Reform and Children's Human Rights]

Claudio Grossman & Daniel D. Bradlow, *Are We Being Propelled Towards a People-Centered Transnational Legal Order?*, 9 AM. U. J. INT'L L. & POL'Y 1 (1993).

Katherine A. Hagen, *Fundamentals of Labor Issues and NAFTA*, 27 U.C. DAVIS L. REV. 917 (1994).

[Symposium: Free Trade and Democratic Values: NAFTA's Effect on Human Rights]

Minasse Haile, *Human Rights in Africa: Observations on the Implications of Economic Priority*, 19 VAND. J. TRANSNAT'L L. 299 (1986).

Louis Henkin, *That 'S' Word: Sovereignty, and Globalization, and Human Rights, et cetera*, 68 FORDHAM L. REV. 1 (1999).

Louis Henkin, *The Universal Declaration at 50 and the Challenge of Global Markets*, 25 BROOK. J. INT'L L. 17 (1999).

[Symposium: The Universal Declaration of Human Rights at 50 and the Challenge of Global Markets]

Laura Ho, et al., *(Dis)assembling Rights of Women Workers Along the Global Assembly Line: Human Rights and the Garment Industry*, 31 HARV. C.R.-C.L. L. REV. 383 (1996).

Paul Hoffman, *Trade Union Rights under Article 11 of the European Convention of Human Rights*, 5 COMP. LAB. L. 149 (1982).

Thomas Hutchins, *Using the International Court of Justice to Check Human Rights Abuses in World Bank Projects*, 23 COLUM. HUM. RTS. L. REV. 487 (1992).

Elizabeth M. Iglesias, *Human Rights in International Economic Law: Locating Latinas/os in the Linkage Debates*, 28 U. MIAMI INTER-AM. L. REV. 361 (1996/97).

Martha Jackman, *From National Standards to Justiciable Rights: Enforcing International Social and Economic Guarantees through Charter of Rights Review*, 14 J.L. & SOC. POL'Y 69 (1999).

Hans de Jonge, *Democracy and Economic Development in the Asia-Pacific Region: The Role of Parliamentary Institutions*, 14 HUM. RTS. L. J. 301 (1993).

David P. Kelly, *Trading Indigenous Rights: The NAFTA Side Agreements as an Impetus for Human Rights Enforcement*, 6 BUFF. HUM. RTS. L. REV. 113 (2000).

Kivutha Kibwana, *Human Rights and/or Economic Development: Which Way Africa?*, 1993 THIRD WORLD LEGAL STUD. 43 (1993).

David Kinley & Rachel Chambers, *The UN Human Rights Norms for Corporations: The Private Implications of Public International Law*, 6 HUM. RTS. L. REV. 447 (2006).

Timo Antero Kivimaki, *National Diplomacy for Human Rights: A Study of US Exercise of Power in Indonesia*, 16 HUM. RTS. Q. 415 (1994).

Nicole J. Krug, *Exploiting Child Labor: Corporate Responsibility and the Role of Corporate Codes of Conduct*, 14 N.Y.L. SCH. J. HUM. RTS. 651 (1998).

Kofi Kumado, *Conditionality: An Analysis of the Policy of Linking Development Aid to the Implementation of Human Rights Standards*, 1993 INT'L COMMISSION JURISTS REV. 23 (1993).

Ernest A. Landy, *The Implementation Procedures of the International Labour Organization*, 20 SANTA CLARA L. REV. 633 (1980).

Paul D. Lall, *Immigrant Farmworkers and the North American Agreement on Labor Cooperation*, 31 COLUM. HUM. RTS. L. REV. 597 (2000).

Deborah Leipziger & Pia Sabharwal, *Companies that Play Hide and Seek with Child Labor*, 1995 BUS. & SOC'Y REV. 11 (1995).

Jerome Levinson, *Certifying International Worker Rights: A Practical Alternative*, 20 COMP. LAB. L. & POL'Y J. 401(1999).

Michael Lucas, *The International Monetary Fund's Conditionality and the International Covenant on Economic, Social and Cultural Rights: An Attempt to Define the Relation*, 25 R. BEL. D. INT'L 104 (1992).

Tarek F. Maassarani et al., *Extracting Corporate Responsibility: Towards a Human Rights Impact Assessment*, 40 CORNELL INT'L L.J. 135 (2007).

Harlan Mandel, *In Pursuit of the Missing Link: International Worker Rights and International Trade?*, 27 COLUM. J. TRANSNAT'L L. 443 (1989).

Jonathan L. Mannina, *The Human Rights Implications of Economic Development: A Case Study of the Huaorani People of Ecuador*, 5 GEO. INT'L ENVTL. L. REV. 117 (1992).

Wade Mansell and Joanne Scott, *Why Bother About a Right to Development?*, 21 J.L. & SOC'Y 171 (1994).

Virginia Mantouvalou, *Servitude and Forced Labour in the 21st Century: The Human Rights of Domestic Workers*, 35 INDUST. L.J. 395 (2006).

Victoria E. Marmorstein, *World Bank Power to Consider Human Rights*, 13 J. INT'L L. & ECON. 113 (1978).

Robert L. Martinez, *NAFTA's Effect on Human Rights at the Border*, 27 U.C. DAVIS L. REV. 979 (1994).

[Symposium: Free Trade and Democratic Values: NAFTA's Effect on Human Rights]

Diane Kroeger May, *Pharmaceutical Crisis in India: Transcending Profits with Human Rights*, 10 WIS. INT'L L.J. 40 (1991).

Brian B.A. McAllister, *The United Nations Conference on Environment and Development: An Opportunity to Forge a New Unity in the Work of the World Bank Among Human Rights, the Environment, and Sustainable Development*, 16 HASTINGS INT'L & COMP. L. REV. 689 (1993).

R.C. McCallum, *Collective Labour Law, Citizenship and the Future*, 22 MELB. U. L. REV. 42 (1998).

Robert McCorquodale, *Secrets and Lies: Economic Globalisation and Women's Human Rights*, 19 AUSTL. Y.B. INT'L L. 73 (1998).

Christopher McCrudden, *Human Rights Codes for Transnational Corporations: What Can the Sullivan and MacBride Principles Tell Us?*, 19 OXFORD J. LEGAL STUD. 167 (1999).

Robert W. McGee, *The Moral Case for Free Trade*, 29 J. WORLD TRADE 69 (1995).

John O. McGinnis, *A New Agenda for International Human Rights: Economic Freedom*, 48 CATH. U. L. REV. 1029 (1999).

Dominic McGoldrick, *Sustainable Development and Human Rights: An Integrated Conception*, 45 INT'L & COMP. L.Q. 796 (1996).

Herbert V. Morais, *The Globalization of Human Rights Law and the Role of International Financial Institutions in Promoting Human Rights*, 33 GEO. WASH. INT'L L. REV. 71 (2000).

Justine Nolan, *The United Nations' Compact with Business: Hindering or Helping the Protection of Human Rights?*, 24 U. QUEENSLAND L.J. 455 (2005).

Justine Nolan & Michael Posner, *International Standards to Promote Labor Rights: The Role of the United States Government*, 2000 COLUM. BUS. L. REV. 529 (2000).

L. Amede Obiora, *Beyond the Rhetoric of a Right to Development*, 18 LAW & POL'Y 355 (1997).

Paul O'Higgins, *The Closed Shop and the European Convention on Human Rights*, 6 HUM. RTS. REV. 22 (1981).

Kaoru Okuizumi, *Implementing the ODA Charter: Prospects for Linking Japanese Economic Assistance and Human Rights*, 27 N.Y.U. J. INT'L L. & POL. 367 (1995).

Joseph Oloka-Onyango, *Beyond the Rhetoric: Reinvigorating the Struggle for Economic and Social Rights in Africa*, 26 CASE W. INT'L L.J. 1 (1995).

Joseph Oloka-Onyango, *Human Rights and Sustainable Development in Contemporary Africa: A New Dawn, or Retreating Horizons?*, 6 BUFF. HUM. RTS. L. REV. 39 (2000).

Diane F. Orentlicher & Timothy A. Gelatt, *Public Law, Private Actors: The Impact of Human Rights on Business Investors in China*, 14 NW J. INT'L L. & BUS. 66 (1993).

[Symposium: Doing Business in China]

Yemi Osinbajo & Olukonyisola Ajayi, *Human Rights and Economic Development in Developing Countries*, 28 INT'L LAW. 727 (1994).

James C.N. Paul, *The Human Right to Development: Its Meaning and Importance*, 1992 THIRD WORLD LEGAL STUD. 17 (1992).

Jordan J. Paust, *Human Rights Responsibilities of Private Corporations*, 35 VAND. J. TRANSNAT'L L. 801 (2002).

Michael D. Pendleton, *A New Human Right - The Right to Globalization*, 22 FORDHAM INT'L L.J. 2052 (1999).

Kathleen Peratis, et al., *Markets and Women's International Human Rights*, 25 BROOK. J. INT'L L. 141 (1999).

[Symposium: The Universal Declaration of Human Rights at 50 and the Challenge of Global Markets]

Jorge F. Pérez-López, *Conditioning Trade on Foreign Labor Law: The U.S. Approach*, 9 COMP. LAB. L. J. 253 (1988).

Jorge F. Pérez-López, *The Promotion of International Labor Standards and NAFTA: Retrospect and Prospect*, 10 CONN. J. INT'L L. 427 (1995).

Richard Wright Perry, *Rethinking the Right to Development: After the Critique of Development, After the Critique of Rights*, 18 LAW & POL'Y 225 (1997).

Ernst-Ulrich Petersmann, *Dispute Settlement in International Economic Law - Lessons for Strengthening International Dispute Settlement in Non-Economic Areas*, 2 J. INT'L ECON. L. 189 (1999).

Ernst-Ulrich Petersmann, *From 'Negative' to 'Positive' Integration in the WTO: Time for 'Mainstreaming Human Rights' into WTO Law?*, 37 COMMON MKT. L. REV. 1363 (2000).

Ernst-Ulrich Petersmann, *The 'Human Rights Approach' Advocated by the UN High Commissioner for Human Rights and by the International Labour Organization: Is It Relevant for WTO Law and Policy?*, 7 J. INT'L ECON. L. 605 (2004).

Ernst-Ulrich Petersmann, *Taking Human Dignity, Poverty and Empowerment of Individuals More Seriously: Rejoinder to Alston*, 13 EUR. J. INT'L L. 845 (2002).

Ernst-Ulrich Petersmann, *The WTO Constitution and Human Rights*, 3 J. INT'L ECON. L. 19 (2000).

Andrew Phang, *Critical Legal Studies, Economic Development and Human Rights*, 1999 LAW & JUST. 122 (1999).

Michael A. Pignatella, *The Recurring Nightmare of Child Labor Abuse - Causes and Solutions for the 90's*, 15 B.C. THIRD WORLD L.J. 171 (1995).

Steven Poe, *Human Rights and US Foreign Aid Revisited: The Latin American Region*, 16 HUM. RTS. Q. 539 (1994).

Balakrishnan Rajogopal, *Crossing the Rubicon: Synthesizing the Soft International Law of the IMF and Human Rights*, 11 B.U. INT'L L.J. 81 (1993).

Paul F. Ramshaw, *Ethical Investment: Retail Ethics and Participatory Democracy?*, 29 CAMBRIAN L. REV. 105 (1998).

Steven R. Ratner, *Corporations and Human Rights: A Theory of Legal Responsibility*, 111 YALE L.J. 443 (2001).

Kerry Rittich, *Transformed Pursuits: The Quest for Equality in Globalized Markets*, 13 HARV. HUM. RTS. J. 231 (2000).

Sumner M. Rosen, *Protecting Labor Rights in Market Economies*, 14 HUM. RTS. Q. 371 (1992).

Seymour J. Rubin, *Economic and Social Human Rights and the New International Economic Order*, 1 AM. U. J. INT'L L. & POL'Y 67 (1986).

John Gerard Ruggie, *Business and Human Rights: The Evolving International Agenda*, 101 Am. J. Int'l L. 819 (2007).

James Salzman, *Labor Rights, Globalization and Institutions: The Role and Influence of the Organization for Economic Cooperation and Development*, 21 MICH. J. INT'L L. 768 (2000).

David M. Schilling & Ruth Rosenbaum, *Principles for Global Corporate Responsibility*, 1995 BUS. & SOC'Y REV. 55 (1995).

Ibrahim F. I. Shihata, *Human Rights, Development, and International Financial Institutions*, 8 Am. U. J. Int'l L. & Pol'y 27 (1992).

Ibrahim F. I. Shihata, *The World Bank and Human Rights: An Analysis of the Legal Issues and the Record of Achievements*, 17 Denv. J. Int'l L. & Pol'y 39 (1988).

Martin Shupack, *Human Rights and the United States-Mexico Free Trade Agreement*, 4 Harv. Hum. Rts. J. 163 (1991).

Robert Bruce Slater, *Companies That Hide Behind the Sullivan Principles*, 1984 Bus. & Soc'y Rev. 15 (1984).

James F. Smith, *NAFTA and Human Rights: A Necessary Linkage*, 27 U.C. Davis L. Rev. 793 (1994).

[Symposium: Free Trade and Democratic Values: NAFTA's Effect on Human Rights]

David M. Smolin, *Conflict and Ideology in the International Campaign against Child Labour*, 16 Hofstra Lab. & Employment L.J. 383 (1999).

Alejandro Sobarzo, *NAFTA and Human Rights in Mexico*, 27 U.C. Davis L. Rev. 865 (1994).

[Symposium: Free Trade and Democratic Values: NAFTA's Effect on Human Rights]

Barbara Stark, *Economic Rights in the United States and International Human Rights Law: Toward an 'Entirely New Strategy,'* 44 Hastings L. J. 79 (1992).

Barbara Stark, *Postmodern Rhetoric, Economic Rights and an International Text: 'A Miracle for Breakfast*, 33 Va. J. Int'l L. 433 (1993).

Barbara Stark, *Women and Globalization: The Failure and Postmodern Possibilities of International Law*, 33 Vand. J. Transnat'l L. 503 (2000).

Henry J. Steiner, *Social Rights and Economic Development: Converging Discourses?*, 4 Buff. Hum. Rts. L. Rev. 25 (1998).

Frances Stewart, *Basic Needs Strategies, Human Rights, and the Right to Development*, 11 Hum. Rts. Q. 347 (1989).

Patricia Stirling, *The Use of Trade Sanctions as an Enforcement Mechanism for Basic Human Rights: A Proposal for Addition to the World Trade Organization*, 11 Am. U. J. Int'l L. & Pol'y 1 (1996).

Johanna Sutherland, *International Trade and the GATT/WTO Social Clause: Broadening the Debate*, 14 Queensl. U. Tech. L.J. 83 (1998).

Rajesh Swaminathan, *Regulating Development: Structural Adjustment and the Case for National Enforcement of Economic and Social Rights*, 37 Colum. J. Transnat'l L. 161 (1998).

Jeffrey S. Thomas, *Should Canadian Labor Be Concerned About NAFTA?*, 27 U.C. Davis L. Rev. 883 (1994).

[Symposium: Free Trade and Democratic Values: NAFTA's Effect on Human Rights]

Ryan P. Toftoy, *Now Playing: Corporate Codes of Conduct in the Global Theater. Is Nike Just Doing It?*, 15 ARIZ. J. INT'L & COMP. L. 905 (1998).

Katarina Tomaševski, *The World Bank and Human Rights*, 1989 HUM. RTS. IN DEVELOPING COUNTRIES Y.B. 75 (1989).

Karen F. Travis, *Women in Global Production and Worker Rights Provisions in U.S. Trade Laws*, 17 YALE J. INT'L L. 173 (1992).

Timothy N. Tripp, *Foreign Investment in China and Its Impact on Human Rights*, 15 BROOK. J. INT'L L. 109 (1989).

Onelia Vera, *Provisions in the U.N. Draft Code within the Context of South Africa*, 2 FLA. INT'L L.J. 285 (1987).

Diana Vincent-Daviss, *Human Rights Law: A Research Guide to the Literature - Part III: The International Labor Organization and Human Rights*, 15 N.Y.U. J. INT'L L. & POL. 211 (1982).

Namita Wahi, *Human Rights Accountability of the IMF and the World Bank: A Critique of Existing Mechanisms and Articulation of a Theory of Horizontal Accountability*, 12 U.C. DAVIS J. INT'L L. & POL'Y 331 (2006).

Christopher Wall, *Human Rights and Economic Sanctions: The New Imperialism*, 22 FORDHAM INT'L L.J. 577 (1998).

Mark A. Warner, *Globalization and Human Rights: An Economic Model*, 25 BROOK. J. INT'L L. 99 (1999).

[Symposium: The Universal Declaration of Human Rights at 50 and the Challenge of Global Markets]

David A. Waugh, *The ILO and Human Rights*, 5 COMP. LAB. L. 186 (1982).

David Weissbrodt & Georgina Mahoney, *International Legal Action against Apartheid*, 4 LAW & INEQ. 485 (1986).

David Weissbrodt & Muria Kruger, *Norms on the Responsibilities of Transnational Corporations and Other Business Enterprises with Regard to Human Rights*, 97 AM. J. INT'L L. 901 (2003).

Robert Weissman, *'Development' and the Denial of Human Rights in Ramos's Philippines* (Fidel v. Ramos), 7 HARV. HUM. RTS. J. 251 (1994).

Christopher Weeramantry, *Human Rights and the Global Marketplace*, 25 BROOK. J. INT'L L. 27 (1999).

[Symposium: The Universal Declaration of Human Rights at 50 and the Challenge of Global Markets]

Erica de Wet, *Labor Standards in the Globalized Economy: The Inclusion of a Social Clause in the General Agreement on Tariff and Trade / World Trade*, 17 HUM. RTS. Q. 443 (1995).

Robert White, *An Agenda of Labour Rights (Celebrating 50 Years of the Universal Declaration of Human Rights)*, 47 U.N.B.L.J. 185 (1998).

Francis Wolf, *ILO Experience in the Implementation of Human Rights*, 10 J. INT'L L. & ECON. 599 (1975).

David Ziskind, *Labor Laws in the Vortex of Human Rights Protection*, 5 COMP. LAB. L. 131 (1982).

§ 3.   Web Sites

Business and Human Rights Resource Centre, http://www.business-humanrights.org.

This site contains links to reports, articles, company policies, and information on lawsuits against companies. It also contains links to information on international standards and guidelines, company statements on human rights, security issues, labor issues, and health issues, as well as several country-specific sites.

FoodFirst, Institute for Food and Development Policy, http://www.food-first.org.

This site contains information on FoodFirst's programs and upcoming events. It also contains a resource library, which has links to sites related to food, agriculture, labor, and development.

International Labour Organization (ILO), http://www.ilo.org.

Contains information on ILO meetings and resources. Of particular interest is the Labour Standards page (http://webfusion.ilo.org/public/db/standards/normes/index.cfm?lang=EN). It also contains a search engine of the ILO website.

International Monetary Fund (IMF), http://www.imf.org.

This site contains links to press releases and publications of the IMF. It also contains information on standards and codes, as well as country-specific information.

Organisation for Economic Co-Operation and Development (OECD), http://www.oecd.org.

This page contains articles and links to country-specific pages, statistics, and contact information. It also contains an alphabetical list of individual topic pages on the site.

Trade Observatory, http://www.tradeobservatory.org.

Global information center on trade, agriculture, and sustainable development.

United Nations and Business, http://www.un.org/partners/business/index.asp.

Describes the misson of U.N. agencies and business. The site also includes business guidelines, news, statistics, and more information.

United Nations, Economic and Social Development, http://www.un.org/esa.

This site contains information on meetings, documents, research, and national governments. It also contains links to individual pages on the site, arranged by topic.

United Nations, Global Compact, http://www.unglobalcompact.org.

The Global Compact is a challenge to world business leaders to enact human rights, labor, and environmental principles. The original nine principles, plus a tenth principle on corruption, are outlined on the Web site. Of particular interest is the Country Information page (http://www.unglobalcompact.org/gc/ilosearch.nsf/search) which allows the user to search several databases related to labor, human rights, and environment, including ILOLEX, NATLEX, Human Rights Treaty bodies, Human Rights Charter-based bodies, and a few more.

University of Minnesota Human Rights Library, Business and Human Rights Links,

http://www1.umn.edu/humanrts/links/business.html.

Collection of links related to business and human rights.

University of Minnesota Human Rights Library, Human Rights Guidelines for Business Links,

http://www1.umn.edu/humanrts/links/conduct.html.

Large collection of sites related to business guidelines and conduct.

World Bank, http://www.worldbank.org.

This site contains links to information on individual countries and regions, events, and services. It also contains links to World Bank publications and newsletters. The research page (http://econ.worldbank.org/) contains a search engine which allows the user to search by topic, project site, or key output.

World Trade Organization (WTO), http://www.wto.org.

This site contains articles, press releases, and information on events. It also contains a full-text keyword search engine and an official documents search engine. The official documents search engine allows direct downloading of individual documents.

See also section F.2. of the present bibliography for a research guide on the International Covenant on Economic, Social and Cultural Rights.

I. Selected Texts

AFRICA, HUMAN RIGHTS, AND THE GLOBAL SYSTEM (Eileen McCarthy-Arnolds et al. eds., 1994).

[Westport, Conn.: Greenwood Press, 272 pp. Discusses briefly human rights philosophy, introduces historical background concerning the evolution of human rights in pre-colonial and colonial Africa, and covers extensively national and international efforts to address human rights issues in Africa.]

THE AFRICAN CHARTER ON HUMAN AND PEOPLES' RIGHTS: THE SYSTEM IN PRACTICE: 1986-2006 (2d ed. Malcolm D. Evans & Rachel Murray eds., 2008).

[New York: Cambridge University Press, 534 pp. Contributions cover African Charter of Human and Peoples' Rights reporting system, interpretation of rights by Commission, prospects for African Court on Human and Peoples' Rights, and role of NGOs.]

T. AKINOLA AGUDA, HUMAN RIGHTS AND THE RIGHT TO DEVELOPMENT IN AFRICA (1989).

[Lagos: Nigerian Institute of International Affairs, 34 pp.]

AMERICAN LAW INSTITUTE, RESTATEMENT OF THE LAW, THIRD, THE FOREIGN RELATIONS LAW OF THE UNITED STATES (1987 & Supp. 1988).

[St. Paul, MN: American Law Institute Publishers, 2 vols. Supplemented annually. Rules that restate generally accepted principles of law, including international human rights law. See 2 Restatement §§ 701-03, 711-13; see also id. at 144-51. Rules are followed by comments, notes, and references.]

AMNESTY INTERNATIONAL USA, THE UNIVERSAL DECLARATION OF HUMAN RIGHTS, 1948-1988: HUMAN RIGHTS, THE UNITED NATIONS, AND AMNESTY INTERNATIONAL (1988).

[New York: Amnesty International USA, 180 pp.]

EVELYN A. ANKUMAH ET AL., THE LEGAL PROFESSION AND THE PROTECTION OF HUMAN RIGHTS IN AFRICA (1999).

[Accra, Ghana: Africa Legal Aid, 180 pp.]

EVELYN A. ANKHUMAH, THE AFRICAN COMMISSION ON HUMAN AND PEOPLES' RIGHTS: PRACTICES AND PROCEDURES (1996).

[The Hague; Boston, MA.: Martinus Nijhoff, 246 pp. Describes and analyzes the work of the African Commission on Human and Peoples' Rights. Provides insight into the structure and mandate of the Commission, the procedures for examining complaints, and the state reporting procedure. Also addresses actual cases.]

ARTICLE 19, PRESS LAW AND PRACTICE (Sandra Coliver ed., 1993).

[London: Article 19 International Centre against Censorship, 307 pp.]

ANTHONY AUST, MODERN TREATY LAW AND PRACTICE (2000).

[Cambridge: Cambridge University Press, 484 pp. Practitioner's guide to treaty practice.]

RICHARD AMOAKO BAAH, HUMAN RIGHTS IN AFRICA: THE CONFLICT OF IMPLEMENTATION (2000).

[Lanham, Md.: University Press of America, 122 pp.]

MASHOOD A. BADERIN, INTERNATIONAL HUMAN RIGHTS AND ISLAMIC LAW (2003).

[Oxford; New York: Oxford Univ. Press, 279 pp.]

PETER R. BAEHR, HUMAN RIGHTS: UNIVERSALITY IN PRACTICE (2001).

[London: Palgrave, 178 pp.]

FAREDA BANDA, WOMEN, LAW AND HUMAN RIGHTS: AN AFRICAN PERSPECTIVE (2005).

[Oxford: Hart Publishing, 407 pp.]

ALBERT KWOKWO BARUME, HEADING TOWARDS EXTINCTION?: INDIGENOUS RIGHTS IN AFRICA : THE CASE OF THE TWA OF THE KAHUZI-BIEGA NATIONAL PARK, DEMOCRATIC REPUBLIC OF CONGO (2000).

[Copenhagen: IWGIA, 142 pp. Presents the case of the Twa, the so-called "pygmies" of Eastern Congo, in the context of emerging and established international norms and principles of indigenous peoples' rights.]

UPENDRA BAXI, THE FUTURE OF HUMAN RIGHTS (2d ed. 2006).

[New Delhi; New York: Oxford Univ. Press, 339 pp.]

ANNE F BAYEFSKY, THE UN HUMAN RIGHTS TREATY SYSTEM: UNIVERSALITY AT THE CROSSROADS (2001).

[Ardsley, NY : Transnational Publishers, 839 pp.]

[This report is the product of a study of the United Nations human rights treaty system commenced in 1999 and conducted in collaboration with the Office of the High Commissioner for Human Rights (OHCHR), with the support of the Ford Foundation. The purpose of the report is to present recommendations for the enhancement of the operations of the human rights treaty system.]

RALPH BEDDARD, HUMAN RIGHTS AND EUROPE (3 ed. repr. 1995).

[Cambridge: Cambridge University Press, 278 pp.]

JOHANNES BINDER, THE HUMAN DIMENSION OF THE OSCE: FROM RECOMMENDATION TO IMPLEMENTATION (2001).

[Wien: Verlag Österreich, 472 pp.]

BROADENING THE FRONTIERS OF HUMAN RIGHTS: ESSAYS IN HONOUR OF ASBJØRN EIDE (Donna Gomien ed., 1993).

[New York: Oxford Univ. Press, 312 pp.]

JURGEN BROHMER, STATE IMMUNITY AND THE VIOLATION OF HUMAN RIGHTS (1997).

[The Hague; Boston: Martinus Nijhoff Pub., 238 pp. International Studies in Human Rights Vol. 47. Demonstrates that international law does not per se demand that foreign states be granted immunity. Extensively surveys international immunity law by state practice and work of learned bodies.]

SEYOM BROWN, HUMAN RIGHTS IN WORLD POLITICS (2000).

[New York: Longman, 195 pp.]

ALISON BRYSK, HUMAN RIGHTS AND PRIVATE WRONGS: CONSTRUCTING GLOBAL CIVIL SOCIETY (2005).

[New York: Routledge, 152 pp.]

THOMAS BUERGENTHAL, DINAH SHELTON, & DAVID P. STEWART, INTERNATIONAL HUMAN RIGHTS IN A NUTSHELL (3d ed. 2002).

[St. Paul, Minn.: West Group, 450 pp. An overview of the doctrinal and institutional framework of international human rights.]

THOMAS BUERGENTHAL & HAROLD G. MAIER, PUBLIC INTERNATIONAL LAW IN A NUTSHELL (2d ed. 1990).

[St. Paul, MN: West Publishing Co., 275 pp. An introduction to the basic principles of public international law including human rights. Research guide at 243-57 includes the key sources of and about public international law.]

THOMAS BUERGENTHAL & DINAH SHELTON, PROTECTING HUMAN RIGHTS IN THE AMERICAS: CASES AND MATERIALS (4th rev. ed. 1995).

[Kehl; Arlington, VA: N.P. Engel, 692 pp.]

BRIAN BURDEKIN & JASON NAUM, NATIONAL HUMAN RIGHTS INSTITUTIONS IN THE ASIA PACIFIC REGION (2007).

[Leiden; Boston: Martinus Nijhoff Publishers, 555 pp. Provides collection of materials to facilitate comparison of national human rights institutions in the Asia-Pacific region; includes prescriptive sections and several comparative tables.]

AGNÈS CALLAMARD, DOCUMENTING HUMAN RIGHTS VIOLATIONS BY STATE AGENTS: SEXUAL VIOLENCE (1999).

[Vanier, Ont.: Amnesty International, 69 pp. The research and publication was sponsored by the International Centre for Human Rights and Democratic Development.]

SONIA CARDENAS, CONFLICT AND COMPLIANCE: STATE RESPONSES TO INTERNATIONAL HUMAN RIGHTS PRESSURE (2007).

[Philadelphia: University of Pennsylvania Press, 200 pp. Empirical analysis of reasons states comply or fail to comply with human rights norms.]

RICHARD CARVER & PAUL HUNT, NATIONAL HUMAN RIGHTS INSTITUTIONS IN AFRICA, Occasional Paper No. 1 (1991).

[The Gambia: Afr. Centre for Democracy & Hum. Rts. Stud., 45 pp. Discussion of national human rights organizations in the Gambia, Tanzania, Togo, Uganda, and Zaire, and analysis of emerging efforts to address human rights issues in Africa. Appendix contains a directory of African national human rights institutions.]

THE CHALLENGES OF CHANGE: THE HELSKINKI SUMMIT OF THE CSCE AND ITS AFTERMATH (Arie Bloed ed., 1994).

[Dordrecht; Boston: Martinus Nijhoff Pub., 463 pp.]

HUMAN RIGHTS IN THE ARAB WORLD: INDEPENDENT VOICES (Anthony Tirado Chase & Amr Hamzawy eds., 2006).

[Philadelphia: University of Pennsylvania Press, 322 pp. Historical and prescriptive essays address current human rights issues in Arab world.]

EDWARD CHASZAR, THE INTERNATIONAL PROBLEM OF NATIONAL MINORITIES (3d ed. 1999).

[Toronto; Buffalo: Matthias Corvinus, 242 pp.]

KENNETH CHRISTIE & DENNY ROY, THE POLITICS OF HUMAN RIGHTS IN EAST ASIA (2001).

[London: Pluto Press, 192 pp. Examines human rights records of several Southeast Asian countries, China, the two Koreas, and Japan; places issues within context of individual countries' political history.]

ANDREW CLAPHAM, HUMAN RIGHTS OBLIGATIONS OF NON-STATE ACTORS (2006).

[Oxford; New York: Oxford Univ. Press, 613 pp.]

ANN MARIE CLARK, DIPLOMACY OF CONSCIENCE: AMNESTY INTERNATIONAL AND CHANGING HUMAN RIGHTS NORMS (2001).

[Princeton, N.J.: Princeton University Press, 183 pp.]

CYNTHIA PRICE COHEN, THE HUMAN RIGHTS OF INDIGENOUS PEOPLES (1998).

[Ardsley, N.Y.: Transnational, 442 pp. Covers the framework of international law, as embodied in the relevant provisions of international conventions and the case law of international tribunals. Also addresses specific issues that arise between indigenous peoples in the United States, Canada, Latin America, Scandinavia, India, and Australia and the states that exercise jurisdiction in their homelands.]

H. VICTOR CONDE, A HANDBOOK OF INTERNATIONAL HUMAN RIGHTS TERMINOLOGY (2d ed. 2004).

[Lincoln, Nebraska: University of Nebraska Press, 536 pp.]

CONFERENCE ON SECURITY AND COOPERATION IN EUROPE: AN OVERVIEW OF THE CSCE PROCESS, RECENT MEETINGS AND INSTITUTIONAL DEVELOPMENT (1992).

[Washington, D.C.: Commission on Security and Cooperation in Europe, 47 pp.]

THE CSCE AND THE TURBULENT NEW EUROPE (Louis B. Sohn ed., 1993).

[San José, Costa Rica: Varitec; Washington, D.C.: Friedrich Naumann Stiftung, 280 pp. Record of a conference organized by the International Rule of Law Institute of the George Washington University in cooperation with the Friedrich Naumann Foundation and the Jacob Blaustein Institute for the Advancement of Human Rights. Conference held May 3-5, 1993, in Washington, D.C.]

SCOTT DAVIDSON, THE INTER-AMERICAN HUMAN RIGHTS SYSTEM (1997).

[Aldershot, Hants.; Brookfield, VT.: Dartmouth, 385 pp.]

INTERNATIONAL LAW AND SOCIETY: EMPIRICAL APPROACHES TO HUMAN RIGHTS (Laura A. Dickinson ed., 2007).

[Burlington, VT: Ashgate, 566 pp. Chapters use qualitative and quantitative methods to analyze core issues of international law and human rights - compliance, development of norms, role of social movements, etc.]

DOCUMENTS OF THE AFRICAN COMMISSION ON HUMAN AND PEOPLE'S RIGHTS, 1999-2005 (Rachel Murray & Malcolm D. Evans eds., 2007).

[Oxford: Hart, 522 pp.]

DO WE NEED MINORITY RIGHTS?: CONCEPTUAL ISSUES (Juha Raikka ed., 1996).

[The Hague, Boston: Martinus Nijhoff Pub., 240 pp. Collection of essays explores important philosophical questions about minority protection as well as related practical and jurisdictional problems.]

ROBERT F. DRINAN, CRY OF THE OPPRESSED: THE HISTORY AND HOPE OF THE HUMAN RIGHTS REVOLUTION (1987).

[San Francisco: Harper & Row, 210 pp.]

ROBERT F. DRINAN, THE MOBILIZATION OF SHAME: A WORLD VIEW OF HUMAN RIGHTS (2001).

[New Haven: Yale University Press, 240 pp.]

TIMOTHY DUNNE & NICHOLAS J. WHEELER, HUMAN RIGHTS IN GLOBAL POLITICS (1999).

[Cambridge, U.K.; New York: Cambridge University Press, 337 pp.]

ASBJØRN EIDE, POCKET GUIDE TO THE DEVELOPMENT OF HUMAN RIGHTS INSTITUTIONS AND MECHANISMS (1989).

[Strasbourg: Council of Europe, 31 pp.]

EMERGING HUMAN RIGHTS: THE AFRICAN POLITICAL ECONOMY CONTEXT, STUDIES IN HUMAN RIGHTS, NUMBER 8 (George W. Shepherd, Jr. & Mark O.C. Anikpo eds., 1990).

[New York: Greenwood Press, 244 pp. Published under the auspices of the Consortium on Human Rights Development. Scholarly articles in part one discuss theories of human rights in the African context, dealing with such issues as the universality of human rights, underdevelopment, and theological perspectives on African human rights. Articles in part two discuss the link between human rights violations and several issues including development, equality, and justice, militarization, refugees, feminism, and self-reliance.]

ENCYCLOPEDIA OF HUMAN RIGHTS (David Forsythe ed. forthcoming).

[Oxford: Oxford Univ. Press.]

8 ENCYCLOPEDIA OF PUBLIC INTERNATIONAL LAW (Rudolf Bernhardt ed., 1985-).

[Amsterdam: North-Holland, 551 pp. Covers human rights, the individual in international law, and international economic relations. Separately-authored articles include titles such as: African Charter on Human and Peoples' Rights, Indigenous Populations, International Commission of Jurists, and Protection. See also the consolidated library edition, ENCYCLOPEDIA OF PUBLIC INTERNATIONAL LAW (Rudolf Bernhardt ed., 1992-).]

ENFORCING INTERNATIONAL HUMAN RIGHTS IN DOMESTIC COURTS (Benedetto Conforti & Francesco Francioni eds., 1997).

[The Hague; Boston: Kluwer Law International, 466 pp. Explores ways in which domestic courts are dealing with international human rights issues in their jurisdictions, identifies obstacles to adjudication and enforcement, and suggests judicial models that may reduce or remove obstacles.]

ETHICS IN ACTION: THE ETHICAL CHALLENGES OF INTERNATIONAL HUMAN RIGHTS NONGOVERNMENTAL ORGANIZATIONS (Daniel Bell & Jean-Marc Coicaud eds., 2007).

[Cambridge; New York: Cambridge University Press, 320 pp.]

EUROPEAN CIVIL LIBERTIES AND THE EUROPEAN CONVENTION ON HUMAN RIGHTS: A COMPARATIVE STUDY (C.A. Gearty ed., 1997).

[The Hague, Boston: Martinus Nijhoff Pub., 420 pp. This study addresses the gap in knowledge of comparative civil liberties with regard to how the Convention operates in other countries and the impact of the European Convention on other European jurisdictions. Examines the domestic laws of leading European jurisdictions and the impact of the European Convention within these legal systems.]

THE EUROPEAN CONVENTION ON HUMAN RIGHTS: CASES AND MATERIALS (Herbert Petzold, 5th ed. 1984).

[Koln: Carl Heymanns Verlag, 529 pp.]

THE EUROPEAN SYSTEM FOR THE PROTECTION OF HUMAN RIGHTS (R.St.J. Macdonald et al. eds., 1993).

[Dordrecht; Boston: Martinus Nijhoff Pub., 940 pp.]

THE EUROPEAN UNION AND HUMAN RIGHTS (Nanette A. Neuwahl & Allan Rosas eds., 1995).

[The Hague; Boston; London: Martinus Nijhoff Pub., 354 pp.]

OSITA C. EZE, HUMAN RIGHTS IN AFRICA: SOME SELECTED PROBLEMS (1984).

[Lagos: Published by the Nigerian Inst. of Int'l Affairs in cooperation with Macmillan Nigeria Publishers, 314 pp. Treats human rights theory and examines human rights situations in pre-colonial and colonial Africa, and in independent African States. Discusses self-determination, racial discrimination and *apartheid*, women's rights, refugee issues, and regional promotion and protection of human rights. Appendices include OAU Convention Governing the Specific Aspects of Refugee Problems in Africa, Monrovia Proposal for the Setting Up of an African Commission on Human Rights, and the African Charter on Human and Peoples' Rights.]

FEMALE GENITAL MUTILATION: A GUIDE TO LAWS AND POLICIES WORLDWIDE (Nahid Toubia & Anika Rahman eds., 2000).

[London: Zed, 192 pp.]

Joan Fitzpatrick, *Human Rights and Forced Displacement: Converging Standards, in* HUMAN

RIGHTS AND FORCED DISPLACEMENT 3 (Anne F. Bayefsky & Joan Fitzpatrick eds., 2000).

[The Hague; Boston; London: M. Nijhoff, 320 pp.]

JOAN FITZPATRICK, HUMAN RIGHTS IN CRISIS: THE INTERNATIONAL SYSTEM FOR MONITORING

RIGHTS DURING STATES OF EMERGENCY (1994).

[Philadelphia: University of Pennsylvania Press, 260 pp.]

JAMES PATRICK FLOOD, THE EFFECTIVENESS OF UN HUMAN RIGHTS INSTITUTIONS (1998).

[Westport, Conn.: Praeger, 168 pp.]

DAVID P. FORSYTHE, HUMAN RIGHTS AND COMPARATIVE FOREIGN POLICY (2000).

[Tokyo; New York: United Nations University Press, 365 pp.]

DAVID P. FORSYTHE, HUMAN RIGHTS AND WORLD POLITICS (2d rev. ed. 1989).

[Lincoln, NE: University of Nebraska Press, 316 pp.]

DAVID P FORSYTHE, HUMAN RIGHTS IN INTERNATIONAL RELATIONS (2d ed. 2006).

[Cambridge: Cambridge University Press, 285 pp.]

DIANA JOYCE FOX & NAIMA ALI HASCI, THE CHALLENGES OF WOMEN'S ACTIVISM AND HUMAN RIGHTS IN AFRICA (1999).

[Lewiston, NY: Edwin Mellen Press, 286 pp.]

THE FUTURE OF HUMAN RIGHTS PROTECTION IN A CHANGING WORLD: FIFTY YEARS SINCE THE FOUR FREEDOMS ADDRESS (Asbjørn Eide & Jan Helgesen eds., 1991).

[Oslo: Norwegian University Press, 239 pp.]

THE FUTURE OF UN HUMAN RIGHTS TREATY MONITORING (Philip Alston & James Crawford, eds., 2000).

[Cambridge; New York: Cambridge University Press, 563 pp.]

C. A. GEARTY, CAN HUMAN RIGHTS SURVIVE? (2006).

[New York: Cambridge University Press, 174 pp. Three essays examine challenges to human rights from war on terror, revival of political religion, and exhaustion of natural resources.]

GENOCIDE AND HUMAN RIGHTS (Mark Lattimer ed., 2007).

[Aldershot, Hants.; Burlington, VT: Ashgate, pp. 571. Collects leading essays.]

WILLEM J. M. VAN GENUGTEN, HUMAN RIGHTS REFERENCE HANDBOOK (2d rev. ed. 1999).

[The Hague: Netherlands Ministry of Foreign Affairs, Human Rights, Good Governance and Democratisation Dept., 203 pp.]

MARK GIBNEY, INTERNATIONAL HUMAN RIGHTS LAW: RETURNING TO UNIVERSAL PRINCIPLES (2008).

[Lanham: Rowman & Littlefield Publishers, 149 pp.]

MARK GIBNEY & STANISLAW FRANKOWSKI, JUDICIAL PROTECTION OF HUMAN RIGHTS: MYTH OR REALITY? (1999).

[Westport, Conn.: Praeger, 207 pp.]

DAVID GILLIES, BETWEEN PRINCIPLE AND PRACTICE: HUMAN RIGHTS IN NORTH-SOUTH RELATIONS (1996).

[Montreal; Buffalo: McGill-Queen's University Press, 339 pp. Analyzes the discrepancy between a government's words and actions. Looks at human rights diplomacy in Canada, the Netherlands, and Norway, and examines case studies of Sri Lanka, the Philippines, China, Indonesia, and Suriname. Highlights the growing north-south rift.]

LAWRENCE O. GOSTIN & ZITA LAZZARINI, HUMAN RIGHTS AND PUBLIC HEALTH IN THE AIDS PANDEMIC (1997).

[New York: Oxford Univ. Press, 212 pp. Examines the impact of AIDS and AIDS-related public health measures on human rights.]

JUTTA GRAS, THE EUROPEAN UNION AND HUMAN RIGHTS MONITORING (2000).

[Helsinki: The Erik Castréén Institute of International Law and Human Rights, 195 pp.]

GUANTÁNAMO BAY AND THE JUDICIAL-MORAL TREATMENT OF THE OTHER (Clark Butler ed., 2007).

[Lafayette, Ind.: Purdue University Press, 187 pp. Philosophical analysis of human rights at stake in Guantánamo.]

ELSPETH GUILD & GUILLAME LESIEUR, THE EUROPEAN COURT OF JUSTICE ON THE EUROPEAN CONVENTION ON HUMAN RIGHTS: WHO SAID WHAT, WHEN? (1998).

[London, Boston: Kluwer Law International, 440 pp. Contains extracts from judgments and opinions on the European Convention on Human Rights delivered by advocates general of the European Court of Justice and the European Court of First Instance.]

NICOLAS GUILHOT, THE DEMOCRACY MAKERS: HUMAN RIGHTS & INTERNATIONAL ORDER (2005).

[New York: Columbia University Press, 273 pp.]

SARA GUILLET, NOUS, PEUPLES DES NATIONS UNIES: L'ACTION DES ONG AU SEIN DU SYSTEME DE PROTECTION INTERNATIONAL DES DROITS DE L'HOMME (1995).

[Paris: Editions Montchrestien, E.J.A., 179 pp.]

JEROEN GUTTER, THEMATIC PROCEDURES OF THE UNITED NATIONS COMMISSION ON HUMAN RIGHTS AND INTERNATIONAL LAW: IN SEARCH OF A SENSE OF COMMUNITY (2006).

[Antwerpen: Intersentia, 443 pp. In-depth treatment of thematic procedures, with more general analysis of UN's work in human rights.]

HURST HANNUM, AUTONOMY, SOVEREIGNTY, AND SELF-DETERMINATION: THE ACCOMMODATION OF CONFLICTING RIGHTS (rev. ed. 1996).

[Philadelphia, PA: University of Pennsylvania Press, 534 pp.]

STEPHEN A. HANSEN, THESAURUS OF ECONOMIC, SOCIAL, AND CULTURAL RIGHTS: TERMINOLOGY AND POTENTIAL VIOLATIONS (2000).

[Washington, D.C.: American Association for the Advancement of Science, 282 pp. This handbook was produced with the goal of developing tools, methods, and resources to help nongovernmental organisations (NGOs) to identify, monitor, and document violations of human rights.]

RAIJA HANSKI & MARKKU SUKSI, AN INTRODUCTION TO THE INTERNATIONAL PROTECTION OF HUMAN RIGHTS: A TEXTBOOK (2d rev. ed., 1999).

[Turku/Åbo: Institute for Human Rights, Åbo Akademi University, 468 pp.]

LOUIS HENKIN ET AL., HUMAN RIGHTS (1999).

[New York: Foundation Press, 1228 pp. Casebook.]

ALEXIS HERACLIDES, HELSINKI II AND ITS AFTERMATH: THE MAKING OF THE CSCE INTO AN INTERNATIONAL ORGANIZATION (1993).

[London: Pinter Pub., 274 pp.]

SHAREEN HERTEL, PROMISES TO KEEP: SECURING HUMAN RIGHTS IN A CHANGING WORLD (1994).

[New York: U.N. Assoc. of the USA (UNA-USA), 50 pp. Briefing book of the UNA-USA Global Policy Project.]

HILDE HEY, GROSS HUMAN RIGHTS VIOLATIONS: A SEARCH FOR CAUSES - A STUDY OF GUATEMALA AND COSTA RICA (1995).

[Dordrecht; Boston; London: Martinus Nijhoff, 264 pp.]

STEPHEN HOPGOOD, KEEPERS OF THE FLAME: UNDERSTANDING AMNESTY INTERNATIONAL (2006).

[Ithaca, N.Y.: Cornell University Press, 249 pp.]

RHODA E. HOWARD, HUMAN RIGHTS AND THE SEARCH FOR COMMUNITY (1995).

[Boulder: Westview Press, 255 pp.]

RHODA E. HOWARD, HUMAN RIGHTS IN COMMONWEALTH AFRICA (1986).

[Totowa, N.J.: Rowman & Littlefield, 250 pp. Discusses various aspects of African human rights, including economic, communal, political, civil, and women's rights.]

COURTNEY W. HOWLAND, RELIGIOUS FUNDAMENTALISM AND THE HUMAN RIGHTS OF WOMEN (1999).

[New York: St. Martin's Press, 326 pp.]

HUMAN RIGHTS: AN AGENDA FOR THE NEXT CENTURY (Louis Henkin & John L. Hargrove eds., 1994).

[Washington, DC: The American Society of International Law (ASIL), 524 pp. Volume number 26 of STUDIES IN TRANSNATIONAL LEGAL POLICY SERIES.]

HUMAN RIGHTS AND DEVELOPMENT IN AFRICA (Claude E. Welch, Jr. & Ronald I. Meltzer eds., 1984).

[Albany, N.Y.: State University of N.Y. Press, 349 pp. Discusses general human rights issues in contemporary Africa, regional responses including the work of NGOs and the Banjul Charter on Human and Peoples' Rights, and presents several views on the "right to development" and self-determination. Appendices contain the Banjul Charter, a summary of basic human rights guaranteed in the Charter and other major human rights treaties, and a list of major African human rights conferences held between 1961-81. Bibliography also included.]

HUMAN RIGHTS AND DEVELOPMENT IN AFRICA: ESTABLISHING THE "RULE OF LAW" (1999).

[Urbana-Champaign, IL: Center for African Studies. 2 v. (various pagings).]

HUMAN RIGHTS AND DISABLED PERSONS: ESSAYS AND RELEVANT HUMAN RIGHTS INSTRUMENTS (Theresia Degener & Yolan Koster-Dreese eds., 1995).

[Dordrecht; Boston; London: Martinus Nijhoff, 757 pp. Contains essays, instruments, and tables reflecting the status of implementation by country and by instrument.]

HUMAN RIGHTS AND FORCED DISPLACEMENT (Anne F. Bayefsky & Joan Fitzpatrick eds., 2000).

[The Hague; Boston; London: M. Nijhoff, 320 pp.]

HUMAN RIGHTS AND GOVERNANCE IN AFRICA (Ronald Cohen et al. eds., 1993).

[Gainesville, Fla.: University Press of Florida, 285 pp. Part I contains scholarly articles that present several theoretical approaches to human rights in Africa, and Part II contains scholarly articles that discuss substantive human rights issues including women's rights, refugees, minority rights, education, and academic freedom.]

HUMAN RIGHTS AND HUMANITARIAN LAW: THE QUEST FOR UNIVERSALITY (Daniel Warner ed., 1997).

[The Hague; Boston: M. Nijhoff, 146 pp. Papers presented at a 1995 Graduate Institute of International Studies colloquium. Covers a wide variety of topics, including Islam and human rights, Asian concepts of human rights, and refugee issues. Projects an integrated approach to ideas shared by three major organizations in the humanitarian law field: the U.N. Center for Human Rights, the International Committee of the Red Cross, and the U.N. High Commissioner for Refugees as well as outside experts on the relationships between the different professional regimes.]

HUMAN RIGHTS AND JUDICIAL REVIEW: A COMPARATIVE PERSPECTIVE (David M. Beatty ed., 1994).

[Dordrecht; Boston: Martinus Nijhoff Pub., 361 pp. Volume 34 in the INTERNATIONAL STUDIES IN HUMAN RIGHTS SERIES.]

HUMAN RIGHTS AND LABOUR LAW: ESSAYS FOR PAUL O'HIGGINS (K.D. Ewing et al. eds., 1994).

[London: Mansell Publishing Ltd., 367 pp.]

HUMAN RIGHTS AS GENERAL NORMS AND A STATE'S RIGHT TO OPT OUT: RESERVATIONS AND OBJECTIONS TO HUMAN RIGHTS CONVENTIONS (J.P. Garner ed., 1997).

[London: British Institute of International and Comparative Law, 207 pp. Collection of essays examining problems of the application of the rules relating to reservations in the Vienna Convention on Treaties 1969 and problems of reservations from a governmental viewpoint.]

HUMAN RIGHTS: CONCEPTS AND STANDARDS (Janusz Symonides ed., 2000).

[Paris: UNESCO, 416 pp. Through essays by human rights experts, analyzes historical and philosophical foundations of human rights. Detailed analysis of civil and political rights.]

HUMAN RIGHTS FIFTY YEARS ON: A REAPPRAISAL (Tony Evans ed., 1998).

[Manchester: Manchester University Press, 237 pp. Radical critique of the current human rights system.]

HUMAN RIGHTS IN AFRICA: CROSS-CULTURAL PERSPECTIVES (Abdullahi Ahmed An-Na`im & Francis M. Deng eds., 1990).

[Washington, D.C.: The Brookings Institution, 399 pp. Discusses African human rights in the context of various conceptions of international human rights, including traditional "western" perspectives, Christian and Muslim perspectives, several African cultural perspectives, and cross-cultural perspectives.]

HUMAN RIGHTS IN INTERNATIONAL LAW: LEGAL AND POLICY ISSUES (Theodor Meron ed., 1984).

[Oxford: Clarendon Press, 566 pp., 2 vols.]

HUMAN RIGHTS IN THE ARAB WORLD: INDEPENDENT VOICES (Anthony Tirado Chase & Amr Hamzawy eds. 2006).

[Philadelphia: University of Pennsylvania Press, 322 pp.]

HUMAN RIGHTS IN THE WORLD COMMUNITY: ISSUES AND ACTION (Richard Pierre Claude & Burns H Weston eds., 3d ed. 2006).

[Philadelphia: University of Pennsylvania Press, 543 pp.]

HUMAN RIGHTS LAW (Philip Alston ed., 1996).

[New York: New York University Press, 559 pp. Provides essays of importance to the subject of human rights law divided into three sections: Human Rights Schools of Thought, Areas, and Legal Cultures.]

HUMAN RIGHTS: NEW DIMENSIONS AND CHALLENGES - UNESCO MANUAL ON HUMAN RIGHTS (Janusz Symonides ed., 1998).

[Paris: UNESCO, 332 pp. Essays analyze obstacles and threats to human rights at beginning of 21st century.]

HUMAN RIGHTS OF WOMEN: NATIONAL AND INTERNATIONAL PERSPECTIVES (Rebecca J. Cook ed., 1994).

[Philadelphia: University of Pennsylvania Press, 634 pp. Part of the PENNSYLVANIA STUDIES IN HUMAN RIGHTS SERIES.]

HUMAN RIGHTS PERSPECTIVES & CHALLENGES: IN 1990 AND BEYOND (K.P. Saksena ed., 1994).

[New Delhi: Lancers Books, 608 pp. Published under the auspices of the Institute for World Congress on Human Rights (IWCHR), New Delhi. Contains thirty-seven articles that were initially prepared as working papers for the 1990 World Congress on Human Rights in New Delhi. Appendices include several addresses from the Congress and the Congress's Final Act, which provides an overall assessment of the human rights situation and a set of recommendations for its improvement.]

HUMAN RIGHTS REFERENCE HANDBOOK (Theo R.G. van Banning ed., 1992).

[Netherlands: Ministry of Foreign Affairs, 181 pp. Sets out European Political Co-operation (EPC) positions on human rights issues.]

HUMAN RIGHTS WATCH, ACADEMIC FREEDOM AND HUMAN RIGHTS ABUSES IN AFRICA, AN AFRICA WATCH REPORT (1991).

[New York: Human Rights Watch, 153 pp. Details human rights abuses committed against members of academic communities in Cameroon, Kenya, Liberia, Malawi, Nigeria, Somalia, South Africa, Sudan, Swaziland, Tanzania, Togo, Uganda, Zaire, and Zimbabwe. Also presents recommendations for African governments, academics, organizations of academics, NGOs, donor governments, and UNESCO to take action that will "encourage the independence and autonomy of academic institutions and academic pursuits." An appendix lists detained African academics.]

LYNN AVERY HUNT, INVENTING HUMAN RIGHTS: A HISTORY (2007).

[New York: W.W. Norton & Co., 272 pp.]

JUDE IBEGBU, RIGHTS OF THE UNBORN CHILD IN INTERNATIONAL LAW (2000).

[Lewiston, N.Y.: Edwin Mellen, 652 pp.]

INDIGENOUS PEOPLES, THE UNITED NATIONS AND HUMAN RIGHTS (Sarah Pritchard ed., 1998).

[London: Zed Books ; Leichhardt, NSW, Australia: Federation Press, 243 pp.]

INTERNATIONAL COMMITTEE OF THE RED CROSS, REPORT ON THE PROTECTION OF WAR VICTIMS (1993).

[Geneva: ICRC, 51 pp.]

THE INTERNATIONAL DIMENSIONS OF HUMAN RIGHTS (Karel Vasak & Philip Alston eds., 1982).

[Westport, CT: Greenwood Press; Paris: UNESCO, 755 pp., 2 vols. Volume I on Principles and Norms of Human Rights includes chapters concerning self-determination and non-discrimination; sources of human rights law; economic, social, and cultural rights; civil and political rights; and human rights in armed conflict. Volume II on International Institutions contains chapters on the U.N., ILO, UNESCO, the International Committee of the Red Cross, the Council of Europe, the Organization of African Unity, and possibilities for cooperation among Asian states.]

INTERNATIONAL HUMANITARIAN LAW AND HUMAN RIGHTS LAW: TOWARDS A NEW

MERGER IN INTERNATIONAL LAW (Roberta Arnold & Noëlle N.R. Quénivet eds., 2008).

[Leiden; Boston: Martinus Nijhoff Publishers, 596 pp. Approaches relationship between humanitarian and human rights law as merger into single set of rules; uses case studies.]

INTERNATIONAL HUMAN RIGHTS: PROBLEMS OF LAW, POLICY, AND PRACTICE (Richard B Lillich et al. eds., 4th ed. 2006).

[New York City: Aspen Publishers, 1,176 pp.]

INTERNATIONAL ORGANIZATIONS AND ETHNIC CONFLICT (Milton J. Esman & Shibley Telhami eds., 1995).

[Ithaca, NY: Cornell University Press, 343 pp.]

INTERNATIONAL PROTECTION OF HUMAN RIGHTS (Louis B. Sohn & Thomas Buergenthal eds., 1973).

[Indianapolis, IN: Bobbs-Merrill, 1402 pp.]

FRANCIS GEOFFREY JACOBS & ROBIN C.A. WHITE, THE EUROPEAN CONVENTION ON HUMAN RIGHTS (2d ed. 1996).

[Oxford: Clarendon Press; New York: Oxford Univ. Press, 469 pp. A completely rewritten edition of the earlier book on the convention. Takes the case law of the European Court as its starting point and offers full consideration of the Commission's case law on questions of admissibility. Explains procedure as well as substantive law of the convention.]

MARK JANIS, RICHARD KAY & ANTHONY BRADLEY, EUROPEAN HUMAN RIGHTS LAW: TEXT AND MATERIALS (2000).

[New York: Oxford Univ. Press, 561 pp.]

KURT JONASSOHN WITH KARIN SOLVEIG BJORNSON, GENOCIDE AND GROSS HUMAN RIGHTS VIOLATIONS IN COMPARATIVE PERSPECTIVE (1998).

[New Brunswick, NJ: Transaction Pubs., 338 pp. Discusses genocide, its development, and its consequences; hunger as a tool of conflict; famines; the Jewish Resistance; as well as prediction, prevention, and intervention.]

THOMAS DAVID JONES, HUMAN RIGHTS: GROUP DEFAMATION, FREEDOM OF EXPRESSION, AND THE LAW OF NATIONS (1998).

[The Hague; Boston: Martinus Nijhoff Pub., 319 pp. Presents a discussion and analysis of the laws governing group defamation and speech inciteful of racial hatred in five countries: Great Britain, Canada, India, Nigeria, and the U.S.]

RIKKE FRANK JØRGENSEN, HUMAN RIGHTS IN THE GLOBAL INFORMATION SOCIETY (2006).

[Cambridge, Mass.: MIT Press, 324 pp.]

CHANTAL JOUBERT & HANS BEVERS, SCHENGEN INVESTIGATED: A COMPARATIVE INTERPRETATION OF THE SCHENGEN PROVISIONS ON INTERNATIONAL POLICE COOPERATION IN THE LIGHT OF THE EUROPEAN CONVENTION ON HUMAN RIGHTS (1996).

[The Hague, London: Kluwer Law International, 576 pp. A five-year study of the law applicable to police in the five countries: Belgium, the Netherlands, Luxembourg, France, and Germany. Discusses the possible impact of the differences on the application of the Schengen Convention. Relevant to practitioners in the field of cross-border criminal law.]

WALTER KÄLIN, GUIDING PRINCIPLES ON INTERNAL DISPLACEMENT: ANNOTATIONS (2000).

[Washington, D.C.: American Society of International Law, 276 pp. Annotations explain the legal basis for the Guiding Principles.]

ARUSA MAHIN KARIM & EVELYN AMOAH-BERTRAND, HUMAN RIGHTS PROTECTION: THE AFRICAN REGIONAL SYSTEM (1998).

[Arcadia, South Africa: NIPILAR, 46 pp.]

MARGARET E. KECK & KATHRYN SIKKINK, ACTIVISTS BEYOND BORDERS: ADVOCACY NETWORKS IN INTERNATIONAL POLITICS (1998).

[Ithaca, N.Y.: Cornell University Press, 228 pp.]

WILLIAM KOREY, NGOS AND THE UNIVERSAL DECLARATION OF HUMAN RIGHTS: "A CURIOUS GRAPEVINE" (1998).

[New York: St. Martin's Press, 638 pp.]

WILLIAM KOREY, THE PROMISES WE KEEP: HUMAN RIGHTS, THE HELSINKI PROCESS, AND AMERICAN FOREIGN POLICY (1993).

[New York: St. Martin's Press, 529 pp.]

TODD LANDMAN, PROTECTING HUMAN RIGHTS: A COMPARATIVE STUDY (2005).

[Washington, D.C.: Georgetown University Press, 231 pp.]

MARK LATTIMER, GENOCIDE AND HUMAN RIGHTS (2007).

[Aldershot; Burlington, VT: Ashgate, 571 pp.]

PAUL GORDON LAUREN, THE EVOLUTION OF INTERNATIONAL HUMAN RIGHTS: VISIONS SEEN (2d ed. 2003).

[Philadelphia: University of Pennsylvania Press, 397 pp.]

LAWRENCE J. LEBLANC, THE CONVENTION ON THE RIGHTS OF THE CHILD (1995).

[Lincoln, NE: University of Nebraska, 337 pp. Volume three of the HUMAN RIGHTS IN INTERNATIONAL PERSPECTIVE SERIES.]

SCOTT LECKIE, WHEN PUSH COMES TO SHOVE: FORCED EVICTIONS AND HUMAN RIGHTS (1995).

[Mexico: Habitat International Coalition (HIC), 139 pp.]

NATAN LERNER, RELIGION, BELIEFS, AND INTERNATIONAL HUMAN RIGHTS (2000).

[Maryknoll, N.Y.: Orbis Books, 183 pp.]

NATAN LERNER, RELIGION, SECULAR BELIEFS AND HUMAN RIGHTS: 25 YEARS AFTER THE 1981 DECLARATION (2006).

[Boston: Martinus Nijhoff Publishers, 228 pp. Explores several aspects of human rights of religion and belief, including proselytism, religion and terrorism, use of religious symbols, international criminal law, and others.]

THE LEGALIZATION OF HUMAN RIGHTS: MULTIDISCIPLINARY PERSPECTIVES ON HUMAN RIGHTS AND HUMAN RIGHTS LAW (Saladin Meckled-García & Basak Cali eds., 2006).

[London; New York: Routledge, 208 pp. Analyzes extent to which legalization shapes human rights theories; provides perspectives from political science, anthropology, sociology, international law, international politics, etc.]

LOUPES G. LOUCAIDES, ESSAYS ON THE DEVELOPING LAW OF HUMAN RIGHTS (1995).

[Dordrecht; Boston: Martinus Nijhoff Pub., 236 pp. Volume 39 in the INTERNATIONAL STUDIES IN HUMAN RIGHTS SERIES.]

JOHN MAHONEY, THE CHALLENGE OF HUMAN RIGHTS: ORIGIN, DEVELOPMENT, AND SIGNIFICANCE (2007).

[Malden, MA: Blackwell Pub., 215 pp.]

MAKING RIGHTS WORK (Penny Smith ed., 1999).

[Brookfield, VT: Ashgate, 254 pp. Essays by human rights experts on experiences and expectations of "rights." Compares South Africa, U.K., Canada and France.]

SUSAN MARKS & ANDREW CLAPHAM, INTERNATIONAL HUMAN RIGHTS LEXICON (2005).

[Oxford; New York: Oxford Univ. Press, 461 pp.]

FRANCISCO FORREST MARTIN ET AL., INTERNATIONAL HUMAN RIGHTS LAW AND PRACTICE: CASES, TREATIES, AND MATERIALS (1997).

[The Hague; Boston: Kluwer, 1356 pp. Casebook.]

IAN MARTIN, THE NEW WORLD ORDER: OPPORTUNITY OR THREAT FOR HUMAN RIGHTS? (1993).

[Cambridge, MA: Harvard College, 24 pp. Published lecture of Apr. 14, 1993, by the Edward A. Smith Visiting Fellow, presented by the Harvard Law School Human Rights Program.]

VOJTECH MASTNY, THE HELSINKI PROCESS AND THE REINTEGRATION OF EUROPE, 1986-1991: ANALYSIS AND DOCUMENTATION (1992).

[New York: New York University Press, 343 pp.]

BERTRAND MATHIEU, THE RIGHT TO LIFE IN EUROPEAN CONSTITUTIONAL AND INTERNATIONAL CASE-LAW (2006).

[Strasbourg: Council of Europe Pub., 124 pp.]

DOMINIC MCGOLDRICK, THE HUMAN RIGHTS COMMITTEE: ITS ROLE IN THE DEVELOPMENT OF THE INTERNATIONAL COVENANT ON CIVIL AND POLITICAL RIGHTS (1994).

[Oxford; Clarendon; New York: Oxford Univ. Press, 576 pp. Excellent description of the committee's work.]

THEODOR MERON, THE HUMANIZATION OF INTERNATIONAL LAW (2006).

[Leiden; Boston: Martinus Nijhoff, 551 pp.]

JULIE MERTUS, THE UNITED NATIONS AND HUMAN RIGHTS: A GUIDE FOR A NEW ERA (2005).

[London; New York: Routledge, 223 pp.]

KURT MILLS, HUMAN RIGHTS IN THE EMERGING GLOBAL ORDER: A NEW SOVEREIGNTY? (1998).

[New York: St. Martin's Press, 256 pp. Examines how recent international practice in the areas of human rights, self-determination, refugees, human migration, and humanitarian intervention is challenging traditional conceptions of sovereignty.]

7A MODERN LEGAL SYSTEMS CYCLOPEDIA (Kenneth R. Redden rev. ed., 1988-).

[Buffalo, NY: William S. Hein & Co., looseleaf. Articles on the Inter-American Commission on Human Rights and the Inter-American Court of Human Rights; humanitarian law (including the role of the International Committee of the Red Cross); and the Western/U.S. and Socialist approaches to human rights. Texts of several human rights instruments and status information are also included.]

DANIEL MOECKLI, HUMAN RIGHTS AND NON-DISCRIMINATION IN THE 'WAR ON TERROR' (2008).

[Oxford; New York: Oxford Univ. Press, 271 pp. Examines whether current legal regimes protect human rights; looks at issues such as military commission trials, racial profiling, and selective immigration policies.]

MONITORING HUMAN RIGHTS IN EUROPE: COMPARING INTERNATIONAL PROCEDURES AND MECHANISMS (Arie Bloed et al. eds., 1993).

[Dordrecht; Boston: Martinus Nijhoff Pub., 338 pp.]

RACHEL MURRAY, THE AFRICAN COMMISSION ON HUMAN AND PEOPLES' RIGHTS AND INTERNATIONAL LAW (2000).

[Oxford; Portland, OR: Hart, 288 pp.]

RACHEL MURRAY, HUMAN RIGHTS IN AFRICA: FROM THE OAU TO THE AFRICAN UNION (2004).

[Cambridge; New York: Cambridge University Press, 349 pp.]

RACHEL MURRAY, THE ROLE OF NATIONAL HUMAN RIGHTS INSTITUTIONS AT THE INTERNATIONAL AND REGIONAL LEVELS: THE EXPERIENCE OF AFRICA (2007).

[Oxford: Hart Publishing, 160 pp.]

THOMAS D. MUSGRAVE, SELF-DETERMINATION AND NATIONAL MINORITIES (1997).

[Oxford: Clarendon Press; New York: Oxford Univ. Press, 290 pp. Examines various political theories of self-determination, the extent to which self-determination has become a legal right, and the historical development of self-determination and minorities.]

CHIDI NGANGAH, THE POLITICS OF HUMAN RIGHTS: A VIEW FROM THE THIRD WORLD (1998).

[Kaduna, Nigeria: Klamidas Communications Ltd., 119 pp.]

INGRID NIFOSI, THE UN SPECIAL PROCEDURES IN THE FIELD OF HUMAN RIGHTS (2005).

[Antwerpen: Intersentia; Holmes Beach: Gaunt, 179 pp.]

NON-STATE ACTORS IN THE HUMAN RIGHTS UNIVERSE (George J Andreopoulos et al. eds., 2006).

[Bloomfield, CT: Kumarian Press, 352 pp.]

MANFRED NOWAK, U.N. COVENANT ON CIVIL AND POLITICAL RIGHTS: CCPR COMMENTARY (2d rev. ed. 2005).

[Kehl; Germany; Arlington, Va.: N.P. Engel, 1277 pp. Analyzes the organizational, procedural, and substantive provisions of the Covenant and the two optional protocols; addresses Human Rights Committee practice and case law.]

TOM OBOKATA, TRAFFICKING OF HUMAN BEINGS FROM A HUMAN RIGHTS PERSPECTIVE: TOWARDS A HOLISTIC APPROACH (2006).

[Leiden, The Netherlands; Boston: Martinus Nijhoff, 247 pp. Applies human rights norms such as rights to life, work, health, and freedom from torture and slavery to trafficking process; identifies obligations to prohibit trafficking, punish traffickers, protect victims, and address causes and consequences of trafficking.]

OFFICE OF THE UNHCR, HANDBOOK FOR EMERGENCIES (2d ed. 1999).

[Geneva: U.N., 405 pp.]

OBIORA CHINEDU OKAFOR, THE AFRICAN HUMAN RIGHTS SYSTEM, ACTIVIST FORCES AND INTERNATIONAL INSTITUTIONS (2007).

[Cambridge: Cambridge University Press, 336 pp. Uses detailed cases studies to examine how rights are enforced within African system.]

DAWN OLIVER & JÖRG FEDTKE, HUMAN RIGHTS AND THE PRIVATE SPHERE: A COMPARATIVE STUDY (2007).

[London; New York: Routledge-Cavendish, 594 pp. Analyzes interaction between constitutional rights, freedoms, and private law in several jurisdictions.]

ON HUMAN RIGHTS (Stephen Shute & Susan Hurley eds., 1993).

[New York: Basic Books, 262 pp. THE OXFORD AMNESTY LECTURES SERIES.]

THE ORGANIZATION OF AFRICAN UNITY, 1963-1988: A ROLE ANALYSIS AND PERFORMANCE REVIEW (R.A. Akindele ed., 1988).

[Ibadan, Nigeria: Vantage Pub., 358 pp.]

THE ORGANIZATION OF AFRICAN UNITY AFTER THIRTY YEARS (Yassin El-Ayouty ed., 1994).

[Westport, Conn.: Praeger Publishers/Greenwood Publishing Group, 216 pp. Assesses OAU efforts in such areas as peacekeeping and conflict resolution, regional promotion of human rights, refugees, and environmental issues. Also discusses OAU relations with other organizations.]

EDMUND JAN OSMANCZYK & ANTHONY MANGO, ENCYCLOPEDIA OF THE UNITED NATIONS AND INTERNATIONAL AGREEMENTS (3d ed. 2003).

[New York: Routledge. 4 vols.; provides basic information on international law, including human rights instruments, organizations, and conferences.]

FATSAH OUGUERGOUZ, LA CHARTE AFRICAINE DES DROITS DE L'HOMME ET DES PEUPLES: UNE APPROCHE JURIDIQUE DES DROITS DE L'HOMME ENTRE TRADITION ET MODERNITE (1993).

[Geneva: Publications de l'institut universitaire de hautes etudes internationales, 479 pp. French language text. Part one examines historical human rights problems in Africa and the processes out of which the African Charter on Human and Peoples' Rights was created. Part two discusses the Charter's material content, examining provisions for individual and peoples' rights, and individual duties, as well as the juridical implications of the absence of a derogation clause. Part three examines the Charter's institutional provisions, dealing with the organization, functions, and procedures of the African Commission on Human and Peoples' Rights, and the related roles of the OAU. Annexes contain the Charter, interior and procedural rules of the Commission, participation of African states in principal international human rights instruments, and a model communication to the Commission.]

OURS BY RIGHT: WOMEN'S RIGHTS AS HUMAN RIGHTS (Joanna Kerr ed., 1993).

[London: North-South Institute, 180 pp.]

JORDAN J. PAUST, JOAN FITZPATRICK, & JON M. VAN DYKE, INTERNATIONAL LAW AND LITIGATION IN THE U.S. (2d ed. 2005).

[St. Paul, Minn.: Thomson/West, 1135 pp. Casebook on international law in U.S. courts.]

R. P. PEERENBOOM ET AL., HUMAN RIGHTS IN ASIA: A COMPARATIVE LEGAL STUDY OF TWELVE ASIAN JURISDICTIONS, FRANCE AND THE USA (2006).

[London; New York: Routledge, 529 pp. Examines how civil, political, social, and economic rights are interpreted and addressed in several Asian jurisdictions.]

PEOPLES' RIGHTS: THE STATE OF THE ART (Philip Alston ed., 2001).

[Oxford: Oxford Univ. Press, 220 pp.]

CHRIS MAINA PETER, HUMAN RIGHTS IN AFRICA: A COMPARATIVE STUDY OF THE AFRICAN HUMAN AND PEOPLES' RIGHTS CHARTER AND THE NEW TANZANIAN BILL OF RIGHTS (1990).

[Westport, Conn.; New York: Greenwood Press. Published under the auspices of the Consortium on Human Rights Development, 145 pp. Provides a brief historical background and an extensive comparison of the Tanzanian Bill of Rights and the African Charter on Human and Peoples' Rights. Bases for comparison include rights and freedoms, individual obligations, and enforcement mechanisms provided in the two instruments. Appendices contain the New Tanzanian Bill of Rights; the African Charter on Human and Peoples' Rights; composition of the African Commission on Human and Peoples' Rights; the Universal Declaration of Human Rights; a summary of rights, freedoms, duties, and obligations under the Tanzanian Bill of Rights, the African Charter, the Universal Declaration on Human Rights; and a table of relevant cases and statutes.]

S.E.M. PHEKO, SOUTH AFRICA: BETRAYAL OF A COLONISED PEOPLE, ISSUES OF INTERNATIONAL HUMAN RIGHTS LAW (1990).

[London: ISAL Publications, 161 pp. Provides historical background concerning British colonialism in South Africa, challenges the notion of international law as the "law of civilized nations," and examines both recognition of international law in relation to South Africa and violations of international law in South Africa.]

THE PHILOSOPHY OF HUMAN RIGHTS (Morton Winston ed., 1989).

[Belmont, CA: Wadsworth, 293 pp.]

CLAUDE PILLOUD ET AL., COMMENTARY ON THE ADDITIONAL PROTOCOLS OF 8 JUNE 1977 TO THE GENEVA CONVENTIONS OF 12 AUGUST 1949 (1987).

[New York: ICRC, 1625 pp.]

THE POWER OF HUMAN RIGHTS: INTERNATIONAL NORMS AND DOMESTIC CHANGE (Thomas Risse et al. ed., 1999).

[Cambridge; New York: Cambridge University Press, 318 pp.]

THE PRACTICE OF HUMAN RIGHTS: TRACKING LAW BETWEEN THE GLOBAL AND THE LOCAL (Mark Goodale & Sally Engle Merry eds., 2007).

[Cambridge; New York: Cambridge University Press, 384 pp. Examines human rights in practice using anthropological studies of human rights work.]

THE PROTECTION ROLE OF NATIONAL HUMAN RIGHTS INSTITUTIONS (B.G. Ramcharan ed., 2005).

[Leiden; Boston: Martinus Nijhoff Publishers, 232 pp.]

B.G. RAMCHARAN, A UN HIGH COMMISSIONER IN DEFENCE OF HUMAN RIGHTS: "NO LICENSE TO KILL OR TORTURE" (2005).

[Leiden; Boston: M. Nijhoff, 854 pp.]

B. G. RAMCHARAN, THE CONCEPT AND PRESENT STATUS OF INTERNATIONAL PROTECTION OF HUMAN RIGHTS: FORTY YEARS AFTER THE UNIVERSAL DECLARATION (1988).

[Dordrecht; Boston: Martinus Nijhoff Pub., 611 pp.]

KENNETH RANDALL, FEDERAL COURTS AND THE INTERNATIONAL HUMAN RIGHTS PARADIGM (1990).

[Durham, NC: Duke University Press, 295 pp.]

ALBRECHT RANDELZHOFER & CHRISTIAN TOMUSCHAT, STATE RESPONSIBILITY AND THE INDIVIDUAL: REPARATION IN INSTANCES OF GRAVE VIOLATIONS OF HUMAN RIGHTS (1999).

[The Hague; Boston: Martinus Nijhoff Pub., 296 pp.]

NINA REDMAN AND LUCILLE WHALEN, HUMAN RIGHTS: A REFERENCE HANDBOOK (2d ed. 1998).

[Santa Barbara, Calif.: ABC-CLIO, 301 pp.]

REFLECTIONS ON THE UNIVERSAL DECLARATION OF HUMAN RIGHTS: A FIFTIETH ANNIVERSARY ANTHOLOGY (Barend van der Heijden & Bahia Tahzib-Lie eds., 1998).

[The Hague: Martinus Nijhoff Pub., 350 pp. Anthology of 50 essays on human rights by world leaders or specialists in the field of human rights.]

RELIGIOUS HUMAN RIGHTS IN GLOBAL PERSPECTIVE: LEGAL PERSPECTIVES (Johan van der Vyer & John Witte, Jr. eds., 1996).

[The Hague, Boston, Mass.: Martinus Nijhoff Pub., 670 pp. Jimmy Carter, John T. Noonan, Jr., and a score of leading jurists assess the religious rights, laws, and practices of the international community.]

NASILA S. REMBE, THE SYSTEM OF PROTECTION OF HUMAN RIGHTS UNDER THE AFRICAN CHARTER ON HUMAN AND PEOPLES' RIGHTS: PROBLEMS AND PROSPECTS (1991).

[Lesotho: Inst. of S. Afr. Stud., Nat'l University of Lesotho, 53 pp.]

A.H. ROBERTSON & J.G. MERRILLS, HUMAN RIGHTS IN THE WORLD: AN INTRODUCTION TO THE STUDY OF THE INTERNATIONAL PROTECTION OF HUMAN RIGHTS (4th ed. 1996).

[Manchester, New York: Manchester University Press, 355 pp. Explains the current guarantees of human rights and how they work. Rewritten and updated to take into account the ending of the Cold War. Includes such issues as the War Crimes Tribunal for the former Yugoslavia, the Convention on the Rights of the Child, and the role of the U.N. High Commissioner for Human Rights.]

GEOFFREY ROBERTSON, CRIMES AGAINST HUMANITY: THE STRUGGLE FOR GLOBAL JUSTICE (3d ed., 2006).

[New York: New Press, 758 pp.]

J. G. MERRILLS & A.H. ROBERTSON, HUMAN RIGHTS IN EUROPE: A STUDY OF THE EUROPEAN CONVENTION ON HUMAN RIGHTS (4th ed. 2001).

[New York: Juris Pub.; Manchester: Manchester University Press, 362 pp.]

MANUEL E. VENTURA ROBLES, SYSTEMATIZATION OF THE CONTENTIOUS JURISPRUDENCE OF THE INTER-AMERICAN COURT OF HUMAN RIGHTS (1996).

[San José, Costa Rica: I/A Court. Vol. 1, 1981-1991.]

NAOMI ROHT-ARRIAZA, THE PINOCHET EFFECT: TRANSNATIONAL JUSTICE IN THE AGE OF HUMAN RIGHTS (2005). [Philadelphia: University of Pennsylvania Press, 256 pp.]

JOHN K. ROTH, GENOCIDE AND HUMAN RIGHTS: A PHILOSOPHICAL GUIDE (2005).

[Houndmills, Basingstoke, Hampshire; New York: Palgrave Macmillan, 352 pp.]

P. J. ROWE, THE IMPACT OF HUMAN RIGHTS LAW ON ARMED FORCES (2006).

[Cambridge; New York: Cambridge University Press, 259 pp.]

RAJKUMARI CHANDRA ROY, LAND RIGHTS OF THE INDIGENOUS PEOPLES OF THE CHITTAGONG HILL TRACTS, BANGLADESH (2000).

[Copenhagen: IWGIA, 232 pp.]

MARK SACHLEBEN, HUMAN RIGHTS TREATIES: CONSIDERING PATTERNS OF PARTICIPATION, 1948-2000 (2006).

[New York: Routledge, 257 pp.]

ALBIE SACHS, PROTECTING HUMAN RIGHTS IN A NEW SOUTH AFRICA (1990).

[Cape Town; Oxford: Oxford Univ. Press, 208 pp.]

DANESH SAROOSHI, THE UNITED NATIONS AND THE DEVELOPMENT OF COLLECTIVE SECURITY: THE DELEGATION BY THE UN SECURITY COUNCIL OF ITS CHAPTER VII POWERS (2000).

[Oxford: Clarendon, 336 pp. Examines the use of force by or under the authority of the U.N. to maintain or restore peace, and predicts likely future developments in the legal framework governing U.N. peace-keeping operations.]

OSCAR SCHACHTER, INTERNATIONAL LAW IN THEORY AND PRACTICE (1991).

[Dordrecht; Boston: Martinus Nijhoff Pub., 431 pp.]

OSCAR SCHACHTER, INTERNATIONAL LAW IN THEORY AND PRACTICE (student ed. 1995).

[Boston: Kluwer Law International, 431 pp.]

HORST SEIBT, COMPENDIUM OF CASE STUDIES OF INTERNATIONAL HUMANITARIAN LAW (1994).

[New York: ICRC; Dobbs Ferry, NY: Glanville Publishers, 145 pp. A collection of some 60 cases in which international humanitarian law applies.]

DINAH SHELTON, REGIONAL PROTECTION OF HUMAN RIGHTS (2008).

[New York: Oxford Univ. Press, 1163 pp. Examines European, Inter-American, and African systems; includes key documents.]

DINAH SHELTON, REMEDIES IN INTERNATIONAL HUMAN RIGHTS LAW (2d ed. 2005).

[New York: Oxford Univ. Press, 502 pp. Provides a comprehensive treatment of the topic of remedies for human rights violations. Gives theoretical framework, historical overview, and practical guide for human rights lawyers, judges, and academics. Includes cases of the Inter-American and European courts of human rights as well as decisions of the African and Inter-American commissions on human rights, U.N. bodies, the European Court of Justice, administrative tribunals, and national courts applying human rights law.]

ISSA G. SHIVJI, THE CONCEPT OF HUMAN RIGHTS IN AFRICA (1989).

[London: Council for the Development of Economic and Social Research in Africa (CODRESIA BOOK SERIES), 126 pp. Discusses several human rights approaches, including universalization, theorization, prioritization, promotion, prevention, and exposition; also critiques "dominant" human rights ideologies such as philosophical idealism and political nihilism, and proposes a "revolutionary" human rights framework based on the right to self-determination and to organize.]

PAUL SIEGHART, THE INTERNATIONAL LAW OF HUMAN RIGHTS (1983).

[Oxford: Clarendon Press, 569 pp.]

SOUTH AFRICA: HUMAN RIGHTS AND THE RULE OF LAW (Geoffrey Bindman ed., 1988).

[London; New York: Pinter Publishers, 159 pp. Discusses the status - under *apartheid* - of human rights, including freedom of movement, speech, association, and assembly, as well as education and access to the professions. Also examines human rights in relation to national institutions such as trade unions, the judicial system, the security system, and the political structure.]

HENRY J. STEINER, PHILIP ALSTON, & RYAN GOODMAN, INTERNATIONAL HUMAN RIGHTS IN CONTEXT: LAW, POLITICS, MORALS (3d ed. 2007).

[Oxford: Clarendon Press, New York: Oxford Univ. Press, 1560 pp. Addresses democracy, self-determination, globalization, and responses to massive tragedies through prosecutions (*e.g.*, of Pinochet) and truth commissions, including those in Chile and South Africa.]

JOHN J. STREMLAU, PEOPLE IN PERIL: HUMAN RIGHTS, HUMANITARIAN ACTION, AND PREVENTING DEADLY CONFLICT (1998).

[Washington, D.C.: Carnegie Corporation of New York, 80 pp.]

STUDIES AND ESSAYS ON INTERNATIONAL HUMANITARIAN LAW AND RED CROSS PRINCIPLES IN HONOUR OF JEAN PICTET (Chistophe Swinarski ed., 1984).

[Geneva: ICRC; The Hague: Martinus Nijhoff Pub., 1143 pp.]

ANNA LENA SVENSSON-MCCARTHY, THE INTERNATIONAL LAW OF HUMAN RIGHTS AND STATES OF EXCEPTION: WITH SPECIAL REFERENCE TO THE TRAVAUX PREPARATOIRES AND CASE-LAW OF THE INTERNATIONAL MONITORING ORGANS (1998).

[The Hague, Boston: Martinus Nijhoff Pub., 780 pp.]

Symposium, *The Hague Peace Conferences*, 94 AM. J. INT'L L. 1 (2000).

BAHIYYIH G. TAHZIB, FREEDOM OF RELIGION OR BELIEF: ENSURING EFFECTIVE INTERNATIONAL LEGAL PROTECTION (1996).

[The Hague; Boston: Martinus Nijhoff Pub., 600 pp. Addresses two questions arising in regard to the current protection of freedom of religion or belief: (1) Why has the U.N. not adopted a legally binding instrument on freedom of religion or belief?, and (2) How can the international community ensure effective protection of freedom of religion or belief?]

THE TENSION BETWEEN GROUP RIGHTS AND HUMAN RIGHTS: A MULTIDISCIPLINARY APPROACH (Koen De Feyter & George Pavlakos eds., 2008).

[Oxford: Hart Publishing, 318 pp. Analyzes current state of protection of group rights, including those of women, school communities, ethnic and linguistic minorities, migrant communities, and impoverished groups.]

A THEMATIC GUIDE TO DOCUMENTS ON THE HUMAN RIGHTS OF WOMEN: GLOBAL AND REGIONAL STANDARDS ADOPTED BY INTERGOVERNMENTAL ORGANIZATIONS, INTERNATIONAL NON-GOVERNMENTAL ORGANIZATIONS, AND PROFESSIONAL ASSOCIATIONS (Gudmundur Alfredsson & Katarina Tomasevski eds., 1995).

[The Hague, Boston: M. Nijhoff, 434 pp.]

LI-ANN THIO, MANAGING BABEL: THE INTERNATIONAL LEGAL PROTECTION OF MINORITIES IN THE TWENTIETH CENTURY (2005).

[Leiden; Boston: Martinus Nijhoff Publishers, 360 pp.]

BRIGIT TOEBES, THE RIGHT TO HEALTH AS A HUMAN RIGHT IN INTERNATIONAL LAW (1999).

[Antwerpen, Netherlands: INTERSENTIA, 417 pp.]

LORENZO S. TOGNI, THE STRUGGLE FOR HUMAN RIGHTS: AN INTERNATIONAL AND SOUTH AFRICAN PERSPECTIVE (1994).

[Kenya: Juta & Co., 295 pp.]

KATARINA TOMAŜEVSKI, DEVELOPMENT AID AND HUMAN RIGHTS REVISITED (1993).

[London; New York: Pinter Publishers, 223 pp.]

KATARINA TOMAŜEVSKI, RESPONDING TO HUMAN RIGHTS VIOLATIONS: 1946-1999 (2000).[The Hague: Martinus Nijhoff, 408 pp.]

U.O. UMOZURIKE, THE AFRICAN CHARTER ON HUMAN AND PEOPLES' RIGHTS (1997).

[The Hague; Boston: Martinus Nijhoff Pubs., 240 pp. An in-depth study of the African Charter on Human and Peoples' Rights, written with the insight of an insider. Assesses the effectiveness of the Charter in its formative years and compares the Charter with other major human rights instruments.]

U.N. CENTRE FOR HUMAN RIGHTS, UNITED NATIONS ACTION IN THE FIELD OF HUMAN RIGHTS, U.N. Doc. ST/HR/2/Rev.4, U.N. Sales No. E.94.XIV.11 (1994).

[New York: U.N., 359 pp. Provides a detailed description of U.N. actions for the promotion and protection of human rights. While it does not include results of the June 1993 World Conference on Human Rights in Vienna, an annex contains the Vienna Declaration and Programme of Action.]

U.N. DEPT. OF PUBLIC INFORMATION, THE UNITED NATIONS BLUE BOOK SERIES (1994-).

[New York: U.N. DPI. The series focuses on the U.N.'s role in resolving conflicts, responding to emergencies and promoting human rights. Each volume includes an introduction by the Secretary-General, a detailed chronology of events, and texts of relevant U.N. documents. Titles include:

Vol. I, THE UNITED NATIONS AND APARTHEID, 1948-1994, U.N. Doc. No. DPI/1568, U.N. Sales No. E.95.I.7;

Vol. II, THE UNITED NATIONS AND CAMBODIA, 1991-1995, U.N. Doc. No. DPI/1450, U.N. Sales No. E.95.I.9;

Vol. III, THE UNITED NATIONS AND NUCLEAR NON-PROLIFERATION, U.N. Sales No. E.95I.17;

Vol. IV, THE UNITED NATIONS AND EL SALVADOR, 1990-1995, U.N. Doc. No. DPI/1475, U.N. Sales No. E.95.I.12;

Vol. V, THE UNITED NATIONS AND MOZAMBIQUE, 1992-1995, U.N. Sales No. E.95.I.20;

Vol. VI, THE UNITED NATIONS AND THE ADVANCEMENT OF WOMEN, 1945-1995 . U.N. Sales No. E.95.I.29;

Vol. VII, THE UNITED NATIONS AND HUMAN RIGHTS, 1945-1995, U.N. Sales No. E.95.I.21;

Vol. VIII, THE UNITED NATIONS AND SOMALIA, 1992-1996, U.N. Sales No. E.96.I.8;

Vol. IX, THE UNITED NATIONS AND THE IRAQ-KUWAIT CONFLICT, 1990-1996, U.N. Sales No. E.96.I.3;

Vol. X , THE UNITED NATIONS AND RWANDA, 1993-1996, U.N. Sales No. E.96.I.20; [Vol. XI, not available yet];

Vol. XII, THE UNITED NATIONS AND THE INDEPENDENCE OF ERITREA, U.N. Sales No. E.96.I.10.]

U.N. OFFICE OF THE HIGH COMMISSIONER FOR HUMAN RIGHTS, HUMAN RIGHTS STUDY SERIES (1989-).

[Geneva: U.N. The series reproduces studies and reports prepared by special rapporteurs on topical issues of human rights. Titles include:

No. 1, RIGHT TO ADEQUATE FOOD AS A HUMAN RIGHT, U.N. Sales No. E.89.XIV.2;

No. 2, ELIMINATION OF ALL FORMS OF INTOLERANCE AND DISCRIMINATION BASED ON RELIGION OR BELIEF, U.N. Sales No. E.89.XIV.3;

No. 3, FREEDOM OF THE INDIVIDUAL UNDER LAW: AN ANALYSIS OF ARTICLE 29 OF THE UNIVERSAL DECLARATION OF HUMAN RIGHTS, U.N. Sales No. E.89.XIV.5;

No. 4, PROMOTION, PROTECTION AND RESTORATION OF HUMAN RIGHTS AT NATIONAL, REGIONAL AND INTERNATIONAL LEVELS - STATUS OF THE INDIVIDUAL AND CONTEMPORARY LAW, U.N. Sales No. E.91.XIV.3;

No. 5, STUDY ON THE RIGHTS OF PERSONS BELONGING TO ETHNIC, RELIGIOUS AND LINGUISTIC MINORITIES, U.N. Sales No. E.91.XIV.2;

No 6, HUMAN RIGHTS AND DISABLED PERSONS, U.N. Sales No. E.92.XIV.4;

No. 7, THE RIGHT TO ADEQUATE HOUSING, U.N. Sales No. E.96.XIV.3;

No. 8, SEXUAL EXPLOITATION OF CHILDREN, U.N. Sales No. E.96.XIV.7;

No. 9, INTERNALLY DISPLACED PERSONS: COMPILATION AND ANALYSIS OF LEGAL NORMS, U.N. Sales No. E.97.XIV.2;

No. 10, PROTECTION OF THE HERITAGE OF INDIGENOUS PEOPLE, U.N. Sales No. E.97.XIV.3.]

U.N. Secretariat, Compilation of General Comments and General Recommendations Adopted by Human Rights Treaty Bodies. U.N. Doc. HRI/GEN/1/Rev.7 (2004), http://www.unhchr.ch/tbs/doc.nsf/(Symbol)/HRI.GEN.1.Rev.4.En?OpenDocument.

[Geneva: U.N. This document contains a compilation of the general comments or general recommendations adopted by the Committee on Economic, Social and Cultural Rights, the Human Rights Committee, the Committee on the Elimination of Racial Discrimination, the Committee on the Elimination of Discrimination against Women, and the Committee against Torture.]

THE UN HUMAN RIGHTS TREATY SYSTEM IN THE 21ST CENTURY (Anne F. Bayefsky ed., 2000).

[The Hague: Kluwer Law International, 1116 pp. This volume compiles the papers presented at a conference held at York University, Canada in 1997, "Enforcing International Human Rights Law: The Treaty System in the Twenty-First Century."]

UNDERSTANDING HUMAN RIGHTS (Conor Gearty & Adam Tomkins eds., 1996).

[New York: Mansell, 656 pp. Collection of essays written by lawyers on a variety of human rights topics.]

THE UNITED NATIONS AND HUMAN RIGHTS: A CRITICAL APPRAISAL (Philip Alston ed., 2d ed. 2002).

[Oxford: Clarendon, 600 pp. Collected essays review the functions, procedures, and performance of the major U.N. organs dealing with human rights.]

UNITED NATIONS UNIVERSITY, THE IMPACT OF TECHNOLOGY ON HUMAN RIGHTS: GLOBAL CASE-STUDIES, U.N. Doc. HRSTD-2/UNUP-821, U.N. Sales No. E.92. III.A.7 (1993).

[Tokyo: U.N. University Press, 322 pp. Studies on the affirmative use of science and technology for the furtherance of human rights, commissioned as a special project by the United Nations University, following a reference to the University by the United Nations Human Rights Commission. C.G. Weeramantry ed.]

UNIVERSAL DECLARATION OF HUMAN RIGHTS: A COMMENTARY (Asbjørn Eide et al. eds., 1992).

[Oslo: University Press, 474 pp.]

THE UNIVERSAL DECLARATION OF HUMAN RIGHTS: FIFTY YEARS AND BEYOND (Yael Danieli ed., 1999).

[Amityville, NY: Baywood Pub. Co., 465 pp. Evaluates fifty years of international action in the field of human rights. Provides substantive overview of international human rights standards and mechanisms, human rights of specific groups, international efforts to promote culture of human rights through institutions and human rights education, regional human rights action, and contributions of health professionals, as well as recent efforts to integrate human rights into other areas of international action.]

UNIVERSAL MINORITY RIGHTS (Alan Phillips & Allan Rosas eds., 1995).

[Turku/ Åbo, Finland: Åbo Akademi University Institute for Human Rights; London: Minority Rights Group, 385 pp.]

GERALDINE VAN BUEREN, THE INTERNATIONAL LAW ON THE RIGHTS OF THE CHILD (2d rev. ed. 1998).

[The Hague: Kluwer Law International, 532 pp. Volume 35 of the INTERNATIONAL STUDIES IN HUMAN RIGHTS SERIES.]

WOUTER VANDENHOLE, NON-DISCRIMINATION AND EQUALITY IN THE VIEW OF THE UN HUMAN RIGHTS TREATY BODIES (2005).

[Antwerpen: Intersentia; Holmes Beach, Fla.: 293 pp.]

P. (PIETER) VAN DIJK, JUDICIAL PROTECTION OF HUMAN RIGHTS IN THE EUROPEAN UNION: DIVERGENCE, COORDINATION, INTEGRATION (1996).

[Exeter: Centre for European Legal Studies, 62 pp.]

FERNAND DE VARENNES, LANGUAGE, MINORITIES AND HUMAN RIGHTS (1996).

[The Hague; Boston: Martinus Nijhoff Pub., 532 pp. Provides analysis of every aspect of language and the law. Presents a theoretical model for language's particular position and relevance in human rights. Includes provisions of close to 100 international multicultural and bilateral instruments involving language rights.]

FRANS VILJOEN, INTERNATIONAL HUMAN RIGHTS LAW IN AFRICA (2007).

[Oxford: Oxford Univ. Press, 670 pp. Covers Pan African Parliament; Peace and Security Council; Economic, Social and Cultural Council, and African Peer Review Mechanism of the New Partnership for Africa's Development, along with jurisprudence under major African human rights instrument, including African Charter on Human and Peoples' Rights.]

JAMES SHAND WATSON, THEORY AND REALITY IN THE INTERNATIONAL PROTECTION OF HUMAN RIGHTS (1999).

[Ardsley, N.Y.: Transnational Pub., 333 pp. Defends the traditional theory of international law – based on a decentralized nation-state system of international relations – as being more appropriate for the analysis of its subject than more recent variants that allow for supranational redress at an increasingly personal level. Critiques the proponents of the international human rights regime for using a legislative mode of reasoning; argues that international law cannot sustain this technique.]

C.G. WEERAMANTRY, JUSTICE WITHOUT FRONTIERS (1997-).

[The Hague; Boston: Kluwer Law International. Two volumes: Furthering Human Rights, and Protecting Human Rights in the Age of Technology. Offers interdisciplinary perspective into the importance of international law and the contributions of the World Court. Selected writings on the topic of justice examine the practical applications of justice in several different contexts: human rights, technology, scientific discovery, international law, and the legal profession.]

JOSEPH WEILER, THE JURISPRUDENCE OF HUMAN RIGHTS IN THE EUROPEAN UNION: INTEGRATION AND DISINTEGRATION, VALUES AND PROCESSES (1996).

[Cambridge, MA: Harvard Law School, 28 pp. Series: HARVARD JEAN MONNET WORKING PAPER; 2/96.]

DAVID S. WEISSBRODT & CONNIE DE LA VEGA, INTERNATIONAL HUMAN RIGHTS LAW: AN INTRODUCTION (2007).

[Philadelphia: University of Pennsylvania Press, 432 pp. Provides overview of human rights as international law; summarizes key rights; reviews national, regional, and international procedures for implementation.]

CLAUDE E. WELCH, JR., PROTECTING HUMAN RIGHTS IN AFRICA: STRATEGIES AND ROLES OF NON-GOVERNMENTAL ORGANIZATIONS (1995).[Philadelphia, Penn.: University of Pennsylvania Press, 356 pp. Part I provides a backdrop for the entire work by describing human rights situations in Ethiopia, Namibia, Nigeria, and Senegal, and discussing strategies with which nongovernmental organizations (NGOs) promote and protect human rights in Africa. Part II presents examples of successful employment of the strategies discussed in Part I, including efforts of the Inter-African Committee on Traditional Practices, the Movement for the Survival of the Ogoni People, the Oromo Liberation Front, the Mouvement Democratique des Forces de Casamance, and the Legal Assistance Center. Part III assesses the future of African Human Rights NGOs and proposes that NGOs expand their impact to areas such as development and documentation of human rights problems.]

MARC WELLER, THE RIGHTS OF MINORITIES IN EUROPE: A COMMENTARY ON THE EUROPEAN FRAMEWORK CONVENTION FOR THE PROTECTION OF NATIONAL MINORITIES (2005).

[Oxford; New York: Oxford Univ. Press, 688 pp.]

MARC WELLER, UNIVERSAL MINORITY RIGHTS: A COMMENTARY ON THE JURISPRUDENCE OF INTERNATIONAL COURTS AND TREATY BODIES (2007).

[Oxford; New York: Oxford Univ. Press, 576 pp. Analyzes international and regional jurisprudence on various minority rights.]

CARL WELLMAN, AN APPROACH TO RIGHTS: STUDIES IN THE PHILOSOPHY OF LAW AND MORALS (1997).

[Dordrecht; Boston: Kluwer Academic Law Pubs., 271 pp. Contains papers to show the development of an important contemporary theory of nature, grounds and practical implications of rights. Of particular interest to legal theorists.]

BURNS H. WESTON & STEPHEN P. MARKS, THE FUTURE OF INTERNATIONAL HUMAN RIGHTS (1999).

[Ardsley, N.Y.: Transnational Pub., 514 pp. Analyzes and assesses emerging domains of international human rights law and practice, including the successes and failures of the Universal Declaration of Human Rights, and explores the possible future of human rights.]

RICHARD WILSON, HUMAN RIGHTS IN THE WAR ON TERROR (2005).

[Cambridge; New York: Cambridge University Press, 347 pp.]

WHAT WOMEN DO IN WARTIME: GENDER AND CONFLICT IN AFRICA (Meredith Turshen & Clotilde Twagiramariya eds., 1998).

[New York: Zed Books, 180 pp. Compiles reports, testimonies, and analyses documenting the human rights abuses targeted at women during the course of recent civil wars in Africa.]

WOMEN AND INTERNATIONAL HUMAN RIGHTS LAW (Kelly D. Askin & Dorean M. Koenig, eds., 1999-2001).

[Ardsley, N.Y.: Transnational Publishers. 3 vols. Comprehensive range of women's human rights issues: promotion of women's human rights, prevention of violations, remedies for violations. Volume 1 analyzes how international human rights law applies to women. Volume 2 looks at various legal instruments, international courts, and other enforcement mechanisms. Volume 3 focuses on the specific regional and cultural contexts of the Middle East, Palestine, Eastern Europe, the United States, Australia, and Africa, as well as the human rights issues that arise for women in those contexts.]

WORLD JUSTICE?: U.S. COURTS AND INTERNATIONAL HUMAN RIGHTS (Mark Gibney ed., 1991).

[Boulder, CO: Westview Press, 178 pp.]

SALVATORE ZAPPALÀ, HUMAN RIGHTS IN INTERNATIONAL CRIMINAL PROCEEDINGS (2005).

[Oxford; New York: Oxford Univ. Press, 280 pp.]

TIYAMBE ZELEZA & PHILIP J. MCCONNAUGHAY, HUMAN RIGHTS, THE RULE OF LAW, AND DEVELOPMENT IN AFRICA (2004).

[Philadelphia: University of Pennsylvania Press, 302 pp.]

TOM ZWART, THE ADMISSIBILITY OF HUMAN RIGHTS PETITIONS: THE CASE LAW OF THE EUROPEAN COMMISSION OF HUMAN RIGHTS AND THE HUMAN RIGHTS COMMITTEE (1994).

[Dordrecht; Boston: Martinus Nijhoff Pub., 272 pp. Volume 36 of the INTERNATIONAL STUDIES IN HUMAN RIGHTS SERIES.]

J. International Criminal Tribunals

For tribunal case law, see D. 5., above. Note: Some of the individual documents of the tribunals, including arrests warrants, indictments, decisions, and judgments, are reprinted in *International Legal Materials*. Comprehensive document collections are also available on the Web: Former Yugoslavia, http://www.un.org/icty; Rwanda, http://www.ictr.org; http://www1.umn.edu/humanrts/instree/ICTR/ICTR_Cases_Index.html, and the International Criminal Court, http://www.icc-cpi.int.

JOHN ACKERMAN & EUGENE O'SULLIVAN, PRACTICE AND PROCEDURE OF THE INTERNATIONAL CRIMINAL TRIBUNAL FOR THE FORMER YUGOSLAVIA: WITH SELECTED MATERIALS FROM THE INTERNATIONAL CRIMINAL TRIBUNAL FOR RWANDA (2000).

[The Hague; London: Kluwer Law International, 555 pp. Deals with jurisprudence of both the ICTY, and, to a lesser extent, the ICTR. Organized by relevant article of the Statute and Rule of Procedure and Evidence. Includes commentary and a digest of judgments, decisions, and orders of the Appeals Chamber and the Trial Chambers. Covers the beginning of the operation of the ICTY through the Furundzija Appeals Judgment and the amendments to the Rules in July 2000.]

KAI AMBOS ET AL., COMMENTARY ON THE ROME STATUTE OF THE INTERNATIONAL CRIMINAL COURT: OBSERVERS' NOTES, ARTICLE BY ARTICLE (1999).

[Baden-Baden: Nomos, 1295 pp. Most of the 51 authors represented in this collection participated in the creation of the Rome Statute.]

AMERICAN BAR ASSOCIATION, SECTION OF INTERNATIONAL LAW AND PRACTICE, TASK FORCE ON WAR CRIMES IN FORMER YUGOSLAVIA, REPORT ON THE INTERNATIONAL TRIBUNAL TO ADJUDICATE WAR CRIMES COMMITTED IN THE FORMER YUGOSLAVIA (1993).

[Chicago, Ill.; Washington, D.C.: American Bar Association; ABA Section of International Law and Practice, 71 pp.]

AMNESTY INTERNATIONAL, FAIR TRIALS MANUAL (1998).

[London: Amnesty International, 187 pp. Guide to international and regional standards for fair trials. Includes standards incorporated into treaties and standards not incorporated into treaties.]

AMNESTY INTERNATIONAL, INTERNATIONAL CRIMINAL TRIBUNAL FOR RWANDA: TRIALS AND TRIBULATIONS (1998).

[London: Amnesty International, 53 pp.]

ANNOTATED LEADING CASES OF INTERNATIONAL CRIMINAL TRIBUNALS (Andre Klip & Goran Sluiter eds., 1999-).

[Antwerpen; Oxford: Intersentia; Hart. Vol. 1 covers 1993-1998 (720 pp.) and includes the leading cases of the Tribunal's first five years. Decisions are reprinted with annotations by scholars in international criminal law.]

HOWARD BALL, PROSECUTING WAR CRIMES AND GENOCIDE: THE TWENTIETH-CENTURY EXPERIENCE (1999).

[Lawrence, KS: University Press of Kansas, 288 pp. Traces the history of war crimes prosecution from the 1899 Geneva Accords up to the Rwanda, Yugoslavia, and Rome tribunals.]

M. CHERIF BASSIOUNI ET AL., THE INTERNATIONAL CRIMINAL COURT: OBSERVATIONS AND ISSUES BEFORE THE 1997-98 PREPARATORY COMMITTEE, AND ADMINISTRATIVE AND FINANCIAL IMPLICATIONS (1997).

[Toulouse; Chicago: Érès; International Human Rights Institute, DePaul University, 290 pp.]

M. CHERIF BASSIOUNI, THE STATUTE OF THE INTERNATIONAL CRIMINAL COURT: A DOCUMENTARY HISTORY (1998).

[Ardsley, N.Y.: Transnational Publishers, 793 pp. Includes the draft statutes of 1951, 1953, 1981, and 1994, along with various related reports, the 1998 Statute, and commentary by the author, who chaired the Drafting Committee of the 1998 Statute.]

M. CHERIF BASSIOUNI & PETER MANIKAS, THE LAW OF THE INTERNATIONAL CRIMINAL TRIBUNAL FOR THE FORMER YUGOSLAVIA (1996).

[Irvington-on-Hudson, N.Y.: Transnational Publishers, 1092 pp. Uses legislative history, international and comparative law sources, and the Tribunal's Rules of Procedure and Evidence to analyze its workings, effectiveness, and significance in the development of international criminal law. Also provides an overview of the conflict in the former Yugoslavia, an article-by-article analysis of the Statute, and annotated texts of the Rules of Procedure, the Rules on Detention, and the Directives for the Assignment of Defense Counsel.]

M. CHERIF BASSIOUNI, THE LEGISLATIVE HISTORY OF THE INTERNATIONAL CRIMINAL COURT (2005).

[Ardsley, N.Y.: Transnational Publishers, 3 v.]

NOTBURGA K. CALVO-GOLLER, THE TRIAL PROCEEDINGS OF THE INTERNATIONAL CRIMINAL COURT: ICTY AND ICTR PRECEDENTS (2006).

[Leiden; Boston: Martinus Nijhoff Publishers, 561 pp.]

ANTONIO CASSESE ET AL., THE ROME STATUTE OF THE INTERNATIONAL CRIMINAL COURT: A COMMENTARY (2002).

[Oxford; New York: Oxford Univ. Press, 3 v.]

THE CRIMINAL LAW OF GENOCIDE: INTERNATIONAL, COMPARATIVE, AND CONTEXTUAL ASPECTS (Ralph J Henham & Paul Behrens eds., 2007).

[Burlington, VT: Ashgate Pub. Co., 283 pp. Collects leading essays on genocide.]

YORAM DINSTEIN & MALA TABORY, WAR CRIMES IN INTERNATIONAL LAW (1996).

[The Hague; Boston: M. Nijhoff Publishers, 489 pp. Based on a Colloquium held at Tel-Aviv University in Dec. 1993. Most of the materials contained in this volume were also published in vol. 25 of the Israel Yearbook on Human Rights.]

KNUT DÖRMANN ET AL., ELEMENTS OF WAR CRIMES UNDER THE ROME STATUTE OF THE INTERNATIONAL CRIMINAL COURT: SOURCES AND COMMENTARY (2003).

[Cambridge; New York: Cambridge University Press, 524 pp.]

Draft Statute for an International Criminal Court (Annex to the Report of the Committee on International Criminal Jurisdiction), 7 U.N. GAOR Supp. No. 11, U.N. Doc. A/2136 at 21 (1952).

MARK A DRUMBL, ATROCITY, PUNISHMENT, AND INTERNATIONAL LAW (2007).

[Cambridge; New York: Cambridge University Press, 298 pp. Systematically assesses modern machinery of international criminal justice.]

Finalized draft text of the Rules of Procedure and Evidence, U.N. Doc. PCNICC/2000/1/Add.1 (2000).

[New York: U.N., 100 pp, http://www.un.org/law/icc/statute/rules/rulefra.htm.]

FORMER YUGOSLAVIA: THE WAR CRIMES TRIBUNAL - ONE YEAR LATER (1994).

[New York, N.Y.: Human Rights Watch/Helsinki, 26 pp.]

FROM NUREMBERG TO THE HAGUE: THE FUTURE OF INTERNATIONAL CRIMINAL JUSTICE (Philippe Sands ed., 2003).

[Cambridge; New York: Cambridge University Press, 192 pp.]

INTERNATIONAL CRIMES, PEACE, AND HUMAN RIGHTS: THE ROLE OF THE INTERNATIONAL CRIMINAL COURT (Dinah Shelton ed., 2000).

[Ardsley, N.Y.: Transnational Publishers, 356 pp. Essays covering all three tribunals, though focusing mostly on the ICC.]

THE INTERNATIONAL CRIMINAL COURT: RECOMMENDATIONS ON POLICY AND PRACTICE: FINANCING, VICTIMS, JUDGES, AND IMMUNITIES (Thordis Ingadottir ed., 2003).

[Ardsley, NY: Transnational Publishers, 212 pp.]

INTERNATIONAL CRIMINAL JUSTICE: A CRITICAL ANALYSIS OF INSTITUTIONS AND PROCEDURES (Michael Bohlander ed., 2007).

[London: Cameron May, 505 pp.]

INTERNATIONAL CRIMINAL LAW: A COMMENTARY ON THE ROME STATUTE FOR AN INTERNATIONAL CRIMINAL COURT (Antonio Cassese ed., 2001).

[Oxford: Oxford Univ. Press, 3 v.]

INTERNATIONAL CRIMINAL TRIBUNAL FOR THE FORMER YUGOSLAVIA, BASIC DOCUMENTS 1995 (1995).

[The Hague: International Tribunal for the Former Yugoslavia, 512 pp. Contains the Statute of the Tribunal, Rules of Procedure and Evidence, and other basic texts including Security Council resolutions 808 and 827, Headquarters Agreement, Rules of Detention, and several others.]

INTERNATIONAL CRIMINAL TRIBUNAL FOR THE PROSECUTION OF PERSONS RESPONSIBLE FOR GENOCIDE AND OTHER SERIOUS VIOLATIONS OF INTERNATIONAL HUMANITARIAN LAW COMMITTED IN THE TERRITORY OF RWANDA AND RWANDAN CITIZENS RESPONSIBLE FOR GENOCIDE AND OTHER SUCH VIOLATIONS COMMITTED IN THE TERRITORY OF NEIGHBOURING STATES, BETWEEN JANUARY 1, 1994 AND DECEMBER 31, 1994, INTRODUCTION TO THE INTERNATIONAL CRIMINAL TRIBUNAL FOR RWANDA (ICTR) (1998).

[Arusha, Tanzania: ICTR, Press & Public Affairs Unit, 9 pp.]

INTERNATIONAL CRIMINAL TRIBUNAL FOR THE PROSECUTION OF PERSONS RESPONSIBLE FOR GENOCIDE AND OTHER SERIOUS VIOLATIONS OF INTERNATIONAL HUMANITARIAN LAW COMMITTED IN THE TERRITORY OF RWANDA AND RWANDAN CITIZENS

RESPONSIBLE FOR GENOCIDE AND OTHER SUCH VIOLATIONS COMMITTED IN THE TERRITORY OF NEIGHBOURING STATES, BETWEEN JANUARY 1, 1994 AND DECEMBER 31, 1994, S.C. Res. 955, Annex, U.N. SCOR, 49th Sess., U.N. Doc. S/INF/59 (1994), *reprinted in* 33 I.L.M. 1602 (1994), statute http://www.un.org/ictr/statute.html.

INTERNATIONAL TRIBUNAL FOR THE PROSECUTION OF PERSONS RESPONSIBLE FOR SERIOUS VIOLATIONS OF INTERNATIONAL HUMANITARIAN LAW COMMITTED IN THE TERRITORY OF THE FORMER YUGOSLAVIA SINCE 1991, YEARBOOK (1995-).

[The Hague: The Tribunal.]

INTERNATIONAL TRIBUNAL FOR THE PROSECUTION OF PERSONS RESPONSIBLE FOR SERIOUS VIOLATIONS OF INTERNATIONAL HUMANITARIAN LAW COMMITTED IN THE TERRITORY OF THE FORMER YUGOSLAVIA SINCE 1991, JUDICIAL SUPPLEMENT (1999-2004).

[The Hague: The Tribunal, http://www.un.org/icty/publications-e/index.htm.]

INTERNATIONAL TRIBUNAL FOR THE PROSECUTION OF PERSONS RESPONSIBLE FOR SERIOUS VIOLATIONS OF INTERNATIONAL HUMANITARIAN LAW COMMITTED IN THE TERRITORY OF THE FORMER YUGOSLAVIA SINCE 1991, BASIC DOCUMENTS (1995-).

[New York: United Nations, http://www.un.org/icty/legaldoc-e/index.htm.]

INTERNATIONAL TRIBUNAL FOR THE PROSECUTION OF PERSONS RESPONSIBLE FOR SERIOUS VIOLATIONS OF INTERNATIONAL HUMANITARIAN LAW COMMITTED IN THE TERRITORY OF THE FORMER YUGOSLAVIA SINCE 1991, BULLETIN (1995-1998) (superseded by the JUDICIAL SUPPLEMENT).

[The Hague: The Tribunal.]

INTERNATIONAL TRIBUNAL FOR THE PROSECUTION OF PERSONS RESPONSIBLE FOR SERIOUS VIOLATIONS OF INTERNATIONAL HUMANITARIAN LAW COMMITTED IN THE TERRITORY OF THE FORMER YUGOSLAVIA SINCE 1991, STATUTE, U.N. Doc. S/25704, Annex (1993), *reprinted in* 32 I.L.M. 1192 (1993), updated statute http://www.un.org/icty/legaldoc-e/basic/statut/statute-feb08-e.pdf.

INTERNATIONAL TRIBUNAL FOR RWANDA: FACTS, CASES, DOCUMENTS (Willem-Jan van der Wolf & C. (Chris) Scheltema eds. 1999).

[Nijmegen, The Netherlands: Global Law Association, 1999.]

INTERNATIONAL TRIBUNAL FOR RWANDA, ICTR QUARTERLY BIBLIOGRAPHY (1999-).

[Arusha, Tanzania: ICTR Library. At ICTR Web site, in "Library" section, http://www.ictr.org. Drawn from the ICTR's own database; contains entries relating to international criminal law.]

INTERNATIONAL TRIBUNAL FOR RWANDA, ICTR YEARBOOK (1997-).

[Arusha, Tanzania: The Tribunal. First yearbook (1994-1996) issued in two parts, French and English.]

INTERNATIONAL TRIBUNAL FOR RWANDA, REPORT OF THE INTERNATIONAL CRIMINAL TRIBUNAL FOR THE PROSECUTION OF PERSONS RESPONSIBLE FOR GENOCIDE AND OTHER SERIOUS VIOLATIONS OF INTERNATIONAL HUMANITARIAN LAW COMMITTED IN THE

TERRITORY OF RWANDA AND RWANDAN CITIZENS RESPONSIBLE FOR GENOCIDE AND OTHER SUCH VIOLATIONS COMMITTED IN THE TERRITORY OF NEIGHBOURING STATES BETWEEN 1 JANUARY AND 31 DECEMBER 1994, U.N. Doc. No. A/52/582 (1997).

[Arusha, Tanzania: The Tribunal, 31 pp.]

JOHN R.W.D. JONES, THE PRACTICE OF THE INTERNATIONAL CRIMINAL TRIBUNALS FOR THE FORMER YUGOSLAVIA AND RWANDA (2d ed. 2000).

[Ardsley, NY: Transnational Publishers, 666 pp. Updated edition of 1998 guide. Includes cases from both the ICTFY and the ICTR, arranged according to the provisions of the Statute and Rules of Procedure and Evidence. Cases are presented with commentary and extracts from the Tribunals' decisions. Rules that have been amended are noted with dates and the reason for amendment.]

JOHN R.W.D. JONES & STEVEN POWLES , INTERNATIONAL CRIMINAL PRACTICE: THE INTERNATIONAL TRIBUNAL FOR THE FORMER YUGOSLAVIA, THE INTERNATIONAL CRIMINAL TRIBUNAL FOR RWANDA, THE INTERNATIONAL CRIMINAL COURT, THE SPECIAL COURT FOR SIERRA LEONE, THE EAST TIMOR SPECIAL PANEL FOR SERIOUS CRIMES, WAR CRIMES PROSECUTIONS IN KOSOVO (2003).

[Ardsley, NY: Transnational Publishers, 1085 pp.]

GEERT-JAN G. J. KNOOPS, AN INTRODUCTION TO THE LAW OF INTERNATIONAL CRIMINAL TRIBUNALS: A COMPARATIVE STUDY (2003).

[Ardsley, N.Y.: Transnational Publishers, 207 pp.]

GEERT-JAN G. J. KNOOPS, THEORY AND PRACTICE OF INTERNATIONAL AND INTERNATIONALIZED CRIMINAL PROCEEDINGS (2005).

[Deventer: Kluwer BV; Hague: Kluwer Law International; 358 pp.]

CYRIL LAUCCI, DIGEST OF JURISPRUDENCE OF THE SPECIAL COURT FOR SIERRA LEONE, 2003-2005 (2007).

[Leiden; Boston: Martinus Nijhoff Publishers, 873 pp.]

LAWYERS COMMITTEE FOR HUMAN RIGHTS, THE INTERNATIONAL CRIMINAL TRIBUNAL FOR THE FORMER YUGOSLAVIA: ESTABLISHMENT, ORGANIZATION, JURISDICTION AND PROCEEDINGS TO DATE (1995).

[New York, N.Y.: Lawyers Committee for Human Rights, 44 pp.]

ROY S. LEE ET AL., THE INTERNATIONAL CRIMINAL COURT: THE MAKING OF THE ROME STATUTE-ISSUES, NEGOTIATIONS, AND RESULTS (1999).

[Boston: Kluwer Law International, 657 pp. Written by several participants in the process of creating the ICC. Describes key issues, divergent proposals, and resolution of differences; also describes the drafting process.]

LEGAL MATERIALS CONCERNING THE INTERNATIONAL CRIMINAL TRIBUNAL FOR RWANDA, U.N. Doc. No. E/Cn.4/1995/7, 28 June 1994 (1994).

[The Hague: ICTR, various pagings.]

KARINE LESCURE & FLORENCE TRINTIGNAC, INTERNATIONAL JUSTICE FOR FORMER YUGOSLAVIA: THE WORKINGS OF THE INTERNATIONAL CRIMINAL TRIBUNAL OF THE HAGUE (1996).

[The Hague; Boston: Kluwer Law International, 70 pp. Explains how the Tribunal was designed to work; describes how victims can institute proceedings.]

Lyonette Louis-Jacques, *International Criminal Court: Resources in Print and Electronic Format*, http://www.lib.uchicago.edu/~llou/icc.html.

[Excellent bibliography that includes Internet and print resources, including articles.]

PAUL J. MAGNARELLA, JUSTICE IN AFRICA: RWANDA'S GENOCIDE, ITS COURTS AND THE UN CRIMINAL TRIBUNAL (2000).

[Brookfield, VT: Ashgate, 166 pp. Critical evaluation of the Criminal Tribunal for Rwanda.]

RICHARD MAY & MARIEKE WIERDA, INTERNATIONAL CRIMINAL EVIDENCE (2002).

[Ardsley, NY: Transnational Publishers, 369 pp.]

THEODOR MERON, WAR CRIMES LAW COMES OF AGE: ESSAYS (1998).

[Oxford: Clarendon Press; New York: Oxford Univ. Press, 336 pp. Collects the author's essays on various aspects of humanitarian law; includes essays on the former Yugoslavia.]

MICHAEL MILDE ET AL., BRINGING POWER TO JUSTICE?: THE PROSPECTS OF THE INTERNATIONAL CRIMINAL COURT (2006).

[Montreal; Ithaca [N.Y.]: McGill-Queen's University Press, 270 pp.]

KRISTINA MISKOWIAK, THE INTERNATIONAL CRIMINAL COURT: CONSENT, COMPLEMENTARITY AND COOPERATION (2000).

[Copenhagen: DJØF Publishing, 127 pp. Covers three issues: necessity of state consent to the Court's jurisdiction, the complementarity of international and national justice system, and the obligation of States parties to cooperate with the court.]

KINGSLEY CHIEDU MOGHALU, GLOBAL JUSTICE: THE POLITICS OF WAR CRIMES TRIALS (2006).

[Westport, Conn.: Praeger Security International, 220 pp. Analyzes political forces behind war crimes trials such as that of Saddam Hussein; argues for regional and national alternatives.]

VIRGINIA MORRIS ET AL., THE INTERNATIONAL CRIMINAL TRIBUNAL FOR RWANDA (1998).

[Irvington-on-Hudson, N.Y.: Transnational Publishers. (Vol. 1, 727 pp.) Vol. 2 contains constitutive and interpretive documents of the Rwanda Tribunal. Analyzes the legal instruments and precedents governing the work of the Rwanda Tribunal, as well as its impact on international criminal law.]

Virginia Morris & Michael P. Scharf, An Insider's Guide to the International Criminal Tribunal for the Former Yugoslavia: A Documentary History & Analysis (1995).

[Irvington-on-Hudson, N.Y.: Transnational Publishers, 487 pp.]

Virginia Morris & Michael P. Scharf, The International Criminal Tribunal for Rwanda (1998).

[Irvington-on-Hudson, N.Y.: Transnational Publishers, 2 v.; 743, 572 pp. Describes the historical and international law context of the Tribunal, the proposals submitted by states and organizations, and the views expressed by members of the Security Council in adopting the Statute. Addresses procedural and evidentiary issues.]

Michel Moussalli, Report on the Situation of Human Rights in Rwanda, U.N. Doc. E/CN.4/2000/41, (2000).

[Geneva: United Nations, 47 pp.]

John Oppenheim et al., Global War Crimes Tribunal Collection (1997-).

[Nijmegen, the Netherlands: Holmes Beach, Fla.: Global Law Association; Gaunt. Vol.1. The Rwanda Tribunal - Vol. 2a. The Yugoslav crisis: background information - Vol. 2b. The Yugoslav crisis: documents - Vol. 2c. The Yugoslav tribunal - Vol. 2d. The Yugoslav tribunal, the cases - part 1 - Vol. 2e. The Yugoslav tribunal, the cases - part 2 - Vol. 2f. The Yugoslav tribunals, the cases - part 3 - Vol. 2g. The Yugoslav tribunals, the cases - part 4 - Vol. 3. The tribunals of the future.]

The Permanent International Criminal Court: Legal and Policy Issues (Dominic McGoldrick & Peter J. Rowe eds., 2004).

[Oxford; Portland, OR.: Hart Pub., 498 pp.]

Mauro Politi & Giuseppe Nesi, The International Criminal Court and the Crime of Aggression (2004).

[Aldershot, Hants.; Burlington, VT: Ashgate, 193 pp.]

Post-War Protection of Human Rights in Bosnia and Herzegovina (Michael O'Flaherty & Gregory Gisvold eds. 1998).

[The Hague; Boston: M. Nijhoff Publishers, 333 pp. International studies in human rights vol. 53. Essays analyze the Dayton Agreement and its complicated system for human rights enforcement.]

Phenyo Keiseng Rakate & Institute for Global Dialogue, IGD Occasional Paper No. 19, International Criminal Justice and Reconciliation: Lessons from the South African Truth and Reconciliation Commission and the International Criminal Tribunal for the Former Yugoslavia (1999).

[Braamfontein, South Africa: Institute for Global Dialogue, 36 pp.]

Florian Razesberger, The International Criminal Court: The Principle of Complementarity (2006).

[Frankfurt am Main; New York: Peter Lang, 201 pp.]

REFLECTIONS ON THE INTERNATIONAL CRIMINAL COURT: ESSAYS IN HONOUR OF ADRIAAN BOS (Herman A.M. von Hebel et al. eds., 1999).

[The Hague; Cambridge, MA: T.M.C. Asser Press, 211 pp. Essays by prominent international lawyers analyze the position of the ICC within the international arena, exploring its relationship to the International Court of Justice, the International Criminal Tribunal for the Former Yugoslavia, and the Security Council. Other essays reflect on parts of the Statute or on the process by which it was created.]

Report of the Ad Hoc Committee on the Establishment of an International Criminal Court, U.N. GAOR, Supp. No. 22, at 17, U.N. Doc. A/50/22 at 17 (1995).

[New York: U.N., 60 pp.]

Report on the Situation of Human Rights in Rwanda (Report of Special Rapporteur), U.N. Doc. E/CN.4/1995/7 (1994).

[Geneva: U.N., 19 pp.]

RETHINKING INTERNATIONAL CRIMINAL LAW: THE SUBSTANTIVE PART (Olaoluwa Olusanya, ed., 2007).

[Groningen: Europa Law Publishing, 213 pp. Essays address key questions of substantive criminal law (command responsibility, mens rea, etc.).]

Revised Draft Statute for an International Criminal Court (Annex to the Report of the Committee on International Criminal Jurisdiction), 7 U.N. GAOR Supp. No. 11, at 21, U.N. Doc. A/2645 (1954).

Rome Statute of the International Criminal Court, U.N. Doc. A/CONF. 183/9 (1998), *reprinted in* 37 I.L.M. 999 (1998).

[Rome: United Nations, 79 pp., http://www.un.org/icc/romestat.htm.]

CHRISTOPH JOHANNES MARIA SAFFERLING, TOWARDS AN INTERNATIONAL CRIMINAL PROCEDURE (2003).

[Oxford; New York: Oxford Univ. Press, 395 pp.]

WILLIAM SCHABAS, AN INTRODUCTION TO THE INTERNATIONAL CRIMINAL COURT (3d ed. 2007).

[Cambridge; New York: Cambridge University Press, 548 pp.]

WILLIAM SCHABAS, THE UN INTERNATIONAL CRIMINAL TRIBUNALS: THE FORMER YUGOSLAVIA, RWANDA, AND SIERRA LEONE (2006).

[Cambridge; New York: Cambridge University Press, 711 pp.]

BENJAMIN N. SCHIFF, BUILDING THE INTERNATIONAL CRIMINAL COURT (2008).

[Cambridge; New York: Cambridge University Press, 304 pp. Uses historical, international relations, and observers' perspectives to explain ICC's origins, dynamics, and challenges.]

SECRETARY-GENERAL, REPORT OF THE SECRETARY-GENERAL PURSUANT TO PARAGRAPH 2 OF SECURITY COUNCIL RESOLUTION 808 (1993), U.N. Doc. S/25704, *reprinted in* 32 I.L.M. 1163 (1993).

[New York: U.N., 48 pp. This report covers aspects of establishing the Yugoslavia tribunal.]

LYAL S. SUNGA, THE EMERGING SYSTEM OF INTERNATIONAL CRIMINAL LAW: DEVELOPMENTS IN CODIFICATION AND IMPLEMENTATION (1997).

[The Hague; Cambridge: Kluwer Law International, 508 pp.]

VLADIMIR TOCHILOVSKY, CHARGES, EVIDENCE, AND LEGAL ASSISTANCE IN INTERNATIONAL JURISDICTIONS: THE JURISPRUDENCE OF THE ICTY, ICTR AND SCSL (2005).

[Nijmegen, The Netherlands: Wolf Legal Publishers, 313 pp.]

VLADIMIR TOCHILOVSKY, JURISPRUDENCE OF THE INTERNATIONAL CRIMINAL COURTS: PROCEDURE AND EVIDENCE (2006).

[The Netherlands: Wolf Legal Publishers, 669 pp. Comprehensive guide to jurisprudence of criminal tribunals for former Yugoslavia and Rwanda, Special Court for Sierra Leone, ICC, and European Court of Human Rights on procedural and evidential matters.]

U.N. International Law Commission, *Report of the Working Group on a Draft Statute for an International Criminal Court*, UN GAOR, 48th Sess. Supp. No. 10, at 255, U.N. Doc. A/48/10, Annex (1993), *reprinted in* 33 I.L.M. 253 (1994).

United Nations Security Council Resolution 827 on Establishing an International Tribunal for the Prosecution of Persons Responsible for Serious Violations of International Humanitarian Law Committed in the Territory of the Former Yugoslavia, S.C. res. 827, 48 U.N. SCOR at 1, U.N. Doc. S/RES/827 (1992), *reprinted in* 32 I.L.M 1159, 1203 (1993).

[New York: U.N., 3 pp.]

SALVATORE ZAPPALA, HUMAN RIGHTS IN INTERNATIONAL CRIMINAL PROCEEDINGS (2003).

[Oxford: Oxford Univ. Press, 280 pp.]

K. Research Guides and Bibliographies

AMNESTY INTERNATIONAL, BIBLIOGRAPHY OF PUBLICATIONS ON HEALTH AND HUMAN RIGHTS THEMES, 1982-1997 (1997).

[London: AI, 49 pp.]

Amnesty International, *Bibliography: Publications on Health and Human Rights Themes: 1985-2005*, http://www.amnesty.org/en/library/info/ACT75/003/1997.

AMNESTY INTERNATIONAL, HUMAN RIGHTS EDUCATION: BIBLIOGRAPHY AND AUDIOVISUAL LIST (1993)

[London, U.K.: International Secretariat, 67 pp. Annotated.]

AMNESTY INTERNATIONAL USA LEGAL SUPPORT NETWORK, GUIDE TO DOCUMENTATION RESOURCES FOR ASYLUM APPLICATIONS (1991).

[London: AI, 37 pp. Prepared by Daniel Honsey, Sonia Rosen, and David Weissbrodt for AI-USA Legal Support Network.]

ASIL Guide to Electronic Resources for International Law: Human Rights, http://www.asil.org/resource/humrts1.htm.

[Other useful chapters in this guide include: Treaties, http://www.asil.org/resource/treaty1.htm; United Nations, http://www.asil.org/resource/un1.htm; and International Criminal Law, http://www.asil.org/resource/crim1.htm.]

JAMES R. BENNETT, POLITICAL PRISONERS AND TRIALS: A WORLDWIDE ANNOTATED BIBLIOGRAPHY, 1900 THROUGH 1993 (1995).

[Jefferson, N.C.: McFarland, 363 p.]

BIBLIOGRAPHY OF INTERNATIONAL HUMANITARIAN LAW APPLICABLE IN ARMED CONFLICTS (2d ed. rev. & updated 1987).

[Geneva: ICRC & Henry Dunant Institute, 605 pp.]

BIBLIOGRAPHY ON THE AFRICAN CHARTER AND THE AFRICAN COMMISSION ON HUMAN AND PEOPLES' RIGHTS: LIST OF REFERENCE WORKS (MONOGRAPHS, ARTICLES, CONFERENCES' REPORTS, THESIS, TECHNICAL STUDIES) THE INFORMATION AND DOCUMENTATION CENTRE (IDOC) ON THE AFRICAN CHARTER AND THE AFRICAN COMMISSION ON HUMAN AND PEOPLES' RIGHTS (1999).

[Banjul, The Gambia: African Commission on Human & Peoples' Rights, 172 pp.]

Bibliography: Human Rights in the African Context, http://www1.umn.edu/humanrts/africa/african.html.

BRIEFING BOOK ON INTERNATIONAL ORGANIZATIONS IN GENEVA (2004).

[Provides a capsule description of various agencies (U.N. and non-U.N.) headquartered in Geneva, and the arms control and disarmament talks that regularly take place in Geneva. Includes organizations specializing in economics and trade, science and communications, law, the environment and wildlife preservation, humanitarian concerns, and other areas. Current version, http://www.genevabriefingbook.com.]

THOMAS BUERGENTHAL & DINAH SHELTON, PROTECTING HUMAN RIGHTS IN THE AMERICAS: CASES AND MATERIALS (4th rev. ed. 1995).

[Kehl; Arlington, Va.: N.P. Engel, 692 pp.]

Charlotte Bynum, *ILO Research Guide*, http://library.lawschool.cornell.edu/WhatWeDo/ResearchGuides/ILO.cfm.

CALS Asylum Case Research Guide, http://www.ll.georgetown.edu/intl/cals/asylumresearch.htm.

[Designed for use in preparing asylum applications in the United States.]

CENTRE FOR HUMAN RIGHTS, UNITED NATIONS REFERENCE GUIDE IN THE FIELD OF HUMAN RIGHTS, U.N. Doc. ST/HR/6, U.N. Sales No. E.93.XIV.4 (1993).

[New York: U.N., 124 pp. Lists human rights materials published by the U.N. by title/subject, document number, and author when appropriate. The guide is divided into several chapters with subheadings. Includes subject index.]

Centre for Islamic and Middle Eastern Law (CIMEL) and the International Centre for the Legal Protection of Human Rights (INTERIGHTS), *Bibliography on Crimes of Honour,* http://www1.umn.edu/humanrts/bibliog/honour.html.

Cynthia Price Cohen & Susan Kilbourne, *Jurisprudence of the Committee on the Rights of the Child: A Guide for Research and Analysis,* 19 MICH. J. INT'L L. 633 (1998).

[Appendix (p.p. 654-728) is a "Guide for Research and Analysis," consisting of several tables that lay out guidelines for submission of country reports, lists of country reports reviewed, and committee conclusions, up to 1997.]

MORRIS L. COHEN ET AL., HOW TO FIND THE LAW 450-513 (9th ed. 1989).

[St. Paul, MN: West Publishing Co., 716 pp. Includes sources for texts of treaties, U.N. resolutions, other documents, and decisions of international tribunals.]

Rebecca Cook, *Women's International Human Rights: A Bibliography,* 24 N.Y.U. INT'L L. & POL. 857 (1992).

Rebecca J. Cook & Valerie L. Oosterveld, *A Select Bibliography of Women's Human Rights (Conference on the International Protection of Reproductive Rights),* 44 AM. U.L.R. 1429 (1995).

COUNCIL OF EUROPE, DOCUMENTATION SOURCES IN HUMAN RIGHTS (1995).

[Strasbourg: Council of Europe, 207 pp. Annotated guide.]

Council of Europe, *Human Rights Education Bibliography of the Documents of the Council of Europe,* http://www.coe.int/t/dg4/youth/Resources/Documents/Bibliographies/HR_Education_en.asp.

DIANA Human Rights database, http://www.yale.edu/lawweb/avalon/diana/index.html.

[This database, which is also several mirror sites, contains bibliographies and research guides.]

GUNNAR FERMANN, BIBLIOGRAPHY ON INTERNATIONAL PEACEKEEPING (1992).

[Dordrecht; Boston: Martinus Nijhoff Pub., 291 pp. Covers academic literature from books, journals, and reports. Includes author/subject index.]

JULIAN R. FRIEDMAN & MARC I. SHERMAN, HUMAN RIGHTS: AN INTERNATIONAL AND COMPARATIVE LAW BIBLIOGRAPHY (1985).

[Westport, CT: Greenwood Press, 868 pp. Bibliographies and Indexes in Law and Political Science; no. 4. Unannotated listing of sources by type of human right, instrument, court, organization, and subject.]

LINDA FRITZ, NATIVE LAW BIBLIOGRAPHY (2d ed. 1990).

[Saskatoon, Canada: University of Saskatschewan Native Law Centre, 167 pp.]

Georgetown University Law Center, Research Guide: *Human Rights*, http://www.ll.georgetown.edu/intl/guides/HumanRightsLaw.cfm.

Georgetown University Law Center, Research Guide: *Refugee Protection*, http://www.ll.georgetown.edu/intl/guides/RefugeeProtection.cfm.

CLAIRE GERMAIN, GERMAIN'S TRANSNATIONAL LAW RESEARCH: A GUIDE FOR ATTORNEYS (1991-).

[Ardsley-on-Hudson, NY: Transnational Juris Publications, Inc., looseleaf. One chapter is devoted to human rights.]

Richard Greenfield, *The Human Rights Literature of Eastern Europe*, 3 HUM. RTS. Q. 136-48 (1981).

Richard Greenfield, *The Human Rights Literature of Latin America*, 4 HUM. RTS. Q. 275-98, 508-21 (1982).

Richard Greenfield, *The Human Rights Literature of South Asia*, 3 HUM. RTS. Q. 129-39 (1981).

Richard Greenfield, *The Human Rights Literature of the Soviet Union*, 4 HUM. RTS. Q. 124-36 (1982).

Guide to Forced Migration Resources on the Web, Forced Migration Portal Project, Refugee Studies Centre, University of Oxford, http://www.forcedmigration.org/webguide.

GUIDE TO INTERNATIONAL LEGAL RESEARCH (2002-).

[Charlottesville, Va.: LEXIS Law Pub. Comprehensive, annually-updated research guide to foreign and international legal materials, arranged by type of source.]

MUNYONZWE HAMALENGWA ET AL., THE INTERNATIONAL LAW OF HUMAN RIGHTS IN AFRICA: BASIC DOCUMENTS AND ANNOTATED BIBLIOGRAPHY (1988).

[Dordrecht; Boston: Martinus Nijhoff Pub., 427 pp.]

Harvard Law Library, *Guide to Human Rights Research*, http://www.law.harvard.edu/library/services/research/guides/international/human_rights.php.

Susan Heintz, *An Introduction to Human Rights Resources on the Internet*, 12 HARV. HUM. RTS. J. 407 (1999).

Jean-Marie Henckaerts, *The Protection of Human Rights in the European Union: Overview and Bibliography*, 22 INT'L J. LEGAL INFORMATION 228 (1994).

MARCI HOFFMAN & MARY RUMSEY, INTERNATIONAL AND FOREIGN LEGAL RESEARCH: A COURSEBOOK (2007).

[Leiden; Boston: Martinus Nijhoff Publishers, 342 pp.]

HUMAN RIGHTS: A BIBLIOGRAPHY (Arthur V. Carrington ed., 2000).

[Huntington, N.Y.: Nova Science Publishers, 435 pp.]

HUMAN RIGHTS BIBLIOGRAPHY: UNITED NATIONS DOCUMENTS AND PUBLICATIONS 1980-1990 (1993).

[Geneva: U.N., 2086 pp., 5 vols. Also in U.N., Human Rights on CD-ROM, *see infra* in this section.]

Human Rights Center, UC Berkeley, http://globetrotter.berkeley.edu/humanrights/bibliographies.

[Bibliographies on numerous human rights issues; *e.g.*, *Refugees* (Molly Ryan comp. 1998), http://globetrotter.berkeley.edu/humanrights/bibliographies/refugeebib.html.]

HUMAN RIGHTS EDUCATION FOR THE TWENTY-FIRST CENTURY (George Andreopoulos & Richard P. Claude eds., 1997).

[Philadelphia: University of Pennsylvania Press, 636 pp.]

Human Rights: Global Issues and Information Sources, 25 INT'L J. LEGAL INFO. 1 (1997).

Human Rights Syllabi for the College Classroom, Institute of International Studies, University of California, Berkeley, http://learning.berkeley.edu/AIUSA-syl/toc.html.

INTERNATIONAL BIBLIOGRAPHY OF REFUGEE LITERATURE (1985).

[Geneva: International Refugee Integration Resource Center (IRIRC), 151 pp.]

International Committee of the Red Cross, *International Humanitarian Law Database, at* http://www.cicr.org/ihl.

[Under "Commentaries," contains bibliographical references arranged by article of treaty.]

Jean M. Jablonski & Debra A. Kellman, *Overview of United Nations Materials Brooklyn Law School Library*, 21 BROOK. J. INT'L L. 537-97 (1995).

Margarita Lacabe, Derechos Human Rights, *Concise Guide to Human Rights on the Internet* (2d ed. 1998), http://www.derechos.org/human-rights/manual.htm.

BHAWANI LOGANATHAN & MANGALIKA DE SILVA, AN ANNOTATED BIBLIOGRAPHY ON WOMEN IN CONFLICT (1999).

[Colombo, Sri Lanka: Social Scientists' Association, 83 pp.]

Lyonette Louis-Jacques & David Weissbrodt, *Bibliography for Research on International Human Rights Law*, 13 HAMLINE L. REV. 673-717 (1990).

Donatella Luca, *A Selected Bibliography*, in THE 1951 CONVENTION RELATING TO THE STATUS OF REFUGEES 633-63 (1991).

[Oxford: Oxford Univ. Press.]

Rita Maran, *The Human Rights of Women: A Reference Guide to Official United Nations Documents*, http://www1.umn.edu/humanrts/instree/women/engl-wmn.html.

Elisa Mason, *Guide to Country Research for Refugee Status Determination*, http://www.llrx.com/features/rsd.htm.

[See also *Annex: Human Rights, Country and Legal Information Resources on the Internet*, http://www.llrx.com/features/rsd_bib.htm.]

Elisa Mason, *Guide to International Refugee Law Resources on the Web*, http://www.llrx.com/features/refugee.htm.

Roy M. Mersky, *The Inter-American Human Rights System: Documents, Publications and Internet Resources*, 25 INT'L J. LEGAL INFO. 112 (1997).

National Implementation Database at the ICRC, http://www.cicr.org/ihl-nat.

[Bibliographical references available under "General Comment," arranged by country.]

STEPHEN C. NEFF, READING HUMAN RIGHTS: AN ANNOTATED GUIDE TO A HUMAN RIGHTS LIBRARY (1997).

[Colombo, Sri Lanka: Nadesan Centre for Human Rights through Law, London: INTERIGHTS, 117 pp. This handbook-style guide is designed to assist human rights activists around the world in developing a good working library on international human rights.]

JOAN NORDQUIST, LABOR ABUSES IN THE GLOBAL ECONOMY: WOMEN AND CHILDREN: A BIBLIOGRAPHY (1998).

[Santa Cruz, CA, USA: Reference and Research Services, 68 pp. CONTEMPORARY SOCIAL ISSUES SERIES No. 51.]

Penny L. Parker, *U.N. Human Rights Documentation: A Guide to Country-Specific Research* (1986), http://www1.umn.edu/humanrts/bibliog/guide.htm.

Kumar Percy & Karen Engle, *Bibliography for Representing Culture, Translating Human Rights*, 41 TEX. INT'L L.J. 529 (2006).

Steven Perkins, *Latin American Human Rights Research 1980-1989: A Guide to Sources and a Bibliography*, 19 DENV. J. INT'L L. & POL'Y 163- 267 (1990).

Steven C. Perkins, *Researching Indigenous Peoples Rights under International Law* (1992-2006), http://intelligent-internet.info/law/ipr2.html.

NINA REDMAN, HUMAN RIGHTS: A REFERENCE HANDBOOK (2d ed. 1998).

[Santa Barbara, CA: ABC-CLIO, 301 pp.]

REFUGEE STUDIES PROGRAMME, DIRECTORY OF RESEARCH ON REFUGEES AND OTHER FORCED MIGRANTS (1993).

[Oxford: Refugee Studies Programme, 184 pp.]

REFUGEE WOMEN: SELECTED AND ANNOTATED BIBLIOGRAPHY (1989).

[Geneva: Centre for Documentation on Refugees, 123 pp. Revised edition of A Selected and Annotated Bibliography on Refugee Women (1985).]

The Rights International Research Guide for International Human Rights Lawyers (2000), http://www.rightsinternational.org/instruments.html.

RIGHTS OF WOMEN: A GUIDE TO THE MOST IMPORTANT UNITED NATIONS TREATIES FOR WOMEN'S HUMAN RIGHTS (2d ed. 1998).

[New York: International Women's Tribune Centre, 148 pp.]

SHABTI ROSENNE, PRACTICE AND METHODS OF INTERNATIONAL LAW (1984).

[Dobbs Ferry, NY: Oceana Publications, Inc., 169 pp. Reference guide to international legal materials.]

Wendy Scott, International, Comparative & Foreign Disability

Law Research (2006), http://www.law.syr.edu/Pdfs/0IntlComp&Foreign Dis06.pdf.

Selected Bibliography on International Human Rights at Fifty, 8 TRANSNAT'L L. & CONTEMP. PROBS. 423 (1998).

Selected Bibliography on the United Nations Convention on the Rights of the Child (Symposium: Implementation of the United Nations Convention on the Rights of the Child), 6 TRANSNAT'L L. & CONTEMP. PROBS. 491 (1996).

SIGI (Sisterhood Is Global Institute), *Violence Against Women Bibliography*, http://www.europrofem.org/material/books/09.book.htm.

JANUSZ SYMONIDES & VLADIMIR VOLODIN, ACCESS TO HUMAN RIGHTS DOCUMENTATION: DOCUMENTATION, BIBLIOGRAPHIES, AND DATA-BASES ON HUMAN RIGHTS (3d ed.1997).

[Paris: UNESCO, 188 pp.]

CHARLES SZLADITS, BIBLIOGRAPHY ON FOREIGN AND COMPARATIVE LAW: BOOKS AND ARTICLES IN ENGLISH (1955-).

[Dobbs Ferry, NY: Oceana Publications, Inc. (Vol. 1- , 1790-Apr. 1, 1953-). Irregular. Parker School Studies in Foreign and Comparative Law. Lists books and articles by subject, country, and author, on a variety of topics including human rights.]

JACK TOBIN AND JENNIFER GREEN, GUIDE TO HUMAN RIGHTS RESEARCH (1994).

[Cambridge, MA: Human Rights Program, Harvard Law School, 228 pp. Excellent guide and bibliography.]

U.N. DEPT. OF PUBLIC INFORMATION, A GUIDE TO INFORMATION AT THE UNITED NATIONS, U.N. Sales No. E.95.I.4 (1995).

[New York: U.N. Dept. of Public Information, 121 pp. Provides brief descriptions of the work and structure of U.N. agencies, departments, and programs, including a listing of their major publications.]

UNHCR, *Human Rights and Refugees: Collection and Dissemination of Sources*, 25 INT'L J. LEGAL INFO. 35 (1997).

U.N., HUMAN RIGHTS ON CD-ROM: BIBLIOGRAPHICAL DATABASE FOR UNITED NATIONS DOCUMENTS AND PUBLICATIONS, U.N. Sales No. E. GV.98.0.9 (1980-).

[Geneva, U.N. Publications. 1980-1998. This CD-ROM contains over 20,000 bibliographical references for the period. Includes 5,000 full-text documents and 95 international instruments. Searches can be conducted in English, French, and Spanish using the on-line trilingual subject thesaurus.]

United Nations Documentation: Research Guide on Human Rights, http://www.un.org/Depts/dhl/resguide/spechr.htm.

United Nations Human Rights Bibliography, http://www.un.org/rights/HRToday/hrbiblio.htm.

University of Minnesota Human Rights Library, *Refugee and Aid Links*, http://www1.umn.edu/humanrts/links/reflinks.html.

University of Minnesota Human Rights Library, Institute for Global Studies, *Asylum and Refugee Resources*, http://www1.umn.edu/humanrts/asylum/refugee_index.html.

Diana Vincent-Daviss, Bibliographic Essay, in Guide to International Human Rights Practice 249-66 (Hurst Hannum ed., 4th ed. 2004).

[Ardsley, N.Y.: Transnational Publishers, 391 pp. Contains sources for texts of international instruments, bibliographies, and research aids, serial publications, practice guides, teaching resources, U.N. documents, regional documents, and works on nongovernmental organization activities.]

Diana Vincent-Daviss, *Human Rights Law: A Research Guide to the Literature - Part I: International Law and the United Nations*, 14 N.Y.U.J. INT'L L. & POL. 209 (1981).

Diana Vincent-Daviss, *Human Rights Law: A Research Guide to the Literature - Part II: International Protection of Refugees and Humanitarian Law*, 14 N.Y.U.J. INT'L L. & Pol. 487 (1982).

Diana Vincent-Daviss, *Human Rights Law: A Research Guide to the Literature - Part III: The International Labor Organization and Human Rights*, 15 N.Y.U.J. INT'L L. & POL. 211 (1982).

Diana Vincent-Daviss, *The Occupied Territories and International Law: A Research Guide* (Symposium on Human Rights and Israeli Rule in the Territories), 21 N.Y.U.J. INT'L L. & Pol. 575 (1989).

GREGORY J. WALTERS, HUMAN RIGHTS IN THEORY AND PRACTICE: A SELECTED AND ANNOTATED BIBLIOGRAPHY (1995).

[Metuchen, NJ: The Scarecrow Press, 459 pp. Magill Bibliographies. Includes a broad range of human rights sources dating from 1982-1994 with detailed annotations.]

David Weissbrodt & Marci Hoffman, *Bibliography for Research on International Human Rights Law*, http://www1.umn.edu/humanrts/bibliog/ BIBLIO.htm.

David Weissbrodt & Marci Hoffman, *The Global Economy and Human Rights: A Selective Bibliography*, 6 MINN. J. GLOBAL TRADE 189 (1997).

WORLD BIBLIOGRAPHY OF INTERNATIONAL DOCUMENTATION (Theodore Dimitriv comp. & ed., 1981).

[Sarasota, FL: UNIFO Publishers, 846 pp., 2 vols. Volume one covers international organizations' activities, structure, and policies. Volume two addresses politics, world affairs, periodicals, and conferences.]

THOMAS D. YOUNG, INTERNATIONAL HUMAN RIGHTS: A SELECTED BIBLIOGRAPHY (1978).

[Los Angeles, CA: Center for the Study of Armament & Disarmament, California State University Los Angeles, 58 pp. POLITICAL ISSUES SERIES; vol. 5, no. 4.]

Guobin Zhu, *Research on Human Rights in China: A General Survey and an Annotated Bibliography of Selected Chinese Language Publications*, 8 CHINA L. REP. 157 (Winter/Spring 1999).

[A few of the listed documents are in English.]

L. Periodicals

ABORIGINAL LAW BULLETIN (1981-).

[Sydney, New South Wales: Aboriginal Law Centre, Faculty of Law, University of New South Wales (vol. 1- , no. 1- , 1981-), six issues yearly.]

ACLU INTERNATIONAL CIVIL LIBERTIES REPORT (1992-).

[Los Angeles: ACLU International Human Rights Task Force (vol. 1- , no. 1- , 1992-), annual.]

ADVISOR (July 1996-2001).

[New York, NY: Lawyers Committee for Human Rights, quarterly.]

AFRICAN HUMAN RIGHTS NEWSLETTER (1990-2004).

[Kombo St. Mary Division, The Gambia: Afr. Centre for Democracy and Hum. Rts. Stud. (vol. 1- , no. 1- , 1990-), quarterly. Each issue contains both English and French language text. French language version presented under separate title: *Bulletin africain des droits de l'homme*.]

AMERICAN JOURNAL OF INTERNATIONAL LAW (1907-).

[Washington, D.C.: American Society of International Law (vol. 1- , 1907-), quarterly. The leading scholarly journal on contemporary issues in public international law. Available on LEXIS from 1980, on WESTLAW from 1982, and on HeinOnline from 1907.]

American Society of International Law, INTERNATIONAL LEGAL MATERIALS [ILM] (1962-).

[Washington, DC: American Society of International Law, published six times a year. Available on LEXIS from 1975, on WESTLAW from 1980, on HeinOnline from 1962. An important resource that includes texts of treaties, international tribunal decisions, and declarations and resolutions of international bodies concerning human rights.]

AMNESTY INTERNATIONAL NEWSLETTER (1971-2001).

[London: Amnesty International (vol. 1- , 1971-), monthly. Contains brief articles relating to AI's current human rights concerns.]

AMNESTY INTERNATIONAL USA LEGAL SUPPORT NETWORK NEWSLETTER (1984-1994).

[New York: Amnesty International USA (vol. 1-11, 1984-1994), published about 2-3 times a year. Covered human rights activities at the U.N.; included notes on current litigation and material of interest to lawyers.]

ANTI-SLAVERY REPORTER (1995- 2001).

[London: Anti-Slavery International, irregular. Continued ANTI-SLAVERY REPORTER (1981-1994).]

ASIA-PACIFIC JOURNAL ON HUMAN RIGHTS AND THE LAW (2000-).

[The Hague; Boston: Kluwer Law International, semiannual.]

AUSTRALIAN INDIGENOUS LAW REPORTER (1996-2006).

[Sydney, New South Wales: Prospect Pub. (vol. 1- , no. 1- , 1996-), quarterly.]

AUSTRALIAN JOURNAL OF HUMAN RIGHTS (1994-).

[Sydney, Australia: International Business Communications; issued by the Human Rights Centre of the University of New South Wales, annual.]

BILL OF RIGHTS BULLETIN (1991-97).

[Hong Kong: University of Hong Kong Faculty of Law (vol. 1- 4, no. 1- 3, 1991-97), published about 3-4 times a year. Edited by Andrew Byrnes and Johannes M.M. Chan.]

BUFFALO HUMAN RIGHTS LAW REVIEW (1998-).

[Buffalo, NY: State University of New York at Buffalo, School of Law, annual. Continues BUFFALO JOURNAL OF INTERNATIONAL LAW. Available on WESTLAW (1998-) and LEXIS (1998-).]

BULLETIN OF HUMAN RIGHTS (1978-1991).

[Geneva: U.N. Centre for Human Rights, quarterly.]

COLUMBIA HUMAN RIGHTS LAW REVIEW (1972-).

[New York: Columbia Law School (vol. 4, 1972-), biannual. Continues COLUMBIA SURVEY OF HUMAN RIGHTS LAW (vol. 1- , 1970-). Available on WESTLAW from 1984 and on LEXIS from 1995.]

CONSCIENCE AND LIBERTY: INTERNATIONAL JOURNAL OF RELIGIOUS FREEDOM (1989-1995).

[St. Albans: International Association for the Defence of Religious Liberty (1st Year- , no. 1(1)- , 1989-1995). French language version presented under separate title: *Conscience et Liberte*.]

CSCE BULLETIN (1993-1994).

[Warsaw: Conference on Security and Cooperation in Europe, Office for Democratic Institutions and Human Rights (vol.1- , no. 1- , 1993-), quarterly.]

DEPARTMENT OF STATE DISPATCH (1990-1999).

[Washington, D.C.: Office of Public Communication, Bureau of Public Affairs, monthly. Formerly known as Department of State Bulletin (vol. 1, 1939-), monthly. Official monthly record of U.S. foreign policy. Contains articles on activities of the President and Secretary of State, treaty information, excerpts of speeches, and an annual index. Available on LEXIS from July 1984 and WESTLAW from 1989.]

DISSEMINATION (1985-1991).

[Geneva: ICRC (no. 1-15, 1985-1991), published three times a year. Provides information on ratification of the Geneva Conventions and Protocols. Similar information is now published every two years in the ICRC report, NATIONAL IMPLEMENTATION OF INTERNATIONAL HUMANITARIAN LAW. The ICRC's database on national implementation is on the Web, http://www.icrc.org/ihl-nat.]

EAST AFRICAN JOURNAL OF PEACE & HUMAN RIGHTS (1993-1995).

[Kampala, Uganda: Makerere University, Hum. Rts. and Peace Centre (vol. 1- , no. 1- , 1993-1995), twice a year.]

EAST EUROPEAN HUMAN RIGHTS REVIEW (1995-2005).

[Den Bosch, Netherlands: BookWorld Publications, twice a year.]

EUROPEAN HUMAN RIGHTS LAW REVIEW (1996-).

[London: Sweet & Maxwell, six times a year.]

EUROPEAN LAW REVIEW: HUMAN RIGHTS SURVEY (1996-2002).

[London: Sweet & Maxwell (1996-), annual.]

FORCED MIGRATION REVIEW (FMR) (1998-).

[Oxford: Refugee Studies Centre in association with the Global IDP Survey/Norwegian Refugee Council, three times a year in Arabic, English, and Spanish. Aims to provide a forum for the regular exchange of practical experience, information and ideas between researchers, refugees, internally displaced people, and individuals who work with them. The Forced Migration Review's Web site is at http://www.fmreview.org. Continues REFUGEE PARTICIPATION NETWORK (RPN) NEWSLETTER.]

GLOBAL JOURNAL ON HUMAN RIGHTS LAW (1996-).

[Holmes Beach, Fla.: Gaunt, Inc. Published by the Global Law Association, semiannual.]

HARVARD HUMAN RIGHTS JOURNAL (1990-).

[Cambridge, MA: Harvard Law School (vol. 3, 1990-), annual. Continues HARVARD HUMAN RIGHTS YEARBOOK (vol. 1/1988-vol. 2/1989). Available on LEXIS from 1993 and WESTLAW from 1990.]

HCHR NEWS (1995-1997).

[Geneva: Office of High Commissioner for Human Rights (HCHR); (vol. 1- , no. 1- , 1995-1997), monthly.]

HEALTH AND HUMAN RIGHTS (1994-2006).

[Cambridge, MA: Harvard School of Public Health (vol. 1- , no. 1- , 1994-), quarterly. Also available on the Web, http://www.hsph.harvard.edu/fxbcenter/journal.htm.]

HELSINKI MONITOR (1990-).

[Utrecht, The Netherlands: Netherlands Helsinki Committee (NHC) (vol. 1- , no. 1- , 1990-), quarterly. Focuses on security and cooperation in Europe.]

HUMAN RIGHTS (1970-).

[Chicago: American Bar Association (vol. 1- , no. 1- , 1970-). Periodical issued by the Individual Rights and Responsibilities Section. Available on WESTLAW from 1987.]

HUMAN RIGHTS: A QUARTERLY REVIEW OF THE OFFICE OF THE UNITED NATIONS HIGH COMMISSIONER FOR HUMAN RIGHTS = DROITS DE L'HOMME: REVUE TRIMESTRIELLE DU HAUT COMMISSARIAT DES NATIONS UNIES AUX DROITS DE L'HOMME (1997-2000).

[Geneva: The Office, quarterly. English and French.]

HUMAN RIGHTS AND CIVIL SOCIETY NEWSLETTER (1995-1999).

[Vienna, Austria: International Helsinki Federation for Human Rights, irregular. Continues PROMOTING HUMAN RIGHTS AND CIVIL SOCIETY IN CENTRAL AND EASTERN EUROPE NEWSLETTER.]

HUMAN RIGHTS BRIEF (1994-).

[Washington, DC: Center for Human Rights and Humanitarian Law, Washington College of Law, the American University (vol. 1, no. 1, spring 1994-). Quarterly.]

HUMAN RIGHTS CASE DIGEST (1990-).

[London: Sweet & Maxwell in association with the British Institute of Human Rights (vol. 1- , pt. 1- , 1990-), bimonthly. Provides summaries of European Court and Commission of Human Rights decisions and judgments and the Committee of Ministers Article 32 and 54 decisions.]

HUMAN RIGHTS EDUCATION: THE FOURTH R (1994-).

[Jonesboro, AR: Amnesty International USA's National Steering Committee on Human Rights Education, AI-USA, published sporadically. Available on the Web, http://www.amnestyusa.org/education/4thr.html.]

HUMAN RIGHTS INFORMATION BULLETIN (July 1996-).

[Strasbourg: Council of Europe, Directorate of Human Rights, semiannual. An update on human rights activities within the Council of Europe. Continues HUMAN RIGHTS INFORMATION SHEET. Available on the Web, http://www. coe.int/T/E/Human_rights/hribe.asp.]

HUMAN RIGHTS INTERNET REPORTER (1976-1999).

[Ottawa: Human Rights Internet, quarterly. Contains an annotated bibliography of new literature; articles on human rights; calendar of upcoming conferences and seminars; international and national human rights developments; and IGO decisions and actions.]

HUMAN RIGHTS LAW IN AFRICA (1996-2004).

[The Hague, Boston: Kluwer Law International, annual.]

HUMAN RIGHTS LAW JOURNAL (1980-).

[Kehl am Rhein; Arlington, VA: N.P. Engel (vol. 1- , 1980-), quarterly. Continues HUMAN RIGHTS REVIEW. Provides articles, decisions, reports, and documentation including texts of resolutions, declarations, and case reports. Issued in association with the International Institute of Human Rights, Strasbourg, France.]

HUMAN RIGHTS MONITOR (1988-).

[Geneva: International Service for Human Rights, quarterly. Reports on human rights developments at the U.N., specialized agencies, and in NGO's.]

HUMAN RIGHTS NEWSLETTER (1988-1992).

[Geneva: U.N. Centre for Human Rights (vol. 1- , no. 1- , 1988-), quarterly. Covers information about the activities of the Centre.]

HUMAN RIGHTS QUARTERLY (1981-).

[Baltimore, MD: Johns Hopkins University Press (vol. 3- , 1981-), quarterly. Formerly Universal Human Rights (vol. 1/1979-vol. 2/1980). Interdisciplinary articles and book reviews addressing all aspects of human rights.]

HUMAN RIGHTS REVIEW (1999-).

[Piscataway, NY: Transaction Periodicals Consortium, quarterly.]

HUMAN RIGHTS TRIBUNE=TRIBUNE DES DROITS HUMAINS (1992-2003).

[Ottawa: Human Rights Internet (vol. 1- , no. 1- , 1992-), quarterly. Reported news of the human rights movement, including NGO and U.N. events.]

HUMAN RIGHTS WATCH UPDATE (1995-1999).

[New York: Human Rights Watch, published ten times yearly. Continues HUMAN RIGHTS WATCH QUARTERLY NEWSLETTER (1991-1995).]

International Committee of the Red Cross, BULLETIN (1976-).

[Geneva: ICRC (no. 1- , 1976-). Highlights current ICRC activities.]

INTERNATIONAL NETWORK ON HOLOCAUST AND GENOCIDE (1995-1996).

[NSW, Australia: Macquarie University Centre for Comparative Genocide Studies, bimonthly. Continues INTERNET ON THE HOLOCAUST AND GENOCIDE.]

INTERNATIONAL HUMAN RIGHTS LAW UPDATE (1994-2000).

[New York, N.Y.: The Aspen Institute, Justice and Society Program, irregular.]

INTERNATIONAL HUMAN RIGHTS REPORTS [IHRR] (1994-).

[Nottingham, U.K.: University of Nottingham (vol. 1- , no. 1- , 1994-), published three times a year. Covers decisions and opinions of U.N. treaty bodies on human rights with respect to individual and state complaints procedures, judgments and opinions of the Inter-American Court of Human Rights, relevant resolutions of the General Assembly and Commission on Human Rights, and texts of newly adopted human rights treaties.]

THE INTERNATIONAL JOURNAL OF CHILDREN'S RIGHTS (1994-).

[Dordrecht; Boston: Martinus Nijhoff Pub. (vol. 1- , no. 1- , 1994-), quarterly. Contains scholarly articles, a section on practice and implementation, and book reviews on children's issues.]

INTERNATIONAL JOURNAL OF DISCRIMINATION AND THE LAW (1995-).

[Bicester, Oxon: A B Academic Publishers, two or three times a year.]

INTERNATIONAL JOURNAL OF HUMAN RIGHTS (1997-).

[London: Frank Cass & Co. Ltd., quarterly.]

INTERNATIONAL JOURNAL OF REFUGEE LAW (1989-).

[Oxford: Oxford Univ. Press (vol. 1- , 1989-), quarterly.]

INTERNATIONAL JOURNAL ON MINORITY AND GROUP RIGHTS (1996/97-).

[The Hague; Boston: Kluwer Law International, quarterly. Addresses legal, political, and social problems experienced by groups which are defined by factors, such as culture, language, race, or religion. Continues INTERNATIONAL JOURNAL ON GROUP RIGHTS (1993-1995).]

INTERNATIONAL REVIEW OF THE RED CROSS (1961-).

[Geneva: ICRC (no. 1- , 1961-), published every two months. In 1999, the REVUE INTERNATIONALE DE LA CROIX-ROUGE and its English edition, the INTERNATIONAL REVIEW OF THE RED CROSS, combined to form this single, bilingual English/French edition: REVUE INTERNATIONALE DE LA CROIX-ROUGE/INTERNATIONAL REVIEW OF THE RED CROSS.]

International Labour Office, OFFICIAL BULLETIN (1928-).

[Geneva: ILO (vol. 1- , 1928-), irregular. Provides information about the activities of the ILO, including inquiries into work conditions in various countries, and decisions of the Committee on Freedom of Association.]

IRISH HUMAN RIGHTS YEARBOOK (1995-).

[Dublin: Round Hall Sweet & Maxwell, annual.]

ISRAEL YEARBOOK ON HUMAN RIGHTS (1971-).

[Tel Aviv: Faculty of Law, Tel Aviv University (vol. 1- , 1971-), annual. Publishes studies on human rights with particular emphasis on problems relevant to the Jewish people and the state of Israel. Includes summaries of judicial decisions, compilations of legislative enactments, and military proclamations relating to Israel and the Administered Areas.]

MEDITERRANEAN JOURNAL OF HUMAN RIGHTS (1997-).

[Padova: CEDAM. University of Malta. Foundation for International Studies, irregular. Chiefly English.]

MINORITY RIGHTS GROUP INTERNATIONAL REPORT (1970-2002).

[London: Minority Rights Group (no. 1- , 1970-), irregular. Series addresses problems facing minorities world-wide. Each issue has a distinctive title. Formerly referred to as MINORITY RIGHTS GROUP REPORT.]

NETHERLANDS QUARTERLY OF HUMAN RIGHTS [NHQR] (1989-).

[The Hague; London; Boston: Kluwer Law International; a co-publication with Netherlands Institute of Human Rights (SIM) (vol. 7- , no. 1- , 1989-), quarterly. Formerly (SIM) NEWSLETTER (1983-87).]

NEW YORK LAW SCHOOL JOURNAL OF HUMAN RIGHTS (1987-).

[New York: New York Law School (vol. 5, pt. 1- , 1987-), annual. Formerly NEW YORK LAW SCHOOL HUMAN RIGHTS ANNUAL (vol. 1/1983-vol.4/1987). Contains book reviews and articles on current issues. Available on WESTLAW from 1990, and on LEXIS from 1993.]

NEWSLETTER (School of Human Rights Research) (1997-).

[Utrecht, The Netherlands: School of Human Rights Research, quarterly. The School of Human Rights Research (established in 1995) is a joint initiative of the faculties of law and of the humanities of Utrecht University, and of the faculties of law of Maastricht University, Erasmus University of Rotterdam, and Catholic University of Brabant.]

NORDIC JOURNAL ON HUMAN RIGHTS=MENNESKER OG RETTIGHETER (1983-).

[Oslo: Norwegian Institute of Human Rights (vol. 1- , no. 1-, 1983-), quarterly.]

THE REVIEW (1969-2001).

[Geneva: International Commission of Jurists (vol. 1- , no. 1- , 1969-), quarterly. Typically contains a "Human Rights in the World" section with a brief report on human rights developments in selected countries, articles, commentaries, and texts of major documents.]

REVUE TRIMESTRIELLE DES DROITS DE L'HOMME (1990-2000).

[Brussells: Bruylant (no. 1- , 1990-), quarterly. In French.]

SOUTH AFRICAN HUMAN RIGHTS AND LABOUR LAW YEARBOOK (1990-91).

[Cape Town: Oxford Univ. Press (vol. 1- , 1990- vol. 2- , 1991), two volumes yearly. Continued by SOUTH AFRICAN HUMAN RIGHTS YEARBOOK.]

SOUTH AFRICAN HUMAN RIGHTS YEARBOOK (1992-1996).

[Cape Town: Oxford Univ. Press; Durban: Centre for Socio-legal Studies, annual. Continues SOUTH AFRICAN HUMAN RIGHTS AND LABOUR LAW YEARBOOK.]

SOUTH AFRICAN JOURNAL ON HUMAN RIGHTS (1985-).

[Braamfontein, South Africa: Ravan Press (vol. 1- , pt. 1- , 1985-), three issues yearly.]

UNHCR, REFUGEES (1984-).

[Geneva: UNHCR (no. 1- , Jan. 1984-), monthly. From 1992 issued quarterly.]

UNREPRESENTED NATIONS AND PEOPLES ORGANIZATION: YEARBOOK (1995-1997).

[The Hague; Boston: Kluwer Law International, annual. Unrepresented Nations and Peoples Organization; edited for the UNPO by Mary Kate Simmons. Other Title: UNPO YEARBOOK.]

THE WOMEN'S WATCH (1987-2000).

[Minneapolis, MN: International Women's Rights Action Watch, Humphrey Institute of Public Affairs, quarterly. Provides information on developments in law and policy with regard to the Convention on the Elimination of All Forms of Discrimination Against Women.]

YALE HUMAN RIGHTS & DEVELOPMENT LAW JOURNAL (1998-).

[New Haven, Conn.: Yale Law School, annual. On WESTLAW and LEXIS from 1998. Available also on the Web, http://islandia.law.yale.edu/yhrdlj.]

YEARBOOK OF INTERNATIONAL HUMANITARIAN LAW (1998-).

[The Hague: T.M.C Asser Press, annual.]

YEARBOOK OF THE EUROPEAN CONVENTION FOR THE PREVENTION OF TORTURE (1997-)

[Nottingham: Human Rights Law Centre, University of Nottingham, annual.]

M. Book and Periodical Indexes

Library catalogs and periodical indices contain listings under the Library of Congress Subject Headings: "HUMAN RIGHTS," "CIVIL RIGHTS (INTERNATIONAL LAW)," and "CIVIL RIGHTS."

Online library catalogs and periodical indices usually provide keyword searching in the bibliographic record of a book or in the title and abstract fields of an article.

CURRENT BIBLIOGRAPHICAL INFORMATION=INFORMATION BIBLIOGRAPHIQUE COURANTE (1971-1993).

[New York: U.N., Dag Hammarskjold Library (vol. 1- , Jan. 1971-1993) (ST/LIB/Ser.K), monthly. Lists authors and subjects of books published by the U.N., specialized agencies, and non-U.N. organizations. Also covers related articles from over 700 periodicals. (UNDOC: A Current Index, principally a list of new acquisitions of the Dag Hammarskjold Library, covers strictly U.N. materials.) Human Rights materials are listed under item 141.]

CURRENT LAW INDEX (1980-).

[Los Altos, CA: Information Access Corp. (vol. 1-, 1980-), monthly with annual cumulation. See also LEGALTRAC below. The electronic version of this index is Legal Resource Index, available on LEXIS, WESTLAW, and the Web.]

INDEX TO FOREIGN LEGAL PERIODICALS: A SUBJECT INDEX TO SELECTED INTERNATIONAL AND COMPARATIVE LAW PERIODICALS AND COLLECTIONS OF ESSAYS (1960-).

[Chicago: American Association of Law Libraries (vol. 1- , no. 1- , 1960-), updated quarterly. Covers selected legal periodicals on public and private international, comparative, and domestic law of countries other than the U.S., the British Isles, and the British Commonwealth. "Human Rights (International Law)" is the search term for articles on human rights. Also available via Web subscription from Ovid (Wolters Kluwer). This database is available on WESTLAW, but not with academic subscriptions.]

LEGAL JOURNALS INDEX and EUROPEAN JOURNALS INDEX (1986-1999).

[Hebden Bridge, West Yorkshire: Legal Information Resources Ltd. These indexes cover legal journals published in the UK and Europe. The print versions of these two indexes was discontinued in 1999. Both are available by subscription on CD-ROM or the Web through Current Legal Information database (produced by Sweet & Maxwell), http://www.sweetandmaxwell.co.uk/online/cli.html. Also available on WESTLAW.]

INDEX TO LEGAL PERIODICALS (1929-).

[New York: H.W. Wilson, Co. Available on CD-ROM from H.W. Wilson Co. and SilverPlatter Information, Inc. Also available on LEXIS and WESTLAW (this file is only available to law school subscribers if they also subscribe to the CD-ROM or Web version of the index. http://www.aallnet.org/products/publications.asp).]

LEGALTRAC (1980-).

LegalTrac on InfoTrac.

[Foster City, CA: Information Access Co. (IAC). The CD-ROM and Web version of Current Law Index plus other sources. Provides extensive coverage of international law journals published in English; indexes over 900 legal and general periodicals. Updated monthly.]

PUBLIC INTERNATIONAL LAW: A CURRENT BIBLIOGRAPHY OF ARTICLES (1975-).

[Berlin: Springer-Verlag (vol. 1- , 1975-), updated twice a year. List of articles in some 1,000 journals and collected works, prepared by the Max Planck Institute; human rights articles are listed under the classification number "14." Available on the Max Planck Institute's Web site, http://www.mpil.de/ww/en/pub/research/details/publications/institute/pil.cfm.]

UNDOC: CURRENT INDEX (1979-1996).

[New York: U.N., Dag Hammarskjold Library (vol. 1- , no. 1- , Jan./Feb. 1979-) (ST/LIB/Ser.M), quarterly as of 1984. Titles and document series of U.N. documents and publications by subject, organization, and title. Includes a list of mimeographed documents published in the official records of the main U.N. organs. A helpful "User's Guide" appears in each issue. For more current information, see READEX United Nations Documents Index on CD-ROM or AccessUN available by subscription on the Web, http://www.newsbank.com.]

N. Electronic Sources

Note: This section lists a few of the most useful sources for researching international human rights. Many of these sources are available only by subscription; however, researchers may be able to access them at a nearby law or university library.

§ 1. Web Sites and Databases

AccessUN (1952-).

[Newsbank. Index to United Nations documents including Official Records, masthead documents, draft resolutions, meeting records, U.N. Sales Publications, and the U.N. Treaty Series citations. Also included is the full-text of several thousand U.N. documents. many law school libraries; subscription information at http://www.newsbank.com. Updated monthly.]

AccessUNDP (1972-1998).

[Newsbank. Fee-based index to a finite collection of United Nations Development Programme Project Reports issued and held by U.N. headquarters between the years 1972-1998.]

Amnesty International, http://www.amnesty.org.

[London. Includes country reports and the latest news releases detailing Amnesty International's activities. News releases are posted to the Web site on a daily basis as they become available. All new reports are added at the end of each working week.]

Annual Review of Population Law.

http://annualreview.law.harvard.edu/annual_review.htm.

[Contains summaries and excerpts of legislation, constitutions, court decisions, and other official government documents from every country in the world relating to population policies, reproductive health, women's rights, and related topics. Produced jointly by Harvard Law School and the United Nations Population Fund.]

CONGRESSIONAL UNIVERSE.

[Bethesda, MD: Lexis-Nexis/Congressional Information Service, Inc. (CIS). Fee-based database containing congressional publications, bills, laws, regulations, member information, and secondary sources that report on the legislative process. Includes indexing and abstracting of congressional publications and the CIS Legislative Histories (1970-present); indexing and abstracting of historical congressional publications (1789-1969) and of transcripts of unpublished hearings (1823-1972). Updated daily.]

Council of Europe, European Court of Human Rights, http://www.echr.coe.int.

[Basic texts, case reports, and news of the ECHR; maintained by the Court.]

Council of Europe, Human Rights Web, http://www.coe.int/T/E/Human_rights.

[Provides information about the human rights activities of the Council of Europe. Maintained by the Directorate of Human Rights of the Council of Europe.]

Derechos - Human Rights, http://www.derechos.org.

[Derechos Human Rights is an international organization working for international human rights. Its Web site provides over 6,000 documents and links. Also provides human rights information in Spanish.]

DIANA, http://www.yale.edu/lawweb/avalon/diana/index.html.

[New Haven, CT. International archive of human rights legal documentation. Project Diana appears under the guidance of the Orville H. Schell, Jr. Center for International Human Rights at Yale Law School. It is designed to be a reference tool for research in human rights law, with online litigation documents and links to reference sites throughout the Internet. Also several mirror sites.]

EUR-LEX, http://eur-lex.europa.eu/en/index.htm.

[Luxembourg: Office for Official Publications of the European Communities. Free database containing full-text coverage of EU legal acts, treaties, binding and non-binding legislation, and case law of the European Court of Justice. Updated daily.]

Europa, http://europa.eu/index_en.htm (English language version).

[Brussels. Europa is the portal site of the European Union. It provides up-to-date coverage of European Union affairs and essential information on European integration. Users can also consult all legislation currently in force or under discussion, access the Web sites of each of the EU institutions and find out about the policies administered by the European Union under the powers devolved to it by the treaties. Updated daily.]

Fourth World Documentation Project, http://www.cwis.org/fwdp.

[The Fourth World Documentation Project is an online library of texts on internationally unrecognized nations, maintained by the Center for World Indigenous Studies.]

HUDOC, http://cmiskp.echr.coe.int/tkp197/search.asp?skin=hudoc-en.

[Strasbourg: European Court of Human Rights. Database of the case law of the supervisory organs of the European Convention on Human Rights. Includes case law of the European Court of Human Rights, the now-defunct European Commission of Human Rights, and the Committee of Ministers. Frequent but irregular updating.]

Human Rights and Constitutional Rights, http://www.hrcr.org.

[Provides news, documents, and links relating to human rights and constitutional rights. Maintained by the Human Rights Institute at Columbia Law School; irregularly updated.]

Human Rights @ igc, http://www.igc.org/igc/gateway.

[Institute for Global Communications (IGC) hosts various progressive organizations, including Peacenet, Econet, and Womensnet. Provides access to alternative news and political analysis, and allows searching for information and Web sites of progressive organizations. Also provides events and calendars, action alerts, and information about volunteers and employment in the progressive nonprofit sector.]

Human Rights First [formerly Lawyers Committee for Human Rights], http://www.humanrightsfirst.org.

[Provides news on the activities of Human Rights First, which is a U.S.-based NGO active in several areas of human rights, including refugee law.]

Human Rights Internet, http://www.hri.ca.

[Provides human rights news, links, and a documentation center, including a collection of full-text reports on various topics.]

Human Rights on CD-ROM.

[New York: United Nations, Centre for Human Rights. The CD-ROM contains citations for approximately 12,000 United Nations documents and publications issued since 1980 on subjects related to human rights. References are drawn from the United Nations Bibliographic Information system. The citations contain the United Nations documents symbol to enable referral to the text of the document. Annual (cumulative). 4th ed. 1999, the last one available, covers 1980-1998.]

Human Rights Watch, http://www.hrw.org.

[One of the major human rights NGOs, Human Rights Watch provides news and documents, including its country reports, at this Web site.]

IHL (International Humanitarian Law) database, http://www.icrc.org/ihl.

[Geneva: ICRC. The IHL database contains 91 treaties and texts, commentaries on the four Geneva Conventions and their Additional Protocols, an up-to-date list of signatures, ratifications relating to IHL treaties, and full text of reservations. The National Implementation database, http://www.icrc.org/ihl-nat, provides data on the implementation of IHL at country level. Both databases are also available on CD-ROM.]

ILOLEX, http://www.ilo.org/ilolex/english.

[Geneva: International Labour Organization. Contains ILO Conventions and Recommendations, ratification information, comments of the Committee of Experts and the Committee on Freedom of Association, representations, complaints, interpretations, General Surveys, and numerous related documents.

Index to Foreign Legal Periodicals: A Subject Index to Selected International and Comparative Law Periodicals and Collections of Essays (1960-).

[Chicago: American Association of Law Libraries (vol. 1- , no. 1- , 1960-), updated quarterly. Covers selected legal periodicals on public and private international, comparative, and domestic law of countries other than the U.S., the

British Isles, and the British Commonwealth. "Human Rights (International Law)" is the search term for articles on human rights. Also available via Web subscription from Ovid (Wolters Kluwer). This database is available on WESTLAW, but not with academic subscriptions.]

Index to Legal Periodicals (1929-).

[New York: H.W. Wilson, Co. Available on the Web from H.W. Wilson Co.. Also available on LEXIS and WESTLAW. This file is only available to law school subscribers if they also subscribe to the Web version of the index.]

International Criminal Tribunal for Rwanda, http://www.ictr.org.

[News, documents, and case law of the Tribunal.]

International Criminal Tribunal for the former Yugoslavia, http://www. un.org/icty.

[News, documents, and case law of the Tribunal.]

International Federation of Red Cross and Red Crescent Societies, http://www.ifrc.org.

[Geneva: ICRC. Information on Red Cross and Red Crescent activities, including those related to humanitarian law. News stories and reports from field operations are posted daily, and other information is added periodically. Also provides access to the IHL (International Humanitarian Law) database; see above.]

International Gay and Lesbian Human Rights Commission, http://www. iglhrc.org/site/iglhrc.

[The IGLHRC (a U.S.-based NGO) site provides news and materials on human rights violations against lesbians, gay men, bisexuals, transgendered people, and people with HIV and AIDS.]

International Labour Organization [ILO], http://www.ilo.org.

[Provides extensive materials on labor issues worldwide. See also ILOLEX, above.]

International Labour Organization [ILO], International Labour Standards and Human Rights, http://www.ilo.org/global/What_we_do/InternationalLabour Standards/lang--en/index.htm.

[Searchable collection of the ILO's human rights standards pertaining to work.]

LEGALTRAC (1980-) (LegalTrac on InfoTrac).

[Foster City, CA: Information Access Co. (IAC). The Web version of Current Law Index plus other sources. Provides extensive coverage of international law journals published in English; indexes over 900 legal and general periodicals. Updated daily. More information at http://www.aallnet.org/products/pub_legal_index.asp.]

LEXIS-NEXIS.

[Dayton, OH: Lexis-Nexis. Major fee-based legal research service. The thousands of LEXIS databases include laws, regulations, and other legislative and administrative documents; cases; briefs; treatises; legal periodicals and indexes; and many other legal resources. The NEXIS databases provide news and business information, including newspapers and magazines, company, country, financial, demographic and market research data and industry reports. Updating varies by database. More information http://global.lexisnexis.com/us.]

Multilaterals Project, Human Rights Treaties, http://fletcher.tufts.edu/multi/humanRights.html.

[Tufts University's Fletcher School of Law & Diplomacy provides the full text of several multilateral human rights instruments at this Web site. Also has links to other full-text collections.]

Netherlands Institute of Human Rights (SIM), http://sim.law.uu.nl/SIM/Dochome.nsf?Open.

[Another source for the full text of human rights instruments.]

OAS, Inter-American Commission on Human Rights, http://www.cidh.oas.org.

[News, rules of procedure, and basic documents of the Inter-American Commission on Human Rights. English version of the site is available.]

ODS [Online Document System], http://documents.un.org/welcome.asp?language=E.

[Offers full-text searching of U.N. documents from 1993-present, with older documents continually added.]

Office of the UNHCR, http://www.ohchr.org.

[New York. Provides searchable Treaty Bodies and Charter-based Bodies database search, a database on human rights education, news, and other documents.]

OneWorld, http://us.oneworld.net.

[Progressive-oriented Web site that contains or links to thousands of documents pertaining to human rights. Also has topical guides on several human rights issues, such as child labor, immigration, and women's rights.]

Organization for Security and Cooperation in Europe (OSCE), http://www.osce.org.

[News and organizational information about the OSCE, along with a library of documents, journals, and decisions issued by various CSCE/OSCE negotiating bodies during different events and meetings, which took place between 1973 and the present.]

PAIS International (1972-).

[Public Affairs Information Service. PAIS International indexes political, economic, and social policy literature. This fee-based database contains abstracts of journal articles, books, statistical yearbooks, directories, conference proceedings, research reports, and government documents from all over the world. Subject headings and abstracts are written in English; some materials in other languages. Available via the Web. Updated monthly. For more information, see http://www.csa.com/factsheets/pais-set-c.php.]

Physicians for Human Rights, http://www.phrusa.org/index.html.

[News and information resources, including a news archive, relating to the activities of Physicians for Human Rights (PHR), an NGO active in international human rights work.]

The Protection Project, http://www.protectionproject.org.

[Paul H. Nitze School of Advanced International Studies, Johns Hopkins University. A legal research project that gathers and disseminates information regarding trafficking and commercial sexual exploitation of women and children. Includes statutes, international instruments, country reports, and many other documents.]

Research/Evaluation [formerly REFWORLD], http://www.unhcr.org/research.html.

[Geneva: UNHCR. Collection of full-text databases containing information on international and national law and practice; current country conditions from a variety of sources including governmental, intergovernmental, and non-governmental organizations; policy guidelines and manuals; as well as an extensive collection of bibliographic references and research contacts.]

ReliefWeb, http://www.reliefweb.int/rw/dbc.nsf.

[Comprehensive source on international humanitarian efforts. Includes directory of humanitarian organizations and a library of reference documents.]

Rome Statute for the International Criminal Court, http://untreaty.un.org/cod/icc/index.html.

[Contains ratification information, documentation such as the statute and draft rules of procedure, and a wealth of information on the creation of the ICC.]

Social Sciences Abstracts (1983-).

[New York: H.W. Wilson Co. Covers the social science disciplines including sociology, anthropology, geography, economics, political science, criminology, and law. Provides bibliographic citations (abstracts since January 1994) to articles from more than 400 English-language social sciences journals and periodicals. Updated monthly.]

UNBISnet (1979-), http://unbisnet.un.org.

[New York: U.N. UNBISnet contains citations to U.N. documents and publications originating from U.N. bodies world-wide and indexed by the Dag

Hammarskjöld Library or the Library of the U.N. in Geneva. Also includes citations to monographs, serials, journal articles and publications of governments, international organizations, commercial publishers and other non-UN sources acquired by the Dag Hammarskjöld and Geneva libraries. Updated daily.]

UNDP, http://www.undp.org.

[The UNDP's primary mission is to decrease poverty. Its Web site contains reports and other information on human rights aspects of its mission, including women's and children's issues.]

UNESCO, http://www.unesco.org.

[Contains documents pertaining to UNESCO's role in promoting human rights through education, science, culture and communication. Includes searchable database of UNESCO resolutions and decisions since 1946.]

UNESCO, Standard-setting Instruments in Human Rights,

http://unesdoc.unesco.org/images/0010/001060/106050e.pdf.

[Excellent collection of human rights instruments and some of the documents related to their preparation.]

UNICEF, http://www.unicef.org.

[Full text of reports on various issues relating to children, including some human rights issues such as child labor.]

United Nations Treaty Collection.

[New York: U.N. Contains over 40,000 treaties from the United Nations Treaty Series. Images of the documents are available as well as a search device. This Web site is free. More information http://untreaty.un.org.]

U.N. (Human Rights main page), http://www.un.org/rights.

[New York. Provides text of treaties and other human rights instruments, a research guide, news, links to related organizations and offices, and many more useful resources.]

University of Minnesota Human Rights Library, http://www1.umn.edu/humanrts.

[Minneapolis, MN: University of Minnesota Human Rights Center. Collection of human rights documents and materials. Over 85,000 documents, searchable and arranged by topic or originating body. Contains a multi-site search device and basic materials in Arabic, Chinese, English, French, Japanese, Korean, Russian, Spanish, and Swedish.]

WESTLAW.

[Eagan, MN: West Group. Major fee-based legal research service. The thousands of databases include laws, regulations, and other legislative and administrative documents; cases; briefs; treatises; legal periodicals and indexes; and many other legal resources. Other databases provide news and business information, including newspapers and magazines, company, country, financial, demographic and market research data and industry reports. Updating varies by database. More information http://westlaw.com.]

Women's Human Rights Resources, http://www.law-lib.utoronto.ca/Diana.

[This University of Toronto Web site contains full-text articles, including annotated bibliographies; documents such as U.N. reports; case law and legislation; and links to other materials on women's human rights.]

§ 2.   Directories

Fulltext Sources Online (1989-).

[Needham, MA: BiblioData. Fulltext Sources Online (FSO) is a directory of periodicals that can be found online in full text through an aggregator or content provider. FSO lists over 40,000 newspapers, journals, magazines, newsletters, newswires, and transcripts. Semiannual; by subscription, http://www.fso-online.com/home_login.cfm?sid=17154199.]

Gale Directory of Online, Portable, and Internet Databases (1993-).

[Detroit: Gale Research. This online database provides detailed information on over 15,600 publicly available databases and database products accessible through an online vendor, the Web, or batch processor, or available for direct lease, license, or purchase as a CD-ROM, magnetic tape, or hand-held product; http://library.dialog.com/bluesheets/html/bl0230.html.]

O. Practice Guides

JOHN E. ACKERMAN & EUGENE O'SULLIVAN, PRACTICE AND PROCEDURE OF THE INTERNATIONAL CRIMINAL TRIBUNAL FOR THE FORMER YUGOSLAVIA, WITH SELECTED MATERIALS FROM THE INTERNATIONAL CRIMINAL TRIBUNAL FOR RWANDA (2000).

[The Hague; London: Kluwer Law International, 580 pp.]

AMNESTY INTERNATIONAL, A GUIDE TO THE AFRICAN CHARTER ON HUMAN AND PEOPLES' RIGHTS (1991).

[London: AI, 68 pp. Explains one's rights under the African Charter, the African Commission's role in safeguarding such rights, and complaint procedures.]

AMNESTY INTERNATIONAL, FAIR TRIALS MANUAL (1998).

[London: AI, 187 pp. Guide to international and regional standards for fair trials. Includes standards incorporated into treaties and standards not incorporated into treaties.]

AMNESTY INTERNATIONAL, SUMMARY OF SELECTED INTERNATIONAL PROCEDURES AND BODIES DEALING WITH HUMAN RIGHTS MATTERS (1989).

[London: AI, 75 pp. Provides brief descriptions, addresses, references to books and articles, and other relevant material for using principal human rights procedures of IGOs and some NGOs.]

DEBORAH E. ANKER & PAUL T. LUFKIN, THE LAW OF ASYLUM IN THE UNITED STATES (3d ed. 1999).

[Boston, MA: Refugee Law Center, 616 pp.]

EVELYN A. ANKHUMAH, THE AFRICAN COMMISSION ON HUMAN AND PEOPLES' RIGHTS: PRACTICES AND PROCEDURES (1996).

[The Hague, Boston, MA.: Martinus Nijhoff, 246 pp. Describes and analyzes the work of the African Commission on Human and Peoples' Rights. Provides insight into the structure and mandate of the Commission, the procedures for examining complaints, and the state reporting procedure. Also addresses actual cases.]

ASSISTING THE VICTIMS OF ARMED CONFLICT AND OTHER DISASTERS (Fritz Kalshoven ed., 1989).

[Dordrecht: Martinus Nijhoff Pub., 258 pp.]

ASYLUM LAW AND PRACTICE IN EUROPE AND NORTH AMERICA: A COMPARATIVE ANALYSIS (Jacqueline Bhabha & Geoffrey Coll eds., 1992).

[Washington, D.C.: Federal Publications Inc., 239 pp.]

ANNE F. BAYEFSKY, HOW TO COMPLAIN TO THE UN HUMAN RIGHTS TREATY SYSTEM (2003).

[Ardsley, N.Y.: Transnational Publishers, 397 pp.]

BRINGING CASES BEFORE THE EUROPEAN COMMISSION AND COURT OF HUMAN RIGHTS (Leif Berg ed., 1997).

[Turku/ Åbo, Finland: Institute for Human Rights, Abo Akademi University, 161 pp. Guide to the legal practitioners and other individuals interested in bringing a case before the European Commission and Court of Human Rights. Tables and Council of Europe documents have been appended in order to form a background to the chapters and to give some additional information on the procedure.]

CENTRE FOR HUMAN RIGHTS, MANUAL ON HUMAN RIGHTS REPORTING: UNDER SIX MAJOR INTERNATIONAL HUMAN RIGHTS INSTRUMENTS (1991).

[Geneva: U.N., 203 pp.]

CENTRE FOR SOCIAL DEVELOPMENT AND HUMANITARIAN AFFAIRS, MANUAL ON THE EFFECTIVE PREVENTION AND INVESTIGATION OF EXTRA-LEGAL, ARBITRARY AND SUMMARY EXECUTIONS (1991).

[Vienna: U.N., 71 pp.]

LAURENCE B. DE CHAZOURNES ET AL., PRACTICAL GUIDE TO THE INTERNATIONAL PROCEDURES RELATIVE TO COMPLAINT AND APPEALS AGAINST ACTS OF TORTURE, DISAPPEARANCES, AND OTHER INHUMAN OR DEGRADING TREATMENT (1988).

[Geneva: World Organization Against Torture/S.O.S. Torture, 92 pp. Explains how to use international bodies in denouncing acts of torture.]

CIRCLE OF RIGHTS - ECONOMIC, SOCIAL AND CULTURAL RIGHTS ACTIVISM: A TRAINING RESOURCE (2000).

[Washington, D.C.: 660 pp. International Human Rights Internship Program. Part I includes information about the substance of economic, social and cultural rights, and about strategies and tools that can be used to protect and promote them. The shorter Part II includes some suggestions for training methods that may be used to convey the material in Part I.]

L. J. CLEMENTS, NUALA MOLE, & ALAN SIMMONS, EUROPEAN HUMAN RIGHTS: TAKING A CASE UNDER THE CONVENTION (2d ed. 1999).

[London: Sweet & Maxwell, 383 pp. Offers practical guidance on the procedures for taking a case to Strasbourg. Every step is detailed with diagrammatic charts. Reference to case law is given to illustrate pitfalls and the likely outcome of cases.]

SANDRA COLIVER, THE ARTICLE 19 FREEDOM OF EXPRESSION MANUAL (1993).

[London: Article 19 International Centre Against Censorship, 284 pp.]

FORCED EVICTIONS AND HUMAN RIGHTS: A MANUAL FOR ACTION (1999).

[Geneva, Switzerland: Centre on Housing Rights and Evictions International Secretariat, 108 pp.]

[Utrecht, The Netherlands: Centre on Housing Rights and Evictions, 58 pp.]

P.R. GHANDI, THE HUMAN RIGHTS COMMITTEE AND THE RIGHT OF INDIVIDUAL COMMUNICATION: LAW AND PRACTICE (1998).

[Aldershot; Brookfield, Vt.: Ashgate/Dartmouth, 522 pp.]

DONNA GOMIEN, SHORT GUIDE TO THE EUROPEAN CONVENTION ON HUMAN RIGHTS (3d ed. 2005).

[Strasbourg: Council of Europe Pub., 182 pp.]

GUIDE TO INTERNATIONAL HUMAN RIGHTS PRACTICE (Hurst Hannum ed., 4th ed. 2004)

[Ardsley, N.Y.: Transnational Publishers, 391 pp. Probably the leading guide to human rights practice.]

HARD CASES: BRINGING HUMAN RIGHTS VIOLATORS TO JUSTICE ABROAD: A GUIDE TO UNIVERSAL JURISDICTION (1999).

[Versoix, Switzerland: International Council on Human Rights Policy, 57 pp. Sets out arguments for the rule of universal jurisdiction, along with ethical, practical, and legal problems that arise in its application.]

HELSINKI FOUNDATION FOR HUMAN RIGHTS, HUMAN RIGHTS MONITORING (2001).

[Warsaw: Helsinki Foundation for Human Rights, 196 pp., http://www.hrea.org/erc/Library/display_doc.php?url=http%3A%2F%2Fwww.hfhrpol.waw.pl%2Fen%2Findex_pliki%2FMonitoring_eng.pdf&external=N]

HUMAN RIGHTS INTERNET (HRI), GUIDE TO ESTABLISHING A HUMAN RIGHTS DOCUMENTATION CENTRE, REPORT OF A UNESCO-UNU INTERNATIONAL TRAINING SEMINAR ON THE HANDLING OF DOCUMENTATION & INFORMATION ON HUMAN RIGHTS (Laurie Wiseberg ed., 1990).

[Ottawa, Canada: HRI, 80 pp.]

HUMAN RIGHTS INSTITUTION-BUILDING: A HANDBOOK ON ESTABLISHING AND SUSTAINING HUMAN RIGHTS ORGANIZATIONS (1994).

[New York: The Fund for Peace (in association with The Jacob Blaustein Institute for the Advancement of Human Rights), 73 pp.]

INDIAN RIGHTS, HUMAN RIGHTS: HANDBOOK FOR INDIANS ON INTERNATIONAL HUMAN RIGHTS COMPLAINT PROCEDURES (1984).

[Washington, D.C.: Indian Law Resource Center.]

INTERNATIONAL HUMAN RIGHTS LAW IN THE COMMONWEALTH CARIBBEAN (Angela D. Byre & Beverley Y. Byfield eds., 1991).

[Dordrecht; Boston: Martinus Nijhoff Pub., 398 pp. Based upon a workshop held in Jamaica in 1987, organized by Interights and the Organization of Commonwealth Bar Associations.]

INTERNATIONAL LABOUR OFFICE, MANUAL ON PROCEDURES RELATING TO INTERNATIONAL LABOUR CONVENTIONS AND RECOMMENDATIONS (1984).

[Geneva: ILO, 34 pp.]

INTERNATIONAL WOMEN'S RIGHTS ACTION WATCH, ASSESSING THE STATUS OF WOMEN: A GUIDE TO REPORTING UNDER THE CONVENTION ON THE ELIMINATION OF ALL FORMS OF DISCRIMINATION AGAINST WOMEN (2d ed. 1996).

[University of Minnesota, MN: IWRAW, 89 pp. A guide to preparing government reports under and using the Convention on the Elimination of All Forms of Discrimination Against Women, http://www1.umn.edu/humanrts/iwraw/publications-index.html.]

ANETTE FAYE JACOBSEN, HUMAN RIGHTS MONITORING: A FIELD MISSION MANUAL (2008).

[Leiden; Boston: Martinus Nijhoff Publishers, 628 pp. Covers basic monitoring techniques for a full range of human rights issues.]

JOHN R. W. D. JONES, THE PRACTICE OF THE INTERNATIONAL CRIMINAL TRIBUNALS FOR THE FORMER YUGOSLAVIA AND RWANDA (2d ed. 2000).

[Ardsley, NY: Transnational Publishers, 666 pp. Includes cases from both the ICTFY and the ICTR, arranged according to the provisions of the Statute and Rules of Procedure and Evidence. Cases are presented with commentary and extracts from the Tribunals' decisions. Rules that have been amended are noted with dates and the reason for amendment.]

GEERT-JAN G. J. KNOOPS, THEORY AND PRACTICE OF INTERNATIONAL AND INTERNATIONALIZED CRIMINAL PROCEEDINGS (2005).

[Deventer: Kluwer BV; Hague: Kluwer Law International; Frederick, MD: distributed by Aspen Publishers, 358 pp.]

PHILIP LEACH, TAKING A CASE TO THE EUROPEAN COURT OF HUMAN RIGHTS (2d ed. 2005).

[Oxford; New York: Oxford Univ. Press, 794 pp.]

TARA MELISH, PROTECTING ECONOMIC, SOCIAL AND CULTURAL RIGHTS IN THE INTER-AMERICAN HUMAN RIGHTS SYSTEM: A MANUAL ON PRESENTING CLAIMS (2002).

[New Haven: Center for International Human Rights, Yale Law School; 473 pp.]

MINORITY RIGHTS: A GUIDE TO UNITED NATIONS PROCEDURES AND INSTITUTIONS (Gudmundur Alfredsson, Erika Ferrer, & Kathryn Ramsay eds., new ed. 2004).

[London: Minority Rights Group International, Raoul Wallenberg Institute of Human Rights and Humanitarian Law, 44 pp. Outlines the procedures currently available for the promotion and protection of minority rights.]

OFFICE OF THE HIGH COMMISSIONER FOR HUMAN RIGHTS AND UNITED NATIONS STAFF COLLEGE PROJECT, HUMAN RIGHTS: A BASIC HANDBOOK FOR UN STAFF, *at* http://www.ohchr.org/Documents/Publications/HRhandbooken.pdf.

OFFICE OF THE HIGH COMMISSIONER FOR HUMAN RIGHTS, ISTANBUL PROTOCOL: MANUAL ON THE EFFECTIVE INVESTIGATION AND DOCUMENTATION OF TORTURE AND OTHER CRUEL, INHUMAN OR DEGRADING TREATMENT OR PUNISHMENT (rev. 1, 2004).

[New York: United Nations, 76 pp.]

OFFICE OF THE HIGH COMMISSIONER FOR HUMAN RIGHTS, MANUAL ON HUMAN RIGHTS REPORTING UNDER SIX MAJOR INTERNATIONAL HUMAN RIGHTS INSTRUMENTS (1997).

[New York: United Nations, 560 pp., http://www.unhchr.ch/pdf/manual_hrr.pdf.]

OFFICE OF THE HIGH COMMISSIONER FOR HUMAN RIGHTS, TRAINING MANUAL ON HUMAN RIGHTS MONITORING, U.N. Doc. HR/P/PT/7 (2001),

http://www1.umn.edu/humanrts/monitoring/index.html.

MICHAEL O'FLAHERTY, HUMAN RIGHTS AND THE UN: PRACTICE BEFORE THE TREATY BODIES (2d ed. 2002).

[The Hague; New York: M. Nijhoff Publishers, 226 pp. Provides up-to-date information on six U.N. human rights treaty bodies: the Human Rights Committee; the Committee on Economic, Social and Cultural Rights; the Committee on Elimination of Racial Discrimination; the Committee of Elimination of Discrimination against Women; the Committee against Torture; and the Committee on the Rights of the Child.]

KAREN REID, A PRACTITIONER'S GUIDE TO THE EUROPEAN CONVENTION ON HUMAN RIGHTS (2d ed. 2004).

[London: Thomson/Sweet & Maxwell, 648 pp. Written for the UK practitioner.]

ADAM STAPLETON & KATHRYN ENGLISH, THE HUMAN RIGHTS HANDBOOK: A PRACTICAL GUIDE TO MONITORING HUMAN RIGHTS (1997).

[Capetown: Juta, 298 pp. Originally published by the Human Rights Centre, Essex University. Written for human rights workers.]

KEIR STARMER & THEODORA A CHRISTOU, HUMAN RIGHTS MANUAL AND SOURCEBOOK FOR AFRICA (2005).

[London: British Institute of International and Comparative Law, 1391 pp.]

BETH STEPHENS ET AL., SUING FOR TORTURE AND OTHER HUMAN RIGHTS ABUSES IN FEDERAL COURT: A LITIGATION MANUAL (1993).

[New York: Center for Constitutional Rights.]

Symposium: International Human Rights, 20 SANTA CLARA L. REV. 559-772 (1980).

[Contains introductory articles on the ECOSOC resolution 1503 procedure, procedures for the protection of detainees, the ILO, UNESCO, the European Convention, and the Inter-American Commission on Human Rights.]

UNESCO, Procedure for Dealing with Alleged Violations of Human Rights (2002), http://portal.unesco.org/en/files/19096/10790144691Booklet_CR.pdf/Booklet%2BCR.pdf.

[UNESCO set up a procedure for the examination of complaints received by the organization concerning alleged violations of human rights in its fields of competence; *i.e.*, education, science, culture and information.]

WOMEN'S HUMAN RIGHTS STEP BY STEP: A PRACTICAL GUIDE TO USING INTERNATIONAL HUMAN RIGHTS LAW AND MECHANISMS TO DEFEND WOMEN'S HUMAN RIGHTS (MARGARET A SCHULER ED., 2003).

[Washington, D.C. : Women, Law & Development International, 197 pp. Designed as a basic and practical guide to the operation of human rights mechanisms and strategies at national, regional, and international levels.]

JANE WINTER, HUMAN WRONGS HUMAN RIGHTS: A GUIDE TO THE HUMAN RIGHTS MACHINERY OF THE UNITED NATIONS (3d ed. 2002)

[London: British Irish Rights Watch, 115 pp. Handbook for NGOs describing the U.N. human rights process.]

P. Congressional Material

Congressional committee reports, as well as past and current federal bills, floor debate (Congressional Record), and selected hearing transcripts, are the Thomas Web site maintained by the Library of Congress, http://thomas.loc.gov/home/thomas2.html.

Another source for locating congressional documents on human rights is the Congressional Web site for GPO access, available on the Web at http://www.gpoaccess.gov/congress/index.html.

Q. Factfinding Methodology

Gudmundur Alfredsson, *Monitoring Minority Rights in Europe: The Implementation Machinery of the Framework Convention for the Protection of National Minorities - With Special Reference to the Role of the Advisory Committee*, 6 INT'L J. MINORITY & GROUP RTS. 417 (1999).

AMNESTY INTERNATIONAL, POLITICAL KILLINGS AND DISAPPEARANCES: MEDICOLEGAL ASPECTS (1993).

[London: Amnesty International, 29 pp.]

AMNESTY INTERNATIONAL NEDERLAND, MONITORING AND REPORTING HUMAN RIGHTS VIOLATIONS IN AFRICA (2002).

[Amsterdam: Amnesty International, 88 pp. http://www.amnesty.nl/documenten/spa/handbook_community_eng.pdf.]

PATRICK BALL ET AL., MAKING THE CASE: INVESTIGATING LARGE SCALE HUMAN RIGHTS VIOLATIONS USING INFORMATION SYSTEMS AND DATA ANALYSIS (2000).

[Washington, D.C.: American Association for the Advancement of Science, 300 pp.]

Thomas Buergenthal, *The United Nations Truth Commission for El Salvador*, 27 VAND. J. TRANSNAT'L L. 497-544 (1994).

[Describes the process the Commission followed in investigating possible human rights violations that occurred in El Salvador between 1980 and 1991.]

KATHRYN ENGLISH & ADAM STAPLETON, THE HUMAN RIGHTS HANDBOOK: A PRACTICAL GUIDE TO MONITORING HUMAN RIGHTS (1997).

[Colchester: The Human Rights Centre, University of Essex. 298 pp.]

Tamar Ezer & Susan Deller Ross, *Fact-Finding as a Lawmaking Tool for Advancing Women's Human Rights*, 7 GEO. J. GENDER & L. 331 (2006).

Thomas M. Franck & H. Scott Fairley, *Procedural Due Process in Human Rights Fact-Finding by International Agencies*, 74 AM. J. INT'L L. 308 (1980).

GUY S GOODWIN-GILL, FREE AND FAIR ELECTIONS (New expanded ed. 2006).

[Geneva: Inter-Parliamentary Union, 214 pp.]

ANETTE FAYE JACOBSEN, HUMAN RIGHTS MONITORING: A FIELD MISSION MANUAL (2008).

[Leiden; Boston: Martinus Nijhoff Publishers, 628 pp. Covers basic monitoring techniques for a full range of human rights issues.]

RICHARD LILLICH, FACT-FINDING BEFORE INTERNATIONAL TRIBUNALS (1992).

[New York: Transnational Publishers, 323 pp.]

GUIDELINES FOR INTERNATIONAL ELECTION OBSERVING (Larry Garber ed., 1984).

[Washington, D.C.: International Human Rights Law Group, 100 pp.]

HANDBOOK ON FACT-FINDING AND DOCUMENTATION OF HUMAN RIGHTS VIOLATIONS (D.J. Ravindran et al. eds., 1994).

[Thailand: Asian Forum for Human Rights and Development (FORUM-ASIA), 140 pp. Based on a documentation/factfinding workshop held in Thailand on October 1-6, 1993. Provides practical suggestions for the systematic collection and documentation of information on human rights violations.]

INTERNATIONAL LAW AND FACT-FINDING IN THE FIELD OF HUMAN RIGHTS (B.G. Ramcharan ed., 1982).

[The Hague: Martinus Nijhoff Pub., 259 pp. Volume one of the INTERNATIONAL STUDIES IN HUMAN RIGHTS SERIES. Provides articles on substantive and procedural law applicable to factfinding by human rights bodies. Annexes include model procedural rules.]

ALLAN MCCHESNEY, PROMOTING AND DEFENDING ECONOMIC, SOCIAL AND CULTURAL RIGHTS : A HANDBOOK (2000).

[Washington, D.C.: American Association for the Advancement of Science, 198 pp.]

MONITORING HUMAN RIGHTS: MANUAL FOR ASSESSING COUNTRY PERFORMANCE (1993).

[Leiden, The Netherlands: PIOOM Foundation, 292 pp. Part I provides background and user instructions, Part II includes questionnaires for assessing country performance, Part III contains a glossary of human rights terminology, and Part IV contains annexes.]

Robert Norris, *Observations In Loco: Practice and Procedure of the Inter-American Commission on Human Rights*, 1979-1983, 19 TEX. INT'L L.J. 285 (1984).

Diane Orentlicher, *Bearing Witness: The Art and Science of Human Rights Fact-Finding*, 3 HARV. HUM. RTS. J. 83 (1990).

Kathleen Pritchard, *Human Rights Reporting in Two Nations: A Comparison of the United States and Norway, in* HUMAN RIGHTS AND STATISTICS: GETTING THE RECORD STRAIGHT 259 (Thomas Jabine & Richard Claude eds., 1992).

[Philadelphia: University of Pennsylvania Press, 485 pp.]

Kersten Rogge, *Fact-Finding, in* EUROPEAN SYSTEM FOR THE PROTECTION OF HUMAN RIGHTS (1993).

[Dordrecht; Boston: M. Nijhoff, 940 pp. Chapter 29.]

A.J. JONGMAN & ALEX PETER SCHMID, MONITORING HUMAN RIGHTS: MANUAL FOR ASSESSING COUNTRY PERFORMANCE (1994).

[Leiden, the Netherlands: Interdisciplinary Research Program on Root Causes of Human Rights Violations, 347 pp.]

HANS THOOLEN & BERTH VERSTAPPEN, HUMAN RIGHTS MISSIONS: A STUDY OF THE FACT-FINDING PRACTICE OF NON-GOVERNMENTAL ORGANIZATIONS (1986).

[Dordrecht: Martinus Nijhoff Pub., 184 pp. Volume seven in the INTERNATIONAL STUDIES IN HUMAN RIGHTS SERIES.]

Katarina Tomasevski, *Sources of Information: Who Determines Which Facts are Relevant in the Field of Human Rights*, SIM NEWSLETTER No. 4, 25-33 (Oct. 1993).

David Weissbrodt, *International Trial Observers*, 18 STANFORD J. INT'L L. 27-121 (1982).

David Weissbrodt & James McCarthy, *Fact-Finding by International Human Rights Organizations*, 22 VA. J. INT'L L. 1-89 (1981).

R. Country Situations

§ 1.   Legal System Information Sources

INTERNATIONAL ENCYCLOPEDIA OF COMPARATIVE LAW.

[Tubingen: J.C.B. Mohr (Paul Siebeck). Contains alphabetically-arranged "National Reports" updated by installments. A report for a country typically provides information on formation of the government, constitutional system (including legislative and judicial structure), sources of law (decrees, orders, court decisions, custom, etc.), and brief history of the development of law, private law (contracts, torts, etc.), commercial law, intellectual property law, civil procedure, and private international law. Each report concludes with a short bibliography of books, articles, and/or periodicals to consult for additional information. The entries are up to date through the early 1970s.]

PATRICK H. GLENN, LEGAL TRADITIONS OF THE WORLD: SUSTAINABLE DIVERSITY IN LAW (3d ed. 2007).

[Oxford: Oxford Univ. Press, 395 pp.]

MODERN LEGAL SYSTEMS CYCLOPEDIA (Kenneth R. Redden ed., 1984-).

[Buffalo, NY: William S. Hein & Co., looseleaf. Provides a description of the political organization, sources of law, legislature, judiciary, and administrative structure of each country.]

University of Michigan Documents Center, Foreign Government Resources on the Web, http://www.lib.umich.edu/govdocs/foreign.html.

[This comprehensive Web site provides links to many Web resources for foreign governments: background information, constitutions, parliaments, laws, and much more.]

U.S. Library of Congress, Country Studies, http://memory.loc.gov/frd/cs.

[Includes extensive reports on 101 countries and regions. Most reports were created between 1988 and 1998, and some countries have been updated since then. Notable omissions include Canada, France, the United Kingdom, and other Western nations, as well as a number of African nations.]

§ 2. Country Reports

AMNESTY INTERNATIONAL REPORT (1962-).

[London: Amnesty International Publications, annual. Documents AI's work for the year prior to the date of issue. Contains substantial information on work in many countries, for the release of prisoners of conscience and against torture, the death penalty, extrajudicial executions, disappearances, and unfair trials for political prisoners. The Amnesty Web site contains many reports by country and by theme, http://www.amnesty.org/en/library.]

AMNESTY INTERNATIONAL: A MAJOR COLLECTION OF PUBLISHED AND UNPUBLISHED RESEARCH MATERIALS (1981-).

[Zug: Inter Documentation Co.]

CANADIAN IMMIGRATION AND REFUGEE BOARD, QUARTERLY REPORTS.

[Ottawa, Canada: Research Directorate, Documentation, Information and Research Branch, Immigration and Refugee Board, quarterly. See also the CIRB's Web site for the full-text of reports, policies, and other information, http://www.irb-cisr.gc.ca/en/index_e.htm.]

CRITIQUE: REVIEW OF THE DEPARTMENT OF STATE'S COUNTRY REPORTS ON HUMAN RIGHTS PRACTICES FOR ... (1983-1996).

[New York: Lawyers Committee for Human Rights & Human Rights Watch, annual. Also known as Critique of DOS Country Reports; beginning in 1990 the Critique became the project of the Lawyers Committee alone).]

FBIS (Foreign Broadcast Information Service) Daily Reports (1979-1996).

[Washington, D.C.: Foreign Broadcast Information Service. FBIS is a microfiche collection consisting of translated broadcasts, news agency transmissions, newspapers, periodicals and government statements from nations around the globe. Use either the print or CD-ROM index to access the documents. The print was continued in part with FBIS Publications on CD-ROM (1997-2000). This CD-ROM may be viewed, and its news may be described and cited in briefs, but copyright permission from the originating source must be obtained before it can be downloaded or printed. FBIS is also continued in part by World News Connection, http://wnc.fedworld.gov as a fee-based electronic service (see below).]

FREEDOM IN THE WORLD (1978-).

[New York: Freedom House, annual. Freedom House Book, annual. Also available on the Freedom House Web site, http://www.freedomhouse.org/template.cfm?page=1.]

HUMAN RIGHTS DOCUMENTS (1983-).

(Microform, Leiden, The Netherlands: IDC. The unofficial depository of Human Rights Internet's NGO human rights documentation. The collection covers a variety of NGO documents from 1980-1993. Use the printed guides to locate the appropriate fiche.]

HUMAN RIGHTS IN DEVELOPING COUNTRIES (1985-1997).

Oslo: Norwegian University Press, annual. Publications from the Danish Center for Human Rights. Covered the human rights situation in such countries as Bangladesh, Botswana, India, Kenya, Mozambique, Nicaragua, Pakistan, the Philippines, Sri Lanka, Suriname, Tanzania, Zambia, and Zimbabwe. Reports were prepared in cooperation with several human rights centers in Europe and Canada.]

HUMAN RIGHTS INTERNET REPORTER (1976- 1999).

[Washington, D.C.: Human Rights Internet.]

HUMAN RIGHTS WATCH, WORLD REPORT (1990-).

[New York: Human Rights Watch, annual. Available in the HRW Web site, http://www.hrw.org.]

INTER-AMERICAN COMMISSION ON HUMAN RIGHTS, ANNUAL REPORTS (1976-).

[Washington, D.C.: General Secretariat of the Organization of American States, annual. Also available on the Web, http://www.cidh.oas.org/annual. eng.htm.]

INTER-AMERICAN COMMISSION ON HUMAN RIGHTS, REPORT ON THE SITUATION IN ...

[Washington, D.C.: General Secretariat, Organization of American States. The publication of these country reports varies. Some are available on the Web, http://www.cidh.oas.org/pais.eng.htm.]

INTERNATIONAL COMMITTEE OF THE RED CROSS, ANNUAL REPORT (1952-).

[Geneva: ICRC. Covers the work of the ICRC in each country where the ICRC has made representations or undertaken activities on behalf of prisoners of war, civilians in armed conflict, or detainees; has supplied medical and other material relief; or has performed other services. The annual reports are ordinarily issued late in the year following the date of the report. The annual reports from 1994 to present are available on the ICRC Web site, http://www. icrc.org/eng/publications.]

INTERNATIONAL HANDBOOK OF HUMAN RIGHTS (Jack Donnelly & Rhoda E. Howard eds., 1987).

[Westport, CT: Greenwood Press, 495 pp. Alphabetically-arranged studies of human rights practices in 19 countries (Canada, Chile, China, Cuba, El Salvador, India, Israel, Jamaica, Japan, Lebanon, Nicaragua, the Philippines, Poland, Senegal, South Africa, Spain, Uganda, the USSR, and the U.S.). Each separately-authored study discusses the historical background of the country as well as civil, political, economic, social, and cultural rights. The introduction provides background information about human rights in general. The appendices contain the Universal Declaration of Human Rights, a ratification chart for human rights instruments, basic economic and social indicators, a selected bibliography, and an index.]

INTERNATIONAL JOURNAL OF REFUGEE LAW (1989-).

[Oxford: Oxford Univ. Press.]

INTERNATIONAL JOURNAL ON MINORITY AND GROUP RIGHTS (1997-).

[The Hague; Boston: Kluwer Law International.]

Kathleen Pritchard, *Human Rights Reporting in Two Nations: A Comparison of the United States and Norway, in* HUMAN RIGHTS AND STATISTICS: GETTING THE RECORD STRAIGHT 259 (Thomas Jabine & Richard Claude eds., 1992).

[Philadelphia: University of Pennsylvania Press, 458 pp.]

THE REAGAN/BUSH ADMINISTRATION'S RECORD ON HUMAN RIGHTS IN ... (1986-1992).

[New York: Human Rights Watch & Lawyers Committee for Human Rights. Beginning in 1990 the Bush Administration Record became the project of Human Rights Watch alone. Reviews implementation of human rights legislation; ratification of human rights treaties; voting record and human rights activities in the U.N.; refugee, asylum, and immigration policy; and policy toward over 20 countries where human rights issues have arisen.]

REFUGEES (1984-).

[Geneva: Office of the United Nations High Commissioner for Refugees.]

REFUGEE SURVEY QUARTERLY (1994-).

[Geneva: UNHCR, Centre for Documentation on Refugees. Continues REFUGEE ABSTRACTS].

UNITED NATIONS DEVELOPMENT PROGRAMME (UNDP), HUMAN DEVELOPMENT REPORT [year] (1990-).

[New York: Oxford Univ. Press. Includes both a Human Development Index (measures life expectancy, educational attainment, and purchasing power) and a Human Freedom Index (rates country performance on 40 aspects of freedom). The first part of the report discusses human development, political freedom, and strategies for the future. The second part contains statistical tables which compare countries over a broad spectrum of human welfare matters. The most recent edition is available on the UNDP Web site, http://hdr.undp.org/reports.]

UNHCR, STATE OF THE WORLD'S REFUGEES (1993-).

[Oxford: Oxford Univ. Press, approximately every two years. The most recent edition is available on the Web, http://www.unhcr.org/cgi-bin/texis/vtx/template?page=publ&src=static/sowr2006/toceng.htm.]

UNICEF, THE STATE OF THE WORLD'S CHILDREN (1980-).

[Oxford; New York: Oxford Univ. Press; annual. Covers the status of children in developing countries, focusing on health and hygiene. The 1996-2008 reports are available on the UNICEF Web site in the Publications section, http://www.unicef.org/publications/index.html.]

U.S. DEPARTMENT OF STATE, ANNUAL REPORT ON INTERNATIONAL RELIGIOUS FREEDOM (1999-).

[Washington, D.C.: U.S. Government Printing Office, annual. The report describes the status of religious freedom in each foreign country, and government policies violating religious belief and practices of groups, religious denominations and individuals, and U.S. policies to promote religious freedom around the world. These reports are also on the State Dept. Web site, http://www.state.gov/g/drl/irf/rpt.]

University of Minnesota, Human Rights Library, Basic Country Condition Research, http://www1.umn.edu/humanrts/asylum/country_conditions.html.

[This site provides a table that includes links for many countries to country reports from the United States Department of State, Amnesty International, Human Rights Watch, the United Nations High Commissioner for Refugees, and Write-Net. More in-depth research on country conditions is available in the country research bibliography, Country Documentation Resources for Refugee and Asylum Cases, http://www1.umn.edu/humanrts/asylum/cond_research.html.]

U.S. DEPARTMENT OF STATE, COUNTRY REPORTS ON HUMAN RIGHTS PRACTICES (1977-).

[Washington, D.C.: U.S. Government Printing Office, annual. Covers human rights practices of nations that receive assistance from the U.S. or which are members of the U.N. Other nations are also included. Provides relevant economic, political, and social information on a country and an evaluation of each country's respect for human rights (mainly civil and political, plus fair conditions of labor) based on its own constitution, legislative measures, and actions towards its citizens. Prepared by the U.S. Department of State for the House Committee on Foreign Affairs and the Senate Committee on Foreign Relations; issued as a congressional committee print. The reports from 1993-1999 are available from the archive of the State Department's Web site, http://www.state.gov/www/global/human_rights/drl_reports.html and from 1999-2006 are at http://www.state.gov/g/drl/rls/hrrpt/.]

WORLD NEWS CONNECTION, http://wnc.fedworld.gov (1995-).

[Washington, D.C.: NTIS. This fee-based service contains the full text summaries of non-U.S. newspaper articles, conference proceedings, radio and television broadcasts, periodicals and non-classified technical reports. See also FBIS Daily Reports above. Many WNC reports are also available on WESTLAW.]

§ 3.   Constitutions

CONSTITUTIONS OF DEPENDENCIES & SPECIAL SOVEREIGNTIES (Albert P. Blaustein & Eric B. Blaustein eds., 1975-).

[Dobbs Ferry, NY: Oceana Publications, Inc., looseleaf. Also available as web subscription.]

CONSTITUTIONS OF DEPENDENCIES AND TERRITORIES (Philip Marc Raworth ed., 1998-).

[Dobbs Ferry, NY: Oceana Publications Inc., looseleaf. Also available as web subscription.]

CONSTITUTIONS OF THE COUNTRIES OF THE WORLD (Albert P. Blaustein & Gisbert H. Flanz eds., 1971-).

[Dobbs Ferry, NY: Oceana Publications, Inc., looseleaf. Also available as web subscription.]

International Constitutional Law, http://www.oefre.unibe.ch/law/icl.

[Provides and links to constitutions, related documents, and constitutional background information as well as country information. Not updated since 2005.]

ROBERT L. MADDEX, CONSTITUTIONS OF THE WORLD (2d ed. 2001).

[Washington, D.C.: CQ Press, 417 pp.]

University of Richmond, Constitution Finder, http://confinder.richmond.edu.

[Arranged alphabetically by country, this index links to constitutions, charters, amendments, and related documents.]

§ 4.   Criminal Codes and Criminal Procedure Codes

AMERICAN SERIES OF FOREIGN PENAL CODES (1960-).

[South Hackensack, NJ: Fred B. Rothman & Co. English-language translations of penal codes of Argentina, Austria, China, Colombia, Finland, France, Federal Republic of Germany (West), Greece, Greenland, Japan, Republic of Korea (South), Norway, Poland, Sweden, and Turkey; criminal procedure codes of France, Federal Republic of Germany, Israel, and Turkey.]

Buffalo Criminal Law Center, Criminal Law Sources on the Internet, http://wings.buffalo.edu/law/bclc/resource.htm.

[This site provides access to criminal law materials throughout the world, including criminal codes, criminal procedure codes, and enforcement codes.]

§ 5.   Other Legislation

CHARLES SZLADITS, BIBLIOGRAPHY ON FOREIGN AND COMPARATIVE LAW: BOOKS AND ARTICLES IN ENGLISH (1955-).

[Dobbs Ferry, NY: Oceana Publications, Inc. (vol. 1- , 1790-Apr. 1, 1953-). Irregular. Lists books and articles by country; codes and statutes available in books and periodicals.]

THOMAS H. REYNOLDS & ARTURO A. FLORES, FOREIGN LAW: CURRENT SOURCES OF CODES AND BASIC LEGISLATION IN JURISDICTIONS OF THE WORLD (1989-).

[Contains citations to sources of law for a variety of subjects as well as information on the sources of codes, legislation, and court reports. Arranged by jurisdiction. Available by subscription on the Internet; see http://www.foreign-lawguide.com.]

§ 6.   Directories

ADRIENNE CRUZ, THE NGLS HANDBOOK OF UN AGENCIES, PROGRAMMES, FUNDS AND CONVENTIONS WORKING FOR SUSTAINABLE ECONOMIC AND SOCIAL DEVELOPMENT (3d ed. 2000).

[Geneva; New York: United Nations Non-Governmental Liaison Service, 372 pp.]

AFRICAN DIRECTORY: HUMAN RIGHTS ORGANIZATIONS IN SUB-SAHARAN AFRICA (1996).

[Ottawa, Canada: Human Rights Internet (HRI); Utrecht, the Netherlands: Netherlands Institute of Human Rights (SIM), 276 pp.]

Directory of Non-Governmental Organizations Associated with the Department of Public Information, http://www.un.org/dpi/ngosection/dpingo-directory.asp.

[New York: U.N. Searchable by the name of the organization, the region where the organization's headquarters is located, or the organization's main area of interest.]

DIRECTORY OF PRO BONO OPPORTUNITIES IN INTERNATIONAL LAW (2d ed. 1998).

[Washington, D.C.: International Law Section, District of Columbia Bar, 42 pp.]

ENCYCLOPEDIA OF ASSOCIATIONS: INTERNATIONAL ORGANIZATIONS (1989-).

[Detroit, MI: Gale Research Co., annual.]

FUNDING HUMAN RIGHTS: AN INTERNATIONAL DIRECTORY OF FUNDING ORGANIZATIONS & HUMAN RIGHTS AWARDS (3d ed. 1999).

[Ottawa, Canada: Human Rights Internet, 213 pp.]

HUMAN RIGHTS CONNECTIONS (1992-).

[Washington, D.C.: American Society of International Law, Human Rights Interest Group. Directory of human rights organizations. Irregular frequency.]

Human Rights Internet Directory, http://www.hri.ca/organizations-data-bank.asp.

[Ottawa, Canada: Human Rights Internet. Searchable database of human rights Web sites recorded by site content, features, geographical focus, key-words/issues, and more.]

THE HUMAN RIGHTS INTERNSHIP BOOK (1999-).

[Winston-Salem, NC: Career Education Institutes, 108 pp.]

IAN NEARY, HUMAN RIGHTS GROUPS IN JAPAN, KOREA AND TAIWAN: A PARTIAL BUT ANNOTATED LIST (1998).

[Colchester: Department of Government, University of Essex, 48 pp.]

PARLIAMENTARY HUMAN RIGHTS BODIES: WORLD DIRECTORY (1990-).

[Geneva: Inter-parliamentary Union. Irregular frequency.]

RESOURCES FOR HUMAN RIGHTS EDUCATORS: A SURVEY OF THE RESOURCES AVAILABLE ON THE INTERNET (1996).

[Ottawa, Ontario: Human Rights Internet, 88 pp.]

WORLD DIRECTORY OF HUMAN RIGHTS RESEARCH AND TRAINING INSTITUTIONS = REPERTOIRE MONDIAL DES INSTITUTIONS DE RECHERCHE ET DE FORMATION SUR LES DROITS DE L'HOMME = REPERTORIO MUNDIAL DE INSTITUCIONES DE INVESTIGACION Y DE FORMACION EN MATERIA DE DERECHOS HUMANOS (1992-).

[Paris: Unesco, 285 pp. Irregularly published; the sixth edition, 2003, is the most recent, http://unesdoc.unesco.org/images/0013/001321/132133m.pdf.]

§ 7. Nongovernmental Organization (NGO) Reports

Several of the numerous NGOs working in the area of human rights produce excellent reports on a range of rights and regions. Some organizations include:

Advocates for Human Rights, http://www.advocates.org [formerly Minnesota Advocates for Human Rights].

10 Fourth Avenue South, #1000, Minneapolis, MN 55415-1012 USA

African Centre for Democracy and Human Rights Studies, http://www.acdhrs.org.

K.S.M.D., Kairaba Avenue, Kombo St. Mary Division, THE GAMBIA

Al-Haq, http://www.alhaq.org.

P.O. Box 1413, Ramallah, West Bank, Palestine, via ISRAEL

Amnesty International, http://www.amnesty.org.

International Secretariat, 1 Easton Street, London WC1X 0DW, UNITED KINGDOM

Anti-Slavery International, http://www.antislavery.org.

Thomas Clarkson House, The Stableyard, Broomgrove Road, London SW9 9TL, UNITED KINGDOM

Arab Organization for Human Rights, http://aohr.org.

91, Al-Marghany St., Heliopolis, Cairo, EGYPT

Article 19, International Centre on Censorship, http://www.article19.org.

Lancaster House, 33 Islington High St., London E1 1IL, UNITED KINGDOM

Center for the Victims of Torture, 717 East River Road, http://www.cvt.org.

Minneapolis, MN 55455, USA

The Egyptian Organisation for Human Rights, http://www.eohr.org.

8/10 Matahaf El-Manyal Street, 10th Floor, Manyal El Roda, Cairo, EGYPT

Federacion Latinoamericana de Asociaciones de Familiares de Detenidos-Desaparecidos (FEDEFAM), http://www.desaparecidos.org/fedefam.

Fedefam 2444 - Carmelitas 1010 - A - Caracas, VENEZUELA

Friends World Committee for Consultation (Quakers), http://fwccworld.org.

FWCC World Office, 4 Byng Place, London WC1E 7JH UNITED KINGDOM

Human Rights First [formerly Lawyers Committee for Human Rights], http://www.humanrightsfirst.org/index.asp.

333 Seventh Avenue, 13th Floor, New York, NY 10001 USA

Global Rights (formerly International Human Rights Law Group), http://www.globalrights.org/site/PageServer?pagename=index.

1200 18th Street NW,

Suite 602, Washington, DC 20036 USA

Human Rights Internet, http://www.hri.ca.

8 York Street, suite 202, Ottawa, Ontario K1N 5S6, CANADA

Human Rights Watch, http://www.hrw.org.

350 Fifth Avenue, 34th Floor New York, NY 10118-3299 USA

Inter-American Institute of Human Rights, http://www.iidh.ed.cr.

Apdo. 10.081-1000, San José, COSTA RICA

International Alert, http://www.international-alert.org.

1 Glyn Street, London SE11 5HT, UNITED KINGDOM

International Commission of Jurists, http://www.icj.org.

P.O. Box 216, 81A avenue de Châtelaine, 1219 Geneva, SWITZERLAND

International Committee of the Red Cross, http://www.icrc.org/eng.

Information Department, 19 avenue de la Paix, 1202 Geneva, SWITZERLAND

International League for Human Rights, http://www.ilhr.org.

432 Park Ave. South, New York, NY 10016 USA

International Service for Human Rights, http://www.ishr.ch.

1 rue de Varembé, P.O. Box 16, CH-1211 Geneva 20, SWITZERLAND

Inter-Parliamentary Union, http://www.ipu.org/english/home.htm.

Place du Petit-Saconnex, C.P. 438, CH-1211 Geneva 19, SWITZERLAND

Interights, http://www.interights.org.

Lancaster House, 33 Islington High Street, London N1 9LH, UNITED KINGDOM

Jacob Blaustein Institute for the Advancement of Human Rights, http://www.ajc.org/site/c.ijITI2PHKoG/b.835983/k.AF53/Human_Rights.htm.

165 East 56th St New York, NY 10022-2746 USA

Minority Rights Group, http://www.minorityrights.org.

379 Brixton Road, London SW9 7DE, UNITED KINGDOM

Physicians for Human Rights, http://physiciansforhumanrights.org.

100 Boylston Street, Suite 702, Boston, MA 02116 USA

Women in Law and Development in Africa (WiLDAF), http://www.wildaf.org.zw.

P.O Box 4622 Harare, ZIMBABWE

ZIMRIGHTS, 38 New Africa House, Box 4111, 40 Union Avenue, Harara, ZIMBABWE

For more information about NGOs, see sections N.2 and R.6 above. See also http://www.umn.edu/humanrts/links/ngolinks.html. The HUMAN RIGHTS INTERNET REPORTER and its human rights directories include entries from the above organizations and many others.

§ 8.   U.N. Documents

The U.N. publishes many reports submitted by U.N. organs and member states detailing countries' adherence to international human rights standards. The Human Rights Council, for example, authorizes working groups, special rapporteurs, representatives, experts, Council members, the Secretary-General, and other envoys to monitor violations or make direct contacts in particular countries, such as Afghanistan, Equatorial Guinea, Iran, Iraq, Myanmar, Palestine (Occupied Arab Territories), Rwanda, and the former Yugoslavia. A list of the Council's country mandates is at http://www2.ohchr.org/english/bodies/chr/special/countries.htm.

In addition, the Commission on Human Rights has established special rapporteurs and working groups on thematic topics (now continued by the Human Rights Council): abuses by mercenaries (1987-present); arbitrary detention (1991-present); arbitrary executions (1982-present); contemporary forms of slavery (2007); disappearances (1980-present); foreign debt (2000-present); freedom of opinion and expression (1993-present); human rights defenders (2000-present); humanr rights while countering terrorism (2005-present); independence of judges and lawyers (1994-present); internally displaced persons (1992-present); international solidarity (2005-present); minority issues (2005-present); racism and xenophobia (1993-present); religious intolerance (1986-present); right to adequate housing (2000-present); right to food (2000-present); right to development (1993-present); right to health (2002-present); rights of people of African descent (2002-present); sale of children, child prostitution and child pornography (1990-present); torture and other cruel, inhuman or degrading treatment (1985-present); toxic waste (1995-present); trafficking in persons (2004-present); right to education (1998-present); transntional corporations and human rights (2005); and violence against women (1994-present). The special rapporteurs and working groups generally produce annual reports discussing human rights violations in many countries and detailing country visits. A list of the Council's thematic mandates is at http://www2.ohchr.org/english/bodies/chr/special/themes.htm.

The Commission on Human Rights has authorized experts on advisory services for the restoration of human rights in countries such as Equatorial Guinea, Guatemala, and Haiti. The reports of those experts provide information on countries receiving advisory services.

The *ad hoc* Working Group of Experts on Southern Africa (1967-1995), the Special Committee Against *Apartheid*, and the U.N. Council for Namibia have also issued specialized reports, but have been discontinued.

Within the framework of the Human Rights Committee, Committee on Economic, Social and Cultural Rights, Committee on the Elimination of Discrimination against Women (CEDAW), the Committee on the Elimination of All Forms of Racial Discrimination (CERD), the Committee Against Torture (CAT), the Committee on the Rights of the Child (CRC), Committee on Migrant Workers (CMW), and the Committee on the Rights of Persons with Disabilities (CRPD), States parties are required to submit periodic reports on domestic developments. Those reports, along with the published conclusions, comments, and decisions taken by the committees, provide indispensable information about the countries.

The Special Committee on Decolonization has received reports from its delegations to dependent territories: American Samoa, Anguilla, Bermuda, British Virgin Islands, Cayman Islands, East Timor, Falkland Islands (Malvinas), Gibraltar, Guam, Montserrat, New Caledonia, Pitcairn, St. Helena, Tokelau, Trust Territory of the Pacific Islands, Turks and Caicos Islands, U.S. Virgin Islands, and Western Samoa.

U.N. documents, listed in *United Nations Documents Index* (1998-) and predecessor indexes, are organized by document symbols referring to the U.N. organ, type of document, session number, and document number. See also the United Nations Documentation: Research Guide for more information about document symbols, basic tools, and indexes, http://www.un.org/Depts/dhl/resguide/index.html. For more information on documents related to human rights, see United Nations Documentation: Research Guide on Human Rights, http://www.un.org/Depts/dhl/resguide/spechr.htm. Document symbols relevant to human rights include:

General Assembly

General Assembly

A/Document for General Assembly plenaryA/INF	Information paper for the General Assembly
A/RES	General Assembly Resolution
A/C.1 through C.6, A/SEC, A/BLR	Main committees of the General Assembly, e.g., the Third Committee (A/C.3) considers social, humanitarian, and cultural matters; the Sixth Committee deals with legal matters. Documents issued only during Assembly sessions.
A/AC.109	Special Committee on Decolonization
A/AC.115	Special Committee on Apartheid
A/HRC	Human Rights Council
A/AC.131	Council for Namibia
A/AC.160	Committee on International Terrorism
A/CONF.144	United Nations Congress on the Prevention of Crime and the Treatment of Offenders

Economic and Social Council (ECOSOC)

E/	Document for ECOSOC plenary
E/AC.57	Committee on Crime Prevention and Control
E/CN.15	Commission on Crime Prevention and Criminal Justice
E/INF	Information papers for ECOSOC
E/RES	ECOSOC resolution
E/C.2	Committee on Nongovernmental Organizations
E/CN.4	Commission on Human Rights
E/CN.4/Sub.2	Sub-Commission on the Promotion and Protection of Human Rights (formerly Sub-Commission on the Prevention of Discrimination and Protection of Minorities)

E/CN.4/WG.15	Working Group on a Draft U.N. Declaration on the Rights of Indigenous Peoples
E/CN.5	Commission for Social Development
E/CN.6	Commission on Status of Women
E/CN.17	Commission on Sustainable Development

Other Major Organs

DC/	Disarmament Commission
S/	Security Council
ST/	Secretariat
T/	Trusteeship Council (suspended operation on November 1, 1994)
HRI/	International Human Rights Instruments
HRI/CORE	

International Covenant on Civil and Political Rights

CCPR/C	Human Rights Committee
CCPR/SP	Meetings of the States parties

International Covenant on Economic, Social and Cultural Rights

ESC/	Committee on Economic, Social and Cultural Rights

International Convention on the Elimination of All Forms of Racial Discrimination

CERD/	Committee on the Elimination of Racial Discrimination

International Convention on the Elimination of All Forms of Discrimination Against Women

CEDAW/	Committee on the Elimination of Discrimination Against Women

International Convention on the Protection of the Rights of All Migrant Workers and Members of their Families

CMW/	Committee on the Protection of the Rights of All Migrant Workers and Members of Their Families

Convention on the Rights of Persons with Disabilities

CRPD/	Committee on the Rights of Persons with Disabilities

International Convention on the Rights of the Child

CRC/	Committee on the Rights of the Child

International Convention on Torture and Cruel, Inhuman or Degrading Treatment or Punishment

CAT/	Committee Against Torture

Functional Symbols

___/Add.	Addendum
___/CONF.	Conference
___/Corr.	Corrigendum

___/L.	Document with limited distribution (often draft resolutions or reports, generally available only at the time of issue)
___/NGO	Document submitted by a nongovern-mental organization
___/PR.	Press release
___/R.	Document with restricted distribution (not generally available to NGOs or individuals)
___/Rev.	Revision
___/SR.	Summary records
___/WG.	Working group

§ 9.   Inter-American Commission on Human Rights

The Inter-American Commission on Human Rights publishes periodic reports on its visits to investigate allegations of human rights violations in OAS member states. Annual reports of the Commission contain updates on the country visit reports or summaries of reports not separately issued. Reports have been prepared on Argentina (1980), Bolivia (1981, 1996), Brazil (1997), Canada (2000), Chile (1974, 1976, 1977, 1985), Colombia (1981, 1994, 1999), Cuba (1962, 1963, 1967, 1970, 1976, 1979, 1983, 1993, 1994), Dominican Republic (1999), Ecuador (1997), El Salvador (1978, 1986, 1994), Guatemala (1981, 1983, 1986, 1988, 1993, 1994), Haiti (1979, 1988, 1990, 1993, 1995), Mexico (1998), Nicaragua (1981, 1984, 1988, 1993), Panama (1978, 1989), Paraguay (1978), Peru (1993, 2000), Suriname (1983, 1985), and Uruguay (1978). A list of country reports and other special reports appears on the OAS website at http://www.oas.org.

OAS member states include: Antigua and Barbuda, Argentina, the Bahamas (Commonwealth of), Barbados, Belize, Bolivia, Brazil, Canada, Chile, Colombia, Costa Rica, Cuba, Dominica (Commonwealth of), Dominican Republic, Ecuador, El Salvador, Grenada, Guatemala, Guyana, Haiti, Honduras, Jamaica, Mexico, Nicaragua, Panama, Paraguay, Peru, St. Kitts and Nevis, Saint Lucia, Saint Vincent and the Grenadines, Suriname, Trinidad and Tobago, United States, Uruguay, and Venezuela. [Cuba is technically a member but cannot participate in OAS proceedings or activities.]

§ 10.   Media Services

Foreign Broadcast Information Service (FBIS) (1979-2005).[Washington, D.C.: Foreign Broadcast Information Service. FBIS is a microfiche collection consisting of translated broadcasts, news agency transmissions, newspapers, periodicals and government statements from eight countries/regions of the world. Use either the print index or the CD-ROM index (1991-August, 1996) to access the documents from 1979-1996. The print indexes and fiche were discontinued in 1996 and replaced by FBIS Publications on CD-ROM (1997-). This CD-ROM may be viewed, and its news may be described and cited in briefs, but copyright permission from the originating source must be obtained before it can be downloaded or printed. The National Technical Information Service (NTIS) of the Dept. of Commerce makes a portion of this database available on the Internet by subscription as World News Connection (WNC), http://wnc.fedworld.gov. Other FBIS material is https://www.opensource.gov.]

LEXIS/NEXIS (online service containing the full-text of news wires, newspapers, and magazines; please refer to the ELECTRONIC SOURCES section of this bibliography, supra).

WESTLAW (for a detailed description; please refer to the ELECTRONIC SOURCES section of this bibliography, *supra*).